THE
NEGRO
TRADITIONS

THE NEGRO TRADITIONS

❄

Thomas W. Talley

Edited, with an Introduction,
by Charles K. Wolfe
and Laura C. Jarmon

The University of Tennessee Press / Knoxville

Frontispiece. Thomas W. Talley, ca. 1930.

Copyright © 1993 by The University of Tennessee Press / Knoxville.
All Rights Reserved. Manufactured in the United States of America.
First Edition.

The paper in this book meets the minimum requirements of the
American National Standard for Permanence of Paper for Printed
Library Materials. ∞ The binding materials have been chosen
for strength and durability.

Library of Congress Cataloging in Publication Data

Talley, Thomas Washington.
    The Negro traditions / Thomas W. Talley; edited, with an introduction,
by Charles K. Wolfe and Laura C. Jarmon. — 1st ed.
            p.   cm.
    Includes bibliographical references.
    ISBN 0-87049-803-7 (cl.: alk. paper)
    1. Afro-Americans—Tennessee—Folklore. 2. Tales—Tennessee.
I. Wolfe, Charles K.   II. Jarmon, Laura C., 1951–   .   III. Title.
GR111.A47T36   1993   92-47011
398.2'089'960730768—dc20   CIP

Contents

✻

LIBRARY
ALMA COLLEGE
ALMA, MICHIGAN

The Negro Traditions

EDITORS' INTRODUCTION

In the early 1920s, Thomas Washington Talley, a chemistry professor at Nashville's Fisk University, began a series of writings about a subject he had been fascinated with since he was a young man: folklore. In a remarkable burst of creativity, he produced three book-length manuscripts in a period of little more than four years. The first of these—and the only one to see publication in Talley's lifetime—was a collection and analysis of African-American folk songs and folk rhymes called *Negro Folk Rhymes (Wise and Otherwise)*, published by Macmillan in 1922. The second was a much more ambitious project designed as a companion volume to *Negro Folk Rhymes:* a huge collection of African-American tales called at one point "Negro Folk Myths" but eventually titled *The Negro Traditions*. It contained sixteen lengthy stories, some of which incorporated still more folk songs and their music; some stories were new versions of familiar tales that were printed by later collectors, but others were unique and distinctive. For a variety of reasons, however, this manuscript did not fare as well as *Negro Folk Rhymes;* it never saw publication during Talley's lifetime and languished in his family's files for years after—a total of sixty-eight years from its completion. It is this manuscript that comprises the present volume. A third book, an analysis of the tales, called "The Origin of Traditions, or The Interpretation of Traditions through Negro Traditions," has also been discovered but remains in manuscript.

A BIOCRITICAL OBSERVATION
CHARLES K. WOLFE

Talley's work is important for a number of reasons. He was, first of all, one of the earliest black scholars to investigate African-American traditional culture. Furthermore, he was himself a member of the nineteenth-century rural black culture he documented, and over and over he added to his work anecdotes and observations drawn from his own childhood and youth. In his "Origin of Traditions" manuscript he noted,

> I was born and reared among the Negro masses whose educational equipment consisted largely of traditions. They planted, cultivated, cooked, ate, and drank in the traditional way. All men born among

such people inherit a love of the past. . . . Born with such a love, I
could not help longing to see and know the dim prehistoric past.

The traditional culture that Talley remembered so vividly was centered in
Bedford County in Middle Tennessee, about forty miles south of Nashville.
Today the area is known as a center of the Tennessee Walking Horse indus-
try, but in the decades after the Civil War it was home to a sizable community
of former slaves, many of whom had come into the area from Mississippi
after the war. A Bedford County landowner and well-to-do former member of
the Andrew Johnson administration began selling small farms to freedmen,
letting them pay off the land in installments; Talley discusses this in the introduction to his story "Why White Overseers of Negro Slaves Had Little Sense."
Two of the land buyers were Charles Washington and Lucinda Talley, the
parents of Thomas Talley, former slaves from Mississippi who bought one
hundred acres shortly after the war. Many of their relatives bought adjoining
farms, and soon they had started their family. Thomas, born in 1870, would
be one of nine children.

Young Thomas Talley grew up in this rich, rural culture, and while
there were bad times—he had to help his father and uncle fight off the
"Night Riders," terrorists who rode through the night trying to frighten off
the new black settlers—there were many good ones: play-parties, husking
bees, church singings, dances. By 1882 Talley had completed six years of
public school, and a few years later he had made his way to Fisk, where he
attended high school and then college and where he began singing with
the Jubilee Singers. By 1890 he had graduated and was back in Shelbyville
teaching in the public school system. After he began work on his M.A., he
left the Middle Tennessee area for a series of jobs at various black colleges
around the South (Alcorn, Florida A&M, Tuskegee) before returning to Fisk
to teach in 1905. He eventually became a senior professor in chemistry and
science, though he maintained his interest in music and folklore and worked
with other Fisk scholars in this area, such as John Work II and William
Faulkner, the noted storyteller (not the novelist). Talley eventually would
retire from teaching around 1942 and would die on July 14, 1952. A fuller
account of his life can be found in the "Introduction to the New Edition" of
Negro Folk Rhymes (Knoxville: University of Tennessee Press, 1991), x–xiv.

Throughout the "Origins" manuscript, Talley describes some of his
prime informants, many of them former slaves whose memories reached
back well before the Civil War. He remembers talking about all kinds of
things, from water witching to seining for fish in the Duck River, but he
especially recalls discussions of language. At one point he notes:

When I as a small boy began at school to study English grammar, and as
I began to use the purer form of English, I was very many times told by
the old ex-slaves, as they listened to my more correct expressions, how

the children of their childhood days expressed themselves. Besides this, I was often told of how one of my great-grandparents, Uncle Harry, a native African (who always declared that Harry wasn't his name) who spoke English of such a broken nature that few could understand him.

Such memories doubtless led Talley to take great pains to reproduce the rural dialect of his childhood and to include in his narratives dozens of details about customs, superstitions, work styles, and family life of nineteenth-century black rural culture.

Talley's personal participation in this tradition also led him to use a methodology different from that of later collectors. With his *Negro Folk Rhymes,* he actively went around soliciting songs and poems, much in the manner of better-known later collectors like Cecil Sharp or John Lomax. In some cases, though, he added to his collection a song he remembered first-hand, and he often illustrated his analyses with personal observations drawn from his travels and youth. With *The Negro Traditions,* however, he did this even more; according to his daughter, Thomasina Talley Greene, he often relied on "stories told to him by his parents or relatives when he was a little boy." In fact, in front of the original "Negro Traditions" manuscript, Talley carefully placed a baby picture of himself, with a caption that read: "One of the Negro children at the age of fourteen months, who listened to the Negro Traditions and in later life had the pleasure of recording them." Thus, rather than a series of transcribed "texts" collected from specific informants, we have in *The Negro Traditions* a set of narratives dating back to the decade 1870–80, taken from rural southern blacks barely a decade removed from slavery—but filtered through the memory and imagination of a fifty-two-year-old college professor who had earned a doctorate at Meharry Medical College and done two summers of postgraduate work at Harvard. What results is the phenomenon of a keen and perceptive intelligence confronting the complex and little-known wellsprings of its own cultural background.

Just as he was a gifted and accomplished musician whose interests ran from Mozart to fiddle tunes, Talley in these stories reveals himself as a skillful, subtle, and innovative writer. Even setting aside the folkloric value of his tales, Talley's manner of presenting and grouping them—as we shall see—reflects both design and structure. Many of his lengthy stories are in fact mixtures of several individual folktales or motifs; all are dramatized with dialogue and local color; and all are surrounded by frame stories. Talley was quite familiar with the works of Joel Chandler Harris—he often refers to him in the "Origins" manuscript—and seems to feel that Harris was his only real predecessor in recounting traditional narratives. In a portion of the "Origins" that was later published in *Phylon* (cf. below), Talley says:

Those who have troubled themselves to know of Negro folk productions, after reading *Nights with Uncle Remus* by Joel Chandler

Harris, will possibly wonder how it happens that I was able at this late date to offer a new collection of Negro folk-lore—entirely passed over by him. The explanation is quite simple: the "Brer Rabbit" stories of Mr. Harris were looked upon by Negroes with few exceptions as fiction pure and simple.

The Negro folk-lore accounts which I have recorded, on the contrary, were looked upon by the large common masses of Negroes as a sort of half and half admixture of fact and fiction. Though very different from the old Greek and Roman stories concerning their gods, they stood in semi-relation to the Negro mind as those old myths stood to the Greek and Roman mind. . . . When Mr. Harris therefore asked ante-bellum American Negroes for stories, he got their stories. He received very, very few of their traditions; and he received these in a very fragmentary way.

"The real Negro traditions," according to Talley, were never told "as a source of amusement pure and simple." When a group of people gathered to visit and exchange experiences, and when somebody described a "mysterious experience" or "some phenomenon queer" to him, it was then that a Negro tradition was brought forth "either as a reminiscence or as something calculated to furnish a theory in explanation of the matter under discussion."

Throughout his manuscript "The Origin of Traditions," Talley offers analysis along these lines for many of his stories. When a reader encounters "Why the Buzzard Is Black," for instance, "he mysteriously walks the paths of the ridiculous from the beginning to the end." But later, upon considering the idea that the snake could paint his body with spots, "he is struck with the possibility . . . that, since very young buzzards are of a light, grey color, there are biological laws holding out the possibility that the primeval buzzard might have been of a very light color." Snakes themselves, he suggests, have acquired their spots as a form of "protective mimicry," and primitive man might have seen snakes evolve to this state—and might have preserved this memory as a sort of etiological legend that gave birth to this story. The thing that impresses Talley about "Cotton-Eyed Joe" is the scene where the main character hollows out the trunk of a tree to serve as a coffin for his child. Talley links this to a discovery, in Alabama, of a Bronze Age gravesite that featured similar "dugout" coffins. Points like this abound in the "Origins" manuscript, which seems to be predicated on Talley's idea that, though the Negro traditions were "unique and characteristic in themselves," they could be used as a "basis of a general study of all traditions," from cultures around the world. Titles of chapters in the "Origins" manuscript include subjects like "The Tradition of Animated Mother Earth," "The Tradition of Creation," "The Tradition of the Flood," and "The Tradition of Animals with Multiple Parts." Modern readers might quarrel with Talley's own assessment of what he has done, but no one can quarrel with his assumption that the "traditions" were more than the charming entertainments Harris saw them as. Indeed, Talley's 1923 definition of "tradition" is remarkably modern: tradition is "whatever has been handed down by word or mouth, and was, at one time, conceived to be either a whole or part truth."

Talley also defended his method of retelling and combining tales, and enriching them with superstitions, customs, songs, and beliefs. "I spent the first years of my life," he reminds us, "among people who told to each other their traditions and who also formulated traditions." When rural blacks told each other a given tradition, "the general plot remained constant; but it was common for an individual to vary portions of the narrative to fit in with other traditions which he might have picked up here and there." The various versions of a particular tradition, therefore, could be compared to "revised editions of school text books." Individual tellers, "while keeping largely to the old, endeavored to so incorporate the new as to make it fit in with whatever might seem more reasonable."

One of Talley's most "literary" devices is his use of a frame story surrounding each tale; sometimes these frame stories are quite lengthy, and, unlike the tales themselves, are always couched in standard English. In his "Origins" manuscript, Talley even defends the authenticity of this age-old practice:

> I have endeavored in recording "Negro Traditions," in this volume, to write such little introductions to each account as would show the conditions under which they usually came to light. But the scenes found there are not imaginary; they are actually among those witnessed by the writer as a child. (I:6)

And, indeed, as he sets his tale through these introductions, Talley mentions dozens of accurate place names from Bedford County in the nineteenth century: Horse Mountain, a few miles east of Shelbyville; Caldwell and the thicket named "Haircane" southeast of Shelbyville; Garrison Fork Creek in the east end of the county; the Duck River, which runs throughout the region; and Ebo, a whistlestop on the old Shelbyville–Tennessee branch railroad. He describes a corn shucking, a group of reapers working with archaic wheat cradles, a play party, a country dance, and other details of rural life.

A Textual Observation
Laura C. Jarmon

Each frame tale contributes a discursive context, manifest in the treatment of such elements as narrative situation, performance occasion, folk motifs, and mimetic idiom. This approach allows Talley to represent the black folktale—tradition—as a dynamic structure in African-American folk culture.

For Talley, narrative situation yields a cohesive context of discourse that enables the tale to function on behalf of its community of users. Like early collectors of African-American folk narratives, Talley employs the frame narrative device; unlike them, however, he uses the frame to link the internal tale and the community, establishing the teller and his audience as members of a cohesive unit subscribing to the internal tale's world view. The cohesion derives from Talley's projection of a narrative in which a black speaker addresses a black audience. Such a homogeneous situation renders a speaker free to express openly attitudes particular to the group itself—casting as superfluous any beliefs extrinsic to the group while affirming beliefs intrinsic to the black folk metaphysic. Freedom of this sort also enables a Talley narrator to draw upon esoteric assumptions and vivify participants performing actions and uttering opinions consistent with a world view that is familiar and normative for both the narrator and his audience. Talley's narrative strategy therefore indulges the functional potential of a tale by compelling cognitive interplay between the internal tale event and the audience's belief system.

This agentive power of the black folktale is insubstantial in the works of such early collectors as Joel Chandler Harris and Charles Waddell Chesnutt: Remus and Julius address white audiences within the frame. Furthermore, these early works were presented to a predominantly white readership. Both audience and readership inhibited the black narrator's creative impulse, in turn, taking a reductionist toll on the tale's capacity to reflect its intrinsic relationship to the African-American folk community. Harris's stories miss the vast repertoire of serious works, "traditions" that Talley establishes in two groups: "historic traditions" functioning as highly conceptual oral records of the past; and "theory traditions" functioning etiologically ("Origin" II:33). Unlike "stories," Talley explains, the traditions "were practically never told by these people as a source of amusement pure and simple" ("Origin" I:373). Moreover, Harris and his fellow collectors were quite unlikely to gain access to the serious works. In the preface to "Why the Irishman Is a Railroad Section Boss," Talley explains of Harris's informants: "They did not tell him all of the story; because no ex-slave at that time was so foolish as to run the risk of incurring the ill will of a white man by going through with a story in which one of that race was held up to ridicule. . . ." Clearly, Talley's other fifteen tales also employ the African-American world view and minimize the opposing stance. Talley's narratives respond to the theoretical shortcomings of works by early collectors.

Talley's response is of vast import for the black folktale as a dynamic communal structure. Talley was the offspring of newly freed slaves and in this respect not much unlike the informants of early collectors. Yet Talley stood in a unique position not only to participate in the cultural milieu that fostered such tales but also to realize their value and reveal it by preserving

xiii / EDITORS' INTRODUCTION

the form as an entity essentially comprised of discursive context, internal tale, and cultural agency. Despite its omission of serious black folk narratives, Harris's work is nonetheless paradigmatic. Along with its successors, it obfuscates the autonomous function of the black folktale as a communal structure, at once purporting the black folktale canon as more or less marginally related to African-American folk culture. By offering his "historic" and "theory" traditions, Talley adds to the existing canon a comprehensiveness and cultural relevancy that other collectors apparently could not give. Talley's attention to narrative situation regains for the black folktale the cohesive context necessary to the structure's function.

Along with the restoration of a cohesive narrative situation, Talley emphasizes the importance of performance occasion, for he establishes the tale as a property of specific occasions appropriate to the narrative performance as an event. These two elements of discursive context establish for the black folktale form an identifiable group of users and a definitive occasion for use. The occasion for use may be either public or private, as illustrated in "How Brer Bar Lost His Judgeship," a theory tradition, and "Riddle Them Right," a historic tradition.

"How Brer Bar Lost His Judgeship" is a lengthy narration the internal tale of which is presented by a fifteen-year-old boy who received it from an older relative. The tale is set in mythic time, "When de sun and moon was married" and enmity arose between them. The tale as a whole does not occur in any well-known collection, yet it is comprised of a wealth of well-known beliefs and superstitions along with several well-known motifs, including the mother's song imitated. One of the central episodes of the internal tale establishes performance occasion as fundamental to the black folk narrative as a dynamic structure. In the episode, Brer Bar has rid the community of Brer Snake's tyranny, and the community honors him with a candy-pulling party. This party is a formal affair including formal dress, dining, music, dance, oration, resolutions, and installation of office: "Dey pulled de candy an' cracked jokes an' tol' tales an' e't ontel dey was almos' ready to pop." Important is the fact that a candy-pulling party is an affair capable of serious import, for on this occasion Brer Bar is installed as "Jedge Bar," the highest office in the community; this occasion is also one appropriate to narrative performance as an event. Several days after his installation, moreover, Jedge Bar undertakes responsibility for tending the community's children, for which service he achieves unlimited praise, and the citizens "ax him out to all de big Barbecues, de big Barn'-Dances, de big Plays, de big Candy-Pullins, de big Sprise Parties, de big Pound Parties, de big Suppers, de big Cake Walks, de big Co'n Shuckins, de big House Raisins, de big Watermillion Feasts, de big Jamborees, an' de big Hullabaloos." These invitations catalog occasions appropriate to narrative performance, and, clearly, the qualifier, *big,* establishes these occasions as both important and public.

"Riddle them Right" specifies not only public occasions but private ones as well. The frame presents a father who reunites with his family after Emancipation and desires most of all to engage them in his favorite pastime, riddling. The frame includes—sequentially—supper, songs, games, riddles, and the pseudo-request for the internal tale as the mother questions the origin of riddles; this family gathering delineates a private occasion for narrative performance. Furthermore, within the internal tale appear thematically related occasions for narrative performance, including use of the riddle as a narrative event to win freedom from slavery, to identify a suitor or win a bride, and to save one's life. As well, there occur riddles of performance, as in the lucky shot, the dumb supper, and the riddle of self-incrimination. The riddling events comprise incidents and episodes arising as narrative performances occasioned by need and operating to make up the tale as a whole. Talley thereby emphasizes the direct relationship between the folktale and the performance occasion, for the occasion calls forth the tale as a tool responsive to a public or private need that is quite frequently more serious than entertaining. Thus performance occasion provides for the black folk narrative a recognizable place in the culture, giving it a boundary within which to function and at once setting up an expectation that such a place be occupied.

As a further operative of discursive context, Talley presents folk motifs as integral to the dynamic role of the black folktale. These motifs are treated exegetically: they respond directly to mysteries within the culture itself. Such causal employment of motifs opposes the much more anecdotal treatment common to other collections. This much is evident, for example, in Talley's only marchen, "The Devil's Daughters or Why the Fish have Fins," a tale type common to European and African-American folklore (Aarne-Thompson type 313; Thompson motif H335.0.1). Talley's use of Jack as Trickster and the Jack and the Devil motif is far and away more comprehensive and culturally relevant than the treatments of Zora Neale Hurston (1935), Julius Lester (1969), Roger Abrahams (1985), and Richard Dorson (1967), treatments that reveal only the merest connection between the tale and its community of users.

Talley's use of the Jack and the Devil motif renders the narrative dynamic in folk culture. Not only is the tale presented as explanatory, but also the frame predisposes the audience to view the tale as moralistic and establishes a cohesive narrative situation the overall tenor of which is cautionary. The performance occasion, furthermore, is dominated by the group's need to arrive at a fully sanctioned interpretation of cosmic phenomena. While the frame presents two generations of men, one older and one younger, who disagree on the meaning of a natural event, the internal tale argues that the older generation's interpretation of the event represents the appropriate cultural world view, and, as such, has the aim of persuading the younger generation toward acceptance of this view. Drama arises from tension between these two generations and their viewpoints.

The frame foregrounds the narrative's emphasis upon the behavior and world view appropriate to the group as a whole. As the narrative begins, a number of male African-American farmers take their dinner, their noon meal, in the field and witness an instance of cosmic ambiguity: it rains while the sun shines. The principal narrator, Uncle Jake, a member of the older generation, remarks on this event by attributing to it the typical folk interpretation that the devil is beating his wife. Jake admonishes the devil: "You Tobe! You stop dat 'ar whuppin' o' Dinah!" Jake's interpretation is immediately challenged by a member of the younger generation, Sib, who states, "Oh come off, Uncle Jake," and asks, "W'ats dis you's a tryin' fer to give us anyhows?" Sib's response denies Jake's knowledge, his veracity, and, ultimately, his belief system. Jake, however, is not alone, for with him are the other members of his generation, as represented by Uncle Harry Ledbetter, for example. Thus Talley establishes between the two generations a conflict of beliefs, one in which the older men employ the etiological internal tale to teach the younger generation principles of their culture's belief system. The conflict becomes highly dramatic when Jake grows irate at the young men's skepticism and insults them, equating them with backwoods Aunt Jemimas and thereby implying their ignorance of cultural views. Jake's insult motivates his generational peers to caution him about his behavior: "Oh you needn' cut setch a hobbin' dash 'bout w'at you knows; caze we knows all 'bout dat too!" While the older generation corrects Jake's behavior, they also affirm his interpretation as a communal norm. Jake responds humbly by offering to drop the subject and is met with the young generation's plea that he deliver the tale and the older generation's approval to do so; however, Ledbetter explains the need for group harmony and cohesion: "We uns jes helt you up a liddle; caze we didn' want no 'Ole Man Know-Alls' around here eatin' wid us." The narrative situation thus presents a black narrator addressing a black audience, but it dramatizes the folktale's regulatory function by revealing that within the black group it is necessary for individuals to observe behavioral codes and respect the communal viewpoint.

Jake's use of the Jack and the Devil motif represents an expansive treatment. Where Hurston, Abrahams, and Dorson have Jack complete two tasks and Lester has him complete three, Jake has him complete seven, two of which do not appear among well-known black collections: uprooting a spring to give the devil a drink, and choosing the hand and body of his fiancée concealed among those of dead women. In addition, although it is common for Jack to succeed aided by the devil's daughter, other black collections do not reveal that the daughter learns her magic with the help of her mother—such betrayal is why the devil beats his wife. It is also not revealed in these collections that Jack and his wife escape the devil by transforming to "mare-maids" and entering the sea—the fish have fins because the daughter, Prissy, is a more powerful magician than the devil and conjures fish to move between themselves and the devil's imps, who perpetually fling at the couple hatchets that lodge in the fish. In addition, although Hurston, Lester, and Abrahams initiate their tales with Jack's gambling and losing to the devil, they do not reveal any motivation for the devil's effort to kill Jack and his wife, whereas Jake employs the gambling episode as motivation for the devil's attempt, as Prissy's magic enables Jack to win against him. Jake also expands action and elaborates personality; he characterizes the devil, for example, by unfailingly referring to him "wid his hawns an' hoofs and snaggle toofs." In addition, Jake emphasizes Jack's success as deriving from his ability to heed to the letter Prissy's directives, and he shows that Prissy ensures her own success by incantation and formulaic action.

Talley's elaboration of black folktale motifs thus extends from the frame through the internal tale itself, in each case revealing the motif as arising in service to the tale rather than standing as the tale itself. Absent a cohesive narrative situation and specific performance occasion, the tale is isolated from both its discursive context and its communal function and thereby rendered dispassionate. When, furthermore, the motifs are unmotivated and just as detached from their cultural milieu, they reduce to static forms more anecdotal than otherwise. The elaborate breadth of tasks, the strict conditions for their successful completion, and the etiological relevance of their outcomes enhance their capacity to regulate culture. Prissy's magic, for example, connotes attitudes toward cultural norms because, although Prissy is a more powerful conjurer than the devil, Prissy and Jack successfully escape him, implying that conjure is a culturally sanctioned practice while bargaining, gambling, and partying with the devil are condemned—Jack's winning at gambling with the devil motivates the devil to attempt to kill them. Moreover, Jack's successful completion of his impossible tasks and their later escape depend upon his faith and forbearance. Talley thereby employs the motifs as indicators of cultural norms of behavior and perception.

Also important to discursive context is Talley's use of mimetic idiom, which particularizes character and reifies action. Such expression lends realism to the narratives, naturalizing them in African-American folk culture. When, for example, Jake feels insulted and offers to drop his tale, he does so in a highly efficient manner:

> I draws in my water-tarrapin head whar deres so many axes in de air
> a lookin' down fer de neck; caze w'en de poo' tarrapin leave his head
> out whar deres sharp folkses, his head mos' in generally drap off an'

he set in de plate at de dinner table! W'en it comes to dat 'ar part of
de progrance; I wants to set in de chair. I draps it all!

Clearly metaphorical, Jake's response is multidimensional: he proffers humility, he insinuates derision, and he threatens. Equating himself with the
"poo' tarrapin," he humbly accepts the terrapin's passivity and garners sym-
pathy. However, his acceptance is only partial, for he ambiguates the phrase
"sharp folkses" and then rejects the terrapin's refusal of volition. By assuming the phrase "sharp folkses" as a metaphoric reference to "axes in de air,"
Jake defuses any potential for the phrase to refer otherwise. Yet given the
broader context of intelligence wherein he has been chastised as an "Ole
Man Know-All," the phrase can easily refer to his critics, in which case he
derides them by insinuating they may not know as much as they think they
do. Furthermore, in proximity to the terrapin as the target of "so many axes
in de air a lookin' down fer de neck," Jake refuses the role of target; rather
than succumb to the terrapin's fate, he rejects the equation of man and
terrapin, instead commanding his power to choose. He refuses to be baited
and manipulated into participating in his own emasculation. Jake therefore
employs folk expression as an efficient means not only of appeasing the
group with his apparent humility but also of successfully returning insult
for insult and compounding his success by threatening to withhold his narrative. Such folk expression mirrors the verbal indirection of group dynam-
ics, showing at once particularities of Jake's personality and standing in the
community and the efficiency with which an esoteric reference system can
overcome disparity.

Jake's metaphor illustrates the power of mimetic idiom as a source of
discursive context. As may be observed, however, such verbal expression
is itself composed of linguistic forms contributing realism, most notably in
the form of dialect. Any reference to dialect relative to the black folk narrative immediately draws attention to the use of orthography as a phonetic
device, a practice long under fire for its subjectivity and invalidity as a scientific process. One wonders, for example, about any purported difference
between the pronunciation of *generally* and *ginerally*. A seemingly arbi-
trary rendering of this sort strengthens charges that dialect spelling tech-
niques lead to unnecessary corruptions, unmotivated exaggerations, and
demeaning images. On the other hand, orthography can effectively delin-
eate speech characteristics. Talley, one notices, employs initial and terminal
elision, as in *'splain* for *explain* and *lookin'* for *looking*. He also employs *d*
substitution for *th* initial, medial, and terminal, as in *dat* for *that,* *brudder*
for *brother,* and *wid* for *with*. Usages of this sort are accurate for many
speakers in the African-American folk community.

Along with such phonetic devices, Talley also presents nonstandard
grammatical forms such as result from indiscriminate pronoun reference,

variable and indiscriminate verb combination and tense marking, word coinages, and malapropisms. He employs word omission that affects syntax, particularly relative to verb tense and phrasal connectives; remarkably, though, such omission is often compensated for by parallelism, antithesis, lexical repetition, and/or redundancy of action and modification. He also uses doubling and redundancy for purposes of intensification, as with the double subject, double negative, or double demonstrative. These dialect features reinforce the reflective power of the mimetic idioms, which are far more telling than what is generally referenced by the label dialect.

Talley invigorates his narratives through other linguistic forms, all contributing to dynamism. The animals come alive through ideophones, and, along with humans, they employ rhymes, songs, riddles, proverbs, incantation, formulaic repetition, chanted prayer and sermon, and all manner of sound to reify their personalities, opinions, and reactions. Throughout, animals imitate human sense and sound, and humans imitate animal behavior, particularly the survival instinct and egoism that motivate much of the violence in the works, albeit such violence accords with natural behavior and thereby achieves distance and objectivity enough to appear less flagrant than coincidental.

Withal, the works in Talley's collection give substantive voice to the African-American folk community: they emerge from the memories of particularized speakers who provide information establishing a normative world view. By granting the narratives the cultural particularities of narrative situation, performance occasion, causal motifs, and mimetic idiom, Talley restores the African-American folktale to its natural habitat and function.

A Note on the Manuscript
❄

Talley's original typescript of *The Negro Traditions,* now in the Special Collections of the Fisk University Library, was completed in early 1923. He apparently worked on his parallel study, "The Origins of the Negro Traditions," at about the same time, for there are references to the latter in some of the introductions to the stories in the *Traditions.* The unpublished manuscript contains numerous references to and interpretations of some of the stories in the *Traditions,* as well as the texts of two further stories, "Why the Negro Is Black" and "The End of Brer Rabbit," both offered as foils to versions by Harris. We have decided, however, not to include these stories in *The Negro Traditions,* as there was no evidence that Talley intended them to be there. Later studies will have to explore in more detail the full nature of the "Origins" manuscript, and its relation to Talley's other work. The "Origins" itself consists of 286 pages of single-spaced type. The first sixteen pages of the "Origins" manuscript were published as "The Origin of Negro Traditions" in *Phylon* (4th quarter, 1942: 371–77, and 1st quarter, 1943: 30–38); the original "Origins" manuscript is also at Fisk.

Talley tried to get his second book published shortly after the manuscript was finished, but for some reason he met a cold reception. In the late 1920s, Talley's own life became much more hectic as he served as a delegate to conferences of black educators and began to work on an advanced degree in chemistry at the University of Chicago. By then, the Depression had hit, and few publishers had money to spend on such a large collection of African-American folklore. After his retirement in the early 1940s, Talley made further attempts to generate interest in the book and prepared his articles for *Phylon.* Nothing came of this either, though, and by the time Talley died in 1952, the manuscript had been all but forgotten. In September 1955, the *Tennessee Folklore Society Bulletin* published "De Wull-er-de-Wust" with a note saying that the story had been found "among Talley's papers after his death." It would be the only one of the stories in *The Negro Traditions* to see print before this collection.

In the 1970s, Talley's daughter Thomasina, along with her husband, the distinguished civil rights leader Dr. Lorenzo J. Greene, rediscovered the manuscript, recognized its significance, and began to try again to get it published. They began working with Gerald L. Davis, then at Rutgers, who also saw the importance of Talley's work and his career, and began work on a biography of him. Davis also began contacting university presses about publishing the manuscript, but again things stalled. Mrs. Greene recalled that some university presses seemed nervous over Talley's use of the heavy dialect in the tales.

Then in 1989, as work was underway for a new edition of Talley's *Negro Folk Rhymes,* and in the course of correspondence about the contracts for the book, Mrs. Greene brought up the "Negro Traditions" manuscript in a letter to Carol Orr, then director of the University of Tennessee Press. Would the press, she asked, be interested in looking at this manuscript as a possible companion volume to *Negro Folk Rhymes?* She soon sent a copy of the manuscript along, and work was soon underway.

As editors, we have been very conservative about changing any of Talley's unusual spelling or phonetics. In an early version of the manuscript, the story "The Negro Slave in the Moon" was unaccountably missing. It appeared in Talley's original typescript of the book, however, so we have restored it to this edition, assuming that he wanted to include it.

There are many other issues about Talley's work that need to be investigated, but our intent here has been merely to get into print this important collection. We offer as apparatus a list of motifs for the stories, as well as a bibliography of African-American traditional narrative, as a starting point for further research. Through such efforts, we hope that Thomas W. Talley can gain some of the recognition due him as one of the country's pioneer scholars of African-American culture.

Charles K. Wolfe
Middle Tennessee State University

Laura C. Jarmon
Middle Tennessee State University

ACKNOWLEDGMENTS

❄

This book would not have been possible without the help and advice of many people. Our greatest debt is to Thomasina Talley Greene for her support and encouragement throughout, and to her son, Lorenzo Thomas Greene, for helping us with inquiries and for making available the Talley manuscripts. We are also grateful to Ann Allen Shockley and Beth Howse at the Fisk University Library Special Collections for their assistance in examining the Talley files and manuscripts. We are grateful to Gerald Davis for sharing his insights and memories about Talley's career. For various encouragements and advice, we also must thank Paul Ritscher, John Hartford, Ralph Hyde, William Griffith, W. K. McNeill, Roby Cogswell, Michael Lofaro, Kip Lornell, Dick Hulan, Vannoy Streeter, Mrs. Fay Bradford, Stephen Wade, Maurine Bronaugh, Gwendolyn Watson, and Leon and Annie Jarmon. Our colleagues and administrators at Middle Tennessee State University were, as ever, supportive. Grants from the Faculty Research Committee, the Gieir Desegregation Fund, and the Faculty Development Fund helped us complete the research for the book. We also would like to thank Mary Dean Wolfe for helping us work through a vast amount of Talley material. Last, but not least, our gratitude goes to Carol Orr, former director, and Meredith Morgan, acquisitions editor of the University of Tennessee Press, for their interest in and support of this endeavor.

CKW & LCJ

THE
NEGRO
TRADITIONS
❄

PREFACE
BY THOMAS TALLEY

It will not be very easy for the general reader to discover the line of demarcation between the Negro Tradition and the ordinary Negro story. The entire difference cannot be stated in a few words. The Traditions, however, are something altogether different from the stories.

Of course, the more intelligent ex-slaves of America placed no credence in the thought content of these Traditions, but the quaint ideas, embalmed, in their narratives, express more or less the peculiar inherited beliefs of the more primitive American Negro ex-slaves.

The little settings given to the individual Traditions are the writer's own handiwork, but the Traditions themselves are the products of the Negro masses and their ancestors. Even the settings are those taken from real Negro life, as the writer witnessed them in his very early childhood days. Thus he is little more than a machine which has registered them that the world may read.

In recording them I have made no attempt at an elegance of literary expression. I felt that, in the years to come, a true record of the language used by those who handed down the Traditions would be of more value. Thus I have recorded them in the language of the American ex-slave. There will not be found in the record therefore any continuously constant characteristic literary style such as is found in most books. The ex-slaves who were picking up their English expressions as best they could did not express themselves systematically. Thus the same individual might speak almost grammatically one moment (other than such as leaving out consonants of words if they were at all harsh sounding) and in the next breath depart from every semblance of good English.

May I be permitted to state that I realize that there are certain terms found in the record such as "Nigger," "Cracker" etc., which are objectionable to us of today. I regret this. But in order to truthfully reproduce the Traditions I had to use the terms, and I know that all will agree that the world ought [to] have the truth.

It is impossible for one who was not born and reared in the midst of the Traditions, and who in addition to this has not carefully thought them through, to understand their deeper import and meaning. All may, however, enjoy their quaint humor and weird pathos, even as have "many thousands gone before". Because of this difficulty in understanding the inner meaning of the Negro Tradition in particular and of Traditions in general, I have written a companion treatise on "THE ORIGIN OF TRADITIONS" and have issued it in another volume, so that those who may wish can know the causes which moved the human mind to formulate them.

I herewith have the pleasure to present to the public the first collection, as such, of the Traditions which had come down to the American ex-slave as a part of his general inheritances from the dim and distant past.

DE WULL-ER-DE-WUST (WILL O' THE WISP)

❄

Near Shelbyville, Tennessee, about a half century ago, a little Negro boy, Henry Hill, had a mother, Betty Hill, who lived alone with him in a one-room cabin in the back yard of a white family to which she had belonged in the days of American slavery. Both the mother and her son associated very little with the other Negroes of the community. Thus when Henry went to attend the Mt. Zion public school, his eyes were opened to a new world.

He had never seen so many books in all of his life, and had never conceived of so large a number of black boys and girls who could read and write. He therefore sat there, on that (his) first day of school, in wonder and amazement.

The teacher took little Henry and gave him a lesson on the alphabet, printed on a large chart which hung on a nail driven into an unhewn log of the cabin's wall. She then left him to study, while she called and gave instruction to her advanced classes.

As class after class was called, Henry was so busy listening to the various recitations, that he studied very little. Finally the teacher called her most advanced pupils for a recitation in Geography. The lesson was on Africa. The teacher told her pupils many things concerning that far away land inhabited almost entirely by Negroes.

Little Henry sat and listened. He had never heard that there was any country in the world other than the one in which he lived. He forgot that there was any such thing as an alphabet to be learned, as he listened to seemingly fairy-like accounts of orange groves, coconut palms, bread trees, naked cannibals, etc.

That afternoon, when he reached home, his mother asked: "Well, Henry, w'at did you l'arn in dat 'ar school to-day? Come, tell mammy; caze she know dat you was done gone an' l'arnt some o' dem A,B,C's."

"Yas, Mammy," said Henry, "I's said all de letters over atter de teacher; an' I thinks, if I keeps on a gwine an' a sayin' de A,B,C's over atter her, I'll git so I can say 'em by myse'f fer a big speech lak dat one w'at we heard Marse Aleck make w'en he took us wid him an' Miss Lizzie down to whar de white folks was a havin' dat big Barbecue. But, mammy," continued Henry, almost breathless from excitement, "I heared dat teacher a tellin' dem tother chilluns de cu'iousest thing you's ever hearn tell of! She say dere was a place somewhars called Affiky, an' nobody dont live dar scacely 'cep' Niggers. She tell de chilluns dat some o' de Niggers over dar was reg'lar "cannonballs;" an' dey calls 'em dat caze dey kills an' eats up people. Mammy, is dere setch a thing as "cannon-ball" Niggers w'at eats one-nudder up or was dat teacher jes a jokin'?"

"Well, Sonny," answered the mother, "dat teacher is so young dat she never did git wid de folkses w'at knowed. I haint never heared dat dere be's Niggers now w'at eats up people an' was got de name of "cannon-balls." My gran'mammy tol' me w'en I was a liddle gal 'bout dem kind of Niggers w'at e't up folkses; but she call 'em "outlandish folks-eaters." W'en she tol' me 'bout 'em, she say dey was all been turned into "Wull-er-de-wusses"; so if dat teacher think dat dey was still now a livin, she's done gone an' git it all wrong. You sees, Sonny, dat teacher is jes natchully too young to a got wid de folkses w'at knowed 'bout de "outlandish folks-eaters"; so she dont know dey was all been turned into "Wull-er-de-wusses" a long time befo' de folks not a livin' was bo'n.

W'en yo' teacher call 'em "cannon-balls", she was a talkin' "Quality talk". I useter hear some o' de big white folks call 'em dat sometimes. I dont know zackly how dey comes to call 'em "cannon-balls", onless it's caze cannon balls kills folks, an' beance dese here Niggers kilt folks dey called dem "cannon-balls" too.

Henry sat for a while pondering over this unexpected learning displayed by his mother; then he addressed her thus: "Mammy, it'll be a long time befo' I git to studyin' Jography; an' dat teacher'll want me to wait ontel I gits to it, befo' I axes her 'bout dem sort of things. Den, you sees, dat she dont know 'bout dis lak you does; an' I wish dat you'd tell me 'bout dese here "cannon-balls" or "outlandish folks-eaters" or "w'atsomever dey is."

"Henry", replied the mother, "folks says 'please ma'ma'w'en dey wants sumpin an' is spectin to get it. I thinks dat you'd better sorter pick up yo' manners, Honey!"

"Yassum, mammy! scuse me!" said Henry. "Please ma'am tell me 'bout it."

"Now dat's sorter lak it!" replied the mother, "I was a 'ginnin' to git skeared dat you was a losin' some o' yo' trainin' by segashuatin wid dem 'ar co'n-fiel' Niggers at de school, today.

Set down over dar, I haint got nothin' to do now fer a while; an' I'll sorter roll 'roun' in my membunce an' see if I caint fetch out de ole into de new.

Away back yon'er one time, de white folks useter go away off somewhars to whar a heaps of Niggers was. (I specks dat it mought a been some place lak dat w'at yo' teacher was a talkin' 'bout.) Dey cotched dese Niggers an' tied 'em an' brung 'em on home wid 'em to sell.

Granny say dat dere wus one pack o' Niggers, over dar whar dey go, w'at e't one-nudder up; an' de "bull tongue" white folks (said the mother, who had heard the expression "bon ton") didn' ketch an' didn' want none o' dem kind o' Niggers.

Well, de nice big white folks went on a ketchin' de nice Niggers, lak we is; ontel, atter while, dey git scace an' hard to git.

Dere was in dem times a ole poo' white buckra cracker, w'at wus too poo' to buy Niggers. He wuked a long time as a overseer; ontel he git 'nough togedder to buy hisself a ole poo' run-down plantation.

W'en he git de plantation; he was too lazy to wuk it, an' he was too poo' to buy Niggers to wuk it fer 'im. W'en he go to settle on it; he take his wife an' his liddle gal, Phoebee, wid 'im.

As de winter come on an' dere wusnt much wuk to be done; he leave his wife an' chile an' go on off to ketch some Niggers fer his plantation. He go away off somewhars over dar whar de Niggers useter live befo' dey was brung 'em all over here.

W'en he git over dar he meet up wid some white mens w'at was out a Nigger huntin' too. Dese here mens tells him dat dere haint no use a gwine a huntin' single-handed; caze, if he do, dem 'ar outlandish folks-eaters'll ketch 'im an' make hash outn 'im.

Den he axes dese here white mens to let him go cahoots an' hunt wid dem dividin' up de game fa'r an' squar' 'twixt an' 'tween 'em. But dese here mens tells him dat de game is a gittin so scace dat dey was skeared dat dey wont git 'nough to go 'roun if dey takes any mo' in de party.

To make deir words good 'bout dere bein' "outlandish folks-eaters"; dey called in a dozen or so of 'em w'at dey wus done took, an' dey showed 'em to 'im. Dey tells 'im dat dey jes keeps dese out dar in de camp an' whups 'em an' makes 'em wait on 'em, whilst dey was a collectin' de good sort o' Niggers to sell. Dey dont try to sell dem "outlandish" Niggers.

He den axed dese here mens if dese here outlandish Niggers kilt an' e't one nudder right dar in de camp.

Dey tells him; No, dey was done broke 'em up from dat by whuppin 'em; but nobody wont buy 'em, so dey jes keeps 'em dar an' uses 'em.

Dis here white man say to de tothers dat dese here "broke" outlandish Niggers wus plenty good 'nough fer him. Den he offer to 'em dat he'll help 'em hunt "good" Niggers; an' w'en de huntin' season was over, he'll take de "broke" outlandish Niggers fer his pay an' take 'em home to his plantation. He put in; dat dey could ketch some mo' outlandish Niggers an' whup 'em in shape fer use instid of de ones he git fer his pay. Dey all tetch an' 'gree on dis.

Well, dey all hunts togedder ontel de end of de huntin season; den dey broke up. Dis here poo' buckra cracker den go home; an' take his "broke" outlandish Niggers along wid 'im.

W'en he git home, he stribit 'em 'roun to wuk on de place. All de Niggers was grown 'cep' one. Dat one was a liddle Nigger gal named Sissy. De grown up Niggers wus all done gone an' git setch cu'ious names

dat nobody caint 'member 'em. So dis here Hill-Billy Mosser an' Missus jes
call all de men-folks, "Daddy", an' all de women-folks, "Mammy".

Dere wusnt nothin t'eat out dar on dat ole poo' plantation; an' de
Niggers hafter all stay out togedder in a ole wore-out barn—dis, dey uses
fer a cabin. Dey had to hunt an' scrap aroun' fer a livin', sorter lak you's
seed de dogs do 'mongst dese here poo' Niggers w'at keep a house full of
'em. W'en dey 'ould ax deir Mosser fer sumpin t'eat; he'd cuss 'em an' give
'em some corn to parch, an' tell 'em to git out an' hunt up sumpin fer
deirselves.

Dey git out, dey do; an' dey kill an' eat dogs, an' lizards, an' grasshop-
pers, an' worms, an' cats, an' ev'rything—'cep 'dey wouldn' eat a black cat.
Dese here outlandish Niggers say dat a black cat wus got seben lives, an'
wus deir bes' frien'. Dey depend on de black cat to save 'em from trouble
in dis worl', an' to fix 'em up a sof'bed to sleep on in de nex' one. Befo'
dey wus at deir Mossers home no time; dere wusnt nothin lef' loose, a
runnin' aroun' dar 'cep' a right coal-black cat.

Befo de fust summer wus over wid, atter deir Mosser wus brung 'em
home; all dese Niggers wus clean gone, never to be seed no mo', 'cep'
one. Dat one wus de Big Black Witch Root Doctor 'mongst 'em. He stayed
an' lived aroun' in de worl', atter de tothers wus all gone, long 'nough to
tell de folks w'at wus become o' all dem w'at deir Mosser brung home wid
'im; den he put in his dispearunce. Dis wus de way it all come 'bout
'cordin' to w'at de Big Black Witch Root Doctor say befo' he wrop hisself
in de winds an' git so nobody caint see him no mo' neider; or as some
tells de loration; W'at he say whilst he wus on de way to his freedom:

De Mosser hisself dont have no nothin much to eat fer his self, an' his
wife, an' liddle gal. So, one day, he riz bright an' early; an' went out a
huntin'. He have powerful big luck' an' he kill an' bring home a whole
satchel-bag full of' squir'ls wid him.

W'en he git home, he call his Niggers; an' he tell 'em to take an' clean
'em an' cook 'em fer 'im.

Dey den axed him if he wouldn' please Sir give dem a liddle bight of
'em to eat; caze it look to 'em lak dey mought jes have a liddle tas'e,
beance dere wus so many of 'em.

He hand it out to de Niggers straight from de shoulder: No he haint a
gwineter do it. Dey can beil 'em done, take de meat offn de bones and
bring dat to him; den dey mought keep de bones an crack 'em open an'
git de morer outn 'em fer deirselves to eat. Den he show 'em his big bull-
whip an' tell 'em: If dey tetches dat meat, den w'at he'll lak a tetchin bofe
de meat an' de blood un'er deir hides won't be nothin.

Well:—De Niggers got some plates from 'im fer to put de game on
atter it git done; den dey took ev'ry-thing off wid 'em down to de old
Barn-cabin to clean an' cook an' fix up fer 'im.

Dey skint an' cleant de squir'ls. Den dey took de wash-kittle, wid legs on it; an' sot it on de big rock hearth which dey was put down un'er de shed. Dey put de squir'ls in de kittle, poured some water on 'em, throwed in a liddle salt, an' set 'em off a beilin'.

De squir'ls beiled away; an', w'en de good scent of de smokin' pot hit de Niggers in de nose, it make deir eyes jump an' deir moufs water. Deir right eyes jump; an', w'en deir right eyes jump, dey all say dat it 'twus bad luck-sign fer 'em all onless dey gits w'at dey wants right away. Dey all tetch an' 'gree dat de onliest way fer 'em to git w'at dey wants an' not to have de bad luck wus fer 'em all to take a liddle tas'e of dat 'ar squir'l. Dey thinks maybe dey can all take a liddle tas'e widout de Mosser a missin it.

So dey tas'es de squir'l. Honey; de good tas'e of dat 'ar squir'l almos' run 'em 'stracted! Dey all sot aroun' de beilin' pot a wushin; an' ev'ry time one would ketch all de tothers lookin off, he'd retch in wid a sharp stick an' take out a whole big piece o' squir'l, an' cram it in his mouf fer anudder tas'e. It keep on dis way—fust one a fo'kin out a tas'e an' den de tother—ontel, w'en de time come fer de squir'ls to be gittin done, dey was tas'ed all away! W'en dey all riz to dip de squir'ls outn de pot-licker an' put em on de plates; dey wus all gone.

Dey all den jes stood dar an' looked at one nudder. Nobody dont 'cuse nobody else; caze dey wus all skeared dat de tothers mought 'cuse dem. Den one o' de Niggers say to de tothers: "W'at's we gwineter do 'bout it?" an' de Big Black Witch Root Doctor make answer; "We caint do nothin onless Phoebee come!"

De tother Niggers ax him w'at he mean w'en he say: "We caint do nothin onless Phoebee come?"

He 'splain to 'em dat he mean: If dey can git hold o' Phoebee on de sly (Phoebee wus deir ole Mosser's gal); dey can cook her an 'sen' her up to her mammy an' daddy to eat in place of de squir'ls. He say; Beance de ole Mosser wus so good as to tell 'em to take out de bones, he caint tell no diffunce in de meat w'en dey sen' it to 'im.

Den dis Big Black Witch Root Doctor make one of 'em go out an' ketch de plantation black cat an' bring her in an' rub her fer good luck. Whilst dey wus a rubbin' de black cat, Phoebee got to studyin' 'bout de good squir'l dinner w'at was a comin'; an' she slip off onbeknowance to her mammy an' daddy to go down to de Barn-cabin to see how it was a gittin on a cookin'. W'en she got down to de Barn-cabin, dese outlandish folks-eatin Niggers kilt her, took up de big stone hearth an' buried her head un'er it, an' den put de rocks all back down over de buryin' place.

Dey den put her on to cook, dey rousted up de fire, dey soon got her done an' ready fer dinner. Den dey took all de meat offn' de' bones, e't some, an' sent a squir'l-measure up to de Big House fer deir Mosser's and Missus's dinner. De Niggers burnt up most of de bones; but dey give a few of de leg-bones an' arm'bones to liddle Sissy (Dese Niggers' liddle gal) to crack open fer to get de morrer outen to eat. De Niggers all think dat de cracked up pieces of bones would make it look to de Mosser lak dat dey wus got deir dinner by crackin up de squir'l bones an' a gittin de morrer outn dem fer to eat. Dis wus w'at de Mosser wus 'spectin' 'em to do.

W'en de dinner wus got to de Big House, de Mosser an' Missus call deir liddle gal fer to come on an' eat wid 'em; but dere didn' no Phoebee come! Den dey calls her some mo', an' w'en she dont answer dey bofe gits mad an' says: If she haint got no mo' sense dan to slip off to de neighbors to play, w'en deres a big squir'l dinner on hand; den she can jes go on an' do widout—dey dont care; Wid dat much said; dey jes sot down an' stuffed deirselves full o' "squir'l". Dey den say dat dey never did have setch a fine dinner in all deir born days; an' bofe of 'em lay down 'cross de bed to take a nap.

Whilst dey wus a sleepin, dey dream dat a bird was a singin' to 'em 'bout Phoebee—sumpin 'bout "Buryin her head an' crackin her bones."

Dey didn' wake up from deir atter dinner nap ontel about midnight. Whilst dey wus a rubbin' deir eyes open, dey thought dat dey heard Phoebee a settin' out on de doo' steps an' a cryin fer to git in de house.

Dey riz an' lit a candle; an' den dey holler to her to dry up dat cryin', dat dey was a good mind not to let her in a 'tall caze she had no business a slippin' off to play widout sayin' nothin'.

Dey onfastened de doo' an' opened it fer her to come in; but as dey opened de doo' de candle go right out. Dey den go back to de fire-place, wid de doo' lef' open, an' light de candle ag'in; but it go right out jes as fast as dey can light it.

Den dey hollers to Phoebee dat dey haint a gwineter bodder along wid no light no longer fer her; dat she can come on in an' go on to bed in de dark, lak she'd oughter fer gwine away widout axin nobody. But no Phoebee dont answer none o' dis here talk from nowhars! Den dey goes back to de doo' an' looks out; but dey dont see nothin but de black night wid a flash, here an' dar, of a lightnin' bug.

De Mosser den go back to de fire place an' job a pine knot in de embers to start up a light. As de light git so it flicker about a liddle over de room; de Mosser an' Missus pull on deir clo'es an' spen' de balance of de night a wakin up deir neighbors an' a ramshackin de plantation a lookin fer Phoebee.

W'en de daylight come, wid no Phoebee foun'; de Mosser an Missus break down a cryin, an' go home an' set out on de pieizzer enjorin de day. De neighbors an' all de tother folks in dem diggins keep up de search all mawnin a lookin' fer her.

Whilst de Mosser an' Missus was a settin out dar, along 'bout dinner time (de time Phoebee was kilt de day befo'), a great big drove o' wren-birds flew up an' lit in a big tree in front of de Barn-House whar de Niggers stayed. De Niggers wus a settin' down dar a lookin' at de birds, an' a wushin dat dey could git 'em to eat; w'en one of de birds busted a loose, an' you never did hear setch a singin' in all your bo'n days! Dis wus de song dat it sung:

(Sing rapidly)

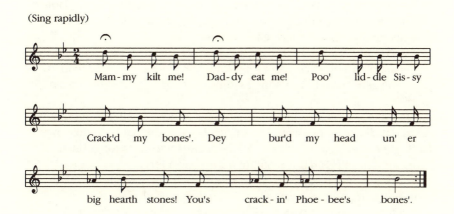

Mam-my kilt me! Dad-dy eat me! Poo' lid-dle Sis-sy
Crack'd my bones'. Dey bur'd my head un' er
big hearth stones! You's crack-in' Phoe-bee's bones'.

Law, Honey! w'en dat 'ar wren-bird sing dis here song; all dem outland-ish folks-eatin' slaves Niggers bucked out deir eyes ontel dey look lak dey wus a gwineter pop outn deir heads! Dey picked up rocks an' sticks an' throwed at de birds, an' hollered: "Shoo—! Shoo—!" De birds 'ould fly a liddle piece outn de retch of de rocks an' de sticks' an' den dey'd open up an' sing ag'in lak dey wus a tryin' to bust deir th'oats open wid deir song.
Dey sing:

"Mammy kilt me! Daddy eat me!
Poo' liddle Sissy crack'd my bones!
Dey bur'd my head un'er big hearth stones!
You's crackin' Phoebee's bones!"

Dem outlandish folks-eatin' slaves Niggers keep on a follerin up an' a rockin de birds; an' dem 'ar wren-birds keep on a singin' an' a flyin' away from 'em.
Bymeby de ole Mosser an' Missus hear de Niggers a hollerin an' a 'shooin' so much dat dey git up an' sorter crawl out to see wat's de matter. By de time dey git out, de Niggers an' de birds wus away off over in de woods, an' de most dey could hear wus: "shoo—!" an' a song—sumpin 'bout "Phoebee" an' "Bones". At las' dey makes up deir minds dat de

Niggers wus jes out a lookin' fer Phoebee along wid de tothers, an' a
hollerin an' a callin her. So dey goes back on de pieizzer an' sets down.

Atter while w'en de Niggers come back de ole Mosser mozey off
down to de Barn-House an' ax 'em did dey find Phoebee.

Dey makes answer: No, dey haint been nowhars a huntin' her.

De Mosser go on away from 'em widout sayin' no mo' to 'em.

W'en de white folkses all come back jes befo' night to de Big House
from deir lookin' fer Phoebee; dey tells de ole Mosser an' Missus dat dey
haint neider seed nor heared tell of her nowhars.

Den de ole Mosser an' Missus tell 'em 'bout deir dreams an' 'bout de
cu'ious actin' of deir outlandish folks-eatin' Niggers; an' deir seemin' to
hear some setch words in a song as "Phoebee" an' "Bones" out dar in de
woods.

De folkses, w'at wus been a huntin' fer Phoebee, tell 'em dat dey wus
skeard dat dey wus so sorrowful dat dey jes 'magine dat outn deir own
heads. Dey thinks dat de Mosser an' de Missus wus all wrong; but dey
makes up deir minds dat it wouldn' do no harm fer to go down to de
Barn-Cabin an' pump de Niggers to see w'at all dey mought git outn 'em.
So dey all starts off fer down whar de outlandish folks-eaters is.

De Niggers seed 'em all a comin' an' dey knowed dat dere was
sumpin a brewin in de air. Dey picks up de black cat, which dey wus
managed to keep 'roun' mongst 'em; an' goes over an' sets down in a
liddle huddle on de groun' in one corner of de Barn-Cabin. De Big Black
Witch Root Doctor tell de tothers to rub de black cat hard de right way fer
good luck; an' to let him do de talkin' 'cep' w'en he scratch on de groun'
by movin' his foot, den dey could talk.

W'en de white folkses git dar dey axes 'em: Is dey seed any thing of
Phoebee any whars.

De Big Black Witch Root Doctor make a scratch by sorter draggin his
big toe a liddle bit on de groun' an' dey all make answer, one atter de
tother, "No Sah!"

Den dey axed 'em: W'at did dey go out in de woods fer to-day.

De Big Black Witch Root Doctor scratch ag'in; an' dey all make answer dat dey wus a tryin to kill some o' de birds so as to git sumpin t'eat.

Den dey axed 'em how it 'twus dat dey wus heared words out dar
setch as "Shoo—!" "Phoebee—! an' "Bones!"

De Big Black Witch Root Doctor keep his foot still so as to close up
de moufs of de tothers; den he bust in lak he wus skeard dat dey wouldn'
git told all 'bout it, an' say: Dey wus a tryin fer to kill some birds fer to
eat. Sissy, deir liddle gal, wusnt big 'nough to go 'long wid 'em; so dey lef'
her behin'. W'en dey git out in de woods, some o' de crowd kep' a
hollerin back to Sissy to keep herself comp'ny by crackin' squir'l bones fer
to git de morrer whilst dey wus gone. Dat wus de reason dat dey hear de

words "Bones". Whilst dey wus out in de woods; some of de Niggers hollered to de tothers dat dey wus skeard dat Sissy mought go an' put in her dispearunce lak Phoebee whilst dey wus gone. Dat wus de reason dat dey heared de words "Phoebee".

Den de Big Black Witch Root Doctor splain furder: Dat, whilst dey wus out dar in de woods, some of de Niggers subgest dat de witches mus'a come along an' tetched Phoebee so dat she turned to a gnat an' j'ined de air gang. W'en dey all wus thought 'bout dis dey wus got power-ful skeard dat Sissy mought go an' do dis here same thing befo' dey git back to de Barn-Cabin.

So dey wus all kep' a hollerin: "Shoo—! Shoo—!" fer to skear de witches away ontel dey could git back dar.

Well—! De white folkses wus all bumfuzzled up by de good luck w'at de black cat wus a givin' de folks-eaters by their rubbin her. So dey tells de Niggers dat dey wus mighty proud to hear dat dey didn' have no han' in Phoebee's gwine; caze, w'en dey did fin' out who took her, dey wus a gwineter hang em up by deir ham-strings, rip de skin offn 'em, den take a knife an onjint 'em! Befo' dey leaves; dey sorter pours into de Niggers' (y)ears fer good measure: Dat dey wus a gwineter pull up ev'ry weed an'comb ev'ry speck of dirt on de plantation a lookin fer Phoebee tomor-row—de ve'y nex' day!

Dey wus done turned deir backs fer to walk away w'en dey say dis an' it 'twus a good thing fer de Niggers dat dem backs wus turned. Dem Niggers wus git taken wid de "All-overs"! Honey, it 'twus black-cat luck dat dey didn' look back; caze, if dey had, dey would a seed dem outland-ish folks-eaters wid deir hair a stan'in' lak hog-bristles, deir teef a clatterin lak tin pans, an' deir knees a knockin' togedder jes lak de rattlin of de bones a shakin in de wind 'twixt de fingers of one of dese here good banjer pickers. All dat talk 'bout "combin ev'ry speck o' dirt" make 'em feel dat it mought mean de"combin" un'erneath dat 'ar hearth; den dat would mean de combin of some folkses heads clean off.

Dat night, de Niggers wus all skeard to death; caze dey wus a thinkin 'bout de white folkses a "combin de dirt" fer Phoebee. Dey make up deir minds right away to put de black cat in a bag—a leavin her head out th'ough a hole in it—to make shore to keep her an' have her on han' to rub fer good luck; make no diffunce w'at come. Dey say dat it look to 'em lak dat dey wus got a long road befo' 'em; so dey think dat dey'd better lie down, an' take a liddle res', an' den git up an' do deir do's.

Dey fix up a big fire on de big rock hearth in de Barn-Cabin, an' den dey lie down to res'. Dey lay dar a restin but dere wusnt no sleepin.

Whilst dey wus a restin, along about midnight, w'en it wus as dark as pitch; de wind 'gin to cry jes lak a liddle chile. Tereckly atter dat; a great big red-eyed wolf, about de size of one o'dese here big flop-(y)eared

Nigger hounds, manage to pull hisself out from un'er de big hearth stones whar Phoebee's head wus buried; an' he sot down on de hearth in front of de fire.

De Niggers; dey looks at 'im, dey looks at one nudder, an' dey lies still. De wolf; he jes sot dar'

Bymeby sumpin else 'gin to squeeze an' pull itself out from un'erneath de big hearth stones, whar de outlandish folks-eatin Niggers wus buried Phoebee's head. Its pullin itself out from un'er de stones of de hearth make a noise w'at soun'sumpin lak a beilin' kittle on legs. W'en de thing, atter so long a time, manage to ontangle itself an' git out; it turn out to be anudder, great big red-eyed wolf, an' it wus as big as a yearlin' calf! It sot down by de tother wolf w'at wus de size of a big dog, an' sot dar.

De outlandish folks-eatin' slaves Niggers look at 'em, lay down low, an' say nothin'.

Terreckly de big yearlin-sized red-eyed wolf say, wid a cracked splintered fence-rail voice, to de big red-eyed dog-sized wolf: "Well! W'at 's we a gwineter do 'bout it?"

Den de big red-eyed dog-sized wolf make answer: "Well—! I reckins dat we caint do nothin ontel Phoebee come!"

W'en dem Niggers hear an' see dis, dey didn' zackly leave; but dey—sorter quiet lak—retched out wid deir hands, pult in deir liddle beslongins, an' fixed em up in liddle fastened-togeder bundles. None of 'em dont say nothin 'cep' de Big Black Witch Root Doctor; an' he jes whisper to de Nigger a holdin' de black cat: Not to let it git away fer nothin'; caze, if he do, dey wus all ruint!

Atter while sumpin nudder 'gain 'gin to pull itself out from un'er de big hearth stones. Its pullin' out make a noise sumpin lak somebody a crackin an' a bustin open bones fer to git de morrer outn 'em!

W'en it git out; it turn out to be anudder big red-eyed wolf, as big as a cow! He step up an' take his place in de line along by de side of de tother big red-eyed wolfs. Atter a liddle, he open up his mouf to say sumpin; an', as he open up, he show his great long white tushes as big an' as long as iron wedges w'at you splits up logs wid. Dis here big red-eyed cow wolf say, wid a voice dat soun' lak rumblin thunder away off yonder: "Well—! W'at 's we a gwineter do about it?"

Honey! Dat rumblin voice shook dat ole Barn-Cabin ontel it look lak dat it wus a gwineter tumble down right on top of de Niggers heads! Dey didn wait to hear no answer. Dey give 'em leg-bail an' toted deirselves away from dar jes a kitin. W'en dey make it to a sorter safe distance; one of 'em hollered back 'twixt an' 'tween his puffin's an' his blowin's: "W'en Phoebee comes; you can tell her, we's gone!"

Well—! Dese here outlandish folks-eatin' slaves Niggers run ontel dey goes across a branch of runnin' water. (You sees, Honey; Hants caint foller nobody across runnin water; so de crossin of de branch got 'em shed of Phoebee's hant.)

Dey makes up deir minds den, dat dey wants to go back up dat way fer a minute or so; caze dey lef' so onexpected dat dey didn' bring 'way all dey want. So dey all turned deir pockets wrong-side-(d)out'ards; caze hants caint bodder folkses wid deir pockets fixed dat a way. W'en dey git deir pockets turned; dey go back an' slip up to deir Mosser's smoke-house an' take off some hog jowls w'at de white folks wus been a savin' up fer starvation times. W'en dey git de hog jowls; dey go on off in de dark, down de big road, wid deir liddle bundles, a rubbin' de black cat de right way fer good luck.

Dey walk down de road about two mile, whar a branch runned across it. Dey waded th'ough dis branch an' kep' on down de road about a mile furder to whar dere wus a big pond by de side of it.

De Big Black Witch Root Doctor stop 'em at de pond; an' make 'em all, walk aroun' de edge of it in de mud an' water, whilst dey rubs de black cat de right way all de time fer good luck. Den he headed 'em all right straight back up de same road ontel dey come back ag'in to de branch dat dey wus waded th'ough an' crossed over. W'en he git dar; he make 'em all leave de road an' wade up dis branch fer a mile or so . Den he calls all his "ducks" outn dé water an' takes 'em on off into a great big swamp, whar dere dont nobody live. W'en dey got away out in de swamp it wus broad day-light. Dey th'owed up deirselves a brush-(h)arbor house, an' put up fer to stay dar a while.

Nex' mawnin de Mosser an' Missus wus a feelin' sorter sick from deir worryment over Phoebee a bein gone. So dey dont get up soon. Dey lies in de bed a waitin' fer de Niggers to cook deir Breakfus an' to roust 'em up fer to come an' eat it. Dey haint got no idee dat de Niggers is all gone; so dey lies up in de bed ontel de tother white folkses comes fer to 'gin deir huntin' fer Phoebee ag'in.

Dese white folkses calls 'em an' dey den sorter pulls deirselves outn' bed. W'en de ole Mosser git up, an' find dat his Niggers haint yit put in deir pearunce; he git so mad dat he clean fergit offn his mind dat he wus ever been sick. So he tells dem tother white folkses dat he want 'em, befo' dey goes anywhars a lookin' fer Phoebee, to come an' go wid him down to de Barn-House to whup his low-downed onfergotten tucky-trotten lazy-rotten Niggers w'at haint yit neider brung him no Breakfus nor stirred a foot to cook him none.

So dey all goes down to de Barn-Cabin; w'en lo an' beholds; de Niggers wus all gone! Dey looks aroun'; an', from de dispearunce of de beslongins, it looked lak dat dey wus moved out.

One of de white mens say right off dat deir gwine away dont make much diffunce; caze he wus got a plenty of big fat Nigger hounds, an' he'd lak to practice 'em up a liddle on ketchin run-aways anyhows! Whilst dey wus a lookin' aroun' in de cabin; dey all notices a heaps of bones all piled up in de corner. Den anudder one of de white mens allows to de Mosser dat it look to him, from de bones piled up dar, dat he haint been a feedin' his Niggers on nothin 'cep'meat, an' he dont see how he wus managed to be able to do dat. De Mosser make answer to him dat he haint give 'em no meat a 'tall; dat he jes give 'em a few squir'l bones to bust open fer to get de morrer outn to eat. Atter a liddle while; one of de mens picked up a bone w'at wus almos' twice as long as his hand. He helt it up an' sayed: Dat wusnt no squir'l bone! Den dey all 'gins to turn over an' ramshack de place. At las' one of 'em turn up de big hearth stones; an' dar wus Phoebee's head!

De Mosser jes fell out; but dey all rubs him, an' he comes back to, atter while. W'en he come back to hisself, he tell 'em: He hate it awful bad dat he didn' starve de Niggers to death; but, beance he fail to do dis, he wus a gwineter give 'em all his whole plantation to help 'im hunt 'em down an' kill 'em'

Dey den took de head up to de house. W'en de Missus see de head; she swoon off an' fall out. No col'water an' no rubbin dont bring her back.

Dat was de las' of her!

Dat evenin' dey took de Missus an' Phoebee's head to de "Big" white folkses' graveyard, whar heaps of de "Big" folkses graves wus all boxed over wid great big high boxes made outn rock. Dey buried 'em dar.

Nex' day de white folkses all come togeder wid deir packs of Nigger dogs w'at dey calls blood-hounds. Dey took 'em an' put 'em on de trail at de Barn-Cabin. Dey follered deir tracks right down de big road smack jam up to de pond. Den dey walks aroun' de pond; an' looks in de water; an' stands an' barks.

De white mens all comes a ridin' up on deir horses. Dey sees de dogs a stannin' 'roun' a barkin at de water! Dey all den say to one nudder dat dis look mighty cu'ious—dem 'ar dogs a stan'in' dar jes a barkin' at de water! Dey sholy mus' a missed de trail' So dey takes de dogs back to de Barn-House fer to trail de course over ag'in. Ag'in, de dogs go a trackin' to de pond; an' den dey stop an' bark at de water!

Well; de owners of de dogs say dat de Niggers wus done gone an' done deir own killin' job fer deirselves; an' so all of 'em can go on home an' res' easy.

De Mosser say dat he wusnt so shore 'bout dat; caze you never could tell nothin' 'bout dem 'ar outlandish folks-eatin' slaves Nigger-Conjers. So he say he think dat dey'd better git a pole an' some big pot-hooks an' drag de bottom of de pond ontel dey rakes out one of 'em, so as to clinch de nail dat dey's in dar dead'

So dey goes an' gits some pot-hooks an' a pole; an' dey drags de bottom of de pond de balunce of de day. Dey rakes out mud; but dey dont rake out no Niggers made outn mud!

De nex day de white folkses come togedder an' talk it all over; an' dey makes up deir minds to try to trace de Niggers up wid de dogs ag'in. Dey all allows dat de third time wus de charm; an' de dogs would jes be bleedged to trail straight.

So dey takes deir dogs down to de Barn-House once mo' an' puts 'em on de track. But dem 'ar dogs dont do nothin but go right straight down dat road to dat pond an' stan aroun' an' bark at de water!

Well—. De white mens all come up an' put deir heads togedder to study it all out. Dey look at ev'rything, up an' down, 'cross an' 'roun'; den dey say dere haint no two ways 'bout it: De dogs wus conjured!

Some mont's atter dat; dem same outlandish folks-eatin' slaves Niggers come up outn de swamps fer to hunt some wa'nuts an' hick'rynuts to eat. Atter dey git de nuts; one of 'em slip up in de white folkses' gyardin fer to git some red pepper an' sage an' so on, fer seasonin' up some swamp rabbits an' mud turkles w'at dey wus cotched up to eat out dar in de swamps. He got de stuff: but, as he dispear from de gyardin into de woods, ole Uncle Moze—de white folkses' house-boy—seed him an' knowed him. Dis out-landish folks-eatin Nigger git 'way easy; but ole Uncle Moze go jes as straight as a arrow an' tell his white folks.

Moze's Mosser take him an' de blood-hounds; an' go an' git de run-away Niggers' Mosser. Den de two white Mossers, on deir hosses wid guns; an' Uncle Moze, on foot wid de blood-hounds, go to hunt 'em up whilst de trail was hot, to kill 'em.

De hounds barks, an' sticks to de trail, an' starts fer de swamps whar de Niggers is. Dem w'at break an' 'take of Phoebee's bones hears 'em a comin' mo' dan heaps o' miles away. W'en dey hears 'em; de Big Black Witch Root Doctor tell 'em all to grab deir bundles, an' pervisions, an' de black cat; an' foller him! He lay it on 'em dat dey mus' keep up wid 'im, do w'at he tell 'em, an' rub de black cat hard in de right way fer good luck! Dey all does w'at he say do.

He leave de swamps; an' make a bee-line fer de "Big" white folkses' grave-yard, whar deir ole Missus an' Phoebee's head was buried. Dey all follers him in a line; an' passes de black cat, as dey goes, from one to de tother, so as to have 'em all rub her fer good luck.

W'en dey gits to de grave-yard gate; de Big Black Witch Root Doctor make 'em all stop. He den make 'em all rub deir footses good wid "goofer" [Goofer means some kind of conjurer's mixture] an' de red-pepper w'at de one stole outn de gyardin, w'en ole Uncle Moze wus seed him. Atter dis, he tell 'em all to go an' hide deirselves in de rock boxes over de graves; an' to stay dar ontel he call 'em by crowin lak a rooster. At las' he tell de Nigger; w'at wus his podner in de gedderin of wa'nuts an' hickry-nuts, an' w'at wus at dat time got de black cat; to come an' hide wid him over de same grave.

De hounds wus a comin'; but dey wus fur 'nough away dat de

Niggers wus all got plenty of time to get hid. De two white Mossers wus tol' Uncle Moze to go on an' keep up wid de hounds through de swamps, an' woods, an' pasters; whilst dey rides along de big road, a keepin' in callin distance w'en de game is treed. Dey says to Uncle Moze: If de dogs ketch some of de Niggers to jes let 'em shake 'em an' t'ar 'em all dey wants to; an if dey goes to roost in de trees, to jes let 'em stay dar ontel dey comes an' shoots 'em offn deir perch.

Uncle Moze keep up wid de hounds an' de white mens foller. De dogs circle through de swamps by de Brush-(h)arbor house; an' den dey turns, hot on de trail, an' makes a straight line fer de grave-yard. De dogs barks an' trails; Uncle Moze keep up wid 'em; de white mens foller 'long de big road on hosses.

W'en dey gits nearly to de grave-yard; de Big Black Witch Root Doctor an' his podner hears 'em a comin'; an' dey rubs de black cat hard de right way fer good luck. At las' de Big Black Witch Root Doctor say to his podner: dat de black cat keep on a lookin' so hard at de wa'nuts an' hick'ry-nuts w'at dey wus geddered; dat he think dat she mean, dat dey should oughter 'vide 'em 'twixt an' 'tween 'em an' not "make no bones 'bout it" ["make no bones about it" means in an unconcealed manner], but jes count 'em out loud 'tween 'em.

So dese here two outlandish folks-eatin' slave Niggers, a lyin' up dar in de grave-yard-box, 'gin to 'vide up de nuts. Dey 'vide 'em dis way; De Big Black Witch Root Doctor would say: "I'll take dis one!" an' his podner would say: "Well; I'll take dat one!" Dis way; dey 'vide all de nuts up 'tween 'em, a takin' one at a time. Dey jes keep de 'vidin' of de nuts a gwine in a reg'lar song lak dis:

(The Witch Doctor)   (The Witch Doctor's partner)

"I'll take dis one!"   "Well; I'll take dat one!"
"I'll take dis one!"   "Well; I'll take dat one!"

Well, atter while, de blood-hounds trail de outlandish folks-eatin' Niggers right up to de grave-yard gate. W'en dey gits dar, an' goes in de gate a sniffin de Niggers new-made tracks; dey drawed a whole passel of dat red pepper up deir noses—dat w'at de Niggers wus rubbed on deir footses—all mixed up wid" "goofer". W'en de pack o' dogs git dat 'ar "goofer" an' red pepper all drawed up deir noses; dey jes turned tail an' runned off a whinin' an' a howlin' down de road towards home!

Uncle Moze see all dis take place jes inside of de graveyard gate; an' it make him feel sorter skittish. So he sorter crep'-crope up to de gate of de grave-yard an' stop an' lissen.

Terreckly he sorter ketch de sound; an' he hear it a gwine, jes a sing-songin':

"I'll take dis one!"   "Well; I'll take dat one!"

"I'll take dis one!"   "Well; I'll take dat one!"

Honey! Uncle Moze retched up an' got his hat; an' he go off down de road jes a kitin' an' a splittin' de wind right behin' de hounds,

De two white Mossers fust met up wid de hounds a whinin' an' a howlin' an' a kickin' up dust towards home. Dey bofe stopped an' looked at de dogs; den dey called an' blowed deir horns fer 'em to stop, but dem dogs dont pay 'em no mind—Dey keeps on a gwine. Dey looks lak dey mought say, if dey could git de time; I haint got no time to tarry!"

Terreckly de Mossers looks up an' dey sees Uncle Moze a comin' jes lak he wus been shot outn a muskit! Dey drawed up deir hosses' reins an' waited to see w'at he wus got to tell 'em. He sail along; an', w'en he git to 'em, he sail on pass 'em lak he wusnt got nothin to say! Dey hails him; but he dont pay 'em no mind. He jes go on a tucky-shufflin' home! Den dey cusses loud at him, an' hollers to him: "Hey dar! You Moze! W'at's you a runnin' fer?" Uncle Moze, he holler back: "Caze I haint got no wings fer to fly wid!"

De Mossers look at one nudder; an', one say: "You dont reckin he's gone stock crazy, does you?" an' de tother one say: "No, I hopes not!" Den dey slapped de spurrers into de flanks of deir hosses an' runned an' cotched up wid Uncle Moze. Dey headed 'im off an' stopped 'im.

W'en dey gits him headed off an hemmed up; dey axed him, sorter brash lak: W'at he wus a runnin fer, lak he wusnt got no sense!

Uncle Moze drapped down on de groun', a pantin an' a puffin' an' a tryin' to ketch his bref. Bymeby w'en he gin to git his wind back, he sorter manage to say—by gittin out one word at a time—: Well—! You's done seed dem 'ar dogs a runnin' an' a whinin'!. Well, dey haint a runnin' an' a whinin' fer nothin!"

"Well, Moze; make 'aste an' tell us w'at's de matter"; de Mossers say to 'im.

Den ole Uncle Moze tell 'em dat de Lawd an' ole Satan was up dar in de "Big" White Folkses' grave-yard a dividin' up de folkses 'tween 'em. He lay out befo' 'em how de dogs wus trailed de Niggers pearuntly right up into de grave-yard; how, w'en dey gits in dar, dey seed de Lawd an' ole Satan a dividin' up de folkses 'twixt 'em; an' how dey jes tucked deir tails an' howled and flewed! Uncle Moze tell 'em dat he jes want to say: Dere haint no mistake 'bout it; caze he wus done crope right up to de grave-yard gate an' hid an' lissened. He wus done heared 'em a singin' dat Jedgement-song:

"I'll take dis one!"
"Well; I'll take dat one!"
"I'll take dis one!"
"Well; I'll take dat one!"

Moze say: w'en he seed w'at wus a gwine on, he didn' know zackly whose hands he mought fall into: so he tol' his footses an' legs to tote de body away, an' dar he wus!

De white Mossers tries to laugh at Moze, but he tell 'em: Dey wus done seed dem dogs, an' dey wus done seed him; an' maybe, if dey dont want to pay all dat no mind, dey mought ride on up to de grave-yard an' see de Lawd an' ole Satan too!

De white Mossers sorter grins an' dey tells Moze to wait dar; dey wus a gwineter ride up to de grave-yard to see w'at kind of a "bugaboo" him an' de dogs wus got up from nowhars. Moze sorter laid down on his elbow to res' hisself an' wait; whilst de Mossers go on off up to de grave-yard.

W'en dey got up to de grave-yard gate, dey drawed up deir reins an' sot on deir hosses an' lissened. Sho 'nough, dey hears de dividin' a gwine on. It jes go in a reg'lar sing-song: "I'll take dis one!"
"Well, I'll take dat one!"
"I'll take dis one!"
"Well, I'll take dat one!"

Dey sot dar an' dey lissened; an' it sorter look to 'em, atter while, dat ole Uncle Moze wusnt maybe almos' gone clean ravin' stracted.

Bymeby, de Niggers up in de grave-yard rock box git about through dividin' de nuts; dey didn' whack up in a eben number 'tween 'em. W'en dis wus de case; de Big Black Witch Root Doctor happen to ricomember dat he drapped two nuts, which he didn' stop to pick up, w'en he was a runnin' in at de grave-yard gate. So he sorter tone off lak one o' dese here big camp-meetin' preachers.

Well, dere's two mo' down yon' er by de gate. You can take dem two; an' dat' ill make it e-ben!

Laws a mussy! Chile, w'en dem white Mossers down at de grave-yard gate hear dis; dey whirled dem nags aroun', an' de way dey whup an' spur 'em away from dar wus a sin! Dey went down dat road lak a blue

streak; an' it wusnt no time befo' dey git to whar Moze wus. Dey didn' hol'
up none; dey jes shot on past him, an' dey hollered as dey whizzed by:
"Look out, Moze! Dey's a comin'! An' w'at 's mo' 'an dat!—De Lawd's done
gone an' tol' ole Satian!—He can have de ve'y nex' two dey comes across!"

Down de road, de Mossers flewed on dem hosses; but w'en ole Uncle
Moze git up from offn dat groun' he wus mo' souppler dan a year ole cat;
an' I tells you, he clattered 'long not so powerful fur behin' 'em!"

Dere wus a bad mud-hole in de road which de folkses wus been a
fixin' up lately by throwin some brush in it. W'en de hosses go to run
through dese brush an' mud; deir footses got all tangled up wid de brush,
an' dey felled an' kilt bofe of de Mossers stone-dead.

Uncle Moze come a wingin' 'long close behin' 'em. He trip up in de
brush an' tumble over in de mud. W'en he go to git up; he see de two
Mossers a lyin' dar dead' But he pult hisself outn dar widout sayin' a
mumblin word, an' he han'-galloped an' single-footed on home.

When he got home; he maked tracks fer de white folkses' house.
When he got dar; he fell in de doo' an' fainted away . De women folkses,
in de Big House, look at him, all smattered all over wid mud an' a lookin'
lak he wus a diein'. Den dey looks out an' sees de hounds all smeared
over wid mud; wid deir tails tucked 'tween deir legs an' a howlin'. Dey
didn' see de men folkses nowhars, an' dey didn' know w'at to do . Dey
wus jes skeared to death!

At las' dey takes de water bucket, an' goes to de rain bar'l, at de corner of de house, w'at dey wus cotched full of water fer to wash de clo'es
wid. Dey dipped up de whole bar'l-full of water, an' pitched it on ole
Uncle Moze, an' dat sorter brung him to.

W'en he 'gin to edge back a liddle on to his senses; he 'gin an'
mumble off a whole lots of cu'ious stuff 'bout de Lawd an' ole Satan. All
dis skeared de women folkses mo' wusser. So dey calls deir tother Nigger
slaves, an' orders 'em to take Uncle Moze on off down to deir cabins; an'
to put him to bed ontel he git some o' his gumption back. Dey tells 'em:
As soon as he git some sense, fer to come up to de Big House fer dem.
De plantation Niggers Say: "Yassum, Missus!" an' took Uncle Moze off an'
put him to bed.

A liddle atter dis, night come on; an' de Big Black Witch Root Doctor
took his podner, an' come from outn de grave whar he wus hid, an' he
crow: "Cou—coucou-cou—!" Den all dem tother outlandish folks-eatin'
slaves Niggers come outn deir graves to 'im. Dey went down de road a
rubbin' deir black cat de right way fer good luck; an' dey seed de two
white Mossers a lyin' dead in de mud-hole. Dey took deir guns offn 'em
wid de satchels of loadin' w'at go wid 'em, an' tote 'em on off. Nex' dey
goes up by de ole Barn-cabin whar dey uster live, an' lug off de big kittle
in which dey wus cooked Phoebee, den dey goes off ag'in 'way down in
de swamps.

W'en de night come on, an' de Mossers wusnt yit back home, an' Uncle Moze wusnt yit got no sense; de women folkses git mighty oneasy. Dey darfo' called up some Nigger men slaves, writ 'em a pair of passes, an' sont 'em off to git some white neighbors to come an' go look fer deir Mossers.

De neighbors went; an' foun' de Mossers, wid deir hosses dead in de mud-hole. W'en dey took 'em home deir wives an' relations almos' go into spasms.

Nex' day, w'en Uncle Moze come to hisself; he lay up in de bed an' tell 'em all 'bout de Lawd an' ole Satan a dividin' up de folkses 'tween 'em. He end it by sayin': It look lak dat ole Satan mought a cotched up wid de Mossers an' a took deir spirits on off wid 'im!

Uncle Moze wus de favoright Nigger 'mongst de whitefolks aroun' in dem diggins; an' w'en dey hear him say dis, dey all go outn de room a wipin' deir eyes an' a sayin he wus done gone stock crazy. He hear 'em a sayin dis an' he call 'em back to 'im.

He call back to deir ricomembunce how dem run-away Niggers look lak dey make de blood-hounds stan' aroun' an bark at de water in de pond. Den Uncle Moze tell 'em dat it was puffeckly clear dat dem outlandish folks-eatin' slaves Niggers wus so mixed up wid de Devil, dat dey could do almos' any thing. He subgest; Since de Lawd an' ole Satan didn' seem to a took no mo' people's bodies atter dey git through wid de gedderin' up of de folkses up dar in de "Big" white folkses' buryin' groun'; dat dey mought bury de two Mossers somewhars else. Den w'en he git well, he'll watch fer de Niggers, find out whar dey is, an' den dey can go out an' shoot 'em down wid silver bullets. [There was a tradition among Negroes that if one shot at the witches with ordinary bullets; they simply caught them in their hands and threw them back at their assailants. Buy witches might be shot and killed with silver bullets.] He add dat he don't think dat dem run-aways can git his skelp; but, if dey does, he love his white folks good 'nough to take it fer his share.

So dey buried de two Mossers, in de "New Buryin' Groun'" un'er de shade of de "moanin'" pine.

W'en de run-away Niggers git back down in de swamps; dey tied deir black cat wid a bundle of love-vines, an' helt a liddle dance aroun' it. Den de Big Black Witch Root Doctor make 'em a speech. He say to 'em:

"Brudders àn' Sisters, dipped an' dyed in de wool wropped up in feller love an' black skins:

Our black cat, wid yaller shiny eyes, have looked de Mossers clean from dis worl' to de nex' one. She beslong to de fambly whar all de kinfolks always has had nine lives; an' all of us w'at wants to keep on a livin', lak we is will lakwise have nine lives. Dey may kill us; but we'll rise from de dead nine times befo' we crosses de black smokin' river.

But you all lakwise knows dat dis—our black cat—wus done gone an' give us good luck an' save us five times from Death w'at wus a wavin to us to come on a sailin' over dat river. Dis is mo' dan half as many times as she wus got lives. Darfo, if you wants to, we can sen' her to de Lan' of Cat-res'whar she'll live happy: an', den, by usin' her bones, turn you all into Wull-er-de-Wusses. W'en you gits to be Wull-er-de-Wusses, you can live happy as long as de worl' stan' an' den go to de Happy Home whar deres Fritter-trees a growin on de banks of Honey Ponds an' ev'ry day'll be Sunday. W'en de Big Black Witch Root Doctor finish up wid his talkin': dey all say dat dey wants to git turned into Wull-er-de-Wusses.

De Doctor say: All right, he'll fix 'em all up into dat; but dey mus' promus him to stick by 'im, atter deir change, so dat he can stay 'roun in de world wid his nine lives, an' help out Niggers w'at gits in trouble. He lakwise say to 'em dat he dont see noways how he can do dis onless dey helps him to git back once mo' to whar all de Niggers is free. W'en he find de way, den he can come back an' git mo' Niggers an' take 'em dar; caze; "De ole sheeps dey knows de road; de young lam's is got to learn de way."

De tother outlandish folks-eatin' slaves Niggers hol' up deir right hands, cross deir hearts, an' hope dey may drap dead; if dey dont stick to him all de way as he trabel to de "Promus Lan'". [Promus Lan' means Land of Freedom].

Den dis Big Black Witch Root Doctor took de big kittle, an' sot it up on nine rocks. Den he poured into dis kittle nine gourds full of clean clear runnin' water; an' make a fire un'er it wid nine sticks of wood, an' kindled it up wid nine dry twigs an' nine leafs. He make 'em all bring up wood an' lay it down in piles of nine sticks; an' he add wood to de fire, nine sticks at a time, ontel de water in it beil.

Den he tell de tothers, w'at wus to git turned into Wull-er-de-Wusses, dat dey mus' form a circle 'roun' de kittle; an' do all he say widout sayin one mumblin word to him an' to nobody else. He say w'en he git through wid de tellin' an' dey git through wid de doin'; dat he'll slap his hands togedder nine times widout sayin' one word. W'en he git through wid de slappin', dey mus all say togedder: "Yisco torbedio Affikan change!" an' den dey'll all be turned into "Wull-er-de-Wusses".

"W'en dey all gits in deir circle aroun' de hot beilin' kittle, de Big Black Witch Root Doctor say: "Take up nine sticks an' tie 'em wid nine strips of bark!"—Dey all do dis.

Den he promp: "Walk aroun' de hot beilin' Kittle nine times!"—Dey all do dis.

Den he say: "I's now a gwineter throw de black cat into de kittle of hot beilin' water; an' you mus' keep her in dar wid yo' bundles of nine sticks ontel de meat draps offn de bones."—Dis took a long time; but dey grip deir teef, an' keep deir moufs shet an' do it.

De Big Black Witch Root Doctor den holler out: "Each an' ev'ry one of you, now souze yo' hands nine times into de kittle of hot beilin' water, w'at de black cat's body is now filled wid all power!"—Dey all bites down hard on deir tongues, an' does dis.

He den say: "Let all de circle of dis new born fambly now take one bone of de black cat outn de hot water, an' put it in deir moufs, an' keep it dar, so dat she'll always be part an' parcel of deirselves. All dem w'at do dis widout utterin' a mumblin word; atter dey gits to be Wull-er-de-Wusses; can turn into w'atsome-ever dey wants to, by sayin' de words ag'in w'at dey say w'en dey fust gits turned into Wull-er-de-Wusses.—De Niggers grips deir teef an' bites deir tongues, an' rumbles 'roun 'mongst de hot water ontel dey gits a bone apiece widout makin a soun'; an' dey puts 'em in deir moufs.

Den de Big Black Witch Root Doctor rake de black cat's skull outn de pot o' hot beilin' water wid a bundle made up of nine sticks tied togedder wid nine strips of bark; an' he put dat in his own pocket.

At de end, he say: "Jine hands in a circle aroun' de kittle!"—Dey jined hands. De doctor den slapped his hands togedder nine times, an' dey all hollered togedder: "Yisco torbedio Affikan change!"—an' dar dey stood, "Wull-er-de-Wusses!"

Dey capered aroun'; a turnin' into white folkses, lions, tigers, b'ars, snakes, an' all dem sorter things—jes a havin all sorts of big fun, a lookin' at one nudder in deir new gifts. Dey jes turned into w'at-some-ever dey wants to by sayin' to deirselves: "Yisco torbedio Affikan change!"

Dey caint talk to de Big Black Witch Root Doctor no mo' w'en dey's along wid 'im, but dey can answer w'en he holler to 'em from away off in de woods whar dey is. Dey can lakwise make signs to 'im w'en dey's aroun' 'im to let 'im know w'at dey's a drivin' at.

Dey go off a piece in de woods from de Doctor, an' he holler: "You's a gwineter set me *free!*" an' de answer come from all de Wull-er-de-Wusses in de woods: "Free-e—ee—!"

Den he holler to 'em: "If de Niggers or de white folkses bothers me; you's a *gwineter kill 'em!*" an' de answer come from all de Wull-er-de-Wusses all aroun': *"Gwineter kill 'em'! Gwineter kill 'em!"*

Den de Doctor take de black cat's skull outn his pocket an' de Wull-er-de-Wusses come back to 'im outn de woods. W'en dey gits back to 'im, he ax 'em w'at dey wants to do fust. Dey all makes answer by p'intin' one finger to Uncle Moze's cabin. (You sees, Honey, deres some low-downed Niggers w'at hates you; if you loves yo' Missus an' Mosser. Dat wus de case wid dese outlandish folks-eatin' slaves Niggers. W'en dey gits to be Wull-er-de-Wusses, dey heared Uncle Moze's words still a trabblin aroun' on de wind, an' a sayin' dat he wus ready to die fer his white-folks; an' dem low-downed good-fer-nothin Devils make up deir minds dat dey wus a gwineter let him do it.)

Uncle Moze wus a settin in his cabin an' a res'in' his bones on his birth-
day. He 'gin to think how his good Mosser w'at got killed in de mud-hole,
useter come down on his birthdays an' bring him a nice big poun'cake an'
some of his own nice britches w'at haint eben got no big holes in de seats
dat needs patchin up; an' he 'gin to cry lak a new-born baby.

Dem 'ar nasty Wull-er-de-Wusses hear him; an' dey thinks dat it was a
good time to begin deir devilment so as to put an end to 'im. So two of de
Wull-er-de-Wusses come outn de big deep woods an' go down to Uncle
Moze's cabin. One of 'em say to hisself: "Yisco torbedio Affikan change!"
an' he turn into a great big black b'ar as big as a hoss. De tother one, by
sayin' dis same thing, jes turned hisself back to natchul Nigger lak he
useter be befo' he git to be a Wull-er-de-Wust. Den de Nigger Wull-er-de-
Wust mounted de big black hoss-b'ar Wull-er-de-Wust an' rid him right up
into de doo' of Uncle Moze's cabin'! De big black b'ar Wull-er-de-Wust
open his mouf an' growl an' show his big long white toofs an' tushes;
whilst de Nigger sot on his back dar in de cabin doo'!

Poo' Uncle Moze wus skeared into lebenty dozen duck-fits an'
spasms; an' he hollered fer dear life. W'en de white folkses heared him
dey runs down to his cabin fer to see w'at wus de matter. W'en dey got
dar, Uncle Moze tell 'em all 'bout w'at wus done gone an' happen. Dey
dont railly b'lieve him; but to make sho, dey looks ev'ry whars, but dey
dont see nothin' nowhars. Dey sorter humor Uncle Moze up de bes' dey
knows how; an' den dey goes on back up to de Big House, a whisperin'
to one nudder dat he look lak he mought be a gwine deranged.

Uncle Moze's wife beslonged to anudder Mosser on a j'inin' plantation. Him an' his ole 'oman wus got a mighty nice lakly-lookin' liddle gal.

One o' dem 'ar mean low-downed Wull-er-de-Wusses turned hisself
into dis liddle gal; an' come over to his cabin w'en it wus a gittin jes a
liddle dark, an' tell him dat her mammy say fer him to come over dar a
liddle while dat night. Uncle Moze go an' ax his Missus fer to go. She say
to 'im: Yes, he wus setch a good Nigger dat she wus a gwineter set down
an' write him a pair of passes w'at he could keep an' go over dar w'en he
git ready. So de Missus go an' git her fine goose-quill pen an' dip it in
some nice poke berry ink w'at she wus jes squez out fresh on dat ve'y
day; an' she writ him a pass. De pass go on lak dis: "To whome it maye
Concerne: Let my Nigger, Moze, pass an' repass to, see his ole 'oman w'en
he git ready. I's a doin' dis wid de hopes o' savin' him from goin' raven
'stracted; but dont you tell him dat dis's in de pass.—His Missus."

Uncle Moze pick up his hat from offn de groun' whar he drapped it
w'en he axed fer de pass; an' he bowed hisself mos' smack down to de
groun' lak de "Big" white folkses does w'en dey's puttin on aires. He den
thank his Missus an' tell her dat she always wus de pruttiest an' bes' thing
dat ever lived or died. She tell him: Dat wus all right; jes to go on an' en-

joy hisself. Dat low-downed Wull-er-de-Wust—a makin' 'tend dat he wus his liddle gal—wus a setin off from dar in de dark a lookin' at it all.

Uncle Moze start off, wid w'at he think wus his liddle gal, to his ole 'omans house. Whilst dey wus a crossin' de woods-lot, de "liddle gal" 'gin to grow. She growed up in a minute as high as a pine-tree; den she looked down on 'im an' grinned, and spit fire all 'roun' 'im!

Uncle Moze run home skeared clean outn his wits. He wusnt eben able to tell w'at happen ontel nex' day. W'en Uncle Moze tell his tale; his whitefolks go over an' see his ole 'oman. Dey axes her 'bout ev'rything, She tells 'em dat she haint never sont nobody over dar atter him. De liddle gal say she was skeared to look outn de doo' atter dark; an' she haint never been nowhars. De Missus say dat was awful cu'ious, caze dere wus sho some liddle gal up dar at de Big House a settin' off a piece from Uncle Moze on de groun' in de dark whilst she wus a settin on de pieizzer a writin' de pass by de light of a candle. Still an' yit de ole 'oman an' de liddle gal jes stan' her down dat dey haint never sont nowhars. De Missus at las' say dat it was all awful cu'ious; but it look lak to her dat her favoright Nigger, Moze, wus 'bout to go crazy. Den she go on back home.

De Wull-er-de-Wusses kep' on a cuttin' up dese sort of capers ontel Uncle Moze die fer de love of his white folkses.

Den de Wull-er-de-Wusses go an' make sign to de Big Black Witch Root Doctor dat dey wus now ready fer to take him whar he'd be free. He ax 'em which way he mus' go; an' dey go an' lay moss on de norf side of de trees, an' make it git pitch dark all aroun' 'em. Den he know dat he wus to trabble to de Promus Lan' by night; an' dat he wus to go in de direction of de side of de trees w'at wus got moss laid over it. He nex ax 'em how fur he'd hafter go befo' he git whar he'd be free. Dey den takes up moss an' wrops it all roun' one of the trees whar he wus. Den de Big Black Witch Root Doctor know dat he mus' keep on a gwine ontel he git to whar de moss is laid all over all de sides of de trees.

So de Big Black Witch Root Doctor tie his liddle bundle o' clo'es on de end of a stick, an' sling it on one shoulder; den he put his ole Mosser's gun on de tother shoulder—de gun w'at he took offn him outn de mud-hole whar de black cat look him off to de tother worl'; an' he sot out on his journey to de Promus Lan' of Freedom. De Wull-er-de-Wusses fed 'im, an' stayed 'roun' about 'im, an' took care un 'im. Dey could give him ev'ry thing he need, 'cep' fire to cook his victuals wid. So, once in a while, he hafter stop in at some slave Nigger cabin, in de dead of night, to git his victuals cooked.

Late one night, he knocked on de doo' of one of de out-o'-de-way slave Nigger cabins of a big plantation; an' de Niggers inside holler out: "Who's dat?"—De Doctor, make answer sorter low-lak: "A Frien'" Den dey gits up an' opens de doo'; an' de Doctor stepped right in.

De slave Niggers stirred up de embers an' sticked in a pine-knot to git a liddle light on de "Frien'". Den dey see dat he wus a rank stranger! W'at wus mo' 'an dat dey sees dat he wus got a gun!

De Doctor shoved de doo' to wid his foot; den he pulled a box ag'inst it, an' sot down on it wid his gun! He cocked dat big muskit an' tol' 'em all to hol' deir tongues. De Niggers look at de gun an' de big bag of loadin'; an' dey jes natchully know how not to say nothin'.

W'en de Doctor git 'em all sorter settled down; he tell 'em dat he haint come in fer to hurt nobody; he wus jes come in fer to have 'em to cook up his week's rations which he wus got in his bundle.

So de slaves Niggers makes up a good fire, an' cooks de victuals Whilst dey wus a cookin' his weeks rations; de Big Black Witch Root Doctor tell 'em all 'bout dis, w'at I's tol' you—'bout whar he come from, how he git over here in dese diggins,—tell 'em all 'bout Phoebee's bones an' de Wull-er-de-Wusses a killin' Uncle Moze. He lakwise took de skull of de black cat outn his pocket an' showed it to 'em! Whilst he wus a showin' 'em de skull; de Wull-er-de-Wusses come to de outside of de cabin, an' fly aroun' it so fast dat de Niggers inside hear de win' almos' a whis'lin' from de flutter of deir wings. W'en he put de skull back in his pocket; dey leaves, an' nobody caint hear nothin'

W'en de victuals wus all cooked done; de Doctor packed 'em up in his bundle. Den he tell 'em; if any of 'em say anything 'bout him to somebody befo' he wus been clean gone fer a whole year or mo', de Wull-er-de-Wusses will come to see 'em jes lak dey wus done been an' gone to see Uncle Moze!

As he go to leave wid his gun an' bundle; he make 'em all go a piece of de way wid him out in de woods; caze he want 'em to hear de Wull-er-de-Wusses for deirselves.

W'en he git 'em away out dar in de woods an' de hills an' de hollows he call out: "You's a gwineter set me *free!* an' de Wull-er-de-Wusses make answer all th'ough de hills an' hollows: "*Free!*" Den he holler out: "If de Niggers or white folkses bothers atter me, you's a *gwineter kill 'em!*" an' de Wull-er-de-Wusses holler back: "*Gwineter kill em!*"

After de slaves Niggers hears tell of all de Doctor's past, an' whar he come from an' de Wull-er-de-Wusses; dey tol' him he mought go right on, an' dey wouldn' never say nothin' 'bout him! A year or so atter dat, w'en de Big Black Witch Root Doctor git good gone, de Niggers w'at cooked up de victuals sorter whispered de news aroun on de plantations; an' dat wus de way my gran'mammy come to know all 'bout dem outlandish folks-eatin' slaves Niggers, an' I haint never hearn tell dat dere wus none of 'em now still lef' in de worl' no whars.

—But I mus' now git up," continued Henry's mother, an' milk de white folkses' cows. Whilst you's gwine to school; if yo' teacher tell you sumpin dat you dont know 'bout, you can jes come to yo' mammy an' maybe she can git it straightened out fer you. I haint never teached no school; but w'en I rolls my wheel of conbersation aroun' de axle-tree of deir un'erstan'in', I haint never seed no folkses yet w'at didn' git it ev'ry bit right!"

"Yassum; mammy, I'll be shore to come right straight to you!" responded Henry, and they arose to finish their tasks of the day.

Cotton-eyed Joe or the Origin of the Weeping Willow

Hen and Perch Stegaul were orphans. Their father passed away when they were babies and the mother followed him to the Great Beyond when her beloved twins were only five years of age. The father and mother had no known relatives, as was the case with many Negro families just after the great American Civil War. They had been sold to their present habitat from far away plantations upon which they were born, while they were as yet in the earliest years of tender childhood; thus all recollection of kith and kin had faded from memory. By their parents' deaths, the boys were left alone in the world.

On the day of the burial of the mother, "Aunt" Mary and "Uncle" Dan Dip, being childless, took the twins to rear as their very own. There was no process of court gone through with in the matter. These good hearted Negroes simply took the children through pity—a thing of common occurrence among those who had just come out of slavery.

George Winrow, another Negro boy of the neighborhood, was an intimate friend of the Stegaul boys. All of the children belonged to poor hard working families, and had no time to visit by day. And since most of the Negro families of that time went to church on Sunday, the custom arose among them of going and spending the night with those with whom they would visit.

One Wednesday evening George Winrow started to the foster home of the Stegaul boys with a view of spending the night with them. It was rainy and rather dark. As he walked along the lonely dirt-road, enclosed on either side by an open rail fence, he heard a peculiar weird groaning. He peeped through the fence on the right side of the road and saw an apparently headless human form, wrapped in grayish-white shrouding, advancing in his direction. "A ghost!" was the thought which immediately flashed across his mind. Now, the common weapon of defense of the Negro boy is a stone. Of course George ran with all his might from the supposed ghost; but, before taking to his heels, he let go a whirring rock in its direction. His swift gait soon brought him to the door of the house of the other two boys. He ran in, and immediately told Uncle Dan and Aunt Mary of the terrible "Hant" which he had just seen.

When George was through with his story, Aunt Mary only said in a somewhat meditative way: "Well, you's bleedged to see hants sometimes."

Uncle Dan, however, lookin at his wife with a countenance of doubt, put in, in a rather quiet way: "I's been a knockin' aroun' down here in dese Low Grounds of Sorrow now, a gwine on more 'an fifty year; an' no hants haint never yit seed fit to give me a chance to lay eyes on 'em."

"Aw! Go hang!" came the words from Aunt Mary—a little provoked. "Didn' you come a runnin' in de house outn breath one night las' Fall w'en you wus been gone over to dat 'ar big corn-shuckin' at ole Zeek Lacy's? Didn' you almos' knock de doo' down befo' I could git a chance to git up an' open it? Didn' you say dat you seed sumpin a walkin' across de railroad, whar Tom Ray wus got killed, w'at look lak a man wid a coffin on him fer a head?"

"Oh yes, but I thinks dat wus jes some o' de neighborhood boys a tryin' to skear me", replied Uncle Dan.

"Well", said the wife, "you sho cut up some awful funny capers an' acted awful cu'ious to a been thinkin n' lak dat.—Go call de boys from a shuckin' de corn down at de crib. Tell 'em dey can stop now an' come on to de house beance George is come fer to stay all night wid 'em. Tell 'em to be sho to put dat cedar torch good out w'at dey's been a usin' to give light to 'em to shuck de corn by; caze we haint got no hankerin atter no burnt up corn-crib."

Uncle Dan called the boys as directed but received no response from the corn crib. A short time afterwards however the two boys—Hen and Perch—appeared on the scene. Perch presented his usual appearance but Hen was draped from head to foot with a number of light gray cotton meal bags. As Hen came into the light it was discovered that his head was covered with blood, and the foster mother burst out with the exclamation: "Laws a mussy, Hen! W'at in de Lawd's worl' is done gone an' happen to you?"

Hen and Perch were aware of the fact that George was intending to come to spend the night with them. They had hidden in the field by the roadside to give him a scare—Hen playing the part of ghost. George's stone, instinctively hurled, had found its mark; and Hen sustained a bloody though slight wound. The twin brothers explained the episode to the foster mother as she washed and dressed Hen's wound . George's heart was filled with sorrow and he broke down in tears. But all the boys were soon reconciled to the happening and went off into a room by themselves to join in an evening of frolicking and fun.

When Uncle Dan and Aunt Mary were alone once more, they sat for quite a while in silence. At last Uncle Dan began the conversation.

"Mary, Honey, dere railly wus a mighty heaps cu'ious about dat 'ar thing a crossin' de railroad dat night whar Tom Ray wus got killed, wid a coffin on fer a head."

"Guess dere mus' 'ave been", said Aunt Mary.

"Well", continued Uncle Dan", you knows I wus brung up sorter aroun' de white folks in de Big House in slavery days. I wus de yard boy. So I wus got to hear de big smart white folks talk to one nudder a whole heaps; an' dey didn' scacely never b'lieve in no hants at all. So I growed up a feelin' maybe perhaps dat dere wusnt no setch a thing".

"W'at does you think about it now?" asked Aunt Mary.

"Dat wus jes w'at I wus a gwineter git aroun' to", explained Uncle Dan. Then he continued as follows: "On de night of de corn shuckin at ole Zeek Lacy's, dey all wus a carryin on about lak common. Dey shucked corn an' singed setch songs as: "Oh rally, aroun' de corn Sally!" "I can whup de one man, doggone de bully man!"

"Ho! my Rinktum, Hi my han'.
Ho! my Rily swing out Miss Dilsie Ann."

De fellers drinked heaps of hard lasses-skimmins beer whilst dey wus a shuckin de corn; an' dey wus got light 'nough in de head dat dey wus jes full of devilment. Sam Smith throwed a (y)ear of corn an' hit Bill Hix in de head wid it fer fun. He didn' aim fer nobody to see 'im; but Bill cotch on to de (y)ear of corn an' deyd lak ter have fowt. But de boys helt 'em an' got 'em all right.

Atter de corn wus all shucked, de boys danced an' cavorted an' de lak fer a while; den dey went in an' sot down to supper. Whilst we wus all a settin dar an' a eatin', we all got to sputin about hants. I sayed dere wusnt no setch a thing as a hant an' de tother boys sayed dere wus. Den I ups an' gives 'em my reasons fer believin de fac' dat all de very biggest white folks claims dat dere haint no setch things; an' dey sholy should oughter know. Den I telled 'em w'at I wus done already tol' you one time about a Nigger w'at drownded hisse'f to death a runnin from his own shadder an' a thinkin it wus a hant. After dat I telled 'em sumpin dat my grandaddy telled me. I dont think I's ever been tol' you about dat, so I'll tell you w'at it wus. Grandaddy say: Away back yonder, his ole Mosser got skeared at nothin. He tell me: Away back dar w'en my Uncle Jerry wus a liddle boy dat de white folks sen' 'im ev'ry evenin' to drive up deir cows home from de paster. Ev'ry day Uncle Jerry play an' fool aroun' so as to be boun' to git home late an' dat wus w'at de white folks hate. De ole Mosser take a hick'ry an' th'ash him but dat dont do no good; so he make up his min' dat he wus a gwineter git him broke from a stayin' late by skearin him.

De road from de cow-paster to de Big House run by a grave yard w'at wus got a rock fence all aroun' it. So ole Mosser call up Uncle Jerry befo' he start him off fer de cows an' tell him dere wus a great big hant up dar in de grave-yard w'at wus named Big Feard. An' if he dont hurry on home wid dem cows befo' sundown dat Big Feard would sho ketch 'im an' pull his (y)ears an' nose off.

So Uncle Jerry go on off up in de woods-lot fer to git de cows: but he play aroun' up dar lak fer common an' den he come a mozeyin along home wid de cows atter dark was set in.

Ole Mosser wus gone an' wropped hisself up in a big white sheet an' wus hud hisself up dar behin' de rock fence to skear him w'en he come along a gwine home. Ole Mosser wus got a pet monkey. W'en dis here monkey seed him wrop up in a white sheet, an' start off fer de grave-yard.; he lakwise wrop hisself up head an' (y)ears in a sheet an' foller along behin' him. Ole Mosser he dont never look back an' so he dont see no monkey. So Ole Mosser go on off up dar in de grave-yard an' squat down behin' de fence to skear Uncle Jerry. De monkey w'at foller him squat down behin' him up dar in de grave-yard too.

Uncle Jerry come along about dark by de grave-yard a drivin de cows. W'en he git benent de rock fence, Ole Mosser riz up from behin' it wid de big white sheet all wound all over him, an' he moan an' groan off: "Woo—! Woo—!"

Uncle Jerry, w'at wus a drivin de cows home, stop an' look at 'im. He wus so liddle dat he wusnt got 'nough sense to git skeared.

He look at Ole Mosser, jes over de fence, a moanin an' a groanin an' a takin on in his big white sheet; an' he look at de monkey right behin' 'im lakwise wroped up in a white sheet. Terreckly Uncle Jerry say "Dar is Big Feard, jes lak Mosser say!—Oh!—an' jes looky! Dar is liddle Feard a stanin' up dar right behin' 'im!"

Uncle Jerry jes keep on a sayin' dis ontel Ole Mosser sorter glance behin' 'im over one shoulder. He seed de monkey in de windin' sheet; an', Mon! w'en he seed dat monkey, he fairly tore up de whole (y)earth a gittin away from dar. He make a bee-line right fer home wid de monkey a markin it off right atter him.

As Ole Mosser runs an' de monkey run, Uncle Jerry gaze in wonderment at 'em an' holler: "Jes look at Big Feard a runnin an' Liddle Feard a runnin atter 'im! Oh—! I railly do believe dat Liddle Feard is a gwineter ketch him!"

Ole Mosser, he sorter look back over his shoulder an' he see dat mon-key in a windin' sheet a comin' atter him lak blue lizards.—Mon! he flewed! It skeard 'im dat bad, dat w'en he git home he fall in de doo' an' take one duck-fit atter anudder ontel he kick de bucket an' dey hafter take 'im out 'an bury 'im.

Atter I wus got through a tellin de boys at de corn shuckin dis here loration over at ole Zeek Lacy's, an' git through a p'intin' out to 'em dat dere wusnt no setch a thing as hants; Kam Rodgers tell one of de beateness tales you's ever hearn tell of to show dat dere wus hants.—Well, w'en he git through; nearly all de tother fellers over dar say dat dey wus done heared dat same thing so much dat dey jes knowed dat it wus bleedged to be de trufe. So atter I come on home from over dar an' seed a coffin-headed man; I 'gun'd to wonder if dere mought not maybe perhaps be some setch a thing as a hant."

"Of co'se deres hants!" interjected Aunt Mary. "But caint you go on an' tell me w'at Kam Rodgers wus tol' you? Den perhaps 'twixt an' 'tween us we mought git you straightened out."

"It's a sorter long loration, an' I dont know whedder or not you'd be amind to take de time to hear it all"; said the husband.

"Well, you go on," replied the wife; "an' if I gits tired, I'll find a stopper aroun' here somewhars, to stop you a drippin an' a leakin at de bung."

"All right!" answered Uncle Dan. "Dis is de way Kam Rodgers tell it: Away back yonder one time dere wus a Nigger by de name of Joe. He wus his Mosser's special favoright house-boy; so he give him his ole clo'es an' fix 'im up ontel dere wusn't no flies on 'im. Joe wus one of dem 'ar high-flyer sky-bugs; an' he didn' have nothin to do wid dem 'ar common corn-fiel' darkies. So he co'ted de likeliest gal on de plantation—I thinks her name wus Lindy—an' she make promus fer to marry 'im.

W'en Joe tell his Mosser about him an' Lindy a gwineter git married, dey wus jes tickled to death; caze in dem days de whitefolkses want likely merlatter Nigger famblies w'at dey could sell fer big money fer house-boys an' house-gals. So dey tells Joe dat dey wus powerful glad dat he didn' go an' mix up rats wid dem 'ar common corn-fiel' Niggers w'at wus as plug-ugly as home-made sin.

De Missus an' de Mosser wus jes natchully crazy over Joe any-hows; caze he wuk lak a bee an' wus as perlite as a basket of chips. Den, Joe wus one of dese here big fine banjer pickers.
He play fer all de big white folkses' dances; an' dey love him an' treat him almos' lak he wusnt no Nigger at all.

So w'en Joe noised it aroun' amongst de white folks dat he wus a gwineter marry Lindy; dey tells him dat dey wus a gwineter fu'nish him wid a weddin' supper. De white folkses' big preacher—de Reverunt Adonijak Green—sont him word dat he wus a gwineter come over an' stay long enough to say de cer'mony fer him.

Well, dey sot de time fer Joe an' Lindy to git married; an' dey axed in all de house-Niggers in dem diggins fer de 'casion.

On de night dat Joe an' Lindy wus to git married; de house-Niggers all come over all bucked an' gagged an' fixed up as fine as a fiddle in deir Missuses' an' Mosserses' clo'es w'at dey wus done put aside an' patched up. De white folks didn' come but eben some of dem sont 'em big fine presents. One sont 'em a hen an' a rooster, Anudder sont 'em a big piggin-full of yaller meller ripe hoss-apples, whilst Joe's Missus an' Mosser give 'em bofe a new pair of shoes an' stockins.

W'en de time come fer de cer'mony to be said; de big white preacher sont 'em over word dat he couldn' come, caze he wus too busy a studyin about gwine to de big camp-meetin' over in Philermadelphy or Philermeryork or somewhars. He say dat he wus awful sorry an' he subgest dat dey git his house-boy, Mansion Green, to say de cer'mony; caze he know it mo' samer dan him.

So Mansion wus picked out to say de cer'mony. He open up by tellin 'em dat it wus his way to 'gin de progrance wid a song befo' he hitch, jine, an' marry his couples. So he axed 'em all to sing. Dey all singed de weddin' song. It go lak dis:

Its hard to love; yes in-deed it is. Its
hard to be broke up in min'. You's all lug'ed up in
some-bod-y's heart, But you hain't gwine ter lug up in mine.

Atter de singin' Joe walk out in de middle of de floo' wid Lindy a hangin' on to his coat-sleeve. Mansion, he git up he do, in his long-tailed bluer w'at his Mosser give him an' he stan' up in front of 'em. He retched into his inside jacket pocket, an' pulled out a pair of his Mosser's specktickles w'at he wus borrowed onbeknowance to him an' brung along wid 'im fer de 'casion. He sot dese out on de en' of his nose an' he look over de top of 'em an' say: "You two jine hands," an' dey hitched up hands. But Lindy give Joe her lef' han'; so Mansion make 'em onhitch an' jine up right. W'en Lindy hitch up wrong wid her lef' han', dey all whis-pered it aroun' 'mongst deirselves in de room dat bad luck wus jes bleedged to come on 'em atter dey git married.

W'en Mansion wus got de hands all fixed up all right; he say off a whole heaps proper lak de white folkses' preacher sumpin 'bout Love all geddered togedder to jine dis man an' 'oman in sunder in de holy bounds of materimony. Atter he git through wid de white folkses' loration; Man-sion make a speech to Joe an' Lindy all on his own hook, to show 'em all dat he wus some stickin-de-mud widout nobody—all by hisself . W'en at las' he go to turn 'em loose all tied up fer man an' wife he say:

I wushes dat you bofe may have;
Jes a liddle tas'e of honey, jes a liddle sip o' wine,
Jes a liddle love to love you so's to keep yo' life a gwine.

Jes s liddle kiss at mawnin, jes a liddle hug at night,
Jes yo' liddle souls togedder 'tel de sun dont give no light.
Jes de hearts dat thump togedder, jes de eyes w'at bat wid pride.
Tu'n an' kiss yo' Honey! Honey. Tu'n an' kiss! Solute yo' bride!

W'en Mansion close up; Joe an' Lindy tu'n an' kiss, an' dey wus married.

All de company walk 'roun' an' shake hands wid 'em jes lak de big white folkses does; an' dey say to 'em dat dey wush 'em much joy .

Atter dat, beance Joe was a banjer picker, dey all got pardners an' helt a big dance. Dey fust danced: "Han's up sixteen circle to de right." Den some o' de finest dancers danced all by deirselves to 'muse de tothers. Dey cut de "Double Shuffle", "Knock dat Mobile Buck in de Head", "Coonj'int", "Cut de Pigeon's Wing", an' dey plays a blowin' out de candle on de floo' wid de win' from deir footses whilst dey dance.

Nex dey all goes in to de Weddin' Supper. Dey wus got a whole shoat w'at deir Mosser give 'em on de table. Dey had lasses, aig-bread, biscuits, batter cakes an' butter too. Joe's Missus lakwise sont 'em over a weddin cake fer a sprise.

It wus got a teen inchy-teeny-tiny chiny doll baked up in it; so dat all de womens dar could take a knife an' cut fer it; so as to know which one wus a gwineter git married nex' by her bein' lucky 'nough to git it out in her sleish.

Dat 'ar cake come might' nigh a bringin' on a big rucus. You see all de womens, one atter de tother, wus a tryin deir hands fer to git de doll; an' one of de gals took a knife an' hoaked a great big sleish outn de middle a tryin to git it. She wus jes stock crazy fer to git dat 'ar doll, caze she wus wild over one of de boys dar; an' she wus got it in mind, if she git de doll, dat it would throw a spell over him so dat he'd hafter marry her befo' de nex season's new moon.—Well; w'en she hoked out de hunk, she didn' git no doll in it. W'en she didn' git nothin', one of de gals, mixed in wid de crowd, giggle an' say dat dis here gal wus bent an' bound fer to be a ole maid; caze she wus cut de whole cake at one lick an' den didn' git no promus fer to marry.

Law, Chile! w'en dis here gal say dat; dat gal w'at hooked de cake git so mad dat she go hot a gunnin', to find an' to fight de one w'at said it. But w'en she go a smellin' through de crowd; bofe dat gal w'at say it an' all dem tothers declar to gracious dat dey don't know who could a ever said setch a nasty lowdowned thing as dat. So de gal hafter cool off an' take w'at wus drapped out on de wind fer her share.

Atter de Weddin Supper; Joe ax diffunt ones fer to make a few scatterin' remarks on de solubious 'casion, den dey all goes home.

W'en Joe an' Lindy git to be man an' wife, deir Mosser give 'em a fine liddle hewed cedar log cabin fer to live in wid de daubin in de chinks all striped off white wid lime; not fur off from de Big House. Some of deir Mussuses' fine Brissles chyarpet wus about wore out; so she give 'em

some pieces of dat to lay down on de floo' to walk on. Bofe Joe an' Lindy
wuked in de big House. Deir Mosser an' Missus wus awful good to 'em
an' dey has a good time.

Dey wus soon have a pretty liddle boy all o' deir own which deir
Missus named Claudius; but dey all call him Claud fer short. Claud wus a
likely chile—jes as sharp as a briar an' as cunnin' as he could be. Eben
w'en he wus jes a liddle shaver of a baby; he could jes mock ev'ry body
an' make folkses bust deir sides a laughin'; Den befo' he wus no size, he
could sing jes lak a mockin' bird. De white folks uster take de chile up on
deir back pieizzer an' give him tea cakes, an' spile him jes to git to hear
'im sing. But dough he wus so speilt; he mind an' do all de white folks tell
'im so dat dey almos' loves him lak he wus one o' deir own chilluns.

Joe an' Lindy wus powerful happy an' dere haint no tellin' w'at
mought a come to 'em if Lindy hadn' a made dat bawk o' givin' Joe her
lef' han' w'en dey wus got hooked up fer man an' wife.

One Sunday atter dinner deir Missus give 'em bofe a pair o' passes an'
let 'em have two hosses so dat dey could go over to anudder plantation to
see some friends o' deirn. Dey rid off down de road all bucked back in
deir stirps an' a lookin' almos' lak dey wus white. It wus awful dry
wedder; an' de branches an' de creeks wus all dried up to liddle mud
puddles here an' dar.

One of dese here branches w'at runned across de road wus got a
liddle kivered over culbert across it, an' de branch wus so dried up dat it
lef' a liddle mud waller un'er dar. So, some hogs wus gone up un'er dat
culbert an' laid down in de mud to cool of. Joe an' Lindy go a ridin' down
de road all rared back in deir stirps of deir saddles an' a actin' lak dey
owned de whole worl'. As dey go to ride over de culbert, de hogs in de
loblolly un'er it jump up an' say: "Boo!! Boo!! Boo!! Boo!!"

Dem 'ar hosses wus jes natchully so skeard outn deir skins dat dey git
taken wid one spasm atter anudder. Joe an' Lindy git ditched an' pitched
an' throwed off. De groun' soon cotched Joe; but Lindy's foot got hung in
de stirp, an' de hoss drug her an' kicked her to death. Some white folkses
soon come along an' foun' 'em—Joe outn his senses an' Lindy dead. Dey
picked up Joe an' took him to his Missus an' Mosser; an' dey told 'em
about Lindy a bein' dead down dar along side of de road.

Joe didn' git back to his senses fer a week. W'en he wus come to an'
wus l'arnt dat Lindy wus dead he go off into anudder loss of his senses an'
stay dar fer anudder week. W'en he wus come to ag'in, de white folks
humor 'im and tell 'im dat he mus' try to git well fer to take care of Claud.
Dis sorter bolster Joe up; an' atter so long a time he git up an' aroun' a
movin' slow by jerks. But he quit his pickin' on his banjer an' he 'muse
hisself by settin' aroun' an' a lissenin to Claud sing.

Dar wus a big tree a growin' in front of Joe's cabin wid limbs on it a comin' all de way down to de ground. Claud would climb from lim' to lim' up to de top of de tree; an' set up dar an' sing.

One day as he sot up dar in de top of de tree a singin'; he 'magine hisself to be a bird. So widout thinkin' he jump out towards de tips of a lim' to sing out dar; an' dat wus de las' of him. Dey all take on over him mighty hard; an' Joe he look lak dat he wus a gwine crazy . He tell de whitefolks an' ev'ry body else dat dey musn' have nothin' to do wid tetchin an' keepin' an' buryin' Claud's body—nobody 'cep' hisself. So his Missus an' Mosser (to humor 'im) tell 'em all to let Joe do lak he please.

Joe go an' git a ax an' cut down de tree w'at Claud fell outn an' kilt hisself. He chopped off de butt cut of de tree; an' hollered it out so as to make a kinder coffin. Den he dug a hole an' buried Claud in it.

Atter dis Joe peerten up an' do all de wuk an' dat sorter thing dat de whitefolks tell him; but he act lak he wus sorter cracked brained. De white folks give him ev'ry thing a tryin' to straighten him out. Dey eben give him money, but he go on actin' cu'ious jes de same. He tell de plantation Niggers dar, dat Claud come back fer to see 'im ev'ry night; an' dat he wus axed him fer to do sumpin but he haint yit maked up his min' fer to do it.

W'en Joe 'gun to talk aroun' lak dis dey all git powerful skeard of him; an' dey give him a wide berth. De cornfiel' Niggers sot to wuk an' tried to plot up some way fer to git his Mosser to sell 'im; but de Mosser he dont pay 'em no mind an' he jes keep on a keepin' Joe.

One day Joe come a walkin up wid a fiddle; an' he hol' it up befo' de Niggers eyes an' tell 'em dat dat wus Claud.

Dey wus all mighty skeard an' skittish of Joe; an' dey sorter keeps deir distance whilst dey looks at de instrument. Atter while dey says to 'im dat dey dont see no looks of Claud 'bout de thing; an' dey dont see no ways how he make out Claud in de fiddle an' de fiddle in Claud.

Joe den tell 'em to jes lissen to a big man whilst he splain hisself. He splain to 'em dat Claud wus been a comin' back ev'ry night an' a axin him to go an' dig him up an' bring him back home, caze he wusnt dead at 'tall. So at las' he wus done gone an' dug him up. W'en he wus got him dug up he wus foun' out dat de hollered out tree-coffin wus done swunk in an' growed into it so dat him an' de coffin all git to be one.

So w'en he wus got it all out; de whole thing look lak a stick o' wood all round-d off on one end wid eyes an' (y)ears on it. Dere wus one liddle lim' on de stick lakwise wid de boys hair a hangin' on it. De hair wus done growed out great long!

Joe tell 'em dat he den call Claud; but dere dont no Claud make no answer. Den he maked up his mind to twis' his (y)ears, an' spit in his eyes to make him answer. He do dis; an' w'en he do it, Claud's neck stretch outn de stick into a great long neck an' his head stretch out so long on de en' of de stick-neck dat de nose bend in; an' it all make a fiddle neck wid its head.

Den de body swunk in, in de middle, whilst all dis stretchin' wus a gwine on; an' de interals come out an' tu'ned deirselves into strings. De (y)ears bofe split in two an' maked four pegs fer to hol' de strings in de head. Whilst dis here makin' of de fiddle wus a gwine on; de lim' wid de boys hair on it drap off an' make de bow. So dar wus his Claud-fiddle an' bow!

Joe say dat he den take de fiddle an' bow up an' play wid 'em; an' Claud den sing fer him lak he wus always done befo' he fall outn de top of de tree. So de fiddle wus Claud an' Claud wus de fiddle; an' he wus come fer to stay wid 'im an' to sing fer him as long as he live.

W'en de Niggers all hears dis; dey look at Joe an' dey sees dat his eyes wus all walled out an' white. So dey right den' an' dar nick-named him "Cotton-eyed" Joe; an' dey wus might' nigh as skeard of him as a hant.

Ev'ry night Joe sot down in his cabin an' runned dat bow over dat fiddle an' lissened to Claud sing. De Niggers keep on a keepin' away from dat cabin an' keep on a tryin to hatch up a plan to git de ole Mosser to sell him. But Joe mind de whitefolks an' do all dey tell 'im; so dey keeps him.

Atter dis, Cotton-eyed Joe's Mosser go away fer a year or mo', an' he take him along wid him. But you'd better b'lieve he maked Joe leave dat 'ar fiddle at home fastened up in his cabin. You see eben de whitefolkses didn' wanter take no chances a luggin' dead-folkses-fiddles about wid 'em. De Mosser sorter maked up his min', off to one side, dat he didn' speshully need Lindy's lef' han' w'at she give Joe w'en she marry him whilst he wus away a knockin' aroun' from pillar to post.

W'en Joe an' de Mosser git gone; dere wus anudder Nigger on de place, named Sol, w'at de Missus took up to de big house fer de house-boy in Joe's place. Of co'se she took him up dar to wuk; but she took him up dar lakwise fer to watch him. Sol wus been a whisperin' aroun' amongst de Niggers sumpin about him a hopin' to run away an' git free; an' de NIGGER BANNERS wus trabbled all de way up to de Big House, an' wus offered de whitefolks a "Pretty" to read 'em right good. W'en de white folkses read in de newspapers 'bout w'at Sol wus got all laid out in his head; he had a mighty heaps o' trouble a keepin' de raw-hides from a lookin' at his back ontel de raw-hide drap offn his back. But Sol wus jes natchully one o' dese here slick talkers w'at could talk all aroun' an' clean by de white folks. He splain so fast dat he make deir heads swim an' he splain it all away .

Still ole Missus wusnt a takin' no chances on Sol's gittin away to de "Promus Lan'". She take him up to de Big House so dat if he go to run away an' take "French-leaf"; she can sen' de bloodhounds right quick to git de "lim'" an' de "leaf" bofe an' bring 'em straight back home.

Sol wusnt none o' yo' sardeens, so w'en he got up to de Big House, he knowed w'at side his bread wus buttered on. W'en he git up dar; he keep ev'ry thing as clean an' as neat as a pin. He do dat wuk faster dan dey can p'int it out to 'im. Den he talk an' tell ole Missus w'at fine folkses dat her an' all her relations always wus. He say to her dat de Lawd's Angels wusnt no mo' pruttier dan her chilluns; an' he hope, w'en she git tired of him, dat she'll give 'im away in de fambly caze it 'twould kill him if he git to de p'int whar he wus bleedged to belong to somebody else.

Ole Missus feel sorter jubous 'bout Sol fer a mont' or so; but by dat time she think dat dere wusnt no setch a Nigger nowhars as Sol on top of dirt. She go off mad wid all de Niggers w'at wus brung news to her 'bout him in deir Banners, a sayin: "Sol wus got holt of a whole heaps of money, w'at he wus a keepin' fer his runaway projick". She maked de Overseer of de plantation flog dem 'ar tale toters ev'ry time one of 'em crook deir fingers.

Sol feel powerful good w'en he git his han' on de upper end of de stick 'mongst de Niggers. He sot up in de Big House an' crowed over de whole yard full of 'em. He wus a banjer picker too; an' he maked up a song an' sung it, an' picked it ev'ry night down at his cabin so as to devil 'em. It was dat banjer song w'at you hears banjer pickers still a pickin' now-a-days. It go lak dis:

1. Oh! Hol' my fid-dle an' hol' my bow, Whilst I knocks ole Cot-ton-eyed Joe. Ole Cot-ton-eyed Joe! Cot-ton-eyed Joe! Whilst I knocks ole Cot-ton-eyed Joe.

2. Oh, I'd a been dead some seben years ago,
   If I hadn' danced dat Cotton-eyed Joe.

3. Oh, it makes dem ladies love me so,
   W'en I comes 'roun' pickin' ole Cotton-eyed Joe.

4. Yes, I'd a been married forty year ago,
   If I hadn' stayed 'roun' wid Cotton-eyed Joe.

5. I haint seed ole Joe since 'way las' Fall,
   Dey say he's sol' down to Guniea Gall.

Well, ev'ry thing move 'long jes as schmove as grease. Sol's Ole Missus eben sometimes give him money; but nobody dont never see him buy nothin, an' dey all dont know w'at he do wid it. W'en de NIGGER BANNERS ax him w'at he do wid it; he in ginerally make answer dat he wus a plantin' it out in de groun' somewhars, caze he wuz hearn tell dat it would grow.

But Joe wusnt sol' down to no Guinea Gall lak Sol wus a singin' it; an' one day de Mosser come back home an' brung Joe along wid 'im. W'en dey got back de Mosser wus a lookin' finer dan he ever look befo' in all his bawn days. An' Joe, he wus got fat an' mo' weller an' mo' smarter dan he wus eben befo' he wus married an' got holt of Lindy's lef' hand. He look lak he love dat Claud-Fiddle mo' samer dan befo'; but he dont talk no mo' about his makin' it outn Claud an' de coffin. Yit de folkses aroun on de plantation wus jes as skeard of him an' dat 'ar fiddle as dey wus befo' he go away an' come back.

W'en de Mosser git home, de Missus tell him all 'bout w'at a good Nigger Sol wus an' how wrong dey wus all been 'bout 'im all de time; an' she close up de palaver by tellin' him dat dey mus' be shore fer to keep Sol fer a house-boy all de time, it make no diffunce w'at come.

Ole Mosser say dat he wus jes bleedged to have Joe. He caint git 'long widout him. An' dey railly didn' need no two house-boys wid all de women suvants dey wus got. But at las' he close up by sayin' dat he reckin dat a extra Nigger or so aroun' de house dont make much diffunce since dey wus got so many of 'em. So de white folkses keep bofe Joe an' Sol fer house-boys .

Well, dey sot in to wuk togedder. Dey wus powerful jealous of onenudder. It wus nip an' tuck a tryin' fer to make a hit wid deir Missus fer bein' de bes' Nigger. It go on dis a way fer a long time, but bymeby it look to Cotton-eyed Joe lak Sol wus a gwineter root him out from un'er de shelter into de cold. So he study an' study w'at to do' bout it. Atter while he maked up his mind dat he wus a gwineter do away wid Sol.

One night Joe's Mosser give him a great big juicy red-ripe watermillion. Atter supper Joe axed Sol fer to stop in at his cabin to jine in wid helpin him to eat it up .

Joe leave de Big House fust an' go to de cabin. W'en Sol got down to de cabin, de watermillion wus cut in halfs, an' dere wus a half a settin on bofe ends of de table.

Dey sot down; each man wid a half a watermillion, an' each man on a end of de table . Jes befo' dey' gins to eat, de cook call Joe an' tell him dat he wus fergot to lock up de smoke-house, an' his Missus say fer him to come an' to lock it up right away an' not to fergit to lock it up no mo' if he know w'at wus good fer him. De cook say dat she wus done gone an' tacked on to dat, Dat he'd better darafter copy atter Sol an' git all his wuk done befo' he walk off to eat watermillion or he mought find hisself a walkin' from de Big House an' de shade to de hoe-handles an' de hot breilin sun in de corn-fields.

Joe jump up an' run to lock de smoke-house doo'. Whilst he wus gone, Sol got up an' tu'ned de table aroun' en' fer en', so dat he'd git Joe's half of de watermillion an' Joe 'ould git his half. W'en Joe wus come back, him an' Sol got down ag'in, an' laughed, an' cracked jokes, an' e't watermillion. W'en dey gits through, Sol git up right away an' go to his cabin to go to bed, caze deir Missus wus tol' 'em bofe to come up to de Big House sooner in de mawnin so as to give it some extra tetches befo' some comp'ny git dar w'at she wus a gwineter have de nex' day.

Nex' mawnin, bright an' early, Sol go up to de Big House fer de extra cleanin' up. He go to wuk lak a bee. W'en he got dar, Joe wusnt yit come; but Sol dont go to wake 'im up caze he want him to oversleep so as to fix up jes one mo' p'int ag'in' him in de Missuses' head. Sol jes wuk away lak a ant a gittin ev'rything spic an' span.

Atter while, a liddle sorter late in de day, de Missus git up an' come down to look aroun' to see how ev'ry thing mought be foun'. She see ev'ry thing jes a shimmerin an' a shinin' but she dont see no Joe.

Bymeby she ax Sol whar wus Joe. Sol make answer, he do, dat he reckin dat Joe wus a takin his gemmun's mawnin nap an' a waitin' fer de wuk to git done, so dat he'd have a nice clean place to set down in an' puff his pipe w'en he git up an' rub his eyes open, an' come over.

De idee of a Nigger a lyin' up in de bed, a sleepin' de daylight away, almos' run ole Missus raven 'stracted. She fust go out on de back pieizzer an' call Joe; but no Joe, he dont answer. Den she go an' git de bull-whup an' call one of de Overseers of de plantation. She hand him dat bull-whup an' tell him to take it an' to go down to Joe's cabin, an' w'en he git dar to whup Joe outn bed, to whup his clo'es on 'im, to whup some water on his face an' hands, to whup him all de way up to de Big House, an' den to lay de lash on de lash ontel he git him good warmed up to wuk.

De Overseer take de whup an' make off fer Joe's cabin to do w'at de Missus tell him. But de ole Mosser overheared some of de directions; dough he didn' git altogedder into de unerstanin' of it all. So he come out an' axed her w'at wus de matter.

Ole Missus wus so mad dat she couldn' hardly talk; but she finally managed to git it out an' tell him 'bout dat "low-downed good-fer-nothin lazy Joe."

Ole Mosser say to her dat dis wus mighty bad in Joe; but dere wusnt no need of killin' a real good Nigger jes caze he do wrong an' sleep too long fer once.

Ole Missus snort an' cavort an' cut up an' say ev'ry thing; but ole Mosser dont pay her no mind. He jes go on off a trabblin down towards

Joe's cabin so as to see to it dat de Overseer dont whup him too hard an' too much. As he go along to de cabin he don't hear nothin'; an' w'en he git almos' down dar, de overseer come outn de cabin lak he wus come out fer to meet him.

"W'at's you done done to Joe?" axed ole Mosser of de Overseer.

"I haint done nothin' to 'im," sayed de Overseer. "Caint nobody do nothin' to 'em now. He's dead and col'!"

Ole Mosser turn as pale as a sheep an' he go in de cabin fer to see. W'en he git in dar, sho 'nough, dar wus Joe dead an' all swelled up as big as any three mens. Lindy's lef' han', retched out to 'im w'en dey git married, wus come an' got 'im!

Ole Mosser go back to de Big House jes a boohooin an' a cryin'; an' tell 'em all dat Joe wus gone. Den all of 'em—white folks, house-Niggers, fiel'-hands, an'all—go down to look him over an' zamine 'im.

W'en dey git through wid de zaminin of him, dey seed dat he wus been pizened. Ole Mosser ax 'em all if any body know what de pizen could a come from.

Ole Missus say she dont see no way how he git de pizen onless he do it on purpose. She tell 'em dat she wus give him some pizen an' some meat fer to pizen de rats wid at de barn; but he knowed dat it wus pizen an' so he couldn' a got it dat a way.

Sol, he jine in an' say dat he stopped in an' e't de watermillion wid Joe w'at his Mosser give 'im jes befo' dey all go to bed; an' he lef' Joe fat an' sassy an' a crackin' jokes.

Dey all den looks up in Joe's cubbard; an' dar wus de meat w'at de Missus give 'im fer de rats wid no pizen on it. Den dey tells Sol dat he mus' tell all w'at happen 'tween him an' Joe befo' he lef' 'im.

Sol make answer dat he didn' do no nothin' but eat watermillion wid Joe lak he wus already done tell 'em. But Niggers wus so cu'ious 'bout puttin conjer mess an' de lak in deir watermillions an' setch things, dat he wus turned de table aroun' whilst Joe wus gone to lock up de smoke-house; so dat, if he wus put some goofer in de watermillion, he would eat it hissef instid of him.

W'en Sol say dis, dey all see dat Cotton-eyed Joe wus put de pizen in de watermillion to kill Sol but Sol wus tu'ned de table on 'im; an' Joe git de pizen hisself . So dey took Cotton-eyed Joe out an' buried him; an' from dat day clean down to dis one, de Niggers is got de word 'mongst 'em dat "So-an-so was turned de tables on So-an-so" Lakwise so long as de Niggers wus in bondage; w'en de house-suvants have deir big dinners 'mongst deirselves, dey always swap deir plates befo' dey 'gin to eat .

W'en dey bury Cotton-eyed Joe, nobody dont want his fiddle, so dey buries dat wid' 'im. His cabin wus hanted an' nobody couldn' live in it. So de ole Mosser tell Sol to lock de cabin up an' to keep de key; an' den perhaps some day w'en he buy a new Nigger, he mought could put 'im in dar to live befo' he wus hearn tell of Cotton-eyed Joe.

Sol lock up de cabin an' tote de keys' but de Niggers all say dat dey could hear Joe's hant in dar a playin' on de Claud-hant fiddle. Some of 'em wus eben say dat dey wus seed him come outn de cabin once in a while wid a coffin on 'im fer a head an' wid a coffin-fiddle in his han'. One time dey wus gone an' waked up deir Mosser fer to come an' see 'em; an' de Mosser got out jes in time to see 'im dis'pear a gwine down de road to whar Lindy wus git kilt. De Mosser go back in de house; but he dont tell ole Missus nothin 'bout w'at he wus seed, caze he dont wanter skear her.

(De Niggers at de c'on-shuckin' las' Fall, over at ole Zeek Lacy's, say dat ev'er since dat time, w'en-so-ever somebody is kilt lak Tom Ray wus; ole Cotton-eyed Joe's hant, wid a coffin on fer a head, walk across de road dar at night once in a while. It sho did look to me lak I seed him walk 'cross de road dar dat night whar Tom Ray wus got kilt.) But I mus' go on wid de loration:

Atter de Mosser hisself wus seed de hant; he kinder 'gin to talk lak he mought t'ar down Cotton-eyed Joe's hanted cabin; an' split up de logs into rails to mend up de fences aroun' de fields wid. But ole Missus laugh at 'im an' poke fun at 'im an' tell 'im dat she railly do b'lieve dat he wus about to git to thinkin' dat dere wus setch a thing as a hant lak de Niggers.

Ole Mosser declar' befo' Gracious he haint got no mind in dat way; an' so as to show her he wusnt a thinkin' lak de Niggers, he let de cabin stan'. But nobody wouldn' never go 'bout dat cabin atter dat' cep' Sol. Sol would go down to it nearly ev'ry day, onlock it, go in an' look aroun' to see dat it wus all dar; den he'd come out an' plug up de doo' wid a padlock an' chain, an' come on away.

At las' one day, Sol an' de tother Niggers—away off by deirselves—git to talkin' 'bout Cotton-eyed Joe's hanted cabin. Dey tells Sol dat it wus fer a great wonderment to dem; dat he'd go down an' go in dat 'ar cabin eben in de broad open day time.

Sol tell 'em dat he wusnt feard o' no noise, an' wusnt skeard o' no hants; an' he'd bet 'im all de big roll o' money w'at he wus saved up fer twenty year ag'in' twenty watermillions dat he could go an' stay in dat cabin all night, if dey wouldn' tell deir Mosser, an' if dey'd wait fer a night w'en deir Mosser an' Missus wus gone offn de place.

De tother Niggers tell 'im dat dey'll take him up on dat bet; but dey puts in dat he mus' git de money an' show it to 'em befo' he go in to de cabin to stay so dat dey'll be shore dat he wus got de money. Dey lakwise promus on deir parts to show de watermillions befo' he go in to stay all night. All de Niggers an' Sol bofe tetch an' 'gree on dese p'ints of de bargain.

Dis wus along in de Spring of de year. So Sol tell 'em, along in de Summer, in de middle of watermillion time: his ole Mosser an' all his brothers always take a day off wid deir wives an' go an' spen' de night wid deir ole rich daddy, a funnin an' a frolickin an' a havin a good time . On dat night, de bet wus on; an' he'd go in an' spen' de night in Cotton-eyed Joe's hanted cabin.

De tothers make answer to 'im dat it wus "a gos'" but dey ax 'im w'at he wus a gwineter do if Cotton-eyed Joe's hant make it too hot fer him.

Sol say: Well, in dat case, he'd hafter run an' try to outrun de hant. If he hafter run, he wus a gwineter run straight across de cornfiel' down de liddle path w'at lead to de big river a mile away. W'en he git away down dar nearly to de river whar dere wus a big log across de path, if he find dat he wus outrunned de hant, he'll set down on de log an' res' his bones an' den come on back home. But if de hant come up wid 'am at de log, he'll run an' jump in de river an' swim across. Dat way he'll git shed of de hant; caze no hants caint cross no runnin' water.

Dese here bettin Niggers tells Sol all right. Den dey gits togedder atterwards to 'scuss how dey wus a gwineter keep Sol from a foolin' 'em; caze dey knows dat he wus got a big stack o' money an' dey wants mo' an' mo' to git it. So dey makes up deir minds an' tetch an' 'gree dat w'en-soever Sol stay in dat 'ar hanted cabin ; dey wus a gwineter tell 'im dat he mus' leave de doo' wide open so dey can see 'im in dar rail good all de time, an' some of 'em wus a gwineter set off in seein distance to see dat he stay in dar lak he say. Den de tothers wus a gwineter strew deirselves somewhars in seein distance along dat corn-fiel' path w'at lead to de river; so as to be shore dat him an' de hant runs a fa'r an' squar' race if it come 'bout dat some runnin' wus bleedged to be done.

W'en dey gits deir plans all made an' deir megs all sot, dey takes 'em to Sol. He tell 'em all right; but he lay it down dat dey mus' be mighty keerful not to let ole Mosser git in to de wind of it; caze, if he do, he wus setch a powerful church man dat he'd bust it all up caze dey wus a bettin'. Dey makes answer to him dat dey'll look atter dat end of de log.

Ev'ry thing go along all right. W'en de day wus almos' come fer Sol's Mosser to go to his daddy's fer to stay all night, an' fer Sol to sleep in de hanted cabin, he go in an' outn de cabin mo' of 'ener dan he wus ever gone befo'.

At las' de night come an' Sol's Mosser an' Missus wus gone on off to stay all night ontel de nex' day. It wus a prutty clear night, an' w'en de sun go down de stars pop outn deir silber sockets an' de moon riz on de clear blue sky. Sol an' de tother Niggers come togedder 'cordin' 'p'intment. De tother Niggers brung along de twenty watermillions an' laid 'em down lak dey say; an' Sol show 'em his big roll of money lak he say, an' den stuff it back down in has Sunday-go-to-meetin' britches pockets.

Sol tell 'em he wus now a gwineter go in de cabin an' leave de doo' wide open. He wus a gwineter cook an' eat his supper in dar; an' den he wus a gwineter lay down an' go to sleep in plain view an' sleep lak a gemmun ontel nex' mawnin. Den he wus a gwineter come out an' take over his twenty watermillions. De tothers make answer to 'im dat seein' wus believin'.

Dey shakes hands wid 'im an' den he goes an' opens de doo'. He leave it open an' go in. He kindle up a big fire in de fireplace, an' 'gin to cook hisself some supper to eat. De tother Niggers takes deir stands out from de cabin an' along by de path w'at lead to de river; so as to watch him an' to watch fer him to see w'at wus a gwineter take place.

Sol sot to wuk an' fried hisself some meat an' cooked hisself some bread. All dis git done all nice . He take it out an' put it on a tin plate. Den he put on some scaly-bark hick'ry tea an a skillet to stew so dat he mought have it to drink w'en he git through eatin'.

He sot down an' 'gun to eat his supper. W'en he git in a good way o' eatin' sumpin nother up in de chimbly 'gin to groan: "Uh—! Uh—! Uh—!" But Sol he play lak he wusnt no skeard. So he holler out: "Hesh up, Joe! You's done took yo' own death fixins lak a man. You's dead, an' I haint never hurted you. So go on 'way an' dont come a bodderin along wid me!"

De tother Niggers set off from de cabin an' look an' lissen, dey do; but dey dont say nothin.

Sol, he eat on a liddle while longer; an' terreckly sumpin-nother up in de chimbly bust out an a great big cry: "Boo—hoo-hoo-hoo-hoo-hoo-hoo-hoo-hoo! Boo—hoo-hoo-hoo-hoo-hoo-hoo-hoo-hoo!"

Den Sol allow sorter pityin lak: "Don't cry Joe! I hopes dat de pizen haint still a hurtin you. I's awful sorry fer you, so please go on off an' don't pester me!"

Da tother Niggers set off an' look an' lissen.

W'en all dis tuck place, Sol 'gin to look lak he don't want nothin much mo' to eat; but he keep on a mincin along an' a makin out dat he wusnt skeard o' no noise.

Terreckly a great big onearthly scratchin on w'at 'pear to be a fiddle take place up in de chimbly. Sol, he holler out: Laws a mussy, Joe! Please dont make yo' liddle dead fiddle-boy, Claud, sing to me! It give me de shivers an' de all'overs! You's about to make me lose all my long years of scrapins togedder of money; so please take yo'self on off an' dont bodder me!"

W'en Joe's dead Claud-fiddle play, an' he heared de grave-yard bones a rattling aroun' in de wind an' a knockin off de chune; Sol git filled up widout eatin' no mo'. He sot dat plate to one side an' he didn' eat anudder bite.

He sot dar fer a while an' ev'ry thing git sorter still; so den he make up his mind to take a swaller or so of his scaly-bark hick'ry tea so as to wash down de bread an' meat w'at wus lodged in his th'oat. You see: Cotton-eyed Joe's hant wus kep' on a hangin' aroun'; ontel it wus a gittin' him whar de wool wus short. He tuck his tin cup an' pewter spoon, an' he dip up a teaspoonful or so of tea outn de skillet a settin on de fire in de fireplace; but befo' he could git de cup in his hand outn de fireplace, Joe's hant drapped a big gob of dirt down de chimbly into it.

Sol holler out: "You stop dat 'ar throwin' yo' mud down de chimbly into my tea!" He den pitch dat 'ar dirt outn his cup back on de floo' of de cabin behin' 'im.

He den dip up a liddle mo' tea, an' Joe's hant throw in some mo dirt. Sol throw dat dirt back on de floo' behin' 'im an' holler out: "Quit dat, Joe! I's jes bleedged to have some tea! De supper is all clogged up in my th'oat an' it's about to choke me to death! It'll kill me if I dont git it washed down somehow!"—So Sol keep on a dippin' up scaly-bark hick'ry tea an' Joe keep on a drappin dirt in it. Sol keep on a hollerin to him, an' a throwin de dirt behin' him in de middle of de cabin floo'.

Atter while dere git to be a great big pile o' dirt in de middle o' de cabin floo'. W'en dis wus so; Joe stopped his throwin' down dirt, an' Sol dipped up a liddle tea widout no dirt in it, an' tu'ned hisself aroun' from de fire-place to drink it.

W'en he tu'n aroun', wid his face towards de pile of dirt to drink de tea; all of a sudden de pile of dirt turn pale, an' jump up offn de floo' an' dar stood Cotton-eyed Joe, gray-white lak blue-john clabber milk, wid a fiddle in his hand an' wid a coffin on 'im fer a head!

Chile! Dey say Sol come outn dat doo' lak he wus been shot outn a muskit. Of de two Niggers dat wus a watchin' him, one whisper to de tother: "Here he come!" an' de tother one whisper back: "Eh-eh—! No-sir-ree—! Yon'er he go!!"

By de time dey wus sayed dis, Sol wus a gwine so fast dat he wus clean outn sight; but dey heared him holler back: "Oh boys! Come an' he'p git Cotton-eyed Joe away from me! I don't want no watermillions an' you can have de money too!" But Honey! dem tother Niggers jes fail to un'erstan' w'at Sol say. Dey thinks dat dey wus got buisness somewhars else, so dey makes tracks away from dar fer deir cabin.

W'en Sol git away down de path nearly to de river whar da big log wus, he look back an' see dat he wus outrun Cotton-eyed Joe's hant an' lef' it behin'. So he sot down dar on da log to pant a liddle an' to res' up an' den to go on back home, jes lak he say he would.

Dar wus two mo' of de Niggers down dar a settin off in de bushes about a stone's throw from de log a watchin' Sol. Dey wus a gigglin an' a nudgin one nudder in de sides an' a whisperin to one nudder 'bout how dey wus a gwineter rake in Sol's money an' den rig him to death 'bout his gwineter put up fer de night in Cotton-eyed Joe's cabin. Terreckly dey seed Joe's big pale gray hant creep up outn de weeds an' set right down on de log by de side of Sol.

Sol squall out: "Laws a mussy, Joe! W'at 's you a doin' here? Is you here sho 'nough?"

Joe make answer: "Yes, I's here; but you sho can do runnin w'at I haint yit hearn tell of neider 'mongst de livin' nor de dead."

Sol answer de hant wid his heels an' as he flewed away he hollered back to de hant: "Yes, but I haint done nothin in runnin compared to w'at I's a gwineter do now!" He made off fer de river lak he say he wus a gwineter do, wid de hant right behin' him. Dar happen to be a rabbit a runnin down dat path along about dat same time w'en Sol wus a trabblin it fer de river. It git all tangled up 'mongst Sol's footses an' he holler out to it:

"Why dont you run, rabbit? If you caint run, git outn de way an' give a good man a chance w'at can!" Sol go so fast dat he split de wind, but de hant keep close up behin' 'im. As dey got to de banks of de river, Sol, he run'd into a liddle bush; an' he wus a runnin so fast dat his whole body got swunked into dat 'ar bush, an' him an' dat 'ar bush git to be all jes one!

W'en de Niggers close up by de log, a gazin' an' a star'in' at Sol an' de hant in de moonlight, see him put in his dis'pearunce in de body of de bush; (Honey!) dey fairly tore up de whole (y)earth a gittin up an' a dustin away from dar! (Chile!) Dey didn' know but w'at w'en Cotton-eyed Joe's hant lose out a tryin to ketch one good man, it mought come back a lookin aroun' fer anudder one. W'en dey gits home:

> Dey jumps in de bed,
> An' kivers up deir head;
> Dont see none a livin',
> Dont want none dead.

Nex' mawnin Sol's Missus an' Mosser come home. De Nigger mens wus all gone out in de fiel' to wuk. Ev'ry thing look to be all right: but w'en de Missus an' Mosser go into de house an' ax de women-suvants how ev'ry thing wus a gittin on, dey makes answer dat ev'ry thing wus all right 'cep' dat "deir" slick 'ceitful lazy do-nothin puttin'-on-aires Sol wusnt yit come outn his mawnin nap fer to do his wuk.

W'en ole Mosser hear dis, he tu'n pale; caze he ricommember 'bout de time w'en he hear sumpin lak dat befo' an' go down an' fin' Cotton-eyed Joe stiff. Ole Missus wus lakwise got dat a tumblin about a liddle bit in her head; so she dont say nothin much neider. So de Mosser an de Missus sorter puts deir heads togedder an' pulls off deir ox-chyart down to Sol's cabin for to see about 'im.

Da doo' wus wide open an' dey peeped an; but dere wusnt no Sol in dar to be seen. Ole Missus, she go on back to de Big House; but ole Mosser, he go on out in de fiel' an' call de fiel' hands an' ax 'em if dey knowed whar Sol wus.

De diffunt ones, w'at wus watched Sol on de night befo', wus jes got through wid tellin' one nudder 'bout w'at dey wus done seed; so dat all of 'em know all 'bout it. But dey haint yit had no time fer to make up 'mongst 'em w'at tale dey wus a gwineter tell deir Mosser. So w'en de ole Mosser ax 'em 'bout Sol, de diffunt ones of de Niggers jes look at one nudder—some a lookin solemcholly an' some a of 'em bein' taken wid de dry grins.

Ole Mosser, he 'gin to git hot under de collar, he do. He hand it out to 'em: If dey dont tell him mighty quick whar Sol wus; he wus a gwineter have de Overseers to strip 'am, an' skin 'em, an' salt 'em, an' pepper 'em.

So one of de Niggers 'gin; an' he tell 'bout Sol from *A* to *Izzard*. He 'gin de tellin' wid de bettin; an' he close it up wid Sol's swunkin hisself inside of de bush.

W'en he git through, ole Mosser ax 'im: Haint he done gone clean raven-stracted crazy, an' 'sides dat w'at in de worl' was ailin him, an' w'at wus he talkin 'bout any-hows?

Den all de tother Niggers jine in an' say dat dis wus de natchul bawn naked trufe.

Ole Mosser look at 'em an' he ax 'em w'at dey wus been a eatin an' a drinkin whilst he wus been gone.

Dey all jes declar to Goodness dat dey haint been a eatin an' a drinkin nothin but ash-cake an' blue-john clabber.

Den he make 'em all come up an' blow deir bref in his face to make shore dat dey wusnt done gone an' fished out some of his good apple brandy an' home-made grape wine outn his cellar onbe-knowance to 'im whilst he wus gone. But he dont smell no licker on 'em. How-some-be-ever he tell 'em dat he wus a gwineter whup de las' one of 'em fer liein to 'im; caze dey knowed dere wusnt no trufe in w'at dey wus a sayin to 'im. But dey all jes turns in an' begs him not to whup' em; but jes to come wid 'em an' 'let 'em show him. So at las' he promus to go wid 'em.

He go, an' dey fust show him de watermillions all piled up in de weeds out in Sol's gyardin—dem w'at dey bet him 'g'inst all his money. Den dey p'ints out to 'im Joe's cabin doo' on-fastened an' lef' wide open. Den dey stands aroun' on de outside an' p'ints out to deir Mosser de skil-let an' dem tother things w'at Sol cook wid, on de night befo', a settin out on de floo' of Joe's cabin; an' dey subgests dat he mought go in an' zamin 'em fer hisself, but he say to 'em dat he dont see no sense in his go a gwine in dar to look 'em over. He can see 'em plenty good outside dar. Den de Niggers tuck him down de path w'at Sol runned over a gwine to de river an' showed him de bush w'at Sol got swunked up in a stan'in' dar by it. De bush wus a liddle willow saplin a settin in de aidge of de water in de river. Its leaves wus so pale an' ashy dat dey wus almos' white; an' all of its limbs wus all drooped over an' a hangin down. Dey all looked at de willow; an' all of 'em—eben de ole Mosser—say dey haint never seed no setch a willow as dat a hangin down all over in all deir natchul bawn days. W'en de wind blow, all de hung down limbs on it swing an' make a noise lak somebody a cryin'; so ole Mosser say dat it look to him lak dat setch a sort of a willow should oughter be called a "Weepin Willow." So dey all 'gin from dat time on to call de bush a "Weepin Willow."

But ole Mosser say to 'em dere never wus no Nigger w'at could pull de wool over his eyes—He haint a b'lievin' in no ways dat no Sol swunk hisself into no bush eben if de bush wus cu'ious lookin'. So he go an' git de blood-hounds an' put 'em on his tracks. W'en he git 'em good a gwine, dey tracks right along de path whar de tother Niggers say dat Sol go. Day tracks him right down to de weepin willow in de aidge of de river. Dar dey stops an' looks at de bush an' barks!

Ole Mosser look at de hounds an' den he look sorter jubous lak at de Weepin Willow, an' he say dat it sorter looked to him lak dat Sol mought a drownded hisself. So he sont de Niggers an' got a whole passel of pot-hooks an' poles. Dey takes dese an' drags de bottom of he river; but dey dont hook up no Sol outn de san' an' de slime. Den ole Mosser git in his dug-out, an' take de hounds wid him across de river, an' up an' down he river fer a mile or so. But dey dont hit no scent of no Sol's tracks nowhars.

At las' dey has to give Sol up an' go on back home. W'en dey gits back dar, ole Mosser tell his Niggers dat he reckin dat dey had better go right down an' t'ar down Cotton-eyed Joe's cabin an' split up de logs into fence rails, lak he wus been a talkin 'bout fer some time befo'.

But dese here Niggers wus railly skeard dat Cotton-eyed Joe's hant mought come atter 'em wid his coffin head; if dey tetches dat cabin. So one of 'em tells ole Mosser: Dis wont never do caze de big sound red cedar logs wus done got too rotten to make rails outn. Anudder one splain dat de logs wus all put up in de cabin so catawampus an' cu'ious an' crooked dat he wus skeard dat dey mought fall down an' kill 'em all if dey eben jes p'int deir finger at 'em, an' look at 'em right hard. Den dey all jine in an' say dat dem logs wus jes natchully so knotty dat nobody couldn' never split one.

Ole Mosser scratch his head an' think a liddle an' den he tell de Niggers to come an' go along wid him down to de cabin; an' he'll set it on fire an' burn it up. He sot it on fire, an' it brung on a cu'ious whirlwind w'at pulled up de blazes almos' clean to de sky. An' whilst it wus a burnin the flames make a cu'ious singin noise lak Joe's dead Claud-fiddle ontel de last of de embers flicker out an' die. Ole Missus come a runnin out w'en she fust seed de cabin on fire, caze she didn' know w'at to make of

it. W'en she got dar an' foun' dat de Mosser wus sot it on fire, she start to
try to laugh at 'im but he shet her up by tellin her dat two Niggers wus
already gone mighty cu'ious outn dat cabin an' he spec dat it mought be
jes about as well to drap it befo' some white folks somehow foller on
behin' 'em.

A liddle while atter dat ole Missus go down to de river
one day to look at de Weepin Willow w'at dey wus all been a tellin her
about. Nobody dont know w'at make her do it; but she tuck up dat ar'
bush an' brung it home an' sot it out in de fambly grave-yard. Some say
dat ole Missus laked Sol, an' she want him in de grave-yard; an' dat wus
de reason dat she brung him home an' sot him out dar; but some say dat
it twusn't dat way at 'tall—she jes laked de Weepin Willow an' sot it out
dar.

Atter dis heaps of liddle Weepin Willows 'gin to pop up here an' dar
in de woods an' de swamps. De folkses say dat dese wus Sol's chilluns an'
dey take dem up too an' plants dem out in de grave-yards. Dat's how
come Weepin Willows to be an' dat's how come dey all to git planted out
in grave-yards."

"Mary," said Uncle Dan, "dis is he loration w'at de Niggers tol' down
at de corn-shuckin dat night at ole Zeek Lacy's an' I wus been a thinkin
'bout tryin to find out whedder or not dere railly be's setch things as hants
lak dey all sayes."

"How's you gwineter find out any mo' dan you's already l'arnt?" inquired aunt Mary.

"Well," said Uncle Dan rather meekly, "De fellers at de' corn-shuckin
say dat de ole 'Red Brick' house down yonder close to town, w'at nobody
caint live in, is hanted. Dey claims dat ev'ry night, at midnight, you can
hear a cu'ious kind o' clock strike three in dar. Den deres three big flashes
of lightnin' inside of de 'Ole Red Brick' w'at light up de house fer a minute
or so as bright as daylight. W'en dis light die out, den it is as dark as pitch
inside, eben if de moon an' stars is a shinin all bright outside. If you
stands outside (Dey say) an' peeps into de pitchy darkness inside, you can
see de hants a playin lak on deir fiddles an' a dancin' all over de house.

"'Big Pete' an' 'Bully' Jim say to me dat day's go wid me down dar
some night to see it all. So I's been a thinkin' dat I'd jes git 'em an' go
down dar an' see w'at I'd see."

When Uncle Dan had placed a plan of investigation before Aunt Mary,
she sat for a few moments looking at him in silent bewilderment, then she
said: "If you's a gwineter go off lak dat a lookin' atter hants; nobody dont
want you a comin' back home here ontel nex' day, caze you's a gittin
ready to git fixed up lak ole Brer B'ar w'en he go out wid ole Brer Rabbit
to git him to show him a man. Yes-sir-ree Bob! I wants to git scused from

a seein' you ontel de time come fer all de hants to quit off walkin' fer de night!"

"How wus dat about ole Brer Rabbit a showin' ole Brer B'ar a man?" asked Uncle Dan. "I haint never hearn tell o' nothin' o' dat kind.—W'at wus it?"

"Well, it wus lak dis", answered Aunt Mary with an aire of one who is desirous of making every thing clear, "ole Brer Rabbit wus a settin' off in de woods one evenin', a tellin' ole Brer B'ar fer w'at a big wonderment Mr. Man wus. W'en he git through wid his splavercations Brer B'ar say to 'im dat he wanter see dis here great big Mr. W'at's-'is-name.

Brer Rabbit try to tell 'im dat he wus skeard dat it 'twouldn' do him no good fer to see 'im. But ole Brer B'ar say if he caint git to see 'im, he jes mus' some how or udder manage to git to put one eye on 'im.

So ole Brer Rabbit at las' say to 'im dat, if he jes mus' git a liddle peep at Mr. Man, he reckin dat he'll hafter take him down nex' day by de liddle trail in de woods whar Mr. Man in ginerally pass along ev'ry mawnin bright an' early.

So nex' mawnin Brer Rabbit take Brer B'ar down by de trail fer to see Mr. Man. He puts ole Brer B'ar down behin' a big log along side of de trail, an' tells 'im dat he'll let him know w'en Mr. Man is about to pass by; den he can put one han' up on top of de log, ease up right easy, peep over wid one eye, lay dat eye on 'im, den drap right back down easy.

At fust Brer Rabbit wus a settin' behin' de log wid him. Atter while Brer Rabbit peep over de log down de trail; an' ole Brer B'ar pop up an' peep over along wid 'im. Dey seed a liddle boy a comin' down de trail through de woods. Brer B'ar say to Brer Rabbit, says he, "Is dat a man?" Ole Brer Rabbit 'spon' "No, dat haint no man; but it's a gwineter be one".

Atter while dey bofe peeps over de log ag'in; an' dey sees a ole man a comin', a walkin' wid a walkin' stick.

"Is dat a man?" says ole Brer B'ar, says he. Ole Brer Rabbit make answer: "No, dat haint no man; but it wus one, one time".

Dey lays aroun' behin' de log a liddle while longer; an' den dey peeps over de log down de trail once mo'. Dey sees sumpin a comin' a way off yonder.

"Is dat a man?" axed ole Brer B'ar, axed he. "Yes, dat's a man;" splained ole Brer Rabbit, splained he; "an' now you can stay right here behin' de log an' peep at 'im jes lak I wus done tol' you. Den you can come down in de swamp an' tell me how you likes him".

Wid dat much said ole Brer Rabbit up an' han'-gallop off. W'en Mr. Man git benent de log whar ole Brer B'ar wus a hidin'; Brer B'ar put his han' up on top of de log right easy an' peep over at 'im lak ole Brer Rabbit wus tol' 'im to do. But jes as he put his han' up on top of de log; Mr. Man seed it, an'—"Bang!!" went off Mr. Man's gun.

Brer B'ar tore off down to de swamp on three footses. Brer Rabbit heard him a comin' an' runned out to de aidge of de swamp to meet him.

"Hey-o, dar!" say ole Brer Rabbit, says he. "Did you seed Mr. Man?"

"Yes I seed him", makes answer ole Brer B'ar answers he; "but I mought almos' wush dat I hadn'. He wus a totin a liddle fence rail on his shoulder, an' w'en I uped an' peeped over de log at 'im, dat rail thundered at one end an' lightnined at de tother, an' it blowed my han' so chug full of splinters dat I's skeard dat my whole fambly wont be able fer to pick 'em all out fer uncteen years or mo'."

"Now," added Aunt Mary, "You's a fixin up fer to git sumpin a heaps wusser dan Brer B'ar; if you's a plannin' up to go a foolin along wid "Big" Pete an' "Bully" Jim, a tryin' to git a peep at de hants!"

"Well Mary, Honey," put in the husband, "I reckins dat it mus' be about bed-time, an' I specs dat I'd better go on to bed an' keep on a gwine to bed ev'ry night about dis time." So Uncle Dan retired for his night's rest, half convinced, but still wondering whether or not there were any such things as "hants" or ghosts in the land of the living.

Why the Jaybird Goes to See the "Bad Man" on Friday

❄

To the east of Shelbyville Tennessee, about six miles distant, flows a creek known as The Garrison. Two Negro boys, Bone Sutton and Skewball Coffee by name, were returning from it, on a beautiful Friday afternoon of an early Spring of the early seventy's of the last century, the one with a large string of fish which he had caught on their fishing trip, and the other empty handed save for the hook and line which he had carried with him. They walked along together, chatting good naturedly, and soon came to the home of the unsuccessful fisherman. Skewball, the unsuccessful fisherman, said as they arrived at the gate: "Say, Bone, de sun is two hours high. Haint no use in yo' hurryin' on home; come in an' let's play a while".

"I's skeard to stop", said Bone, "I's skeard my fish mought spile".

"Oh, no dey wont", answered Skewball. "I'll git my mammy to put 'em in a topped tin bucket an' hang 'em down in our well whar dey'll keep cool whilst we plays."

This plan was agreed to by Bone; and when they had gone into Skewball's home, the ex-slave mother—Aunt Jinsey Campbell—was kind enough to hang the fish as suggested and the boys went out to play.

Soon there was a veritable din of sounds, from without, issuing forth from the throats of jaybirds. The boys were robbing their nest.

Aunt Jinsey quickly sprang to her feet, and running to the cabin door, cried out: "You, Skewball! Come here to me, Sah!"

Skewball dropped the nest and eggs upon the ground which he had procured, and walked with dropping head to his mother; while Bone, rather disconcerted, followed many steps behind him.

"Skewball didn' I tell you not to never rob no mo' birds' nesses?" said the irate mother. "How many times is I gwineter hafter skin you befo' you gits some common sense in dat stubble head o' yourn? I thought I had you broke off from de sin of breakin' up birds' nesses; an' now here you is a t'arin' 'em up again, an' a fixin up fer mo' bad luck fer us all!"

The mother wasted no more words, but proceeded immediately to administer the form of corporal punishment characteristic of that time. Then turning her attention to Bone, she said: "I's a gwineter tell yo' mammy so's she can tan yo' hide an' l'arn you some sense too! I knows she dont want no jaybirds a totin' sand down to de Bad Man fer to burn you wid, an' I's a gwineter tell her!"

"Oh, Aunt Jinsey!" said Bone. "My mammy haint never telled me not to rob no birds nestes! I haint never hearn tell of no Bad Man a burnin' you wid sand fer dat! I dont never do nothin' w'at my mammy tell me not to do."

"Well! Well! Well!" slowly murmured Aunt Jinsey. "Yo' mammy is sho a powerful cu'ious 'oman not to a never tol' you w'at a turble thing it 'twus to break up birds' nesses."

"Well, she haint never tol' me nothin' 'bout dat," said Bone, "an' you mus' tell me so's I wont be a doin' nothin' wrong an' a gittin' bad luck. I wants you to take half of de fish w'at I wus cotched, caze I wants you an' Skewball to have some; an' den I mus' be a gittin on home. But befo' I goes; I wish dat you'd tell me how it got to be a sin an' bad luck fer to break up birds' nesses."

Aunt Jinsey, pleased with the boy's liberality, felt constrained to oblige such a good-hearted youngster and said: "All right, Honey, set down on de box dar. I's almos' fergit a lots of de fac's I's hearn 'em all tell 'bout how it all happen; but I'll tell you all dat I can call back to my membunce.

But atter I tells you how an' why it git to be a sin an' bad luck fer to rob birds' nesses, an' how it all come 'bout dat de jaybirds totes sand down to de Bad Man on a Friday; I dont want you to be lak Skewball over dar. Why—! De mo' I tells him about de Bad Man an' his bu'nin' up folks wid hot sand; de mo' it look lak he wus mo' bent an' bound to go down to 'im. Sometimes w'en I looks at Skewball, I's skeard dat eben all my good seasoned hick'ries haint a gwineter save 'im.

Aunt Mary Shaker comed over here one day an' told me: jes atter I wus got through wid chestizin Skewball 'bout meddlin wid birds' nesses an' a gittin bad luck; dat Skewball telled her boy, Bill, dat he sorter think dat I wus a "ole fogey".

Honey, it wus in de mawnin w'en she tol' me all dat an' Skewball wus gone a huntin'. He didn' git back ontel night, an' it 'twus a good thing; caze, if I hadn' a got time to cool off, I reckin I sho would a skint him alive, an' a salted de hide an' a hung it up in de sun to dry."

"Oh, Aunt Jinsey," remarked Bone, "I wouldn' never say nothin' 'bout you fer nothin'".

"Ve'y Well, Honey", said Aunt Jinsey, "I'll splain it all to you den.—My granmammy come from away back yon'er befo' Bargro Times [Bargo Times = The time of England's passing of the Embargo Act for their American Colonists]. She wus de one w'at tol' me all about it. She say dat her folks come from away back in de times w'en de folkses wus all black an' dey could talk wid de birds. Her folks an' de birds wus good friends an' go to see one-nudder jes lak Brer Rabbit an' Brer Ter-pin an' dem useter go to see King Deer's daughter an' Miss Meadows an' de gals.

Well, my granmammy wus de funniest liddle ole gray-headed dried-up lookin' 'oman dat you ever did see; an' de bes' way dat I can tell you 'bout dis whole thing is to tell you 'bout her. My granmammy say w'en she wus a liddle gal she had a mammy an' daddy same as folks now-a-days. She wus at dat time so liddle dat she wusnt yit l'arnt how to talk wid de birds, but her folkses w'at could talk wid 'em tell her all 'bout how de jaybird come to go down to de Bad Man on Friday.

W'en I axed her how dere come to be white folkses, she say she dont know zackly. She tell me w'en she was a liddle pickaniny, she went to sleep one night, an' w'en she woke up de nex mawnin she wus in a great big cu'ious house a floatin aroun' in some water, an' almos' all de folkses aroun' her wus white. She say dese here white folkses couldn' talk; dey jes make signs. Atter so long a time dey all l'arn to talk: but dey never did know nothin 'bout birds an' dem sort o' things lak her daddy an' mammy."

Granmammy say dat her mammy say: 'Way back yonder in dem days de birds an' de folkses wus de best of friends. Dey do all dey can fer one-nudder an' live in peze an' homny [peze an' homny = peace and harmony].

Honey, in dis here worl', dere is good folks an' dere is bad folks; an' dere always has been good folks an' bad folks. Dere wus some bad folks a livin' w'en de folks an' de birds wus all good friends. Dese bad folks set out, jes lak de bad folks now, to tilt de fryin' pan, to th'ow de fat in de fire, to turn over de tea-kittle a hangin' on de potrack, to put out de fire befo' de ash-cake git done a cookin', an' to flavor up ev'ry thing wid "lye" in ginerally. Dese here bad folkses 'gin to slip aroun' an' steal an' eat some o' de birdses' eggs jes lak ole Ake, dat ole pourakin [pourakin = One of the names given to the poorer white people of the South by the antebellum Negro], slip out in yo' co'nfiel' yo' daddy's ras'in' (y)ears fer to eat.

De birds watch an' watch; but dey dont seem to be able somehow to ketch up wid no rogues so as to git 'em took bofo' de Jedge fer deir devil-ment. De good folkses lakwise try to ketch de rogues w'en dey wus got time to stop wuk fer to watch; but de bad folkses wus got time enough an' to spare to lie down an' go to sleep w'en de good folkses wus a watchin'. Leaswise dese good folkses dont ketch no rogues a stealin' eggs.

But de birds knows dat it's folkses a stealin' deir eggs; caze dey could smell whar deir hands tetch de nes' w'en dey git de eggs out. (An' if you's noticed, clean down to dis day, if you puts yo' hands in de wild birds' an' guineas' nesses; dey quits dat nest.)

Bymeby de Jaybird subgest to de tother birds dat dey call all de folkses an' de birds togedder to see w'at dey can fin' out an' to see w'at dey can do towards keepin' peze an' homny.

Dey all come togedder; an' whilst de tothers wus a settin on de groun', de Jaybird sot upon de lim' of a big tree above 'em so dat he could act fer a cheersman of de meetin'. He tell 'em all w'at he wus called de meetin fer; den he ax de folkses to do deir talkin fust.

De folkses fer de most part say dat dey haint got no nothin to say much, 'cep' dat de ones w'at done de egg-stealin' should oughter have deir backs whupped raw an' den salted an' peppered.

Nex' de Jaybird ax de birds to do deir talk-in'.

Brer Peafowl git up fust caze he wus 'bout de bigges' an' fines' lookin' one 'mongst 'em. Of co'se he want to save his eggs; but de bigges' thing in Brer Peacock's mind wus to show off his fine clo'es. He git up, an' he take so much time a primpin up an' a spreadin' out his big-eyed tail fer 'em; dat de tother birds 'gin to git mad befo' he git his likely tale a gwine. W'en he git his speech to de p'int whar he aim to warm her up an' pour some gravy on her; de tother birds 'gin to scrape deir footses 'roun' mongst de san' an' gravel an' dey raise setch a hubbub dat it didn' look lak Brer Peacock wus a gwineter git no hearin'. But bymeby he manage to git hisself heared; caze Brer Peacock wus got one o' dese here hallelujah-preacher-voices an' he know how to make use of it mo' samer dan his tail finery. W'en he git hisself oncorked good, dey wus jes bleedged to hear 'im. He subgest to 'em dat dey call up all de folkses an' smell deir hands; an' den dat dey go an' smell deir robbed nesses, an' in dat way dey can pick out de ones w'at wus been a tetchin de nesses an' a stealin de eggs.

All enjorin' Brer Peacock's speech, Brer Owl wusnt zackly one of dem w'at keep as still as a lam'; but w'en he see w'at fine plan Brer Peacock wus put befo' 'em, he feel sorter shame. So Chile, ole Brer Owl pop up an' de way he scold dem tother birds 'bout scrapin' deir footses wus a sin. He tell 'em dat wus de reason dat de birds dont git 'long no better; dat w'en dey wus got fine smart folks, dey haint got sense 'nough to lissen to 'em an' 'spect 'em.

Ole Brer Rooster git up behin' 'im an' say dat de whole compoodle of de birds wus ready to perfess an' polergize to Brer Peacock fer not knowin' dat he wus got so much sense. He tell 'em dat he wus been a whisperin' aroun' 'mongst de tothers whilst Brer Owl wus a talkin' an' dey'd all tetched an' greed dat dey would show Brer Peacock clean down to his chilluns' chilluns how much dey 'spect him by always givin' his folkses de highes' tree to roos' in.

Den he tu'n to Brer Pèacock, an' scratch out his foot 'hin' 'im, an' bow sorter low an' say: dat heaps of de scratchin' jes happen caze most of de folkses dar wus so poo' dat dey hafter scratch fer a livin'. Dey wus done scratched so much dat it wus sorter hard fer 'em to keep deir footses still long 'nough fer to hear a fine long-winded speech. He lakwise put in fer sorter good measure dat whilst he wus a whisperin' 'roun' 'mongst de tothers dat it seem to him lak he heared some of 'em say dat dey eben seed Brer Owl move his big clumsy footses whilst Brer Peacock wus a speakin'. An' some of 'em eben go so fur as to say dat if Brer Owl hadn' a got his long crooked claws hung in de groun'; he mought a maked mo' noise wid his footses dan all de balunce of de bunch, an' a 'sturbed Brer Peacock's speech along wid de tothers widout knowin' it. At las' Brer Rooster subgest dat dey all shake hands, look over an' fergit de wrong time o' foot-scratchin, an' 'gin to smell de hands of de folkses to find out w'at ones do de stealin' of deir eggs. Dey all 'gree to dis.

Nex', de birds all line up on a long rail fence; an' Brer Cheersman Jaybird 'nounce to de folkses dat dey wus ready to have 'em swing down de line an' let de birds all smell deir hands. Ole Brer Hawk didn' git on de fence, caze he say he put his eggs in setch a high tree dat no mens caint never climb up dar an' git 'em. So he dont need no nosin aroun' into tother folkses' business. So Brer Hawk tell 'em dat he'll set off up in de top of a big tall tree to watch an' see dat some of de mens dont slip off an' run away widout gittin smelt.

De folkses 'gin to go down de line, lettin de birds smell deir hands. De smellin go on all right ontel atter while de Niggers w'at wus been a stealin an' a eatin de eggs have deir time to come fer to pass down de line. De fust one w'at go down de line, onbeknowance to de birds, go an' rub his hands wid pods of red pepper. W'en some o' de birds smell his hands; dey gits taken wid a sneezin spell an' sneeze deirselves clean offn de fence down on de groun'.

Brer Hawk wus a sorter actin Jedge as well as Perleesmun. So he holler down from de top of de tree fer dis Nigger to stop. Brer Hawk sorter jump aroun' from one lim' to anudder so as to git a good look at dis Nigger on all sides. Den he scratch his head an' think fer a while: den he holler down dat he dont know zackly w'at's de matter but sumpin mus' be wrong. He say dat it look to him lak dat dis Nigger's hands wus so cold dat jes de smellin of 'em makes folks git taken wid de Ipizoodic. So he holler down dat he think dat dey'd better heat up a big pot o' hot water right away to dip dis here Nigger's hands in so as to show 'em out an' fix him so dat he wont give ev'ry body setch a bad col' w'at smell him.

De dry-land birds bring sticks an' trash, de water-birds bring water; an' so dey git deir big kittle o' hot b'ilin' water. Den dey called fer de Nigger wid "col'" hands fer to come for'd an' stick 'em in de hot water. (Chile! you wus heared folkses a sayin dat "Mistah So-an-so is in hot water", haint you?—Well dat's whar dat ole sayin comed from.) Dis here Nigger wid peppered-up hands w'at steal bird-eggs hafter scald his hands good. An' he daresant make no noise 'bout de scaldin' neider; caze, if he had, de birds would a seed which way de win' wus a blowin'. He jes whistle while he scald 'em an' say: "Oh, Mussy! It sho do make yo' fingers ache w'en you thaws 'em out all frez up!

"W'en de tothers w'at wus been a stealin de eggs see how deir podner fare; dey 'gins to wash deir hands in a branch w'at wus a runnin' close by, so as to git off de scent of de red pepper, de Heaben-tree leaves, de gyarlic, de dog-fennel, de chyarn, an' heaps o' udder bad-smellin things w'at dey wus been a rubbin on deir hands to fool de birds. Brer Hawk seed 'em a washin' but he didn' stop 'em; he jes holler down: "I's a markin down in my head all dem w'at is a changin' an' a doctorin-up deir smell"!

Well, atter dis de birds git settled on de fence once mo'; an' go on wid de smellin'. W'en de smellin' of de hands git over wid it wus about night;

an' de birds an' de folkses didn' have no time fer to finish up de job by gwine an' smellin de nesses an' a pickin out de egg-eaters by de smell a bein de same in bofe places. So dey all stops off ontel de nex' day to finish up deir pickin out of de rogues.

But dey all say dat dem w'at act so funny a runnin an' a washin deir hands sorter condemn deirselves: so dey'd better slap 'em in jail ontel dey finds out fer shore. Well, dey slapped 'em down in a dungeon an' rolled a big rock over on top of de doo' an' den dey go on off some fer de night.

Dat night a big rain comed up an' washed all de scent offn de birds' nesses. So w'en dey all meets de nex day, de big plan fer ketchin de egg-eaters by smellin wus plum flammogasted. De birds all sot aroun' fer a while. Den dey allows: Of co'se dey haint got all de proofs togedder but it look lak dat de mens w'at go an' wash deir hands mus know sumpin 'bout de eggs.

So dey calls 'em all out an' axes 'em: W'at make 'em go to de branch, on de day befo', an' wash deir hands in dat 'ar branch.

De Niggers all make answer dat dey wus all col-handed jes lak de one w'at had to put his hands in de hot water. So w'en dey see how de hands hurt if dey thaw 'em out in hot water; dey go to de branch to thaw 'em out in col' water, so dat it wouldn' hurt so bad, an' so dat dey'd be ready to be smelt widout hurtin' de birds.

De birds say dat look mighty cu'ious caze dey haint never hearn tell befo' of no frez-handed folkses. It look to dem lakwise dat mens wid dem kind of hands would eider warm 'em up by blowin deir bref on 'em or by stickin 'em down in deir pockets.

But de egg-eaters say dat deir moufs wus lakwise col' so dat dey couldn' blow deir hands warm; an' dey wus clean fergit it offn' deir minds dat dey wus got pockets caze dey dont never hardly have nothin scacely to put in 'em.

Dar wus whar dem egg-eaters miss deir footin'. De birds say dat gemmuns wid col' moufs should oughter have 'em, warmed up. Dey say dat dey wus broke all de young dogs, w'at didn' know no better, from a suckin eggs by bustin hot eggs in deir moufs. So dey makes up deir minds dat by bustin hot eggs in dese here men's "col'" moufs, dey can hand out a double dose of bitters at one swaller; an' w'at-some-ever de trouble mought be, it 'twould chuore 'em. If deir moufs is jes col', it'll warm 'em up; if dey wus been a eatin de eggs, it'll burn 'em an' break 'em.

So dey h'et up an' busted hot eggs in deir moufs! Dat wus w'at de fust Niggers got fer breakin up an' a robbin' birds' nesses.

Atter de "bustin" dey all went on off home. De Niggers w'at git de burnt moufs hafter set 'roun an' eat milk an' mush fer a mont'. W'en de news git out dat deir moufs wus all lined wid sores from de burnin of de hot eggs; all de birds knowed dat de "col'-hand", "col'-mouf" business wus all put on. Dey knows dat dese wus de scounters w'at wus been a stealin deir eggs but dey couldn' prove it. So dey comes togedder an' fixes up fer good de "smellin-out" fer a law to ketch egg-stealers. Den dey say dey wus a gwineter salt an' pepper an' kill de fust one dat dey smells out.

W'en dese lazy Niggers wus got well; dey still didn' want to do no wuk. So dey calls a meetin' all on deir own hooks to 'scuss w'at dey wus a gwineter do. At las' de Nigger w'at wus burnt an' scalded say dat he jes mus' eat 'nough eggs to git back at dem birds if dey kills him de nex' minute. But he add dat he wus done gone an' got a plan; caze dere never wus no smart man whar dere wusnt anudder one w'at wus jes a liddle bit smarter.

De tothers wid de burnt moufs says all right, dey wus ready fer de plan jes so long as it 'twusnt one of dem 'ar kind w'at call fer han'-scaldin, mouf burnin, an' hot egg bustin on de tongue.

De burnt handed Nigger den tell 'em dat dis wus easy. He declar to gracious dat his burnt hands talk to him so much whilst dey wus a gittin well dat he jes had to promus 'em to git up a plan to keep 'em outn hot water. Dis, he say, wus de plan: Jes take a liddle stick an' rake de eggs outn de nes'; den throw de stick away an' pick up de eggs an' leave. Dat way dere wouldn be no scent lef' fer de nose to git no holt on 'cep' de wind.

Dis sound good an' all dem egg-eaters take up de plan. W'en dis took place, de birds all git de liddle end of de bargain; so dey called anudder meetin of bofe de birds an' de folkses. Dey tells de folkses dat it look lak dat de Niggers w'at steal bird-eggs wus done gone an' turned deirselves into witches or conj'ers; caze dey comes an' gits deir eggs an' dont leave no smell behin' 'em.

De good folkses say, beance dat wus so, dey dont see no way fer to help 'em; 'cep', if de birds'll spare a few eggs, dey'll try to git ev'ry body to feel dat dey wont steal w'at dey can git far' an' squar'.

Ole Sis Turkle-dove git up an' moan off dat she dont lay but two eggs a year; an' if she give 'way one egg, w'en de tother one hatch out, it wont mate off wid nobody an' atter while it grieve itself to death. So if she give 'way one egg a year de whole Turkle-dove name'll die out.

Brer Buzzard, Brer Hawk, Brer Jaybird, an' 'bout all dem tothers git up atter Sis Turkle-dove an' say: Dat same dog wus done gone an' bit deir folkses.

At las' ole Sis Hen an' a few mo' of 'em w'at lay almos' any time say dat dey wus willin' to let de folkses eat deir eggs in de bad wedder caze w'en deir chilluns hatches out in dem times dey most in ginerally drawed up an' died. But if dey does dis de folkses mus' cross deir hearts an' hope dey may drop dead if dey dont keep deir promus not to never eat no eggs at no other time. Dey say lakwise dat de folkses'll hafter let 'em live in de house an' feed 'em an' wait on 'em an' clean up fer 'em in de bad wedder, if dey gives 'em de eggs to eat.

De folkses study over all dis promisin an dey thinks maybe dat it wus tolerbus good rough rocky road outn a mighty bad mud-puddle; so dey crosses deir hearts an' 'gree. Dem bird-egg stealin Niggers lakwise cross deir gizzards an' promus.

Well, de folkses take in Sis Hen's folkses; an' den all of 'em 'gun to love an' to eat eggs. De ones w'at wus been a stealin git deirselves plantations jes lak de tothers. Dey eben try to keep mo' chickens dan de good folkses w'at didn' do no egg-stealin. But it wus in de bargain dat dem w'at took chickens wus to feed 'em. Dese roguish Niggers wouldn' wuk, an' dey didn' have no feed; so de fowls all up an' lef' 'em.

Now w'en Sis Hen's folkses leave dese lazy good-fer-nuthin egg-stealers; dey wus strapped an' hongry; so dey goes to stealin' an' a eatin' de birds' eggs ag'in.

De birds call a meetin of all de folkses an' birds ag'in; an' lay out de troubles in public meetin'. But de good folkses didn' jes zackly see de egg-stealers lak dey useter atter dey git to eatin an' a likin de eggs deirselves. So dey say to de birds dat dey wus a gwineter keep deir words onbroke an' whole, but dem an' de bad folkses mus' scratch out deir troubles 'twixt an' 'tween 'em.

Den de birds git up a meetin all by deirselves to 'scuss w'at to do. W'en dey all got dar, Brer Hawk riz an' tol' 'em: Since he wus about de onliest one 'mongst 'em w'at wus saved his eggs; he guess he mought loan 'em all a liddle o' his kind o' sense, if dey wus stout 'nough to put it on deir heads an' tote it off wid 'em. He tell 'em dat dey mus' stop deir puttin' deir eggs 'roun' down on de groun'. Dey mus' eider put deir nesses up so high dat de folkses caint git to 'em, lak he do; or dey mus' hide 'em some'ars whar dey caint be foun'.

De birds all make up deir minds to foller w'at Brer Hawk subgest. Brer Crow an' Brer Owl an' dem say dat dey wus a gwineter put deir nes up high. Brer Sap-sucker an' his browd say deir eggs wus a gwine inside of a holler tree. Some say dat dey wus a gwineter fix 'em up an' hide 'em one way an' some say anudder—all 'cep' Brer Jaybird.

Brer Jaybird say dat he wus a gwineter fight it out an' he want all dem tother birds to he'p 'im out. Dem tother birds make answer dat dey'll he'p 'em fight; but dey wus a gwineter always run away fust an' hide deir eggs, caze:

"Dem w'at fight an' runs away,
May live to fight anudder day."

Brer Jaybird say dat all rogues wus cowards so he hain't a gwineter hide his eggs. He's jes a gwineter tell dem bad folkses dat he dares 'em to do it, w'en dey comes fer to git his eggs; caze he haint never seed no cowards w'at you couldn' back out w'en you double dares 'em. Dat end it wid de birds.

Bymeby, one Friday, dese here egg eaters start out a huntin' an' dey comes right smack up on Brer Jaybird's nes'. So w'en dey starts to git his eggs he hollers out:

"Do-it! Do-it!
I dares you! I dares you!
I dares you! I dares you!
Do-it! Do-it!"

Well, Honey, dem 'ar bad folks "done it" fer Brer Jaybird all right. Dey swiped all his eggs an' th'owed his nes' down on de groun'.

De Jaybird ax dem tothers fer why dey didn' come over an' he'p him lighten his troubles.

Dey make answer to him dat dey did he'p. Didn' dey holler w'en he holler; an', in dat way, didn' dey do lak dey promus? De Jaybird couldn' 'spute dis. So he didn' say no mo' to 'em, but jest sot down an' cried two whole days widout stoppin. On de third day, on a Sunday, he quit off his cryin an' 'gin on his thinkin'. He think two whole days. On de third day, on a Tuesday, he make up his mind dat he want to see de Bad Man; to try to git him to 'gree to git de bad folkses, an' take 'em down to de Bad Place, an' burn 'em up wid fire, an' smoke 'em dry wid brimstone.

So he git his provisions togedder; an', bright an early Wednesday mawnin, he 'gin to dig right straight down th'ough de groun' to git to de Bad Place.

He dig two days widout stoppin'. On de third day, on a Friday, he git down to de doo' w'at open up into dem red hot ridgions.

He knock on de doo', an' de Bad Man come an' open it a liddle an' look out. He wus jes stonished to see Brer Jaybird a stan'in' out dar at de doo'—big as life an' twice as natchul! He rub his eyes an' look at Brer Jaybird ag'in to make shore dat his mawnin toddy wusnt got him a seein' double. Den he pinch hisself to see whedder it wus him or wus some-body else. At las' he make up his min' dat he wus hisself an' dat de tother one wus Brer Jaybird alive. Den he say:

"Jaybird, you can cut loose an' sing
Dat you's my pet, dat's one sho' thing.
You can git w'at you wants w'en you shows yo' face
From de worl' dat's above, down in de Bad Place."

De Jaybird tell de Bad Man all his troubles wid de dem low-downed egg-eatin Niggers, w'at wouldn' keep deir word; den he ax him fer to he'p him.

De Bad Man wus jes tickled to death wid de Jaybird; caze he wus de fust bird w'at wus ever make his way down to de Bad Place alive. So he tell 'im dat he'll do all he can fer him.

Fust word dat he say wus dat de Jaybird mus' go back; an', atter dat, hide his eggs jes lak de tother birds.

Brer Jaybird make answer dat he'll do dat.

Den de Bad Man tell 'im dat he caint do much to de bad folkses ontel dey dies an' falls in his hands. So he mus' go back an' make it so hot fer 'em in de worl' dat dey'll cuss a plenty an' fall to him w'en dey dies; den he'll fix up all de balunce.

De Jaybird tell 'im dat he wus willin' but he de didn' see w'at a liddle man lak him could do along side of great big mens, 'cep' to dare 'em. He wus done done dat an' los' a whole fambly!

De Bad Man tell 'em dat he'll splain de plan: Fust an fo'most he mus' come back on a Fridays to find out de wuk dat he wus got cut out fer him to do. But for jes now, he mus' go on back to de worl' an' hide his eggs lak he wus told him. De Devil caint have no chilluns w'at dont mind 'em. Atter he wus done w'at he wus tol' 'im; so soon as he notice a change, he mus' come back on a Friday an' let him know.

De Jaybird hide his eggs lak de Devil wus tol' 'em. Wen de egg-steal-ers couldn' find no eggs much fer to eat, an' it look lak dey wus a gwineter pe'ish to death, dey planted a crop, den dey planted a apple orchard, a peach orchard, an a plum orchard.

Dis wus a bran' new move. So de Jaybird go down on a Friday to de Bad Place fer to tell de Bad Man w'at wus done gone an' took place.

De Bad Man tell him dat now wus his time for to take a turn. He mus' go back an' tell all de worms dat he's gwineter eat up all of 'em w'at wont bore into dem fruit trees an' spile all de fruit. He's a gwineter pick deir heads off an' swaller down all de worms an' bugs w'at wont go an' eat up dem crops. He mus eben tell some of 'em dat it wont be good fer 'em if dey dont go up into dem egg-eater's houses an' live in deir meal-bar'ls an' eat holes in deir clo'es.

De Jaybird come on back an' do all de Bad Man tell 'im. Mon! dem worms an' bugs soon e't dem bad egg-eaters outn house an' home. W'en dey seed ev'ry thing dat dey wus got a gwine to rack; dey gits awful wicked, an' dey sw'ars a heaps wusser dan dey wus ever swared befo'. De Bad Man hear 'em away down dar in de Bad Place; an' he grin caze dey wus a gittin nigher down to whar he chunk de fire, w'en dey comes to got deir hire.

Dem egg-stealers sorter 'gin to live down on de lower end of Starva-tion Lane. So, den dey makes up deir minds to 'gin to hunt birds fer a livin. Den de Jaybird go down to de Bad Place on a Friday an' tell the Devil 'bout de "New Huntin' Dogs".

De Bad Man lissen to it all; den he retches his hand in an' took out a red coal of fire from de place whar his heap wus a blazin de hottest. He spit on it an' put it out. Den he take it an' make a black mark on bofe side of de Jaybird's head. "Now"; says de Devil, says he; "Wid dese marks on you no nothin' caint te'ch you nor hurt you. Go back, dance befo' de "Huntin' Dogs", eat deir fruit an' deir corn; make 'em cuss still mo' wusser!"

So De Jaybird come on back an do lak de Devil wus tol' 'im. One day, w'en one of dese here egg-stealers went a huntin'; Brer Jaybird fly out an' light right in a tree in plain view befo' 'im. Dis here Nigger leveled his gun an' pulled down on 'im.

De Jaybird sorter flop over in de tree on de tip end of de lim' an' hang dar lak he wus been dead. So dis here bad bird-nes'-robben' Nigger drapped his gun an' clum up de tree fer to git him. W'en he wus clum out on de lim' a liddle so as to git close 'nough to retch out his hand an' git him; dat lim' busted off, an' down he come! De lim' wus all rotten. De Nigger got all broked up!

Brer Jaybird flew off an' hollered back as he go:

"Do-it! Do-it!
I dares you! I dares you!
I dares you! I dares you!
Do-it! Do-it!"

Dis here fall dont jes simpully git dis egg-eater all broke up, but it git him all took wid de rheumaties atter he 'gin to git sorter half way over it; so dat he cuss still mo' wusser.

One day his ole 'oman, Aunt Mary, wus a feelin a liddle sorter poo'ly. He tell her dat he think dat a liddle Jaybird soup would fetch her aroun' about all right ag'in. It wus on a Friday; but de grabbed up his gun an' he wobbled off to de wood dis time fer to hunt fer Jaybirds on purpose.

Brer Jaybird see him a huntin an' hear him a cussin his rheumaties; an' laugh an' go to he'p him. He fly an' light in de big open road right in front of him.

Dis here bird-nes'-robbin Nigger say; "Uh-huh! You haint up in no tree dis time!"—an' wid dat, he raised his gun an' cracked down on 'im!

Mon! Dat ole gun kicked mo' harder den a red-eyed mule. It split his chin an' he tumbled over back'ards. W'en he fell, dat head of hisn hit a great big sharp rock; an' dat finished 'im!

De Jaybird flopped off an' hollered back:

"Do-it! Do-it!
I dares you! I dares you!
I dares you! I dares you!
Do-it! Do-it!"

W'en dis Nigger die; de Bad Man come up wid all his Imps an' git 'em, caze he rob bird's nesses and wus so sinful.

De tother egg-stealin Niggers some an' pick up his kyarkiss outn de road, to take it home fer to fix it up to bury it. Dey wus all awful skeard dat he wus gone to de Bad Place: case whilst dey wus a luggin him some, dey seed a whole heaps of cu'ious bad signs.

As dey totes de body down de road home, a lizzud crawled right along on de rail fence by de side of it. It keep right up wid 'em all de way to his cabin.

A big swamp rabbit started to cross de road in front of 'em but he buckled up his (y)ears an' looked at 'em, den he turned aroun' an' runned in de direction whar de graveyard wus, lak he wus skeard clean outn his senses. When dey git almos' home dey comed across some gooses, an' de ole gander raised his head an' blowed at 'em lak he wus done seed sumpin w'at was about to come over an' ruin all his liddle folkses. W'en dey goes across de cowlot so as to take a liddle nigh cut to git home quicker; sumpin come along lak a liddle breeze an' rattle de leafs, on de trees. Mon!—Dem ole cows heisted der heads an' tails in de air lak dey wus seed sho 'nough hants, an' dey runned off lak ten packs of dogs wus atter 'em. Den—all along de route, dem Jaybirds keep up deir racket, a hollerin':

> "Do-it! Do-it!
> I dares you! I dares you!
> I dares you! I dares you!
> Do-it! Do-it!"

I tells you dem 'ar bird-egg stealers wus mo' skearder dan a rusty toad-frog wid a snake atter him; w'en dey seed all dese things whilst dey wus a totin dat dead Nigger home.

Dat night w'en dey wus a settin' up wid de body, deir 'possum dogs howls lak dey wus seed sumpin w'at dey wish dey didn' see. Den a screech owl come an' he trimble off a long lonesome song. He eben 'fuse to go away w'en dey jobs de handle of de shovel in de fire in de fire-place.

Honey, dem 'ar egg-stealers wus ve'y nigh skeard outn deir skins an' dey sot dar wid dat dead Nigger's body dat night an' dey didn' eben sing: "W'at's dis dat crawl all over my frame, is it death?" But whilst dey wus a settin dar an' a turnin' it all over is deir minds; dey thinks dat dey wus jes about ready to quit dat egg-stealin' business.

Well, de nex' day, dey buried him; but buryin' him didn' keep the tothers from a worryin' 'bout him—'bout whar he wus gone an why he wus done gone dar.

Dem egg-stealers wus so all troubled an' broke up in mind; dat dey come togedder to sleep an' take deir rest de nex' night. Dey wus so skeard dat dey daresant sleep apart. An' w'en dey all gits to bed in de room; dey wus so scrouged up dat dey couldn' scacely turn over.

Whilst dey wus a lyin' dar on de pallet, dey kep' a pine torch a burnin'; caze dey didn' know w'at mought walk in 'mongst 'em, if it git dark in dar. Dey caint sleep none; but atter while dey all doze off into a liddle snooze. Whilst dey wus a dozin dey 'gin to dream.—It 'twusnt eben zackly a dream, Honey! Dem 'ar Niggers float off in de sperit; an' de Devil's Imps come an' ketch 'em all!—Dey ketches 'em, an' puts 'em all in a cage, an' takes 'em on down to de Bad Place. Whilst de Niggers wus a gwine down in de cage; dey hears sumpin all de time a floppin an' a flyin aroun' it. Dey caint see it, but dey hears w'at-some-be-ever it wus holler out.

"Do-it! Do-it!
I dares you! I dares you!
I dares you! I dares you!
Do-it! Do-it!"

W'en de Niggers git down to dem ridgions w'at wus a smokin wid brimstone; de Imps take 'em an' hang 'em up over de Burnin' Lake o' Fire by a stran' o' hair. Dem red sparks wus jes a flyin' up outn de Lake o' Fire, an' a threatenin' to burn dat stran o' hair in two ev'ry minute. Of co'se, if dat one stran' of hair git singed in two, de Nigger'll drap right straight down in de fire an' dat'll be the end of 'em. De Imps fly aroun' de cage wid deir flamin' torches; an', sorter kelless lak, dey almos' lets de torches bresh de one stran o' hair by which dey wus a hangin'. De Imps laugh an' tell dem egg-eaters: Dat dey mus' hang up dar fer a whole hour; an', if no sparks dont burn away deir hangin' contrapsion in dat time, dey mought take 'em back to de worl' an' let 'em loose fer one mo' chance.

Whilst dey wus a hangin up dar a wishin dat deir lifes was at least one mo' hour shorter; dey hears de soun' of a pitiful crier, an' he moan out: "Oh—! Oh—! Oh—! Please dont th'ow no mo' hot sand on me!—I caint see whar you gits so much sand no ways!"

Dem egg-eatin Niggers in de cages sorter peep out down in to de fire below, an' dey sees deir podner, w'at wus got killed a huntin' Jaybirds on a Friday, down dar in de fire. Dey jerks deir heads back, an' lies flat down on dem betrayin' stomachs of deirn wid deir faces buried in deir hands. Dey lies dar a hopin' dat de Bad Man wont move an' stir up dem embers much fer a couple of hours or mo'. Dey hears de Devil—(Honey, scuse me! I means de "Bad Man". I's skeard dat I's been a callin him by dat tother name, w'en I knows dat I should not oughter be callin him dat to chilluns.)—Dey hears de Bad Man jes a "Whah-whahin!" an' a tellin dis here egg eater w'at wus got kilt dat de reason he wus got so much sand down dar, dat him an' de Jaybirds wus close friends' an' dey comes down to see him on a Fridays an' brings him jes dead oudles of sand. Dey brings it to him fer to heat up red hot an' to pitch on all de folkses w'at breaks up de birdses nesses.

De Bad Man say to dis here dead egg eater, beance he wus already done got 'em, he'll tell him all 'bout it. Den he cut loose an' tell him all 'bout how de Jaybird wus done come down to 'im; an' all 'bout de 'rangements w'at he wus done maked wid him.

W'en dis here dead egg stealer beg de Bad Man to let him go back, an' tell de tothers an' deir chilluns so dat dey wont come down to Hell— (Scuse me! Honey, I was meanin to say "down dar to de Bad Place". It haint never nice to use dat 'ar bad word. My mammy didn useter know how to git th'ough brushin my back if I used dat tother bad word instid of de "Bad Place". So you musn' never use dat word onless you gits to be a preacher an' preaches 'bout it. Den you mought say it.)—W'en de Bad Man hear him ax to go back to de worl', he bofe "whah-whahed" an' "guf-fawed". Den he says to 'em: "I caint do dat fer my liver, my liver doesnt suffer sitch!" Den he laugh some mo' an' say dat he caint let him go caze he want to git all dem tother egg stealers. He put in 'sides dis, dat he mought lose him, if he let him go back; caze he mought freeze up in a cold onfriendly worl' atter livin' down dar in setch a fine warm corner. Den he "whah-whah" some mo', an' say dat he dont see whar no freezin wus a gwineter do him no good.

De dead bird-egg eatin' Nigger say: Yes it 'twould do him heaps of good; caze he would jes take a minute or so, an' sing 'em a liddle song, an' w'en de egg-eaters in de worl' 'gin to sing it over to deirselves, dey'd see w'at he wus a drivin at.

De Bad Man tell 'im: No, he wusnt a gwineter let him go back to de worl'; caze he wouldn' have dat to happen fer almos' nothin'. But he put in along wid dis, dat he haint heared no singin' fer a long time; caze singin' wus done gone outn style down in dem parts. Yit an' still he lak to hear a liddle singin once in a while. So he tol' de Nigger if he'd sing de song real good whilst de smoke from de fire wus a chokin' him up, he wont th'ow but a liddle of de hot san' on 'em w'at de Jaybirds wus brung; he'll save up de balunce, as it pile up, fer dem tother egg-stealers w'en dey comes down dar.

(Law, Chile! dem 'ar snoozin egg-stealers, a floatin aroun' outside o' deir bodies, wus skeard stock stiff up dar in dat case, a hangin' over de Bad Place; but dey caint come back into deir skins an' wake up). Dis wus de song dey heared dat egg-stealer sing, dat he say dat he would sing if he jes could only some back to dis worl':

* I have written this note as G# through this song because that is the best of which the Caucasian scale will admit. In the Melody as sung by the antebellum Negro, the technically scientific Gb was the note used — a note lower in pitch and giving an impression of sorrow. The other Negro intervals were also just a little different but it cannot be shown on our music scale.

Atter dis song git sung, de hour git to be over; an' since de hair w'at de cage wus a hangin by wusnt got singed in two, de Imps come an' onfasten de cage an' take de egg-stealers back to deirselves an' dey wakes up. Dey gits awake a liddle befo' day; but dey kivers up deir heads an' dey lays dar jes a shiverin' an' a shakin' an' a quakin'.

W'en it git to be good broad open daylight, dey all gits up but dey dont say nothin' to onenudder 'bout whar dey wus been in deir floatin' aroun'; caze dey wus skeard if dey tells it befo' Breakfus it mought come to be true all de time fer shore.

Dey gits deir clo'es on; an' one of 'em stirs up a liddle meal an' water an' makes a ash-cake. W'en dey raked it outn de fire, it wus all burnt; but dey all say it dont make no diffunce much, caze dey dont feel so mighty hongry noways.

Atter dey swaller down some ash-cake an' some water an' de Breakfus wus all th'ough wid; one of de Niggers say to de tothers dat he was done gone an' had de cu'iousest dreams or sumpin else, las' night, dat he ever did have.

Dey all ax him w'at it wus.

Den he tell 'em all about de Imps a takin' him down to de Bad Place; about all of dem a bein' in de cage wid him; about de Jaybirds; an' 'bout all de balunce.

W'en he git th'ough; all of 'em sot dar puffeckly still, fer a while, wid deir eyes all bucked out lak de staves on a meal bar'l. Terreckly one o' de tothers say dat he wus done had dat ve'y same spearunce. Den all of 'em say dat de Imps wus done gone an' took 'em off an' brung 'em back ag'in. Den dey all sot dar ag'in puffeckly still fer a long time lak dey wus skeard dat de Imps mought come up atter 'em bowdaciously in de broad-open daytime.

At las' one of 'em say dat he wusnt never a gwineter break up no mo' birds' nesses no mo'; dont make no diffunce whar he go. De tothers say dey wus done got th'ough wid all dem sort o' doins too.

Den all of 'em say dey wus skeard dat some o' deir chilluns, away off yander, mought take up de sin of breakin up birds' nesses. So one of 'em subgest dat dey git de "Shorten" gals to sing de song dat dey wus done heared whilst dey wus a hangin in de cage by a stran' o' hair over de smoke of de fire an' brimstone of de hot lake of de Bad Place—git 'em to sing it to de chilluns, so dat evrybody would always know not to never break up no birds' nesses.

So dey gits de Shorten gals to sing de song to de chilluns. W'en de chilluns hears an' learns de song, dey goes an' makes up a chune all of deir own to sing to de words back to de Shorten gals. W'en de chilluns git to de sponse dey sings: "I loves dem Shorten gals! I loves dem Shorten gals! Oh, have mussy on my soul!"

"You's heared ev'rybody a singin dat song an' I thinks I heared you a

whis'lin' it las' week," said Aunt Jinsey, Addressing Bone. "So you sees I
give Skewball a good whuppin an' a dressin' down 'bout breakin' up dem
Jaybirds' nesses to try to keep him from a gwine to de Bad Place whar
dey totes sand ev'ry Friday fer de Bad Man to heat up an' th'ow on him
an' all de balunce w'at goes down dar w'en dey dies."

With the story finished, Bone said: "Well, Aunt Jinsey I haint a
gwineter need no switch to make me let Jaybirds' nesses alone.—But I
mus' be a gwine home now."

When Bone had said this, Aunt Jinsey arose and drew the bucket
containing the fish from the well. She took one for herself and Skewball,
in accordance with Bone's kind offer, and handed the others to him.

Bone ran home—arriving there almost breathless. He went hurriedly
into the room where his mother was; and, after handing her the fish, began: "Oh—! Mammy, I stopped at Aunt Jinsey's, an' Skewball broke up a
Jaybird's nes', an' Aunt Jinsey whupped him, an' she tell me 'bout why she
do it to keep de Jaybirds from a totin san'—"

"Wait—! Wait dar!" interrupted Bone's mother. "Baby, did dat ignant
Bargro 'oman tell you all dat trash?—Dat sho do beat me!—Baby all dat
sort o' stuff dat you hears; you mus' jes let go in at one (y)ear an' come
out at de tother. W'y—! If a rabbit cross de road in front of one of 'em,
dem 'ar gooses'll make a cross mark on de groun' an' spit on it befo' dey
walks on by de place whar de rabbit go over! I sho caint see how dey
haint come to have no mo' sense dan dey is! I can see how dey mought
think if de rabbit a gwine across de road wus bad luck, dat de fixin up
sumpin lak de Lawd's cross mought help 'em; but, Baby, I caint see how
dey thinks de Lawd would lak deir spittin on his cross!

Now you go an' set down an' res' yo'se'f whilst mammy fries yo' fish
fer yo' supper; an' dont you never pay no 'tention to de tales w'at dese
here ignant Niggers tells to skear deir chilluns to death instid o' talkin
sense to 'em!"

With these assurances and instructions, Bone was once more a Sutton
in word, in thought, and in deed.

Skewball was living in another atmosphere but he somehow felt that
the ideas and ideals there were those of an "old fogey". The "hickories"
applied to the back did not drive his conviction from the brain, and he
grew up, in spite of them, to a strong stalwart intellectual manhood.

THE HEADLESS MAN

❄

One cold hazy September afternoon, in the early seventies of the last century, a little Negro boy by the name of Bone Sutton, who lived in Bedford County, Tennessee, secured permission from his parents to go and spend the night with his little friend Jim Brim. His parents did not permit him to go until a little while after the night had fallen, and until after he had eaten his evening meal because they were firm believers in the old Negro adage:

"Eat yo' supper befo' you comes,
Dont eat too much of de breakfus fine;
Dat way you'll have mo' better frien's,
An' dey'll ax you over anudder time".

With the supper over in the Sutton home; Bone pulled together and buttoned his coat, put on his home-made gray-jeans cap and was off for a visit and for the night. A half hour's walk down a lonely country dirt-road brought him to the Brim home. When he arrived at the yard gate, he stopped and called, after the custom of those days: "Hullo—! Hullo—!"

The dogs of that home were the first to respond to his call, and so lustily did they bark that the voice of the caller for the night was completely drowned to hearing.

"Uncle" Crocket Brim—the head of that home—had already gone to bed and was peacefully snoring away in the arms of sleep. The home was a newly built one, and the one-room cabin in which the family lived had had only an opening, closed by a roughly made wooden shutter, for a window. This primitive window they had left open during the warm summer months, and thus through it they had received an abundance of fresh air and light. But as the cool frosty nights of September descended this opening admitted uncomfortable chilling blasts and gusts of wind. The wife had therefore insisted that the husband should go to town and purchase a sash fitted with glass, to be placed in this opening, so that she might have her "window" closed and still receive the much needed light from without.

Uncle Crocket, after saying much to her about "jes a puttin' on aires an' a wanting sumpin fer to look lak de white folks an' de big Niggers", had gone and gotten the window sash; and had brought it home. When he arrived his wife insisted that he must nail it in at once; "caze one of dem 'ar high-folutin Sutton niggers wus a comin' over dar 'fer to stay all night wid her boy Jim, an' she want 'em to see dat dere wus mo' Blue-tailed Flies in de worl' sides dem."

Her husband demurred much concerning his lack of skill, as a farmer, in the use of hammer and nails. He begged that she wait until he could secure a carpenter, but Aunt Lize—his wife—would hear nothing of this. So Uncle Crocket, in sheer personal self-defense, undertook to nail in the window sash. Though a reasonably good tiller of the soil, he wus almost utterly helpless in the matter of driving a nail. But after smashing all his fingers on both hands with the hammer, he managed to get the glass sash tacked into the opening.

Angry because of his wife's insistence, he had swallowed a few bits of food and had gone to bed at dusk of dark leaving the information that he "didn' want nobody fer to bother him no mo' fer no nothin' dat night— nothin' fer to show off wid; neider to dem 'big-Ike' Suttons, nor to nobody else".

Thus as the dogs raised such a din when Bone called, Aunt Lize did not dare to arouse him to go out and see what was the matter. So she stepped to the door, opened it just a little, and peeped out. She saw the dim outline of Bone at the gate in the pale moonlight. Whereupon she threw wide the door and cried out to the dogs; "You Tige—! You Rule—! You ole pant'ers, you! If you dont shet off yo' coon-snappers an' possum-grabbers, an' come here an' go up un'er dis here house; I wont git through wid knockin' de ha'r offn you wid green hick-ries befo' de trees gits tired of growin' 'em!"

Even these ferocious wolf-like dogs seemed somehow to recognize the meaning of the stern command and the dire threat of Aunt Lize. With bristles still raised, they sullenly lowered their tails, crept back to the cabin, and crawled underneath the floor. Then she stepped outside, a few feet in front of the door, to see that all wus well and bade Bone to come in. He came, they shook hands, and all concerned entered the cabin. Once inside and seated, the conversation ran as follows:

"Honey, wont you let Aunt Lize git you a liddle bite o' supper?"

"No, Aunt Lize", said Bone, "I wouldn' choose a mouffull. I wus done e't ontel I was jes as full up as a tick; I was done so stuffed up wid supper at home jes befo' I lef'."

"I's jes bound fer yo' mammy a doin' lak, dat!" Said Aunt Lize. "She should oughter a let you a e't supper wid Jim an' breakfus too. You tell her, w'en you goes home tomorrer, dat I sayes, de nex' time you comes;

"Come on over to de house of a frien',
Big pot hashed in de skillet; den
De mo' you eats, de mo' we'll lak it.
Jes wanter hear yo' liddle mouf smack it!"

"Mighty much obledged to you, I'll be shore fer to tel her", said Bone, with a hearty quiet chuckle.

"Look here Bone!" joined Jim in the conversation. "Say, wusn't you skeard fer to be a comin' over here in a gray-grizzly moonlight lak dat out dar to night?"

"Skeard o' w'at?" asked Bone, somewhat puzzled by his question.

"Skeard dat ole Caesar mought come a rattlin down de road on his wa'nut-wooden hoss, an' wid his noggan* [*noggan = head] all off, an' a axin you sumpin all 'bout his head!"

"You hush all dat up now, Jim!" broke in the mother. "Bone's folkses let on lak dat dey dont b'lieve in nothin' lak dat; an' I don't spec dat he's ever hearn tell of it".

"I sho haint! W'at's it all about anyhows?" anxiously inquired Bone.

"Mammy wus done spoke, so it's all over wid," answered Jim—"But look out dar! Dont you see how cu'ious de moonlight look to-night?"

Aunt Lize' though a little displeased that her son, Jim, should suggest any thing further concerning the matter, inasmuch as she had spoken, did not raise objection, because she wanted to make sure that Bone should be duly impressed with the fact that she had gotten a new glass window sash fitted into the opening in the side of her cabin.

It wus on an evening when a deep haze had overspread the skies and the pale moon alone gave its half-dimmed light to the silent land-scape. In Bone's home there had never been any occasion to suggest that the tint of the light on one moonlight night might differ from that on another. Thus as he gazed through the little window out in to the silent starless half moon-lit night, his imagination did all the rest. Though he had only occasionally heard of the existence of ghosts through his little playmates, as he looked out on the quiet pale gray landscape, the whole seemed to him somehow very mysteriously transformed into one huge hideous goblin.

"Laws a Mussy!" said little Bone. "I don't know w'at you's a talkin' 'bout; but I sees it! Caint you tell me 'bout w'at-some-ever it is?"

"I caint", answered Jim. "Don't know it all too good noways. You'll hafter git on de good side of mammy dar, if you's a gwineter git dat 'ar loration."

"Bone", put in Aunt Lize, "I could a handed you over some supper, caze I knows w'at kind o' eatin' fixins yo' mammy want you to have; but I's skeared she mought not lak it, if I dishes up to you how Caesar hunt fer his head so dat he can git into Heaben".

"Oh yes she will lak it", was Bone's prompt assurance; "an' 'sides dat she wont know nothin' 'bout it. You tell me! My mouf's sewed up wid a rawhide string w'en I gits home. Dis is a case whar you wont hafter mop up de floo' atter you spills de milk. I'll lick it all up clean; an' dat'll be de en' of it".

Aunt Lize much pleased with the boy's expression, and desirous of his good will that she might cultivate through it a somewhat closer relation with the family to which he belonged (at that time considered aristocratic for Negroes) said:

"Well, Bone, you always wus a mighty nice liddle boy. You's fermiliar an' haint scornful lak heaps o' folkses dat I knows. An' since you sayes dat de tails's dead as soon as it fall offn de dog; I reckins dat I can whirl in an' tell you 'bout it.

Ole Caesar don't ride a lookin' fer his head on all of de nights; he jes ride on de gray grizzly nights lak dis one. You jes set still an injoy yo'self a lookin' out through my new winder; an' I'll try to tell you all about it.

As I wus a sayin' jes a liddle while ago, I don't spec dat you's ever hearn tell of de loration; and yit agin I specs you has. Haint you never hearn folkses a talkin' an' a sayin' dat 'So-an'-so's a losin his head 'bout So-an'-so'?

Bone made answer to this question that he had.

"Well, dat's whar dat ole 'sayin' wus come from. Caesar lose his head 'bout a prutty yaller gal; an' den he missed gittin de gal an' Heaben too."

It all happen on dis wise: Away back yon'er one time dere wus a prutty yaller Nigger gal named Sindy. She wusnt zackly a slave an' she wusnt zackly free. Her own Mosser wus her own daddy; an' so she wus sorter 'twixt an' 'tween'.

Her daddy never did have no white wife. He got to lovin' a Affikan gal w'at wus his slave; an' dis gal git to be his wife all 'cep' dey wusnt yoked an' pinned togedder in de white-folkses' way.

Dis here white man wus named Marse Hector Dilldine; but ev'rybody called him 'Marse Heck' for short. W'en Marse Heck's mammy die; dis here Affikan gal w'at wus named Venie wus powerful good to 'im. She jes set aroun' an' studied all day w'at to do fer to make Marse Heck feel good an' to please 'im. Den she wus one of dese here prutty Affikan gals. Of co'se her ha'r wus de kinky nappy kind; but she keep her on hand one of dese here wool chyards, an' w'en she git through wid a greasin' it an' a chyardin' it, it look lak a prutty fluffy moss on a log along a swif' runnin' branch, in de deep cool shady woods. Her face wus as round an' as plump as a peach; an' her skin was copied its color an' look from de wings of de ches'nut-colored butterflies w'at you's seed a showin' deir finery on de flower beds in de middle of June. Her teef wus lak de inside of a mussel shell an' she keep 'em as white as milk a scrubbin' 'em off wid a hick'ry-stick toof-brush. Marse Heck jes go crazy over dis here Affikan gal w'at wus his own slave, an' his own wife; an' dis here gal, Sindy, wus his an' Venie's gal.

Venie's gal, Sindy; 'bout who Caesar lose his head; wus as prutty as a speckled pullet. She wus a gold yaller, wid de red of de rose laid on her cheek.

'Sindy wus a beauty,
Ev'rybody know;
Coal-black eyes a sparklin',
Ha'r hung down befo'".

Marse Heck wusnt none o' yo 'half-strainer would-if-you-could poo'
white Crackers. He wus owned a great big plantation wid droves of
Nigger slaves on it as thick as black-birds. He wus alredy got mo' Niggers
dan he know w'at to do wid; but he go aroun' wid his pockets chugged
full o' money, an' nearly ev'ry time he go to town he come back home a
bringin' a new Nigger or so wid 'im.

One day he go off to one o' dese here great big Nigger auctions an'
he bid in one of dese here big strappin double-j'inted Nigger boys. Atter
he wus got him bought an' wus handed over de spondoolics fer him; he
find out dat dis here boy wus jes floated over from Affiky an' he caint talk
no talk w'at nobody can un'erstan'. He try to sell him back to somebody
on de spot fer half price; but dey all jes laugh an' say dey dont want 'im.
So he hafter take him on home wid 'im.

W'en he git home wid de boy; his wife, Venie, bein' a Affikan 'oman,
felt powerful sorry fer 'im; caze she herself ricomember w'en she wus
lakwise a long ways from home an' in dat same fix. So she ax Marse Heck
fer to let her keep him up dar wid dem in de Big House ontel he l'arn
how to talk. Now Marse Heck love Venie so much dat w'at-some-ever she
say prutty much go. So he tell her: All right. She can rig up a place fer him
to stay up in de garret of de Big House. She can fix an' give him a plate of
sumpin t'eat ev'ry day atter dey all gits through; an' beance him an' Sindy
wus about de same size, she mought let Sindy play wid 'im an' l'arn him
how to talk an' to act lak de tother folks. W'en Sindy wus got him bridle-
wise an' broke in; dey could hitch him out to wuk wharsome-ever dey
wants to.

Dey den give de boy de name, Caesar, an' started him out; an' de
progrance w'at Marse Heck was laid out slip along lak it wus greased.

Marse Heck wus got a Nigger man fer a house-boy w'at wus named
Uncle Jake: an' dough you mought call him a 'Jack-leg' preacher now-a-
days, he wus a whoppin crackin' good preacher fer dem times. Uncle Jake
had a wife named Aunt Becky; an' she wus her Mosser's cook. Aunt
Becky beslonged to de church jes lak her ole man; but she wus jes about
de smartest 'mongst de conj'er womens in dem diggins.

Uncle Jake an' Aunt Becky wus lakwise got a powerful fine lookin'
boy by de name of Bob. He wus about de same size as Caesar. So whilst
his mammy an' daddy wus a wukin up aroun' de Big House; he stay
aroun' an' punch up de fires an' bring in de water an' make hisself handy
in ginerally. W'en he wusnt got nothin fer to do; he'd whirl in an' play wid

Sindy an' Caesar, so dat all three of de chilluns grow up a playin' togedder.

Caesar wus jes as bright an' as smart as you make 'em; but whilst he wus a l'arnin' how fer to talk, he make all kinds of awky-gawky mistakes. He maked one powerful big one wid Uncle Jake an' Aunt Becky; an' dey never did git over it. It jes natchully rubbed 'em sore un'er de saddle an' atter dat w'ensoever dey looks at Caesar, dey jes feels lak kickin' 'im.

It all happen dis way: Marse Heck always twice ayear fix up an' have Uncle Jake to preach a big sermon on "Suvants obey yo' Mossers". De time o' year come aroun' fer one o' dese here sermons jes befo' Caesar l'arn how to talk good an' to know w'at all folkses wus a sayin' to 'im.

All de week befo' de Sund'y fer de preachin' of de big sermon; Marse Heck have anudder Nigger fer to come up an' do wuk fer de house-boy whilst he load up Uncle Jake's flint-lock leather muskit wid grape-shot fer to fire off de big Gospel Gun wid. By de end of de week Uncle Jake wus got it all fixed up in flopper talk lak de white folks an' wus ready fer to turn 'er loose on de plantation Niggers down in de Brush-harbor Church on a Sunday night. Dey wus to have de big sermon at night so dat all de Niggers could git dar easy, 'sides a whole flock of 'em from de j'inin' plantations. Marse Heck kilt four or five big shoats an' sont 'em all to his corn-fiel' darkies so dat dey'd have a fine Sund'y dinner befo' de big sermon. He lakwise sont 'em word dat he wusnt a gwineter lay down no rules 'bout deir gwine to bed Sunday night atter de big sermon. Dey could jes get up an' injoy deirselves all dey wants to. He kilt fer hisself an' Venie, a lamb; an' beance Uncle Jake wus to preach de sermon, he give him a fore quarter of de lamb fer him an' his folkses' dinner. Uncle Jake axed Marse Heck if he mought not skin de sheep-head an' take dat along wid him too fer him an' his fambly; an' Marse Heck tol' him yes.

De fresh meat wus all kilt an' stribited 'roun' 'mongst de slaves on de Sadday evenin' befo' de Sund'y fer de big sermon. W'en dey all gits up on a Sund'y mawnin, an' Uncle Jake 'gin to think 'bout dat 'ar fo' quarter of lamb an' de tothers 'bout dat 'ar good ole fresh hog-meat; dey didn' wait fer no dinner time to come. Dey git it all cooked by a liddle atter sun-up; an' dey e't an' e't ontel dey e't it all up. Some of 'em git so stuffed dat dey didn' need no mo' fer to eat fer three long days; an' dere wusn't no fresh meat lef' 'mongst de Niggers on dat 'ar plantation w'en Sund'y dinnertime got dar.

In de evenin' jes befo' time to go down to de big Brush-harbor Church fer de preachin'; ole Uncle Billy (anudder big Nigger preacher on a j'inin' plantation) sont Uncle Jake over word dat he wus a gwineter bring a big jug of molasses-skimmins beer along wid 'im to church; an' stop by his house on de way home fer to let him sample it whilst he sample an' taste over some of his ole 'oman's good cookin'.

Now Uncle Jake an' his folkses wus done e't up ev'ry thing in his cabin 'cep' a liddle meal an' flour an' de sheep-head; an' Marse Heck didn' give out no reg'lar rations to his slaves 'cep' on a Mond'y mawnin. So him an' Aunt Becky sot aroun' dar an' maked a wonderment of w'at dey could do to git sumpin t'eat fer de visitin' preacher, Uncle Billy.

At las Aunt Becky say dat she could put on de sheep-head to beil an' drap some flour-dumplins in 'mongst it fer to cook up along wid it. Den she could go an' git Marse Heck fer to let Caesar stay dar in deir cabin, an' push up de fire an' watch de cookin'; caze Caesar wusnt yit got un'erstan'in' 'nough fer to know nothin 'bout sermons. Dat way she could git de supper to cookin'; an' den dem an' deir Bob could go on to church an' ev'ry thing would be neat an' scruptious an' bumptious an' all right.

So she go an' git de Mosser an' Venie fer to let Caesar come an' stay lak she say. Atter dat w'en she git de sheep-head an' dumplins on a cookin'; her an' her ole man an' her boy put on deir things an' goed on down to do Big Brush-harbor Church. Jes befo' dey lef' for de church; Aunt Becky say dey dont need nothin fer to make de supper slicker-dandy 'cep' some fried meat. So she b'lieve dat she'll git Caesar fer to go over to her ole daddy's cabin 'twixt de stirrin' of de fire an' de cookin' of de sheep-head an' borry a few sleishes of bacon from 'im ontel deir Mosser hand out de rations de nex' mawnin; den she'll pay him back. Aunt Becky's ole daddy wus named ole Uncle Paul, an' he wus so ole dat he couldn' go out to church at night no mo'; caze he threaten fer to break up de meetin' wid his snoozin an' snorin. He wus so stingy dat he'd skin a flea for his hide an' taller; darfo' he wus always a saving sumpin outn his rations an' wus always got sumpin of ev'ry thing on hand. So ole Aunt Becky an' ole Uncle Jake an' Bob go on off to church an' leave Caesar dar fer to look atter de cookin' of de sheep-head an' to do de borryin' of de meat from ole Uncle Paul. As dey go out of deir yard gate Aunt Becky holler back to Caesar an' tell 'im: if sumpin start to go mighty wrong, for to come down to de Big Brush-harbor Church an' let her know 'bout it.

W'en Uncle Jake rolled up to de Big Brush-harbor Church all loaded down wid his big sermon; de Niggers wus dar from ev'ry whar jes a swarmin aroun' it lak flies aroun' a honey jug. He elbow his way up through de big crowd to de log-pile flatform w'at he wus to preach to de waitin' congergation from. He mount up on it an' look aroun' to see w'at he could see.

Dey wusnt got no nothin' for to light de Big Brush-harbor Church up wid 'cep' two big blazin' pine-knots—one in de front an' one in de back of de church; an' de thickness of de black Niggers in dar wus jes about put all dat light out.

But ole Uncle Jake slap his hands togedder so as to git deir notice; an' he open up de meetin', he do. He say, sorter white folks lak:

'I looks aroun' dis pulpit here,
An' I sees my Bible gone
I speck some feller's tuck it home
Fer to strop his razzer on.
I don't know whar de hymn-book are
To tell you w'at to sing:
So Sisterin raise yo' voices high
An' tackle anything.'

W'en de slave Niggers heared all dis here finery dey didn' zackuly know jes w'at to make of it. Dey sot dar jes a liddle, an' looked at de Sister w'at most in ginerally led 'em in de singin' an' waited fer her to start up de song. But de Sister w'at most in ginerally led de songs dont start up no nothin caze she don't know zackully w'at to make of dis here fine langridge neider. Atter a liddle; one of de Sisterin, a settin by her, nudge her in de short-ribs an' whisper: 'Dat 'ar mean long meter!' So de Sister w'at most in ginerally lead de songs start off an' all de tothers jine in wid her:

'So Sis - ter'n raise yo' voi - ces high,
An' tack - le a - ny thing'.

W'en de Niggers maked dis here big blunder, it
sorter vex Uncle Jake; so he holler out:

'You stubborn geese, you 'gins to bawl,
W'en dat 'ar haint no hymn at 't all!'

Den all de Brush-harbor Church full o' Niggers sail in an'
sing right out behin' 'im:

'You stub - born geese, you 'gins to bawl,
W'en dat 'ar haint no hymn at all.

W'en ole Uncle Jake seed dat his new tall green hick'ry kindlin' wus 'bout to put de Gospel fire clean out; he retched aroun' an' handed over some ole dry pine an' cedar: He say; 'Sisterin, sing some song dat you all likes, please.'

Den de Sister w'at most in ginerally lead de songs un'erstan' him; but she wus so flusterated dat she couldn' think o' no nothin' fer to sing. Atter while, one o' de Brudderins bust out and sing: 'Chilluns, we's all a gwineter git free; w'en de Lawd shall appear.' Dis here song come zackuly hind-part befo' fer ole Uncle Jake's sermon but he git up an' start her off anyways.

De law fer de big preachers in preachin' in dem times wus dat dey mus' git up two big shouts enjorin of de sermon—one somewhars in de middle an' one somewhars on de end. So Uncle Jake wus got it in mind fer to git dese here two big shouts by de Niggers so dat dey'd all go away an' say dat he wus preached a jolly-whopper!

Honey, I haint a gwineter keep you up here all night a tellin' you 'bout ole Uncle Jake's big sermon. I's jes a gwineter tetch it light here an' dar an' ev'ry whar in spots so dat you can git some thought 'bout it. He didn' preach nothin' jes zackully lak his Mosser wus done tol' 'im; caze he want de two big shouts an' he wus jes bleedged fer to git 'em.

He didn' start off dat 'ar sermon a talkin' lak preachers does nowadays. He 'gin it a 'sing-songin''; an' w'at he don't sing-song off, he shout off. He preach it sumpin lak dis:

'My Brudders an' my Sisters,
As I comes out here tonight,
You will somewhars fin' my tex'
Down 'twix' de lids of de Bible.
De fust thing in dat Bible
Is ole man Ginerations.
An' it closes down de top
Wid ole man Regerlations.
Ole man Ginerations fust,
Ole man Regerlations las'
Ole man Paul, he come a tween
Fer to keep us from a gittin mean;
Caze w'en slaves gits mean, you knows,
Down to de Devil straight dey goes!
An' dey goes down darde fas'er
W'en dey dont obey deir Mosser.
'So my tex' fer you to-night is:
'Suvants, obey yo' Mossers'.

Ole Uncle Jake preach off a whole lots lak dis an' stack up de gravy on it. Den he preach off a whole heaps mo' 'bout: Not slippin' off at night widout axin yo' Mosser, an' a gwine whar you should not oughter go; a whole heaps about plowin' as many corn-rows an' a pickin' as much cotton as yo' Mosser tell you; a whole heaps 'bout not stealin' Mosser's chickens an' tuckys, an' about eatin' jes de corn ash-cake an' de rashers of bacon dat yo' Mosser give you ev'ry week; an' he pile up de mou'nful doanful gravy mighty thick an' high on top of dis.

Ole Uncle Jake git a whole passel of 'Amens!' an' 'Preach-its!' fer all dis here kind of good 'vice; but he dont git no big shoutins.

But ole Uncle Jake wus jes bleedged fer to git dem two big shoutins; an' he wusnt yit git one. So he 'gin to tell 'em 'bout all de good things de Niggers wus a gwineter git, w'at obey deir Mossers, atter dey goes up in Heaben. He telled 'em all 'bout how dey wus a gwineter put on long white robes; an' turn aroun' an' drink goose-berry wine fer ten thousan' year. Dis here warm up de Brudderin an' Sisterin considerbul. Den he tell 'em how dey wus a gwineter draw dem golden slippers on dem feet; an' git up an' eat honey an' milk ten thousan' mo' year. Dis here git de sperit in 'em mighty hot an' dey wus jes de nex' doo' to de shoutin somewhars in de middle of de sermon. Den ole Uncle Jake roll it off to 'em:

W'en you gits a-way o-ver yon' er in de Hea-ben, wid all dem good ole—— beans an' collards an' cab-bitch.

W'en he say all dis; one of de Sisterin, a b'arin' witness moan off:

'Uh————————! I smells 'em now!'

W'en dis here took place; all de whole Big Brush-harbor Church-full
o' Niggers busted a loose a shoutin'; an' it wus a good thing dat dere
wusnt no nothin in dat 'ar church but a dirt floo', caze if dare had a been
dey would a shook it smack out!

Well—Dis here maked one shout fer ole Uncle Jake; an' he sorter talk
along an' let 'em cool down so as to git ready fer to make a start fer to git
up his second an' last big shout to his jolly-whopper sermon.

All de thing w'at brung on de fust big shout run along de road of
obeyin' yo' Mosser, an' gittin to Heaben, an' all de good things dey wus a
gwineter git w'en dey got dar. De tother part of de sermon wid which he
hope to git up de last big shout go along dat same road back'ards.

So he 'gin to warm up an' tell 'em 'bout w'at'll become of dem w'at
run aroun' from pillar to post widout axin deir Mossers; an' dem w'at go
to Mosser's hen-house an' bring off Mosser's tuckies an' sing over 'em:

'Dis here chicken are our pickin'
Caze he are our bird.
Got him las' night, long 'bout midnight,
So's I wouldn' git heard.

Fedders burnin', interuls turnin'
Over in de fire.
White folks caint peep whilst dey's dead sleep
An' I gits my hire.

Whilst its cookin', I sets tookin'
Jes a liddle nap.
Needs some res' to do my bes'
A weedin' of de crap.

Day's a breakin' an' I's takin'
Up dat chicken-stew.
Sun all rised; I mought git sprised
'Fo' I gits all through.

Give dat ash-cake dat haint half-bake
To my possum dog:—
Chicken Bones, 'long wid de pones;
I haint got no hog.

Oh, dis here chicken are our pickin'
Caze he are our bird.
Hush yo' fuss! Ole Mosser'd cuss,
If he mought git word.'

Atter ole Uncle Jake git dis all moaned off, he oller out: 'Oh, My Bruderin an' my Sisterin, I sees some o' you a settin' right in here tonight w'at I's heared a singin' dat 'ar song! An' w'at I wants to leave wid you tonight is: Don't you never sing it no mo'; caze de Devil hisself hate dat song!'

He baste dis all up wid a whole heaps o' gravy; but de slave-Niggers dont answer up wid no "Amens" much.

Den he go back an' bait up his hook an' line wid anudder kind o'worm. He sorter hand it out to 'em lak dis:

'It wus jes de tother day,
Dat I looked at Mosser's fences.
All dem fences, dey needs fixin;
An' I needs a heaps o' rails
Fer I wants dat fence pig-tight,
An' I wants dat fence hoss-high;
An' I wants dat fence bull-strong,
W'at dey caint jump 'les dey fly.
But you knows you caint git rails
Onless you splits 'em wid a mall-er;
So I goes out in de woods
Fer to git a good soun' mall-er.
I picks me out some hick'ry trees,
From which I wus to cut dat mall-er;
But ev'ry mall-er dat I cut-er,
Wus holler an' rotten in de butt-er.
Dat's de way 'tis wid you Niggers
W'at wont wuk an' wont pick cotton.
W'en we looks you through an' through,
You's all lazy, holler, rotten!
An' I's jes jes out here tonight,
To tell you lak I's tol' you befo',
W'en dese good Niggers gits over yon'er,
Dey's gwine inside an' shet de doo'!

W'en ole Uncle Jake preach off all dis: he git some liddle hallelujahin' from dem w'at think dey wus powerfully bent an' bound fer de Promus Land; but he dont git no genuwine shoutin'. So he hafter load up his gun an' cock it an' prime it ag'in.

'Bout dis time de Nigger boy, Caesar; w'at dey wus lef' up at de cabin fer to look atter de cookin' of de sheep-head an' dumplins an' borry some bacon; come a runnin' up to de Brush-harbor. He wus been over fer to see Aunt Becky's ole stingy daddy fer to borry de meat lak he wus been told. But ole Uncle Paul tell Caesar to go back an' tell Jake an' Becky dat he wusnt a gwineter loan 'em no mo' meat ontel dey pays back w'at dey wus already owed him.

So Caesar go on back down to ole Uncle Jake's cabin fer to stir up de fire an' to keep de sheep-head an' dumplins a cookin'. W'en he git dar he make it fer a wonderment aroun' in his mind 'bout w'at he should oughter do 'bout not gittin no meat from ole Uncle Paul to fry. Atter while he say to hisself dat it wont do no good fer him to go down dar to de church a botherin an' a tellin' Aunt Becky about it; caze his walkin' down dar wont make ole Uncle Paul's meat walk down to de cabin. So he'll jes stay dar an' git some fresh pine-knots an' put up un'er de pot a hangin on de pot-rack in de fire-place; an' make de sheep-head an' dumpling hurry up an' beil deirselves tender. So he go out an' git some fresh pine-knots, an' chunk up de fire, an' stick 'em up un'er de pot.

Mon! It maked one o' dese here roarin'-joker fires! It 'twusnt no time befo' dat sheep-head an' dem dumplins wus a beilin so hard dat dey wus a runnin' out over de aidges of de pot into de fire; an' it beil over so much dat it look lak it wus a gwineter put de fire clean out'

W'en Caesar see all dis here beilin an' squenchin of de fire, he didn' know jes w'at to make of it; caze he never wus seed no pot over dar whar he come from beil over ontel it look lak it wus a gwineter put de fire smack out. So he think he'd better run down to de Brush-harbor an' see Aunt Becky an' tell her 'bout it. He git down dar at de church jes at de time ole Uncle Jake wus ready fer to pull de trigger an' tu'n loose de last big load of Gospel buck-shot on de plantation darkies fer to git up his last big shout.

W'en Caesar git dar, he dont see no Aunt Becky in de big crowd; an' she wus so filled up wid de sperit of de 'casion dat she dont see him. He stan' dar jes outside of de Brush-harbor a lookin' wid bofe his eyes an' mouf wide open.

Atter a liddle ole Uncle Jake 'gin to warm up wid his sermon fer to git dat 'ar last big shout. But he caint keep from a lookin' at Caesar all de time an' a wonderin' fer why he wus come a runnin down dar instid o' stayin at de cabin an' lookin' atter de cookin' lak dey wus done told him to do. So whilst he wus a gazin' an' a lookin' hard at Caesar, he holler out:

'But come now my 'loved Brudd'rin,
Let us hear dis matter's 'clusion.
Let us hear! Let us hear! Let us hear!
W'at did Paul say? W'at did Paul—say!'

Now, Caesar, he didn' know no nothin' 'bout no preachin' an' he don't no un'erstan' w'at ole Uncle Jake is a drivin' at. So he squall out back to him: 'Paul says you haint a gwineter git no mo' meat outn him, ontel you pays back all dat w'at you already owes him!!'

W'en Caesar wus hollered out dis; all de Niggers looks aroun', an'
'gins to sorter giggle. So ole Uncle Jake holler off sorter lak he wusnt a
payin' him no mind: 'Yes, my Brudderin an' my Sisterin', all dem w'at
giggle in de Big Brush-harbor Church is gwineter git tumbled over in de
fire, an' turned about an' about, an' burnt clean up!'

Den Caesar, he holler back: "Dere haint a gwineter be no fire, onless
Aunt Becky hurry up an' run home; caze de sheep-head is a buttin' all de
dumplins an' water outn de pot, an' a puttin' de fire smack out!!"

'Bout dat time Aunt Becky put in her pearunce in Caesar's neighbor-
hood wid a great big top of a sapplin' in her hands. W'en he seed her a
comin' wid all dem switches, all fastened up togedder; he didn' know jes
zackuly w'at wus wrong, but he knowed it wus jes 'bout time fer him to
be a gwine. So he put out fer home wid Aunt Becky atter him. She run'd
an' he run'd; but he outrun'd her. W'en he land at de Big House yard; he
dont look towards no Uncle Jake's cabin, he make tracks fer de Big House
wid Aunt Becky right behin' 'im.

W'en Caesar git to de Big House; he find Marse Heck an' Venie, an'
deir prutty liddle gal a settin out on de pieizzer. He run up an' ole Mosser
step out an' stop Aunt Becky from a pouncin' on 'im wid her tree-top.
Aunt Becky an' Caesar bofe 'gin to try to splain deir troubles to Marse
Heck all at one an' de same time.

Marse Heck stop 'em an' shet 'em up; den he telled 'em: "One at a
time; an' dey'd hold out mo' longer'" W'en he git 'em dried up, he fust tell
Caesar dat he can splain; an' Caesar set to wuk an' rattled off a whole lots
of sumpin 'bout 'de sheep-head a buttin' all de dumplins outn de pot.' At
las' ole Mosser stop him; caze he caint make neider no heads nor no tails
outn w'at he's a talkin' 'bout.

Den he telled Aunt Becky to splain her side of it. So she go through
an' splain ev'ry thing w'at she wus done tol' Caesar to do: an' den how
he come down dar a hollerin his foolishness an' a breakin up her ole
man's big meetin'.

W'en Aunt Becky git through Marse Heck sot down a minute fer to
sorter study de riddle out. Terrecky he bust loose an' laugh so loud an' so
long dat all de ole Niggers on de plantation, w'at wus too ole fer to go out
to de night meetin', lef' deir cabins an' come a hobblin up dar to see w'at
wus de matter.

Venie (Marse Heck's wife) wus done seed de trouble long 'go; an'
wus done been in de Big House an' got a great big dish full o' cold victuals an' brung 'em out. She say to Aunt Becky dat she un'erstan' all of
poo' Caesar's troubles; caze she wus one time been through wid it all.
Den she handed her de big plate full of cold, good eatins an' say: 'Now
take dat, an' don't be mad wid poo' ignant Caesar!'

Aunt Becky take de dish full o' good victuals; but she try fer to git
Marse Heck jes to strop Caesar jes a liddle anyhows fer breakin' up de

meetin'. But ole Mosser tell her dat a storm w'at's over wid haint a gwineter blow down no mo' trees; so he haint a gwineter do nothin', an' he haint a gwineter let no nothin' be done to him. So dat settled it.

De meetin' down at de Big Brush-harbor Church broke up; an' de Niggers went home, an' laughed 'most all de balunce of de night 'bout w'at wus done gone an' tuck place down dar, an' went on to wuk de nex' day.

Atter dat Caesar sorter manage fer to make it aroun' to whar he could pass de time o' day wid Aunt Becky an' Uncle Jake; but dere never wus no mo' love to be lost 'tween 'em. All atter date w'en dey looks at him, it jes natchully rub 'em sore un'er de saddle; an' dey wants to pitch 'im, an' ditch 'im, an kick 'im. Atter while Caesar, an' Bob, an' Sindy all growed up fer to be young mens an' womens. Marse Heck maked Caesar his Nigger Overseer on his big plantation; he maked Bob his carriage an' yard boy an' fixed it up fer him to look atter an' 'tend to his big Blood-hound w'at wus named Sub; he didn' make Sindy do nothin' but set aroun' de Big House wid her mammy an' look prutty.

Sindy an' Caesar 'fessed 'ligion an' wus mighty big church members; but as Bob growed up he got to be powerful wicked.

Bofe Caesar an' Bob love Sindy; an' ev'ry time dey wus got a minute off, dey wus aroun' on deir knees a beggin' her fer to take 'em in outn de rain.

Sindy don't care notin 'bout Bob caze he git to be so wicked; but she love Caesar mo' samer dan he love her. She git him a pair o' passes ev'ry Sund'y from her daddy an' go off somewhars to meetin' wid him.

Of co'se Bob wus up dar at de Big House fer de yard an' carriage boy, an' he git in mo' talks wid Marse Heck dan do Caesar. At las' one day he telled Marse Heck all 'bout how much he love Sindy an' how much he want her fer a wife.

Marse Heck telled him: Well, one time he railly wus got it in mind fer to send Sindy off an' git somebody fer to mark her off an' an' gragerate her, an' maybe fer to set her free. But he reckin dat he wus done gone an' put it off too long an' it wus now too late. So he mought knock aroun' Sindy, an' he'd sorter he'p him wid a good word now an' den; an', 'twixt an' 'tween 'em, dey'd finally manage fer to git a cabin rigged up fer de two of 'em.

But Caesar wus been a puttin' in his words wid de gal. He tol' her dat he love her, an' she tol' him dat she love him. She promus him dat she'll marry him if her daddy say so.

So Caesar go up one Sadday atter dinner to see Venie—de gal's mammy—at de Big House; whilst Marse Heck wus gone off to town to buy some whisky fer to make hisself some mint-julep wid an' some cloth fer to make his Niggers some clo'es. Caesar say to hisself dat he wus a

gwineter see Venie; caze she wus been one time so dat she didn' know
how to talk, an' he think she mought be willin' fer to talk fer him whar he
didn' know zackuly how to talk.

He sit up dar at de Big House an' he see Venie. He sorter fumble an'
bumble aroun' caze he wus so shame-faced; but at las' he manage fer to
tell her dat he love Sindy mo' harder dan he do hisself, an' he want to
give hisself to her.

Venie tell Caesar dat she wus willin'; an' she wish an' hope dat Marse
Heck will let him marry Sindy caze he look so much lak her own daddy
w'at de white folks kilt jes befo' de wus brung her over her to whar it wus
so cold dat de folkses wus bleedged to w'ar clo'es. She promus dat she'll
see Marse Heck dat ve'y night an' talk it all over wid 'im an' den let him
know. So Caesar leave an' go on off to his cabin.

Dat night atter supper, Sindy say to her mammy an' daddy dat she
wus sleepy an' she git up an' go on off to bed. She knowed w'at her
mammy wus a gwineter talk wid her daddy 'bout, an' she want to git
gone.

Marse Heck go in de parlor an' set down; an' Venie go an' git his pipe
an' fill it wid baccer an' light it an' ax him if he dont wanter smoke an'
injoy hisself. He tell her dat he don't care if he do; an' he take de pipe an'
puff away on it lak one o' dese here steam-engines.

Whilst he wus a puffin away; she go an' git some o' de whisky an'
flavor it all up wid honey an' mint. So jes as he git ready fer to lay de pipe
aside she brung dat in, an' telled him to taste dat down liddle by liddle an'
see if it don't jes fit de th'oat of de sweetest an' de bes' man in de worl'.

Marse Heck take de tumbler an' he drink it down a drap at de time.
W'en he git through, he telled Venie: Dat wus de best thing dat he wus
ever tasted in all his live-long days. He say to her dat she wus de sweetest
an' de bes' thing dat God hisself ever wus drapped down outn Glory. An'
beance she wus so prutty an' so sweet dat she mought ask fer w'at-some-
ever she want in de whole big world—eben her own freedom—an' he'd
give her all she ax fer.

Venie say to 'im: 'Oh Marse Heck don't you never talk 'bout givin' me
freedom. W'en de day come dat I mus' leave you; may de good Lawd
p'int dat out as de day fer my body to go to de lonesome graveyard. I
caint live widout you. I jes wants to live fer to make you happy ontel you
dies; an' den I wants to die so dat I can foller along in seein' distance of
you. But Marse Heck I wus jes got one thing fer to ax you fer; an' I's so
glad dat you's already promused fer to give it to me—Yes jes one thing.
Caesar love Sindy an' Sindy love Caesar. Let Caesar have Sindy fer a
wife—he's de spit an' image o' my own daddy! Dat's all I wants, Marse
Heck; dat's all.'

W'en Marse Heck wus heared w'at Venie want, he wus powerful sorry
fer his promus; an' he ax her if sumpin else wont do her jes as well. He
put in dat he wus jes about got it fixed out in his mind dat Sindy an' Bob
would make a sorter prutty match team fer to hitch up togedder.

Venie tell Marse Heck no; no tothin' else wont answer lak dat. Den
she up an' at him fer to tell her fer why he dont want Caesar to have
Sindy fer a wife.

At las' he say to her dat he'll tell her. He hisself likes Caesar mo'
samer dan Bob. But Caesar wus so black dat if Sindy tuck him fer her
man, all deir chilluns would be black. If she choose Bob fer her man den
deir chilluns would be somewhars 'tween a dusky yaller an' a light brown.
He tell her: Now, dat she know dat he love black; he think it wus de
pruttiest color in de world, an' he love her mo' dan he love his own heart.
But most of de big white folkses love to have yaller Niggers fer de house
suvants. So he wus jes been a thinkin' dat, maybe some day, Sindy's
chilluns mought hafter git sold. If dey did git sold he sholy wouldn' want
'em to git sold fer no cotton field hands an' corn-crib darkies: an' dis
mought take place, if dey wus good black. So dat wus de reason he want
Sindy to git jined up wid Bob instid o' Caesar.

Den Venie say to 'im, wid her clear black eyes a swimin' wid water:
'But Marse Heck, you wus done promused me; an' you never wus failed
in yo' life to give me w'at you wus promused.

Marse Heck den maked answer: 'Venie w'at I wus promused, dat will
I do. But let dis go in de bargain: Dey mus' wait ontel nex' Chrismus Day;
an' if dey dont git broke up deirselves by dat time, den dey can be man
an' wife, an' I'll give 'em a lamb fer deir weddin' feast.'

W'en Marse Heck wus maked dis here promus, it wus in de summer;
an' a long time till Chrismus. Venie telled Caesar an' Sindy w'at deir
Mosser wus promused an' dey wus bofe as happy as June crickets, caze
dey say dat all deir Mosser's oxens couldn' pull 'em apart an' break 'em
up.

But w'en dey wus a handin' out all dis here big talk; dey didn' know
dat Aunt Becky—Bob's Mammy—wus de biggest Conj'er in all dem parts.
W'en it wus leaked out dat Caesar wus to git Sindy fer a wife instid o' Bob
an' Bob go an' tell her; She say to 'em 'nev' mind Honey, Yo' mammy
haint yit los' her hand.'

Dar wus a big Live-oak tree up in Marse Heck's yard, close by a liddle
house whar he kep' his big Blood-hound an' he have his slaves to cut his
winter wood an' rank it up un'er dat tree in de summer fer him to burn in
de winter. De wood fer de nex' winter wus already been cut an' piled up
un'er dat tree. Caesar go up to see Sindy ev'ry night. He always ax her fer
to leave de Big House an' go an' set out on de wood un'er dat tree an'
talk wid him dar befo' dey bofe goes to deir houses to go to bed fer de

night. He say dat he love to set an' to talk un'er dat tree wid her; caze it
put him in de mind of one of de big trees close to his own mammy's
house away off dar whar he come from. W'atsomever Caesar want,
datsomever Sindy want to do. So atter while she tell 'em dat he needn'
come to de Big House at 'tall—jes to come in de evenin an' set down
un'er de big tree an' wait fer her; she'll be dar bye an' bye. So dey meets
ev'ry evenin' jes atter it grow dark to talk an' to love one-nuder ontel bed-
time; an' den go 'way an' think 'bout an' dream 'bout one-nudder ontel de
nex' night.

Ev'ry night w'en dey goes out un'er de big Live-oak tree to live an' to
love; Bob would slip out an' set behin' de blood-hound house an' watch
'em. At fust his mammy try to 'suade him not to do dis; but w'en she find
dat she caint stop 'im, she tell him dat she'll go 'long an' watch wid 'im an'
throw spells on 'em fer to break 'em up. One night she tuck along some
soday in one cup an' some vinegar in anudder one. An' whilst Sindy an'
Caesar wus a settin on de woodpile a injoyin deirselves; Aunt Becky keep
a puttin' her han' on de Soday cup an' a sayin': Dis is Sindy. Den she'd put
her hand on de vinegar cup an' say: Dis is Caesar. So she jes sot dar a
sayin' over an' over: 'Dis is Sindy—Dis is Caesar! Dis is Sindy—Dis is Caesar!' Terreckly she up an' pour de Caesar-cup into De Sindy-cup an' it
spew up lak it wus fit to bust! Den she pour it all out on de ground an'
kiver it all over wid dirt.

Den dey sot dar an' peeped at Caesar an' Sindy. An', Honey, it didn'
zackuly break 'em up; but dey sot dar all de balunce of de evenin' an' jes
looked at one-nudder an' dey couldn' say ne'er anudder word ontel dey
riz to say good-bye fer de night.

Ole Aunt Becky go wid her boy, Bob, night in an' night out fer to
watch an' to conjer Caesar and Sindy; but somehow nothin dont look lak
it wuk lak it should oughter. So she telled Bob fer to watch whar Caesar
step on de groun' an' to go an' git some o' de dirt outn his track w'at he
wus stepped on. Den she want him to go up in de grave-yard an' git some
dirt from a new-dug grave, an' to bring bofe o' dem dirts to her. Bob do
dis.

Aunt Becky tuck de dirt w'at come outn Caesar's track an' mixed it up
wid de dirt w'at come from outn de new grave in de graveyard; an' mixed
'em up togedder wid goofer water. She den tuck dis death-drap at de
dead hour of midnight an' buried it un'erneath de doo'-step of Caesar's
cabin. In a mighty few days, Caesar got down turble sick.

Venie an' Sindy maked Marse Heck sen' away off lebenty mile to
town an' git a sho' 'nough Doctor w'at wus white fer to come an' tend on
Caesar. Atter while, de doctor he come a ridin' up on saddle bags. He
light, hitch his horse, an' go in. He look Caesar over an' leave him some
white powders fer to take an' den he tell 'em dat he'll be back in about a

week. At de end of a week, w'en de doctor come back to Caesar, he wus a heaps wusser. De doctor den say dat Caesar wus somehow managed fer to git mo' blood jes natchully beslonged to him. So he sharpened up his lances an' drawed about a tea-cup full of blood outn him. Den he go on off fer to be gone anudder week. W'en he come back dis time; he tell 'em dat Caesar wus bound to die; he hate it powerful bad, but all de biggest of de white folks wus bleedged fer to lose money sometimes by deir finest Niggers a lyin' down an' a diein'.

Atter de doctor git gone, Marse Heck go an' tell Venie w'at he say; but he tell her not to tell Sindy caze he dont want no funerl cryin a gwine on aroun' dar befo Caesar git dead. Venie tell him, All right.

Marse Heck wus got a 'oman amongst his Niggers w'at wus named ole Aunt Millie. Aunt Millie wus a big Yarb an' Root doctor. W'en de slaves on de plantation git sick; she would go in de woods an' git some stuff an' beil it up in a kittle, an' give it to 'em an' git 'em well. So as soon as Marse Heck git outn de room from a tellin' Venie dat Caesar wus bound to die; she maked up her mind fer to go an' see Aunt Millie.

She go over an' see Aunt Millie an' tell her 'bout Caesar. She den say to her: If she know any way, an' can he'p poo' Caesar; she wus whar she could an' would he'p her in w'at-some-ever way dat she want to be he'ped.

Aunt Millie telled her dat she wus turble glad dat she wus come; caze she wus knowed all along all 'bout w'at Caesar need fer to make him well; but she couldn' say nothin' whilst Marse Heck wus got de big white doctor a comin' a strewin his blue-mass here an' his calamy dar. So now she wus a gwineter git him all right.

Venie tell Aunt Millie dat she wus jes overjoiced fer to hear dat! An' now fer her to hurry up an' fix up some root medicine fer Caesar so dat she can hurry up an' take it over to 'im befo' he turn in an' die.

Aunt Millie maked answer dat Caesar dont need no medicine. He wus jes conjured. Ole Aunt Becky wus done gone an' done it all, a tryin' for to git him outn de way so dat her boy, Bob, mought git Sindy fer a wife. She say to Venie dat w'at wus needed wus dis: To go up into de grave-yard an' dig down into a ole grave ontel she git down to clay. Den git two big double hands-fulls of dat clay an' bring it to her; an' she'll chuore Caesar well wid it.

Venie telled her dat she wus skeard fer to go up dar, an' to go a diggin' down in dat 'ar grave-yard by herself. She dont know w'at she mought not see!

Aunt Millie say she mus' manage fer to go somehow or Caesar's cake's all dough.

So Venie leave Aunt Millie an' go off a tryin' to study some way fer to git dat 'ar ole grave-yard clay widout goin' atter it. At las' she maked up her mind dat she caint git it dat way. Den she think 'bout tryin' fer to git Marse Heck fer to go; but she say to herse'f dat he'll jes 'poo-poo' it all off an' say it haint nothin' but ignant Nigger mess an' walk on off an' leave her. At las' she maked up her mind dat she wus a gwineter tell Sindy all 'bout it (dough ole Mosser wus done tol' her not to); an' maybe she mought go wid her to de grave-yard fer de clay; if not, den she caint do no mo'.

So she go home an' git her a grubbin' hoe an' call Sindy; an' tell her to come an' go wid her out in de woods, she wus got sumpin' fer to show her out dere. You see, she take her away off dar fer to tell her so dat if she cut up an' squall w'en she hear it all; Marse Heck wont hear her. An' she plan fer to keep her out dar, if need be, ontel she git her hushed up befo' she bring her back. Dat way nobody wont know nothin' 'bout her tellin' her.

W'en she git Sindy away out in de woods an' tell her; she didn' make no noise. She tell her mammy to jes hand her dat grubbin' hoe an' she'll go to dat 'ar grave-yard an' git dat 'ar clay all by her lone self. Her mammy maked answer to her: No, No; she wus a gwineter go along wid her an' dey'd live an' die togedder.

So dese here two womens went up to de grave-yard. Sindy digged down in de ole grave an' fingered up de clay wid her own two hands an' tied it up in her apron. W'en dey gits dat clay, dey goes on 'way; an' goes right straight down to ole Aunt Millie's cabin. Sindy give her de clay.

Ole Aunt Millie say to her: 'Law' Honey! Did you grabble dis clay out wid yo' own hands?—Well, dont be oneasy; caze w'en I lays clay over Caesar's heart picked up wid hands of love; dat heart an' dem hands is bleedged to live an' to die togedder!'

Den Aunt Millie take de clay-dirt an' go over to Caesar's cabin; an' Venie an' Sindy foller 'long behin' her.

W'en dey gits to de doo' of de cabin; Aunt Millie stop an' take up de steps an' scrape out all de new grave-yard dirt w'at Aunt Becky wus put un'er dar at de dark hour of midnight. She den kindle up a brush-heap fire out in de yard; an' take dis dirt on a shovel an' throw it on de fire. All de time she throw de dirt on de fire she keep on a sayin' over to herse'f:

'Come Devil, go Devil
Back down to de fire'
Dar's whar you come from;
Stay down dar, you liar!'

By sayin' dis an' usin' de fire: she git shed of all of ole Aunt Becky's conjer mess.

Den she put de step back down an' went in fer to fix Caesar up. He wus all outn his head an' a tryin' fer to show 'em de big black dogs an' big red-eyed snakes a runnin' aroun' all over his cabin. Aunt Millie up an' allow to 'im dat wus all right, she wus a gwineter run 'em all off an' make him well. She knowed dat dey wus in dar eben if she couldn' see 'em.

She go outside of de cabin an' see three big hogsheads full of rain water a settin' out dar, w'at dey wus all cotched up fer to wash deir clo'es wid. She go an' dip her hands in all three of de hogsheads full o' water an' den hold 'em up over her head an' mumble off sumpin to herself. W'en she git through wid dis she go back in de cabin an' tell de Niggers w'at wus a lookin' atter Caesar fer to go out dar, an' bring in a whole tub-full of dat water which she wus fixed up; to bring it in, to lay Caesar down on de naked floo'; an' take a gourd an' dip up an' pour out de whole tub-full of water on him: Den to dry him an' put him back in de bed.

De Niggers do all w'at ole Aunt Millie say; an' w'en dey put Caesar back in de bed he say dat de snakes an' de dogs wus all gone outn de cabin an' he almos' feel lak a new man. Den Aunt Millie give him three swallers of sweet milk; an' mixed up her own grave-yard clay wid vinegar an' laid some of it on his head an' some of it on his stomach; an' he went on off to sleep an' slep' lak a new-born baby. She den telled de Niggers w'at wus a lookin' atter Caesar: Dat dey mus' pour a tub-full of dat water, w'at she wus fixed up, on him three times a day; dat dey mus give him dem three swallers of milk three times a day; an' dat dey mus' keep some o' dat clay, w'at she wus brung 'em, on his head an' stomach all de time.

De Niggers keep up de remedy w'at Aunt Millie wus lef' 'em. In a week Caesar wus a settin' up in de bed. In two weeks he wus a sittin up in a chair. In three weeks he wus a walkin' aroun' in de yard an' a wantin' to go up at night to see Sindy ag'in.

All de time while Caesar wus sick an' on de way to de bone-yard, ole Mosser kep' on a tryin' fer to git in a good word wid Sindy fer Bob. But Sindy would sorter grin an' tell him dat he musn' talk about dat now; since he wus done promus her off to Caesar. Ole Mosser would say dat Caesar wus so low, dat he don't think dat he's never a gwineter to be no mo' count no mo'. Den Sindy would make answer: Yes, but he wusnt nigh dead yit.

W'en Caesar git up an' git to gwine up to see Sindy ag'in ev'ry night at de wood-pile un'er de big tree; Bob an' his mammy—Aunt Becky—'gin to go out an' set 'hind de dog-house an' watch 'em ag'in as fer common. Old Aunt Becky keep all her Caesar conjer mess a gwine red hot an' still a heatin', fer to break 'em up. Her stuff dont look lak it break 'em up; but it keep 'em a feelin' so cu'ious an' oneasy dat it look lak dat dey caint injoy deirselves no mo'.

As I wus done telled you, Caesar git to be a mighty good 'ligious man. An one night whilst him an' Sindy wus a talkin' it all over out dar on de wood-pile, un'erneath de big tree by de Blood-hound house; dey bofe thinks maybe it would be a good thing to pray to de Lawd over it. So dey promuses one-nudder to pray to de Lawd ev'ry night 'bout it all.

Sindy say over her pra'rs to herself up dar in de Big House; an' she say 'em so low dat nobody caint hear 'em onles it 'twus de Lawd, so she dont git in no trouble 'bout 'em. But w'en Caesar prays he pray away out loud down dar in his cabin so dat ev'rybody w'at wus a passin' 'long dat way could hear him.

One night Marse Heck wus a passin' 'long dat way by de cabin whilst Caesar wus a prayin'. So he crope aroun' in de chimbly corner on de outside fer to lissen to 'im an' hear w'at he wus got to say. Caesar wus jes a moanin' an' a sing-songin' off de pra'r; an' he pray sumpin lak dis:

'O Lawd! Dar's me an' Sindy! We's yo' 'umble chilluns! Bless us, an' bin' us, an' tie de Devil 'hin' us so fur he caint never fin' us!—Dar's Bob! Oh Lawd, kill 'im dead! Lawd, I don't mean to kill 'im dead sho' 'nough; I means to kill 'im dead in his sins an' cussin', an' fix 'im up jes lak you wants 'im!—Dar's Marse Heck! Lawd, make his heart sof' w'en he look at me an' Sindy! But, O Lawd, w'en he look at Bob, make his heart so hard dat it wont never move no mo'. 'Caesar keep on a gwine on lak dis ontel he wus down dar on his knees nearly a hour widout gittin' through wid prayin' fer all de Niggers on de plantation an' de hosses an' de hogs an' all dem things.

Whilst ole Mosser wus a setin' out dar a lissenin to all dat prayin'; he 'gin to feel powerful cu'ious. He say to hisself: Spose Caesar's Pra'r should git answered, an' he look at Bob, an' his heart git so hard dat it wouldn' never move no mo', and he drop out dead as a doo'-nail! He say to hisself dat sumpin mus a be done to break dat up an' make Caesar somehow sorter partly take dat 'ar pra'r back.

Jes as ole Mosser wus got all dis thought through his head; Caesar bring his pra'r to a close. He close it up sumpin lak dis: 'Now, O Lawd! I's done axed you! It's fer you to give or not to give! But, O Lawd, if you caint gimmy Sindy, den jes come an' take poo' Caesar home! Amen!'

Jes as Caesar close his pra'r lak dis; ole Mosser sorter moan off low from de chimbly corner outside, so as to make hisself soun' lak he wus away off yon'er; 'Oh Caesar! Oh, poo' Caesar! I wants you now; jes come on outside, an' I'll take you on to yo' Heabenly Home!'

Caesar hear dis; an' he holler back, in one o' dese here screechy voices lak a 'oman: 'Dat you Lawd?—Haint no Caesar here! He's away off somewhars out in de woods, a possum huntin'! If you'll hurry on out dar right away you'll be shore fer to find 'im!'

Some folkses w'at tell de loration say dat Caesar talk lak dat, all fine lak a 'oman, so as to fool de Lawd. But some say dat it all come so sudden an' skeard him so bad; dat it jes natchully change up his common way of talkin'. Some say one way an' some say de tother; an' you caint tell but maybe dey all mought be right.

Ole Mosser go on off from de chimbly corner a laughin to hisself 'bout w'at he wus done. He go on home an' go to bed' but he dont tell Venie an' Sindy nothin' 'bout it.

De nex' day he got to talkin' wid Bob, an' he telled him w'at he wus done gone an' done 'bout Caesar: an' dey bofe jes whahwhahed! Atter dey git through; Bob go off an' tell all de corn-fiel' darkies out dar whar Caesar wus a overseein' 'em. W'en dese here Niggers git holt of it you couldn' hear nothin' but: 'Is dat you Lawd?—Haint No Caesar here!'—Well, it almos' rig Caesar clean outn his life.

One day Caesar go up to de Big House whilst de Mosser wus away to see Sindy an' Venie. He tell 'em bofe all 'bout de pra'r, all 'bout w'at de Mosser wus done, an' all 'bout how de Niggers wus a devilin' him to death 'bout it. Venie sot dar fer a while an' study it all over; den she tell Caesar not to come up to de wood-pile, dat night, fer to see Sindy. She wus got some eintment fer to pour in Marse Heck's (y)ears an' she want Sindy along wid her w'en she do it. Atter dat night; he can come up ev'ry night lak he do fer common. Caesar tell 'em all right, an' go off to his cabin.

Dat night w'en Marse Heck wus come home an' wus had his supper; Venie fixed up his pipe fer him an' atterwards brung in de mint-julep lak she wus done on de night w'en he promus fer to let Caesar have Sindy fer her ole man. W'en he wus got through wid his good swallers; she den axed him w'at wus dis here tale 'bout Caesar dat de Niggers wus got a passin' aroun' over de plantation wid him all mixed in wid it.

Den Marse Heck sot in an' tol' her all 'bout Caesar's long pra'r, an' w'at he wus done an' how Caesar back clean outn a gwine to Heaben w'en de time come fer him to go. Den he drapped back in his chair an' laughed ontel he wus red all over.

W'en he git sorter whar he could stop laughin' long 'nough to lissen; Venie telled him: Well, she wus got sumpin fer to tell him; an' she wus kep' Sindy dar so dat he could ax her 'bout it if he want to. An' den w'en he git through wid axin her; he mought go over an' ax ole Aunt Millie so dat she can straighten out all de tother tangles w'at haint clear to him.

Venie 'gin. She tell Marse Heck all 'bout Caesar's gittin conjured by ole Aunt Becky an' Bob! She tell 'im all 'bout de conj'er-mess w'at Aunt Millie wus raked out from un'erneath de doo'-steps of Caesar's cabin; an' wus burnt up! She telled him all 'bout her gwine up to grave-yard with Sindy; an' Sindy a gittin' out de ole grave-yard clay wid her own hands! She lay out to him all 'bout de three hogsheads of healin' water w'at ole Aunt Millie wus gone an' fixed up! She telled him all 'bout de healin' water a drivin' de big black sperit dogs an' red eyed snakes outn Caesar's cabin'.

She telled him 'bout de three swallers of milk an' de bindin' of de grave-yard clay on Caesar's head an' stomach; an' how it make him feel lak a new man! W'en she wus got through wid all dis; she telled him dat he ricomember dat de big white doctor wus done said dat Caesar wus bleedged fer to die, but now he see dar he wus still alive. Den she say to 'im: if he dont hurry up an' git shed of ole Uncle Jake, an' ole Aunt Becky, an' Bob; dat she'll bet dat dey'll have him a trabblin outn de Big House feet-fo'most de fust thing he know'

W'en Venie git through, ole Mosser wus jes stonished. He knowed 'bout Caesar a bein' sick nigh onto death, an he knowed 'bout ole Aunt Millie a chuorin him up atter de doctor wus gin him out; but he didn' know nothin' 'bout no conjer-business a gittin all mixed in wid it. It wus sorter late in de night; but he say he think maybe he'd better go over an' git ole Aunt Millie outn bed an' question her a liddle. So he go over to ole Aunt Millie's an' beat on her doo' ontel he git her rousted up. W'en he wus managed fer to git her wid her eyes open, he 'gin an' ax her all 'bout Caesar. Den she go through de same great big long rig-a-ma-role dat Venie wus handed over to 'im; an' tacked on about twice as much mo'. W'en he git through wid her de mawnin star wus a risin' an' it wus a pushin' along towards daylight.

So Marse Heck maked up his mind fer to go on back home an' take a liddle nap; an' put off de balunce of de axin' ontel atter his snooze. Nex' day w'en he git his eye-lids sorter proped open, he got out 'mongst his Niggers fer to sorter smell out w'at all wus gone an' tuck place. He axed de Niggers, w'at wus looked atter Caesar w'en he wus sick, w'at dey wus done fer him. Dey maked answer dat dey done nothin fer him 'cep' to pour a liddle water on 'im, an' give 'im three swallers of sweet-milk three times a day, an' lay some clay-dirt on his head an' stomach—all lak ole Aunt Millie wus done tol' 'em to do.

W'en he git through wid all his nosin aroun' he go on back up to de Big House; and tuck Venie an' Sindy into de parlor, an' shet down all de winders an' doo's. He tell 'em dat he wus got sumpin fer to tell 'em but it wont do to let none of it git outn de room, caze if it did dere wusnt no tellin' w'at mought happen! W'en he git 'em in de room, wid ev'rything bang up tight, he telled 'em dat he wus done seed dat ole Beck, an' ole Jake, an' ole Bob wus de bigges' Devil conjers in de worl'! He wus a gwineter fix up an' sell 'em right away! But it wont never do fer to let 'em git nowhars in de wind of it; caze, if dey do, dey mought jes go out an' shake a bush an' kill ev'rybody an' ev'rything on de whole broad planta-tion wid deir Mosser throwed in fer good measure! He say he wus a gwineter wuk de sellin' dis a way: He wus gwineter send word to de Court-house an' Papers dat he wus got three of de finest Niggers fer sale dat dey ever laid eyes on; but he wusn't a gwineter tell 'em which ones

dey wus. Den since Chrismus wus jes a week off; he wus a gwineter sen'
'em word fer ev'rybody to come over on a Chrismus Day, fer de buyin,
about three hours by sun. He wus a gwineter have it dar an' give 'em all
de good whisky dey wants fer to drink. Den he wus a gwineter sell dese
here three big fine Niggers to de one w'at offer de mostest fer 'em; if dat
wusnt but one shinplaster.

Venie an' Sindy telled him dat dey wus powerful glad fer to see dat
he wus got so much good hard common sense: Fer him to jes go on an'
fix up to git shed of dese here snakes in de grass, a watchin fer to bite
you w'en you pass; an' dey'll jes keep on a lyin' low, an' feed dat poo' ole
pitiful crow, till his head go off befo' he know. So de Mosser go on off to
town an' send word to de Court-House an' de Papers a bout his projick,
w'at he wus got on foot.

It wus de week a leadin' up to Chrismus Day, w'en Caesar wus to git
Sindy fer his wife. So dey meets ev'ry night out on de big wood-pile, un'er
de big tree, by de big Blood-hound house. Bob go an' set behin' de
Blood-hound house ev'ry night, an' watch 'em; an' he take ole Aunt Becky
along wid 'im fer to conjer 'em apart an' break 'em up.

It go on lak dis all de week up to de night befo' Chrismus Day. Dat
night, befo' Caesar an' Sindy git out un'er de big tree; ole Aunt Becky
taked some pepper an' salt an' goed out dar an' sprinkled it all over de
wood whar dey most in ginerally sot. As she siftered her conjer-dust over
de wood an' on de ground, she sayed over an' over to herself:

'Dat salt, it's good,
Dat red-pepper burns;
So she haint hisn,
An' he haint hern!'

Ole Aunt Becky git it all strewed aroun' thick an' good; an' den she start
back to her cabin whar Bob wus. W'en she got dar she met Bob a comin'
outn de doo' fer to go down behin' de Blood-hound house fer to watch
Caesar an' Sindy. So she turned aroun' an' went on back wid 'im. By de
time dey gits back behin' de Blood-hound house; Caesar an' Sindy wus
already comed an wus a settin on de wood-pile.

Caesar an' Sindy sot dar, an' sob an' Aunt Becky watch 'em. De lovin
couple dont git no peace o' mind; caze ole Aunt Becky wus strewed
down dat conjer-dust so thick dat it wus altogether onsettled 'em! So atter
dey wus been dar jes a liddle while Caesar telled Sindy: Well, tomorrer,
she'd be hisn an' he'd be hern; so he speck he'd better let her go on home
an' go to bed, an' den he'll go on off an' snatch a liddle res'. He kiss her
good-bye, an' telled her to run along; an' atter he see her go inside o' de
doo' of de Big House, he'll move on off home.

W'en Sindy go inside an' close de doo' to de Big House; Caesar start fer to leave de wood-pile. Den all of a sudden, befo' ole Aunt Becky or anybody else know it, Bob jumped an' tu'ned loose de big Blood-hound an' sayed: 'Sick-'im! Sick-'im!'

Dat ole Blood-hound, *Sub,* wus as big as one o' dese here big yearlin' calfs; an' w'en he go at any body, he make right straight fer deir th'oats! W'en Caesar see *Sub* a comin', it make his woolly ha'r oncurl an' stan' up straight on its ends! But he grabbed up one of de big sticks of wood on which he wus been a settin, an' landed it squar' on dat dog's head. He plumped him so hard dat he tumbled over on de groun' so dead dat he couldn' eben whine.

But, by de time de Blood-hound hit de ground, Bob wus up an' on Caesar wid de ax w'at wus a lyin' out dar by de wood-pile fer to split kindlin' wid. He hissed out 'twixt his gritted teef: 'You ole tar-black Scullion! If *Sub* caint git you, I can!' As he say dis: he hit Caesar an' he fell. As Caesar strike de ground; Bob passed anudder saveigus lick, wid de ax, at his head. He missed his mark, an' chopped de head clean loose from de body.

Ole Aunt Becky wusnt a spectin nothin lak dis fer to happen; and by de time Bob wus got Caesar's head clipped off, she wus a makin' tracks fer her cabin widout layin' in no scuses. W'en Bob look up an' see dat dere haint nobody dere 'cep' him; it come to him lak a flash dat he'd better take Caesar clean on off an' hide 'im so as to cover up w'at he wus done done! So he grabbed up de bloody head an' tuck out wid it to de woods. W'en he wus been a runnin' through de woods an' de cane-brakes an' de thickets for some time, he comed across a big holler tree. He pitched de head inside of dis big holler tree an' den went a trottin back atter de body.

W'en he wus got almos' to whar Caesar's body wus, de thought come a runnin through his head lak dis: Mosser wus put him in charge of dat 'ar Blood-hound; an' dar wus dat 'ar Blood-hound a lyin dead! If de dog's a lyin' dar dead in de mawnin, an' dere haint no Caesar dere; den de question'll come: Who killed dat 'ar dog? If he tote off an' hide bofe Caesar an' de Bloodhound; den Mosser'll go an' git some mo' heaps o' Blood-hounds fer to track 'em up; an' he can jes see dem fool dogs come a trackin' right up to his daddy's doo'! Terreckly he stop hisself an' set down fer to make up his mind w'at fer to do. At last, he maked up his head fer to go back an' git Caesar's head, an' put it along wid de body, an' leave it all dar togedder. But den; he wusnt kep' no track of hisself whilst he wus a runnin through de woods an' abouts; an' so he dont know whar dat head is! So at las' he maked up his mind dat dere wusnt nothin fer to be done but to wash his hands right good in de branch down dar in de woods an' den go on home.

So he go back down out into de woods ag'in to de branch an' wash his hands good. Den he wipe his hands on de ha'r of his head; an' go on off home fer to git in de bed.

It wus Chrismus mawnin. Ole Uncle Jake, w'at went to bed early, rousted up his ole 'oman an' telled her fer to let's git up. She telled him: All right but to lie dar right still fer a while ontel she whisper an' tell him w'at Bob wus done gone an' done.

Ole Uncle Jake lay dar an' ole Aunt Becky whisper it in his (y)ears— all 'bout w'at wus done gone an' happen to Mosser's big fine dog, an' how Bob wus done gone an' kilt de dog-killer. Uncle Jake whisper back to her: If dat wus de case; dey'd better roust up Bob sorter quiet lak, an' fix up togedder w'at dey wus a gwineter say to Mosser.

So Uncle Jake got up an' lit a pine-knot an' stuck it in de chimbly-jam so as to make a liddle light in de room. Den he walk over to Bob's lounge-bed in his stockin'-feets so as not to make no noise an' sorter shake him to wake him up. W'en he shake him; Bob pop up in de middle of de bed an' say as he git sorter half awake: 'You Caesar! Don't you hit *Sub!* You ole Hellion!'—Uncle Jake shake him a liddle mo' an' say powerful sof'-lak: 'Sh—! Sh—!' W'en Bob sorter git his eye-lids half-propped open; dey 'gins to subgest to one-nudder w'at it wus best fer to do. At las' dey makes up deir minds dat it wus best fer dem to git back into deir straw-beds an' stay dar ontel all de Niggers on de plantation flock up to Marse Heck's at day-break fer to git deir Chrismus gifts. W'en dey wus all flocked up dar; dey would find de dog an' Caesar bofe dead. Den w'en Mosser call dem; dey'll jes say dat Bob wus chained de dog up at dusky-dark an' comed on home; an' dey wus all done gone to bed befo' moon-rise. So dey all gits back in de bed fer to carry out deir progrance.

As soon as de Chickens 'gins to crow fer de light; de plantation darkies all hops outn bed. As soon as de dey 'gin to break, dey all maked a bee-line fer Marse Heck's House fer to git deir Chrismus Gifts. Dey all goes jes a runnin' an' a bouncin' an' a pouncin' fer to see who can git dar fust; so dey haint got no time fer to look whar deir footses is a gwine. A whole gang of 'em run'd right on past Caesar's dead body widout not seein' no nothin'. Terreckly one of 'em, in runnin', stumped his toe on Caesar's foot; an' he fell 'kerblam!' right over on de body! Mon! Dat 'ar Nigger riz a givin' a squall lak somebody wus done gone an' stuck a pitch-fo'k through 'im! He jes kep' on a gwine; an' as he pass de tother Niggers on his way to de woods, an' dey see him all kivered over wid blood; dey all scattered an' runned in ev'ry direction lak sheeps.

Atter while some o' de older colder Nigger heads go an' look. Dey sees Mosser's hound a lyin' dar wid his head all smashed. Dey sees Caesar a keepin' comp'ny 'long wid him wid no head on him at 'tall. So dey goes up to de Big House fer to git Marse Heck.

Marse Heck comed an' looked de land over; den he sent off some of de slaves right away fer to tell ole Aunt Becky an' ole Uncle Jake an' Bob to come up dar. Dese here Nigger slaves go on off down to de cabin; an', atter beatin' on de doo' almos' hard 'nough fer to break it down, manage to git dem inside fer to say dat dey reckins dat dey mought be awake. Atter so long a time; de three of 'em sorter pull on deir clo'es an' go a mozeyin up to whar Marse Heck wus. W'en dey gits dar; Marse Heck ax Bob w'at wus dat 'ar dog a doin' outn his House out dar on de ground wid his head smashed.

Bob maked answer: He dont know!—Who wus it dat foun' him out dar lak dat?

Den dey telled him how one of de Niggers wus stumbled an' fell an' run'd off to de woods all bloodied up; an' how, w'en dey wus looked, dey foun' bofe de dog an' Caesar.

Bob say he dont see no way onless de Nigger w'at run'd to de woods wus a runnin' so hard dat he tromped on Sub's head an' mashed it; an' den got so mad at Caesar fer letin' him do it dat he cut off his head an' tuck it off to de woods to throw it away.

About dat time de Nigger w'at runned off to de woods wus got over his skear an' wus jes a comin' back. He heared w'at Bob wus done sayed an' he hollered out: 'No, I haint done nó nothin'! I couldn' a cut off nobody's head! I haint eben got no pocket-knife!' W'en he say he haint got no pocketknife, he turned his pockets wrong-sid'out'ards to show 'em he haint got none.

Marse Heck look aroun' a liddle; an' he find de bloody stick an' de bloody ax. Den he say to ole Uncle Jake; since he mos' in ginerally handle de ax, a splittin' wood an' a bringin' it into de house, dat he'd lak fer to hear w'at he mought have to subgest 'bout it.

Uncle Jake say: he don't know, it all jes bang his time! He dont see no way dat it could a happened onless Caesar tuck de hound out an smashed his head; an' den de hound turned 'round an' bit his head off an' chawed it up an' swallered it down!

Ole Mosser say dat wont do; but jes as he say dat Sindy walked up, an' w'en she see Caesar dead, all bloody widout a head, she scream an' fall ought jes lak she mought widout doubt turn out an' die!

Marse Heck stop his zaminin of de Niggers an' pick her up an' tote her off to de Big House. W'en he git up dar wid her; she look lak ev'ry bref was a gwineter to be her las' one. So he sont word down to de plantation darkies fer to take Caesar's body an' wrop it up in a ole quilt, an' fasten it up in one of de stalls down at de stable ontel he git time fer to come back an' to talk wid 'em some mo'. An' he say fer 'em lakwise to git a hoss, an' to mount him, an' not to spare neider whup nor bridle, an' to git de big white doctor from town fer Sindy right away.

About de time one of de Niggers wus a ridin' off fer de doctor an' de
tothers wus a wroppin up Caesar's bloody body; a big crowd of white
mens, w'at de Court House an' Papers wus told fer to come out to Marse
Heck's fer to buy slaves an' drink whisky, come a ridin' up. Dey seed de
Niggers a rollin' up Caesar's bloody body widout a head; an' dey stopped
fer to ax 'em who kilt him.

W'en dey wus axed; de Niggers maked answer dat dey dont know.
But dey sayes dat it look to dem lak dat somebody wus done gone an' so
conjured up dat bloody ax an' big bloody stick, w'at dey see a lyin' down
dar on de ground, dat 'twixt an' 'twen 'em, dey wus busted de dog's skull,
an' cut off Caesar's head, an' knocked it to de back-sides of nowhars!

Dese here white mens feels sorter skittish w'en dey hears all dis: but
dey goes on up to de Big House whar Marse Heck wus. Dey gits dar an'
walks on in de house. W'en dey gits in dar dey finds Venie an' Marse
Heck a pourin' Camfire, an' Turbentime an' ev'ry thing all over Sindy a
tryin' fer to save her. But atter dey wus been a standin' aroun' de bed fer a
liddle while, dey heared Sindy mumble off: 'W'en I lays de clay over
Caesar's heart, picked up wid hands of love; dat heart an' dem hands is
bleedged to live an' to die togedder.' Den de cream-colored lips an' de jet-
black eyes fall half-open an' she wus gone.

Venie leave de room an' bust out in a great big cry. She ricomember
w'en Aunt Millie wus a paddlin up de grave-yard clay wid vinegar fer to
save Caesar dat she say: 'W'en I lays de clay over Caesar's heart, picked
up wid hands of love; dat heart an' dem hands is bleedged to live an' to
die togedder.' Aunt Millie wus put de charms on too strong; an' now her
chile all—all she wus got—wus gone!

De white mens say to Marse Heck dat dey dont b'lieve dey chooses
fer to buy nothin jes now; ontel he git his Niggers sorter in hand. As dey
mount up to ride off; dey ax him if dere is sumpin dat dey mought do fer
'im. He telled 'em, yes; W'en dey meets de doctor along wid his Nigger fer
to tell him not to come no furder: Sindy's dead: He'll pay him de nex' time
he come to town. De slave-buyers den ride on away.

Dey all jest sot aroun' on Marse Heck's plantation on dat Chrismus
Day. Dey dont say no nothin, an' dey dont do no nothin'—all 'cep' ole
Uncle Jake, ole Aunt Becky, an' Bob. W'en dey gits back down into deir
own cabin dey notices dat Bob's ha'r look lak dat it wus done gone an'
turned a sandy-brownish black color; an' w'en dey zamine it close dey
sees dat it was Caesar's blood w'at Bob wus wiped off on dere w'en he go
to dry his hands atter he wash 'em in de branch of runnin' water out in de
woods. Dey washes 'an dey washes Bob's head but dey caint git dat 'ar
murder-blood offn his ha'r! At las' dey takes some soot outn de chimbly,
an' mixes it up wid some grease, an' greases his ha'r wid dat; an' dis sorter
kiver up an' hide de blood.

De nex' day dey takes Caesar an' Sindy an' buries 'em in de same grave. Ole Mosser telled de slaves fer to lakwise bury de bloody stick an' de bloody ax along in de grave wid 'em; caze he wus skeard dat dey mought have some of Caesar's blood on 'em, an' Caesar'll need all w'at beslong to him to go along wid him un'er de groun'. De slaves do ev'rything jes lak Marse Heck say.

Atter dey gits Caesar an' Sindy buried; *De Powers* comed dat night an' got deir sperits, an' tuck 'em up to de gate of Heaben fer De Keeper to let 'em in. W'en dey wus got dar De Keeper stopped 'em so as to turn 'em in one at a time. Caesar step back fer to let Sindy go in fust.

W'en Sindy wus walked up to de gate fer to go in; De Keeper hollered out: 'Is dere anybody inside or outside o' Heaben w'at haint willin' fer to let Sindy go in?' De good sperits inside an' de sperits outside, a waitin' fer to git in, say dey dont mind if she go on in. So he opened de gate an' turned her in.

Den Caesar walked up to de gate fer to go in. De Keeper hollered out: 'Is dere anybody inside or outside o' Heaben w'at haint willin' fer to let Caesar go in?' Den all de good Sperits inside holler out: 'We caint have 'im in here; We caint have 'im in here, caze we caint never count him in our number! W'en we counts we sayes: so many an' so many heads of Good Sperits, so many an' so many heads of hosses, an' so many an' so many heads of ev'rything. W'at-some-ever haint got no head we caint never count in our number. He'll hafter go back to de world an' git his head!"

De Keeper of De Gate telled Caesar dat he wus powerful sorry; but he'd hafter go back wid *De Powers* to whar his head wus got buried, so dat dey can git his head fer him. Den he can come on back an' git into Heaben.

Caesar telled De Keeper dat he dont know whar his head is. Bob wus took it away off somewhars; no tellin' whars. De Keeper say: den he'd hafter go back an' keep on a showin' hisself to Bob ontel he show him whar de head is. An' if Bob die widout showin' him whar de head is; den he mus' keep on a showin' hisself to de tother folkses in de world on de gray-grizzly moonlight nights ontel some of dem show him whar it is; onless dey can make Bob tell 'em w'en he come up dar. W'ensoever he find his head, *De Powers* will fix a head on him; den he can git into Heaben.

But Caesar say to De Keeper dat he caint walk on an' on forever a lookin' fer his head; caze dat would tire him all out, an' break him down.

De Keeper maked answer: Den, fer him to go an' take de big black-wa'nut stick an' de ax outn his grave wid de blood on it; an' draw a stick outn de stick an' a ax outn de ax. Den he mus' take de ax outn de ax an' shape de stick outn de stick into a great big black wa'nut-wooden hoss.

Den he can ride dat great big rattlin black wa'nut-wooden hoss all de time, an res' his weary bones; whilst he's a lookin' fer his head.

So Caesar comed on back to de worl'; an' he 'gin to ride dat big black rattlin' wa'nut-wooden hoss an' to show hisself to Bob on ev'ry gray-griz-zly moonlight night a tryin fer to git him to show whar he wus done gone an' put his head. But w'en Bob hear de big black wa'nut-wooden hoss a comin' an' ketch a glimpse of Caesar widout a head; he tear out home, an' run' in, an' run un'er de bed. Den Aunt Becky would turn her apron-pockets wrong-side out'ards an' throw salt in de fire; an' Caesar would hafter go on off an' let 'em a lone.

At las', Bob tuck to stayin' in altogedder at night; dat way he sorter manage fer to git shed of Caesar. Atter while w'en summer comed on, Bob 'gin to go out a liddle once in a while in de evenins; an' he telled his mammy an' daddy dat it look lak dat ole Caesar wus got 'nough sense at las' fer to let him alone an' not bother 'long wid 'im.

Bymeby Chrismus Eve come ag'in: an' all de Niggers on Marse Heck's plantation make it up fer to go out a huntin' dat night an' ketch 'nough possums fer 'em all to have possum meat to eat wid sweet taters fer Chrismus Day. Dat evenin' atter it git dusky dark: de whole drove of 'em met togedder up dar close by ole Mosser's House. Bob wus along mixed in wid de balunce of de crowd. Terreckly dey all blowed deir cow-horns an' started off wid a pack of possum dogs towards de woods.

On de way to de woods; dey starts to pass by Marse Heck's stables an' de stall in which dey wus fastened up Caesar w'en he wus all bloody an' wus lost his head. As dey goes to pass by dat stall, dey all hears a rattlin' sound lak de bones of a banjer picker a knockin' togedder. Dey all stopped. As dey stopped, Bob hollered out: 'Looky! Looky! Cae—sar!' Den he tumbled over stone-dead!

De tother Niggers all tuck to deir heels an' brung deir selves up at deir Mosser's back doo'. Ole Mosser come out to see w'at in de worl' wus de matter wid 'em. Dey tells him to jes come an' go wid 'em an' see. Marse Heck go along wid 'em down to de stables; an' dar he see Bob a lyin' all stretched out cold!

W'en Marse Heck wus seed dis he telled 'em: Well, he caint have no dead folkses a lyin' on his plantation fer two Chrismuses, one atter de tother: To git de hoes an' a shovel an' come on an' let's bury him. Some of de Niggers den sayed to 'im dat dey wus skeard to go away off up to dat grave-yard at night. Marse Heck maked answer dat he wusnt a gwineter send no one or two fer to bury him; he wus a gwine hisself, an' take de whole tillion of 'em along wid him fer to do de job, an' no hants caint bother 'long wid no crowd lak dat.

So Marse Heck have 'em to git four hick'ry poles an' tie 'em togedder in a square wid bark. Den dey laid poles on dis here square so as to make a flatform. Den dey laid Bob on dat flatform. Dey nex' all lit deir pine-knot torches; an' started off wid deir hoes an' shovel fer de grave-yard, wid Marse Heck at de head. Some of de Niggers toted de flatform wid Bob on it in de middle of de crowd.

As de wound deir way through de deep woods towards de grave-yard; de hants w'at wusnt yit got into Heaben, caze some of deir parts wus missin', seed 'em a comin'. W'en dey seed dat crowd dey scooted back down un'er de ground an' stayed dar. W'en Marse Heck an' his band git up to de grave-yard; he have 'em to dig out a hole right quick by de torch lights; an' drap Bob in an' rake de dirt over him. Den he take 'em all back home wid him an' give 'em a good big drink apiece from his whisky bar'l. Den he tell 'em to go on a huntin'; caze it wus jes about de time of night fer de big possums to be a comin' out. De Niggers blowed deir cow-horns once mo'; an' tuck deir dogs on off a huntin'.

Beance Bob wus buried at night; *De Powers* comed right off an' got him an' tuck him up to de Gate of Heaben to see if he mought git in. Caesar's hant see Bob a gwine; an' it go a tripsin an' a trolippin right along behin' him up to de gate.

W'en Bob wus got dar; De Keeper of de Gate look out an' see 'im wid his head still all sandy-brown wid Caesar's blood. He stan' dar a minute an' look at him; an' at las' he holler out: 'Is dere anybody inside or outside o' Heaben, w'at haint willin' fer to let Bob go in?'

Den Caesar holler from de outside: 'I caint let him go in' I caint let him go in; caze he wus done gone an' chopped my head off an' hid it so dat I caint git into Heaben. I caint let him go in; 'til he wipe out his sin, by showin' me w'at he wus put my head in!'

De Keeper of de Gate den axed Bob whar wus Caesar's head.

Bob say he dont know. He wus put it somewhars out in de woods in a big holler tree; but he wus done gone an' clean clear fergit it offn his mind whar an' which it 'twus.

Den De Keeper say to Caesar dat he caint make Bob show him de head w'en he dont know whar it is. Yit an' still he'll leave it to him to order w'at he want done to Bob. W'at Caesar order, dat will De Keeper do.

Den Caesar say: 'Let my blood be on his head, blood-red; an' blood-red on de heads of his chilluns' chilluns! Let him an' all his folkses w'at come atter him dig holes in all de holler trees so dat I can look in dem fer my head! Let 'em keep on a diggin', day in an' day out, ontel I finds my head! Den fer fear dat some (y)other man on earth mought cut down an' split dat holler tree wid my head an' tote it away befo' I finds it a lookin' in through de holes; let me ride a big black rattlin' wa'nut-wooden hoss on all de gray-grizzly moonlight nights at de crossroads an' in de by-paths, an' ax all de folkses a passin' by fer my head! Let all dese things be, ontel I gits into Heaben an' be happy once mo' by de side of my Sindy!'

De Keeper of De Gate of Heaben telled Caesar all right. So he turned Bob into a red-headed pecker-wood bird; an' him an' his chilluns' chilluns is still a diggin'out holes in all de holler trees, so dat Caesar can look in 'em fer to see if his head be in dar. Den; on de gray-grizzly moonlight nights (lak dis one); he mounts his big black wa'nut-wooden hoss, an' axes ev'rybody dat he meet up wid fer his head.—He's a ridin'; an' he's a gwineter keep on a ridin' forever a lookin' fer his head or ontel he find it!"

Aunt Lize had finished her long and weird Tradition. Bone sat speechless as he looked out into the pale moonlight and thought how narrowly he had probably escaped seeing so gruesome and so terrible a specter. No word was spoken; but Aunt Lize again broke the silence by saying: "Well, I reckins I'd better fix up fer to let you chilluns go to bed."

So saying, she arose, took her long clothes line from a box, and so tied it across the room as to divide it into two sections—leaving one bed in each section. She next pinned sheets on this line so that they served temporarily to divide the room into two neat little compartments. Then she assigned the two boys to the compartment with the unoccupied bed; while she herself shared the other, already taken by her husband.

WHY THE BUZZARD IS BLACK

It was a beautiful Saturday's afternoon of an early summer day in the early seventies of the last century when two Negro boys, strolling through a thick woods of Bedford County Tennessee, accidentally met upon a slight elevation known there as Horse Mountain. Their greetings and conversation proceeded as follows:

"Hullo, Buck. I haint seed you in a coon's age."

"W'y! "Hullo, Bill! It sho do seem lak dat I haint seed you since de woods 'us bu'nt over. Set down here on dis here log an' tell me 'how you wus'".

"Aw! Now git out Buck wid yo' high-folutin questions—'How you wus?' I s'pose you can see dat I's fat and sassy; an' so I'll jes say: I 'wus' in de cornfiel' ontel daddy tuck a notion to go down to town dis evenin', an' tol' me dat I mought take de dog an' go a huntin'. Aw' You'd jes a oughter a been dar w'en he started!"

He saddled up our ole sor'l mule, Beck, fer to ride so as to save his Sunday-go-to-meetin' shoes from a w'arin' out. He saddled 'er an' den he mount up, he do. W'en he mount ole Beck she sorter hump up in de back, she do; an' den he gouge 'er in de flanks wid his toe-nail heel an' holler out to 'er: 'Here! You come up here, you ole huzzy you! I haint a gwineter put up wid none o' yo' foolishness now! Does you hear me?'

He rid out an' started down de hill towards town. W'en dey gits down nearly to de branch at de bottom of de hill, all of a sudden ole Beck kick up an' daddy he sail right over her head lak a kite; but de ole man land spang flat-footed on de groun'. Well, dis here make him as mad as a bald hornet w'en you job in her nes' wid a long pole an' run. He lit in on 'er wid his switch an' poured two or three pot's full o' hot hick'ry tea on dat mule's back. W'en he git sorter to de holdin' up p'int, he blow a liddle so as to ketch his win' an' git cooled off a liddle. Den so as to make ole Beck ricomember an' not fergit who he wus; he tuck her back to de top of de hill, so as to begin de journey over ag'in, an' so as to let her act lak a good mule should oughter act.

He mount up ag'in he do, an' ole Beck move off down de hill mo' quieter an' mo' innocenter dan a one day ole lam'. But w'en she git to de branch, at de bottom of de hill, which are now dried enough to make a fair sort o' mud-hole; all of a sudden ole Beck buck 'im up in de air ag'in, but as he sail over her head lak a buzzard he grabbed her by de (y)ears, an down dey bofe tumbled into de loblolly! De las' w'at I seed un 'em wus a muddy man a kickin' at de muddy mouf of muddy mule."

"Humph!" said Buck after a little laugh. "I thought you sayed dat yo' daddy wus done pick up an' go to town."

"Well" responded Bill, "I s'pose he did if mammy ever got de mud raked offn him. I hurried up an' lef' caze I wus skeared dat he mought git outn de notion o' goin' to town an' den I couldn' a got no chance to go a huntin'."

At this point their conversation was arrested because their attention was attracted by the barking of a dog, a short distance away, by which one of them was accompanied. Thinking that the dog had found a squirrel, they started in his direction. They had not proceeded far before they were met by the animal seemingly fleeing from the "unseen". He fell panting at their feet, rolled over a few times, and vomited.

"Humph!" said Buck, "W'at's de matter?"

"It 'taint no matter 'tall!" replied Bill,—"Jes 'fresh cut'."

They stood, for a while, quietly peering first through the tangled thickets of the wild wood and then towards the clear blue of the sky.

At last Bill raised his hand slowly and pointed to a large bird gracefully sailing over head.

"Dat haint nothin' but a buzzard! W'at's he got to do wid it?" said Buck.

"Well!" responded Bill with an air of erudition, "Perhaps he haint got nothin' to do wid it 'tall; an' den perhaps he's de 'chief queen an' bottle washer'. Ole Uncle Jock Hunter tol' me one time: Dat w'en sumpin-nother go a botherin' aroun' a buzzard-nes'; dey jes up an' vomit on dat sumpin-nother, an' dis make dat sumpin-nother so sick dat dere haint never no need o' doin' it over no mo'. So I 'spect dat dis here dog wus been a bodderin' along wid dat 'ar buzzard's nes'."

"Humph!" replied Buck, "I doubts dat, I doubts dat muchly.

"Well!" retorted Bill, "You knows dat de white folks all calls Kyernel Clay Thunderbu'g de buzzard or'tor. Miss Jane Rittenberry, whar I helped to clean house las' week, tol' me dat dey wus all done name 'im dat caze he puked up cuss words on all dem tother folkses w'at wus a tryin' to git de place w'en he wus a runnin' fer to git to be Jedge. Now, if de white folks calls folkses buzzards w'en dey throws up sumpin on dem tother folkses w'at you caint see, den dey mus' know w'at dey's a talkin' about w'en dey tells you 'bout de kind w'at you can bofe see an' smell."

"Oh, sho!" said Buck, "But seein' 's believin' wid me. S'pose you sorter amble 'long ahead th'ough de bushes. I'll foller 'long behin' an' stick to yo' back ontel yo' face beat black. Dis a way, we'll see if we caint find some trace o' dis here wonderful buzzard-nes' w'at you's a lookin right straight at w'en a buzzard flies over yo' head an' yo' dog vomit; even if it dont happen to be nowhars in existence."

"Dar you goes ag'in, an' dat's all right!" replied Bill. "Dat haint nearly half as bad as yo' thinkin' you seed a hant dat night w'en I laid behin' de fence on de big road an' groaned whilst you wus a gwine home. W'y! you didn' even stop w'en you git home. You run'd un'er de bed an' got yo' head all hung up 'mongst de bed-cords an' it tuck de whole fambly to ontwis' you and drag you out."

"Hants! Well, hants an' buzzards' nests is sumpin diffunt," said Buck. "S'pose you ramble aroun' an' fin' a buzzard-nes'; den we mought knock off eben."

With this much said the two boys set out through the thickets and underbrush, Bill ahead, and Buck following at a safe distance behind. After walking for some time over the rocky ground, looking in each hollow stump, under each little bush, and under each little rocky ledge, they stopped for a little rest. Buck started towards the decaying log of a fallen tree, that he might be seated there during the interim of their search. He had not gone far before he gave a leap backwards of three or four feet uttering simultaneously a loud shriek to the syllable "Ou—!"

Bill ran quickly to him and gazed anxiously towards the spot whence he had jumped; then, looking at his companion with a somewhat disgusted countenance, he said: "Oh, shucks!—Nothin' but a spotted adder snake! I thought you'd seed sumpin. Let 'im 'lone, dere haint no harm in 'im. Come on an' let 's set down on de log caze I knows we 's a gwineter find a buzzard-nes' now.

"How does you make dat?" asked Buck.

"I dont make it 'tall!" answered Bill. "Ole Uncle Jock Hunter had it all mixed in wid dat same perlaver he wus a handin' us out 'bout buzzards. He say: One time de buzzard an' de hawk have a big fallin' out. In dem days ole Brer Buzzard's eggs wus white an' ole Brer Hawk see 'em a long ways off. Dem eggs look so pretty an' dey look so good in Brer Hawk's eye dat he up an' dove down an' got one an' e't it.

Now, ole Brer Buzzard caint count much but he know wid all his layin' dat he should oughter git more' an one egg in his nes' . So de nex' time he go down to Mr. Mans house to git some calamus root to give his chilluns w'en dey wus sick wid de cramp colic; he call by fer to see Brer Spotted Adder. He call in an' tell Brer Spotted Adder all about his troubles.

Ole Brer Spotted Adder kinder lick out his forked tongue an' whistle th'ough his teef an' say: "Law, Brer Buzzard! Dat 's dat low-downed outdacious, good-fer-nothin', unfergotten, tucky-trotten, buck-eyed, pop-eyed, wall-eyed hawk! De reason I move outn de hills an' come down here to live wid Mr. Man wus to git 'way from dat ole Scounter [Scounter = Scoundrel].

W'en I lived up dar in de hills I got some brown mud an' black dirt an' sticked 'em on me so as to make myse'f brown an' black spotted. But now, atter I 's moved down here, I gits myse'f nice red an' yaller clay to rub up wid. Dough I keeps a liddle brown so 's my ole frien's lak you'll know me; I spots myse'f up down here all red an' yaller ontel eben Brer Butterfly sometime git taken wid de jealousies.

You has to spot yo'se'f up brown w'en you lives up dar in de hills, Brer Buzzard. W'en I wus a livin up dar, befo' I tuck to spottin up my chilluns, ole Brer Hawk could see 'em 'way off yonder. He 'ould sail over, scoot down, an' tote' em away up high in de air an' drap 'em. W'en he drap 'em, he kill 'em. Of co'se he say dat he wus jes a playin' wid 'em an' a givin' 'em a ride; but it kill 'em. I sees lakwise dat Brer Hawk always manage to come down an' eat 'em atter dey git dead; an' so I jes knowed dat he wus a killin' em on purpose.

Spottin' up my chilluns all black an' brown help some but I 's done moved down here. You see Mr. Man an' Brer Hawk haint on no good speakin' terms: so he dont pass down by dis way much an' my chilluns gits 'long tol'able well."

"Well! Well! Well!" say ole Brer Buzzard, "You's sho a mighty smart man Brer Spotted Adder. I caint move down here caze it 's too cramped up fer me down here in town; but I wonder if I couldn' git you to come up an' spot up my eggs wid brown so as ole Brer Hawk caint see 'em so good." Ole Brer Spotted Adder allow dat he don't mind helpin' a frien' an' so he go an' spot 'em up fer 'im.

So ole Uncle Jock Hunter say w'ensoever you finds a spotted adder, 'way off from de stables an' de house, up in de hills an' abouts; he's been up dar a spottin' up buzzard-eggs brown. Darfo' w'en you finds a spotted adder lak dat one w'at you wus jes now a squallin' 'bout; deres in generally buzzards' nests not so fur away.

After this "wise" explanation as to how Bill knew that a buzzard's nest was somewhere near, the two boys arose and resumed their search. In a short while Bill came to a low hollow stump. After peering within he turned and said to his companion in a low voice: "Dere it is in dere an' de young buzzards is done hatched out. Look at 'em quick an' let's git 'way from here befo' ole Miss Buzzard come an' drench us wid some of her 'Heaben-tree puffume'."

Buck crept up rather cautiously; and looking within, turned to his friend with a half offended look and said: "Dem haint no young buzzards! W'at's you tryin' to gimme?"

"Great Jehosaphat 'liver me!" exclaimed Bill. "I heared de boys an' gals a singin' at de big play de tother night dat ole man "Know-All" wus dead; but dey sho hadn' never seed you caze, if dey had, dat song would a been so broke up dat dey would a had to throw it all away.—Dem's buzzards all right!"

"But dey caint be buzzards!" retorted Buck. "Buzzards is black an' dem 'ar young birds in dar is might' nigh white'. White haint no black an' nobody haint never hearn tell of no white buzzards!"

"Well, come on an' let's git away from here", said Bill, as he quickly and silently slipped away, followed rather unwillingly by Buck. "Come on! I's skeared ole Miss Buzzard mought come along an' give us bofe a plain proof dat I haint got no hankerin atter. I's done seed young buzzards befo'. Ole Uncle Jock Hunter showed 'em to me. He say dat de young buzzards takes off deir white dress an' puts on a black one w'en dey begins to git about half grown. W'at's furdermo' he say dat all de buzzards—young an' ole—useter be white; an' dey layed white eggs. He splained it all in dat same confab whar he told 'bout de spotted adder a spottin' up de buzzard-eggs brown.—Buzzards white! Eggs white! All white!"

"Bill," said Buck, "fellers makes mistakes sometimes an' you mus' sorter overlook my short comins. But I wish you would tell me how ole Uncle Jock know all dis an' de whole balunce of de tale of how de buzzards wus once all white an' now dey is black."

"Now!" said Bill, "I didn' ax him how he know. I haint never hearn tell of ole Uncle Jock a sleepin' aroun' un'er no ash hoppers an' a drinkin' down no lye; an so I jes lis'en to him spectable lak widout axin a whole passel of questions."

"Well let's have de tale dat he tol!" said Bill.

"All right! I'll try to tell you de balunce of w'at Uncle Jock sayed" answered Bill. "I speck dat I'll leave out a lots of de facts, but I'll do de bes' I can; den you can ax ole Uncle Jock all about it fer yo'se'f de nex' time you see him."

"Uncle Jock say, "Way back yonder one time, somewhars, Mr. Man didn't wuk hard lak we does now. He make liddle crops but not much crops. So de animuls didn' live aroun' him much caze he didn' have big fields o' corn an' he cut deir rations short. Perhaps ole Sis Hen stay aroun' 'im a liddle to git some crumbs fer her chilluns an' ole Brer Spotted Adder hang aroun' him to git away from ole Brer Hawk.

Uncle Jock say how-some-be-ever dat eben in dem times Brer Dog an' Brer Hoss wus done make up deir 'greements wid Mr. Man fer to live wid 'im. Brer Dog keep de things from a bodderin' Mr. Man whilst he sleep at night an' hunt a liddle fer him in de day time; so he give him his board an' keep fer dis. Brer Hoss 'gree to tote Mr. Man if he'll wait on 'im an' feed 'im. Dis look all fa'r an' squar', so him an' Mr. Man strack a bargain.

In dem days all de birds wuk fer deirselves an' dey whirl in an' raise crops togedder. Dar wus ole Brer Jack Sparrer an' all his fambly an' kinfolks; dey picks off an' sows de seed. Dar wus Brer Robin an' all his relations; dey worms de crops an' picks off de bugs. In wormin' de crops dey hafter take a heaps of bugs in deir moufs: an' so, to make de job mo' easier, dey mince 'long ontel dey gits deirselves a likin' to eat 'em. An'

den; dar wus Brer Pattridge an' his kin-folkses, dey scratch in de seed.
Brer Jack Sparrer's folks sow de seed so thick dat de crops wouldn' be no
'count if dey come up dat way; so whilst Brer Pattridge's folks scratch in
de crops, dey jes eats up 'nough of de seeds to make de crops thin 'nough
to grow good w'en dey gits up. W'en dey wus a makin' de crops; de birds
sing, dey do, lak dey wus a gwineter bust deirselfs wide open lak Niggers
a wukin on de 'struction gang on de railroad w'en dey sings:

> "Wukin on de railroad,
> Dollar an' quarter day.
> Dollar fer my baby,
> Quarter t' throw away."

'Cose dey wus got to have a leader fer de chunes; an' dey handed all dat
part o' de progrance over to ole Brer Mockin' Bird, caze dey hears him a
singin' all de songs from de clouds to de canefields an' de cane breaks;
dey darfo' knows he can lead songs to suit everybody.

Ole Brer Buzzard, Brer Hawk, Brer Crow, Brer Owl an' Brer Eagle an'
deir relations wus de big folks in dem days an' dey didn' do much work.
Dey sorter managed to live offen de crops o' de tother birds by head-work.

De birds git long monstus well considerin' dat dey wus got to keep up
ole Brer Buzzard an' all dem tother big bugs free fer nothin' in one way or
anudder. But bymeby a bad crop-year come on. Dere wusn't no rain an'
de crops all fail. It make Brer Fish Hawk an' all his folks sing;

> "De water's all muddy an' de creek's gone dry.
> 'Twusnt fer de tadpoles we'd all die."

It hit all de birds hard an' dey live from han' to mouf but it hit de big
folks lak Brer Buzzard, Brer Hawk, an' Brer Eagle, an' folks of dat kind mo'
samer dan de liddle folks; caze dem 'ar big people didn' raise no crops on deir
own hooks. As de liddle song sayes w'at de liddle birds make up 'bout 'em:

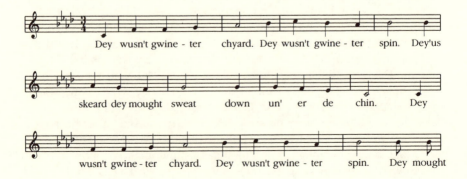

sweat down un'er deir chin.⸺ Dat ole mould-y ash-cake, it's up dar on de she'f. If you wants sump-in else, you go git it yo' se'f! Wants sump-in else? Wants sump-in else? Sump-in else? Go get it yo' se'f!⸺

Whilst all dese here big folks wus about to starve; ole Brer Buzzard sail aroun' an' ax 'em all in to a confab 'mongst deirselves, so's to kinder talk over how dey mought kinder make buckle an' tongue meet.

Dey helt deir meetin' at night away out in de top of a big tall cyprus tree—way out in de middle of a great big swamp, whar none of dem 'ar liddle birds caint go much. Dis wus caze dey didn' want none of dem liddle birds aroun' an' caze lakwise dey didn' want de big Bird Jedge to know nothin' 'bout it—an' dis wus de caze dat dey helt deir meetin' at night. De Bird Jedge, he had to see to it dat all de birds do right—big an' liddle—but dat Bird Jedge, lak all de tother good folks, stay home an' sleep at night. So dey holds deir confab at night lak dem dough-faced Ku-kluxes w'en dey wus a gwineter fix it up to do deir meanness.

Dey makes ole Brer Owl de moderator of de confab, caze he could see mo' better an' mo' plainer at night, an' darfo' could splain de twisted an' kinked-up p'ints mo' better dan any of de tothers. Dey all 'scusses how poo' dey wus an' how all of 'ems wife an' chilluns look lak dey wus bent an' bound to starve an' die.

    Dey 'scuss it up,
    Dey 'scuss it down.
    Dey 'scuss it through,
    Dey 'scuss it 'roun'.

You see: Dese here big folks' scuss deir livin' in de same directions dat de liddle folks wuk deir crops so as to make deirselves have good luck.

Well, at las' ole Brer Hawk up an' say dat he wus been a watchin' Mr. Man as well as keepin' one eye on some of his fine fat good-lookin'

chickins. He say dat he notice dat some of Mr. Man's folks once in a while
fowt wid one nudder; an' sometimes some o' de folks e't up some o' de
folks w'at git killed in de skummishin. Brer Hawk den throw in dat he
dont scacely know whedder or no dat dis wus wo'thy of de gemmuns
'tention; but he jes drap it in dat dey mought pick it up an' chaw on it to
test de flavor.

Fust: Dey all say dat Mr. Man was powerful smart, den dey say dey
wus a gwineter do lak him. All of 'em tetch an' gree 'cep' ole Brer Crow.
He flopped out an' lef' de meetin' a singin'.

"Jaybird jump from lim' to lim',
An' he tell Brer Rabbit to do lak him.
Brer Rabbit say to de cunnin' e'f:
You wants me to fall an' kill myse'f'.

"So if you' s noticed," said Bill with a show of much learning, "crows eats
eggs but dey don't scacely never eat no birds an' setch lak. But to go on
wid de loration: Ole Uncle Jock say dat dey all lef' dat meetin' a tetchin
an' a 'greein' to eat dem tother birds jes lak dem some mens eat dem
tother mens; an' to wipe deir moufs an' say nothin'.

Nex' day dey all 'gun to ketch an' eat de liddle-fry birds. Brer Hawk
an' Brer Eagle an' dem fly so fast w'en dey ketch somebody an' dey wus
lakwise so onsarten in color dat de tother birds don't hardly know who
an' which it wus. But w'en ole Brer Buzzard make a dive down an' ketch
'em dey all know him an' who it 'twus caze he wus de onliest big white
man amongst 'em. So dey all goes an' tells on 'im to de big Bird Jedge.

De big Bird Jedge up an' call all de birds togedder an' tells 'bout de
big lawsuit befo' 'im. He den call fer Brer Buzzard an' dem w'at 'cuse him
to come forward.

Dey all come up an' ole Brer Buzzard come up an' 'ny it all but de
liddle birds prove by ev'rybody dat one of de birds a doin' de ketchin wus
a big white man. Since ole Brer Buzzard wus de onliest big white man
'mongst 'em in dem times, dey condemns him.

W'en dey condemns 'im, ole Brer Buzzard den up an 'fess an' he
vomit on de tother big birds w'at wus wid 'im. He tell on Brer Hawk, Brer
Eagle, Brer Owl an' all de res'. Den dey condemns all of dem 'ar big folks.

W'en dey condemns 'em de Jedge say dat de law wus to fix 'em up so
dat dey couldn' do it no mo'. De liddle birds want 'em all kilt caze dey
wus been a killin' udder folks. De Jedge say dat he'll kill 'em, if dat wus
w'at it take to stop 'em: but he wus bleedged to go in 'cordance wid de
p'ints of de law. He den ax how dey ketches de liddle birds; an' all dem
liddle birds say dat de ketchin wus done wid deir long moufs an' sharp
claws.

Den de big Bird Jedge sorter clear his th'oat an' look over his specks an' say dat he sentence 'em all to have deir moufs an' claws broke.

He call in Brer Yaller Hammer an' order him to do de job whilst de tothers of de liddle birds stan' aroun' an' see it well done.

Brer Yaller Hammer was all so glad w'en dey see dem bills an' claws all broke up dat dey almost jump "Juba"; caze dey thinks dat all deir troubles wus over wid. Brer Mockin' Bird tell 'em dat dey mus' have a song togedder befo' dey parts. He make up de song an' lead it; an' dey all cackles an' sings it. It wus dat liddle song dat you hears 'em sing at plays sometimes.

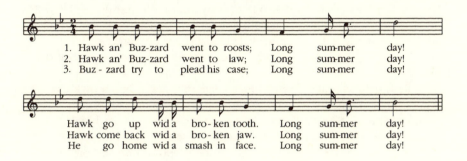

Well, dey dances an frolics aroun' an' den dey goes home. But de hawk an' buzzard an' all dem tothers wid broke up bills an' toes git well. You see; Dat's de reason hawks an' buzzards an' dem kinds o' birds is got crooked bills an' claws. W'en de bills an' de claws grow back togedder atter dey git broke; dey grow back crooked.

W'en dey git well ag'in, dey 'gins to ketch de liddle birds ag'in on de sly. So dem liddle birds goes ag'in to de big Bird Jedge to git him to sorter sweeten up deir cup of troubles. De Jedge tell 'em dat money make de mar' go an' he caint git up no big lawsuit ag'in widout a big pile of it.

Wid de bad crop year all dem liddle birds wus strapped; so dey hafter give up de idee of takin' dem big birds down to de court house an' jail. Dis make all dem liddle folkses mighty mad; an' w'en dat big Jedge's time git out, dey votes not to have no mo' big mens to be a runnin' deir shibang. Since de big birds wus all sore from deir broke toes an' moufs; dey say dat no Jedges at 'tall wus plenty good 'nough fer dem. W'en de Bird Jedges played out; de birds take up de law "Ev'ry man fer hisself, an' de Devil ketch de hindmos'.

Wid no nothin' lef' fer to stop 'em, dem big birds git too big fer deir britches. Dey say 'mongst deirselves dat dey wus so big an' smart dat dey could give Mr. Man one, an' den beat him at his own game. So dey sot out to l'arn him a thing or two. Dey fust 'gin to show him who dey wus by totin' off almos' all his fine fat chickens.

De little birds run aroun' to Mr. Man an' turned deirselfs wrong-side-out'ards an' tol' him who it wus a stealin' his chickens. Mr. Man tell 'em dat he wus mighty much obliged to 'em, an' he swar' by de p'int of his knife dat he wus a gwineter lie in wait fer 'em.

At'er while ole Brer Hawk an' Brer Eagle an' Brer Buzzard an' deir folkses come a flyin' down "Flippity-flappity, Flippity-Fappity!" Mr. Man, he crack down on 'em, he do, wid all his big guns. He kilt a few but dey gits away fer de' mostes' part caze dey flies so crooked. But dar was ole Brer Buzzard an' his folkses—so fine, so white, so sticked up!"—dey puts on aires an' sails down in a straight line fer Mr. Man's fine juicy fat pullets, an' he sen' nearly half of 'em to de bone-yard an' Buzzard Heaben.

Den de big birds hol' anudder meetin' to Sweeten up an' season deir troubles.

Ole Brer Owl make de fust big speech an' say dat he's a gwineter hunt at night altogedder an' he think dat'll wrop up an' stop up an' chuore up his sore toes. Brer Eagle say dat he think dat he'll go a fishin' fer hisn an' leave Mr. Man some whars out on de dry lan' by hisself. Ole Brer Hawk say dat he wus a gwineter hunt in de wood to find sumpin good; an' at some time of his own pickin he mought dart down an' git a chicken.

Ole Brer Buzzard say dat he wus done put on aires widout failin' till he caint fly 'tall widout sailin'. So he caint noways do no good; a sailin an' a ketchin in de wood. Dem trees dey stan' in dar so thick; dey'd bus' his head open lak a brick. He caint in no ways hunt out in de clearin's; caze he wus so fine an' white dey could see him out dar at night an' git outn his way wid all deir might. So he ax all his big frien's an' 'quaintunces right den an' dar; if dey wont sorter take him an' his folkses in outn de rain, an' de cold; an' put a liddle bite of victuals in deir moufs.

De tother big birds tell ole Brer Buzzard dat dey can sorter take deir frien's in over night so long as dey comes 'long one at a time an' leaves befo' breakfus; but dey haint yit never hearn tell of nobody a thinkin 'bout takin' all deir frien's in de fambly. Den dey all sorter give 'im "de laugh" an' tell him dat folkses wus got to pay fer bein' white an' a puttin' on aires. So dey stretched deir wings, broke up de meetin' an' went home.

Ole Brer Buzzard went on home too; an' w'en he tell de remnants of his fambly dat he didn't git no promus of no grub at de meetin; deir heads hung down, deir wings hung down, deir tails hung down, an' dey hung down all over.

Fer de nex' few days it look lak dat all dat fine white Buzzard Fambly wus a gwineter peg out an' die. Old Brer Buzzard couldn' sleep a wink fer nine days an' nine nights; caze he think so hard 'bout his dead chilluns an de outlook fer all de balunce of de fambly to be a gwine to 'em soon.

At las' one night he sorter doze off, an' he hear his dead chilluns a callin' to him from Buzzard Heaben.

Ole Brer Buzzard, he git up he do, an' 'gin to walk in his sleep. Now, w'en folkses walks in deir sleep dey can walk whar dey caint walk w'en dey's awake, an' dey can go any whars. De dead chilluns' sperits call him, an' ole Brer Buzzard walk. Ole Brer Buzzard walks an' a follerin de call o' de dead chilluns, he walk right down to de smokin' lake w'at divide off dis worl' from Buzzard Heaben.

W'en he git down dar on de banks of de smokin' steamin' waters; de sperits of de chilluns sail back from Buzzard Heaben close to de banks of dis here worl', an' balunce deirselves in de fumes over de lake, an' talk to him so as to he'p 'im outn his troubles. Dey sense it into 'im dat all deir troubles wus come to de fambly caze dey wus so proud dat dey wus all white an' wus all bucked up in white all de time. Dey tells him dat all deir troubles can soon git to be over wid by sheddin' off deir white duds an' a puttin' on black clo'es, an' a waitin' on de Lawd.

Ole Brer Buzzard say to 'im dat he dont mind none o' dis, dat he wus puffeckly willin' to wait on de Lawd; but he didn' see no way fer him to git no black clo'es for hisself an' de balunce of de fambly, caze it wus done been a awful bad crop year an' nobody wusnt got no money.

De sperits make answer dat de way to do dat wus fer 'em all to dye up deir white clo'es black.

Ole Brer Buzzard say to 'em dat he haint never dyed up nothin' in all his bo'n days, he dont know nothin 'bout dye, an' he dont see no way how he wus a gwineter tu'n his white gyarment into a black one.

De sperits tell 'im dat it wusnt much trouble to de dat.

Brer Buzzard ax 'em to 'splain to him how to do it.

De sperits make answer dat dey'll tell him how to do it but he must be mighty keerful to do jes zackly lak dey tells 'im caze, if he dont, he mought land in Buzzard Heaben befo' his time. Dey tells him to retch out his head over de edge of dis here lake w'at divide de livin from de dead an' git a liddle of de black water an' pour it all over hisself an' dat'll dye his coat a midnight black. But dey pintedly tells him dat he mus' be shore to hol' his bref w'en he go to git de water; caze jes one whiff of de smoke from de lake'll make him wall his eyes, an' gap open his mouf fer de las' time.

Ole Brer Buzzard done w'at his dead chilluns' sperits tell him, an' he got dyed dead black all right; but de nasty fumes offn' de dirty black water make all de fedders fall offn his head: so he walk on back home in his sleep all bal'-headed an' black. W'en he git back home his folkses don't scacely know him. He tell 'em all whar he wus been an' it almos' skear 'em to death. Den dey all dream an' walk in deir sleep down to de lake an' git as black as midnight an' as red-headed as lightnin'.

Now w'en dey wus all got bal-headed an' black, dey sails out an' sets down side by side on a dead lim' of a dead tree to wait on de Lawd lak de sperits wus done tol' 'em to do.

Bymeby ole Brer Hawk come a floppin' by an' he holler out: "Hullo! Cousins! How in de worl' did you all manage to git so black an' bal-headed an' rusty un' crusty?"

Den all de buzzards up an' make answer: "Dat's for us to know an' fer you to fin' out'!"

Den Brer Hawk say: "W'at's you all a doin' a settin up dar all red-dened up an' blacked off any ways?"

"Humph" de buzzards make answer, "We's a waitin' on de Lawd!"

Brer Hawk sot dar fer a minute an' say to hisself: "Waitin' on de Lawd! Who ever heared of de lak?" Den he busted out in one of dese here big guffaw laughs an' it make dem buzzards mo' sore an' mad dan dey wus black an' red.

Whilst he wus a settin dar an' a laughin' he spied one of ole Mr. Man's big fat yaller-legged chickens w'at look to be fur 'nough away from de house fer safe nabbin. So ole Brer Hawk make up his min' to try his han' at "raisin" it. He heist his wings an' flop 'em an' go! He cotch de chickin an' riz wid his claws stuck through its head. As he git into de edge of de woods, a sailin along, he look back an' holler to de buzzards: "Dis is de way de big folkses waits on de Lawd!" Jes as he say dis he wus a sailin' right over Mr. Man's head who wus out in de woods a squir'l huntin'. "Bam!" go off Mr. Man's gun's an' "Bop!!" go Brer Hawk wid his chicken down on de groun'.

Ole man Buzzard sorter pull hisself togedder lak he wus a wakin' up outn a snooze; he stretch his wings out an' pull 'em back togedder ag'in lak he wus a tryin' 'em to make right shore dat dey wus still dere; den he up an' say: "Chilluns! It sorter looks lak w'en you waits on de Lawd dat you gits two at a time instid o' one. Let's sail down in de style an' look 'em over."

Dey all comes down a slippin an' a slidin through de a'r to whar Brer Hawk wus done drapped, an' shore 'nough dar wus two—bofe a Hawk an' a chicken'. Dey gobbled 'em bofe down befo' you could say "chick-a-needle"; an den dey flops aroun' an' sails back to de perch on de dead tree ag'in to wait on de Lawd.

Whilst dey wus a settin' dar dey whispers a liddle bit 'mongst deirselves; but dey dont talk loud caze dey wus skeard dat de Lawd mought hear 'em. Some of 'em says Dat liddle bite wusnt 'nough to fill deir half-hollers. Heaps of 'em say dat it 'twusn't scacely 'nough to make 'em feel dat dey wus smelt grub fer a mont'. But dey all say dat day haint a gwineter grumble an' be onthankful to de Lawd fer leavin' 'em down in de bes' worl' dat dey's ever seed. So dey dries up an' sayes liddle prarers an' goes on a waitin' on de Lawd ag'in.

Atter while Mr. Man open up his stable doo', an' his big fine fat hoss bounce out lak a Injun-rubber ball; jes a cuttin up an' a caperin' an' a dancin'. He let him out into de paster whar de buzzards wus all a settin on de dead lim' waitin' on de Lawd.

De hoss raise his tail high in de air, kick up his heels lak greasy lightnin', den hol' up his head an' snort an' say to de buzzards: "Dont you wish you wus me? If you wus me, you wouldn' be a settin up dar an' a starvin'."

De buzzards make answer to him, dey do, dat dey wusn't aroun' a wushin; caze it wus de ole sayin' in deir fambly dat: "If you wush in one han' an' spit in de tother, it haint never no trouble to see which one git full fust".

Now dis here hoss w'at wus a doin' all dis big talk wus named Tony. So Tony up an' nicker back to 'em: "Humph! W'en you says dat you spits in de tother han', dat should oughter mean dat you're a fixin' up to git a good grip on a ax handle or a hoe handle or a plow handle or sumpin! Dat mean w'en you wuks fer w'at you wants you's mighty apt to git it! Dat's jes common hard hoss sense; but you all's jes a settin up dar an' dont look lak dat you's got no notion o' wukin nor doin' nothin' else! Dat's de reason dat you's a starvin now. You has to keep:

"A cuttin an' a charvin,
To keep from a starvin."

"Well," say de buzzards, "dat's you' trouble, Tony. It take a heaps more 'an hoss sense to see how to git on down here in 'dese low grounds of sorrow'."

Tony den tell 'em if dey's been a eatin apples offn de knowledge-tree, an' if dey wus done git qualified to structify him 'bout wuk wat folkses does w'at you caint see; den he draw in his Noggen an' quit.

Dis here answer sorter wool de buzzards an' git away wid 'em; an' dey says off sorter kellas lak: "Well! We's a wukin an' a waitin' on de Lawd!"

Law! Chile! W'en dey say dis, Tony tu'n a loose an' give 'em one o' dem dar hoss laughs w'at you can hear fer fully a mile; an' he holler back up dar to 'em dat de "Fool-killer" sholy mus' be dead or mus' a got tuck wid de 'ralysis.

It keep on a gwine on lak dis ontel de buzzards say to 'im dat dey dont see no diffunce 'tween waitin' on de Lawd an' a waitin' on Mr. Man, 'cep' dat it wus mo' better to wait on de Lawd. Dey allows to him dat de Lawd wus done already give 'em a liddle snack an' dey wus got a pow'rful strong feelin' dat a fine dinner wus som'ars already on de road to 'em. Den lakwise dey p'ints out to Tony dat de Lawd let de buzzards sail aroun' wharsoever dey will; but Mr. Man tie him up in de house an' w'en he let him out he keep him fastened up in a paster.—"W'y!" say ole man Buzzard: "Tony, Mr. Man wont eben let you go inside his gyardin, 'cep' w'en he's got you hung on to de end of a plow an' a doin' de part of a good clod-hopper."

Dese scatterin' remarks sorter act fer a stopper to Tony's mouf. At fust he wus sorter wool-gethered an' his tongue wus all bridled up fer a answer. But at las' he fish up fer his gag on his side of de questions "Pshaw! Brer Buzzard I jes jumps de fences w'en I wants to go whar I pleases. Mr. Man sorter holler aroun' an' spew over; but he caint do nothin'. I goes in dat 'ar gyardin w'en I innerpenunt please."

Den ole man Buzzard tell Tony dat it wus mighty cu'ious dat he dont never want to go in de gyardin whar dere's so much fine greens an' full sweet roas'in (y)ears; an' he put on to all o' dis dat he sho would lak to see 'im jes make a motion lak he wus got eben a notion o' gwine in dat 'ar gyardin of Mr. Man's. "Eh-eh! No-no!" say ole man Buzzard, "You knows w'at side yo' bread's buttered on! You knows better dan to try to go in dat 'ar gyardin of Mr. Man's."

Dis git down so fur un'er Tony's shirt nex' to his hide dat he sorter think dat he wus jes bleedged to do sumpin to bolster up his end of de oggifyin; so he holler back to ole man Buzzard an' his folkses; "Jes watch me an' I can show you mo' better dan I can tell you how I does!" Wid dis said, he raise his head an' tail an' start off wid one o' dese here fancy han'-gallops towards de gyardin, w'ich wus all fenced in wid dese here tall pine pickets all sharpened off to a p'int on de ends. On de way to de gyardin he look back an'—a pokin' fun—he holler back to 'em: "Jes look at ole 'Black-bal'-skinny-red-head' a settin an' a waitin on de Lawd! 'tel he git dead!" Den he bug-jump in de air, a handin' 'em out a sample of how he wus a gwineter clear dem gyardin pickets.

He reach de gyardin fence an' raise hisself in de air wid a lunge—his nose an' (y)ears bofe p'inted towards de fine roas'in (y)ears an' good ole greens—den;—den he come down right spang on top o' de pickets! Dat wus de en' o' Tony.

Ole Brer Buzzard sorter grin an' stretch his neck up high an' look aroun' at his hongry relations an' say: "Chilluns, de sperits sho wus done gone an' tol' us right! Who would a thought; w'en we wus a talkin' to Tony, an' a sayin' dat we had feelin' dat a big dinner wus on de road to us from de Lawd; dat de fine, fat, slick, sassy caperin', taperin', Tony wus hisself dat dinner? Come along, we mus' now jine in de feastin' w'at beslongs to us an' to our chilluns' chilluns caze we wus made up our minds to wait on de Lawd. I's a gwineter sing a new song. I'll sing de "call" an' you mus' sing de "sponse".

Atter ole man Buzzard make his gran' speech, dey all sail down one by one an' light on Tony. Ole Brer Buzzard stood on his head an' led de "calls" whilst de tothers perched on his back-bone an' rattled an' picked off de "sponse". Dis wus de song:

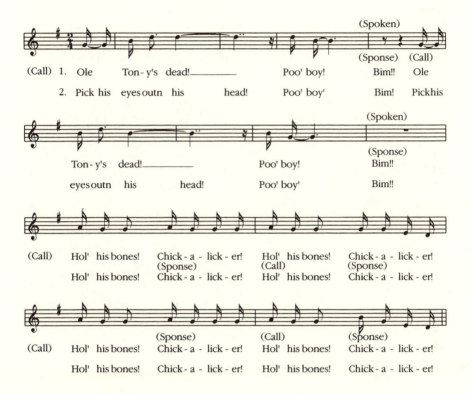

Well, dem 'ar buzzards go on a singin' an' a stuffin' ontel dey caint wrop deirselves aroun' no mo'; den dey flies back to deir perch on de dead lim to go on a waitin' on de Lawd. Lots an' gobs of hosses an' cows an' varmints starved to death caze it wus a bad crop year; an' ole Brer Buzzard an' all de remnants of his fambly git mo' dan dey can jes natchully 'stroy by jes a settin' aroun' an' a waitin' on de Lawd.

All de young buzzards is still white lak dem you's jes done seed dar in de stump, but dey all takes back atter deir great gran'daddies; an' w'en dey's about half grown; dey walks in deir sleep; walks down to de smokin', b'ilin', hot lake 'tween dis worl' an' Buzzard Heaben; dyes deir gyarments a midnight black; gits a bald red head; an' den comes back to set on a dead lim', an' wait on de Lawd along wid de rest of de Buzzard Fambly.

W'en Brer Hawk's relations, w'at wus lef' behin' w'en he drap dead wid Mr. Man's chickin, see Brer Buzzard an' his folkses a gittin on so good a waitin on de Lawd; dey gits begrudgeous an' one of 'em 'gun to steal his eggs. But Brer Spotted Adder he'p him outn dis lak I wus done already tol' you—leaswise dat's w'at ole Uncle Jock Hunter say w'en he wus a tellin' 'bout buzzards an' how dey git to be black."

With Bill's story finished, Buck sat quietly bewildered that such won-derful information should have floated around in the world and not have come earlier into his possession. Being kindly disposed and inclined to pass on all "good" things to others he said: "Well, Bill; dat 'ar loration beats all dat I's ever hearn tell of. You come over tomarrer Sunday an' tell mammy an' daddy 'bout it. Come along 'bout dinner time.

Dat ole brown hen o' ourn crowed dis mawnin; an' mammy cotched her, wrung her head off, an' throwed de head over de house three times to keep us all from a havin' bad luck. She's a keepin' de kyarkiss fer to make a big chickin pie for tomorrer's dinner. Come over an' tell 'em all 'bout buzzards; an' eat an' laugh yo'se'f ontel you's in misery".

"I'll sho be dar!" said Bill.

"Good-bye, Buck"; "Good-bye, Bill" and the boys parted.

THE NEGRO SLAVE IN THE MOON

In the early seventies of the last century; two Negro families, the Muggins and the Rivers, lived near each other, about four miles to the east of Shelbyville Tennessee. Very close to their homes was a picnic ground upon which lay a little circle covered with a deep layer of saw-dust. On this circle occasional old-fashioned "bran" dances were held by the Negroes of the community. In the interims the children of the two families were accustomed to meet on this spot in the late summer afternoons and play characteristic Negro plays such as "Jing-jang", "I'm going out on the Anchor Line", and "Rule over."

On the particular afternoon of which I am now writing, all the children of the two families, nineteen in number, had congregated here. As the sun went down and it tints of red, gold, and purple faded from the skies in the west, a full moon, already standing about twenty degrees above the horizon in the east, flooded the landscape with a mellow light. Such was the beauty of the twilight that the children lingered and extended their period of play instead of returning to their homes at the time of the sun's going down, as was their custom.

Two of their number, Johnny Muggins and Pate Rivers, were only about three years of age and were thus too young to take part in the plays with the older children. These two children played together apart from the others, now heaping up piles of dirt, now running and catching at eachother, or doing whatever else fancy might dictate.

As the golden twilight silently began to fall over all, Johnny and Pate sat on a small log of a fallen tree, near where the plays were being carried on, and gazed almost constantly at the full face of the silvery moon. Johnny occasionally whispered a few sentences in Pate's ears, and both then resumed their careful continuous looking at the moon. Finally, they arose and ran twenty or thirty feet, forward and back—always looking steadfastly at the moon; then they sat down once more only to keep up their careful constant gazing, breaking the apparent monotony by occasional whisperings.

When the playing of the larger children was finished, the two groups separated, each going to its own home. At home, both families were served by the mothers with wholesome plain suppers and the groups gathered around their respective firesides for a little evening chat before retiring for the night. The mothers in the respective families remained in the kitchen to clear away the dishes before joining the main group. In the

Rivers home, little Pate left those talking around the fireside and rejoined his mother just as she was finishing up the cleaning after the meal. He addressed her thus:

"Mammy, I's done gone an' had de goodes' time in de worl' dis evenin'!"

"Is you, Baby?" said his mother. "Well mammy's mighty proud to hear dat! W'at did you do?"

"Oh, me an' Johnny digged in de dirt an' den we looked at de moon!" replied Pate. "An' mammy, Johnny telled me all 'bout dere wus a man up dere a burnin brush on de moon! I looked an' looked fer him but I couldn' see 'im; but mammy, I could see de brush-piles! De brush-piles wus throwed up in great big heaps; an' you knowed dat de man wus a burnin' 'em, caze w'en you looked at one of de brush-piles an' wait awhile an' den look back ag'in, dat brush-pile wus done gone, an' dere wus anudder one piled up on de moon at anudder place. An', mammy, Johnny telled me too: dat if I'd run an' watch de moon; I'd see de man make de moon run an' keep up wid me! An', mammy, I runned an' tried it; an', sho 'nough, de man make de moon run an' keep right up wid me!"

"Well, Baby," said the mother, "I's glad you had setch a good time. Now, I's th'ough wid de cleanin'. Let's us go in an' set wid de tothers!"

"Oh no, mammy!" answered Pate. "I dont want to hear nothin' 'bout w'at dey wus got to say. Let's us dont go in. Johnny sayed dat his mammy telled him all 'bout how de man git to be up dar in de moon. Please m'am, stay out here an' tell me 'bout it too, caze I wants to know jes as much as Johnny."

"Well," said the mother, affectionately placing her hand upon his head, "Will you be a good liddle boy an' go right on to sleep w'en I gits th'ough, if I tells you?"

"Yas 'am!" promptly replied Pate.

"Well", said she, "come git in my lap an' keep still an' I'll try to tell you 'bout it."

When Pate was comfortably placed in her lap, she began as follows:

"Baby, dis here thing 'bout a man a bein' up dar in de moon is a tale I heared telled away back yonder in slavery days. I dont spect dere wus much trufe in it. You musn' put too much pennunce in tales. Sometimes dey's so, an' sometimes dey haint so. Of co'se a man ought be up dar in de moon, an den ag'in he moughtn't. W'en I looks, I sees sumpin up dar w'at look lak brush-piles, an' I's noticed dat de moon'll foller you aroun'; but whedder it all come 'bout lak dey all tells; I caint say. But how-some-be-ever de tale run lak dis:

"'Way back yonner in slavery days dere wus a Nigger boy named Sam, w'at git to lovin' a likely-lookin' Nigger gal, named Lize. Dey jumped de broomstick an' wus married; so fur as dere wus setch a thing as marryin' fer Niggers in dem times.

Sam an' Lize wus bofe church members. Dey come 'long an' git deir 'ligion right in de good ole fashion way. Dey mourned lak dey'd oughter at de mourners' bench, deir heads got wet wid de midnight dew, an' de Good Sperit wus poured out all over 'em. Dey almos jes as good as took 'em in de white folkses church; dey did let 'em go down to it once an' a while an set on de backmost seat an lissen to de big white preacher. Sam an' Lize wus Methodis, bofe warp an' fillin beat up wid a double shickel. You see, Honey, if dey had a been Babtis, lak I is, dey never would a fell from grace; an' dere never would a been no man up dar a pilin' an' a burnin' brush on de moon.

Well—, Sam an' Lize wus jes as nice as a bucket o' peaches an' as perlite as a basket o' chips to deir whitefolks. W'at dey wants, dey prays fer, an' axes deir Mosser an' Missus, an' dey gits it.

De fust liddle tilt w'at Sam an' Lize have wid deir Mosser come from deir prayin' so loud one night dat dey wake up de liddle white chilluns, w'at go to bed wid de chickens; but dey somehow manage to git dat all shmoved over.

Sam wus de house-boy an' Lize wus de house-gal. Dey dress up so fine in deir Missus' an' Mosser's ole clo'es dat all dem tother Niggers on de plantation git green-eyed. W'en dey gits a pass from deir white folks an' goes off to church on Sunday; dey looks as slick as a peeled onion an' lak dey wus jes been dusted off an' took outn de ban-box. Dis sorter pinch off all de good feelins of de cornfiel' hands fer 'em; an' it speshully rile ole Uncle Billy, a Nigger overseer. Dat Nigger, Uncle Billy, wus a wantin to git outn de cornfiel' altogedder, away from de clod-hopper class. It wus him w'at at las' ruint Sam an' Lize.

W'en Sam an' Lize wus a wukin aroun' deir white folks in de Big House, an' Lize 'ould start to lif' sumpin heavy; Sam 'ould run an' stop her, an' lif' it hisself. W'en he git th'ough wid his wuk at night, an' fin' Lize still a wukin, he'd sen' her on off over to deir cabin, an' finish up her wuk hisself. Sometimes his Missus cotch him a doin' dem sort o' things, an' she sorter git atter him; but, in ginerl, he'd tell her dat Lize wus a liddle sorter poo'ly an' ailin' an' so he wus jes a lendin a liddle hand on account o' dis.

Bymeby one day, Uncle Billy sorter git a chance to talk about Sam an' Lize to de Mosser an' Missus. He tell 'em dat Sam wus done gone an' speilt Lize so much by doin' all her wuk; dat she wus 'ginnin' to think dat she wus jes 'bout free an' as good as de white folks.

Atter Uncle Billy leave, de Mosser an' Missus 'gin to think over w'at he say; an dey talks it over 'bout Sam an' Lize. Dey allows: if Lize wus got so swelled up, dat it wus done got leaked out 'mongst de Niggers dat she wusnt a doin' nothin an' wus got too big fer her britches; dey reckins dat dey'd better look into it.

Of co'se, Baby, all dis time, dere wusnt nothin wrong wid neider Sam nor Lize. Sam jes love his wife so much dat he wus jes natchully crazy over her; an' he wuk hisself to death to save her all he can. As fer ole Uncle Billy, he wus jes a totin lye-bones wid de hopes o' gittin Sam outn de Big House an' a gittin hisself in.

De Mosser an' Missus, dey watch Sam an' Lize. Now, Honey, folkses mos' in ginerally finds w'at dey's a lookin fer; an' dat wus de case dis time. It look to dem lak Lize wus speilt, an' lazy, an' wusnt a doin' nothin'.

So, one day, de Missus say to de Mosser dat she guess dat she'd better fix up a liddle scuse to give Lize a liddle light breshin so as to let her know fer shore dat she beslongs in a Nigger's place. She didn' aim to give her no whuppin much—jes a liddle to take her down a peg or so an' make her gnaw on 'umble pie.

De Mosser tell de Missus dat wus zackly de way to do. W'en meat look lak it mought spile; it 'twusn't no mo' 'an good common sense to sprinkle a liddle salt on it an' try to keep it.

So de ole Missus sot out an' give Lize more wuk dan two or three womens could do. Eben wid Sam a helpin her she couldn' git nowhars in sight of de end of de row. Sam help her on de sly, but w'en night come de wuk wusnt hardly half done.

De Missus den come in at de end of de day; an' say: Lize wus a good-fer-nothin lazy huzzy, an' she wus a gwineter th'ash her wid dat raw-hide dat she wus got in her hand.

Sam tell his Missus: No, please ma'am dont do dat. He'll stay dar an' see dat de wuk's all done good an' nice, if it take all night.

De Missus tell him to git outn de way befo' she tan his hide too!

Sam say to her dat it wus all right fer her to whup his back ontel it wus red, if she want to; but, please ma'am, let Lize go on to deir cabin, caze she wus done wuked herself sick.

De Missus allows to him; to shet up an' git outn de way. Whilst she wus a tellin 'im dis, she hauled off an' give Lize a keen cut wid de raw-hide.

Befo' Sam jes natuchully know w'at he wus a doin; his han' flew out an' smacked his Missus flat down on de floo'! He hadn more 'an done it, befo' he would a give all dis worl' ('cep' Lize) an' a good part o' de nex' fer to take it all back; but it wus too late! De flamin torch wus done come; an' poo' Sam wus done tol' de gyardin of Eden good-bye in spit o' hisself.

He knowed if his Mosser come an' foun' him about de Big House dat he'd kill 'im. He knowed lakwise, if his Mosser wus got his guns, dat he'll shoot at all de spots whar he hear tell dat he is an' whar he mought a passed by. So he grabbed up all his Mosser's guns an' run'd off down to his cabin wid 'em an' went in an' barred de doo'.

W'en de Mosser come an' hear w'at wus took place; he fergit all 'bout dat he ever beslonged to no church. He rip an' he rar, he cuss an' he swar, he snort an' he cavort; but his guns wus all gone off a visitin down to Sam's cabin. Lize didn' go off wid Sam w'en he run off wid his Mosser's guns down to de cabin. She stayed up dar at de Big House a wukin. De ole Mosser wus so hot in de collar dat he pick up a great big stick to beat her up wid; but de ole Missus stop him. She tol' de Mosser dat Lize wus took all she give widout a mumblin word an' she didn' raise no finger an' didn think no sass. So de Mosser let Lize alone.

De night passed. Nex mawnin de Mosser got up an' started out to git up a whole passel of white mens to help take Sam outn de cabin an' kill him.

As he wus a gwine down de road; he met a white Nigger trader wid a whole gang o' Niggers, all handcuffed an' chained togedder, a takin' 'em off down to Orleans fer to sell 'em.

He hail dis Nigger trader an' tell him 'bout his troubles. Den he ax him if he caint takes jes a liddle time, long 'nough to help kill Sam.

De Nigger trader say dat he wus jes in a liddle sorter hurry; but he guess he could spare time 'nough fer dat. But railly, as he look at it, he dont see no good sense in killin off five hundred good silver dollars at one time. He'll give him dat much fer Sam an' sell him to a hide-splittin Mosser so fur away from dar dat de buzzards couldn' smell 'im.

De Mosser say to de trader: But dat Nigger, Sam, wus done gone an' laid his black dirty hand on de Missuses 'red rosy cheek; an' nothin but his life should oughter take de mark off.

Den de trader laugh an' say to 'im dat a dead Nigger mought put on a stink but he never would take off no stain. Five hundred dollars would do dat a heaps mo' better.

De Mosser stan' aroun' a liddle while an' study; den he say: it look to him dat Sam wus easy wo'th a thousan' dollars, if he wus a gwineter sell him at 'tall. But de trader say dat he think it ought to be wo'th sumpin to a body to git good riddance of bad rubbish.

De Mosser den oggify to him dat he reckin dat he'd better talk wid de Missus befo' he sell 'im.

De trader butt off to 'im dat womens dont know nothin much fer common, much less w'en dey's been hit; an' if he'll let him have Sam fer de five hundred, he can jes put it away onbeknowance to ev'rybody wid his tother rusty dollars, an' tell all de folks dat he wus jes fixed it up wid him to take Sam off an' kill him.

De Mosser sorter study it all over, an' make up his mind dat it wus about as good way as he see outn de bad mix-up. So he give de trader a Bidder sale dar in de middle of de road an' took de change; den dey went back up to de house fer Sam.

W'en dey gits in about hollerin distance of de cabin; de trader sont one of his Niggers up to de cabin. Dis Nigger whisper th'ough de auger hole in de doo' fer de latch (lak he wus been tol') an' tell Sam dat he can eider come out an' go on off wid his new Mosser or stay dar in de cabin an' die.

So Sam come out, an' go on down an' git handcuffed wid de tothers, an' go on off wid 'em.

De Mosser tell de tother Niggers, beslongin to him, befo' his wife, Dar went Sam to de bone-yard. He didn' keer to dirty his own hands wid killin him, so he wus a lettin somebody else do dat; but de nex Nigger on de plantation, w'at eben show lak he mought have some notion o' kickin up his heels, he wus a gwineter tar an' fedder an' burn him up hisself!

W'en Lize see Sam dispear down de road, han'cuffed an' boun' fer de bone-yard ('cordin to w'at de Mosser said); she fall out in a faint.

W'en de Mosser see dis, he say dat he know w'at wus good fer faintin Niggers. Dis time de Missus couldn' stop him; he lit in an' he whupped her ontel he couldn' make use of his arms no longer. But, through it all, Lize jes lay dar still in a faint lak she wus been dead. Atter while w'en he wus all wore out wid de floggin; he ordered de tother Niggers to take her down to deir cabin an' look atter her. Dey took her down dar, an' at las' brung her to by pitchin col' water in her face; but she wusnt no 'count fer two or three mont's atter dat.

W'en Sam wus gone, de Mosser an' Missus make Uncle Billy de house boy an' move him up into Sam's cabin—up in de whitefolkses' yard—Uh-uh—!Chile, I tells you, Uncle Billy strut aroun' lak he wus de bigges' dog in de bone-yard an' he Head of de Patterrollers! Who but him?

Atter while w'en Lize got better, de Missus took her back up to de Big House to wuk. Ole Uncle Billy dont want her up dar, an' he tell his whitefolks dat he wus skeared dat she mought conjer him an' pizen him; but dey jes laugh at him an' take Lize back any ways. How-some-be-ever day didn' take her back right in de house; dey put her to cookin' out in de kitchen. Dis hurt ole Uncle Billy a heaps wusser; caze he wus' always made a practice of goin out dar, an' a stuffin' hisself full o' de white folkses' good victuals. Wid Lize out dar fer de cook, Uncle Billy wus skeared to tetch de white folkses' victuals; an' he hafter eat ash-cake an' milk three times a day lak de tother Niggers on de place.

In about two or three mont's, two of de Mosser's chilluns took sick wid some sort of lingerin' disease. Deir skins turned brass-colored an' dey look lak dey wus been sprinkled all over wid copper; an' de doctors say dat dey dont know what's ailin' 'em. Dey died.

Atter dis anudder one of de chilluns took sick. It wus jes kivered all over wid knots w'at wus de shape of toad-frogs. W'en it wus wet rainy wedder; dese here frogs would hop back'ards an' for'ards un'er de skin; an' de chile 'ould jes holler an' scream lak it was a gwine into spasms. De doctors couldn' tell neider head nor tail of de ailment; an' dat chile lakwise die.

One day atter de funerl, whilst de Missus wus a settin out on de pie-izzer sorrowful an' lonesome; Uncle Billy went up dar whar she wus. He sot down on de floo' on de aidge of de pie-izzer, an' he tell her: He caint lie down an' he caint set up, he caint sleep an' he caint stay awake fer thinkin 'bout her chilluns. He say dat he jes natchully love all de fambly an' he hate awful bad to see 'em all die; so he wus done make up his mind to come an' tell her w'at wus a gwine on.

He tell her dat Lize wus gone an' drapped a spider in de dumplins; an' dat wus w'at wus de matter de wid de chilluns w'at died wid brass an' copper skins. He lakwise tell her dat Lize wus gone an' kilt a toad-frog an' dried 'im an' powdered 'im up. She fed dese toad-frog powders to de chile w'at died wid frogs all over 'im He tell de Missus dat w'en de chile eat dese powders, ev'ry grain of it turned to a frog; an' dese new made frogs, a crawlin' aroun' un'er de skin, kilt it. Den he take a dead dried-up toad-frog outn his pocket, an' show it, an' say dat he foun' it down by Lize's cabin whar he now stay.

Lize over-hear w'at ole Uncle Billy telled her Missus; an' she slipped off from de kitchen an' went down behin' Uncle Billy's cabin, whar she uster live, to pray whar she uster pray an' git all she axed fer.

De Missus call ole Mosser an' tell him w'at Uncle Billy say an' show him de dried-up toad-frog. He jes grabbed up his bull-whip an' went out to look fer Lize. He went to de kitchen, but she wusnt in dar; den he go a lookin' fer her about de yard. He find her down on her knees behin' Uncle Billy's cabin: an' w'en he see her wid her eyes shet, a wukin her mouf an' a sayin' nothin'; he think she wus down dar a practicin' up her "hoodoo." He jes lit in an whupped her all over.

Nex' day she wus sick, nex' day she wus sicker, nex' day she died. She died a prayin'.

Atter Lize wus dead, one night, along about midnight; Uncle Billy heard a cu'ious noise in de cabin whar he wus a sleepin'. He waked up an' seed a great big black yaller-eyed cat a settin in de corner by his fire-place.

He sot up in de bed to look at it; caze he knowed dat he wusnt got no black cat, an' he dont see how none should oughter git in dar, wid de doo' all barred an' de batten winder shetter all fastened up. De cat look at hi an' say: "Well! Dere haint nobody here but you an' me. De frog's all dried away! Come an' let's pray!"

Uncle Billy drapped back down in de bed lak somebody wus struck him 'twixt de eyes wid a sludge hammer; an' he kivered up head an years. But he hear dat cat in dar all de balunce of de night, a meowin: "Well!

Dere haint nobody here but you an' me! De frog's all dried away! Come an' lets pray!"

Nex day, Uncle Billy tell his Mosser dat de cabin of Sam an' Lize's wus hanted an' he dont want to try to sleep down dar no mo'. He tell him all 'bout de big black yaller-eyed cat a comin' home an' w'at it say all de night long.

De Mosser make answer to 'im dat nobody wusnt skeared o' no cats w'at wus got good sense. He tell 'im dat he can sleep in dar dat he mus' live in dar.

Uncle Billy make answer dat he wus skeared to live in dar. But his Mosser give him a gun—a great big muskit, an' tell him to stay dar an' to shoot all de cats w'at come. He stick in fer good measure: If mo' cats come dan he can kill, jes to come up to de Big House atter him an' he'll come an' fix 'em.

So dat night Uncle Billy tuck de gun home wid 'im an' sot it down in his chimbly corner. He maked up his mind not to go to bed but to set up. He sot up dar a singin' an' a whis'lin 'wid his doo' an' winder all barred up tight.

Ev'ry thing wus a gwine on all right; an, once an a while, Uncle Billy sorter nod a liddle so's he'd be fresh an' fine, jes offn de vine, fer his nex day's wuk. Whilst he wus a noddin a liddle, along about midnight, de barred doo' jes swung wide open; an' in stepped a liddle tiny black cat. Soon as it git in, de doo' shet an' bar up tight right behin' it.

Uncle Billy wus so stonished at de openin an' de shettin of de doo'; dat he clean fergit offn his mind to grab de gun an' shoot at de cat. So it walked right in an' sot down by de fire 'twixt him an' de gun. Dar it sot!

Uncle Billy didn't wait fer de cat to 'gin de confab dis time. He up an' say sorter brash lak to it: "Well, I's here! An' I reckins dat you can set over dar an' stay here, if you keeps yo' mouf shet an' 'haves yo'se'f." De cat, she jes sot dar an' she say nothin'.

Uncle Billy den retched an' got de shovel an' poked up de fire to make it give him a liddle mo' light on de subject—a liddle mo' light on dis here cat w'at come home w'en you haint zackly lookin fer it.

W'en he git th'ough wid his chunkin up de fireblaze; he looked to see how his gun wus a gittin along wid de cat a settin by it. He see de cat mo' samer dan de gun an' it 'pear lak dat cat wus some-how done gone an' growed a liddle bigger! It look almos' as big as a dog.

But Uncle Billy wus done fix up his head dat he wus a gwineter stick 'er out. So he lit his pipe, an' he smoke, an' he look off altogedder in anudder direction, an' he play 'tend dat he haint a studyin' 'bout no cats an' he haint skeared o' none o' 'em neider. Atter while he sorter glance outn de corner of one eye over towards de gun to see how de cat wus a takin it. Mon! W'en he look, he see dat de cat wus done gone an' git as big as a b'ar!—Den de big B'ar-cat 'gin "Well! Dere haint nobody here—." Law, Honey, Uncle Billy didn' wait fer to hear no mo'! He runned into de doo' an' knocked dat smack down a gittin out; an' he holler as he go: "I haint here no longer! I haint here no longer!

As he runned, he looked back to see if de B'ar-cat wusnt a comin'. Whilst he wus a runnin' an' a lookin' back'ards; he runned his head in a big tree an dis stopped him. His Mosser heard de noise; an' he jumped up outn bed, an' runned down dar. He got dar, jes as Uncle Billy wus drawin his las' breath. De Mosser holler out: "Hello! Uncle Billy, W'ats de marter?"

Uncle Billy dont make no answer, but he mumble off: "Let's—pray!—I haint here no longer!—Den he wus gone.

Nex' day dey wrops Uncle Billy up in a windin' sheet an' buries him; but, atter dat, de tother Niggers on de plantation say dey caint sleep in hearin' distance of Sam an Lize's cabin in de yard not fur off from de Big House. Ev'ry night, in de middle of de night, dey hears somebody a moanin off: "Let's—pray—!" an' den dey hears somebody else holler out: "I haint here no longer!"

De Mosser say dat he dont never neider hear nor see nothin'; but somehow he buy anudder plantation, an' move off, an' take all de Niggers away wid him. Dey hadn' been moved off no time befo' de lightnin', enjorin a big storm, struck de Big House an' burnt it up. Whilst it wus a burnin up, it set fire to de Nigger cabins an' burnt dem all up too. Dat wus de way of de gwine of Sam an Lize's cabin.

De Nigger trader w'at bought Sam took him 'way off south on de tother side of Orleans. He sell all de tothers of de flock of Niggers w'at he wus got along wid 'im, 'cep' Sam, caze he wus got a riccommend fer each an' ev'ry one of 'em from deir one-time Mosser. He couldn' git shed o' Sam widout no riccommend, so he had to keep him hisself.

So dis here new Mosser take Sam out on his liddle ole woods-lot plantation, w'at he wus a buyin wid his liddle extra money, to break him in an' git him ready fer sale. Of co'se he know all 'bout his slappin' his tother Missus an' so he set to wuk to make him 'umble. De fust thing dat he do wus to take him over to de "New Buryin-groun'" [graveyard] an' show him a whole lot full o' Niggers w'at he wus done whupped to death an' buried fer sassin him.

Sam look at de graves an' he say: "Oh, Mosser, I haint a gwineter give you no trouble in no ways! I's got 'ligion an' I wouldn' do nothin wrong fer nothin, if I knowed it. I jes make dat mistake, dat time, befo' I knowed it; all caze I loved Lize, my 'oman, so much. If you'll jes go back an' buy her fer yo' slave an' bring her to live along wid me; I'll wuk fer you all my bo'n days, day an' night, widout a mumblin word."

His Mosser look bramble-briars an' daggers at 'im! Den he say: "Look here, Sam! (Den he use all de cuss words dat he's ever hearn tell of since

he wus a boy!) Don't you never open yo' head ag'in to me 'bout dat
Nigger wench o' yourn no mo'! W'en I thinks 'bout your hittin yo' Missus
'bout dat low-downed good-fer-nothin thing; I caint hardly bring myse'f to
do nothin but skin you alive an' bury you right here 'mongst dese here
tother no 'count impident Niggers!" W'id dat much said, he whirl aroun'
an' give him a couple o' keen cuts wid his cat o'nine tails; an, Sam, he
sorter draw up an' say nothin.

Atter dis Sam's Mosser set him to doin' a task of double wuk ev'ry
day. He had to wuk a way late in de night to git it done; but w'en he go
to his cabin fer de night; he always go out un'er a certain big tree to pray
befo' he go to bed. He most in ginerally prayed one o' dem' 'ar long hallelujah prayers; but he always end 'em all in de same way. Dis wus de way
he end 'em: "Now, Lawd, rain down yo' power lak unto millstones, break
up Mossers heart, make him buy Lize from up in Ferginny an' bring her
down here to whar I is".

Of co'se, Sam's new Mosser keep up wid 'im; caze he wus a "breakin
him in". He sot off hid, at night, a lissenin to de long prayers. Atter while
he wus heared dat part 'bout "rainin' down power lak unto millstones"
ontel he wus got sick of it; so he make up his mind dat he wus a gwineter
manage to cut dat part out. He darfo' go an' fill up his pockets wid a
whole lots of gravels; an' go an' climb up in de top of Sam's prayer-tree,
one night, befo' it wus time fer him to go out dar to pray.

Bymeby Sam go out to de tree to pray as fer common. W'en he git
through wid his great long prayer, an' 'gin to say dat part! "Lawd, rain
down yo' power lak unto millstones"; his Mosser throwed down great big
hands fulls of gravels on de top of his head. Sam stop an' look up, all
skeared to death! He seed his Mosser but he didn' know 'im in de dark.
He trot away from dar; an' as he jolt along, he holler back: "Lawd! Caint
you take no jokes neider?"

Somehow or nudder de Niggers on de plantation git in de wind of w'at
took place 'tween Sam's prayer an' de gravels; an' dey rigged him so much
'bout de Lawd a hurryin up an' a answerin his prayers, dat he quit off prayin
altogedder. (Baby, dar wus whar Sam lose out. W'en folkse quits prayin, all
deir guidin fer good leaves 'em; an' dat wus de way it wus wid Sam.)

Sam quit off prayin' an' it 'twusnt no time befo' he pearuntly haint got
no good sense. Sometimes he wus got jes as good sense as any of de
balunce of 'em; an' den ag'in sometimes he go aroun' a mumblin to de
trees, an' de bugs, an' ev'rything else—a mumblin sumpin 'bout Lize.

One day, he wus a gwine aroun' a mumblin sumpin 'bout "Lize" an'
"Mosser" an' "whuppin" to ev'ry thing. One of de Niggers on de place
hear him a doin' dis, an' jes sorter say to 'im in passin off de time of day:
"Sam! W'en Mosser bothers you; you jes cuss him out, an' he wont whup
an' pester you no mo'. Dat's de way I does, an' he jes lets me alone.

It 'twusnt no time atter dis befo' Sam's Mosser come along; an' Sam whirl in a' cuss him to all he can think of, jes as soon as he laid eyes on 'im. His Mosser wus jes stonished! He jes look at 'im an' go on off widout sayin nothin to 'im. Atter while he come back, an' brung a whole pile of white mens wid 'im; and' dey took Sam an' tied him 'cross a bar'l an' whupped him wid in a inch o' his life.

One day, w'en he wus a gittin a liddle better from de whuppin, an' his head wus a liddle sorter clear, he up an' say to de Nigger w'at wus a lookin atter him: "Seems to me dat I heard you say dat you cussed Mosser w'en you git ready!"

Dis here feller answer sorter sof' lak "Yes—yes; but I cusses him away off down yon'er, clean outn hearin, in de back of de woods-lot. It wus fer a wonder dat Mosser didn' kill you w'en you cust him to his face; caze he's one of dese here Devil's Snuff-boxes in a hornet's nes', w'en he git mad. Dont you never cuss him no mo' to his face onless you's got yo' head un'er a dead-fall wid de triggers all ready knocked a loose."

Atter while Sam git up from a bein' beat up by his Mosser so as he can sorter git aroun' ag'in. W'en he git up he go aroun' a heaps mo' wusser dan he useter a talkin to ev'rything. One day he come 'cross a tearpin down in de hoss-lot; an', atter mumblin sumpin to it, he went jes a runnin up to de Big House whar his Mosser wus. W'en he git dar, he find his Mosser a settin out on de pieizzer. He holler out to 'im: "Oh, Mosser! Come here an see! I's done gone an' foun' a tearpin w'at can talk!"

His Mosser say to 'im: "Go on off from here, Sam, wid yo' blasted fool-ishness! Dere haint no tearpins w'at can talk! I's skeared dat you's a gwineter use some mo' of yo' onwisdom to buy some mo' of dat w'at you dont want."

But Sam keep on a contendin dat dere wus a tearpin down dar w'at could talk, an, dat it say: "Nigger, you talks too much!"

W'en it look to his Mosser dat he jes couldn' git shed of Sam in no way widout gwine; he git up an' go wid 'im to see de tearpin.

W'en dey got down in de lot, dar sot a sho 'nough tearpin. Sam walk up to 'im an' sorter kick out his foot towards him an' say: "Now! You talk, Sah!" But de tearpin jes drawed hisself head an' all, into his shell; an' shet up mouf, soul, an' body.

Sam's Mosser look lak he was a liddle sorter put out; an' he whirled aroun' an' give him a couple o' keen cuts wid his cat o' nine tales an' walked off.

Dat evenin' w'en Sam wus a gwine to his cabin, he met up wid his Mosser ag'in an' he say to 'im: "Sam, w'at did you want to try to fool me 'bout dat tearpin fer?"

Sam make answer: "Mosser, I wusnt a foolin you. Dat wus jes a mean ole tearpin. He talk a plenty w'en he wus up dar in de bar, a helpin' me to feed de hosses; an' he jes keep on a sayin: "Nigger, you talks too much!"

Well, Sam's Mosser leave him; an' as he let his mind run to fust one thing an' den de tother, it 'gin to sense into 'im dat Sam wus a liddle onsettled in de head. So he make up his mind to stop him from a doin' hard wuk out in de fiel' fer a while.

Sam's new Mosser wus a great man fer huntin'. He hunt squirls, deers, an' all kinds o' varmints. He need somebody to lug home de game w'en he kill it; so he take Sam along to do dis. 'Sides dis he think a liddle airin out in de woods mought help to dry out some o' de wet kinks in Sam's mind.

De white folks in dem diggins had a big Huntin' Band; an' Sam's Mosser wus one o' de big mens in it. Dis here Huntin' Band 'ould meet at de end of ev'ry week fer a big Barbecue; an' at dis Barbecue dey gived a big prize to de man w'at wus killed de mos' game enjorin de week an' a prize to de man w'at do de bes' shootin.

All de Huntin' Band bring de scalps of w'at dey kills enjorin de week along wid 'em; an', so by countin' de scalps, dey knowed who wus to git de prize fer killin de mos' game. As fer de bes' shootin' an' gittin dat prize; ev'ry man tol' his own tale. De man w'at tell de bigges' tale 'bout his fine shootin, an' prove it by his Nigger w'at wus 'long wid 'im at de time; git de tother big prize.

At de end of de week, Sam an' his Mosser go to de big Barbecue of de Huntin' Band. Dey took deir scalps along. De Jedges count de scalps; an' Sam's Mosser wus got de mostes' scalps, so dey give him de fust prize which wus a brown jug of apple brandy.

Den all of 'em tells deir big tales 'bout deir fine shootin' enjorin de week. One say dat he shot a wild turkey in de eye a hundred yards off. Anudder say dat he shot de lim' offn a tree on which a squir'l wus a settin; an' den he run a' cotched de lim', squir'l, an' all befo' dey hit de groun'. One say one thing, an' one say anudder; an' all of 'em prove it by deir Niggers, w'at wus along wid em.

At las' it come Sam's Mosser's turn to tell his big tale. He up an' say dat he shot a deer th'ough three times at one shot wid de same bullet. De tother mens w'at wus de Jedges say dat it look lak dat Sam's Mosser's tale call fer de top of de pot. But dey say dat de tale dat he tell wus so cu'ious dat he mus' prove all de "ins" an' "outs" about it. Den all de tother Mossers lay it on dat he mus' lakwise prove it all good an' well by dat Nigger of hisn befo' he clamp his "grippers" on dat tother prize an' tote it of too!

De Mosser say dat he mought could prove it by Sam; but he wusnt got sense 'nough to take a junie-bug to water, tied to a string, as dey all too well knows. So Sam's Mosser an' de tother Mossers 'gin to spute an' ogify w'at dey wus a gwineter to do 'bout it. Whilst dey wus red hot wid deir twis'in' up of de p'ints, Sam break in an' say: "Yes Mosser did do it!"

Den dey all stops an' axes Sam how in de worl' his Mosser manage to do dat! Sam splain it: Dat de deer wus a scratchin his (y)ear wid his behime foot. So Mosser shot; an shot 'im th'ough de behime foot, de (y)ear, an' de head all at one "crack". Dat make it dat he shoot him th'ough three times wid one bullet at one shot.

De white folkses all jes cracked deir sides a laughin' at Sam; an' widout sayin' no mo', dey passed over de tother prize to Sam's Mosser which wus a big round gourd full of 'simmon beer! Den dey all go off to have a good time. Dey wrapped deirselves aroun' whole great big chunks of Barbecue, dey cracked jokes, dey pitched hoss shoes, dey runned races, dey boxed, an had a big time in ginerally. Den dey all broke up an' went home.

Dat night Sam's Mosser talk wid his Missus 'bout w'at Sam say 'bout de "deer-tale"; an' dey close up de talk by sayin' dat Sam wus got bushels of sense—De fact wus dat he wus got so much sense dat he wus done fooled 'em all into thinkin' dat he wus a fool. Den his Mosser say dat he wus a gwineter set him back at hard wuk lak de tother Niggers.

So, de nex' day he put Sam to wuk in de gyardin; an' he go on off an' hunt all dat day ontel night as fer common. De nex' mawin a follerin; he go out to see how much wuk Sam wus got done befo' he go off huntin' fer de day. W'en he look, he didn' see no wuk done at 'tall scacely an' all of his big fine onions wus pulled up an' gone!

He go up to Sam's cabin to git atter him 'bout not wukin. W'en he walk in de cabin; he find Sam a settin down on top of de onions pulled up outn de gyardin an' piled up in de middle of de floo'. His Mosser look at him an' he git mighty mad; but he haint got no cat o' nine tails along wid 'im to th'ash 'im wid. So he tell him dat he'd better git outn dar an' clean dat whole gyardin, dat day, if he didn' want to git kilt w'en he come home dat night. Den he say dat he wus a gwineter whup him 'bout stealin' dem onions anyhows an' den he goes on off.

W'en de Mosser come home dat evenin'; he go by an' look over in de gyardin to see how Sam wus a comin' on wid de wuk. W'en he look over de fence, dere wusnt no Sam dar.

But de Mosser look away over 'cross de cornfiel' an' he see Sam a comin. He had a pole swung over his shoulder an' sumpin wus a hangin down tied on to end of it. W'en he got dar he throwed de pole down, wid de sumpin on de end of it in front of his Mosser; an' he say: "Mosser! Here's de man w'at's been a stealin yo' onions! Whew—! Smell him bref! Dat 'ar feller dar say, he pile! He pile 'em up, so dat Lize can have plenty of 'em to eat w'en you goes an' buys her an' brings her down here to me!"

Sam's Mosser look an' see dat de thing on de end of de pole wus a pole-cat; an' w'en he hear him say all dis, he know dat he wus done gone clean 'stracted. So he dont neider whup him nor do no nothin to 'im no mo'.

Den his Mosser think maybe he mought git Sam straightened out by makin' 'tend somehow dat he wus a gwineter buy Lize fer 'im. So he tell Sam to go up in his big woods-lot, an' clean up a nice new groun', an' burn de brush, an' raise a fine big crop; den he'll sell de crop an' take de money an' buy Lize fer 'im.

Sam didn' have no sense; but w'en he hear de words, "Lize" an' "newgroun'", dat wus jes 'nough to set him wild at wuk. He wuked an' burnt brush all de week; den he wuked an' burnt brush on Sunday. His Mosser beg him, an' try ev'ry way to stop him from wukin on Sunday; but Sam dont seem to know how to quit. His Mosser is done maked up his mind dat he haint a gwineter whup him no mo'; so he haint got no way to stop him. So Sam go right on a burnin' brush on Sunday jes as same as Monday.

He wuk mawnin an' evenin, nobody caint stop him; an' he grow weaker an' weaker. One day, a cu'ious feelin come on 'im; an' he quit off wukin an' went away out in de woods to a big sink hole whar de water in it wus so deep dat folkses wus let nine bed-cords down in it widout tetchin de bottom. He laid down by dis sink-hole fer to take a rest.

It 'twus on dat self same day dat Lize died; an' whilst he wus a lyin' dar he seed her spirit wid de Angels up in de air a motionin' to him to come. His right mind come to him fer a liddle while; an' it look lak dat all he wus ever done passed befo' his eyes. He think how good de Lawd uster to be to 'im w'en he prayed; an' so he start to pray. He 'gin: "Good Lawd—!" den his mind sorter slip a notch an' he sorter half-way 'member his cussin; den he 'gin over ag'in an' say: "Good devil—!" Den his mind went an' he say nothin'.

But his mind come back ag'in; an' he ag'in 'gin wid de words: "Good Lawd." His mind start to leave him ag'in. He feel it a gwine, an' he wuk hard to keep it; an' whilst he wus a kickin' aroun' on de groun', he tumbled off into de big sink-hole. His body go down an' his spirit come up.

W'en he come up, dere wus Lize an' de Angles a waitin' fer 'im; but ole Satan's Imps soon put in deir pearunce too.

De Head Angel axed de Imps w'at dey wus come fer.

De Imps make answer dat dey wus come fer Sam.

De Head Angel den splain to de Imps dat dey wusnt got no place fer no prayin' man down in de Bad Place.

But de Imps make answer day dey wus heared Sam cuss mo' samer dan he pray.

De Head Angel ogify to de Imps; dat dis wus caze Sam wus gone stracted; an' dat Uncle Billy wus at de bottom of runnin him crazy. De Head Angel put in: As he look at de turnin' of de coffee-groun's in de Cut of Time; he see Uncle Billy wus due to come over in a few days; an' it look to him dat it mought be fa'r an' squar' fer dem to take him to balunce up de cussin w'at wus been laid on Sam's scale-pan.

De Imps make answer dat dey'll take Uncle Billy an' glad to git 'im to eben it all up 'bout de cussin; but dey thinks de Scales of Jestice calls fer sumpin to be done 'bout Sam's burnin' brush an' clearin' up new-grounds on Sunday.

De Head Angel say dat he think dey mought take Sam's Mossers fer to pay dat debt; w'en dey leaves deir plantations an' Niggers an' comes over.

But de Imps make answer dat Sam's Mossers wusnt due to come over fer some time yit; an' whilst dey wus a waitin fer 'em, dey mought change an' go to prayin, den dey'd lose de whole debt.

De Head Angel say he reckin dat wus so. He wus willin darfo' to give his sayso to lettin Sam pay off some of de debt; if de Bad Man an' his Imps'll take deir chances of gittin de balunce outn Sam's Mossers. But he put in: Right dont wrong nobody. It 'twus right fer Sam not to go to no Bad Place, an' he wusnt a gwineter let him go dar! But since Sam burnt brush on a Sunday; he reckin dat it wus right fer him to burn mo' brush to pay up a part of de debt.

So de Head Angel took Sam an' put him up on de moon to burn brush an' give light to de folkses on de (y)earth. He hafter make de moon foller an' keep up wid folks w'en dey runs; caze it's his wuk to see to it dat de light from de burnin' brush git to de folkses an' do 'em good. In dat way he pay off part of de debt.

Some says dat Lize stayed too, an' is up dar wid him on de moon; but he love her so much dat he still do all de wuk jes lak he try to do at his Mosser's house. So you never does see her up dar.

Dem w'at tells de loration says dat de Head Angel lef' word wid Sam to burn Brush ontel Jedgment Day. On dat day w'en de sun quit shinin, an' w'en de Lawd rolls up his blue coverlid wid de stars in it, he'll call at de moon fer Sam an' Lize, an take 'em on to de Good Place whar de Fritter Trees grow by de Honey Ponds an' dere haint no partin' no mo'."

When mother Rivers had finished her weird story, she looked to see just how profoundly it had impressed little Pate, her baby; and found that he had fallen soundly asleep.

"Well—!" she lowly gasped in half amazement; then she softly arose, carried him to his little trundle-bed, and tucked him away snugly for the night.

HOW THE BEAR LOST HIS JUDGESHIP

❄

About a mile to the southeast of Caldwell Tennessee—a little station on a branch railroad which finds a place only on the largest railroad maps—lay a tangled wildwood, about a half century ago, known among the resident Negro people as the "Haircane". The word "haircane" is a corruption of the English word "hurricane". The trees and undergrowth in this forest were so dense that one, in passing through it by crooked by-paths, could rarely see more than fifty feet away. The bushes and trees were so interlaced and twisted together that the woods uniformly presented the appearance of a recently storm-swept area. It was for this reason that the Negroes dubbed it the "haircane" (hurricane).

A Negro boy, about fifteen years of age, Andrew by name, was walking along a half beaten trail leading to this woods when he met his friend Isacc with a bucket of blackberries which he had gathered from Nature in order that his mother might preserve them for the winter season which was as yet distant.

"Hullo, Ander! Whar's you gwine?" said Isacc.

"W'y, hullo, Ike!—I's a gwine to de haircane fer to look fer our cow an' ca'f," replied Andrew.

"You'd better keep outn dar", said Isacc, "you haint no Barlow knife wo'th a whole good dime dat somebody is a comin' a lookin' fer if you gits lost."

At this goodnatured sally Andrew only smiled and added by way of reply: "I knows dat I haint no Barlow knife to be looked fer, an' I haint as sharp as some folks tries to be; but I's been in dat haircane huntin' 'nough dat I'll bet I's whetted up sharp 'nough to cut my way out from all de lost corners in it to de openins. W'en once I gits in de openins, I knows how to strike a bee-line home.

Go take yo' berries to yo' mammy an' ax her to let you go wid me to help hunt fer de cow an' ca'f. If she look lak she was a gwineter say "no," tell her dat I he'ped you find yo' hosses las' week, an' dat one good turn deserves anudder."

Isacc readily agreed. In a very short while he had carried the berries home—a short distance away, secured the desired permission, and was back by Andrew's side ready to join in the search.

"W'at did you bring yo' ole dog 'Brinjah' along wid you fer? You mus' think dat you caint go nowhars widout lakwise gwine a rabbit huntin'," said Isacc.

"I didn't bring no Brinjah fer to hunt fer no rabbits dis time," answered Andrew. "I brung him 'long fer to hunt fer de calf!"

"I dont see no sense," said Isacc, "in havin' a dog along fer to hunt fer de cow an' ca'f. You jes finds yo' cow an' ca'f, an' drives 'em on home. You dont need no dog 'cep' whar you's a gwineter ketch sumpin' an' tote it home. Now if you's got in yo' head to ketch dis here cow an' ca'f, an' lug 'em home; den I's skeared dat I wont make no kind o' podner fer you in dat sort o buis'ness. De buis'ness is altogedder too big fer a many of my surbilities."

"Oh, hesh up, Ike!" replied Andrew. "You's wusser dan one o' dese here pot-metal guns w'at always a gwine off half-cocked an' a gittin busted. You see our cow's ca'f is jes a day ole. I wus kelless 'nough to leave de gate onbarred las' night; an' de cow tuck dis baby ca'f an' go off to de haircane. W'en de cows wus got baby ca'fs wid 'em in de woods, dey takes 'em off an' hides 'em. So w'en you 'as foun' yo' cow, you haint foun' yo' ca'f. But if you's got yo' dog along; you can sick 'im on de cow, an' she'll go right straight to de ca'f. Den you 'as foun' 'em bofe, an' you drives 'em on home."

Dat's mighty cu'ious!" remarked Isacc. "I wonders why cows hides deir baby ca'fs."

"Railly," answered Andrew, "I scacely thinks dat dere dont nobody know; but some o' de folks claims dat dey knows, an' dey's got a long cu'ious loration 'bout how it all happen. Dey say dat de cows commence a doin' it to hide 'em from de b'ars!"

"Now Ander," said his companion, "I'll foller you 'roun' all day—cow or no cow—if you'll jes tell me de loration. I's jes crazy 'bout dem ole sayins', an' I can set up all night a lissenin to 'em."

"Well, Ill try to tell you whilst we's a walkin' 'long," replied Andrew, "but you mus' keep you' eyes skinned fer de cow. You see, I caint tetch an' 'gree wid you w'en you says 'cow or no cow'. I's already had a mighty heaps o' trouble 'bout lettin' 'em out; an' I mought have a whole peck mo' 'bout not lettin' 'em back in dis evenin'."

"I'll skin my eyes an' thighs, my nose an' toes, my chin an' shin, widout gittin' 'em back 'g'in; if dat'll do any good," came the assurance from Isacc, "Go on wid de loration."

Andrew dropped his head for a few moments, as if trying to recall something most profound; then raising it slowly he began: "Way back yonder one time, de sun an' de moon wus married; an' de moon wus de sun's wife"—

"Hol' on dar!" interrupted Isacc. "I tol' you dat I wanter hear de loration 'bout de b'ars an' de cows. I didn' ax nothin' 'bout de sun an' de moon away off up yonder."

"Now den!" said Andrew. "I close down my apple cellar doo', an' lay a great big rock down on top of it. Ole Aunt Betsy Turbentime tol' me all

'bout how it 'twus an' she 'gin wid de sun an' moon. I's almos' already
clean fergit it offn my mind. I dont eben scacely know it day way an' I
knows dat I dont know it no udder way."

"Oh!" replied Isacc apologetically, "I jest thought dat you didn' know
w'at I was a axin fer. Scuse me an' crack away wid de loration."

"Well", said Andrew, "to go on wid de loration: Way back yonder one
time de sun an' moon wus young an' dey co'ted 'roun' lak de boys an'
gals does now a days. Mr. Sun wus monstus good-lookin' an' he grin
aroun' at de gals mo' samer dan a possum. De gals all git mo' sticked on
him dan Brer Rabbit wus on dat 'ar 'ceitful Tar-Baby. [For a full understanding of the figure here used, read "Brer Rabbit and The Tar-Baby" by
Joel Chandler Harris.]

Miss Moon, she wus jes as pretty as a speckled pullet; an, she git de
pick an' choice of all de fellers. So, of co'se, she pick on Mr. Sun caze he
wus de cock o' walk w'en it come to bein fine lookin'.

Dey jumped de broomstick back'ards an' got hitched, jined an' married; an dey have de stars fer deir fambly of chilluns. Dey git along as
lovin as two peas in a pod an' at home dey wus "jes as snug as a bug in a
rug". De ole man wus a mighty good provider. Dey all git a plenty to eat;
an' dey wus all fat an' roun'-faced. Dey had de animuls aroun' on de earth
to play an' caper so as to 'muse de chilluns; an' so dey wusnt no trouble.
Ev'ry thing wus lovely an' de goose honk high. [The figure in this sentence is borrowed from the passage of wild geese in their migration—their
high flight providing safety.]

Bymeby, w'en dey 'gin to git ole, ole Miss Moon git blotched faced; an',
of co'se, she wus oncommonly homely. Ole man Sun git mo' better lookin
as he git older. But de mo' better he look de mo' wusser his wife look.

Ole man Sun go aroun' wid his good looks; an' he grin at ev'ry body
an' ev'ry thing. Ole Miss Moon say she think her ole man should oughter
be settled 'nough to quit his grinnin' 'roun' at de gals.

Ole man Sun say dat he think dat he wus ole 'nough to grin at who
he pleases; an' if de ole oman dont lak it, she can jes lump it.

Den ole Miss Moon tell him 'to go to grass an' eat mullin'. Dis jes
broke ev'ry thing up; so dey wus parted.

W'en dey git parted, de chilluns go wid deir mammy; so now ole man
Sun journey 'cross de sky by hisself an' ole Miss Moon an' de stars journey
'cross de sky by deirselves.

W'en Miss Moon an' de star-chilluns leave Mr. Sun, den de tother gals
('oman lak) dont want him neider. So dey moves clean off to anudder
place to whar Mr. Sun caint see 'em an' nobody else. Den Mr. Sun want
Miss Moon an' de star-chilluns to make up wid 'im; but dey wont do it.

Den Mr. Sun say dat he wus a gwineter stop all de animuls from a
caperin 'cep' w'en he's aroun' jes fer spite; so dat de chilluns wont have

nothin' to 'muse 'em an' dey'll cry an' be heaps o' trouble to de ole 'oman. But de animuls wus mo' used to de ole 'oman an' de chilluns dan dey wus to him. So his plan didn' wuk at fust 'cep' in case of Mr. Big Snake. Mr. Sun's grins warm up Mr. Big Snake an' make him feel good an' soupple. So he wus jes natchully crazy 'bout ole man Sun.

Mr. Sun tell Mr. Big Snake dat if he'll jes git de tother animuls not to run aroun', eat, cut up, caper, an' play 'cep' w'en he's aroun'; dat he'll give him power to charm all de tother animuls, an' he wont draw no water from de river an' make it rain 'cep' w'en he want it.

Mr. Big Snake 'gree; an' he make all dem tother animuls do lak Mr. Sun want 'em 'cep' ole Brer Mink, Brer Possum, Brer Cat, Brer Coon, an' a few udders. So de animuls stay wake an' cut up an' caper in de presence of de Sun; but dey goes to sleep w'en Miss Moon an' de Star-Chilluns is aroun'.

W'en it come to pass dat de Star-Chilluns haint got nothin to play wid an' to lok at to 'muse 'em; dey give ole Miss Moon so much trouble dat she git all worried out an' pale. De Star-Chilluns lakwise fret an' fume so much dat dey gits all sick an' pale.

W'en Mr. Big Snake git his power to charm de tother animuls an' to regerlate de rain; he 'gin to make use of it right away. Fust of all, he charm 'em so an' make 'em all think so much of him dat dey wus always got him out a eatin' a big dinner somewhars.

One day old Sis Cow ax him over to her house an' she give him some of her big fine white-head cabbages fer dinner. Den, so as to make him a scrumptious meal, she give him a big bowl o' sour buttermilk to drink along wid de pot-licker to wash down the green roas'-in-(y)ears w'ich she lakwise have fer de feast.

Well, Mr. Big Snake e't an' drunk his fill; but he didn' more an' hardly git it all stuffed down 'im befo' he tuck de wo'st case of cramp colic dat you's ever hearn tell of. Dey drenched him wid catnip tea, but dat didn' do him no good. Dey gits him some peppermint, but dat didn' he'p 'im none. Dey give him sage tea, an' ho'hound, an' cherry bark, an' poplar bark, an' sassfac, an' dog fennel, an' pennyr'yal, an' fodder tea, an' sycamo' tea, an' snake root, an' slickry-ellum bark, an' groun' ivry tea, an' calamus root, an' life-everlastin' tea; but none o' dem things didn' seem to reach his case. Den dey rubbed him wid May-apple root grease, an' Jimson weed salve; but dis look lak it make him bloat up mo' bigger, an git mo' weaker an' wusser. So den dey wropped him up in bran poultice, wid red-oak bark, wid roasted polk root, an' wid green leaves wet wid vinegar; but wid all dis, Mr. Big Snake got mo' lower, an' he look lak he wus a gwineter make a die of it. It look dat dey wus bound to lose 'im, an' dey didn' know w'at to do; so dey slaps a mustard plaster on his head, den he look lak he wus bofe a gwineter die an' a gwine crazy all de same time.

By dis time might' nigh all de animuls wus done heared Mr. Big Snake a squirmin an' a twisin an' a rollin an' a moanin an' a groanin, wid dat 'ar cramp colic. So dey wus all come over to see w'at dey could do; if it twusnt nothin but to set up, drink coffee, an' sing over his dead body all night befo' de day on w'ich dey preach over him an' lay him away to res'.

W'en dey all git dar an' se how de lan' lay; dey all say dey dont see nothin mo' to be done—all 'cep' Brer Horn Toad, an' he subgest dat dey sen' fer Brer Snake Doctor. (De Snake Doctor, Ike, is dat 'ar big fly w'at de white folks calls a Drag(o)on fly; but de right name is Snake Doctor. Dey gits a heaps o' things wrong w'ich we uns caint tell 'em 'bout w'at knows better. You mought call 'im a Snake Feeder; caze ole Aunt Betsy Turbentime say dat dey bofe doctors an' feeds snakes, w'en dey gits sick or hurt. I guess all dis mus' be so' caze I's seed dese same flies, wid my own eyes, a settin aroun' on de bloody head of a snake dat I kilt. Dey looked lak dey wus a tryin to clear off de blood, an' do sumpin fer him.)

Well, dey all sends for Brer Snake Doctor; an' he come jes a buzzin an' a bulgin. W'en he git dar he sail up, light on 'im, an' look 'im over.

De tother animuls holler to Brer Snake Doctor dat dere haint no need a zaminin aroun'; caze he haint got nothin but cramp colic;—to hurry up an' give him sumpin!

Brer Snake Doctor make answer, he do, dar wus whar dey wus all wrong!—Dey dont unerstan Brer Big Snake's 'fliction!—He wus got a complercation o' troubles!—He wus got ev'ry thing 'cep' de Death-Rattles.

W'en dey all hears Brer Snake Doctor say dis, some of 'em gits outn dey way to give him a liddle mo' room; de tothers all hesh up deir moufs, an' try to hol' in deir brefs, caze dey's all powerful skeared dey mought ketch some of dar "Complercation". Bymeby Brer Snake Doctor up an' stick his sharp mouf into Mr. Big Snake an' put sumpin in 'im jes lak you sees sho 'nough doctors stick needles in folkses' arms an' den put sumpin in dar.

W'en he do dis, Mr. Big Snake curl hisself up an' go to sleep. W'en he wake up ag'in he wus about well but he wus mighty sore an' stiff. Atter he git so he can sorter wobble about ag'in, he go over to see Brer Snake Doctor to talk over his case wid him.

Brer Snake Doctor tell him: Of co'se he'll come over an' do all he can fer 'im w'ensoever he mought git sick; but it wus heaps mo' better an' mo' cheaper to hobble 'roun' trouble dan to hobble th'ough it.

Ole Brer Big Snake ax him w'at he mean by dis.

Den ole Brer Snake Doctor splain dat he mean dat ole Mr. Big Snake musn't eat no mo' clabber, an' cabbage, an' pot-licker; in fac', dat he'd better not pester 'long wid no mo' veg'ables. He tell him dat he mought take a few swallers of sweet milk once in a while but never no butter-milk. (You see dat's de reason daddy rushed me off to de woods to git our cow back. Aunt Betsy Turbentime say dat w'en de ca'f is liddle an' de cow is in de woods; de snakes is apt to tie deirselfs aroun' her behin' legs an' suck de milk. I caint say about dis, caze I haint never seed it. Bit I does know w'en yo' cow is in de woods at setch times, an' you lets her stay dar; w'en you gits her back home, her bag is in ginerally as hard as a rock an' all sp'iled).

Well, how-some-ever all dis may be; de loration goes dat Brer Snake Doctor tell Mr. Big Snake dat he musn' eat no mo' veg'ables.

Mr. Big Snake say dat he hate awful bad to eat dem tother animuls; but he sho wus done got 'nough of cabbage an' colic. Den he allow since ole Sis Cow an' dem wus been a feedin him up on veg'ables, an' wus done got him so dat he caint eat nothin much but meat, since dey wus de 'casion of it; he reckin dat it wus fa'r an' squar' fer him to eat any of 'em w'at wus liddle 'nough for him to swaller. As fer Brer Horn Toad: He subgest sendin fer de doctor an' save him; so he haint a gwineter eat up de Doctor an' his kinfolks—He's a gwineter leave dem outn his calkerlations.

Now, it twusnt no time befo' Mr. Big Snake git hongry. So he go an' climb right close up to Sis Bird's nes'. W'en he git up dar, he lick out his forked tongue an' charm her. Fust she fly aroun' him at a distance; den she fly a liddle closer an' a liddle closer. An' den—"Zip!"—he grabbed her an' swallered her down! Nex' he swaller her eggs an' den he come on down.

Some one of de birds seed him do dis (I think Ole Aunt Betsy say it wus de Snake-Bird); an' it fly aroun' an' tell all de animuls how Mr. Big Snake wus a usin' his powers to charm, fer to ketch folks an' make hash outn 'em. Den all de animuls, w'at wus liddle 'nough fer to git cotched an' e't up tuck to deir heels w'en dey seed him a comin'. (You's noticed, Ike, dat all de liddle frogs, lizards, an' de lak runs from snakes. Aunt Betsy Turbentime say dat dis wus de reason dey does dat.) Dey tuck to deir heels so dat Mr. Big Snake dont git no chance much fer to charm 'em an' ketch 'em.

W'en de ole folks git to runnin; den Mr. Big Snake take to eatin deir chilluns—de baby rabbits, foxes, pigs an' de lak. W'en he 'gin to eat deir chilluns; it stir up all de ole folks, an' make 'em put deir heads togedder to find out sumpin to do to stop it.

De animuls all tetch an' gree dat dere haint no nothin to be done 'cep' fer de next one w'at meet up wid Mr. Big Snake to kill him or die a tryin. So dey sont word to him dat de nex' one, w'at meet him, want to give him an' his head a good knockin down an' a quaintunce wid de end of a good long stick.

De fust one w'at happen up wid 'im wus Brer Fox. He bristle up, a' light into 'im. But Lawd, Honey, it 'twusnt no time befo' Mr. Big Snake wus got him choked down an' e't up. Brer Tucky gobbler see dis an' he run through de woods an' gobble: "He's swallered-swallered Brer Fox! He's swallered-swallered Brer Fox!"

W'en de tother animuls all hear dis, dey looks for Brer Big Snake whar dey knows dey's sho not to find 'im. One day how-some-be ever, ole Brer B'ar—"big awky-gawky"—start 'cross de woods an' stumble rought up on 'im.

Mr. Big Snake spring for'd an' wrop 'im from head to heels quicker dan a wink. Brer B'ar want to bite but his mouf is all bound up. He want to cut an' scratch wid his sharp claws but dey wus all rooled up in a bundle. Brer B'ar wus as stout as a mule, an' as saveigus as a bulldog w'at you's been a feedin up on raw meat an' gun powder fer a mont'; but Mr. Big Snake wus got de choke holt on 'im, an' it look lak he wus on de way to de "Promus Lan'!"

Dey wus a fightin on de top of one hill, so all dem tother critters gethered deirselves togedder on anudder hill as fur off as dey could git so as to see it all through. Den dey hollered over: "Oh you! Kill 'im Brer B'ar! You's big 'nough an' stout 'nough to whip 'im!

We's a stanin at yo' back,
You jes beat his face black.
Do sumpin! Shake 'im's w'at we shout,
Befo' we 'gin to give you out!"

Ole Mr. Big Snake hear 'em a hollerin; an' he loosen up a liddle so as to git 'nough of hisself to raise up his head high 'nough to see if dem tother critters wus about to come an' he'p Brer B'ar. Dis here of de choke holt sorter let ole Brer B'ar ketch his bref, an' he holler back: "Don't you never gimme out, ontel I's dead an' laid out!"

Wid dis much flung back to 'em; ole Brer B'ar laid down, an' shet his eyes, an' 'gin to roll over down de hill mo' faster dan de chyart wheels behin' a pair o' run-away oxes. Of co'se Mr. Big Snake was bleedged to roll over wid 'im. But dis here Mr. Big Snake didn' shet his eyes; an' de whirlin an' tu'nin' make him git taken wid de swimmin in de head. W'en he git taken wid de swimmin in de head, he lose his grip on Brer B'ar; an' Brer B'ar onroll him.

W'en Brer Bar do dis, whilst Mr. Big Snake wus a lyin all stretched out on de groun' wid de swimmin in de head; he jumped right on top of 'im in de middle. Den he brung all four of his footses togedder in one place, an' stuck his claws in up to de toes; an' den he stretch out lak he do w'en he go to sleep! Dat wus de las' of Mr. Big Snake.

W'en all dem tother animals sed w'at Brer B'ar wus done done; dey come over jes a flyin to tell him how fine he look a fightin; an' to study out w'at dey can do to show him w't a big man dey all thinks he wus.

Brer B'ar tell 'em all to stan' back an' give 'im elbo room; caze he haint yit got through a settlin' up marters wid Mr. Big Snake. He call to deir membunce how Mr. Sun wus done give Mr. Big Snake power bofe to charm an' to regerlate de rain. He say: Cose, dey all knows how Mr. Big Snake wus done gone an' 'buse his charmin gifts; an' dey mus' now look out dat he dont so die as to keep all de rains away, dry up de creeks, kill all de crops, an' pe'ish 'em all to death.

He splain to 'em dat Mr. Big Snake wus familious lak wid his frien', Brer Horn Toad; an' he tell him all 'bout de rain regerlatin buis'ness, caze he save his life by subgestin dat dey sen' fer Brer Snake Doctor dat time w'en he wus so sick from eatin' dem white-head cabbages.

Mr. Big Snake tell Brer Horn Toad: W'en-so-ever he stop wavin his tail to Mr. Sun befo' de Sun go down; Den Mr. Sun ketch de sign an' let it rain right away an' reg'lar. But if Mr. Sun go down whilst Mr. Big Snake's tail wus still a movin an' wavin; den Mr. Sun would let it rain wid as many days 'tween de showers as Mr. Big Snake wus long, ontel he git some furder news from him.

Den some-how Mr. Sun wus lakwise got it fixed up so dat Mr. Big Snake's sperit would pass outn his body through his tail instid o' his mouf an' nose, w'en he die. He fix it up dis way so dat; if Mr. Big Snake git kilt; it 'twould take his sperit ontel sundown to git outn him through de tail, beance it wus all closed up. Dis bring it 'bout dat de tail would keep on movin ontel sundown atter he git kilt. Dis bein de case; atter Mr. Snake was dead—his body bein powerful long; de rains would come so fur apart dat de crops would all die an' all de animuls would git pe'ished to death.

Darfo, Brer B'ar say he mus' t'ar Mr. Big Snake's tail off an cut it up to sossage size. Wid ole Brer B'ar it wus tetch an' go. So it 'twusnt no time befo' he git dat tail off an' he cut it in pieces so liddle dat de ants couldn' pick 'em up.

Well, dem tother animuls wus dat proud caze Mr. Big Snake wus dead, dat dey didn' know how to haive deirselves. Dey wus proud dat Brer B'ar wus so smart; caze, he if hadn' a been (from w'at ole Aunt Besty Turbentime say), dey never wold a had no mo' rain. From w'at Aunt Betsy say, Mr. Big Snake mus' a been as long as ten or a dozen or mo' bed-cords; an' you well knows, Ike if it 'twus dat long 'tween de showers, dere never would a been no mo' showers—much less rain.

Wid Mr. Big Snake's tail all fixed up by Brer B'ar, it 'gin to cloud up a liddle. Dem tother animuls crowd aroun' Brer B'ar an' want to do sumpin fer him right den an' dar to show him how much dey loves him fer gitin Mr. Big Snake outn de way. But he tell 'em dat dere haint no time fer nothin lak dat den; caze de rain clouds wus already a gittin black an' a big rain storm wus a comin' wid a howl n' a growl an' a whoop.

Brer Mus'rat say dat sumpin wus bleedged to be done; so he wus a

gwineter give a big candy pullin down at his house de nex' night fer Brer
B'ar. He ax 'em all to come over an' be dar; dey can bofe have a sweet
time, an' make up deir minds w'at to do fer Brer B'ar who wus done done
so much fer dem. Dey all say dat dis wus 'greeable.

Brer B'ar say dat he wus still skeared dat Mr. Sun mought look down
from de sky nex' day; an' l'arn w'at wus happened to Mr. Big Snake, an'
cut off de crops an' starve 'em any ways. Brer Tumble-but come 'long
'bout dat time; an' he subgest dat dey tu'n Mr. Big Snake over on his back,
belly up, an' den Mr. Sun wont know him.

Dey all say dat dis wus a good idee, an' dey forms a long line, 'side o'
Mr. Big Snake's body, to turn it over wid a pull all togedder. Brer B'ar he
give de word. He holler out: "Hee—oo!"; an' dem tothers all answer wid a
pull togedder on de body: "Hee—!" Mon! dey jes maked dem woods ring
a tu'nin de body:

"Hee-oo!"
"Hee-oo!"
"Hee-oo!"
"Hee-oo!"

Dey gits Mr. Big Snake all tu'ned over, den dey pat an' dance:

"Go kill dat snake an' hang 'im high,
Go tu'n his belly to de sky;
Storm an' rain come by an' bye."

Den dey lit out fer home, so as to git dar befo' de rain'; an' so as to
sleep an' dream 'bout de big candy-pullin down at Brer Mus'rat's fer Brer
B'ar de nex night.

Well, on dat night w'en dey go home, it rained out hoe-handles an'
poured down pitchforks; an' if ole man Nora's Ark had a been about
somewhars, it 'twould a got all de top clean washed offn it. But it clear off
de next day in plenty a time fer Brer Mus'rat's candy pullin fer Brer B'ar.

Brer B'ar go over to Brer Mus'rat's house sorter early; so's he'll be dar
to shake hands wid de diffunt ones w'en dey comes in at de doo'. He git
dar an' he knock on de doo'.

Brer Mus'rat tip over to his doo' an' peep out through de auger hole
in it, through which he wus got a chain runned to fasten it up wid a padlock. He peep through; but de hole is so liddle dat he caint see who it 'tis.
So he holler out: "Who's dat?" An' ole Brer B'ar make answer: "A frien'."

Den Brer Mus'rat ondo de doo' right quick an' open it, an' say: "Laws
a mussy! Brer B'ar! No, you railly mus' scuse me, caze I wus been a livin
aroun' so much of late 'twixt de devil an' de creek, caze dat ole hacient

Big Snake wus a livin; dat I done go an' fergit it offn my mind how to open my doo' at night eben to my friends. W'y! dat ole scamp wusnt above comin' right in behin' yo' friends to crack you an' de friends too w'en you cracked de doo'!"

Brer B'ar step in an' 'spon': "Well, Brer Mus'rat! De dog's dead an' de tail's col'; an' I reckins dat we can now all have a liddle peace o' mind. Leave de doo' wide open caze we's all friens an' free once mo'."

Brer Mus'rat leave de doo' open an' Brer B'ar start 'cross de floo' towards one o' de rockin' cheers.

Mon! Brer B'ar wus all fixt up! He wus all bucked in one o' dese here long-tailed bluer Jim-swingers. He had on a pair o' dese here big water-p'oof boots—dem all red an' fork-ed at de top; an' w'en he step across de floo', dey cries out: "Wah-tah! Wah-tah!"

Brer Mus'rat wus got his eyes all bucked a lookin' at de fine fixins; but, w'en he look from Brer B'ar down to de rockin' cheer fer which he wus bound, he see dat dis wus a gwineter be de las' of dat 'ar cheer. Brer Mus'rat wusnt a hone-in to lose dat 'ar rockin cheer; an' den he lakwise think, if a big man lak Brer B'ar set down sorter sudden lak on de floo' wid some pieces of cheer un'er-neath 'im, it would shake de pillars of his house; an' den he didn' know w'at mought happen.

Brer Mus'rat sorter pull his wits togedder un'er his thinkin' cap; an' den he jerk his clo'es box out from un'er de bed, an' slap a pillow down on it. Den he call out: "Wait, Brer B'ar! Wait! A big man lak you musn' set down on no common cheer! He mus' set on a sofa! Here's one I's done made all by myse'f fer you!" Al dis hit Brer B'ar zackly in de right spot, caze he wus already ginnin to feel his oats. So he make one o' dese here low-scrapin perlite bows to Brer Mus'rat an' set down on de box.

Den de animuls 'gin to come in to de candy-pullin'. Brer Possum, he come in fust an' brung along a whole great big jug full o' 'simmon beer wid 'im! Ole Brer B'ar jump up an' shake hands wid him an' ax him? "How's yo' corporosity seem to segashuate?" An' ole Brer Possum make answer: "Mo' supious combunxious 'cordin' to de contrax of yo' popular-ity!" (Dat was jes de way, Ike, dat ole Brer B'ar wus got o' sayin': "Howdy do?" an' de way Brer Possum wus got o' answerin': "I's Well!")

Dis wus de way ole Brer B'ar meet 'em all an' de way dey meet him, 'cep' once in a while whar he try to play antic. Of co'se he know all of 'em but some time he make out lak he dont. W'en Brer Coon come in he say to him: "W'at mought be yo' intitlements?" an' ole Brer Coon up an' say: "I ties up to de double bow-knot of Zip Coon." Brer B'ar say to ole Brer Mink: "W'at mought be yo' entrimmins?" an' ole Brer Mink up an' 'spon': "I stitches up to de fine bindin' of Gray Mink!" Dey go on lak dis ontel dey all gits dar.

Brer Mus'rat pass aroun' de lasses candy on a fine tin plate to 'em all. Den he give 'em all some of de butter w'at Sis Cow sont over fer de 'casion; so's dey mought grease deir hands to keep de lasses candy from a stickin to 'em, whilst dey wus a pullin it. Dey pulled de candy an' cracked jokes an' tol' tales an' e't ontel dey wus almos' ready to pop.

Den somebody subgest dat dey play some. Dey all git up an' form two lines an' swing dat song: "Sugar lo' tea". Den dey forms a ring an' plays de "Sweet Pinks Kissin' song". Ev'ry body wus a feelin' good an' ev'ry body got a kiss 'cep' it wus old Brer Polecat. De gals all say dat his bref smell too bad! Brer Polecat wus mighty fine lookin' an' it look to him lak de gals mus' be a liddle nigh-sighted. So once in a while he'd wave his pretty long white striped tail an' start in deir directin; but Mon, de gals fairly run from 'im!

At las' ole Brer Mus'rat jump up on de table an' rap wid his walkin stick fer 'em all to git still an' set down. W'en dey wus all sot down, he open up wid a big speech an' say: "Fello-po-citizens an' gemmuns an' ladies one an' all. In de injoyments of dis here 'casion, we's 'bout to fergit 'bout dat we's all a living. We's a slippin' off from our membunce how Brer B'ar wus done 'livered us from de hongry belly of de saveigus serpunt. We mus' now all resolute sumpin fer Brer B'ar so's he wont fergit us in dis worl' neider in de nex'."

W'en ole Brer Mus'rat git through, dey all say to Brer B'ar dat dey polergize fer not praisin up de pony fust; but dey wus now ready to do 'nough an' a heaps mo' besides.

Brer B'ar say to 'em dat it make no diffunce w'at time o' night de meal come in de bar'l so long as it 'twus dar by Breakfus time.

Brer Mus'rat call on 'em all to stop deir foolin an' to git down to peas an' puddin in de marter.

Ole Brer Possum riz up an' say dat Brer B'ar wus more 'an welcome to take all de 'simmons from offn his 'simmon trees dat he want. Liddle Miss Fox say he could come aroun' an' see her an' take more 'an half o' de grapes offn deir vines; caze, since de ole man wus got kilt in de fight wid Mr. Big Snake, dey caint scacely miss de grapes offn de vines w'at de tothers of de fambly eat. All de tother animuls lakwise make Brer B'ar more 'an welcome to take all o' deir victuals dat he want so dat he could live widout doin' no wuk lak de whitefolks.

Brer Mus'rat speak from offn' de table ag'in an' tell 'em dat he wus mighty much pleased wid all dis; but it look to him lak dat Brer B'ar should oughter have sumpin to mark him off from all de tother common folks.

Den Brer Dog riz up an' tol' 'em all dat he wus been stayin a good part of de time up dar aroun' in Mr. Man's house.

He say: Up dar de folkses wus got reg'lar names fer de big mens an' he think dey'd oughter give one o' dese here names to Brer B'ar.

He tell 'bout one o' de mens up dar w'at jes set 'roun' an' make all de tothers pay him money an' den sen' 'em on off to jail. Dey all called dis big man "Square".

Now, of co'se de animuls lak to run aroun' an' dey dont want no look into no jail house; so dey makes up deir minds right off an' tells Brer Dog dat his name wont never do at 'tall.

Den he tell 'em dere wus anudder one up dar w'at drunk lots o' whisky an' got drunk' an' de folkses wus all named him "Kyernel".

De animuls all sorter lak de drinkin' idee; but dey wus skeared dat a big drunk man lak Brer B'ar mought be sorter hard to handle. So dey tells Brer Dog dat dey thinks dat dey's druther not name him "Kyernel".

Den Brer Dog say dere wus anudder one up dar w'at jes ride aroun' a big plantation an' dey call him "Jedge", dough he dont never do nothin an' he dont hardly never go 'bout town an' nowhars else. W'en he wusnt a ridin' aroun'; he jes set up on his pie-izzer, bresh back his long white whiskers, an' smoke his long-stem cob pipe. De folkses up dar look lak dey call him "Jedge" caze he wus jes natchully de bigges' man in de whole bandittio.

De animuls all 'gree right off dat dis 'ould a fine name to mark 'im off wid as de biggest man 'mongst 'em. So dey named 'im Judge B'ar. From dat time on all de balunce of de evenin' ontel dey go home; it wus "Jedge" B'ar on dis side, it wus "Jedge" B'ar on dat side, an' it wus "Jedge" B'ar on ev'ry side.

Befo dey breaks up fer de night, Jedge B'ar make 'em a big long speech an' he say a whole heaps o' dem big jawbreaker words w'at none of 'em caint un'erstan'. He tell 'em 'long twixt an' 'tween de big words dat he wus a gwineter live up to de perfessin of his big name by gwine aroun' on de do-nothin' job lak de big man w'at wus named "Jedge". He allow dat de most nothiness job dat he know of fer a man wus fer him to look atter de chilluns. So dey all mought tell deir chilluns w'en dey go home dat dey could look fer him to come aroun' an' take 'em out fer play a liddle while ev'ry day. At las' dey all come 'roun' an' bow to "Jedge" B'ar an' go home.

Atter dat Jedge B'ar take de chilluns out reg'lar to play ev'ry day; an' all de tother animuls say dere never wus setch anudder man on (y)earth as "Jedge" B'ar. Dey ax him out to all de big Barbecues, de big Barn-dances, de big Plays, de big Candy Pullins, de big Sprise Parties, de big Pond Parties, de big Suppers, de big Cake Walks, de big Co'n Shuckins, de big House Raisins, de big Watermillion Feasts, de big Jamborees, an' de big Hullabaloos. Dey all say dat nothin caint go on onless Jedge B'ar is dar fer 'em to scrape deir footses an' bow to.

W'en Jedge B'ar's Relations see w'at a big man he wus done git to be; dey all jes quit home an' comed an' settled down aroun' 'im. You see dey gits to be some stick in de mud by claimin to be some blood-kin to 'im. All of 'em say dey wus powerful close kin to 'im. None of 'em wus furder off from his fambly tree dan cousin. One day Jedge B'ar say to one of 'em;

dat he didn' have no ricomembunce of none o' his furdest off kinfolks a claimin kin wid dis here B'ar's furdest off kinfolks. Dis here tother B'ar make answer to Jedge B'ar an' say: He wus kilt a toad-frog an' wus put dat toad-frog in a ant-heap ontel de meat wus all cleaned offn de bones; den he put dat toad-frog's wush-bone un'er his pillow on a Friday night, an' he dremt dat de wife of de great-gran'-daddy of his great-gran-daddy's uncle wus married to de great grand-nephew-uncle of Jedge B'ar's great-gran'-aunt; an' he added, dat dis should oughter at least make 'em mighty close cousins. Jedge B'ar stan' aroun' a while an' scratch his head an' study it through; den he say to dis B'ar dat he never wus much on countin out things, but he reckin dat "cousin" would make it somewhars about in de neighborhoods of right.

You could always know w'en Jedge B'ar wus a gwine down de road; caze as he pass by de B'ar houses dey would all holler to 'im. It wus: "Hullo, Cousin Jedge!" It wus: "Howdy-doo, Brer Jedge." It wus: "Jedge!" "Jedge!" "Jedge!"

Atter de Jedge's relations git to living aroun' him; dey tells him an' de tother animuls dat he wuk too hard to be a actin' lak Mr. Man's Jedge—dat he jes should oughter walk aroun' an' be a sort of big Overseer, an' let de tother Bars take care of de chilluns an' dem tother things.

Of co'se de tother Bars wus got in mind de gittin of deir sumpin (d)eat fer nothin' jes lak Judge B'ar; but none of dem tothers dont see which way de win' is a blowin'. So all de tother animuls clip in an' say: "Jes any thing to make Jedge B'ar big" an' de Jedge say: "Jes any thing to please his relations".

Now, w'en Jedge B'ar take in all his kinfolks in his business; dar wus whar he step in de quick-sand, sink up to his eye-balls, an' lose sight of all dat wus a gwine to 'im. Ole Aunt Betsy Turbentime say: dat folkses an' bars is jes alike w'en it come to dis; dat w'en folkses tries to take all deir relations into deir business, de Devil hitches up his wagin an' team an' comes fer to git 'em all.

De ole Bad Man didn' zackly come an' git Jedge B'ar hisself; but he sho did come an' git all dat big name away from 'im. Aunt Betsy say dat it all happen in dis way:

W'en dere wusnt nobody a takin' part of de crops an' provisions fer nothin 'cep' Jedge B'ar, an' w'en de animuls wus all a contendin 'mongst deirselves dat Jedge B'ar mus' he'p hisself to some of deir provisions fust; he wus jes natchully got mo' dan he can say de Blessin over. But w'en de whole B'ar Compoodle 'gin to eat an' drink offn jes one po'tion, dey didn' have 'nough to go aroun'; an' de Jedge an' all de res' of 'em wus jes as poo' as Job's tucky an' hongry 'nough to eat dirt.

Of co'se, enjorin all dese hard times fer de B'ars, dey wus a takin care of de chilluns of de tother animuls. Dey look longin-lak at de chilluns all slick an' a rollin' aroun' jes as fat as dey can waller. So at las' some o' de B'ars git so hongry, whilst dey wus a takin care of de chilluns, dat dey slip off to one side once in a while an' eat one.

Den dem tother animuls go to Jedge B'ar an' say to 'im dat it wus mighty sildom how some of deir chilluns go an' put in deir dispearunce an' caint be found by nobody nowhars.

Jedge B'ar ax 'em to take cheers an' be seated an' he'll call in de tother b'ars, wat wus been a lookin' atter de chilluns, an' pump 'em to see w'at he can draw outn 'em. He call de b'ars all in an' ax 'em 'bout de los' chilluns; an' he tell 'em dat he wus a gwineter tu'n 'em all off if dey caint splain sumpin 'bout de goin' of 'em.

One B'ar say dat he wus been hearn tell of a heaps o' hants a bein' aroun'!

Jedge B'ar say dat wont do; caze de hants mought skear 'em to death, but dey could find 'em atterwards.

Anudder B'ar say dere wus heaps o' sinkholes abouts; an' maybe perhaps de chilluns mought 'ave fell in dem.

Jedge B'ar say dat wont do neider; caze Brer Mus'rat an' Brer Mink wus bofe done look in de bottoms of all de sinkholes fer 'em.

At las' one of de Bars say dat he dont see nothin' else 'cep' de "Boogers!" mus' 'ave cotch 'em an' e't 'em up.

Jedge B'ar tell him dat dis soun' a liddle mo' reasonable; caze dough he haint never seed no "Boogers" in his whole life, his mammy used to tell 'im w'en she put 'im to bed at night, if he didn' keep his eyes shet an' go right on to sleep, dat dey would sho git 'im an' eat 'im up. He put in dat he never did open his eyes to see 'bout 'em caze he never wus ig to go a skeetin' down "Booger-red-lane"; but he know dat ev'ry thing dat his mammy say wus so.

De animuls a settin dar an' a lissenin, an' w'at lose deir chilluns, want to know of dese B'ars w'at "Boogers" wus an' w'at dey wus lak.

Jedge B'ar say he dont know; but one of dem tother B'ars w'at wus been a doin' de eatin of de chilluns say he know. He say dat one git atter him w'en he wus liddle, an' might' nigh cotch him; an' it skeared him so bad dat it tu'n some of de hairs white all over his body. Dat was de reason he was a gray B'ar instid of a black one.

De tother animuls say dat he mus' go on an' tell 'em all about 'em; so dat dey can be on de lookout an' save deir chilluns as much as dey can.

Well, dis here B'ar say dat "Boogers" wus great big black ugly wooly things bigger dan Sis Cow; dat dey wus got moufs an' throats big 'nough to swaller a rain bar'l; an' dat dey jes make a business o' ketchin an' swallerin bad chilluns. Den he say de wustest thing 'bout Boogers wus dat dey all had on big witch-coats; an' by w'arin' dese here coats, dey can dis'pear right in broad-open daytime right befo' yo' naked eyes, an' melt away into de wind. Dis B'ar splain to 'em darfo'; if somebody wus big 'nough, an' stout 'nough, an' could git to 'em befo' dey melt into de wind; he mought kill 'em wid a club, but nobody nowhars in de worl' could do dis.

Atter de tother animuls hear dis B'ar splain 'bout "Boogers"; dey makes up deir minds to let all de B'ars go, to hide deir chilluns, an' to look out fer 'em as best dey can. But dey tells Jedge B'ar if he'll jes look up an' kill de "Boogers" dat dey wont stop wid callin him "Jedge". Dey'll call 'im Gineral, Kyernel, an' all dem tother big names dey can hear tell of.

W'en de animuls let de B'ars all go, it sen' 'em all to de Poo' House; an' dey watches out mo' sharper dan ever befo' to ketch an' eat up de chilluns, w'en dey can git a chance.

Miss Pig hid her chilluns in a great big bed of leaves. Miss Fox hid hern in a hole in de groun'. Miss Possum toted hern aroun' wid her on her back.

Ole Sis Cow's chilluns wus so big dat she couldn' do no good a hidin' 'em 'cep' in de thick bushes of de tangled up woods So she take hern off an' hide 'em in dar; an' tell 'em not to answer nobody w'at calls 'em, an' not to come to nobody 'cep' her.

She tell her baby dat, w'en she come an' call him, she'll sing a song; an' dat way he'll know her call from de Boogers' call, an' from ev'rybody elses'. She hide her baby an' l'arn him de song so dat he'll know it. Dis wus de song:

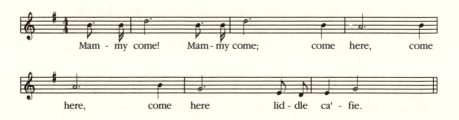

Mam - my come! Mam - my come; come here, come here, come here lid - dle ca' - fie.

Dis way Sis Cow, Sis Pig, an' all de balunce hide deir chilluns so good dat de B'ars live from han' to mouf in Hongry Holler all de time. Jedge call all his kinfolks togedder an' subgest dat dey he'p 'im to hunt up an' kill de "Boogers". Dem tother B'ars sot 'roun' an sung off to him.

Let's wuk togedder,
An' we'll all git fat.
Dat wukin apart
Make us poo' as a rat.

Den ole Jedge B'ar cotch on to it dat dem tother B'ars wus de "Boogers" w'at wus been a eatin up de chilluns. He wus awful sorry dat de tother B'ars wus done gone an' do dis, but he make up his mind dat he'd better wuk wid his own folks caze blood wus heaps thicker dan water an' birds of a fedder mus' flock togedder. So he 'gin to eat up de chilluns too.

Him an' Sis Cow wus always been mighty good friends; so, he know her song. One day w'en his mouf was a waterin an' his paunch was a pinchin him; he ax one of dem tother B'ars to go wid him to dinner, caze he wus a gwineter call Sis Cow's ca'f an' eat it up. Dey bofe goes 'long togedder, an' lays 'roun', an' watches ontel Sis Cow gits some distance off from whar dey thinks de calf is. Den dey goes togedder to dat spot an' ole Jedge B'ar clear up his th'oat sorter keerful lak; an' den he open up an' sing Sis Cow's song. Sho 'nough, w'en he do dis, here come de ca'f jes a runnin' to 'em.

Ole Jedge B'ar an' de tother B'ar grab it. It holler a liddle but dey soon stop dat an' e't it up. Ole Sis Cow, away off at a distance, sorter think dat she hear her baby whimper an' she go back to see 'bout it. She git dar so quick dat de two B'ars dont git no time to run away; an' so dey runs an' hides behin' a great big rock. She see a few of de hairs of her baby scattered aroun', an' she might strong dat de Boogers wus done got it. But Sis Cow think maybe dey haint yit git time to eat it. So she call it; an' say to herself, if it answer wid de "Boogers," she'll go to it. Den de "Boogers" 'll eider hafter eat bofe of 'em or neider of 'em wont go on de Booger-table. So ole Sis Cow open up an' sing: "Mammy come! Mammy come; come here, come here, come here liddle ca'fie."

Den ole Jedge B'ar in order to skear Sis Cow sing back lak he wus de Head-man 'mongst de "Boogers" a answerin':

Chile! Sis Cow know ole Jedge B'ar's voice; an' she make right straight fer dat rock, whar dey wus a hidin', wid her tail up an' her hawns down. She onkivered 'em; an' she rund her hawns into dat B'ar w'at wus wid ole Jedge B'ar an' rip him wide open. Whilst she wus a doin' dis de ole Jedge rund an' got away.

W'en she at de insides of de B'ar w'at she rip open, she seed some of de pieces of her chile; den she knowed all 'bout who de "Boogers" wus. She sen' fer all dem tother animuls an' tell 'em all 'bout de B'ars a bein' de "Boogers"!

De animuls wus all blue mad an' dey chew up an' spit out on de ground de 'greements to call ole Brer B'ar "Jedge". An so ole Brer B'ar lose his Jedgeship by mixin up his kinfolks in his buisness—leaswise dat's w'at ole Aunt Betsy Turbentime say. De animuls all name him over an' call him: "Ole Rag Tag an' Bob Tail."

W'en de animuls all know dat de B'ars wus de "Boogers"; dey den know how to plan to run an' to keep outn de way. Dey keep outn de way so good dat "Ole Rag Tag an' Bob Tail" hafter go to de nex neighbor; so de B'ars 'gin to gedder an' to eat his co'n. An' he put it all in his co'n-crib; so dat put a en' to de hash a comin three times a day in misery from dem quarters.

Den de B'ars git turble mad an' say dey wus a gwineter git eben wid Mr. Man by ketchin an' eatin up his liddle boy. So de next time Mr. Man's liddle boy wus a comin home from de mill, a ridin a turn o' meal on a hoss; dey got atter him.

He whup up de hoss an' de hoss run an' de B'ars run atter him. He laid de whup on de hoss mo' harder an' de hoss go jes a t'arin down de road; but w'en he look back he see dat de B'ars wus a gainin on him. He looked back an' he whupped de hoss mo' harder still. Den de hoss stumbled an' th'owed him an' de bag o' meal off on de groun'; an' so de B'ars git right up on 'im an' dey wus 'bout to ketch him. Dar wus a big tree close by him on de side of de road. He wus a good climber; so he clumb away up in de tip-top, close out to de tip end of de limbs, whar de parts wus so liddle dat de B'ars couldn' hug 'em to climb 'em. De hoss run on off home an' lef' him an' de meal bag an' de B'ars all togedder.

De B'ars come up, dey do, an' eat up all de meal outn de bag on de groun'; den dey look up at de boy in de tip-top of de tree an' say:

"We'll sharpen our teef!
We'll dull 'em ag'in!
We'll git you by an' by;"

and den dey 'gins to gnaw on de tree.

De B'ars gnawed away ontel atter while de tree wus half gnawed down. W'en de boy see dat de tree wus half down, he wus skeared to death.

De B'ars look up at him an' say:

"We'll sharpen our teef!
We'll dull 'em ag'in!
We'll git you an' by."

Dis liddle boy had two dogs; one of 'em wus named Fisherman, an'
de tother one wus named Beaver; an' he knowed dat de onliest chance fer
his life wuṣ to call 'em. He most in ginerally called 'em wid a song; but he
wus so fur from home dat he didn't see no chance day dey could ever
hear 'im if he sing away off dar. But he whoop out dat song on de winds
wid de hope dat de dogs mought maybe perhaps hear it. Dis wus de
song:

Here, Fish-er-man! Here, Beav-er! Hear poo' Ton-y hol-ler!

At fust de dogs didn' hear no song; dey wus too fur off. De B'ars dey
keep on a gnawin an' a sayin':

"We'll sharpen our teef!
We'll dull 'em ag'in!
We'll git you by an by!"

De col' chills run all down Tony's back whilst he lissen to de gnawin'
an' look at de bottom of de tree a growin' thinner; but he keep on a
singin moanful an' downful dat song:

"Hear Fisherman! Hear Beaver!
Hear poo' Tony holler!
Eat b'ar-meat, all night long,
Crack skull-bones fer yo' supper!"

W'en de hoss, w'at drapped Tony an' de meal, got home; an' his
daddy see bofe de meal an' de boy gone, he break off down de road to
see w'at wus become of 'im. De two dogs foller along wid 'im. Terreckly
de dogs git close 'nough dat dey ketches a liddle whiff of Tony's singin':
an', Mon! Dey sailed off down de road lak a streak of lightnin'. Dey got to
whar Tony wus jes befo' de B'ars gnaw out de las' splinter to make de
tree fall.
Dey cotched one of de B'ars an' kilt him as dead as a hammer. (Some
say 'twus ole Jedge B'ar). De tother B'ars got away. Tony clumb down' an'
atter his daddy pet him up a liddle, dey tuck de dead b'ar an' went home.
W'en dey git home an' talk it all over; dey all loves dem dogs so much
fer savin Tony's life day dey make up deir minds not to eat none of de
B'ar-meat but to save it an' feed it all to Fisherman an' Beaver.

Dey sot up late dat night a talkin' 'bout Tony's bein' saved an' 'bout b'ars in ginerally. De ole 'oman say dat she wus been a hearin tell ever since she wus a liddle gal dat if you kilt a wild varmint an' dragged it home dat de mate to it 'ould trail it up an' come dar too.

Tony up an' say dat he wus done gone an' git 'nough spearunce wid b'ars fer one day; an' he wus a gwineter climb up de ladder into de loft of de cabin, an' go to bed. So he clumb up an' tu'ned in on de pallet fer de night.

His daddy—ole man Abe wus his name—say he haint skeared o' no noise an' he dont ax nothin no odds; an' he jes wish dat he could git a chance at one of dem b'ars w'at wus atter his boy, caze den somebody else would sho have b'ar-meat to eat 'sides de dogs.

He den riz up from his cheer, sorter lazy lak, an' say dat he wus fergit to fasten up de co'n-crib doo'—dat he guess he'd better go an' fasten dis, an' den come back an' lay down fer a liddle snooze.

He go to de doo' an' onbar it, an' pull it back a liddle—den he give one o' dese here onearthly yells, run back an' lit out up de ladder fer de loft. Whilst he wus a gwine up de ladder, in walked a b'ar! It skear de ole man so bad dat he pult de ladder up behin' him in de loft. Dis lef' his ole 'oman (Aunt Sookie Ann wus her name) down dar by herse'f wid de b'ar.

Ole Uncle Abe holler down to his wife, he do: "Oh Sookie, dar's de pitchfork over dar in de corner of de room! Grab it an' run it th'ough dat b'ar befo' he climb up here an' git our poo' liddle Tony! Be quick, Sookie, fer Lawd's sakes or we's all gone!"

Befoe' de ole man git th'ough wid his splavercations; de ole 'oman was done got de pitchfork an' used it on de b'ar, an' he wus dead.

Den de ole man an' Tony come down. De ole man say to his wife: "Law Honey, jes look w'at a big b'ar we wus done killed!"

She say to 'im dere haint no "we" in dis thing! I kilt dis b'ar; an' if you dont hesh up an' herry up an jerk de hide offn him; I's a gwineter use de tother end of dat 'ar same pitchfork on you, caze you skint up dat ladder to de loft an' pult it up behin' you!"

De ole man dry right up an' say sorter 'umble-lak: "Honey, I didn' mean no harm! I jes got a liddle woolgethered an' rattled. It's so dark in here dat I caint see a wink; but I jes thinks so much of you dat I can skin de b'ar in de dark, if you says so.

De ole man fumble aroun' in de dark; an' he git a knife an' 'gin to skin de b'ar. W'en he wus a skinnin' fer a while, he say: "Honey, I's got de hide clean off down to de head; but dere's sumpin so cu'ious 'bout de head dat de skin wont slip over it. Spose we kindle up de fire a liddle an' throw on a pine-knot; den we can see how to finish de skinnin', an' maybe we can cook a liddle tas'e o' b'ar-meat to eat befo' we lies down ag'in fer a liddle res'."

Dey kindle up de fire an' pitched on a pine-knot.

As de room 'gin to light up a liddle so as de ole man could see; he raise up his hands lak dey wus been whar day wusnt got no business, den he say in a whisper; "Laws a mussy, Sookie Ann, jes look w'at you's done done! You's kilt ole Uncle Calup Weather's big pet black horned sheep!"

Aunt Sookie Ann say to 'im: "Now look here, ole man, you's done already said dat we uns kilt de b'ar. Of c'ose I got a liddle mad, an' spoke up a liddle sorter crabit, caze my fedders wus a liddle ruffled; but I knowed all de time dat you was a sayin right. Fer didn' you holler down from de lof' an' tell me whar de pitchfork wus?—An' didn' you lakwise say to kill 'im to save Tony?"

"Yes", answered ole man Abe, "I wus a liddle upset an' I specks I mought 'ave spilt out sumpin w'at I didn' zackly mean.—Well, I'll tell you w'at we'll do. We'll jes eat up dis sheep an' say nothin'. Den at Chrismus Time, I'll give Calup dat big black ewe o' mine fer Chrismus Gif' w'at he wus a been tryin' to trade me outn fer mo' dan a year. But we mus' tell all de neighbors bout de b'ars—w'at dey'll do, an' w'at dey wont do—caze if we don't dey wont think dat no b'ars cotch an' e't up dis here pet sheep."

Dey put dat sheep away; den dey goes 'roun' an' tells all de folkses setch big skeary b'ar-tales dat dey all run if somebody open deir mouf lak dey wants to say "b'ar". De tales spread lak wild fire; an' ev'ry body got to be skeard of b'ars.

Ole Aunt Betsy Turbentime say dat folkses runs from b'ars caze dey wus hearn tell o' dese big b'ar-tales; an' b'ars runs from folkses caze dey thinks dey hears Tony's dogs a comin'; an' all de whole layout of de business come 'bout caze Jedge B'ar lose his Jedgeship by takin' all o' his kinfolkses into his business. It lakwise got all de animuls to hidin' deir liddle babies out in de woods.—But look!" said Andrew, changing de conversation, "Dar's my cow!"

In a few moments the boys had their dog barking at the heels of the cow. She lowered her head in a half fighting attitude, and backed away slowly into the deeper and more tangled woods. In a short while she stood by her calf, stopped, bade the dog and all others defiance.

Andrew called the dog away, then went towards his cow holding out a little salt in one hand as a peace offering. The boys and the cow were soon on good terms again, and she walked home quietly in front of them closely followed by the calf over which she kept an ever watchful eye.

"Well, Ander!" said Isacc when they were once more at the former's home, "If you knows some mo' lorations lak de one you's been a tellin' me; I hopes dat you' ll let yo' cow git out ev'ry day an' come by an' git me to go an' he'p you find 'er."

"I dont know 'bout lettin' dis here cow out no mo'" replied Andrew, "caze my daddy wus got too many good seasoned hick'ries by de chimbly

jam in de house an' he know how to use 'em. But I can come fer you; an'
we can play or do sumpin fer a good time; den I can hand out some mo'
to you jes lak ole Aunt Betsy Turbentime hand it out to me."

"So long, Ander!" "Good-bye, Ike!" and the boys parted.

WHY THE IRISHMAN IS A
RAILROAD SECTION BOSS
❊

(PREFATORY NOTE. This Tradition—full of Negro wit and humor—is most unusual even for one of its kind. Perhaps those who do not read my treaties on "The Origin of Traditions" must necessarily remain at a loss to understand why the Negroes should have formulated such a tradition.)

Fortunately for me, in this generation where those have largely passed away who heard the story, Joel Chandler Harris, in his introduction to "Uncle Remus," wrote: "There is an anecdote about the Irishman and the rabbit which a number of Negroes have told me with great unction, and which is both funny and characteristic, though I will not undertake to say that it has its origin with the blacks."

Following this statement, Mr. Harris gives nearly a page in outlining this supposed story which will be found to be only one Negro version of one of the scenes in "Why the Irishman is a railroad section boss." Mr. Harris has left this witness that it was current among Negro ex-slaves.

They did not tell him all the story, because no ex-slave at that time was so foolish as to run the risk of incurring the ill will of a white man by going through with a story in which one of that race was being held up to ridicule, though, even at the same time, the relator felt that there was probably much truth in the explanation being offered.

Many years ago, one midsummer Saturday afternoon, Nat Ray, surrounded by his sons, sat beneath the shade of a large oak standing in front of his cabin near Ebo on the Shelbyville, Tennessee Branch of the Nashville, Chattanooga, and St. Louis Railroad. The Ebo there, in the early seventies of the last century, was only a kind of level spot where the little local railway train could be flagged and boarded, or where a passenger might get off. The Ebo of today differs only from that of the olden times in that the primeval forests thereabouts have given way to cleared cornfields, and the railroad officials have constructed a crude platform crossing from which their patrons may board the train.

Nat and his sons had just cut open two large red ripe watermelons and were seating themselves for a feast when the passing little local train blew, stopped, and let off a passenger. The homeward path of this passenger naturally carried him by Nat's house.

As he came near the cabin, Nat exclaimed: "Looky! If dat haint Bully Gooden!—Hello, Bully! Whar in de worl' did you come from?"

"W'y, Hello, Uncle Nat!" answered Bully. "I's come from whar dey drives de spikes; Whar dere haint nothin' lef', 'cep' dem Big Ikes!"

"De same ole seben an' six; de same ole Bully Gooden!" goodhumoredly remarked Uncle Nat. "Come by, an' drap down in de shade, an' cross up yo' legs so as we can see how you looked whilst you wus a ridin dat ole puffin' snortin' blowin' "iron-hoss" [Iron-hoss = Railway train] to death a gittin here. We wus all done heared dat you wus done gone so fur off las' Spring dat you couldn' git back ontel de wild geese [Wild geese = this expression means Fall of the year—the time when the wild geese migrate south] come a flyin' in a p'int to show you de way. But here you is!"

"Yes, here I is," assuringly came the reply from Bully as he looked longingly at the freshly cut black-seeded redmeated watermelons.—"Humph! Dem 'ar watermillions looks mighty good. Dont dey tas'e mighty good?"

"Come up an' cut yo'se'f a sleish, an' try 'em," came the much desired reply from Nat. "If you likes watermillions, I's got a couple o' mo' of 'em in de house un'er de bed. So jes you eat yo' fill!"

"If I likes 'em?" laughingly came the words in an echo from Bully. "Does you ricomember dat time las' summer w'en I wus so sick wid w'at de Doctor say look sumpin lak de Yaller Janders?"

"Yes," responded Nat.

"Well," continued Bully, "de Doctor, he tol' me dat I wus jes boun' to die! Den I tol' him dat he mus' jes sorter patch me up fer a liddle while anyhows ontel along towards Fall. He tol' me dat he hate might bad fer to see me go; but folks w'at go to de right place wus a heaps better off a settin' down a res'in' an' a feastin' on milk an' honey an' wine. But I tol' him dat it didn' make no diffunce w'at come or go; I wanted to git patched up fer a mont' or so, caze if I wus jes bleedged to die, I didn' want to go right in de middle of watermillion time! Well, Suh! Dat 'ar Doctor jes laugh an' tel me dat I wus gone stock crazy to be a studyin' 'bout watermillions, caze if I got patched up an' tetched one it 'twould kill me deader dan a load of grape-shot! Dat 'ar giggle of hisn maked me sorter mad, an' I fergit clean offn my mind dat I wus got sick. So I ups an' laid it off to 'im dat he wus all wrong; caze I never wus seed no watermillions w'at hurted me 'cep' de ones I wanted an' couldn' git.

Den he look solemn an' tell me dat I'd better stop so much runnin' of my mouf an' do some studyin' 'bout de Pearly Gates an' Gol'en Streets. So I tells him sorter pitiful lak; if I's boun' to go, I reckins I'd better pay him off, caze I didn' want no debts a hangin' 'roun' over my ole 'oman atter de funer'l.

He wus been a comin' fer to see me two or three times a day fer a couple o' weeks or mo'; so I knows dat I mus' a owed him all de stray change dat I wus got along wid all de ole 'omans wash-pans an' pots put in fer to make up de diffunce. He look at me lak he rially mought feel a liddle sorter sorry fer me, an' say dat he hate to charge me at 'tall; but I can jes give him a couple o' dollars, an' dat'll make it eben if he dont hafter come to see me no mo'.

I retched my han' un'er my pillar an' pult out my ole money stockin' an' handed him de two dollars.

Atter he leave de house an' git on his hoss, I tells my ole 'oman to run out an' say to 'im dat I wus sont him word dat he need' come back no mo' ontel I sont fer him.

Honey! I haint ever sont fer dat Doctor no mo'. I jes sont fer Ole Uncle Sandy Hughes an' got him to fix me up a bottle of bitters made outn wil' cherry bark, poplar bark an' sasferreller. I drunk down a liddle of dis along an' I 'gin to git better right away. In about a week I 'gin to chomp on watermillion—a spittin it all out 'cep' de juice; an' you needn' b'lieve it onless you wants to, but dem watermillions an' bitters chuored me soun' well!"

"Well," said Nat, "de doctors dont know it all. Dey comes aroun' a strewin' deir blue-mass here an' deir calimy dere an' dey kills mo' dan dey chuores. I'd a heaps druther 'pend on yerbs an' roots dan to put penunce on dem. But whar is you been?"

I's been away out yon'er a wukin on de Iron Mountin railroad," replied Bully.

"Well, well, well, well!" said Nat. I's heard a heaps 'bout dat 'er place; an' I's powerful glad dat you's here. I wants to ax you 'bout dem big flop-(y)eared Dutch railroad Bosses. I's hearn tell dat dere's dead oudles of 'em out dar."

"No! Dey dont have no mo' of dem big flop-(y)eared Dutch out dar no mo' nowhars," answered Bully. All de big Bosses out dar now is Irshmons. I tells you dem Irshmons caint hardly talk so dat you can know w'at dey wus a sayin'; but (Lawsy Mussy!) you caint hardly find nobody w'at can beat 'em a cussin!"

"Is dat so?" said Nat. "I caint see no ways how dey wus l'arnt 'bout railroads so dat dey can see to 'em a gittin fixed; w'en dey caint hardly talk wid folks."

"I caint hardly zackly see into dat neider," said Bully; "but I heard a Missip Nigger out dar on de railroad in Arkansaw a 'splainin it all. He tell all 'bout how it come 'roun' dat de Irshmons knowed all 'bout railroad tracks so day dey git de job of bein' Bosses; an' it all come right back to me de minute I laid eyes on red ripe watermillions w'at wus all mixed in wid it."

"I dont see how yo "Missip Nigger git de railroads mixed in wid watermillions widout bustin 'em up," jokingly replied Nat. "Is dat de way he fix it up; an' did he git de Irshmons in jes in time to git 'em e't up jes befo dey got dar?"

"No, dat wusnt it!" said Bully. "Dis wus de way it 'twus: All us wuk-hands chipped in one night an' bought a lots of watermillions fer a feast.

We managed to wrop ourselfs aroun' all of 'em 'cep' one. We wus jes dat stuffed dat we couldn' eat no mo'. So we all maked up our minds dat we'd give de lef'-over watermillion to de man w'at cold tell de bes' loration a splainin sumpin dat none of de tothers dont un'erstan' nothin' 'bout. You see, we all say dat it look lak de lef'-over watermillion should oughter go to de smartest man.

Dis here Nigger from Missip git de fust clip at de rigamarole; an' he tol' setch a big long loration dat all de tothers of us say dat it 'twus too late fer us to start up onless we wus all a gwineter set up all night. So we jes handed him over de watermillion. If it hadn' a been so late; of co'se I could a beat him han' over fist, an' a throwed in one or two of dem tothers fer de gougers. He wus one o' dem 'ar norrer-gauge injines w'at puff an' blow a whole heaps harder dan dey can pull. But he hand out a right good loration 'bout how de Irshmons git to be railroad sexion Bosses. I specs heaps dat he say mought perhaps not a been so; but den ag'in perhaps maybe it mought all a been so, caze dem Irshmons is sho cu'ious folks!"

"S'pose you light in an' tell us de rigamarole loration; whilst we's a slippin' dese here 'millions down de 'red lane', said Nat. "We dont know nothin' 'bout Irshmons, an' we wants to git some notion 'bout 'em."

"Well, here she go," replied Bully. "You can jes pull her down wid de bell-cord; if you gits tired of hearin' her pop off steam, a gwine up grade, whilst she's makin' fer de station. Dis here Missip Nigger claim dat he sleep in a caboose nex' to de sexion Bosses; an' he hear 'em a tellin' deir spearunce one night atter he go to bed. He say w'en you gits it all togedder; it wus 'bout lak dis:

De Irshmons comed over here in pairs; an' in ev'ry pair, one wus named Pat an' de tother wus named Moike (I knows dat dis here part of de loration mus' be so; caze dese wus all de names dat all de Bosses of dat persuasion wus got dat I's been seed.) Well, de splainin' go; dat Pat an' Moike wuked togedder on de plantation over dar in de country whar dey come from. Dey didn' git no nothin' much fer to eat over dar 'cep' w'at tuck sick an' died.

Some chickens died; an' de Mosser on de plantation give 'em dese to eat. A hog died an' he fed 'em on dat. A goat died an' he cooked dat up fer 'em. At las', one Saddy night, de Mosser's mudder-in-law died; an' Pat an' Moike jes throwed up deir jobs an lef'!

Dey went on down on a Sunday mawnin to a place whar a boat wus tied up, a gittin 'ready fer to come from dar over de water to 'Orleans. De conducter man wus all ready an' wus jes wantin to say: "All aboard!"; but he couldn' git nobody fer to wuk on Sunday, an' load up de baggage chyar of his boat. So Pat an' Moike went to dis here conductor man; an' tol' 'im dat dey's wuk or do any thing else fer to git away from eatin' a dinner w'at wus bein' cooked up fer 'em out dar on de Moser's plantation!

De conductor man lissen to w'at dey say, an' he dont zackly know w'at to make of 'em; but he tell 'em: All right; jes any thing fer to git de ingine un'er head an' a gwine.

Pat an Moike soon trucked on de baggage, de conductor pulled de bell-cord, an' dey pulled out fer 'Orleans.

W'en dey git sorter good started; de conductor man fin' Pat an' Moike a lookin' lak dey wus skeared to death. He ax 'em w'at wus de matter. Dey say to 'im dat de ingine wus a makin' setch a sizzlin' swishin noise dat dey wus skeared dat it was a gwineter blow up!

Den de conductor man laugh an' tell 'em jes fer fun dat dere wus powerful heaps of danger of dat!

W'en dey hears dis; dey gits so skeared dat dey takes awful sick' an w'en-some-ever dey eats a liddle bite, day goes right straight an' empties it all out o' doors.

W'en dey gits over to 'Orleans; dey gits off. De conductor man on de boat tell 'em dat he want to keep on a hirin' em; but dey tells him: No, dey wus a gwineter go back out into de country an' look fer some sort o' place w'at dey wus been used to. W'at wus mo' dan dat: Dey declar' dat dey wus a gwineter go along on de railroad whilst dey wus a huntin' fer a job. No mo' boat fer dem!

De conductor man tell 'em dat he dont see no sense in runnin' off from a good boat job an' a walkin' down de railroad a lookin' fer anudder one. W'at wus de matter wid 'em any ways?

Pat an' Moike starts on off; an' dey hollers back to 'im as dey goes: "If you gits blowed up on de railroad, dar you is! But if you gits blowed up on a steam-boat, whar is you?"

Atter Pat an' Moike wus done said dis; dey totes dem mail, a walkin' down de railroad track towards de country a lookin' fer a job. W'en dey gits out in de country a piece; dey sees a man a settin' up in his house on de side of de road. His house wus got all de top done gone offn it. He wus one o' dem 'ar rich Mossers w'at wus lef' as poo' as Job's tucky w'en de war come an' sot all deir Niggers free. I dont know zackly how poo' Job's tucky wus; but some says dat he didn' have but one fedder lef' in his tail, an' dey had to prop him up 'long side de fence to gobble. Well, dat wus de way it 'twus wid dis here onetime rich Mosser; he didn' have nothin lef' 'cep' de walls of his house, an' he wus too lazy to put a kiver back on top of it.

So dese here Irshmons, beance dey wus a lookin' fer a job, go to dis here Mosser an' ax him fer why he dont kiver his house? He wus too shamed to tell 'em dat he wus too lazy. So he jes tell 'em: W'en it rain, it 'twus too wet to kiver it; an' w'en it 'twus dry, his house wus jes as dry as anybody's.

Dey tells him dat dey would lak to git de job o' throwin' a roof on over his head fer 'im anyways.

He make answer dat his money tree wus sorter all shriveled up; but if dey'd whirl in an' kiver de house, he'd scratch aroun' an' try to git 'em a liddle bite to eat. Den he say: He mought eben be willin' to go aroun' to de neighbors an' put in a good word fer 'em w'en dey git through; dat way, dey could git hired fer chyarpenters an' make bushels of money.

All dis soun' good to Moike an' Pat; so dey makes up deir minds, den an' dar, dat dey wus a gwineter go into de chyarpenter buisness. Dey goes out, an' dey cuts down a big straight white-oak tree, an' dey rives it up into some boards; an' den dey climbs up on top of de house an' 'gins to spike 'em on.

Dey sorter straddle 'long over de strippin an' de rafters; an' git on de fust course of boards. Den Moike say to Pat dat he wus a gwineter set down on his pile o' loose boards, to keep 'em from a slipin' an' a slidin' offn de house back down on de groun'. So he straddle his pile o' loose boards an' 'gin to spike on de nex' course.

Terreckly Moike's pile o' boards take a scoot an' head fer de groun'. Of co'se dey dont mean no harm; but dey sorter takes Moike 'long wid 'em fer comp'ny. W'en he hit de groun'; Pat sot up dar on top of de house fer a while an' lissen fer 'im. Atter while; when he dont hear no steam a shootin' off, an' no bell, an' no whistle; he crope to de aidge of de roof, locked legs aroun' a rafter, an' sorter lent over an' peeped down. He seed Moike a lyin' down dar all querled up lak he wus laid out! So he holler down: Hello, Moike! Is you dead? Moike he squall back to 'im: "No! I haint no dead; but I's spetchless!"

Pat clumb down offn de house, an' rubbed Moike a liddle; an' he got all right. Leaswise it look dat a way; caze 'bout dat time de Mosser called 'em in to set down wid de fambly to dinner, an' Moike he e't mo' an' all de tothers put togedder.

W'en he fall offn de house, he sorter bruise up his nose an' face. Dat's de reason dat all de Irshmons wus got a red nose an' face. W'en de folkses at de table sorter joke Moike 'bout eatin' so much; he hand 'em back dat he wus jes sorter fillin' out de mashed-in bruised places. So you sees: 'Bout all de Irshmons is full-faced.

Atter dinner, Moike say to Pat dat he jes natchully wusnt nailed togedder fer no chyarpenter; an' whilst his ingine wus all fired up, he wus a gwineter pull out fer de nex' station. Pat say: He reckin dat he wont be lak no pig; so he'll blow de whistle an' roll on too.

W'en Pat use dat word "pig", Moike 'gin to swell up an' git mad; caze he think Pat wus a talkin' 'bout his eatin' setch a big load.

But Pat shmove it all over. He allow dat he dont mean dat 'tall. W'at he mean wus dis: Over dar whar he come from he notice, w'en he feed de pigs on hot slop an' one would run up an' stick his mouf in an' git burnt; all dem tothers, a follerin 'long behin' 'im, didn' pay it no mind.

Dey all jes runned up an' sticked deir moufs in an' got burnt too. He splain to Moike dat he mean: One good man a ridin' through de air on a board in de broad-open daytime should oughter be plenty an' 'nough to make de tothers not hanker aroun' fer dat same thing w'en dey wusnt yit growed no wings. Wid dat much said; de ingineer an' de firesman gits deir heads togedder, pulls deir bell-cord, an' goes a puffin' off to de nex station.

De railroad from 'Orleans out to dis place, whar Pat an' Moike wus already gone, wus all fulled up an' shmove an' make good walkin'. But from dis place on, it 'twusnt all fulled up 'tween de cross-ties; an' de gwine on foot wus rough. So dey makes up deir minds to take to de dirt-road an' go through de country a huntin' a job.

About dat time, it 'twus gittin 'long towards night; an' it 'twusnt no time befo' dey 'gin to hit into de swamps. Dey come to a liddle branch a runnin' across de road; an' dere wus a liddle sand on bofe sides of it. Dey start to cross—Pat a leadin' de way. All of a sudden, Pat sunk right down; an' he look to Moike lak he wus a takin' a runnin' start to go down through de groun' clean to de Bad Place! Moike wus so stonished dat he hafter wait fer to ketch his bref befo he can pull his mouf open. By dat time, Pat wus waist deep in de quick-sand an' a gwine on down!

Says Moike, says he: "Faith an' Be Jazzus, Pat! An' w'at's you a doin'?" Pat makes answer, he do: "I haint a doin' nothin'! Some blarsted tother thing is a doin' it all!"

Den Moike say: "W'at 's you a lookin' fer down dar anyhows? An Pat holler back jes as he wus a gittin in de sand over his mouf: "I's a lookin' fer de way out! Grab an' pull de way I's a lookin'!"

Moike grab Pat by de hair jes as he wus a gwine down outn sight, an' pull him out; whilst he grumble 'bout him a bein so rough wid his head.

W'en dey gits outn de quick-sands; dey makes up deir minds to go back an' do all deir trabblin on de railroad. But it wus a gittin dark, so dey looks aroun' fer some place to sleep. Dey seed a ole empty cabin; but it had one o' dese here hewed slab-board floors w'at wus so rough you couldn' do no good a sleepin on it. So dey makes up deir minds to put down some brush on de groun' outside, den pile up some leaves an' grass on top of dis; an' sleep on 'em. Dey fixes up deir bed an' lies down.

W'en it git black dark, dem big swamp gallinipper skeeters come a zoonin aroun'. Dey say: "Cuzzeen—! Cuzzeen—! Cuzzeen—!" Pat an Moike haint never hearn tell o' no skeeters. Dere wusnt none in dat place over dar whar dey come from; an' dey dont know w'at to think of 'em.

Pat say to Moike: "W'at's dat?"

Moike make answer dat he dont know; but he hear 'em a sayin' "cousin", an' so it 'peared lak dey mought be de sperits of deir dead kinfolkses.

Pat say: If dat's it, he wus a gwineter set in an' stop 'em. So he holler out: "I dont want no segashuatin aroun' wid you dead kinfolkses! You go on back down to whar you come from, an' stay dar ontel I comes to see you in de broad-open daylight!"

W'en Pat git through wid his hollerin, he say to Moike dat he guess dat wus 'nough to make de deadfolkses stay in deir places—bofe dem w'at wus got gumption an' dem w'at wusnt! Den dey stretches out on deir bed fer a liddle snooze.

Terrackly dem big gallinipper skeeters 'gin to sting an' bite 'em lak wild fire. Moike den jump up an' say to Pat: "you's done gone an' ruint ev'rything! You's maked yo' kinfolkses so mad dat dey wus jes bent an' bound to eat us up!"

Den Pat whisper an' subgest dat dey slip in de ole tumble-down cabin an' hide 'hin' de doo'. So dey jumps up an' scoots away on deir tiptoes to hide behin' de doo' in de cabin.

W'en dey gits behin' de cabin doo', dey keeps mo' stiller dan a mouse. Atter while Moike peep out 'tween de doo' an' de doo'facin'; an' he seed de big lightnin' bugs—sumpin dat he haint never seed nor hearn tell of befo'. He look an' he look; an' he see deir lights jes a flashin ev'rywhars! He look at Pat but he dont say nothin'. At las' Moike nudged Pat in de short-ribs an' say: "We mought jes about as well git outn here from behin' dis here doo' an' fight it out lak mens wid de sperits of yo' dead kinfolkses; caze dey's done gone an' got torches an' lanterns, an' dey's a gwineter find us!"

So dey comed on out an' fou't at de skeeters ontel a hour or so befo' day. Of co'se, skeeters quit deir botherin you atter dat time o' night; an' Moike an' Pat den say dey wus done whupped de sperits of deir dead kinfolkses an' dey lies down an' sleeps ontel daylight.

W'en day wus comed on, dey maked deir ways back to de railroad an' started on off a walkin up de rough on-eben track. At fust, dey missed de cross-ties in deir steppin; an' dey stumped deir toes an' got powerful jarred up in deir walkin'. Dey wobbled aroun' so much in deir shufflin' 'long dat dey struck up 'g'inst de rails an' cut up deir footses an' ankles.

It go on dis a way so bad dat dey hafter study 'bout how fur de rails an' crossties wus apart an' how all de spikes wus set an' all dem things. Den dey walks along de railroad widout no mo' trouble.

Whilst dey wus a walkin' on up through Lousanner; dey seed folkses a wukin in de sugar-cane fields an' de rice swamps. So dey axed one of de plantation Capuns fer a job. He tell 'em dat he'll hire 'em to wuk in de rice swamps. But dey make answer to 'im dat dey wus done gone an' git 'nough of de water whilst dey wus a comin' over from whar dey come from. Den he say he'll hire 'em to wuk in de sugar-cane fields. So dey sot in to wuk. Dey cotched holt of some of de blades of fodder on de cane stalks; an' it cut deir hands jes lak a knife. Den dey tells de plantation Capun dat dey dont want no mo' wuk in dem diggins. Dey dont want to live aroun' no place whar de corn out in de field toted knives to cut up folkses wid. So dey pulled out up de railroad; widout blowin no whistle an' widout ringin' no bell; a sayin': Dey wus done clean through wid farmin'!

Away up de railroad in Lousanner; dey meets up wid one o' dem 'ar coal-black Guinea Niggers an' dey axes him w'at de plantation Capuns pay out de mostes' money fer ev'ry year. Dis here Nigger scratch his head an' study fer a while; den he say dat it look to him lak, since de Niggers wus all done gone an' got free, dat dey wus always a spendin out deir money fer mules. Den Pat look at Moike an' say dat dere wus plenty of open woods ev'rywhere aroun' dar; an' he think dat dey mought git rich by raisin an' sellin mules an' widout no wukin on no plantation an' nothin else.

Den dey axes dis here Guinea Nigger whar folkses gits de mules to raise; an' he make answer: He haint never seed none raised—All of 'em wus jes brung down dar to Lousanner. He tell 'em dat dey wus all raised away furder on up de railroad; an' he wus hearn tell dat de mules wus hatched outn great big yaller mare aigs bigger dan water-buckets; an' dat dey had to set on dese here aigs nine days fer to hatch 'em out. He tell de Irshmons lakwise dat he wus hearn tell dat dere wus great big woods-fulls of dese here hatched out young mules furder on up de railroad.

Pat an' Moike tell de Guinea Nigger dat dey wus mighty much obliged to 'im fer w'at he tell 'em. Den dey walks on off up de railroad a sayin' to one nudder dat dey wus a gwine into de mule-raisin' buisness.

Whilst dey wus a crossin' a railroad bridge over a big river, dey looks up an' dey sees de chyars a comin'! Dey didn' have no time fer to git off; so dey jes rolled offn de bridge an' landed on de jeists of de pillars un'er it to git out of de way of bein' runned over. Atter de train wus gone by; dey hafter study dat bridge from top to bottom befo dey git outn whar dey was gone to. It took 'em so long to git out; dat, w'en dey did git out, dey knowed ev'ry spike an' rail of wood w'at beslonged in railroad bridges, an' how it should oughter git set up.

Well dey gits out at las'; an' goes on down de railroad a whirlin' deir drive-wheels ontel dey gits to Missip whar dat 'ar Nigger come from w'at tol' me dis here loration away over in Arkansaw.

W'en de Irshmons got up dar in Missip; dey seed a great big cornfiel' all kivered over wid great big yaller punkins bigger dan a big cedar piggin. "Looky!" says Moike to Pat, an' Pat to Moike. "Jes looky! Jes looky! Dar dey is! We's gone an' foun' de mare-aigs. Now all we's got to do is set on 'em, an' hatch out, two at a time, an raise 'em; den we's rich.

So dey goes an' gits 'em a nice punkin apiece; an' hunts up a fine shade tree on de side of a hill, wid a branch a runnin by, down at de bottom of it. Dar dey sot down on de punkins to hatch 'em out! Dey sot 'em day an' night—skeared to git offn 'em. Pat say to Moike dat he wus so hongry dat he think dat he mought eben stomach a sleish of his ole Boss's mudder-in-law, if he had her dar. But dey say to one nudder dat it wont never do to git offn de aigs befo' de nine days wus up; caze dey mought git col', an' spile, an' not do no good a hatchin'.

W'en de nint' day open up, an' it wus 'bout time fer de aigs to hatch; de Irshmons wus almos pe'ished an' starved to death fer a drink o' water. Dey looked at de liddle clear branch o' water a runnin' along at de bottom of de hill; whilst dey wus a waitin' fer de mules to pip through de shells, an' come out. Deir moufs jes watered fer a drink!

Pat up an' say to Moike dat he jes knowed dat dey could run down dar an' git a drink of water, an' git back befo eider de aigs could git col' or de mules kick outn de shells. Moike say: Dat same min' struck him. So dey promus one nudder to count three, den run down to de branch, gulp down a swaller of water, an' git back befo' da "aigs" can git a chance to git col' an' let dem long-(y)eared songsters die in de shell.

Pat 'gin to count: "One!—Two!—Three!" an' off dey flewed to de branch. Dey got dar an' drunk right quick; den dey goes back, jes a bug-jumpin', [buck-jumping] up de hill. W'en dey got started back; dey looked an' seed de punkins a rollin down de hill. W'en Moike see dis he holler: "Hurry up Pat, an' let's ketch de 'aigs' befo' dey gits broke an' we gits broke along wid 'em always fer good!" Jes as Moike say dis; bofe of the punkins in deir rollin', hit a big holler stump an' busted open.—Dere wus two o' dese here big long-(y)eared spider-legged swamp rabbits in dat 'ar stump; an' as de punkins busted open, dey jumped out an' commenced to run off.

Moike see 'em an' he holler out: "Pat, dar de young mules is all hatched out! Call 'em! Dey's about to git away!"

Den Pat busted a loose wid a reg'lar song, a callin' 'em! He sing it over an' over. Dis wus de song:

Well, Pat an' Moike stan' dar an' look at deir fine "young mules", jes hatched out, ran clean off! Den Pat say to Moike dat dey should not oughter a never bothered along wid no nothin w'at wus a gwineter wuk on no plantation nohows. Dey should oughter a got enough of dat over dar whar dey come from! So dey makes it all up dar an' den dat dey wusnt never a gwineter wuk on no plantation no mo'; an' dey haint a gwineter wuk wid no nothin' w'at wus a gwineter wuk on no plantation.

So dey pulls out wid deir ingines wide open up de railroad a countin crossties. W'en dey wus stepped some miles furder up de railroad; dey

met up wid one o' dese here Jew peddlers. Of cose, you knows dat nobody caint look bad 'nough an' caint have no nothin' 'nough but w'at a
Jew peddler think he can sell 'im. De ole sayin' sayes: "You caint git no
blood outn a tunnup"; but de man w'at make dat up, he haint never come
across no Jew peddler.

Well; dis here Jew peddler, he stop Pat an' Moike right in de middle of
de railroad tracks widout flaggin' deir ingines an' widout axin whedder dere
be's mo' trains in front of 'em or mo chyars behin' 'em. He onrolled de big
bundle w'at he wus a totin' on his back an' spread it out on de railroad. He
haint got no nothin' fer to sell much 'cep' some ole black bross watches an'
chains an' finger rings. But he talk so fast 'bout de watches an' dem tother
things; dat it look lak Pat an Moike haint a gwineter git no mo' chance to
blow deir whistles nor to run deir chyars no furder.

At las' dis here Jew slow up his Lightnin' 'Spress long 'nough to ax Pat
an' Moike how many watches dey wants. Den dey makes answer dat dey
thinks dat dey wants 'em all from de way he talk 'bout 'em; but dey haint
got no nothin' to buy wid at dat time fer de present.

De Jew tell 'em: But dey'd hafter buy right dar an' den; caze nobody
else haint got none but him.

Pat an' Moike say to 'im: If nobody else haint got none, dey don see
whar he git hisn from.

De Jew make answer dat he could easy splain all dat. He tell 'em dat
he raise hisn from one or two stray watches w'at he pick up aroun' in de
swamps; so dey'd better buy right den caze dere wusnt no mo' no-whars.
Den dis Jew put in: If dey'd buy right den an' dar—beance he wus been a
knowin' 'em so long—dat he'd fork over de watches to 'em fer half price.

Pat an Moike tell dis here Jew day dey sho wus in love wid him fer
offerin to let 'em have de watches fer half price, caze he wus knowed 'em
so long. An' now; beance dey haint got no money, an' de quaintunce wus
done tuck away half of de price; dey would rattle on off up de railroad,
an' by de time he meet up wid 'em ag'in, dey hoped de quaintunce would
git long 'nough fer him to pass 'em over de watches fer nothin'. So dey
puffs on away from dar a countin' crossties an' lef' de Jew behin'.

Dey wus a walkin' along de railroad a palaverin' about gwine into de
watch business an' a tryin to hatch out an' cook up a plan fer to git into it.

Bymeby dey come 'cross one or two pieces of dem 'ar liddle rusty
chains w'at dey uses to fasten de padlocks on to freight chyar doors wid.

Pat says to Moike, says he: "Moike! If here haint de chains jes lak dem
w'at dat Jew frien' o' ourn is got! Now; let us look out an' see if we caint
find one or two stray watches lak him! Den we can go into de business of
raisin watches an' git rich."

Bymeby as dey walks along de railroad through de swamps' dey sees
one o' dese here liddle ole mud turkles off a liddle piece from a bayou.

Moike, he holler out: "Pat! Dere's a watch!" Pat tuck out atter de liddle turkle an' cotch 'im. De turkle pulled his head in; but Pat jes fastened de chain on to his tail—dat freight chyar chain w'at he wus done foun'—an' rammed him down in his jacket pocket.

"Now!" says Pat to Moike, says he, "we's got a big fine watch an' we can go into de watch raisin' business mo' samer dan dat Jew; an' de nex time we sees him, we can give him one instid o' him a givin' us one caze he wus been so good as to tell us all 'bout 'em."

As dey walks along, dey meets up wid a white man; an' he says to Pat: "Mawnin, Kyernel! W'at time o' day is it by yo' time piece?"

Pat pull out de turkle; an' he look at it jes a kickin' its footses, an' a clawin', an' he say: "It's half pas' a quahtah in de mawnin an' a scratchin lak de Devil an' all his Imps towards dinner time."

Dis here white man laugh jes fit to split his sides, an' w'en he manage to git hisself stopped fer a minute, he say: "Lawsy mussy! Look here feller, dat 'ar haint no watch; dat 'ar haint nothin but a mud turkle!"

'Bout dat time, de turkle nab Pat aroun' de thumb. He wus mighty liddle, but he wus got de grip in de jaws; an' w'en he shet down, he make Pat see stars in de broad-open daytime! Pat, he holler; an' de turkle bite an' blow! At las' Pat, he manage to shake 'im loose; an' de turkle runned an' jumped into de bayou.

So Pat an' Moike's ingines puff on off up de road, a blowin' to one nudder 'bout watches. Moike say to Pat dat de watch dat he throwed away looked zackuly lak de ones w'at dat 'ar Jew wus had.

Pat make answer dat it look dat way to him too; but it didn' feel dat way w'en he got his thumb cotched up in de case.

Moike den tell Pat dat he wus skeared dat dis here white feller w'at dey wus met wus done fooled 'em; an' dat he wus a gwineter wade into de bayou, atter dey wus gone, an' git de watch out fer hisself.

About dat time, dey met up wid anudder white man; an' dey stops him an' tells him all 'bout de Jew an' his watches. Den dey tells him dat dey found a watch an' chain jes lak dem w'at de Jew had; but w'en dey looked at de time o' day an' go to put it up, it cotched Pat's thumb an' almos' cut it off, an' den dey throwed it into de bayou.

W'en dis here white man hear dis, he bust out an' almos' kill hisself a laughin' too. He tell 'em: Dere haint nobody w'at sticks deir thumbs inside of de watch case w'en dey goes to shet it up! Of co'se, if dey does dat, dey'll break de glass crystial an' cut deir thumbs. He allow dat he wus powerful sorry dat dey wus throwed deir watch away. Den he subgest dat dey mought go back, an' wade aroun', an' feel over de bottom of de bayou, an' perhaps dey mought git deir watch back ag'in. Den he leave 'em.

It wus den about night; but Pat an' Moike maked up deir minds to go back an' look in de bayou to see w'at dey mought see. W'en dey got dar de sun wus done gone down' but de moon wus away up high an' a shinin'.

Moike look in de bayou an' he see de moon down dar in de water, an' he say: "Dar it is Pat! De water is done washed it off ontel it shine mo' pruttier dan de Jew's watches.

Pat say: "Yes, I sees it a layin' right down dar flat on de bottom; but I's skeared dat de water is so deep dat we caint never git it out."

About dat time a great big bull-frog in de bayou holler out: "Knee-de-deep! Knee-de-deep! Knee-de-deep! Knee-de-deep!"

Pat say: "Moike! W'at's dat?"

Moike tell him dat he dont know; but he think dat dey mus' be some sorter of sperits ag'in, caze he dont see nothin'.

Den dat ole frog, he holler out ag'in, he do: "Knee-de-deep! Knee-de-deep! Knee-de-deep! Knee de-deep!"

Well, Pat den say dat he think dat dey mus' be some sort o' good sperits; caze, whilst he wus a wonderin' how he mought git de watch out an' how deep de water wus, dey wus a tellin' him how deep de water wus an' wus a sayin' dat it wus jes "knee-deep". So Pat tell Moike dat he wus a gwineter wade in an' git his watch—dat he wus! He step in;—an' (Chile!) de fust step he took, landed him in water away over his head! Pat scrambled aroun'; an' churned up an' splashed up de water lak he wus a gwineter kick it all outn de bayou. But atter while he manage to drag hisself out on de banks jes a drippin' wid water.

He look back at de water. It wus all got muddy from his kickin'; an' he couldn' see de moon down dar no mo'. Den he straighten up jes as mad as "brinjah" an' he hollered an' ripped out: "You good-fer-nothin' lowdowned mus'rat polecat kinfolkses; sperits; I hates you! If you'd a he'ped me, so dat I wus got in de watch buisness, I mought 'ave give de preacher sumpin fer to bail you outn de Bad Place [Negroes often used a stronger term here than "Bad Place"] whar you is. But now, you can jes stay dar! Me an' Moike is a gwine into some udder buisness an' I haint a gwineter spen' out one blarsted red cent on you!

Dey built up a fire, an' dried Pat off; an' dey slep dar dat night. Nex mawnin dey say: "All aboard", an' put out up de road a countin' cross-ties. Whilst dey wus a walkin' on de railroad through de swamps, sooner in de mawnin; an' a seein' all kinds o' varmints a runnin off from de sides of de road into de cane-brakes an' woods' Moike subgest to Pat dat dey go into de huntin' business.

Pat say dat dey haint got no guns.

Moike say: Dat dont make no diffunce. Dey can hunt b'ars; an' w'en dey finds a b'ar-den, Pat can jes go in an' git de young b'ars whilst he stay outside wid a big stick an' look atter keepin' de ole b'ars away. Dat way dey can ketch an' sell de young b'ars, make big money an' git rich. Dis all soun' good to Pat; so dey lef' de railroad track right away fer a day's hunt in de woods.

Dey soon foun' some b'ars tracks in de mud an' de slime of de swamps; an' dey follered 'em right spank up to a b'ar's den. So Moike tell

Pat to go right in an' git de young b'ars; an' he'll go an' git a big stick to keep de big ole b'ars off, should dey chance to come.

Pat, he go into de den, he do; an Moike, he start off fer to git de big stick. Moike didn' mo' 'an git good started atter de stick befo' he look up an' see de ole big b'ar a makin' fer de doo' of de den whar Pat wus inside a doin' de ketchin. So he lef' off de stick; an' lakwise runned fer de den right behin' ole Miss B'ar. But ole Miss B'ar beat him to de doo' jes by a liddle bit; an' start inside whar Pat wus. Moike got dar jes in time to ketch her by de tail as she wus a gwine in. Dar dey wus! De b'ar a scratchin an' a growlin' an' a pullin' fer to git in; an' Moike a settin back, a brakin' an' a scotchin' an' a gruntin' fer to keep her out.

Pat wus a ketchin up de young b'ars inside; but he hear setch a racket dat he look up fer to see w'at wus de matter. De doo' wus all stopped up; an' it wus got so dark in dar dat he couldn' scacely see nothin'. So he holler out: "Who's dat da'ken de hole?" Den Moike he blurt out back: "If dis here tail-hol'-break; you'll see who da'ken de hole!"

'Bout dis time, ole Miss B'ar 'gin to sorter feel lak she wus somehow got a big block chained on to her tail; so she sorter turned 'roun' to see 'bout it. Mon! W'en she see w'at it 'twus; she go atter Moike lak a bald-hornet go atter a "Block-head" w'at wus done gone an' punched into her nes' wid a short pole. But Moike wus some runner, he wus; an' in de short chase w'at foller, he managed to piece out de distance 'tween him an' de ole lady; den he clumb a tree.

Ole Miss B'ar wus a stan'in' un'er de tree a growlin'; w'en she chanced to look back down towards de den, an' seed Pat a comin' outn it. Chile! She raised dem bristles o' hern, an' tore off down dar to see about 'im.

W'en Pat look an' see ole Miss B'ar a comin' wid her tongue a lollin' an' her white teef a shinin'; he dont see nothin' 'roun' dar w'at can save 'im 'cep' a great big tall slippry ellum tree w'at haint got no limbs on it ontel you gits up to de tip-top. He wus powerful skeared dat he couldn' climb dat tree; but he know dat he mus' eider go up a slippry white tree or down a slippry red lane.

He ricomember 'bout some o' his folkses over dar in dat country whar he come from a prayin'. So he maked up his mind to pray a liddle befo' he try de tree. So he pray lak dis: "Oh Lawd, h'ep me! An' if you wont he'p me, den dont he'p de b'ar, an' let me git to a good stick, an' I'll show you one of de pruttiest fights dat you's ever seed in yo' life!"

W'en his prayers git over wid' he look an' see de b'ar almos' to 'im, an' he skint up dat tree lak one o' dese here long'tailed blue lizards.

Wid bofe of 'em treed; ole Miss B'ar jes rack back'ards an' for'ards 'tween de two trees, a roarin' an' a clawin' an a growlin'; but Moike an' Pat clinched deir limbs an' sot steady on deir perches. De b'ar kep' dis up ontel along 'bout leben o'clock; w'en a great big rain storm come up.

W'en dis come on' ole Miss B'ar heist her umbersol an' go into her den fer to let de shower pass. Whilst she wus in dar; Moike an Pat blow down offn deir roosts an' fly off towards de railroad.

De rain soon pass off; an' as de Irshmons rattle 'long towards deir good ole railroad; dey vow dat dey haint a gwineter try to make no livin' by huntin'. On de way to de railroad, Pat subgest to Moike dat; whilst dey wus off from de railroad, an' de b'ar an' de rain wus bofe gone; dey mought try deir luck a fishin' a liddle: an' if deir luck wus good at dis, dey mought take it up fer a business. Moike say all right. So dey took off deir rag galluses an' tied 'em togedder fer fishin' lines. Den dey bent some pins fer hooks an' stuck dem on de end of de galluses. Den dey sot down an' throwed de ends of deir lines into de creek fer to fish.

Dey sot dar, an' dey sot dar; but de fish didn seem to git no hankerin to go takin' no snacks aroun' de Irshmons galluses. Dey dont do no bitin'. So Pat an Moike sot deir poles out; an' whilst dey wus a settin dar, bofe of 'em went to sleep. Whilst dey wus a snorin an' a nappin; de water in de creek riz from de rain w'at wus fell, runned out from de banks, an' got all aroun' 'em.

Atter while dey woke up; an' dar dey wus wid water all 'roun' 'em! Moike ax Pat w'at he think dat dey'd better do.

Pat tell him dat he clum dat slippery-ellum tree an' got 'way from de b'ar by prayin'; so he subgest to Moike dat he pray dis time, caze he dont want to be a axin de Lawd for too much all on de same day. Den Moike pray lak dis: "Oh Lawd, I haint never been called on you, now a gwine on forty year; an' if you'll jes he'p me outn deep water, I wont call on you fer might 'nigh forty mo'. I wont be lak my brudder John a dingdongin aroun' atter you night an' mawnin."

W'en de prayers git over wid; dey tries de water. Dey bofe gits a good soun' duckin'; but dey manages to flop deirselves out in de mud on de banks. W'en dey gits out; dey p'ints deir ingines right straight fer de railroad tracks. W'en dey gits dar; dey dont eben stop at de startin' place; dey pulls right off up de tracks a countin' crossties. Dey keeps on a gwine; an' dey dont stop fer no flaggin, an' no red lanterns, an' no tarpeters ontel dey git away up dar in Arkansaw close to whar I's been a wukin.

W'en dey gits up dar in Arkansaw, dey come across some white mens a fightin' game chickens. At de sight of dis, Moike an' Pat pult de bell'cord of deir lightnin' spress an' blowed, an' stopped; caze dey haint never seed nothin lak dis befo' in all deir bawn days.

Dey axes de mens w'at dey wus a doin'; an' dey splains it all to 'em as bes' dey can. Dese here mens den ax de Irshmons w'at dey wus a doin'. Dey makes answer dat dey wus a tryin' to find some sort of business fer to go into. W'en de mens finds out dat Pat an Moike wus done walked all de way from Orleans to Arkansaw a lookin fer a buisness; dey almos' turn in an' pop deirselves wide open a laughin'.

At las' one of de white mens tells 'em dat "De Rollin' stone dont never gether no moss"; an' de way fer to git a business wus jes to quit off trampin' an' to go on to wuk.

Pat an' Moike tell 'em dat dey wus puffeckly willin' fer to go to wuk. Den dey starts an' goes over an' tells 'em dat dey wus done tried chyarpenterin, fahmin, hoss-raisin, watch-gittin, huntin', an' fishin; but some how or nudder nothin dont go noways right. Dey say: It jes look lak ev'ry time dey tetches sumpin, dey gits burnt an' ev'ry time dey opens deir moufs, dey gits deir footses into it.

Dis here white feller wus awful tickled; but he sorter helt in, caze he wus a liddle sorry fer 'em. So he tells 'em dat dey mought try deir hands a raisin game chickens; an' ev'ry time dey gits a good blue-game rooster, he'll fork 'em over a ten-dollar bill fer him.

De Irshmons den ax him how dey mus' do fer to raise 'em.

He tell 'em; dat wus dead easy! De blue-game hens laid de blue-game aigs. Dey mus' jes go an' git dese here blue-game aigs; hatch 'em out, an' raise de blue-game chickens.

De Irshmons say: All right, dat wus puffeckly plain 'nough fer any-body. Den dey walks on off a liddle piece up de railroad to whar it cross over a river. W'en dey gits dar; dey sees one o' dese here bluish colored wild ducks rise outn a big clump of weeds an' fly away.

Pat say: "Moike, jes looky! Dar goes a blue-game hen; an' she dont look lak dat she beslongs to nobody!"

"So it is!" say Moike. "An' I jes bet dat she's got a nes' somewhars down dar in de weeds by de water!"

Pat subgest dat dey go an' look; an' so dey goes. Dey fumbles aroun' in de weeds by de water; an' atter while dey comes 'cross de wild duck's nes'. Dey look at de bluish colored aigs; an' den dey looks at one-nudder. Den Pat grin at Moike an' allow: "Dar dey is! Jes w'at dat feller sayed! Blue-game aigs laid by a blue-game hen!"

So Pat an' Moike took dese here aigs, an' wropped 'em up in some ole rags, an' put em in some ole empty oyster cans w'at dey wus picked up an' built 'em up a fire, an' sot 'em by it to warm 'em up an' hatch 'em out.

Atter dey wus kep up de fire an' turned de cans aroun' fer a mont'; some of de aigs hatched out. W'en dey git 'em hatched out; dey wus jes tickled to death; so dey tuck em fer to show to de feller w'at dey wus a aimin fer to sell 'em to, w'en dey git grown.

W'en dey gits to whar de feller wus, dey hollers out to 'im: "Jes come an' look here, podner; we's got dem fine blue-game chickens all done hatched out, w'at we's a gwineter raise for you!"

De feller make answer: "You is? How does dey look?"

Den Pat say, "Dey's de kind w'at's hatched outn blue-game aigs laid by a blue-game hen! Dey's got setch broad wide mouves; dat w'en dey gits grown an' ketches holt on to anudder rooster; de jar of ten claps o' thunder couldn' shake 'em a loose! An' dey's a gwineter have setch great big wide flat foots, dat de Devil an' all his Imps couldn' up-t(h)rip 'em!"

Well, w'en Pat say all dis; de feller didn' know jes zackly w'at to make of 'im. So he walk over an' peep in de bucket whar de "chickens" wus. Den he jes fell out on de groun', an' kicked, an' helt his sides, an' jes hollered!

De Irshmons didn' know jes zackly w'at wus de matter; but dey knowed somehow dat it wus all wrong. So dey jes dumped out all deir young ducks on de groun'; an' took deir ingines a puffin, wid full steam on, up de railroad, a countin' crossties.

W'en dey got some miles furder on up in Arkansaw; dey come across a railroad Floatin' Gang of Niggers (lak de one I beslong to), w'at wus had one o' dese here big flop(y)eared Dutch fer a Sexion Boss. Dis here big flop(y)eared Dutch Boss wus jes been got killed; an' all de big Head-mens of de railroad wus come out dar fer to look atter gittin his body off home.

He wus met wid a turble accident; an' it all happen on dis wise: De rule wus; fust, Dat de Niggers should dig up dirt an' fill up de flat-chyars. Den dis big flop(y)eared Dutch Railroad sexion Boss wus to go an' git in de Caboose an' wave out his big red hankcher to de ingineer to pull off down to de place whar dey wus a fillin' in wid dirt fer de new railroad. Dis plan wuk all right fer a long time.

But one day, w'en de chyars wus all loaded, an' de Niggers wus all aboard; de big flop(y)eared Dutch Railroad-sexion Boss waved his big red hankcher to de ingineer befo' he git on de Caboose.

De train started off; an' w'en de Caboose come along de big fat flop(y)eared dutch Sexion-boss jumped on. He broke it right smack jam in two, right in de middle! W'en dis tuck place; of co'se, de behind half of de Caboose runned over him an' kilt him!

Pat an' Moike got dar; an' dey halted deir ingines fer to look over de wreck. Dey lissens; an' dey hears all de big Head-mens a talkin. Dey hears 'em say dat dey wus jes bleedged to have some mo' Railroad-sexion Bosses; an' dey wus jes bleedged to have 'em right away. But dey all allows dat dey dont want no mo' of dem kind of Bosses w'at wus so big an' fat dat dey wus a gwineter break de Cabooses in two w'en dey jumps on 'em.

So Pat an' Moike goes up to de big Head-mens of de railroads out dar; an' tells 'em dat dey'd lak powerful well fer to git dat job of being Sexion Bosses. Dey says dat dey's done walked deirselves lean, an' its been so long since dey's eben hearn tell of good grub dat dey dont think deir bodies will ever ricomember no mo' how to git fat.

Dese here mens den ax Pat an' Moike is dey ever done wuked on de railroad.

Dey make answer "no". Dey haint never wuked on no railroad a' 'tall!

Dese here big mens give 'em a liddle grin; den dey tells 'em "Dey's awful sorry", "Dey caint take em on", "De Railroad-sexion Bosses wus got to know ev'rything 'bout railroad tracks."

Pat an' Moike contended wid 'em; dat dey does know ev'ryting 'bout railroad-tracks; an' dey ogify dat dey stands ready fer to prove it, if dey'll jes give 'em a fair chance.

De big Head-mens of de railroads den say: All right! Dey'll give 'em a chance!

Den Pat an Moike (in order to show 'em dat dey knows w'at dey knows) offers dat dey'll walk wid 'em down de railroad tracks all blind-folded up; an' dey'll p'int out to 'em all de crossties w'at's loose, an' ev'rything else w'at's done gone an' went wrong wid de whole buisness!

Dese big Head-mens takes 'em an' tries 'em; an', sho 'nough, de Irshmons p'ints out, blindfolded, ev'rything w'at's done gone on off wrong wid de railroad-tracks. You see dey'd done walked de railroad so much dat dey could tell ev'rything 'bout de bed by jes lettin deir footses tetch it!

Den de Irshmons tells 'em: To take off de blindfolds; an' dey can p'int out to 'em ev'ry place whar de rails haint gauged up right, widout usin' no gauge but deir eyes. Dey does dis; an' de white mens a gwine behin' de Irshmons, a medjurin an' a markin', finds out dat de Irshmons wus always right.

Den dey tells dese here big Head-mens dat dey can tell 'em all 'bout railroad bridges. An'—Mon!—De Irshmons takes 'em an' talks to 'em an' shows 'em 'bout bridges ontel it make deir heads swim!

De big Head-mens den says to de Irshmons right den an' dar dat dey wus hired fer Bosses, an' as many mo' as dey can find an' git lak 'em.

So dis here Missip Nigger, away over dar in Arkansaw, say dat de Irshmons keep on a trampin up from Orleans to Arkansaw an' a knockin' de big flop-(y)eared Dutch outn deir jobs; ontel almos' all de railroad sexion Bosses out dar now is Irshmons."

"Well! Well! Well!" said Nat at the conclusion of Bully's account: "Of co'se perhaps it mought be jes a tale; but yit it dont soun' altogether onreasonable, an' it mought be so."

"Yes, dere's heaps of things in dis here worl', w'at's so, dat some folkses dont believe," responded Bully.—"An' now, Uncle Nat, I mus' be knockin' along towards home so as to pull into de station befo' night, I's mighty much obliged fer yo' fine treat; an' I gives you a thousan' thanks ontel you's better paid."

"You's mo' dan welcome, Bully," came the gracious reply. "An' any time w'en you's a passin', jes stop in an' have some mo' watermillion, an' tell us some mo' 'bout dem Irshmon Bosses out dar in Arkansaw, whar you's been."

"Thank you, I Will!—Good-bye Uncle Nat."

"Good-bye" said the older man; and Bully disappeared down the little country by-way singin the Negro banjo song:*

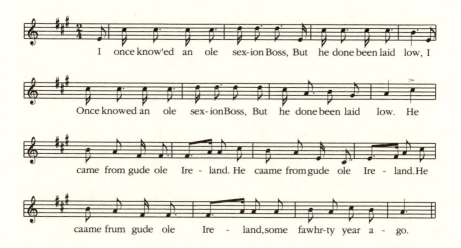

I once know'ed an ole sex-ion Boss, But he done been laid low, I

Once knowed an ole sex-ion Boss, But he done been laid low. He

came from gude ole Ire - land. He caame from gude ole Ire - land. He

caame frum gude ole Ire - land, some fawhr-ty year a - go.

* The other stanzas to this song are found in "Negro Folk Rhymes" by the writer of this treatise. The notes above were so respaced in the time allotted to them in each measure that they fitted all the Rhyme perfectly.

WHY THE PREACHER
DRESSES IN BLACK

(NOTE. In giving this Tradition, the antebellum Negro always uttered the words, ascribed to the various fowls in the different passages, in imitation of each as it is heard in the barn-yard.)

A few years after the close of the great American Civil War, two Negro men, Bunk and Shed Upgar by name, sheltered themselves from the scorching rays of a summer's noonday sun underneath the shade of a giant sycamore tree on the banks of the limpid waters of Duck river. They were very happy as they sat down on the carpet of green for their midday meal surrounded by their three sons. They with the help of these sons, had just finished "layin in" the large field of waving green corn spread out before them. In this corn, they had earned a half interest as a reward for its planting and cultivation.

The two men were brothers (a thing which was not always true of Negro ex-slaves with the same family name); and had only recently come into possession of their freedom through the Proclamation Emancipation. They had moved into their present surroundings from a community nearly fifty miles away.

During the War of the Rebellion, these Negro men had forsaken their former master's plantation by night, and had made their way to the Northern army. Because of this and because of the fact that one of them, much to the knowledge of his former owners, had accompanied details of Northern soldiers on some of their reprisal raids against Bushwackers; [During the Civil War, a few Southern white men—not soldiers—occasionally waylaid and shot Northern soldiers from ambush by night. They were called "Bushwackers"] both men were persona non grata—a class whose lives were in constant jeopardy—in and about their former homes. Thus they had moved here.

When they reached this community a few years prior to the little scene which I am presenting, they were not able to rent land, because they could not bring forward some white man (as was customarily demanded in the South at that time) who would vouch for them as desirable tenants. They had therefore worked at first as day-laborers at a sawmill; but they both longed to till the soil in the open fields where they might listen to the songs of the birds and behold the beauties of Nature as they were wont to do as they went about their day of accustomed toil.

While working at the saw-mill, it fell to the lot of Bunk, the more diplomatic of the two brothers, to haul the lumber from the saw-mill to rebuild a frame mansion on the ashes of one consumed by the flames of Northern army raiders during one of their sorties of retaliation against Bushwackers. Bunk, through his "gift of gab", had made the owners acquaintance while engaged in his hauling; and by continuously holding up this Southern Colonel's own "great and good" qualities before the possessors face, he had gained his good will and had secured an agreement to raise this crop of corn on his plantation. He had taken his brother Shed in as a helper; but the two brothers were in reality partners in this, their new venture. Shed—outspoken, scrupulously truthful, and undiplomatic—could never have been openly acknowledged as partner in the crop without nullifying the whole contract which was only a verbal one.

Though unlettered, these two Freedmen were serious minded. Their desire to rise in the world had choked out of their lives most of the sparkling good nature so characteristic of the race to which they belonged. But on that day, as they looked at their first fine growing crop of corn, all their better nature came to the surface, and the inherited spirit of Negro wit, humor, story, and song asserted itself once more.

When they were seated upon the grass, they spread a few old newspapers (brought along for that purpose), opened two home-made "split" baskets, and laid out their dinners together to be shared in common. There came from those dinner-baskets nearly every common vegetable known to the kitchen-garden besides a fried chicken and a generously large piece of barbecued pork.

After asking the Blessing of God upon their food, they began to eat. Between the two men and their three sons was kept up a constant roll of riddles, and jokes, and witticisms, as they ate. Finally Bunk said: "Brer Shed, w'en you tuck out all dem chicken fixins an' gravy; you put me in de mind o' ole Uncle Adonijah Millsaps—de Nigger preacher, w'at uster live on ole Gran'sir' Upgar's plantation befo' he git sold to Kyernel Millsaps an' make de darkies shout deirselves clean outn deir shoes w'en he open up good."

"How's dat?" asked Shed.

"Well," said Bunk, "you know all us slave-Niggers useter w'ar homespun, sorter dyed up wid red-oak bark an' copperse. Not long ago, ole Uncle Adonijah wus up here fer to 'gin a visit of a couple of weeks or so 'mongst his folks an' relations. He come along de road all fixed up in one o' dese here long black preacher-duster coats, an' one of de liddle Niggers (Tip was his name) up an' ax him how it 'twus dat all de preachers git to eat so much chicken an' w'ar black clo'es w'at look so diffunt from all dem w'at beslong to de tother Niggers.

Ole Uncle Adonijah tell him dat he'll splain all dis to 'im if he'll git somebody to give 'em bofe a invite to a big chicken dinner on de nex

Sunday. Tip is a good liddle chap. I's always felt sorry fer 'im caze he
haint got no folks nowhars. De white folks in slavery days wus done
buyed an' sol' him so much dat he dont have no thought whar he come
from nor whar he's a gwine. So I sorter takes him in almos' lak he wus
one o' my own chilluns.

W'en I hears ole Uncle Adonijah say dis; I tells him dat bofe him an'
Tip was got a invite to come over to de chicken dinner in my cabin on
de nex Sunday. I do dis bofe caze I likes Tip, an' den Sunday is 'bout my
onliest day to have a liddle fun, an' I wanted to hear him tell how de
black clo'es buisness come 'b out 'mongst de preachers.

Well, you never did jes hear sitch a tale as dat 'ar preacher-man tol'!
You see: At de las' big meetin' of de preachers fer to git churches, de
head-Bishop didn' give him none to preach at. Mon! Dis make him sore
as a hosses' shoulder wid de fistalo;' an' I specs he put a whole lots in
de loration w'at didn' never beslong in dar at no time. If you had a
heard him a gittin it off; you never would a thought dat he wus a
preacher hisself! W'en he quit; I sorter thought dat it wus a good thing
dat de Lawd, atter killin "Nias an' Saffire, lef' off his killin of de tothers
w'at stretch de threads in de blanket of trufe ontel dey haint no 'count
no mo'."

"Now, Brer Bunk," interrupted Shed, "since de preacher hisself ruint
de blanket' we'd lak to git you to open it up jes 'nough to let us git a
liddle peep at it. We dont mind laughin' a liddle bit eben if we is a feelin'
sorter bad(?) caze we's a gwineter quit plowin' a while an' set up in de
shade."

"If you haint in no hurry fer to git home," replied Bunk, "an' haint got
no mo' wuk fer to do to-day an' can stay; I dont mind to gun out de
loration to you lak it wus gun out to me."

"Ole man Wuk is dead, an' stay is our names to-day," said Shed.
"Crack away wid it!"

"All right!" said Bunk, as they all settled down to quiet and
exspectation; Dis is de way dat ole Uncle Adonijah, de preacher, git it off.
He tell us dat de preachers useter w'ar homespun jes lak de tother
Niggers; 'cep' dat it wus white an' wusnt dyed up wid red-oak bark an'
copperse. De black clo'es an' de chicken eatin come 'round in a 'culiar
sort o' way.

One time, dere wus a preacher w'at de head-Bishop 'p'int to be de
preacher over three churches. He wus to preach at ev'ry one of 'em once
a mont'. W'en he go to one of his new charges; one of de sistern (ole
Aunt Donie Maggin wus her name), an' her ole man (ole Uncle Cudger
Maggin; ax him home to deir house to dinner.

Dis here preacher wus named Elder Thunderholler; an' he tell 'em dat
he wus a comin', an' bring de Reverunt Sweetsinger along wid him, caze

he wus setch a fine songster an' he'p him so much in Stracted Meetins
[Protracted Meetings or Revivals.]

At de 'p'inted time dey bofe dress up in long white-duster coats, white
cotton britches, white raw-hide shoes, an' white hats. Heistin up deir
umbersols fer to keep off de sun; dey started off fer sister Maggin's house.
(All de preachers in dem days an' time go bucked up lak dat in white.)

Dey walked five or six mile through de hills an' woods; an', at las',
dey come in sight of de house whar dey wus to git dinner. W'en dey wus
about a mile off from de house; de chicken rooster flop hisself upon top
of de fence, stick out his head lak he wus a tryin to push it off, clapped
his wings, an' crowed an' sayed: "I's-got-hasty-news—!"

Den de young rooster flop his wings an' crow back to 'im: "W'at's-de-
hasty-news—?"

Nex de young rooster say: "I-don't-b'lieve-w'at-you-say—!

So de ole rooster say: "Well-dey's-comin-dis-a-way—!"

By dis time all de tother fowls on de place gun to notice dis here
'spute 'tween de two chicken rooster; an' beance so many of 'em wus
already done lost deir heads to de preachers, dey kinder 'gin to look
aroun' to see w'at wus w'ich.

Ole Sis Guinea Hen riz an' flew up into de top of a tree to see fer
herself w'at wus a brewin' in de wind. W'en she git up dar, ole man
Guinea Rooster see her stretch out her neck an' look so skeared dat she
caint say nothin. Den he knowed dat de fowl-destroyers wus a comin' in
her direction. So he dont ax her at 'tall if dey're a comin'; he jes holler:
"How—! many-many-many-many-many-many-many-many? How—! many-
many-many-many-many-many-many-many?"

An' his ole 'oman jes answer him an' say: "Couple-of-'em! Couple-of-
'em! Couple-of-'em! Couple-of-'em!

About dis time, ole man Chicken Rooster flop his wings an' crow out
ag'in: "Preachahs-come-dis-a-way—!

Den ole Sis Puddle Duck, widout stoppin fer to look, ketch holt of
her ole man's han' an' take out in a run fer dey river. As she wobble along
towards a safe place, she holler to her ole man, "Run-run-run-run! Run-
run-run-run-run-run-run-run!"

Ole man Drake shuffle along a tryin' to keep up wid her; an' as he go,
he say in a half whisper: "Keep-still! Keep-still! Keep still! Keep still!"

At las' ole Brer Tucky Gobbler say to his ole 'oman—ole Sis Tucky
Hen—dat he think dat she'd better fly up on de hoss-stable an' see 'bout
all dis here racket w'at de chickens an' guineas an' ducks wus a keepin'
up. He tell her dat de guineas holler an' keep up so much noise 'bout
nothin, dat he caint hardly never put no pennunce in w'at dey say. As fer
ole Sis Puddle Duck, she squall out lak dat 'mos' any time so as to skear
her ole man an' to make him stop wuk an' go a fishin' wid her. Ag'in, as

to ole man Rooster; he sometimes stan' 'roun an' practices up how he wus a gwineter let de tothers know 'bout de preachers a comin'; so, he dont know 'bout botherin long wid w'at he say neider.

Ole Sis Tucky Hen up an' spon to her ole man dat she reckin dat she'll hafter fly up an' look 'bout de preachers, caze she wus promused fer to mind him w'en she wus jumped de broom-stick back'ards wid 'im. She tell him: Sometimes, w'en she wus been a wukin an' a scratchin' fer de chilluns all day, an' wus come home as all tired out as a plow hoss an' as poo' as a louse, an' look an' see him so fat an' lazy dat he caint fly; she almos' wush dat de preachers would come an' git him!

About dis time, ole man Rooster sorter break into de Tucky-fuss by crowin out ag'in: "Here-de-preachers-come—!"

Ole Brer Tucky Gobbler wus sorter mad 'bout w'at his ole 'oman say; so he play biggity, an' holler out: "Doubtful-doubtful-doubtful-doubtful!"

"Yes—!"

"Doubtful-doubtful-doubtful-doubtful!"

But by dis time; all de hens, an' de pullets, an' de fryers, an de young rooster wus a runnin towards de woods an' a hollerin back: "Watch! Watch! Watch! Watch! Watch-out—! Watch! Watch! Watch! Watch! "Watch-out—!"

W'en ole Sis Tucky Hen see all dis here flusteration a gwine on; she 'gin to feel sorter *jubous [*Jubous = doubtful—A corruption of the English word "dubious"] 'bout ev'rything a being, all right. So she riz an' flew to de top of de stable. Mon! Dem feet of hern didn' mo' an' tetch de top befo' she flop dem wings faster dan a hummin' bird an' go a sailin' to de woods. She lit a mile off from dat 'ar place in less dan no time. W'en she hit de groun', she hit it a runnin' an' she holler out as she move on:

"Fly-fly-fly-fly-fly-fly-fly-fly!"
"Fly-fly-fly-fly-fly-fly-fly-fly!"

W'en ole Sis Tucky Hen's chiluns see her a gwine; dey dont neider ax no questions nor make no scatterin' 'marks. Dey jes tells deir feet an' wings to tote de body away.

Ole Brer Tucky Gobbler dont yit see nobody a comin'; but he say to hisself dat he mought git lonesome if he come to happen to have de preachers fer comp'ny all by hisself. W'en dis mind strike him; it hit him so hard dat he cleared hisself fer de woods mo' faster dan a race hoss. W'en he git out dar; Sis Tucky Hen sorter look him over, an' say dat she think dat he look better wid half of de fat runned offn him anyhows.

Ole man Rooster look aroun' an' he see ev'rybody gone but him. Uh-uh, Honey!—He drapped offen dat fence lak somebody wus busted him up in de head wid a rock; an' w'en dem feet of hisn tetched de ground, dey kicked him mo' harder towards dem woods dan dey kicked 'im later on towards Chicken Heaben, as he los' his head on de road to de pot.

Ole Aunt Donie hear all de rattle an' de cackle of de chickens, ducks, guineas, an' tuckys; an' she look out an' see de preacher-comp'ny a comin'. She wus got a boy by de name of Zack w'at didn' have all in de head dat you mought be a lookin' fer. So she say to him: "Now, Zackie! You mus' jes set 'roun' an' dont say nothin w'en de preachers gits here. I dont want 'em to know dat you dont know nothin'; maybe go off an' tell folks dat you haint got no sense. Preachers is mighty smart folks. Dey knows de onknowable, an' says de onsayable. If you jes opens yo' mouf; dey finds out right off, all dat you haint."

Zack answer: "Mammy; I haint a gwineter say nothin! I's a gwineter look lak I's skeard dat I mought eben git de notion to say sumpin."

"Well now," Aunt Donie say to herself, "I's got dat much all fixed up." Den she holler form de kitchen to de ole man in de tother room: "Cudger! Oh—, Cudger! Run out an keep de dog offn Parson Thunderholler an' Elder Sweetsinger. Dey's almos' up to de front yard gate; an' dat ole dog o' ourn is jes a barkin' at 'em lak he wus done gone de tother half-crazy. Run quick, caze he mought snap one of 'em".

De ole man riz up sorter spry-lak, an' runned outn de doo'; an' dar wus de dog jes a pitchin' an' a r'arin' an' a t'arin'. He bark out:

"Go-back! Go-back! Preach-preach-preach-preacher, go back!"
"Go-back! Go-back! Preach-preach-preach-preacher, go back!"

As de ole man runned out to keep off de dog; his boy, Zack, runned out 'hind' him. Ole Uncle Cudger squalled out to de dog: "You, Rattler! You ole Scounter! Git back un'er dat house!" Wid dat, he whizzed a whole passel of rocks at 'im, an' he scooted back un'er de floo' of de cabin. He runned away up un'er dar nex' to de chimbly as to git outn de way of de chunks an de clods an' de rocks; but he sot up un'er dar, wid his bristles all a stan'in' on ends, an' he jes keep on a coughin' up: "Go-back! Go-back! Preach-preach-preach-preacher, go back!"

Whilst de ole man wus a chunkin' an' a rockin' de dog un'er de house; Zack kep' on a gwine ontel he git clean down to de gate whar de preachers wus. He wus done hearn tell of 'em so much; dat he want to git a look at 'em.

W'en he git down dar, an' meet de preachers; dey say to 'im: "Howdy-doo! My liddle Brudder!"

Zack, he dont say nothin'.

Den de preachers sayed to 'im: "Honey! You mus' be skeard un us! We's holy men, shod wid de pripiration of de Gospel; an' kivered up wid de gyarments of Righteousness.—W'at's yo' name?"

To all dis; Zack dont answer nothin'.

De preachers, dey keep on a axin questions; an' Zack, he keep on a sayin' nothin'. At las' dey gits sorter mad, an' dey sayes: "Boy! You sho is a fool!"

Mon! W'en de preachers say dis, Zack tuck out fer de house lak sumpin wus atter him; an' he didn' fetch up ontel he landed in de kitchen whar his mammy wus. He put in his pearunce dar just a puffin' an' a blowin'; an' his mammy say to 'im: "Zackie—Honey—, Did dat ole lazy daddy of yourn hafter go an' make you run an' keep de dog offn de preachers atter I wus done told him to do it? I didn' want you a keepin' off no dog from no parsons; caze I knowed dat dey would be a talkin' to you, an' a axin you questions, an' a makin' you talk; an' den dey'd find out dat you didn' know nothin'."

"Mammy!" says Zack, says he, "I haint never hearn tell o' no folks smart lak dem preachers! I haint runned no dog an' I haint said no nothin'. I's done done w'at you tol' me to do; but dat didn' do no good, caze dey jes look at me an' say dat I wus a fool!"

"Well, well, well!" says Aunt Donie, says she, "Dat sho is awful cu'ious! Dere haint no tellin' w'at all de preachers dont know!—Now Honey! You stay out here in de kitchen. I's a gwine in fer to talk a liddle while wid de parsons befo' I goes to git de dinner all ready. I's done got all de dinner cooked 'cep' de chicken. Whilst I's gone; I wants you to ketch three big fryin' chickens—two fer de parsons an' one fer us—scald 'em, pick 'em, an' cut 'em up. Den you come an' call me; an' I'll come an' fry 'em befo' you can say chick-a-needle. Den we'll set de table wid dat big red tablecloth an' eat our big dinner. Whilst we's a eatin', I wants you to keep all de flies fanned off wid dis here tucky-wing; but dont you say nothin', an' atter de preachers gits through an' leaves de table, mammy'll let you eat ontel you caint eat no mo'."

W'en de ole 'oman git through a handin' out to Zack w'at she want him to do; she give him a buiscuit, an' go off to talk wid de preachers.

W'en she git in dar; dey shakes hands wid her an' says: "Howdy-doo, ma Sister!" an' she make answer: "Jes sorter tolerbul, thank you!" Den she lay in a whole heaps o' 'scuses to 'em 'bout ev'rything she wus got 'cep' her ole man an' de boy. But de preachers answer an' tell her: "Dat dont make no diffunce. Heaps of people would live on de backsides of nowhars to git setch good eatins as dey'd hearn tell wus laid out at de Magginses."

Den Aunt Donie allow: "Brer Thunderholler, I knows dat yo' church mus a been a jollywhopper down dar whar you come from befo you wus come out here in de sticks fer to preach over an' take charge of our liddle waitin' congergation."

Brer Thunderholler make answer: "Yes ma Sister; four big churches instid o' three liddle ones lak I's got now. De Bishup wus got to shift us 'round a liddle; caze it wont never do fer one hoss to graze over de bigges' an' bes' paster all de time. You see; he mought git so fat dat he mought kick up on de wrong place.—But de fines' of dem four churches was Brown's Corner!"

Den Aunt Donie ax 'im: "Brer Thunderholler, wont you please jess tell us a liddle sumpin' 'bout dat 'ar Brown's Corner? We's always powerful glad to hear 'bout big things an' dem 'ar tony places."

"Well, ma Sister," say Brer Thunderholler, "Down dar, de folks is got mo' rusty dollars dan Chyarter is got oats! W'en dey takes up a collection; de treasure caint hardly hold it widout poppin' wide open, an' de treasurer-holder caint hardly tote it off. W'en dey sings; you mought almos' think dat Gable wus come down wid his singin band of Angels, a singin de song of Moses an' de Lam'. W'en de church-flock go a picknickin'; dere's so much barbecue lef' over, dey caint hardly haul it all off wid deir double teams of oxes. An' w'en dey shouts—Well, dey jes shouts lak dey wus a gwineter t'ar deirselves all to pieces!"

W'en Elder Thunderholler say all dis, dey all sot dar sorter still fer a while; Den ole Uncle Cudger Maggin up an' say: "Well, folkses; Sometimes I's up, an' sometimes I's down, Sometimes I's almos' flat on de groun'. But I's a gwineter ax de good Lawd; if he dont never let me die an' git to Glory Land; dat he'll jes let me fetch up an' live somewhars abouts in de neighborhoods of Brown's Cornder".

Elder Sweetsinger wus one o' dese here kind o' parsons w'at dont talk much; He take out all o' hisn a linin' off an' a singin' through his nose lak de white folkses. Dat wus de reason dat he wusnt got no church. But he manage to go 'roun' an' git his feed an' keep by singin'. But w'en he hear how Elder Thunderholler's talk stir up ole Brer Cudger; he want to take some part, so dat he can go away an' brag to de tother preachers 'bout his rousement powers w'en he pay visit to folks. So he up an' put in : "Yes, yes; Brudder an' Sister Maggin; Elder Thunderholler had de bes' patients' an' de mos' waitin'es' congregation at Brown's Corner dat I mos' ever did see! Dey never wus ready to quit off wid one sermon. 'Sides dat; dey always wanted two or three big mens lak me to lay up de gaps, atter de tother big Elders git through wid deir splavercations.

I haint never seed nobody never git tired of no preachin' out dar but once. Dat wus one Sunday w'en ole man Elder Bluedarter preach. Brer Bluedarter wus one of dese here preachers w'at dont want nobody a gittin up an' a preachin' atter him; caze he wus skeard dat dey mought outpreach him, an' make de members shout mo' louder dan him. So w'en he start to preach' he try to preach all day.

On dis here Suday w'at I's a talkin' 'bout now; he preach on de Prophets. Well—! He 'gin to preach; an' he preached an' he preached! He preach on Moses an' tell all 'bout him. He tell 'bout de Hebrew an'

Shebrew chilluns. He preach over Abraham, Isacc, Jacob, an' all de balunce of 'em; an' den he go back to tetch on 'em ag'in. Den he hitch up Malchiar; an' he look lak he never wus a gwineter turn him a loose from de Gospel plow. Of co'se, w'en he git to de end of de row, all de members of de church 'spected him to onhitch his hosses an' go to supper. But instid o' doin' dis; he jes pulled his hoss 'roun—'Haw!'—an' looked down anudder weedy middle an' sayed: "But Brudderin, w'at place is we a gwineter give to Matthew, Mark, Luke an' John?"

W'en he look lak he wus 'bout to start to bust out de weeds from dese here middles; ole Brer Ahaz Williams riz'. He riz an' walked outn de doo'. As he wus a gwine out; he hollered back sorter half-vexed-lak: "You can jes give dem my place!" Dis make all de members giggle so much dat it look lak it mought break ev'rything up; so he helt up an' stopped."

W'en de Reverunt Sweetsinger git through, dey all bust out in a great big laugh. Den Elder Thunderholler put in fer good measure: "Yes! Yes! Yes! Dem folks at Brown's Corner is mighty fine folks. Dont no grass grow on de tops of deir heads neider. De nex' time dat de deacons see me, atter dat Bluedarter-preacher lef'; dey tells me dat dey hopes dat I wont chance to git holt of no mo' preachers w'at'll git up dar an' talk 'bout de Prophet Joner a swallerin de whale."

About dis time; ole man Cudger's son Zack come a runnin' into de room 'bout halfway outn bref. His mammy say: "Zackie, Honey, I tol' you to call Mammy. You shouldn' oughter come an' break in w'en de Elders is a talkin'." Den she say to de preachers: "You mus' all please scuse Zackie! He's been a runnin' so hard to ketch de chickens fer dinner dat he sorter fergit to pick up his manners."

"No, no, no!" Zack say. "No, no, no, no! Mammy, I haint been a runnin' no chickens. De chickens, an' de ducks, an' de guineas, an' de tuckys, an' de dog is all done gone an' got lost; an' I caint find 'em nowhars."

Ole Aunt Donie look sorter sorrowful an' say: "Well, dat jes beats all! It look lak dat ev'rybody an' ev'rything knows de preachers. I wonders whedder or not dat tale wus true w'at ole Aunt Jane, de Fortune-teller, telled me. I wus jes a liddle gal w'en she telled me all dat 'bout preachers an' chickens. I jes laughed an' didn' pay it no mind w'en she tol' it to me.— Elders; I'll jes hafter give you de bes' dat I's got in my hand; an' you'll hafter come back ag'in to eat offn my shelf lak I wants you to. I wus aimed to have fried chicken; but somehow dey's all strayed off to nowhars."

De preachers sorter console her an' say: "Sister, dont do no worry! We's glad to be here if we dont git a mouf-full."

Den ole Aunt Donie go out an' put up w'at she wus got cooked, an' call 'em in to dinner. Dey sot down to de table an' axed de Blessin'. De table wus jes strewed wid gyardin truck. Dey had good ole greasy beans, an' collards, an' cabbitch, an' all dem good things. Den dey passed aroun' de 'simmon beer an' reasin puddin wid reasins all strewed in 'mongst it.

W'en Aunt Donie go to help de plates; she ax de preachers w'at dey'll have, an' dey bofe makes answer "Reasin puddin". So she rolled 'em off almos' a plateful apiece. Den she axed 'em w'at mo' dey'll have; an' dey makes answer "Nothin mo' fer de present, Mam. Thank you."

Dey gobbled down de Reasin puddin, an' passed back deir plates ag'in. Aunt Donie ax 'em w'at dey'll have; an' dey makes answer ag'in, "Reasin puddin".

Den Aunt Donie say: "Dese here tother things here is mighty good. Wont you take some o' dem. But dey answer her an' say: "Sister Donie; Dat 'ar Reasin puddin is plenty good 'nough fer us!" So Aunt Donie jes raked deir plates off full o' Reasin puddin dis time, an' pass it over to 'em.

Now w'en dese here preachers see all dat good Reasin pudding hot an' smokin on deir plates; dey wus got some tother business befo' 'em, an' dey haint got not time to waste away a talkin'. So dey says to Aunt Donie' so as to keep de conbersation a gwine; "Sister Donie, s'pose you turn in an' tell us w'at dat 'ar Fortune-teller 'oman wus told you 'bout de preachers an' de chickens. Some of dem 'ar folks w'at deals wid chyards an' coffee grounds an' de Devil, n' tells Fortunes, mos' natchully in ginerally knows 'bout dis here world. You see dey wus done give up Heaben; an' so dey gits a big holt on de earth.

Aunt Donie answer an' say: "Well, dis here 'oman say dat she wus de sebunth daughter of de sebunth son, born on de sebunth day of the sebunth month of de sebunth year atter her mammy an' daddy wus got hitched jined an' married. So she say dat she could see ghoses an' hants an' setch things in de broad open daytime. She lakwise know all dat de animuls say to one-nudder; an' she could look all de way over into nex' year jes lak she see back into yistiday.

She tell de loration 'bout chickens an' preachers lak dis:

'Way back yonder, one time, de sperits an' ghoses of dead folkses w'at wus bad got tuck wid a notion dat dey want to come back from de Bad Place to see how ev'rything wus a gittin along in de worl'. (Of co'se you knows; Good folkses w'at goes to Heaben dont want to come back.)

Dese here sinful ghoses want to come back wid deir heads on so dat dey'll look natuchful. De Keeper of de Ghoses say dat he dont know 'bout dat.

Den de sinful ghoses tell de Keeper dat; if he'll allow 'em to go back; dey'll set a good zample fer to git a heaps mo' folkses to come on down to de Bad Place w'en dey dies. 'Sides all dis; dey'll skear a heaps mo' of 'em to death an' bring 'em on back down dar wid 'em.

De Keeper of de Ghoses den go an' tell de Bad Man w'at de ghoses say; an' ax him w'at to do 'bout it.

De Bad Man, he sot down an' cut chyards, he did; an' he look at dem. Den he turned a cup wid coffee grounds in a saucer an' he look to see which a way de grounds lay. Den he cross de pa'ms of his hands wid a silver dime; an' he look at de lines outn de corner of one eye to see in w'at direction dey shimmer. Den he take up his iron-handled shovel; an' he stir up, de coals an' embers to see w'at way de sparks fly.

De Devil do all dis a tryin to tell his own fortune, so as to know w'at to do 'bout lettin 'de ghoses go back to de worl'. But, Chile, He mought as well a been trying to git a platefull of buzzard grease offn a buzzard! Of co'se, de Bad Man is a big Conjer an' Fortune-teller. He hafter be all dis to know 'nough to lead folks astray; but dere never wus no Conjers an' Fortune-tellers w'at could tell deir own fortunes. He set down an' he think on de signs; an' den he think some mo'; but all about dat he wus a thinkin' wus hindpart befo'. De chyards an' coffee-grounds an' sparks an' embers all git so mixed up togedder dat he wus befuzzled an' fell sorter jubous. At las' he tell de Keeper of de Ghoses dat he mought choose a hant-walkin night, an' let de Ghoses go out wid deir heads on; but he must keep de most of 'em back down dar at home ontel he see how marters wuk.

Bymeby one night, atter de sun wus done gone down, an' tuck a liddle nap; he git up along towards midnight, an' start back 'round behin' de hills to de place whar he most in ginerally riz de nex' mawnin. On his way to de risin-place, he make up his mind to light his lamp fer a liddle while so as to snuff de wick an' git it ready to burn bright de nex' day.

He lit his lamp down behin' de hills; but whilst he wus a gittin de wick snuffed, some of de bright light shined up over de hills through de pitch dark almos' up to de top of de sky. De milky night clouds haint never had no light on 'em befo' dat time. De warm light speilt de white milk clouds an' turned 'em all into blue-john, red, yaller, spotted, an' all dem tother sorts of colors; an' de sky wus all streaked up wid 'em.

Some of de folkses an' wild varmints, w'at wus a prowlin' aroun' late, see it; an' dey runned home an' waked up all de tothers fer to see de sights. Dey looks at de light an' de clouds; an' ev'rything look so skeary dat dey all draw up an' git taken wid de cold shivers. All of 'em sot aroun' still lak death; an' none of 'em dont make no sound 'cep' de dogs. Dese here dogs jes tuck deir tails 'tween deir hind leggs; an' dey howls once in a while lak dey wus a livin' down in a lonesome valley on Jedgment Day.

W'en de Bad Man's Keeper of de Ghoses see all dis, he think dat it wus a good time fer to let out a few of de sperits an' let 'em come back to dis here worl'. So he turn out some of 'em wid deir heads on; an' tell 'em dat dey'd better not come back dar widout skearin' sumpin to death an' bringin' it along wid 'em. He declar dere wusnt no scuse for not doin' dis w'en ev'rything wus already skeared half to death.

So de ghoses sot out on deir journey, an' come out on de face of de earth. W'en dey gits out, dey dances a reel to de moanin chunes whistled by de friskin' winds through de wavin tree-tops. Bymeby, dey all quits off deir frolickin an' dancin'; an' goes fer to skear some folkses to death, so as to take 'em back down to de Bad Man lak dey wus promused.

Dey goes to de folkses houses, an' de doo's all swing wide open' an' dey walks right in.

In dem days, de folkses wus all Niggers, an' wus all black. Some of de waked-up Niggers wus done gone on back to bed, an' wus a lyin' dar awake. De tothers wus still a settin up, a peepin' through de cracks in de side of deir house at de cu'ious lookin sky, a lissenin to de dogs a howlin an' de wind a whislin de lonesome reel to which de ghoses wus a dancin'.

W'en de doo's fly open an' de ghoses walk in; de Niggers, w'at wus in de bed, jes kiver up deir heads, to make mighty sho, to miss "Ole Ned".— But dem 'ar "smartie" Niggers, w'at wus a settin up an' a lookin' an' a tryin' to know ev'rything!—Whar wus dey?—Well, dar dey wus!

Dey look at de ghoses an' git mo paler an' mo' skeader. Den dey tries to sing, lak you's hearn some Niggers do now-a-days, w'en days a gwine along a liddle narrow foot-path in a dark woods at night, an' a tryin to keep deir courage up. But dese here "smartie", biggitty Niggers' tongues sorter fall back an' git hung in deir th'oats w'en dey manages to git deir moufs open. Deir song sound lak de talk o' folks w'at's so low sick dat dey wus done got tuck wid de death-rattles. De singin' sound so funny dat it make all de ghoses grin an' show deir milk-white teef. Den des here pale skeared Niggers hush deir fuss an' git mo' paler an' mo skearder! De cold sweats rund down deir backbones an' drapped offn 'em!

Bymeby de Niggers all tuck a notion dat dey mought sorter talk off deir skeardness wid de ghoses. So one of 'em sorter mumble off to de hants, lak he wus got sumpin all hung up in his wind-pipe! "How is times in yon'ers worl'? How is times in yon'ers worl'?"

De ghoses dont answer nothin'; but dey hits down deir long bony scorched-up hands a rattlin' on de chairs an' tables an' things; an' ev'rything deir hands git down on gits great big holes burnt down through 'em.

W'en dis hittin' an' burnin' tuck place; it skear all dem smartie Niggers so bad, w'at wus a settin' up, dat dey turned plum white. De hairs on deir heads lakwise git skeard white an' straight an' stiff. Yit an' still; dese here white Niggers didn' die so dat de ghoses could git 'em an' take 'em back down wid 'em to de Bad Man.

Some says dat dese here skeard Niggers wus a beginnin' of white folks; but some say dey wus a beggin of dese here albiners wid gray eyes w'at dance aroun' lak dey wus a gwineter pop outn deir head. How-some-ever dis may be; all dese here Niggers wus lef' skeard to death, an' sick, an' no 'count.

W'en de ghoses leave an' git good gone; de Niggers in de bed onkiver deir heads an' set up. Dey look at de white skeard sick Niggers; an' makes up deir minds day maybe dey should oughter git outn bed an' loan a liddle helpin hand to 'em. So dey gits up.

Dey thinks maybe dat dey'd better fust make a liddle chicken soup fer 'em. But w'en dey goes out to ketch de chickens fer soup, dey takes de white Niggers along wid 'em. Dye takes 'em 'long caze dey thinks a liddle fresh air wont de 'em no harm; an' lakwise to so fix it up dat if de ghoses should happen to start back, dey could run off an' leave 'em to carry on a confab wid 'em whilst dey once mo' runnd to git in bed an' kiver up de head.

Well, dey comes outn de house jes befo' day; an' dey didn' see no nothin of de ghoses. So dey walks out towards de tree whar de chickens wus a roostin'. As dey walk towards de trees, de ole rooster tuck his head out from un'er his wing an' see 'em a comin'. Den he crow out: "Here-some-whitefolks-come—!"

Now all dese here chickens wus black; an' dey haint never seed nothin but black folks in all deir bawn days. W'en dey seed dese white Niggers a comin'; some o' dese black chickens jes stuck deir heads un'er deir wings; an' dey dont git no mo' skeard an' haint no mo' bothered. Dem an' deir chilluns jes keep on a bein' black. But dere wus some "smartie" black chickens w'at keep on a lookin at de white Niggers ontel dey gits skeard white. Some o' dese here white skeard chickens git tuck wid de palsy an' fall offn de roost on to de ground. De Niggers jes picked dem up to use fer soup. Some of de tother skeard white chickens clinched deir toe-nails so deep in de limbs of de trees day dey wus jes bleedged to stay dar whar dey wus. So dese an' deir chilluns keep on a livin' white. But lots of dese here white chickens flewed all up into de speilt milk clouds an' git deir fedders all colored up wid de red an' yaller an' blue water an' so on. From dese chickens; all de chickens of so many colors, dat you sees, wus come. Lakwise, ever since dat time; chickens wus been a crowin' always jes befo' day, caze dey wus thinkin 'bout how dey wus hearn tell how dey wus got all deir prutty colors.

Well; "to cut off a long dog's tail short"; w'en daylight begin to break de Niggers wus a makin' soup fer de sick no 'count Albiners, an' de ghoses wus back down to deir house a tryin to git back in.

De Bad Man sorter crack de doo' a liddle, an' look out at 'em. He see dat de ghoses haint skeard nobody to death; an' brung 'em back wid 'em. So he tell 'em dat dey caint never come back in' caze dey wus fell through wid w'at dey un'ertuck to do. He lakwise tell 'em dat he wus a gwineter let his tother ghoses go out an' come back n from time to tome, jes so as to make 'em wush dat dey had a home to go to somewhars.

But later on, w'en de Bad Man turn out his tother ghoses; he make 'em leave deir heads at home. Dat way, he know 'em from de tothers; an' he know who to let back in, w'en dey comes a knockin' on de doo'. Dat's de reason some ghoses, w'at you sees, is got heads an' some haint got none.

Atter dis, as time go on, de whitefolks gits well;but as dey thinks 'bout de ghoses an' de Bad Man, dey wants to make shore not to never go down dar whar dey wus come from. So all dese white folks git to be preachers. But dese here white preachers e't up so many of de chickens whilst dey wus a gittin' well, dat de chickens take to de woods w'en-so-ever dey see one of 'em a comin'. De chickens lakwise tell all de tother kinds of fowl; an' so, dey runs an' hides too w'en dey sees de preachers a comin'.

De black Niggers sorter lak de preachers an' de preachin'; but dey dont want all dey's got to run off an' leave 'em. So dey tells de white Niggers wid deir white hair dat dey mus' move off to deirselves.

Now, w'en de white Niggers wus gone; de black ones say dat dey dont see no tother way but dat dey mus' have some preachin' to keep 'em in de good way. So dey sorter comes togedder, each to each; an' dey p'ints some 'mongst 'em to preach.

Den; so as to make 'em look a liddle lak de white preachers, an' so as to put 'em in de mind of ole times; dey tells dese here black preachers dey mus' wear white clo'es (lak dem w'at you's a wearin'; Brer Thunderholler an' Brer Sweetsinger.) "I's almos' clean fergit it offn my mind;" says ole Sister Maggin, says she; "how de fowls l'arnt dat dese black mens, all fixed up in white, wus preachers; but, I thinks, dey says dat de house dog foun' it an' tol' 'em. So dey sayes, w'en de black preachers is a comin', all fixed up in white, de chicken rooster always flies upon de fence an' crows twice. Fust he crows out: "I's-got-hasty-news—!" Den, atter dis, he crows off: "Preachers-w'arin-white-shoes—!" Dey sayes as soon as de rooster do dis; all de fowls run an' hide, makin' deir scatterin' 'marks as dey goes. W'en dey all gits away off dar in de woods; de guinea hen flies up in de top of a big tree, an' watches fer de preachers to leave. De chicken rooster axes her once in a while from de groun' below if de preachers is gone. W'ensoever she tell 'im dat de preachers wus gone; he crow it out to de tother fowls, den dey all goes back home".

—Well, ole Uncle Adonijah, de preacher w'at wus at my house say: W'en ole Sister Donie Maggin reached dis p'int in her loration; dey all heared a rooster crow away off somewhars about a mile in de thickets of de woods. Dey wus all through wid deir eatin an' pult back deir chairs; an' sot dar a lissenin to de fowls a hollerin away off over in de woods.

Terreckly, de ole chicken rooster crow out: "Is-de-preachahs gone—?" an' ole guinea hen make answer from de top of de tree: "Not-yit! Not-yit! Not-yit! Not-yit!"

Den Brer Thunderholler an' Brer Sweetsinger say: "Look here, Brer an' Sister Maggin, we caint neider talk no un'erstan' no fowl langridge; but

dem critters sho do son' lak dat one of 'em ax "Is de preachers gone?" an'
de tother one soun' lak it go on to answer: "Not yit!"

"Well"; says ole Sister Maggin, says she: "my chickens an' things is all
pets, an' it look mighty sildom [Sildom = queer] how dey wus done gone
an' put in deir dispearunce in de woods."

Dey scuss it up an' dey scuss it down. At las' Brer Thunderholler tell
'em dat de bes' way fer to jedge 'bout a puddin wus to eat a big hunk of
it; so he guess dat de bes' way fer to learn 'bout de fowls wus to try 'em.
Den he sorter put in wid a flatterin' tongue: Dere wusnt nobody from
nowhars w'at wouldn' feel lak he wus a roostin on high an' a eatin apple
pie, if he could jes git to come twice to de Magginses' fer dinner. So he
say, if dere wusnt no objection, he'd put on black clo'es, an' come back
ag'in fer dinner on de next Sunday atter preachin. Dey all 'gree to dis.

Atter dis, de preachers tell 'em all good-bye 'an start off fer home. As
dey put in deir dispearunce over de hill, ole Sis Guinea Hen wus a
watchin 'em from de top of a tree; an' she call off to de fowls: "Preachahs-
gone! Preachahs-gone! Preachahs-gone!"—an' all de fowls come outn deir
places of hidin' in de woods an' come on home.

On de nex' Sunday, de preachers come back to de Magginses' ag'in
fer dinner. Dis time dey wus all rigged out in black clo'es instid o' white.

W'en dey gits to de gate dey hollers: "Hello!" Ole Rattler, de dog, wus
a lyin out in de front yard a dozin in de shade of a big oak tree. He wake
up lak he think dat dere wus some pressin' business on hand. But w'en he
see somebody all fixed up in black clo'es; he jes stretched out an' went on
back to sleep. De chickens an dem tother fowls sorter stretch up deir
necks, an' look at 'em; but, Law Honey! dere wusnt no cacklin', an' no
gobblin, an' no runnin off, an' no nothin else 'mongst 'em. W'en dey sees
somebody a comin' in all diked up in black; dey jes go on a scratchin', an'
a singin' an' a bug-huntin'.

De preachers keep on a hollerin' "Hello!" ontel bymeby ole Uncle
Cudger Maggin come a mozyin outn de house lak he wus jes sorter a gittin
over wid a bed spell of rheumaties atter a col' rainy day. W'en de preachers
sees him dey says: "Looky here Brer Maggin, you dont come out to keep
no dog off lak you was overly anxious to put our names in de pot."

Ole Brer Maggin, he up an' 'spon': "Oh yes, Elders, we's done got yo'
names writ down in de coffee pot; an' we's a gwineter hash de skillet an'
lid, an' put de big ubben inside of de liddle one fer one. I wus jes a settin
back in dar a watchin dat dog an' de fowls; how dere haint no barkin', an'
no cacklin, an' no nothin a gwine on lak dere wus w'en you all come over
fer dinner all bucked up in white."

Well, dey went on up to de house—de ole man an' de preachers. De
ole 'oman an' Zack called up de fowls; an' killed a whole passel of 'em,
an' spread a great big feast fer de preachers. Dey had fried chicken, dey

had stewed chicken, dey had b'iled chicken, dey had stuffed chicken. Dey all e't ontel dey stuffed deirselves clean through. Dey laughed an' cracked jokes 'bout how dey wus done gone an' folled de dog, de chickens an' all de balunce of 'em; by bein' all dressed up in black clo'es.

De dog wus a settin on de floo' 'round de table, a lissenin to it all. At fust he didn' have no good feelin' 'bout it; but atter dinner he git so much chicken, an' pie, an' hog jowl, an' tunnup greens, an' de lak to eat w'at wus de preachers leavins dat he feel lak dat he wouldn care if de preachers would come to see 'em ev'ry day.

So de dog, he go out an' splain to ole chicken rooster w'at wus done gone an' happen. He tell 'im dat dem preachers wus monstus fine folks; caze w'en you stays aroun' 'em dey feeds you fat! He say to 'im dat he lakwise hear his Marse an' Miss Maggin say dat all dem w'at walks in de ways of preachers gits de fat of de lamb whilst dey lives an' never does die. Instid o' diein dey goes to a Good Place whar dey jes keeps on a livin always.

Ole Brer Rooster study over all dis w'at ole Brer Dog was told 'im; an' he make up his mind to call all de fowls togedder to 'vide up wid 'em all he know. He jump up on de fence an' flop his wings fer to git deir notice. Den he crow off: "All-you-fowls-run-here—!" an' all de fowls come jes a scootin' to 'im.

W'en dey all gits crowded 'round' him, he open up. He tell 'em dat de two preachers wus done been dar, an' e't up four or five of 'em!—Den dey all gits skeared to death an' starts to run. But de rooster call on 'em not to run; caze de preachers wus done gone, an' he wus jes called 'em to tell 'em 'bout it.

He ax 'em all to set down an' sing a song wid 'em so dat he can fust preach de funerls of de dead chickens' an' enjorin of de meetin git 'em to un'erstan' all 'bout de preachers. Dey all sot down.

Ole Brer Rooster sorter clear his th'oat to give out de hymn chune. He 'gin to line her off:

"An is I bo'n to die, to lay his body down."

But de chickens all instid o' 'ginnin' de singin, all bust out in a great big cry! Dey blubbered an' boohooed back to 'im:

"No! We's a gwineter take dese wings of ourn,
An' fly to worl's onknown!"

Ole Brer Rooster see dat de Funerl idee was a gwineter break up de meetin; an' so he tell 'em dat he think dat dey'd all should oughter better put off de Funerls ontel nex' winter, w'en de craps wus all put in, an' de neighbors could git time to come over an' shout enjorin de preachin. Dey all 'gree to dis.

Den de ole rooster tell 'em dat he want to splain jes a liddle to 'em how de preachers wus managed to git in dar an' eat ev'rybody up widout nobody knowin' it. He say to 'em (from w'at Brer Dog say); de preachers wus all done gone an' changed deir natchur. It now 'pear dat dey haint bad at 'tall; w'en you wus managed to git a look inside of 'em. Dey wus awful good!

He sing off dat dey all ricomember dat de preachers useter have ev'rybody killed fer to make soup outn 'em; but now he wus l'arnt from Brer Dog: All dem w'at walks in de ways of preachers gits to a Good Place whar dey never dies! He den splain to dem dat it wus puffeckly clear dat de onliest way to "walk in de ways of preachers" wus to let 'em swaller you down an' take you 'long wid 'em.

De fowls all sing off: Dis is de finest thing dat dey's ever hearn tell of. Dey all vows: Darafter w'en de preachers comes; dey wus a gwineter hang aroun' de kitchen steps to git swallered down fer de journey to de Promus Lan'.

De nex' time dat de preachers come; de ole rooster manage to know 'em, an' he crow out lak befo':

"Here-de-preachahs come—!" Den all de chicken hens crowd aroun' de kitchen doo' an' sing off: "Take-me—! Take-me—! Take, take, take, take, take-me—!" De guineas all sot on de fence close by an' sung off: "Pot-rack! Pot-rack! Pot-rack! Pot-rack!" De ole gobbler stan' around de kitchen doo' an' say: "I's-ready-ready-ready-ready!"—In one way or anudder de fowls al try to let 'em know dat dey wants de preachers to take 'em down an' take 'em 'long 'roun'.

W'en Brer Thunderholler an' Brer Sweetsinger see how de fowls all hang aroun' to git killed an' e't up w'en dey goes bucked up in black clo'es instid o' white; dey spread de news! So atter dat de tother preachers lakwise dress up in black. Leaswise dat's w'at ole Uncle Adonijah, de preacher, say; w'en he wus a tellin de loration at my house on de Sunday dat he took dinner wid me."

With the story finished; the men and their sons mounted their horses and started for home. As they rode away, Shed said to Bunk: "Well, Bud, dat loration wus 'nough to make a rabbit laugh an' fergit dat he haint yit git set fee from de hounds.

If dis here corn crop turns out good, an' ole Bill Gold-bug will pay w'at he sayes dat he'll pay fer it; I hopes by dis time nex' year, we can set down an' tell tales an' lorations aroun' a table on a liddle spot of land w'at we can call all our own."

THE PARROT OVERSEER

"Hullo, Rube!"—"Hullo, Calup!" These were the mutual greetings exchanged by two Negro boys, on a bright crisp sunshiny day of early spring, as one of them carrying a bucket was making his way toward Horse Mountain in Bedford County, Tennessee.

"Whar's you gwine!" asked Rubin of Caleb who was carrying a bucket.

"I's a gwine to gedder up de water from de sugar-trees w'at I's done bored over yonder on de Mountain. Come go wid me", came the cordial crude invitation from Caleb.

"I dont care if I does", replied Rubin, 'caze I knows you wont mind to let yo' ole podner drink his fill of sugar-tree water. So, here I comes!"

"Come right on!" said Caleb. "You's mo' dan welcome to drink ontel you's as full as a tick; jest so long as you'll look but not to let it slosh out on me from yo' oncorked leather jug. W'at's de new up yo' way anyhows, Rube?"

"W'y nothin' much; 'cep' de funniest fambly of Niggers, you's ever laid eyes on, is jest moved up dar in Dog Town. Chile! you caint hardly un'erstan' nothin' dey sayes, dey talks so funny".

"Whar did dey come from?" asked Caleb.

"Oh, I dont know!" said Rubin. "Dey come from 'way down Souf somewhars. I caint tell no heads nor tails of de name w'at dey calls de place whar dey uster live. De ole man of de fambly (Uncle Boast Patty) say it wus a place whar de white folks in slavery times have monkeys an' keep parrots fer Overseers on de plantations ontel a witch Nigger turn in an' break it all up."

"Parrots fer Overseers? Gee-whiz-za-kin! Come on here Rube, an' tell me 'bout dat. I haint never hearn tell of no nothin lak dat in all my whole lifetime;" said Caleb.

"I dont know whedder I can git it straight or no"; answered Rubin. "I stayed aroun' ole Uncle Boast fer a whole half a day a tryin' fer to l'arn it, but I's skeared I didnt; so you'll jes hafter take it de best I can tell it".

"Dat's all right"; said Caleb. "W'at you knows, you can tell me; an' w'at you dont knows, you can jes leave out.

You jes go right on a talkin,

Whilst I goes right on a walkin.

I'll pour de sugar-tree water in de pail; whilst you pours out de loration of de tale.

W'en you's emptied out de tale, den I'll empty in de pail; Dat'll fill you to yo' hair, an' I thinks dat'll be fair. Dont you?"

"Look here, Caylup, you's a sight!" said Rubin; "so here's de tale, as good as I can make it out from w'at ole Uncle Boast Patty say:

Away back yon'er in slavery times; one o' dese here trashy half-strainer poo' white Crackers dress up lak he wus one of de Blue Bloods; an' he manage to marry in 'mongst white fambly w'at wus prutty well fixed up wid Nigger slaves. Uncle Boast say dis here feller manage to marry de gal by gittin her to run away wid 'im. De gal's daddy swelled up at fust an' ripped an' cust; but atter while he git sorter suaged down an' make up wid 'em, an' give 'em a home an' a liddle plantation out on de aidge of town an two Niggers—John an' Mandy—to wuk fer 'em an' wait on 'em.

W'en de gal 'ould go over to see her folks; dey'd always give her 'nough liddle change to keep her 'spectabul an' keep de pots a hangin' on de pot-rack in de chimbly.

One day, w'en she wus at her daddy's house; her sister up an' axed her w'at her husban' wus give her fer a present w'en dey wus got married, an' she make answer: "nothin".

Den her sister tell her dat she wouldn' stay hung on to no man w'at wusnt give her nothin but his good-fer-nothin-no-'count name.

Atter de gal's sister say dis; she go back an' tell her husban' w'at wus done got said. Dis here sort o' talk sorter rubbed her ole man in a tender spot un'er de collar. So he up an' say to her: "Honey, I's a gwineter go an' show 'em dat I knows how to give you presents right! I's a gwineter go an' buy you a big, fine, prutty, yaller cat fer a pet!"

Den de ole 'oman make answer: "Oh Sug'! Dont git no cat! De ole maids is all got yaller cats fer pets; an' dey gits so dey whines jes lak 'em w'en dey talks. No, no! You dont want to git no cat fer yo' liddle Honey-bug dumplin'. Does you Sug?"

Den he answer up an' say: "Sweedy Bunch, all dat wus kinder skipped my recomembunce. No! I haint a gwineter git no cat! I's a gwineter git you a fine Feist dog fer a pet present!"

Den she say to 'im: "Oh, Sug! Dont git no dog! De Niggers is all got dogs fer pets; an' 'sides dat, dey gits you mighty full o' fleas. Git me sumpin else."

"Well," says he, "I's got a dollar or so; an' I's a gwineter go down to whar de boats comes in an' buy you bofe a monkey an' a talkin' parrot. Den I reckins dat dey'll all git green-eyed; caze dere haint many, eben of de Big Bugs w'at's got a monkey an' a parrot."

Den she make answer: "Oh Sug', dat'll be jes fresh an' fine, offn de vine, one half a dime!. W'en you gits 'em; I's a gwine right over to git sister an' dem to let 'em hear my parrot talk an' see my monkey cut up his capers. Den dey'll all look foolish 'bout sayin dat you never did give me nothin but you bumptious scrumptious name."

So dis here feller go on off down to whar all de boats comes in; an' he fin' some mens down dar w'at wus got bofe monkeys an' parrots to sell. He didn' have no change much; an' de mens tells him dat dey dont think dat dey's got nothin at dat price of his money. But dey looks aroun' fer a long time 'mongst deir truck; an', at las', one of 'em tells him dat he wus got a young monkey w'at he mought let him have, an' one parrot w'at talk too much fer to suit most folks fer deir money.

De Cracker [Cracker was a name applied by Negroes to the poorer class of white people in the South] make answer to dis here man an' tell him dat dere never wus no parrot w'at could talk too much fer to suit him an' his wife. So he buyed de monkey an' de parrot an' tuck 'em on home wid 'im. W'en he got dar, his wife jes go wild over de presents; an' she call John an' Mandy an' tell 'em to feed an' git 'em to feelin' good so dat dey'll show off w'en her folks come over to see 'em.

Den she run on off to git her mammy an' daddy an' sister to come over an' see de presents w'at her husban' wus give her, an' to hear de parrot talk. Dey all come on over; an' w'en dey got dar dey made a great miration over de presents, an' tell her, now dat her husban' wus a sorter actin' lak he wus some stick in de mud all by hisself. Dey say dat de monkey wus mighty liddle, but he'd outgrow dat; den dey tells her; Let's hear de parrot talk.

So she holler out to de parrot: "Pollie! Pollie! Pollie! wanter cracker?" But dat ole parrot bird sorter look at her an' turn his head away. Den she say: "Poo' Poll, Poo' Poll! Pollie wanter cracker?" But Chile! dat ole bird jes shet his eyes an' sticked his head un'er his wing an' went on to sleep.

Den she tu'n 'roun' an' look at her husban' an' say to 'im: "Sug! Dey's weaved you a coat widout seams, an' euchered you outn a weeks rations, an' sol' you a Poll Parrot whar de cat wus done gone an' got its tongue".

Her mammy an daddy an' sister feel sorter sorry fer her husban'; caze dey sees dat he wus a tryin' to do sumpin, an' ketch as ketch can. so dey all chips in an' "praises up de pony". Dey tells her dere haint no tellin' w'at de parrot mought do atter while if dey keeps on a feedin' an' a tendin' to 'im right. If he dont 'gin to talk in duetime, dey mought split his tongue; caze eben a crow'll lern how to talk if you splits its tongue. Atter while de gal's folks goes on off home.

Well, de parrot an' de monkey stay aroun' dar fer better 'an a year. Dey bofe gits big an' fat an' sassy. De monkey jes git full of pranks an' antics; an' he try to do ev'rything dat he sees folks a doin'. But dat ole Parrot jes sot aroun' an' looked prutty, an' sticked his head un'er his wing, an' slep all de time; an' he dont say nothing'. So de gal wus always a pushin it up un'er her husban's nose dat dem mens down dar on de boat sho did cheat 'im w'en dey sol' 'im dat 'ar parrot fer a talker.

At las' one night, dese here whitefolks give one o' dese here "high-fly" parties; an' about all de "Big Ikes" popped in fer to have a dance 'mongst 'em. De "Big Ikes" comed in all bucked an' gagged wid ev'ry foot up an' toe-nails a draggin. Dey had fer deir musicianers one o' dese here big whitefolkses' bands wid some of deir fiddles as big as a barn-doo'. Dey hung up de parrot cage in de parlor-room an' sticked flowers all aroun' de cage fer to make it look prutty.

W'en de "Big Ikes" all got dar, dey went an' looked at de flowers an' de parrot' an' dey tells de Missus dat dey looks powerful prutty! So she thanked 'em an' put on all sorts of cat-fish aires to show 'em dat she wus still some of de "bit-to-do", eben if she wus done gone an' got hitched up wid a "half-strainer". Den dey all axes her to make de parrot talk fer 'em. She make answer to 'em dat de parrot caint neider talk nor say nothin; dat it wus jes one of dem kind to set 'roun an' look prutty whilst it 'twus awake.

De parrot jes kep' on a settin' dar; an' he sticked his head un'er his wing an' looked lak he wus pearuntly gone to shet-eye town. All de "Big Bugs" tell de missus day dey never wus seed setch a prutty parrot in all deir borned days; but it look to dem awful cu'ious dat it couldn' neider talk nor say nothin'. De Missus den tell 'em dat it was one o' dese here fine sort w'at wusnt picked up ev'ry day by Tom, Dick, an' Harry. Dat kind didn't need to be no gabbler. Chile! w'en she tell 'em all dis; dey all tuck a good look at 'im, so as to git de way of hew he hang an' to buy one lak him for deirselves. You see: Dem w'at wusnt jes zackly de bigges' 'mongst 'em thinks; if dey gits a bird lak dis; it would make 'em look lak dey wus some of de red bricks.

Well, de white musicianers start up; an' dey all 'gin to dance. Dey prances 'roun' an' scrapes an bows to onenudder. De ole parrot sorter looked at 'em a liddle outn de corner of one eye; den he sticked his head back un'er his wing an' went off to sleep. De white musicianers make de folks step aroun' lak dey wus a marchin 'roun' de walls of Jericho. Dey makes 'em swing corners an' twis' deirselves into all sorts of figgers; but dat ole parrot jes sot an' slep' wid his head un'er his wing, an' dont pay 'em no mind.

Atter while, w'en dey wus sorter dance deirselves down; dey brung chairs an' sot deirselves aroun' de room fer to eat down some 'freshments. W'en dey wus all git settled down to chawin deir victuals good; de Missus riz to give 'em a speech. She say: "Ladies an' Gents, Fellerpercitizens, an' friends: I's glad to see you here tonight a flippin de light fan-fastes' toe! An' whilst you's a eatin' here; I's brung over, from my big rich daddy's plantation over dar, some Nigger fiddlers an' banjer pickers an' some Nigger dancers to 'muse you. Dese here dancin' Niggers is so soupple dat dey can jump up in de air an' crack deir heels togedder three times befo' dey tetches de floo'. Dey can lie on de flat o' deir backs, an' knock off a jig wid deir footses on de floo' widout movin' deir bodies. An' w'en dey dances: 'Juba', 'Nigger, Nigger nebber die".—Well, I jes caint tell you 'bout it! You'll hafter see it fer yo'selves. So I'll stop an' de Niggers'll show you de res'."

W'en she git through; ole Uncle Joe—de fiddler, an' ole Uncle Ned— de banjer picker come in wid de dancin' Niggers. Dey wus all bucked up an' rigged out in red an' blue calico suits w'at de white folks wus fixed up fer 'em. Dey turned up de banjer strings a liddle an' chuned de fiddle an' put some rawsum on de bow. Den dey started up wid deir dances.

De Nigger musicianers open up wid:

Oh! De Ram blow de h'on an' de Sheep shell co'n. An' he sen' it to de mill by de buck-eyed whip-por-will Ole Joe's dead an' gone but his hant blows de ho'n. An' his houn' howls still from de top of dat hill.

Uh-uh! Chile! Dem Niggers dance so hard dat dey makes de whitefolkses' floo fairly talk un'er deir footses. W'en dey gits to fiddlin' an' de floo' gits to shakin'; dat ole parrot pulled his head out from un'er his wing, an' by de time de fust dance wus through wid, he wus a settin up straight on de perch wide awake an' wid his eyes stretched lak half moons.

Well, de whitefolkses, w'at wus dar a lookin on, jes laugh fit to kill deirselves an' guffaw lak dey wus 'bout to die a laughin' an' tell de Niggers to go on an' give 'em anudder shufflin hop an' a breakdown.

Den de Niggers 'gin to play an' knock off wid deir heels an' toes:

Bring a-long yo' hot co'n, Bring a-long yo' col' co'n, But
I say bring a-long, Bring a-long yo' Jim-my-john.

Some loves de hot co'n, Some loves de col' co'n,
But I loves, I loves dat Jimmy-john.

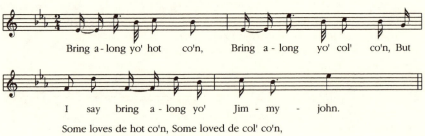

Bring a-long yo' hot co'n, Bring a-long yo' col' co'n, But
I say bring a-long yo' Jim-my - john.

Some loves de hot co'n, Some loved de col' co'n,
But I loves, I loves dat, Jimmy-john.

W'en dey 'gins dis dance, de ole parrot wus a settin up straight an' a watchin ev'ry move! De Niggers wus jes a dancin away an' a knockin' it off! An' w'en dey gits to dat part w'at goes: "But I say, I say, bring on yo' jimmy-john"; de ole parrot busted in an' hollered out: "Home once mo'! Bring in de whisky an' de brandy an' de beer!—Play dem chyards fair, you ole Cuss! I's done winned all de money from dat 'Son-of-a-Gun'! Hand it over; you ole Jail-bird!—Ha—! Ha-ha-ha-ha-ha-ha-ha-ha-ha!"

Den de ole parrot jes tu'ned a loose an' cust lak a sailor! An' Mon! It mightnigh broke up dem whitefolkses party. De Missus jes fall over an' faint; caze she wus done tol' 'em all dat de parrot couldn' say nothin'. So, of co'se, dey all thinks dat de Missus wus been a carryin' on drinkin' an' cussin' an gamblin' in de house. In dat way dey thinks de parrot wus done gone an' l'arnt all dis. Some of de "Big Bugs" sorter whisper 'roun' mongst de "Gold Bugs": Dat wus w'at gals gits w'at runs away an' mixes deirselves up wid de poor-Achan Trash.

Dey all got up an' got deirselves off home fer to make room fer de doctor.

De Missus wus sick in de bed all de nex' day. Her husban', he go 'roun' he do fer to see de "Big-Ones" w'at wus dar dat night. He splained to 'em dat he buyed de parrot offn a boat; an' dat de parrot mus a l'arnt to talk 'bout whisky an' dem things an' cuss down dar; but de folkses dont say much. Dey thinks dat it powerful cu'ious w'en dey ricomembers dat de Missus wus tol' 'em dat de parrot couldn' say nothin' 'tall.

Atter dis; de parrot go right on ev'ry day a talkin' an' a cussin' an' a hollerin' 'bout whisky. So de Mosser an' Missus make up deir minds dat dey wus a gwineter do sumpin fer to break him up from dat.

So dey calls in deir Niggers, John an' Mandy, an' tells to take de parrot outn de cage an' duck 'im in a tub of water ev'ry time he talk 'whisky' or cuss. De Niggers do dis an' sorter break de parrot, but it make him hate de very pearunce of 'em.

Well, dis ole parrot wus jes as smart as he could be. He talk an' he say ev'rything; so his Missus an' Mosser make him a Overseer fer to tell 'em ev'rything w'at John an' Mandy does He jes hated de Niggers fer dippin' him in dat 'at tub o' water; an' de Niggers git so dat dey jes hates him caze he blab out ev'rything dat dey do, an' a whole heaps dat dey dont do.

One day w'en de parrot wus might 'nigh broke from his cussin, a powerful big rainstorm come up. All de young chickens on de place git drenched an' almos' drowned. De ole parrot set 'roun' an' holler: "Lazy Niggers! Git up de chickens! You lazy Niggers, git up dem chickens!"

Aunt Mandy, she pick up de liddle chickens; an' bring 'em in an' lay 'em befo de fire fr to dry 'em off. De ole parrot, he sot aroun' he did an' he looked at de wet chickens; den he break out: "Ha! ha! ha! ha! ha! ha! ha! ha! ha!—You hollers 'whisky' an' 'dams' too!—Ha! ha! ha! ha! ha! ha! ha! ha! ha!"

Aunt Mandy jes hate de ole parrot an' dis give her a scuse. So w'en she heared him say 'whisky' an' 'dam', she had her chance; an' she grabbed him an' souzed him in a tub of water ontel she wus almos' drownded him. Den she tuck him outn de tub an' laid him befo' de fire to dry along wid de tother chickens.

Atter while de Missus come in de kitchen. Mandy wus jes a gittin ready to eat some o' de hot buiscuits w'at she wus done gone an' cooked fer de whitefolks. W'en she wus heard de Missus a comin'; she laid de biscuits on a chair, an' kivered em up wid de dish-rag fer to hide 'em from her. W'en de Missus got in dar de ole parrot hollered out: "Niggers try to drown de Overseer! Niggers try to drown de Overseer!" Mandy, she splain to de Missus, dat de parrot wus been a usin' his "bad" words ag'in. Den de ole parrot squall out: "Say, say chicken say dat! Say, say chicken say dat!"

De Missus sorter look de lan' over; but it 'pear lak dat 'twixt Mandy an' de parrot she caint git nothin' 'bout deir troubles straight. So she say dat she reckin dat she'll say dat de water-dippin' days wus over wid fer de parrot. She tell Mandy w'en de parrot say sumpin w'at wus wrong; dat she can come to her 'bout it, instid o' dippin an' duckin' him.

Den de Missus start fer to set down in de chair, wid de hot biscuits an' dish-rag on it, fer to hand over to Mandy her walkin papers 'bout lettin' de chickens all get drenched in de rain. W'en she go to set down; de ole parrot squall out; "Hot! Biscuits burn Missus! Hot! Biscuits burn Missus!" De Missus stop an' look at de chair; den she raise up de dish-rag, an' dar wus de biscuits! She haul off an' give Mandy a few liddle "love" licks wid her switch; an' den she take up de parrot un'er her arm an' take him along wid her into de parlor to dry.

Atter dis, de Missus fix up a great high perch in de kitchen fer de parrot, whar Mandy an' John caint git 'im. So he sot up dar on dis; an' watched 'em an' made it hot fer 'em. De Missus lakwise fix him a perch out on de back porch whar he can set out in de cool, on de do-nothin' stool, an make hisself at home.

One day de Missus wus a settin out on dis back porch wid de parrot; an' a man come 'long down de ally wid wood to sell. De man holler out: "Nay wood today?" an' de Missus maked answer. "Yes! Pitch it in from de alley over into de back yard; an' come to de back doo' an' git a dollar." De man throwed de wood in, an' come an' got de dollar, an' driv' on off.

Atter dis, de Missus go in de parlor; an; she call Mandy fer to clean off de wall picters whilst she set aroun' an' watch fer to see dat wus done right. De Mosser, he leave an' go off out to de field whar he wus sont John to wuk. He wanter sorter see to it dat John dont let no grass grow un'er his feet; an' dat he move 'roun' 'mongst de corn rows lively 'nough to make his salt an' a liddle bit over.

Whilst all dis wus a gwine on; anudder man come down de alley wid a load of wood. He holler out: "Wood to-day! Wood to-day?" De ole parrot out on de back porch hear him; an' he holler out; "Yes! Pitch it in from de alley over into de back yard, an' come to de back doo' an' git a dollar." So dis man stop, he do, an' pitch in de wood, an' go to de back doo', an' call de Missus fer to git de money. She say to de man dat she haint never tol' him dat she want no wood at no time! She tell him to go an' git his wood an' take it on off wid him an' be quick 'bout it. W'en she want wood, she wus got a mouf fer to let him know wid!

De man wus awful mad; but he didn' say much, caze he dont want no mix-up wid no 'oman whar he caint turn loose an' fight. So he load up his wood sorter stubborn-lak, an' clucked to his hoss an' driv' on off wid his mouf poked out.

Atter while anudder man come down de alley a hollerin': "Wood-today! Wood today?" De ole parrot ag'in squall out; "Yes! Pitch it in from de alley over into de back yard, an' come to de back doo' an' git a dollar." De man stopped an' throwed de wood over, an' went to de back doo' fer to git de dollar.

De Missus den handed it to him red hot offn de fire-coals dat she haint never tol' him neider dat she want no wood. She blurt out, to 'im dat

he wus stock crazy if he think dat he wus a gwineter make her buy wood
by comin' along an' throwin' it over de fence She give him to know
widout usin' Sunday-go-to-meetin; words; day she want him to git hisself
an' his wood bofe away from dar an' be quick 'bout it. She sorter act lak
dat she mought "boot" him, eben if she wus a 'oman!

Well, dis here man wus blue mad; but he tuck his wood, an' driv' on
off, caze he didn' want to do no nothin fer to break into jail.

Atter while anudder man comed down de alley a hollerin' "wood"; an'
he git fooled dis same way. De Missus flung a lots of sass at him an' sont
him off wid a sore toe.

Bymeby, de three mens w'at de parrot wus made a fool outn sell out
deir wood; an' dey all driv' deir hosses down to de waterin' place so as to
give 'em some water an' den go on home. W'en dey meets down dar; one
of 'em gits to tellin' de tothers 'bout his gittin fooled up by a 'oman into
throwin' in his wood into her back yard fer a dollar; an' den w'en he go to
git de money, her a makin' him reload de wood, an' a drivin' him off lak
he wus some of de low-downed scrapins of de earth. De tother two mens
looked at him, an' den dey all looks at one nudder; den one of de tothers
say: dat same flea bit him; den de las' one of 'em say: he wus managed to
swaller down dat same kind of bitter mouf-full too.

About dat time anudder man come 'long w'at lived aroun' dar; so dey
up an axed him 'bout de folks w'at live in dat house. Dey wants to know
of him whedder dey wus crazy an' gone clean deranged or not.

Dis man tells 'em; No, dem folks wus all right. De 'oman's ole man
wus a sorter half-strainer Cracker; but de 'oman herself wus got a daddy
wat wus as rich as Gundy, an' as smart as you make 'em. Dere wusnt no
fools up dar; all of 'em wus got sense. W'en de man git through wid tellin'
'em dis; he go on off.

De three mens scuss it some mo'; an' den dey makes up deir minds to
tie up deir hosses, an' go back an' see 'bout w'at dey can find out 'bout
dis here cu'ious callin' out fer wood an' den not takin it. W'en dey gits to
de alley; one of de mens goes down it to de back of de house by de back
gate. He seat hisself dar to wait an' to watch. De tother two mens den
starts down de alley a hollerin': "Wood to-day! Wood to-day?"

De ole parrot out on de back porch holler back to 'em: "Yes! Pitch it
in from de alley over into de back yard, an' come to de back doo' an' git a
dollar." De man w'at wus a settin' by de back gate see him an' hear him.

W'en de tother two mens git down to whar he wus a hidin'; he p'int
out to 'em de fly in de'lasses. So one of de mens tells de tothers fer to
watch out fer him; an' he'll slip in to de back porch an' git dat parrot fer to
settle up wid him. Perhaps w'en dey gits him; dey can send 'im to whar
de rain dont fall an' de wind don blow, an' he wont need to holler out to
nobody no mo' fer to pitch over wood an' come an' git a dollar.

De parrot, he haint yit l'arnt to keep outn de way of whitefolks; he jes stay outn de retch of Niggers. So dis here white man tipped up to 'im, an' grabbed him 'roun de neck, an' squez down on his goozle so as to cut his wind off an' keep him from hollerin. He tuck him on wid him to de alley. W'en he git dar, all three of de mens wrung an' wrung on de ole parrots neck; but it wus so long an' tough an' stringy dat dey couldn' wring de head off. But dey wrings ontel dey thinks dat he wus about got good dead; an' den dey pitches him down dar in de alley, an' goes an' gits deir hosses, an' makes deir ways on home.

Atter while de Missus come out from whar Mandy wus a cleanin' in de parlor, an' she miss de parrot. She call him; but he no answer. She look ev'ry whars; but she no see 'im. Den she call Mandy an' ax her whar she think he wus. Mandy say she dont know; but she spec he wus done gone an' git so smart dat he wus off some'ars a lookin' atter de neighbors' business.

De Missus laugh at w'at she say; an' tell her to ketch an' kill two chickens fer dinner. Den she say; w'en she git through wid dat, she can go an' look fer de parrot.

Mandy ketch de chickens whilst de Missus wus a standin' dar an' a lookin' at her. She wrung deir heads off an' pitched 'em over into de alley. De ole parrot wusnt dead; an' he wus jes a comin' to hisself, an' a gittin his senses back w'en de chicken heads come a fallin' over de fence. W'en he see de chicken heads tumble into de alley, he holler out: "Oh, Missus! De Niggers is a wringin ev'rybody's heads off, an' a slingin 'em over in de alley! Dey's wringed de Overseer's head off an' slung it out here too!"

W'en de Missus hear dis, she didn' hardly know how to believe her own (y)ears; she wus jes stonished, an' tuck Mandy an' went out into de alley fer to see w'at she mought see. Dar she found de ole parrot wid his neck half twisted off! De ole parrot look at Mandy, he do, an' he squall out: "Niggers kill de Overseer! Niggers kill de Overseer!"

Mandy say to her Missus; Not to whup her; caze she wus been along wid her all mawnin, an' knowed dat she wusnt been a bodderin along wid no parrot. She wus been a cleanin an' a scrubbin de things in de parlor all day right un'er her naked eyes.

Her Missus tell her dat she know dat wus so; an' she wusnt a gwineter tetch her. But she say, she know who done it. It 'twus dat good-fer-nothin Nigger John; an' she wus a gwineter make de Mosser skin him alive, much less tetch him! She know jes zackly how it git done: John wus axed his Mosser fer to come back over home fer to git a drink of water, an' whilst he wus dar he do his sneakin' meanness.

All de time dey wus a totin de parrot to de house, an' a talkin wid onenudder; he kep' up de squallin an' de hollerin: "Niggers kill de Overseer! Niggers kill de Overseer!" De Missus rub de ole parrot's neck fedders down de shmove way a' say to 'im: "Nev' min', Pettie, somebody else is a gwineter kill dem too, if dey dont watch out!"

Bymeby John an' his Mosser come back from de field. De Missus go out to meet 'em jes a puffin an' a blowin' an' as mad as blue lizards! She didn' wait fer nobody to say nuthin'. She jes bust in an' spew out: "Sug'! I wants you jes to skin John dar; caze he wus almos' wrung our parrot Overseer's head off; w'en he come to de house fer to git hisself a drink of water dis mawnin!"

John tu'n an' look at his Mosser's bull-whup an' he trimble mo' samer dan a leaf.

De Mosser fust look at John an' try to figger out how he manage to git away from him an' stay wid 'im all at de same time! Den he walked up an' grabbed John in de shirt-collar an' John 'gin to holler: "Please, Mosser! Please dont whup me; you knows dat I haint been nowhars!"

But dere wusnt no use in John's hollerin; caze de Mosser wus jes a tryin to find out whedder it mought be a fact dat sometimes he wus gone clean off w'en he look dat he wus still dar. So he turned John a loose widout tetchin him wid a whup. Den he tu'ned to de Missus an' telled her dat John couldn' a tetched de parrot in no way; caze he hisself wus been a settin down dar un'er a shade tree all mawnin—a watchin John an' a wukin him. He haint been nowhars to git no water. He den ax her to splain herself.

De Missus tell him all 'but de parrot; whar she find 'im an' wha't he say. De Mosser say dat he hate it awful bad; but he haint a gwineter whup John, caze he know dat he haint had no hand in de wringin' an' de twistin' off of no parrot's head dis time. So dey let John go on to de kitchen to whar Mandy wus.

De pet monkey wus out in de kitchen whar Mandy wus. Mandy an' John love de monkey an' de monkey love dem. Dat monkey wus jes as smart as he could be; an' he try to do ev'rything dat he see John an' Mandy do. Mandy wus a pickin de two chickens w'at she wus killed fer de white-folks; an' de monkey would jump up on de chair by de side of her, an' pick some fedders offn de chickens too. Atter while at monkey git so smart dat he could pick a whole chicken all by hisself.

De day's troubles 'bout de parrot a gittin his head twisted off blow over atter dey caint find out in no way who done go an' do it. In about a mont' or so de parrot git all right ag'in; an' he fly aroun' through de house an' he tell ev'ry blessed thing John an' Mandy do. W'at wus mo' dan dat, he wus got sense 'nough not to eat nothin' w'at John an Mandy give him. So dey caint send him to de bone-yard by de way of his stomach. He lakwise keep outn deir retch; w'en dey wus got sumpin in deir hands wid w'at dey mought "accidently" hit him. Well,—he sho did make dem two Niggers wush dey dey wus dead or dat sumpin else wusn't a livin'.

One day deir Mosser an' Missus go off fer to see deir kinfolks. Dey takes deir parrot Overseer an' locks him up in de "Big House"; caze dey wus skeard dat somebody else mought git him an' wring his head off lak dey do befo'. Dey says to deirselves:

Once, it haint always,
Twice, it haint forever,
But w'en de head once git off,
It dont never come back, no never!

W'en dey gits de parrot fixed up in de "Big House"; dey tells John an'
Mandy to keep outn dar, it dont make no diffunce w'at come or go from
'bove or b'low. Lasly dey tells 'em to kill two chickens an' git 'em ready fer
deir supper w'en dey comes back home. Den dey leaves.

Of co'se John an' Mandy haint a gwine into de "Big House"; caze dey
knowed dat de ole parrot would tell on 'em; an' dere wouldn' be none of
'em lef' scacely atter dat w'en deir Missus an Mosser come home. But dey
sets aroun' out dar in de kitchen an' dey whispers to onenudder an' wushes
to onenudder dat dey knowed some way fer to go away wid dat ole parrot.

At las', Mandy whisper to John dat she wus got a plan; an' jes fer him
to set aroun' an look at it wuk! She go out, she do, an' she ketches de two
chickens fer de whitefolkses supper. She kilt 'em an' scalded 'em an' got
'em ready fer de pickin'. De pet monkey wus on hand as fer common, to
help out wid de pickin'. Mandy 'gin to pick de chickens. De pet monkey
want to lend a hand in de pickin; but she wont let him. W'en he try to git
to pick she push 'im away. She kep' dis up ontel de monkey got full of ig
[ig = eagerness] fer to pickede chickens; den she tuck him outn de
kitchen; an' tuck him up to de "Big House", an' put him in through a
winder w'at de whitefolks wus lef' heisted up w'en dey went away.

W'en de pet monkey git in dar; he see de parrot, an' he grab 'im an'
pick all de fedders offn' him jes as clean as yo' hand!

'Long towards night de Missus an' de Mosser comed home. W'en dey
wus got dar an' onlocked de doo', an' stepped in; w'at should dey see but
de ole parrot wid all his clo'es pulled offn him. De ole parrot sot up on a
perch an' he looked down at his Missus an' Mosser; an' den he looked at his
clo'es all strewed aroun' all over de floo'. Den he squall out: "Monkey raise
ole Ned, Missus! Monkey raise ole Ned, an' dere haint no fedders lef'!"

Well, de whitefolks knowed dat dey wus lef' de winder up, an' locked
all de doo's; an' wus tol' de Niggers fer to keep out. So dey caint blame
dem. But dey thinks dat dey'd better call John an' Mandy anyhows; an'
sorter look 'em over.

John say to 'em dat it wus jes awful; an' Mandy chune up lak she wus
a gwineter cry 'bout it. Dey say dat dey missed de monkey outn de
kitchen; an' dey wus went fer to look fer 'im in de alley, caze dey wus
skeard dat somebody mought a tuck him, an' wrung his head off, an'
throwed him out dar, jes lak dey wus done de poo' liddle helpless
innercent parrot, one time. W'en dey didn' see 'im out dar; dey think dat
he wus all right, an' 'ould come back home atter while.

De Missus an' Mosser sorter study it all over a liddle' den dey tells John an' Mandy dat dey reckins dere haint nothin' dat can be done 'bout it. But dey mus' see to it darafter dat de monkey stay out in de kitchen all de time.

Mandy an' John tell 'em dere haint nothin' in de worl' dey wont do fer to please 'em! You sees, Mandy an' John wus jes tickled to death; caze whar de monkey is, dar de parrot haint also! De monkey an' de parrot sorter turn onenudder's stomachs; so, de parrot live in de "Big House" an' de monkey live in de kitchen.

John an' Mandy wus dat proud dat dey jes natuchully dont hardly know how to 'have deirselves.

> Parrot in de "Big House",
> Monkey in de kitchen;
> Wus 'nough to save de Niggers' backs
> From many a many a switchin'.

But dat ole parrot git well from de pickin'; an' he grow hisself a new crop of fedders. He den sot aroun' in de "Big House" a talkin' an' a tellin his Missus ev'rything w'at he could see; but he couldn' see nothin much.

Along in de spring of de nex' year, Johns Mosser tell him fer to go out into de aidge of town to de fiel' w'at de Missus' ole rich daddy wus give 'em; an' to plow out de new corn crop. De Mosser hisself stay aroun' out in dat fiel' an' keep him a gwine. But de Mosser soon take a big bad cold, an' go on off home sick. W'en he wus got down sick; John, he sorter mozeyed aroun' an' tuck it easy.

De Missus go down dar, an' see dat dere wusnt much wuk a gwine on; an' she come back an' tol' de Mosser 'bout it. He tell her dat he know jes zackly how to fix dat. He's a gwineter send de parrot Overseer down to watch John, an' keep him a stickin' to de hoe. He sont word to John by Mandy fer to come dar. John, he come. W'en he git dar, de Mosser he tell 'im dat he wus a gwineter send de parrot Overseer fer to watch 'im; an' fer ev'ry time he stop wuk, he wus a gwineter seed fer de patterrollers an' have 'em come an' give him fifty lashes.

John walk on off, a gwine to de field, wid his head a hangin' down; an' de ole parrot fly along wid 'im, away up over his head, an' he holler out: "Walk up dar! Git a move on you! I's a gwineter give you fifty lashes!" Chile, w'en John hear dis, he know dat de ole parrot mean business, an' he sho pearten up his gait.

W'en he git down in de fiel' an' 'gin to plow; de ole parrot flew along an' kep' up wid 'im from one een to de tother of de corn rows. W'en de hoss would git to de en' of de rows; de ole Parrot would holler to 'im: "Come here, Sah!" an' de hoss would wheel an' turn befo John could git a chance fer to take de plow outn de groun an' scrape de dirt offn its p'int. Mon! De parrot almos' wuk John to death! Ev'ry evenin' w'en John take out de hoss an' go to de house; dere wus one of dem patterrollers a settin' up der a waitin' fer to see if his Mosser dont want to git him flogged. De patterroller wus a mushin fer de job; caze he git a half a dollar an' a big drink of whisky fer ev'ry Nigger-floggin' dat he give.

But ev'ry evenin de ole parrot come home an' tell de sick Mosser dat John wus a doin' sorter tolerbus; so dat de patterroller's job dont git quite ready fer him. Along towards de end of de week, at dinner time one Friday, John git de corn all plowed over an' almos' cleaned out. He come up to de house an' he tell de Mosser dat de corn wus as clean as a dog's toof.

De Mosser make answer: Dat treein' had de right sort of a bark to it fer big game. An' now he want him to take his ole muskit, an' go out to de woods, an' kill him a jaybird fer to make him some jaybird soup. He say dat he think dat he wus cotched de croup along wid his tother sick-nesses, an' jaybird soup wus good fer croup.

Now Chile! Mind you ! Dis wus on a Friday evenin' w'en folks sayes dat de jaybirds is all jes come back from de Bad Place whar dey's been to tote sand in deir moufs—dat sand w'at de Bad Man heat up red hot an' sifter on de naked backs of all dem dat bothers 'long wid dem sort of birds!

John, he 'gin to say to his Mosser dat he wus hearn tell dat it wus awful bad luck fer to hunt jaybirds on a Friday; an' he wus powerful skeard dat de soup wouldn' do him no good if he git it on dat day. Den he close up by axin if dere wusnt some tother time or some tother bird w'at nought be jes as good.

His Mosser look at 'im, he do; an' den he say to 'im; If he dont go an' git dat 'ar jaybird lak he tell 'im, he'll sen' an' have a hundred patterrollers come an' w'ar deirselves out on 'im!

Den John tell 'im ; Yassir! He always wus jes crazy to git w'at-some-ever his Mosser want fer 'im, eben if dat sumpin wus salt widout no salt in it. But he ax his Mosser: If he fail to git de jaybird, wont he let him jes keep on a huntin' day an' night ontel he ketch one, instid o' ketchin de cat-o-nine-tail.

De Mosser make answer: Since he wus now a talkin an' a actin' lak a good Nigger should oughter; he reckin dat he'll keep de lash offn him so long as he'll keep it offn hisself.

Well, dis answer sorter fix John up. He make up his mind dat he wus a gwine a huntin'; but he wusnt a gwineter kill no jaybirds on Friday, bad-luck day. He go an' git de gun an' start to load it. Jes as he wus a startin' to do dis; his Mosser holler an' tell him dat heaps of jaybirds used to be out dar in de woods jes back of de ole grave-yard at de back side of de ole sedge field.

Law, Chile! Dat wus jes lak knockin John in de head wid a maul an' a crackin his noggan; [noggan = head] caze he knowed dat it wus bad luck to be a shootin' 'roun' 'mongst a graveyard, onless you shoots wid silver bullets. But John he jes kep' on a answerin' 'umble-lak "Yassir!"

In de room whar he wus a gittin an' a loadin' de muskit; he notice his Missus' silver thimble a lyin' in dar on de bed. He grabbed up de thimble an' rammed it down in his britches' pocket; den he go out de doo' an' call his Mosser's two dogs an' pull out from de Big House. He go down in de hoss-lot by de stable whar dere wus a great big broad-axe w'at dey wus used to hew logs wid. He tuck dis broad-axe, an' cut up de Missus' silver thimble into slugs. Den he put a silver slug or two in 'mongst de shot an' finished up de loadin' of de gun.

W'en he git de silver slugs mixed in 'mongst de shot in de loadin' of de gun; it fix him up so dat he could shoot aroun' de graveyard widout de hants a gittin' atter him. Den, eben if a witch should happen to bother' long wid 'im; he could shoot de witch too. You see: If you shoots at de witches wid common lead shots an' bullets, dey jes laughs an' ketches 'em in deir hands; den dey comes an' throws 'em in yo' eyes an' puts 'em out! So dis here sort of loadin' in de gun fix John up so dat he can be as sassy as a jack-sparrer.

W'en he git dis all fixed, he make a cross mark on de ground an' spit in it; so dat w'en he go back to his cabin, lak he wus a fixin to do, it wont give him no bad luck. Den he go back to his cabin an' git hisself some sweet taters, an' cram 'em down in his pockets; an' he lit his cob pipe so as to have some fire along wid 'im. You see: John haint got no huntin' of jay-birds on Friday in his head! He aim to go up dar in de woods 'hind de grave-yard an' kindle up a fire an' roast an' eat sweet taters. He think, maybe, if a rabbit or a pattridge come along an' pester him whilst he wus a roastin' an' a eatin sweet taters, he mought shoot at it; but he haint got no notion of shootin' at no jaybirds on no Friday! So, off goes John wit gun, dog, taters, an' pipe; to de woods up back of de ole grave-yard.

W'en he git away off out dar in de woods; he stop un'er a big tree, gedder up some dry trash, drap some embers outn his pipe in de trash, an' git hisself up a fire. W'en de fire git burnt down fur 'nough to make some red hot coals, he opened up de coals an' put de taters fer to roast. Den he set down, he do, an' say to hisself dat huntin wus all over fer dat Friday anyhows. He think to hisself w'en he go home, he'll sho go mighty late. Den, so as to rub de whitefolks de right way, he's got his mind fixed up fer to tell 'em he's a gwineter go a huntin' fer jaybirds befo' day de nex mawnin.

John sot down, he did, an' looked at de fire; an' he cotched de good smell of dem roastin sweet taters a callin' him from outn de ashes an' de embers. He sot dar a wushin dat dey'd hurry up an' git done; w'en (all of a sudden) he hear somebody wid a liddle ole cu'ious cracked up voice: "Hullo dar!"

Dis skear john mighty much at fust; caze he think maybe his Mosser wus riz up outn dat sick bed to watch him. If dat wus so; he mought need to git in de bed hisself a liddle later on, w'en de patterrollers git through wid deir shakin of deir hands aroun' him. He look aroun' ev'ry which a way; but he dont see nobody.

So he sorter settle down ag'in wid his mouf a waterin' an' a makin a wide open sign to de taters fer to hurry up an' git done. Nothin' dont pester his mind much 'cep' how to keep de whitefolks all right w'en he git back home. He knows dat de hants caint bother him; caze he wus got dem silver thimble silver slugs in dat muskit! As fer de witches;he can fill dem full of silver slugs too; an' dat'll b e de las' of dem lakwise, if dey tries to fool aroun' wid him—a carryin' on wid deir segashuatin'. But whilst he wus a rumblin all dis aroun' 'mongst his mind; dat same somebody say ag'in: "Hullo dar!"

John look aroun' ev'ry which a ways ag'in, an' he dont see nobody; but at las; he look up in de tree un'er which he wus a cookin', an' he see a Nigger a settin up dar on a lim'.

John say "Hullo" back to 'im; an' ax him w'at he wus a doin up dar in de tree.

Dis Nigger answer an' tell 'im dat he wus a "runaway" Nigger; an' he wus jes a hidin up dar an' a waitin fer night to come on, so as to go on furder towards Freedom. He den ax John if he dont want to go 'long wid 'im.

John tell him dat he'd lak to go mighty much, if he jes had some way fer to take Mandy along wid 'im. Of co'se John haint yit altogedder make up his mind to try fer Freedom; but he jes natchully likes dis here Nigger w'en he hears him a handin' out talk 'bout Freedom. So he rake de taters outn de fire; an' ax him to come down outn de tree an' take a bit of 'em along wid 'im.

De Nigger thank 'im an' tell 'im dat he will; but dat John mus' fust drive his dogs off, caze he wus monstus skeard of dogs. He drapped John a liddle switch down outn de top of de tree; an' telled him to him 'em a liddle light tap apiece wid it fer to make 'em go away.

John took up de switch an' give bofe of de dogs a liddle light tap wid it. W'en lo, an' beholds! Bofe dogs git turned into rocks!

John stand dar an' look stonished wid his mouf dropped wide open. He see right off dat de feller in de tree wusnt no Nigger 'tall; he wus a witch! John sorter git taken wid de palsy. Of co'se he wus sorter skeared of de witch; but de gun would look atter dat end of de stick. His troubles wus: He knowed dat if he go back to de white folks widout dem dogs, dere moughtn't no hide git lef' on his back atter dem hired patterrollers git through, how-some-be-ever befo' you could say "tucky" de thought come to John dat de gun mought fix up ev'rything 'bout de dogs too. So he grabbed de gun an' cracked down on de witches' legs wid de silver thimble slugs.

W'en John shoot; he wing de witch so bad dat he tumble smack down on de groun' an' he caint git away. John load up de gun right quick ag'in wid de silver thimble slugs; an' den he tell de witch dat he's a gwineter turn loose anudder load of silver into 'im an' finish 'im, if he dont bofe bring de dogs back from de rocks an' den fix up "Nigger John" so dat he'll be a witch too.

Of co'se de witch haint in no big hurry fer to git dead; so he whistle de dogs right back outn de rocks. Den he take a liddle red bag outn his britches pocket an' ontie it an' take a liddle white sumpin outn it w'at look lak a gravel. He hand dis over to John; an' dat put 'im in de fambly an' maked him a son of de witches.

W'en de witch got through wid doin' dis; John went an' cut a switch, an' rubbed it wid his liddle white gravel rock. Den he hit de witch wid de switch, an' all de silver slugs bounced outn him. He wus well ag'in! De witch den leave; but befo' he go, he shake hands wid John, beance he wus done made his way into bein' a part of de fambly.

John den pick up de gun an' call de dogs an' walk on off home, a full-blooded genuwine witch! He go back home by his Mosser's stable; an' he pick up a liddle fryin' smotherin chicken an' kill it. He take dis along wid 'im on up to de whitefolkses' house. He take it; an' witch 'em up so dat dey dont know de chicken from a jaybird! De Missus take de chicken an' make some fine "jaybird" soup outn it fer de Mosser.

Den John go on down to de cabin to whar Mandy wus. He lorate to her all 'bout his shootin' de witch, his witchin' an' foolin' de whitefolks, an' ev'rything. He tell her dat dey wus a gwineter live now jes 'bout lak dey wus free.

Mandy tell John dat dis soun' so good dat she jes caint hardly believe her own (y)ears.

John den make answer dat he wus a gwineter show her. Den he reckin dat she mought believe her own eyes. Wid dat much sayed, John stepped up in front of de fire-place whar dere wus a big fire a burnin' an' a waitin' fer Mandy to git supper. He took de liddle white rock, w'at put 'im in de witch fambly, an' stuck it inside of his mouf. Den he say:

"Over de thick,
An' down de thin;
Through de key-hole,
An' back ag'in!"

Atter John say dis, he jump right spang in de fire! He flame up an' blaze; an' go a roarin up de chimbly lak a piece of paper w'at you lights an' turns a loose in de fire-place!

Well; Mandy wus jes about to bust out in a big cry; caze it look to her lak dat John wus done gone an' come to dat p'int whar dere wusnt no use in sayin: "Ashes to ashes, an' dust to dust." But as she go to lift up her big blue cotton apron to wipe her eyes; sumpin shot in from de outside through de key-hole in de doo'. It lodge right in a chair an' look lak a grain of sand. Terreckly de grain o' sand 'gin to swell. It swell an' it swell, an' it twis' an' shape up; an' dar wus John ag'in!

Mandy look at 'im an' talk to 'im a liddle; but she railly wus skeared dat he wus some sort of hant. At las' John manage to talk prutty 'nough to git her to put her hands on 'im. Atter she zamine him rail good all over; she sorter half-way make up her mind dat it mought be him. She den tell him dat she always did know dat he wus de smartest as well as de pruttiest thing dat ever lived or died.—An' now, fer him to set in an' witch up de whitefolks right away so dat dey caint hear an' so dat dey caint miss deir fowls; an' go up to de hen-house an' git her a big fat chicken hen to bile up an' make into a big juicy pie fer dem. Dey got de hen an' maked up de pie an' e't it all; an' dey has mo' fun dan a flock of mouses a runnin aroun' in a locked up corn-crib whar de cats caint git in.

W'en dey git through wid deir frolickin', it wus might'nigh midnight. John tell Mandy dat he mus' go out at midnight an' know up some stirrups in de hosses' mains an' tails an' take a ride through de air on 'em. He splain to her dat de white witches rides brooms; but de Nigger witches rides on de hosses' mains an' tails—dat dey jes witches de hosses an' dey sails aroun' through de air jes lak he sail up de chimbly an' back through de keyhole.

He ax Mandy w'at place she think dat he should oughter go whilst he wus out a ridin'. She make answer to 'im dat she dont hardly know; but she think dat he had better go somewhars an' fix up some ways to git shed of de ole parrot Overseer an' all of his kind. If he dont do dis; it'll keep him so busy a witchin up de whitefolks, to which dese parrots totes deir tales, dat nobody caint git no rest an' no peace of mind.

John tell Mandy "All right". So he go out an' mount de horses' tails; an' go a sailin' aroun' through de air. He twis' hisself aroun' a liddle an' turn hisself into a big witch hawk; den he go an' stop in de top of a tree whar a whole heaps of hawks wus a roostin'. He wake dese here hawks all up an' tell 'em dat he wus come to have a liddle confab wid 'em.

Atter John witch up de hawks a liddle; dey tells him to jes go on an' talk w'at he want done, an' dey'll do it. John tell 'em fust, dat he want one of 'em to come down tomorrer mawnin bright an' early; an' git de ole parrot Overseer an' take 'im on home fer dinner. One of 'em say dat he'll do dat. Den he tell 'em dat he want 'em to send word to all de hawks ev'rywhars to ketch up an' eat up all dem kind of parrots w'at make Nigger Overseers. Dey all say dat dey'll send word.

De nex' mawnin, bright an' early, John go off from de house lak he wus a gwine out to de field to wuk. De ole parrot Overseer riz in de air an' follered him. He flew 'long over his head an' hollered down to 'im: "Walk up dar! Git a move on you! I's a gwineter give you fifty lashes; if you dont walk mo' lak you wusnt a seein' Lazy Lawrence! 'Bout dat time, de hawk come along an' grab him; an' scoot off a sailin' home wid him fer his dinner.

De parrot Overseer know dat John hate him, an' dont want him to have no good times. So, as he hang down from de hawks claws, he holler out to John: "John, I's a ridin'! John, I's a ridin'!" He think dat his hollerin dis will make John chunk de hawk an' make him drop 'im; caze he know dat no John wouldn' want him a ridin' an' a havin' a fine time. But John make answer back, he do; "Ride on! Consarn you! Ride on!"

De ole parrot Overseer see dat dis wusnt a gwineter wuk. So he holler back to John: "You go on to de Bad Place! [Much harsher terms were used in these places by Negroes who were non-church members. The Christian ex-slaves used the terms which I have recorded] You go on to de Bad Place!" But John, he up an' answer back, he do: "I haint a gwine! I's skeared dat dere wont be room 'nough fer you an' yo' relations, if I goes down dar! I's a gwineter stay away, so as to give you all a plenty of room to turn over in de hot embers!"

By dis time de hawk wus done squez down on de ole Overseer's goozle an' cut off his wind; an' wus a takin' a liddle tas'e of 'im, to see how much mo' flavorin' he'd need befo' he go on de table.

Atter dis, de hawks cotch up an' e't up all dem kinds of parrots w'at de whitefolks could take an' make Nigger Overseers outn—leaswise dis wus de loration dat ole Uncle Boast Patty tell me as fur as I wus able to git it from his kind of talkin'. He lakwise put in dat John an' Mandy, atter dis, never did have no mo' trouble; an' dey live offn de fat of de lam'."

By the time that Rubin had finished this somewhat lengthy story, Caleb had safely gathered the sap from the sugar maples into a pail. Rubin drank himself "full up to the neck"; then—the dinner hour of each being near—they shook hands, "good-bye", and each turned his face homeward.

THE COURTING OLD WOMAN

Samps Nickerjack had just returned from Shelbyville, Tennessee, to his little country home located out about four miles on the Murfresboro pike. Most of the country folk, many, many years ago, customarily went from this community to the town, on each Saturday afternoon, to purchase a week's supply of such commodities as could not be gotten directly from the farms. While there, the Negroes commonly collected themselves into group acquaintances. Some of these groups discussed the most serious phases of their life problems, while others met only to crack jokes and to while away the hours as pleasantly as possible. Samps Nickerjack was, by nature, a unit of one of the latter groups, and as he comfortably seated himself once more at home in his cabin, he addressed his wife thus:

"Law', Mag, you couldn' guess fer de life of you, who I wus done gone an' seed down in town dis evenin'!"

"No, I dont spec I could", answered the wife. "Who wus it?"

"It wus Bud Stone, w'at wus sold offn ole Grandsir' Stone's plantation, 'way back yonder w'en he wus chilluns;" replied Samps; "an' none of us knowed w'at wus become of 'im atter dat. He come from somewhars away down Souf, an' he's a lookin' up his folkses. He's a gwine up to Vinegar Hill to see his mammy an' daddy to-night w'at he haint heared from sice he got sold away from 'em. Perhaps you ricomembers dat his mammy try to let on lak dat she wus a gwine stracted w'en he git sold; an' de Niggers over dar say, dat de Overseer brung her aroun' by tannin' her hide ev'ry day fer a week."

"Yes, I ricomembers it all", said the wife; "an' it wus been so long ago dat it sho do soun' cu'ious to eben hear tell of Bud. How do he look, how do he 'ear, an' w'at do he say 'bout hisself?"

"He's jes lak he wus w'en he wus a boy", answered Samps. "He's dat full o' foolishness an' jokes an' tales dat you dont know w'en he's a talkin' sense an' w'en he haint. Whilst he wus wid us he take up all de time a tellin' us 'bout his ole Missus 'way down dar whar he come from; but he stick in so much foolishness dat we didn' know jes zackly w'en he wus a standin' out in de sun wide awake, an' w'en he wus a noddin' wid his footses in de moonlight an' his head in de lye [lye = lie or falsehood. This figure of speech wus common among antebellum Negroes] un'er de ash-hopper."

"Well"; said Mag, who had just gotten their evening meal ready and put in on the table; "come on to supper, an' tell me all 'bout w'at Bud say—foolishness an' all."

They were soon seated. After the plates had been served, Samps gave Bud's story of his old Mistress, in the far South, as follows:

"Bud say: Atter he wus been sol' to de Nigger trader, offn ole Gradsir' Stone's place; dat de trader keep him a walkin' Souf fer a good mont' befo' he sol' 'im. One day w'en dey wus a walkin' along a dusty dirt-road by a big plantation; a liddle ole hooked-nosed dried-up lookin Cracker 'oman seed 'em a passin', an' hailed 'em from de Big House on it. She telled de Nigger trader dat she want to buy a Nigger; vidin he wus got one w'at could cook an' wash an' iron an' plow an' make hisself handy in ginerl.

Now, Bud wus been a cookin' fer de crowd along de road; an' de trader tell her dat he wus got de very artickul dat she wus a lookin' fer! He talk to her so fast an' so slick, dat she dont git no time fer to do nothin' but to draw out her ole stockin wid de chink [Chink = money] in it to pay fer him wid. He wus soon her Nigger; an' de rest o 'em pull out an' leave him dar.

W'en he git up to his new home an' stay dar fer a liddle while; he find out dat his ole Missus wus onetime been a poo' ole maid. But her ole rich bachelor uncle wus done gone an' kicked de bucket an' died an' lef' her rich. He wus lef' her a big plantation wid ev'rything on it.

De ole dead Uncle, w'at leave her rich, wus one time owned heaps of slaves; but he make up his mind jes a liddle while befo' he die dat he'd sell out ev'rything an git bushels of money an' jes go off somewhars an' live easy all de balunce o' his days. He wus jes sold off all his slaves, an' wus a fixin to sell off de plantation an' de balunce of his things; w'en he laid down an' died.

So w'en Bud's ole Missus come to take over her plantation; she wus got stock an' ev'rything else 'cep' Niggers. Bud say: W'en he fust git dar; he hafter cook, wash, iron, feed de stock, an' do ev'rything. His ole Missus almos' wuk him to death; but atter while she buy some mo' slaves an' he sorter git a let-up. Bein' wid her fust sorter make him a favoright wid de ole Missus; an' she take him almos' ev'rywhars wid her an' always keep him aroun' her.

One day, soon atter she wus done buyed Bud, she tell him to git up a couple o' hours or so befo' day de nex' mawnin, to ketch her hoss an' put a saddle an' bridle on 'im, to ketch hisself up a mule an' bridle it to ride along wid her; caze she wus a gwineter go to town. She wus a gwineter go down dar an' buy things an' fix up so dat de poo'-Achan ole bachelors an' white trash out in her diggins would know dat she wusnt none of deir kind. Of co'se she wus a ole maid; but atter she git rich, she wus a lookin' fer a young fryin' chicken. She wusnt a castin' 'bout fer no ole tough long-spurred dung-hill roosters fer to git hitched up wid.

Well, dey gits up away befo' day de nex' mawnin—away befo' de mawnin star 'gin to shine. Dey started to town; her a ridin' a hoss an' saddle, an' Bud a ridin' a mule a follerin on behin'. It wus so fur to town dat dey didn' git dar ontel dinner time.

W'en dey git down dar de ole Missus buy a dime's worth of cheese an' crackers. She skins de cheese, an' hands Bud over de skins wid a han'full of' crackers; an' she tells him: Dat'll stay on his stomach ontel dey gits back home. Den she e't de cheese an' de balunce of de crackers.

Nex, she go 'roun' to de stores, she do; an' buy herself a big fine pair o' new gaiters, w'at you could hear a cryin' almos' a mile away w'en she walk in 'em! She got her some fine cloth fer to make herself a dress wid, w'at wus got prutty big checks on it almos' as big as yo' hand. She buyed her a umbersol an' almos' ev'rything w'at you mought think of.

De ole Missus wus one-eyed; so she go aroun' an' git herself a glass eye to fix dat up wid. She wus lakwise bal'headed; an so she go 'roun' an' git herself a whole box full of false hair to fix dat up wid. De ole Missus' teef wus a gittin as scace as hen-teef. So she go 'roun' to a toof-dentis' an' git her some false teef. All dis take so long dat dey hafter git a place fer to stay all night, an' go home de nex' mawnin. W'en dey gits ready fer to go; she makes Bud git on de mule, an' loads him all over wid bundles an' boxes an' den starts off.

W'en dey gits almos' home dey ketches up wid Long Jim Skimson—a white man w'at wus a ole bachelor. All de folkses called him Long Jim; caze he wus so tall dat his head wus outn de county. He know Miss Jane; an' he wus sorter in a notion o' settin up to her, beance she wus done turned in an' got rich. He wus a walkin' down de road at de time to ole Zip Ivory's plantation to see if he could git de job of bein' de Overseer fer de Niggers over dar. W'en de ole Missus cotched up wid 'im; he tipped his slouch-brimmed Lon'on-troop-sailor hat, an' scratched his toe eight or ten foot behin' 'im an' say: "Mawnin, Miss Jane! I wus jes a thinkin' 'bout you! You knows de ole sayin' 'bout dat!"

"Now look here, Long Jim", broke in ole Miss Jane, "if you haint got no nothin better fer to hint at dan 'If you thinks 'bout de Devil, his Imps'll 'pear' you can pick up yo' walkin' papers an' tote yo'self on off."

Long Jim, he up an' 'spon', he do: "Law, Miss Jane! I wusnt a thinkin no nothing of dat 'ar kind! I dont know dat I's ever jes heard it jes zackly dat way. By my ricommembunce it go dis way: 'If you thinks 'bout de Angels, you's a gwineter hear de flutterin' of deir wings'."

W'en Long Jim manage to stick in sumpin 'bout de Angels (Bud say); his ole Missus reddened up in de face lak a beet, an' her long crooked nose git to lookin' lak a pod o' red pepper. Terreckly she say: "You sees, Mr. Jim, we womens has to thump de watermillions an' look at de curls once in a while to see whedder dey wus green or ripe. Yo' polergizin' an' perfessin' is 'cepted; an' de wind are a blowin' from de Souf, an' a bringin' de flowers back wid 'em ag'in.

Atter Miss Jane talk all flopper lak dat; her an' Long Jim go on off down de road—him a walkin', her a ridin', an' Bud a follerin along behin' on de mule. Long Jim wus dat tall; as he go down de road a walkin by de side of ole Miss Jane on a hoss; dat his towseled up head strike a dead level, an' one wus jes as tall up from de groun; as de tother.

Long Jim roll off all kinds of big courtin' words to Miss Jane; an' she draw back her mouf an' try to giggle lak she wus a gal. She put on a whole heaps of aires; an' at las' she hol' her pocket hankcher in her hand an' chaw it wid her mouf jes lak sho 'nough gals does now days w'en dey wus sorter in de notion of sayin' "yes." W'en Long Jim see dis; he think dat it 'twus jes 'bout time to call fer ole Miss Jane fer his wife, an' rake in all her new-got rich beslongins fer hisself. So he say to her: "Miss Jane, I knows you an' you knows me.

If you'll jes draw de iron of my arms into chains,
An' pass 'em 'bout you back to me;
I'll go git de preacher, an' we'll lock up togedder,
An' den we'll throw away de key."

W'en Long Jim say all dis; ole Jane git mo' redder in de face dan befo'.

Den she say to 'im: "Jim, I likes you right good: an'; if you wusnt a gitin' along to a time of life; dat w'en I looks in yo' mouf dat it pear lak all de chairs wus 'bout fell outn yo' parlor; I thinks dat you mought suit me an' we mought make it. You see, w'en folkses gits rich, it make 'em git young. I mus' spark aroun' wid some of de young fry fr awhile; an' den, if dey dont seem zackly fer to fill my fryin' pan, we mought talk ag'in 'bout fastenin' up all our pigs in de same pen."

Long Jim den make answer to her dat it dont look to him lak dat she need none o' dem 'ar young fry on her big plantation aroun' 'mongst her rusty dollars. She need a big tall settled man, a sho 'nough man, w'at can look all over her plantation from one en' to de tother.

Ole Missus tell 'im dat she wusnt so sho 'bout dat. She think dat if she jes could see de right man, dat she herself mought could furnish de age.

Long Jim say to her dat she'd better look out; caze he wus done heard it sayed a whole heaps o' times, dat gittin rich sometimes turned folkses' heads so much dat it twis' 'em clean smack off.

W'en Long Jim say dis, he make Miss Jane fightin' mad. He wus befo' dis got a sort of walkin' papers w'at make him keep up wid a hoss a gwine along de road; but w'en Miss Jane git mad she hand him a bran' span new set w'at took him so fur off dat Bud say dat he haint never hearn tell of 'im since. As he go to leave her in de road, an' take to de woods; she holler out to 'im: "No! I dont want no ole mens! I's already got w'at can do all dey can do. I's got a parrot w'at can cuss; I's got a taller candle w'at can smoke; an' I's got a cat w'at can stay out all night sometimes w'en I dont want it to do it. Dat's all you ole mens can do; an' you's stock crazy, if you thinks dat we rich womens is a gwineter git hitched up wid yo' kind."

Bud say; w'en all dis took place; he jes couldn' he'p hisself, an' he laugh out a liddle. Den ole Miss Jane, she look back, she do, an' she holler out to 'im: "Nigger! W'ats dat you's laughin' 'bout?" Den Bud tell her dat he wus jes thinkin' 'bout w'at her tother Niggers wus sayed 'bout Bal-headed Jerry w'at she wus jes bought a day or so befo';—Dat wus fer why he laugh. De tother Niggers say: W'en Bal'-headed Jerry come, all de flies on de plantation go light right on his slick noggan fer to shake hands wid 'im; an' dey all slipped up an' busted deir brains out. W'en dis took place; de flies' brains got so mixed up wid Bal'-headed Jerry's brains dat he wusnt got 'nough sense on de change of de moon to lead a blind goose to water.

Ole Missus git 'nough of her good humor back, over w'at Jerry say, to make her give a couple of dry grins.

Den dey git solemcholly ag'in; caze it look to her lak sitch sassy Niggers as dem mought git up a Nigger-risin'. So she say to Bud: "W'en you goes down to de Nigger quarters, w'en you gits home, Bud; you tell dem tother Niggers dat dey'd better mind out not to say nothin' 'g'inst dat deir Missus do or buy. If dey dont watch out somebody's back mought git mixed up wid sumpins brains an' limbs; an' dat wont be so funny.

Bymeby dey gits home. De tother Niggers puts up de hosses an' feeds 'em; an' Bud go on off to his cabin. Atter he git hisself a liddle snack of victuals; he go down to de Nigger quarters, an' he tell 'em dat dey'd better dri'e mighty slow in talkin' 'bout w'at Miss Jane buyed in de way of bald-headed Niggers if dey wants all de hickries to stay on de trees whar dey beslongs. Dey makes answer to 'im: All right, deir moufs wus sewed up good an' tight widout thread; caze dey wusnt a gwineter have no words a spillin' outn 'em w'at mought call fer de ole Missus to come aroun' an' whup 'em togedder wid her hick'ry needles.

Miss Jane res' herself up ontel de nex' day; den she got in fer to make up all her fine'ry w'at she wus got down town. Whilst she wus a settin dar an' a sewin'; who should come over fer to see her but Billy Biggerots w'at wus de pick an' choice of all de poo' white trash in dem diggins, in dem times. Miss Jane wus powerful glad to see 'im come a courtin; caze she figger out dat he wus got de looks, an' she wus got de spondoolics, an' 'twixt an' 'tween 'em dey wus got all dere wus a gwine. [Spondoolics = money. The Negro formulated in his mind this word as follows: "spon"—something that brings response; "doo"—something which does things; "lics"—something with which one may strike a blow.]

Ole Miss Jane wus so fixed up wid her glass eye an' her false teef an' her false hair dat her own Niggers didn' scacely know her! An' Mon! W'en Billy look at her an' think 'bout all dem riches she wus got; he think dat she wus pruttier dan a speckled pullet. He sot upd ar, he did, an' he fust rolled lovie-dovie eyes at her; an' den he sputter off love words to her lak water a runnin' down a ditch atter a big summer rain storm. He almos' good as ax her to have 'im; an' she almos' good as say "yes". Bymeby he riz to go home; an' she tell 'im as he leave dat he mus come back an' eat dinner wid her nex' Sunday.

He go away, an' as he go along de road home; he go a singin. Dis wus de song:

2. How ole is yo' gal, Billy Boy, Billy Boy?
   How ole is yo' gal, charmin Billy?
   She's jes about sixteen, an' she's fine 'nough fer a queen.
   She's a young thing an' caint leave her mother.

3. Did she ax you to set down, Billy Boy, Billy Boy?
   Did she ax you to set down, charmin Billy?
   Yes she axed me to sit down, wid her hand put on my crown,
   She's a young thing and caint leave her mother.

4. Can she make a cherry pie, Billy Boy, Billy Boy?
   Can she make a cherry pie, charmin Billy?
   She can make a cherry pie, quicker 'an a can can wink her eye.
   She's a young thing and caint leave her mother.

W'en Billy git away over de hills, a gwine towards home; he meets up wid Long Jim Skimson, w'at ole Miss Jane wus already sacked an' put over in de corner. Long Jim say to 'im: "Hullo Billy! Whar is you been?

Billy, he make answer, he do: "I's been over a cuttin aroun' de rich Miss Jane! An' I tells you Jim; w'en I looks at de big plantation an' de Niggers, an' dem turns an' looks at dem prutty eyes of hearn, an' dat long hair an' dem prutty white teef; I thinks dat we'd make a mighty prutty matched team a holdin' hands an' a pullin on de same single-tree in front of de preacher."

Of co'se Long Jim wus sore caze Miss Jane wus done laid him offn her co'tin' job; but w'en he hear all dis he git so tickled dat he give one o' dese here hoss-laughs. Den he say: "Lawsy-mussy, Billy! You haint a studyin' about marryin' dat ole 'oman, I hopes, w'at's been in de storm long 'nough fer to be yo' great-granmammy befo' you wus born, is you?"

Billy make answer an' say to 'im, he do, dat he dont see no ole-time looks 'bout Miss Jane. He wus jes git mistaken in his las' year's bacon!— "W'y!" says he; "Dat 'oman's hair is as brown as a ches'nut, an' so long dat she can set down on it. Her teef is so prutty an' clean an' nice an' white dat dey looks lak fresh skined grains of lye hominy. Her eyes is as prutty watery blue lak de sky on a warm sun-shiny day in de middle o' May."

W'en Billy wus sayed all dis, Long Jim looked at him sorter puzzled; den sayed to him: "Look here Billy, I thought dere mus' be sumpin wrong w'en you telled me dat you wus done been over dar fer to see Miss Jane an' w'en I heared you signing 'She's a young thing an' caint leave her mother.' I dont see no way to splain you' fix onless you wus got some o' dem 'ar Niggers o' hern to make up some o' deir conjer mass an' strew it 'roun' you.—W'y Billy! Miss Jane haint got no long brown hair w'at she can set down on. She's slick bald-headed 'cep' a liddle patch in de kitchen on de back of her head. As fer teef; I knows dat she haint got no mo' 'an two or three, if she wus got dat much. De fact is: I haint seed her wid no teef at 'tall fer many a day. An' so fur as eyes is concerned; dat 'ar 'oman is one-eyed in one eye, an' moon-eyed in de tother."

Well, Billy an' Long Jim stan' up to one-nudder an' ogify de p'ints all over Miss Jane. Long Jim wus a tryin fer to tell Billy dat he wus got conjer-tricked by ole Miss Jane's Niggers an' Billy wus a tryin to show dat he wusnt no sitch a thing. At lat' dey lef' one nudder an' went on home.— Long Jim a feelin' sorry fer Billy a bein' hoodooed an' Billy a feelin lak he dont know how he feel.

W'en Billy git home, he think to hisself dat Long Jim wus jes git taken wid de jealousies caze he think dat he wus about to marry off rich. But den ag'in he think dat it wus kinder cu'ious dat Long Jim would come along an' spin setch a big long yarn dat it would break in two in de middle from its own weight befo' nobody could git no chance fer to tie it on to nothin'. So he set aroun' home dar, he do, an' he think an' he think; an' he think, an' den he think some mo'. At las' he say to hisself dat he reckin dat he should oughter sorter zamine into Long Jim's sifter-water-bucket tale; dough he think dat it look powerful foolish an' onreasonable.

Den he 'gin to ax hisself how he wus a gwineter zamine into de thing an' see w'at wus right. He say to hisself dat he wus been a lookin right straight at Miss Jane; an' if his eyes wus so hoodooed dat dey didn' see w'at dey did see; he didn see no way of telled de head from de tail of de buisness. He dont see no way dat he can fumble wid her hair; caze all de women folks gits powerful mad if you towsels dat up. He lakwise dont see no way fer to fix up a scuse fer to be a tetchin aroun' wid her eyes an' teef.

At las' he struck up on a plan. He make up his mind to borry a hoss fer to ride over fer to see her nex' Sunday w'en he wus to go to eat dinner wid her. W'en de Niggers onsaddle his hoss an' put 'im up to feed, he'll make 'me hang de saddle on de stable doo'; an' den he'll go on off up to de house an' ax Miss Jane if she can see de brass tacks a stickin in de saddle away down dar on de stable doo'.

So de nex' Sunday w'en he go to dinner at Miss Jane's; he do all dis. Atter her an' him wus been a settin out on de pie-izzer fer a while a courtin' an' a carryin' on; he say to her: "Janie, Honey, can you see de stable?" an' she make answer: "Yes, Sweet-heart!"

Den he say to her: "Honey, can you see de liddle brass tacks a stickin' in my saddle a hangin' on de stable doo?" an' she say: "Yes Sweetheart, I sees de stable an' de saddle an' de tacks; but I dont see de stable doo'."

Billy, he sot dar, he did, an' he didn' say much. He wus a doin' a liddle bitsy thinkin on his own hook. He think dat it wus mighty cu'ious 'bout her seein de tacks an' de saddle an' not seein' de doo'. At las' he say to her: "Honey, yo' eyes mus' be diffunt from most folkses. W'y! I can see de doo' a heaps better dan I can see de saddle an' de tacks."

Ole Miss Jane see w'ich a way de wind wus a blowin' an' she make answer, she do, "Well, w'en I wus a poo' Yap, I couldn' see good; but now since I wus got rich, my eyes wus got so dey can see de liddlest things mo' samer dan de biggest ones."

Atter dis, she scuse herself from Billy fer a minute, an' go into de house to Bud (so Bud say); an' she tells him dat she wus a gwineter send 'im up in dey hay loft over de stable fer to git her some hen-aigs fer din-ner. She dont want him to go right den; but to wait n' go w'en she call an' tell 'im out offn de pie-izzer. Dere wus jes one udder thing dat she want him to do; an' dat wus dis: To take a liddle fine sewin needle along wid 'im, an' stick it in de gate-post, as he go into de hoss-lot to de stable an' to be shore to leave dat needle stickin dar. At las' she tell Bud dat she never wus done hit 'im ne'er a hick since she buyed 'im; but if he should hap-pen to leave off de stickin of dat 'ar needle in de gate-post, she sho would have to send fer de patterrollers in dem diggins fer to come an' try deir hands out on 'im. Bud say, he tell her "Yassum!" Dere wusnt no danger of him fergitin to do w'at-some-ever she tell 'im, an' all dat she tell 'im.

W'en de ole Missus git through wid Bud she go back out on de pie-izzer whar Billy wus. She sot dar an' talked a liddle while wid 'im, den she hollered out: "Oh Bud! Is you been an' git de aigs yit fer yo' Marse Billy's dinner?"

Bud make answer: "No Mam, Missus!"

Den she say to Bud: "Go down to de stable right away, look up in de hay-loft, git some fresh hen-aigs, an' hurry up an' git de dinner ready."

So Bud take de needle an' start off fer de hay-loft down at de stable. He sticked de needle into de gate-post as he go into de hoss-lot, went on an' got de aigs, an' den come on back to de house.

Atter while Miss Jane say to Billy: "Look 'way down yonder at de gate-post of de hoss-lot gate! Does you see w'at dat is a stickin' in de gate-post?"

Billy look an' he look; he squinch his eyes an' he squinch his eyes. At las' he make answer to her dat he dont see no nothin' a stickin in no gate-post nowhars.

Den Miss Jane tell 'im dat she see sumpin; an' dat "sumpin" wus a sewin needle a stickin up in de post as big as life an' twice as natchul.

Billy declar' to "Gracious" dat he dont see no nothin'; an' he dont see how nobody else could see sumpin as liddle as a sewin' needle away off down dar to "Never".

Miss Jane make answer to 'im: Well, dat fine rich womens wid fine rich eyes could see lak dat!

Billy say to her dat he caint see no ways how dat git fixed up an' take place.

At las' she tell 'im to come an' go wid hr down to de post at de hoss-lot gate; den he can see fer hisself whedder w'at she say wus fer a fact or not. So dey bofe gits up an' goes down to de post to zamine it. Shore 'nough! Dar wus de needle a stickin' in it.

Billy hurry up an' pull de needle outn de gate-post, he do' an' he zamine it, an' roll it 'round ' mongst his fingers to make shore at his eyes wusnt in 'clipse an' de Imps wusnt a makin' 'im see w'at he didn' see. He look, an' he feel, an' he zamine; an' he wus jes bleedged to think dat de needle wus dar onless he think dat it 'twusnt him a lookin' an' a feelin'. So he make up his mind dat it must be dar shore 'nough.

Dey takes de needle, an' walks on back towards de house. Whilst dey wus a walkin' back; Billy, he tell her dat she must sorter overlook his axin her so many foolish questions about her seein'. He tell her 'bout de long rig-a-ma-role w'at dat "Lowdowned" Long Jim tell 'im 'bout her. He say to her dat she wus de pruttiest thing dat ever trod de dirt; an' he love her mo' harder dan a mule could kick. He declar' dat he never would a axed her no nothin' 'bout seein', 'cep' dat he wus done heared some of de "Big" folks say dat love wus blind; an' he lover her so much dat he wus a wonderin' if he could see wid his eyes at 'tall. How-some-be-ever, he see dat he wus done lost part of his sight from lovin' her so much, by his not seein' de needle sticked in de gate-post; an' he hope she wont go an' drap him if he turn an' go stone-blind from lovin' her.

Miss Jane make answer dat Long Jim wus jes sore un'er his hoss-collar caze she give 'im his walkin' papers w'en he come aroun' a wantin' fer to marry her. She say to Billy dat she wont drap 'im 'tall onless dat he show dat he wus 'bout go git ole an' stiff in de j'ints; an' she dont see no sign of dat yit eben dough he look lak he mought be a liddle on de blind order w'en it come to lookin' fer a needle in a gate-post. Billy, he thank her, an' about dat time, de Niggers call 'em bofe into dinner.

Bud say dat dey had de table fixed up jes as prutty as a speckled pup. Dey eben had de blossoms of "Ole Maids" an' "Bachelor's Buttons" all stuck up in a tumbler of water in de middle of de table lak de "Bigges'-to-do." Dey had it all spread up wid one o' dese here prutty big red table clofs an' white chiny dishes; an' de iron knives an' forks wus been rubbed up wid ashes by de Niggers ontel you could see yo' face in 'em. At de head of de table, dar wus a great big white chiny milk pitcher; an' it wus all filled up wid fine think blue-john clabber fer dinner.

W'en Miss Jane got to de doo' of de room whar de table wus set, she wus a walkin' jes in front of Marse Billy. All of a sudden she run an' leave 'im. She runed up to de end of de table whar de big white milk pitcher wus a settin'; an' all of em sorter stan' still to see w'at she wus up to. W'en she git up to de end of de table, she holler out: "Scat!!" An' den she haul off an' slap de milk-pitcher, milk an' all, off on de floo'; an' she break an' spill ev'rything to flinders!

You see (Bud say) dat de ole Missus couldn' see good; an' she think dat de milk-pitcher wus her big ole white cat done jumped up on de table an' she wus runned an' whirled in to slap 'im off. W'en she wus seed how wrong she wus; she busted out in a great big cry; an' Billy, he busted out in a great big laugh, an' went an' got on his hoss an' rid off home.

Atter dat, Billy an' Long Jim go aroun' through dem parts an' say so many cu'ious things 'bout Miss Jane dat de tother young white mens wus sorter skeared to go to see her; but de women folks sorter pay her a liddle mind, beance she wus a new comer an' beance her ole rich Uncle wus lef' her rich. Dese here women folks subgest dat she take to gwine to church on a Sundays. Some of de womens likes her right well. So dey tells her: If she'll go out to church, de mens'll see dat dere haint nothin' cu'ious 'bout her, den she'll git mo' beaux dan she can knot-up wid. How-some-be-ever dey tells her: She jes mus' git a fan; caze all dem bit "High Flies" out dar took bought fans wid 'em to church instid of tucky wings.

She tells de womens dat she wus got ev'rything 'cep' a fan; an' she wus a gwine to town to git dat too right away. So de nex' mawnin she git Bud outn de bed away befo' day. She order him to git dat hoss an' mule ready fer to go to town. W'en dey wus got ready fer to go; Miss Jane ricomember dat she wus done gone an' clean fergit it offn' her mind about de name of de thing wa't she want to buy. But she mount her hoss an' start off; an' Bud he foller 'long behin' her a ridin' a mule. Dey fust rid by one of de neighbors' houses fer to ax de name of de thing w'at she wus a gwineter buy downtown.

Dey gits dis neighbor up outn de bed; an' she tells Miss Jane dat de name of de thing wus a "fan".

Miss Jane thank her; an' den she rid on 'way. She stick de switch to her hoss fer to make 'im go, an' as he hard-trot an' jolt her up an' down; she say along wid his heels, as dey slap de ground, "Fan-fan! Fan-fan! Fan-fan! Fan-fan!" She keep dis up all along de road so as not to fergit w'at she wus a gwine to town to buy.

Atter while dey day 'gin to break, an' de folkses here an' dar 'gin to stir aroun'; an' one de way, dey met a ole speckled-faced dried-up lookin' white man. He wus cross-eyed; an' so he wus jes bleedged to hold Miss Jane up an' ax her, if she knowed somewhars he mought git de job of bein' de plantation Overseer.

She tell 'i dat all de "Big" folkses up her way wus got Overseers 'cep' her. Up to a few weeks ago, she didn' have no slaves much; an' she wus jes been sorter a usin' her Nigger Bud dar fer to kinder overlook de tother Niggers. But countin' up de batch w'at she wus buyed a day or so ago; she wus now got up'ards of forty slaves, an' she reckin dat she wus a gwineter hafter have some sort of a Overseer.

He tell her dat his name wus Skimpy Ben Blesson; an' he'd love mighty much fer to git de job. Den he handed her over his ricommends; an' ole Missus read 'em. As she read 'em dey go lak dis:

"Dis are Skimpy Ben Blesson. He are overseed our plantation over an' over. He dont whup an' lash much fer common; caze one straight look at a Nigger outn his off cross-eye are enough in ginerally fer to make 'em git up an' skeedadle. But w'en dem eyes of hisn fails fer to wuk de charm; he know how to make sound green limbs fall on seasoned black backs mo' faster dan de rotten ones fall off on de sof' ground enjorin of a big sowclone.

W'en you hires Mr. Blesson fer a Overseer: de worms, an' bugs, an' ants, an' de lak dont never bother 'long wid yo' crop much; caze w'en any one of 'em see Mr. Blesson a comin' dey hollers out to de tothers: 'Look out! Here come Skimpy Ben's big foot!' an' dey all gits up an' leaves yo' plantation so as not to git all de stuffin mashed outn 'em.

We haint got no time to tarry an' tell you 'bout all setch good qualities as his bein' able fer to drink a whole gallon of peach brandy; an' yit not to git so tipsy dat he caint foller de Niggers an' make 'em go still mo' faster still. He haint never scacely good drunk 'cep' w'en he git to lyin' on his face in de furrows in 'twist de corn-rows. An' eben den, he seem to know w'at his big last meal of victuals is a drivin' at.

All de folkses down here wus loved so much dat dey wus nick-named him 'Whisky-bottle'. Wid de white ladies, he are as gentle as a lam', an' as lovin' as a houn'-dog; an' so he are a great favoright wid dem. To llarn all his good qualities; you'll jes hafter hire 'im! Hire 'im an' see!"

Bud say w'en ole Missus see all dis writ down in black an' white; she up an' hire 'im right den an' dar, an' sont 'im on off out to de plantation. Bud say dat he dont blame ole Missus much fer doin' it; caze w'en he hear de ricommends, an' look at Skimpy Ben's eyes an' footses, dey all sho did look lak dey beslonged in de same goober-pea shell.

All dis here segashautin an' palaver take so long dat; w'en Miss Jane git through wid Skimpy Ben an' start on de balunce of de journey; she wus done clean fergit offn her mind ag'in w'at she wus a gwine to town fer to buy. She axed Bud w'at de name of de thing wus; but he wus been a studyin' so hard 'bout Skimpy Ben's gross-eye a lookin' straight at 'im, an' 'bout how his "grubb-grabbers" could make de limbs fall on salves' backs, dat de word "fan" wus don fluttered clean away from him too. So he tell Miss Jane dat he dont know.

Of co'se he knowed all 'bout fans befo' he git sold Souf, an' atter so long a time he ricomember de word; but he wus skeard fer to tell Miss Jane, caze she mought think dat he wus a tryin fer to play antic, an' den she mought p'int him out dat evenin' fer de fust one fer Skimpy to try out his limbs on. So he jes "Keep yo' seat Miss Lize Jane an' hol' on to de train." [A quotation from a Negro secular song.]

Miss Jane, she rid on down de road, she did, towards town; jes a studyin' an' a tryin fer to think of de name of de trick dat she wus a gwine atter. Bymeby, she holler out to Bud: "Oh! I's got de name ag'in now! De name is "Flip-flap-cooler!" Bud, he jes make answer, "Yassum Missus!"

Atter dat, as de ole hoss go a hard-trottin' down de road; Miss Jane wus jes bent an' boun' not to fergit dat name no mo'. So as his footses hit de groun, she say along wid 'em: "Flip-flap! cooler! Flip-flap! cooler!"

Bymeby dey gits to town, an' hitches deir nags an' goes to de stores. Ole Missus walk into de fust store, she do; an' she holler out to de store-keeper: "Is you got any Flip-flap-coolers here?" Dis man make answer: "No, I haint got no setch a thing as dat!"

She go into de nex' store, an' she call out in dar: "Is you got any Flip-flap-coolers here?" an' dis man say lakwise dat he haint got no setch a thing. Den she go into a whole heaps of stores; an' she say dis same thing, an' she git dis same answer.

At las' she go into a Jew-store—one o' dem 'ar kind w'at keep ev'rything from hoss-hames to hankchers. She holler out to de Jew: "Is you got any Flip-flap-coolers here?"

De Jew, he look at her an' think fer a minute; den he say to her: "Yes, I specs I is; an' if I haint I's got sumpin else w'at's jes as good!" But Miss Jane tell de Jew dat she dont want no nothin' else w'at's jes as good. She want a genuwine Flip-flap-cooler! De Jew ax her: W'at kind of a thing a Flip-flap-cooler wus. But whilst he wus a axin her dat; he wus a pullin' down an' a layin' out on de counter hats, umbersols, hoes, hoss-collars, chains, hame-strings, an' ev'rything else so as to make shore fer to sell her—w'atever else he do.

W'en ole Miss Jane see dis Jew a pullin' down an' a lyin' out ropes an' coff' pots an' all dem things befo' her; she git mad. So as he ax her w'at a Flip-flap-cooler wus; she best in an' answer him an' say:

"Good Gawd-a-mighty man;
Dont you know?
'Sunday-go-to-meetin' 'thing!
You do jes so."

W'en she say de words; "You do jes so", she fan her face wid her hands. Den de Jew say: "Oh yes, you did vant a fan!" An' ole Missus say: "Yes, I reckins dat wus de name; caze it sound sorter lak Flip-flap-cooler."

De Jew give her one of his prutty big broad grins; an' go an' git down a whole big arm-full of fans. Dey wus all dem big pa'mleaf kind as big as a parlor table top. He den tell her dat he wus a gwineter sell her one cheaper dan ev'rybody else in de worl'; if she jes wont tell nobody 'bout it. W'en he git de pa'mleaf fans all spread out befo' her, he tell her: Beance it wus her; he'd let her take one along fer a dollar, but she musn tell nobody caze dey wus worth four or five time dat much! He sell her de fan in a liddle o' no time; an' her an' Bud wus soon on deir nags a gwine back home ag'in. Dey got back home away up in de night; but Bud didn' mind dat, caze ole Missus wus so proud dat she wus got dat pa'mleaf fan, an' feel so good 'bout it dat she give him some biscuits fer his supper instid o' corn cake w'at so rough dat it scratch his th'oat as it go down.

Atter dey wus got back home, ev'rything go on as about fer common' 'cep dat de Overseer make it mighty warm fer dem comfield darkies an' keep 'em on de jump. Skimpy Ben live up to his agreements, an' his ricommends. Bud say he keep outn trouble wid de Overseer caze he wus de House Boy.

Ole Miss Jane go on out to church on a Sunday an' she kep' her big pa'mleaf fan a gwine in de hopes dat she'd ketch a beau. She roll dat glass eye an' she show dem false teef an' she pin on dat false hair so as to ketch some of de young fry fer a husband; but dey scoots aroun' an' keeps outn her retch. W'en she wus kep' up a tryin' dis fer 'bout a year; she give outn de notion a ketchin de young bucks, an' 'gun to try to trap up some of de ole ones w'at wus sorter a gittin stiff in de j'ints. But de ole mens look lak dey wusnt much in a notion of gittin hooked up on her long crooked nose.

Dey had a powerful preacher in dem times out dar in de white folkses' church. His name wus Parson Hezekiah Ezekiel Loky. W'en he git warmed up; he pull off his coat lak de Nigger preachers; an' he preach lak he wus a gwineter t'ar hisself all to pieces.

He make a whole heaps of tellin folks dat dey can git anything if dey prays an' axes de Lawd fer it. So ole Miss Jane think over w'at dis here preacher say, an' she 'gin one night to pray fer a husban'. She pray away an' she pray away a axin de Lawd fer to giver her one.

Atter while a great big ole whoop owl outdoors holler out: "Whoo—! Whoo—! Whoo-whoo-whoo—!" Ole Missus stop her prayin' an' lissen fer a while; but she dont hear no mo'. So she 'gin to pray away 'gin fer a husban'. Atter while de ole owl outside holler ag'in: "Whoo—! Whoo—! Whoo-whoo-whoo—!" She stop prayin', she do, an' she holler back to de owl: "Anybody Lawd, jes so he wear britches!" Wid de prayers all finished, she go on to bed an' go to sleep.

De nex' day, she wus a settin out on her pie-izzer all fixed up wid her big pa'mleaf fan in her hand; w'en ole crosseyed Skimpy Ben, de Overseer, come up fer to talk wid her. He fust chat wid her 'bout de wedder an' de wuk on de plantation; but atter while he manage to drap dis an' lay out to her how prutty she wus a lookin'. An' befo' he git through good wid tellin' her dis; he wus a tellin' her 'bout his wantin' fer to marry her.

Bud say dat ole Skimpy would a married anything fer a plantation; an' dat wus fer why he wus a settin up to ole Miss Jane. She look at his ole speckled face an' cross—uped eyes, an' she think to herself dat a liddle beauty sleep wouldn' hurt 'im; but she ricomember over de ole sayin' dat "Prutty wus dat prutty does". She lakwise run over in her mind 'bout de prayin': an' she think dat Skimpy's comin' to her on de very nex' day look lak dat de Lawd mought a sont 'im. So Miss Jane tell Skimpy Ben, de Overseer, dat she'll marry him.

Skimpy, he go down town, he do, an' he git a couple o' pairs of licenses fer de preacher to git him an' ole Miss Jane togedder. Dey axed in all de neighbors an' dey got married. Bud say dere wus a whole passel of folkses dar; an' de preacher tell de couple dat it wus de custom in dem parts fer de bride an groom to lead de 'sembled congregation in de singin' of a weddin song. So he tell 'em to start up de song.

Skimpy, he say to Miss Jane, he do: "Ole 'Oman, you lead de song." She say back to 'im, she do; "Ole man, you knows I caint sing. You can sing. So, you lead de song."

Skimpy Ben, say, he do, "I would lead de song; but I dont know w'at I should oughter sing."

Miss Jane make answer, she do: "Oh, I can give you de song to sing! Sing dat song dat go dis way:

'Dis is de way I long has sought;
An' mourned all caze I foun' it not.'

Well, Skimpy cleared up his th'oat an' tried to lead off de song through his nose; but dere wus so much gigglin dat he didn' do no good much, an' he had to dry up.

At las' dey called 'em all to co me to de weddin' dinner. Miss Jane she tell 'em all dat dey'd hafter wait fer a liddle while ontel she bresh an' fix herself up some fer gracin up de table. She den go into anudder room to wash her face an' so on' an' she take her husban', Skimpy Ben, along wid her. Skimpy wus been a livin as de Overseer on de plantation; but he haint never seed no Miss Jane git ready fer dinner.

W'en she got off into de room, she retched up an' pult off dat false hair o' hern an' 'gin to comb it; an' Skimpy he stood dar a lookin' at her bald head wid eyes stretched ontel dey wus de size of y o' straw hat. Nex' she retched up an' pult out dat glass eye o' hern an' laid it in a cup o' water; an Skimpy looked lak he wus jes stonished. Den she retched in her mouf an' pult out de false teef an' laid dem out fer a scrubbin. Skimpy wus jes flammergasted, an' he say: "Ole 'Oman, haint dere none of you dar at 'tall; or is you all simpin else?"

Dis make Miss Jane powerful mad, an' dey 'gin to fuss. Bud say dat dey would a parted right den an' dar; if de ladies an' gemmun waiters hadn' a come to git 'em bofe to come on in to dinner atter dey wus done got tired of waitn' fer 'em.

Well, dey git through wid de weddin' an' 'gin to live togedder; but Bud say dey wus jes a jowerin all de time lak cats an' dogs. Skimpy tell Miss Jane dat she wus done gone an' go stock crazy, caze she wus got rich. Miss Jane tell Skimpy dat he wus come from nothin' from nowhars; an' dat he wus a gwine back whar he come from.

W'en Skimpy's friends an' poo' relations come aroun' him; he'd take 'em wid 'im all over de whole plantation an' brag. He'd tell 'em: Jes look at *my* crops, jes look at *my* hosses, jes look at *my* cows, an' so on. Ole Miss Jane heared all dis; an' she tol' Skimpy dat she want him to dry-up his talkin' to folkses 'bout *my* "so an' so". She lay it out to 'im dat ev'rything aroun' dar wus hern; dat she mought let him say *ourn*, an' dat wus jes about as fur as she wus a gwineter let dat thing go.

Skimpy tell her dat dere wusnt no 'oman from nowhars w'at could drive his wagin fer him; an' dat wus all dere wus about dat! Ole Miss Jane make answer dat she wusnt a tryin to drive no wagin of hisn from nowhars; she wus jes a leadin' her own hosses aroun' by deir own halters.

W'at wus mo' dan dat: She wus a gwineter cork up dat jimmyjohn onless he stop it up hisself.

Skimpy try to stop de fuss by sayin:

"Needles an' pins, needles an' pins;
W'en a man marry his troubles begins."

But Miss Jane go right on wid her part of de squabble ontel Juvember.

Ev'rything sorter worry 'long ontel Skimpy's friends an' relations come to see 'im ag'in. He take 'em as fer common over de Missus' plantation, a showin' 'em "his" so an' so. Den he bring 'em to de house; an' he take 'em into de parlor whar Miss Jane wus a settin'. He sot down on de sofa widout pullin' off his hat; he cross up his legs an' he go on a talkin' 'bout "*his*" fine hosses, "*his*" fine cows, "*his*" fine crops, an' "*his*" fine so an' so.

All of a sudden, ole Miss Jane haul off an' take a swipe at Skimpy's head wid de handle of de broom a settin in dar in de corner. She take 'im by sprise! How-some-be-ever he dodge; an' she miss his head, but she git his hat. De hat hit de floo' an' rolled un'er de sofa; an' Skimpy, he tumbled down an' rolled un'er dar behin' it.

Ole Miss Jane stan' up in de middle of de floo' an' wave de broomstick, an' holler un'er dar to 'im: "You come out from un'er dar, Sah! I haint got started wid givin' you w'at's a comin to you yit! Come out from un'er dar!—W'at's you doin' un'er dar anyhows?"

Den Skimpy make answer, sorter 'umble lak, away up un'er de sofa; "Honey! Dont be rough wid me. I's jes down un'er here a lookin fer 'our' hat."

By dat time, de tother mens, w'at wus dar fer to see Skimpy, wus grabbed hole of Miss Jane's broom; an' dey wus a swingin' on to it an' a beggin' her fer to have a liddle pity. She scuffle aroun' an' tell 'em to turn loose; she want de tother end of de broom to git de balunce of de trash outn de house. Whilst dey wus a holdin', an' scufflin, an' a sputin, an' a ogifyin; Skimpy he jumped out from un'er de sofa an' runned clean off.

Atter Skimpy git away an' de mens wus got Miss Jane aroun' to whar it wus safe fer to turn loose of de broom handle; dey leaves an' goes fer to look fer 'im. Dey wants to find out how it happen dat his ole 'oman git so handy wid de broom; w'en he wusnt a doin' nothin but a setin up an' a talkin' cross-legged. Atter dey wus been a ramblin aroun' through de woods fer a week or mo'; dey comed across him. Dey tries to talk wid him; but dey caint git no nothin outn' him 'cep':

"No wife to quawl,
No chilluns to bawl;
How happy dat man, w'at keep bachelor-hall."

"W'en Bud Stone got to dis part of de loration," said Samps, "he tell us dat he mus' be a gwine so as to git up to Vinegar Hall by night; but he say to us dat he wus a gwineter tell de balunce of w'at he know 'bout it all to de fust one w'at axes him over fer to stay all night, an' eat supper an' breakfus wid 'em."

At the conclusion of this part of the story, Mag, the wife, laughed heartily. She then said: "Samps, I thinks you'd better go right over to Vinegar Hill in de mawnin; an' ax Bud fer to come down an' stay a day or so wid us, de very fust time dat he git a chance fer to run off a liddle while from his mammy an' daddy."

WHY THE CAT AND THE DOG ARE ENEMIES

A few years ago after the Proclamation Emancipation, a few Negro families moved and settled in a little community about four miles southeast of Shelbyville Tennessee in a place commonly known as "The Bend of the River". They had apparently made a long journey thither; but as one looked at their possessions, consisting of scanty clothing, a few quilts, and many dogs, he could easily see that the largest task involved in the moving was the calling of the canines and the putting out of the fires.

In this community lived Aunt Ritter Motty and her little daughter Ferinie. It was late in the afternoon; and the mother and daughter were engaged in roasting an ashcake which was to be used as part of their evening meal. They had already stewed a rabbit for their supper which their industrious house-cat had brought in for herself during the morning only to have her owners take it and give her a cup of butter-milk as a substitute. As the ash-cake finished cooking, the mother pulled it from the ashes still partially wrapped in thick semi-charred brown paper. She unrolled it from its entanglements, rinsed off the adhering particles of charcoal and ashes with clear water, placed it on a tin plate, and the supper was ready.

Just as they seated themselves to partake of the meal, they heard a loud barking of their dogs in the thick woods a little more than a hundred yards distant.

"Dar now!" exclaimed the mother. "We's about to have mo' good luck in one day dan Chyarter's got oats!—De cat burng in a rabbit dis mawnin; an' dem 'ar dogs o' mine (I bounds you) is done gone an' treed a great big possum right at de house befo' de sun can git a chance fer to go down an' leave 'possum-light'. You run 'long to 'em, Honey; caze you's good an' soupple. Mammy'll git de ax an' come right on behin' you. I dont reckin dat it'll take us long fer to git 'im; caze de biggest possums climbs de liddlest trees. Jes a lick or two from a 'oman will bring him down to whar de dogs'll make him lay down an' play lak she been dead.—Humph! Rabbit fer supper an' possum fer breakfus! Somebody come hold me! I hopes Gable wont blow his hawn whilst all dese good eatins is a flotin' aroun!"

The child set out for the dogs as directed; and the mother, after getting her ax, followed at no very great distance behind. The child, upon reaching the sapling around which the dogs were barking a little in advance of her mother, cried out at the top of her voice: "Run, Mammy! come here quick!" to which came the answer: "Oh hesh up, Ferinie, an' don git so flusterated! Folks would think dat you never wus laid no eyes on no big possums befo' in yo' whole life."

By the time that this sentence was finished, the mother had reached the sapling. Looking up, she saw to her surprise her own pet cat perched among the topmost branches instead of the large o'possum of her imagination.

"Great punkin-bugs alive, Ferinie!" said the mother in disgust. "Haint you got sense 'nough fer to know yo' own pet cat from a possum?"

"Yassum!" came the reply. "But I jes thought you wouldn' want no nothin a botherin 'long wid yo cat w'at brung you in a great big rabbit to eat."

"You's mighty right!" answered Aunt Ritter; and gathering up stones, she hurled them with a precision that sent the yelping curs through the underbrush seeking a place of refuge and of safety.

With the dogs gone, Ferinie and her mother coaxed the cat down from the sapling; and picking it up, they carried it to the cabin, gently and fondly stroking down its fur. When there, they took down a rusty tin bucket top, poured into it a cup of milk and set it on the floor for the cat; then they seated themselves once more for their evening meal.

"Mammy", asked Ferinie, "w'at make de dogs always a runnin' an' a fightin' de cats; an' de cats always a runnin' from an' a spittin' at de dogs?"

Aunt Ritter looked at her child for a few moments rather perplexed, and then answered: "Chile, am it possible dat you's done growed up to be dis big, an' I haint tol' you an' nobody else haint never done tol' you how cats an' dogs come to fall out an' git to be inimies?"

"No 'am! Nobody haint never done tole' me nothin' 'bout nothin' o' dat kind"; replied Ferinie.

"Well, Honey, deir big fallin' out took place away back yon'er befo' de stars fell. [This has reference to the meteoric shower of 1833 which covered the southern part of the United States, when the Negroes thought that the end of the World had come.] Some say it wus away back yon'er a coon's age befo' folkses git to be white. My great-granmammy uster tell me 'bout it w'en I wus a heaps liddler dan you is now. My great-granmammy git to be so sole dat she couldn' do no wuk fer our ole Mosser; an' she wus so crooked up wid de rheumaties dat nobody wouldn' buy her. So ole Mosser took all us liddle strips of chilluns away from our own mammies; an' sont dem on off to de cotton-fiel' to wuk. Den he hands all us liddle chilluns over to my great-granmammy fer to raise. She uster feed us an' tell us a hole heaps 'bout how cats an' dogs come to fall out an' setch things.

"Now Mammy," interrupted Ferinie, "please tell me 'bout de cats an' dogs a gitin a hatin onenudder."

"All right;" responded the mother. "You's been a right good gal to-day; so whilst we's a eatin, I'll try to tell you if my ricomembunce dont give out on me.

I thinks my great-granmammy useter 'git it dis way: Away back yon'er one time, de animuls all live off by deirselves away from de folkses, out in de woods. Brer Dog an' Brer Cat walk aroun', dey do, an' see Mr. Man's big fine house; an' dey sayes to onenudder dat dey wants a big fine house too. Brer Dog, he up an' say, says he, dat dey can all git w'atsome-ever dey wants; if dey'll all jes put deir heads along side by side, an' pull togedder. Brer Cat say dat he 'gree wid Brer Dog all 'cep' he dont see no use in axin ev'rybody to come to de meetin' to build de house an' to live in it.

Brer Coon, Brer Rabbit, Brer Fox, Brer Benjermun Ram, Brer Monkey, Brer Polecat, an' Brer Possum all come 'long 'bout dat time a gwine home from a meetin; at de Big Brush (H)arbor Church; an' dey all stops an' jines in de confab. Dey all scratches deir heads a liddle; an' dey say fer de mostes' part dat dey dont see no need o' no house nohows at 'tall.

Dey sot aroun' dar in a circle scussin; an' Brer Fox he up an' say day dey caint build no house wid 'em all a pullin' apart, an' gee, an' haw all at de same time. So he move, vidin he could git a second dat dey make Brer Dog de Cheersman of de meetin; an' take up deir tother troubles w'at needed to be tended to 'mongst 'em.

Brer Benjermun Ram 'ject, he do. He say dat he jes natchfully hate Brer Dog caze he wus been a runnin' his chilluns lately; an' darfo' he dont want him fer no Cheersman.

Brer Cat make answer to dis day dey could scuss all dat w'en dey got de meetin to gwine. An' w'at wus mo'; if dey would jes pass his motion, an' make Brer Dog de Head Comolloger of de meetin;' He'll make a motion right away dat Brer Benjermun Ram wont 'ject to.

Brer Benjermun tell 'em: All right. If dat wus de case; he'd jes drive his ox-chyart to one side of de road, an' let deir wagin an' team go by. So Brer Cat driv' his wagin by; an' dey made ole Brer Dog de Head of de meetin'. As Brer Dog go to take his seat in de middle of de circle; he make 'em a crackin big speech, an' tell 'em if his hunkers dont fill up de seat of de Moderator, dat he'll rattle 'roun' in it 'nough to fill it up wid noise.

Now Brer Dog an' Brer Cat wus big friends; an' wus so thick dat you couldn' stir 'em wid a stick in a kittle of hot b'ilin water. So w'en dis here Brer Dog git through wid his speakin'; he wunk his off eye at Brer Cat, an' tol' him now wus de time fer him to make his moves w'at Brer Benjermun Ram wouldn' 'ject to.

Brer Cat riz up sorter slow lak, he did, an' he scratch his bead lak he wus a thinkin' w'at in de world he could motion for. Bymeby he say sorter meek lak; "Brer Moderator Cheersman; I moves you, I do, vidin I can git a second; since Brer Benjerman Ram is setch a fine big propintickler Stick-a-ma-stew; dat we all now votes to send him to Heaben.

Law, Chile! Dis here make Brer Benjerman Ram so mad dat he riz an' blated out: "I'll die fust!" Den he walked on off an' lef' de meetin'.

Atter Brer Benjermun Ram wus got off; Brer Cat, he riz, he did; an' he say: "Brer Moderator Cheersman an' Gentlemuns! I wants to polergize an' perfess dat I haint never hearn tell o' no place w'at wus mo' better dan Heaben. If I had a jes knowed of somewhars w'at wus better; Brer Benjermun Ram mought still be 'mongst us, a helpin us along wid his red-eyed wrinkled thoughts. But his name's done b'iled outn de pot; an' I reckins dat we'll hafter wag 'long widout him de best we knows how. An' now Brer Moderator Cheersman", say ole man Cat, "I sees from de case of Brer Benjermun Ram dat all of us mought git a liddle hot. So I specs dat we's a gwineter need some water to keep our th'oats from a gittin dry in de splavercations. So I motions you, vidin I can git a second, dat de ugliest man in our Compoodle go to de spring an' fetch us a big gourd full of cold water."

Chile! Befo' de tothers could git a chance to jine in wid Brer Cat's motion; Brer Monkey wus on his footses on his tip-toes jes a hollerin. He wus jes sizzlin hot, an' he bark off, blue mad: "Brer Moderator Cheersman (all 'cep' ole Tom Cat); I's jes riz to tell you all dat I haint a gwineter lug no gourds of water on my head up here to dis crowd fer nobody!"—Wid dat much handed out to 'em; Brer Monkey fergit dat he wus ever had a notion of bein in de meetin, an' he walk off, a darin' Brer Cat fer to make anudder motion whilst he wus in hearin distance of de meetin'. None of 'em look lak dey wants to git a mix-up wid ole Brer Monkey; so dey sot dar an' waited ontel he got outn sight an' outn hearin'.

Den Brer Coon, he git up, he do' an' he subgest dat Brer Cat sorter hold up wid his motionin, caze ev'ry time he make a motion he kill a member. Wid dem sort o' carryin's-on; dey soon wouldn' have nobody lef' fer to scuss an' vote one nothin'. All de tothers tetch an' 'gree wid Brer Coon; an' say de time wus come fer to git down to business.

Brer Dog, de Cheersman, tell 'em all right. Den he say to 'em dat de fust thing dat dey mus' do was to make up deir minds how dey wus a gwineter vote.

Brer Coon, he den helt up his prutty long tail wid rings all 'roun' it; an' he swish it aroun' an' look how fine it look. Den he up an' say, says he: "Gentermuns; I thinks de pruttiest way in de world fer us to vote is fer us all to hold up our prutty long bushy tails, an' let de Cheersman count 'em."

Brer Fox den throwed up his prutty long red bushy tail an' swished it an' hollered out: "I seconds Brer Coon's motions!"

W'en dis took place; ole Brer Possum riz. Mon!—Chile, he riz wid all his bristles a stan'in on ends! He squall out: "Brer Moderator Cheersman; Brer Coon's move are a grand insult to de whole possum gineration fro de liddlest to de biggest! We wus hard wukin folks w'at eben w'ars all de ha'rs offn our tails a totin' our chilluns aroun' an' a takin' care of 'em; whilst Brer Coon's folkses an' Brer Fox's folkses leaves deir youngsters at home an' go a sharadin aroun' a segashuatin wid de Sons an' Daughters of Rest. If Brer Coon hand out any mo' of his scatterin' remarks an' hints of hisn 'bout ugly tails; let me tell 'im, dat de whole possum gang will lay way fer him an' clean de ha'r offn dat tail of hisn if its de last ack befo' Jedgment Day! I's a gwineter leave yo' ole half-strainer meetin'; an' I jes knows dat Brer Rabbit over dar, w'at haint got nothin 'cep' a liddle bunch o' white hair fer a tail wh'ar de tail should oughter be, is a gwine too. I knows dat he's too smart a man to stay 'roun' here what he caint git no vote an' wont have no say-so."

'Bout dat time Brer Billy Goat come a passin' by an' a gwine down de road. Ole Brer Possum look up an' see him. Den he open up ag'in wid his ogifyin an' he say: "Furdermo', dar go Brer William Goat. You all is got to have him up here wid you befo' you can settle up a heaps of de neighbor-hood sputes an' troubles. Jes look at Brer William Goat, if you wants to see w'at a bad moves Brer coon are a makin'!—W'y Sah; Brer William Goat jes natchully hol' up his tail all de time. W'en he come into yo' meetin' he'll jes natchully be a votin' all de time wid his holdin' up of his tail; whilst we tothers is jes a gittin' good warmed up to scussin our troubles. If you passes Brer Coon's move; den Brer William Goat will outvote de whole neighbor-hoods an' take off ev'rything wid 'im in his own way.—But I's gone!" says ole Brer Possum, says he. An' he walked away; an' Brer Rabbit, w'at haint got no tail, crope on off behin' 'im. Dis dont leave nobody in de meetin' 'cep' Brer Cat, Brer Coon, Brer Fox, Brer Polecat, an' Brer Moderator.

'Bout dis time Brer Polecat speak up an' say dat it look lak dat Brer Coon, Brer Cat an' Brer Fox had oughter sorter better keep still, since dey wus about to bust up de whole meetin' wid deir clumsy moves. He subgest dat all dat wus needed fer to fix things up wus fer to go an' git Brer William Goat. Dey could den stop all de clumsy moves w'at wus bein made; caze dey could let Brer William Goat make all de moves, an' den his votin all de time would jes be votin' to make de moves an' not to pass 'em. Brer Polecat added: W'en Brer William Goat wus made de moves, he would still always have 'nought votin' a gwine on left to second de moves.—Perhaps in dat way dey can git 'long widout t'arin' up de meetin'.

W'en Brer Polecat say dis; Brer Cat, Brer Coon, an' Brer Fox all sorter look at onenudder sorter jubouslak. Den Brer Polecat ax 'em w'at wus de matter wid dis here plan of hisn.

Brer Cat pull out his big red pocket hankcher, an' open it, an' wipe his nose; den he say sorter hesitatin' lak: Railly, Brer William Goat smell too bad fer to ax him in to de meetin'.

Law, Chile! Dis here talk about "smell" he't Brer Polecat whitehot; an' dere haint no tellin w'at he wouldn' a done, if all dem tothers hadn' a rund off from dar to anudder meetin' place over by Brer Fox's house. Dey had to go lak greased lightnin'; an' leave him dar wid plenty o' room aroun' 'im! Whilst dey wus a rattlin off an' a totin' deirselves away through de brush an' de bushes; ole Brer Polecat flung great big rocks at 'em, an' hollered to 'em: "Come back here an' fight! You ole bare-faced cowards!

W'en you talks 'bout me an' Brer William Goat; I's here to give you to know dat you's a tryin' to talk about yo' 'betters'. I's a gwineter git de las' one of you; an', w'en I does git you, I's a gwineter give you a wallupin w'at folkses calls 'fer-git-me-nots'."

W'en Brer Cat, Brer Coon, Brer Dog, an' Brer Fox git over to de nex' meetin' place; dey sorter zamine onenudders coats to see whedder Brer Polecat's rocks wus hit some of 'me or not. W'en dye finds out dat dey wusnt yit got hit; Brer Cheersman Dog subgest dat he think dat dey'd better git down to talkin' over w'at dey mought do towards makin de neighborhood better right away, caze it look to him alk, w'en dey 'gins to scuss, dat sumpin always almos' in ginerally happened.

He den knocked down a log wid his stick fer to git deir 'tention. Nex' he tell 'em dat dey can take deir turns in speaking deir minds. He wus a gwineter hear 'em all talk—de man wid de longest mouf to talk fust, de man wid de nex' longes' nex', an' so on ontel dey all gits through.

Brer Fox's mouf was longer dan Brer Coon's an' Brer Cat's; so he git up fust fer to tell w'at it would take fer to fix up his troubles.

Brer Fox say: "Brer Moderator Cheersman; You knows dat we's all got de 'greements not to bother an' not to hurt onenudder. At our big meetin' whar de Riperzinters of all de neighborhoods wus dar, we all votes fer dis. You ricomembers dat we wus made up our minds dat dere wusnt no sense in de Dog fambly a runnin' de Fox fambly, w'en dey dont eat none of 'em atter dey ketches 'em.

Now Brer Moderator Cheersman; De tother night, w'en de Fox fambly give a big grape-eatin' party an' barn-dance; who should be a hollerin:

"I'll kill you! I'll kill you! You owes me! You owes me!"

but a whole passel of Brer Cheersman Moderator Dog's folkses over dar. Well, it tore de party clean up; an' all de Fox fambly had to run home so fast dat it give 'em de Palsy in de knees fer a mont' atterwards. I wants darfo' to ax Brer Dog here to wash up his promus, an' show us dat it's clean; an' den I wants him to go home an' wash off his relations wid some hick'ries ontel dey sings a new song, an' let dis be de song:

I haint a gwineter bite at yo' heel,
An' you haint a gwineter bite at mine;
Fer dat's de way de Devil do,
An' we haint none o' his kind.

W'en dis here speech git handed out an' over, Brer Dog look aroun' an sorter sheepish-lak an' he say: "Railly, Brer Fox, dem 'ar dogs wusnt none of yo' good fust class Dogs. Dey wus jes a few of dem 'ar low-downed houn' dogs w'at dont come to de meetins whar we p'ints Riperzinters fer to meet wid de tother folkses w'at make de laws."

"Brer Moderator Cheersman!" ole Brer Coon break in.

"Dry up, Brer Coon!" say ole Brer Dog, de Cheersman, "Nobody musn' say nothin' ontel Brer Fox git through wid his say; caze he's de biggest 'pup' now in de Bone-yard." Ole Brer Dog talk lak dis a praisin up de pony so as to shmove Brer Fox down an' make him let de runnin' of de Fox fambly slip outn his membunce.

But ole Brer Coon stand his ground; an' he wont let his mouf be sewed up. He holler out to de Cheersman: "Dat's jes de reason I's a scussin now. Dere haint no use o' makin' no two bites at one mouf-full of watermillion!"

Brer Fox den jine in an' say to Brer Moderator Cheersman dat he'll jes set down fer a liddle while an' let Brer Coon talk; since it look lak dat de same flea mought a hopped on bofe famblies at one jump. So den de Moderator tell Brer Coon dat he can say on.

Brer Coon den up an' say dat on dat very same night w'at Brer Fox wus a talkin' 'bout; him an' his folkses wus a havin a big play an' Simmon Supper. W'en dey git ev'rything a gwine wid a wheel an' a turn, Brer Dog's folkses come a bustin over de hill towards whar dey wus—a sayin:

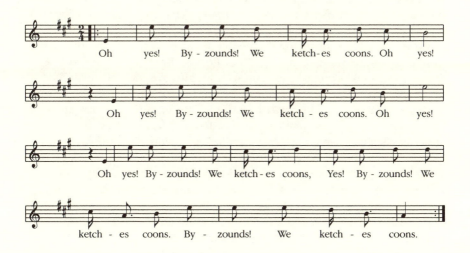

Well, Brer Coon say dat dey don hafter all run home lak Brer Fox's folkses; caze dey could all climb. So dey jes all clum trees.

Den de dogs all come an' got right up un'er de trees whar him an' his folkses wus; an' dey could see 'em all good. Brer Coon den declar to "Goodness" dat he eben put on his specks an' looked at 'em; an' dere wusnt ne'er a houn' dog in dat whole crowd down dar un'er dat tree. Furdermo', one o' de dog's Head mens in dat crowd sorter looked in de moonlight lak Brer Cheersman Moderator!

Brer Dog see dat Brer Coon an' Brer Fox wus jes 'bout cotch up wid his sly doins, an' de sly doins of his folkses; so he make up his mind to play big an' to play too in his answer to 'em. So he shet his eyes an' raised his bristles from een to een, den he give a long grumpy growl. But w'en he open his eyes ag'in to hand out his part of de scussion; Brer Fox an' Brer coon wus outn sight behin' de furdest hill. Dey wus took a glancin look at Brer Dogs long white teef; an' told deir footses to tote de body away.

Brer Cat den open up an' say: "Brer Dog, dont look so saveigus! Ev'rybody else is done heared deir folkses a callin 'em home 'cep' me; an' if you keeps on a havin' dem rabiddy crabbidy looks, I mought jes natchully hear cu'ious kinds of callins w'at would take me off home or up a tree or somewhars else too."

W'en Brer Dog hear dis, an' it look to him lak dat he mought be on de road to gittin a meetin all by hisself; he drapped his bristles an' grinned a liddle, so as to make Brer Cat feel a liddle mo' at home whar he wus. Den he allow to 'im: "Brer Cat, dont be oneasy on account of w'at ole man Fox an' de ole man Coon say. You knows dat we wus all got our Riperzinters togedder no long 'go; an' we all 'gree not in no way hurt onenudder. I's a gwineter keep dat promus. You ricomembers lakwise dat we all says dat we wus a gwineter pay up all we owes.

Brer Cat tell ole Brer Dog dat he ricomember all dat.

"Well!" wen on ole man Dog. "Brer Fox an' Brer Coon wus out one Sunday a ketchin a bref of fresh air an' a lookin' over deir crops. Whilst dey wus a walkin aroun'; dey found a great big rock wid a whole passel of cu'ious marks on it. So dey sont fer Jedge Buzzard fer to come an' look at de marks; an' tell 'em w'at dey means. Jedge Buzzard come an' looked at de marks, an' tol' 'em dat it wus "writin"; an' dat de "writin" say: "Turn me over an' see w'at's un'er me."

W'en Jedge Buzzard tell 'em dis; dey bofe turns 'roun an' axes him w'at he think mought be un'er dar. De Jedge make answer dat he dont know; but he spec dat somebody, w'at wus dead, wus done gone an' buried a great big pot o' money un'er dar! De writin' mus' have been put on de rock so dat de relations mought know whar fer to find de money.

Jedge Buzzard den charge 'em a hoss fer tellin 'em all dis an' flop on off home.

Dis wus de fust part of Brer Dogs tale to Brer Cat. De balunce of it run lak dis: W'en Brer Fox an' Brer Coon hear tell of a big pot of money;

dey almost go clean 'stracted fer to git dar 'ar rock turned over. Dey grabs holt on it to turn it:

> Dey grunts an' dey strains;
> Dey puffs widout gains!
> Dey pulls an' dey blows,
> Till dey t'ars off deir clo'es!'

But dat ole rock, it jes lay dar; an' it wont budge.

Den dey goes an' gits a han'stick; an' puts de een un'erneath fer to prize dat 'ar col-headed rock off, w'at kiver up an' keep so much money warm; but it dont move. Den dey jumps up an' sets down bodaciously on de han'-stick to turn it over offn de money; but it jes laid dar lak it wusnt in no hurry to git up an' give it over to Brer Fox an' Brer Coon.

At las' dey makes up deir minds fer to go an' git somebody else to help 'em turn dat ole rock offn dat money. Brer Dog say dat he come along 'bout dat time; an' dey axed him fer to lend a hand in deir new bit git-rich projick. Brer Dog tell 'em dat he'll whirl in an' help, vidin dey'll hash up de money wid 'im w'en dey gits it. But Brer Fox an' Brer Coon say dat dis wold be altogedder too much; caze nobody would give a whole ham of meat to somebody jes to git him to help 'em hang up a hog.

Brer Dog claim dat it go on lak dis ontel it look lak he wusnt a gwineter git no job at 'tall; so he telled 'em dat he'd help 'em turn de rock over fer a dollar. Brer Fox an' Brer coon say dat de dollar wus hisn jes as soon as he rig up a plan fer to make de rock move.

Brer Dog look aroun', he do, an' he tell 'em dat deir trouble wus dat deir han'-stick wusnt long 'nough.

Dey makes answer to 'im dat if dey gits a han'-stick w'at's longer dat dis; dey caint reach up to de end of it to pull down on it.

Brer Dog den tell 'em dat dis wus de plan: Hang a bag on one end of de han'-stick; den short heel de tother end un'er de big rock on a liddle rock. Den walk up de han'stick from de ground to de bag an' drap rocks in it ontel de rocks in de bag prize up de big rock w'en dey walks up de long han'stick. Dat way dey can turn de big rock right over.

Dey all 'gree to tote de rocks up de han'stick an' drap 'em in de bag. Dat way, in a liddle o' no time, dey got de big rock turned over. W'en dey got de big rock turned; dey didn see no money un'er it. Dey didn see no nothin' but some mo' cu'ious marks scratched on de tother side w'at wus den turned up.

Brer Fox up an' allow dat de money mus' be dar some-whars; caze Jedge Buzzard wus done read on de top side: 'Turn me over an' see w'at's un'er me'. Brer Coon put in dat he reckin dat he'd better oughter go an' git Jedge Buzzard ag'in fer to come an' make out de marks on dis un'erside; den dey'll know fer shore jes whar de money is. So he rack off atter him. He see Jedge Buzzard an' he promus 'im dat he'll come over in jue time; so he rack on back to de rock fer to wait fer 'im dar.

Atter while Jedge Buzzard come. He lit on de rock an' he look; but he dont see no money. Den he put on his specks an' sot 'em on de end of his nose an' looked good at de marks on de bottom of de rock. W'en he wus zamined all de marks real good; he riz an' flopped hisself up in de top of a big tree an' sot dar a sayin' nothin'.

Bymeby Brer Fox an' Brer Coon ax de Jedge w'at de marks on de bottom of de big rock say.

Den Jedge Buzzard sorter stretched his neck out long an' drawed his head back in, so as to git his wits 'bout 'im; an' he sorter half whisper down to 'em: "De rock say; 'Turn me back an' let me be'."

W'en dey hears dis; Brer Fox an' Brer Coon gits taken wid de dry grins; den dey gits sorter taken wid a mad spell. It look to 'em lak somebody mought a been playin' a trick on 'em. Dey feels a liddle lak fightin; but dey looks at Jedge Buzzard a roos'in' too high fer a squabble. Dey looks at Brer Dog; but dey sees him all down in de mouf caze he's all mixed in wid it. Den lakwise dey thinks dat he mought be a liddle too big fer liddle mens lak dem to tackle.

'Bout dat time, Brer Dog say dat he put in: "Gemmuns, you can hand me over my dollar fer helpin' you; an' den I guess I'll be a knockin' 'long towards home." Brer Dog tell Brer Cat dat w'en he axed 'em fer de dollars dey tol' 'im dat dey'd hafter step off a liddle piece to one side to fix up 'nough money 'twixt an' 'tween 'em fer to pay him. Dey walks on off a liddle piece an' talks a liddle bit in a whisper; den ole Brer Coon send de pay back to 'im wid dese here words: "Brer Dog! Jest git Jedge Buzzard up dar to set you down a order fer dat dollar, den take it an' bury it in de groun' lak dat 'ar big rock; an' de fust big rain dat come a sloshin' down'll settle it!" Whilst dey wus a sayin' dis; dey wus jes a lammin de ground a gwine through de woods an' a gittin' away.

By de time Brer Dog see w'at wus a takin' place, dey wus outn sight; but he tell dat he call out to 'em: "Say! I wus thought dat you wus gemmuns of yo' word!" Dey heared w'at he wus said, four or five hills away, an' dey flung back some mo' sass an' say: "You thought lak Young's Niggers dat buckeyes wus biscuit, dat puddle ducks wus ridin' hosses; an' dey started to ride 'cross de river an' got drownded!"

W'en Brer Dog git through wid his tellin of Brer Cat ev'rything; he say he dont blame him fer runnin' Brer Fox an' Brer Coon all he want to, caze dey dont pay deir debts, 'cordin' to promus. He lakwise tell Brer Dog dat dere wus some mo' folkses up dar in dat 'ar big meetin' w'at made promuses w'at wus brickle lak pie-crus'. So he wus almos' made up his mind fer to drap all de 'greements w'at wus make down dar too.

Den Brer Dog, he open up an' say: "Law, Brer Cat, you dont meant to tell me dat some o' dat 'Trash' w'at wus in dat meetin is a owin' you too an' wont pay you?"

"No, not zackly", say ole Brer Cat, "but dey's been doin' w'at's wusser!"

"W'at you mean?" axed ole Brer Dog.

"I means dat dey's been a stealin'" says ole Brer Cat, says he.

"W'at—? Cut loose an' tell me how it 'twus", says ole Brer Dog.

"Well, here's de way it 'tuws", say ole Brer Cat. "Some o' dem 'ar ole twisted-moufed slu-footed crooked-toed birds got to grabbin' an' totin' off my baby-chilluns w'en I wusnt a lookin'. So I makes up my mind fer to set a dead-fall fer to ketch 'em an' eat 'em. I sot de dead-falls an' cotch 'em; but who should come 'long an' eat 'em up befo' I could go an' git 'em but ole man scale-tail Rat, an' his folkses. Atter dat wus took place; I jes put aside de promuses made at de Riperzinters meetin an' I's been a pitchin' rat-hash at my chilluns three times a day in mis'ry."

"You sho is a actin' wid sense", say ole Brer Dog, "an' I's a gwineter copy right atter you an' ketch an' eat ole Brer Rabbits folkses; caze he stole a good pair o' shoes from me an' runned right off wid 'em befo' my eyes whilst I wus a callin' to 'im right along: "Come-back! Come back!" I's lakwise maked up my mind fer to run ole man Fox's an' ole man Coon's folkses fer fun, caze dey dont pay deir debts. But I's a gwineter run ole man Rabbit's folkses fer pot-fixins caze dey steals." [For a fuller explanation of this escapade on the part of "Brer Rabbit", read Joel Chandler Harris' Negro story: "Why Mr. Dog Runs Brother Rabbit."]

"Bully fer you! Bully fer you!" hollered out ole man Cat. "Now, you see so, Brer Dog, we mus' shake hands an' be big friends; caze wid de combine of you an' yo' folks a ketchin on de ground an' me an' my folks a ketchin in de trees, we wont have no empty kittles a hangin' on col' pot-racks". Wid dis much said; dey shake hands, cross deir hearts, an' hope dey may drap dead if dey dont always be de best of friends.

Atter dis, Brer Dog's folks an' Brer Cat's folks hunts in cahoots. De Dog fambly ketch w'at live on de ground; an' de Cat fambly ketch w'at live 'bove de ground. Dey wus got de whole world by de nose holt wid a down hill pull. Dey gits mo' to eat dan dey can 'stroy; an' dey lives togedder in pease an' hom'ny.

Dey ketches up so much of de game dat Mr. Man up dar in his big fine house once in a while fin' his stomach a pinchin' him to wake 'im up an' tell 'im dat a liddle mo' grub wouldn' do 'im no harm. It go on lak dis ontel times git so tight dat Mr. Man sent fer Brer Dog's an' Brer Cat's folkses to come up to see 'im.

Dey goes over, an' Mr. Man axes 'em to set down on his pieizzer. He tell 'em dat he wus been a lookin' at how well dey wus a gittin on; but he wus jes been a thinkin' dat all dey lacked fer to make ev'ry day lak Sunday, a settin down an' a eatin' chicken-pie fer Breakfus, wus to live up in a fine house lak hisn. So he tell 'em dat he wus jes natchully gone an' think so much of 'em dat he wus called 'em in to give 'em a invite fer to come up an' live wid 'im.

Brer Dog an' Brer Cat tell Mr. Man dat dey wus been a wantin' fer to live in a big fine house fer a long time; an' dey wus been a tryin' fer to git dem tother animuls fer to whirl in an' build one. But it wus already come to dat pass dat de mo' dey talked wid dem tothers 'bout buildin' up ; de mo' dey studied how fer to t'ar down. So dey dont care if dey do live wid 'im, if dey can strike up a 'greeable bargin. At las' dey axes him w'at it'll take to fix it up fer bed an' board.

Mr. Man make answer dat he jes thought dat he'd let dem do de huntin; an' he'd take care of de provisions an' de saltin' of 'em down. By saltin' of 'em down; w'en hard times comes a knockin' on de doo'; he'll have plenty fer to keep 'em all fat an sassy. He tell 'em dat his pay'll be w'at he eat. Deir pay'll be to live an' sleep at de big fine house.

Brer Cat an' Brer Dog make answer dat dis all sounded good; but dey would all hafter giver deir consent, an' fix up some way so dat none of deir folkses couldn' never fergit it.

Mr. Man tell 'em: In ginerally w'en his folks wus had a meetin'; deir Riperzinters jes nodded deir heads w'en dey meant "yes", an' shook deir heads w'en dey meant "no". So he subgest dat dey give deir consent wid de motionin' of de head.

Brer Dog an' Brer Cat tell Mr. Man dat deir folkses dont never make no 'greements lak dat. Dey always wagged deir 'greements wid deir tails.

Mr. Man tell 'me dat he haint got no way fer to jine in wid 'em in fixin' up no promus lak dat; so he subgest dat ev'ry man make his own promus in his own way. Dey all 'gree to dis. So Mr. Man, he sot still, he did' an voted "yes" to livin togedder by noddin' his head. Brer Dog riz up an' voted "yes" by waggin his tail; an' Brer Cat sot down an' tapped "yes" on de pieizzer floo' wid his tail.

Brer Dog den allow to 'em: Now day dey wus promused fer to live togedder; he dont see no way how dey wus a gwineter fix it so day dey wont never fergit dat promus offn deir minds, since none of de bunch can write it down.

Brer Cat subgest dat dey git ole Jedge Buzzard to come over an' mark it down on sumpin' fer 'em.

Mr. Man tell 'em dat he jes caint let no Jedge Buzzard come into his house; caze w'en he come, all of him dont leave de place fer a whole month.

Brer Cat an' Brer Dog den ax him how dey wus a gwineter do.

Den Mr. Man say dat dey'll do dis way: Dat he wont only nod his head fer "yes" to dese 'greements; but he'll nod his head fer "yes" fer all de promuses dat he mean to keep; dat Brer Dog wont only wag his tail fer "yes" to dis promus, but dat he'll wag his tail all de time fer ev'rything whar he's willin'; dat Brer Cat wont only tap his tail for "yes" to dis progrance, but dat he'll tap his tail down fer ev'rything whar he's ready fer to jine in. So by his noddin', an' by Brer Dog's waggin', an' by Brer Cat's tappin all de time; dey caint never fergit de promus dat dey make onenudder to live togedder in de Big House.

Brer Dog make answer: Dat wus all right. Brer Cat jine in wid 'im. All of 'em den say dat it wus all right. So eben nowadays, atter dey wus done broke deir promuses to onenudder, in one way or anudder; dey still keeps up deir noddin an' deir waggin an' deir tappin'.

W'en dey gits dat Man-cat-dog Combine all fixed up; it 'twus "Hite out, Little One! de Witch-Booger'll ketch you!" fer all dem tother varmints. Wid Brer Dog a ketchin on de ground, Brer Cat a bannin' in de trees, an' Mr. Man a bossin' de job; dey piled up de Big House jes' full o meat.

Brer Dog an' Brer Cat sot aroun' all fat an' slick, dey did. Whilst dey sot aroun' an' wus a thinkin 'bout Brer Fox, Brer Coon, an' dem tothers w'at useter give 'em trouble out in de woods; dey maked up a funny song to sing 'bout 'em.

De song go lak dis:

Atter dey sing de song an' "Wha! Wha!" Mr. Man pass out de victuals. One day, Brer Dog ax Brer Cat aroun' to dinner; an', de nex' day, Brer Cat call Brer Dog in fer a snack. Dey all eat offn de same plat; an' dey wus so thick dat you couldn' drive a peg in 'tween 'em.

Dey wus always got plenty to eat; so Brer Dog an' Brer Cat sot aroun' an' bit liddle bites, an' e't slow, an' put on mo' aires dan a peafowl w'at strut aroun' widout lookin' down at his footses.

All dis keep up ontel it look to Brer Fox, Brer Coon, an' all dem tothers lak dey wus a gwineter git clean e't up hide an' hair. So all deir

folkses 'gin to move away off down in de swamps an' about; whar Brer
Dog an' Brer Cat caint find 'em so good.

W'en dis took place; de meat quit flowin' so revunt into de Big
House; an' Mr. Man's smoke-house poles look lak dey wus a gwineter git
empty. So he call in Brer Cat an' Brer Dog an' tell 'em dat dey mus' go a
huntin' down in de swamps to keep dem smoke-house poles from a lyin'
up so straight 'tween de jeists.

Mr. Cat say to 'im dat he wus born so tony dat he never wus been
known to git his footses muddy; so he jes caint hunt down in de muddy
swamps. Brer Dog say dat he caint go down dar neider onless Mr. Man go
along wid 'im. He wus skeared if he git down dar by hisself dat he mought
git lost. If he git lost down dar; w'en he howl, de sound'll go right along de
water in de bayous an' branches, an' nobody wont never hear 'im out on de
hills. Wid all dis a gwine on; he mought die an' miss hesself. Mr. Man ax 'em
den: If dey caint do dis, wat is dey a gwineter do fer to pay fer bed an' board.

Ole Brer Cat make answer: Since he spize all of ole man Rat's folkses an'
dey eats up Mr. Man's things; he'll manage to ketch up, an' keep all dem
away. 'Sides dis he'll hunt a liddle stray game w'at mought come aroun' 'bout
de Big House. Brer Dog den jine in, an' say: He'll make his victuals an' clo'es
by gwine a huntin' wid Mr. Man enjorin de day; an' he'll set up an' see to it
dat nothin' dont pester him at night w'en he want to sleep.

Mr. Man tell 'em: Dat wus all right fer bofe of 'em, but dey'll hafter git
deir sumpin t'eat atter he wus got his fill.

So dey starts off wid deir new 'rangements. Mr. Man would eat his
dinner, an' put w'at wus lef' over on a tin plate, an' put dat down on de
ground fer Brer Dog an' Brer Cat to eat together. W'en dey wus got deir
grub, dey sot down to eat as fer common—a chawin slow an' a puttin' on
aires. Atter dey gits through; bofe of 'em feels lak dey wus got setch a
liddle dat it didn' fill deir half-holler.

Brer Cat go on away an' drap off to sleep; but ole Brer Dog sot down
to rummage through his head so as to try to make out how he wus a
gwineter make buckle an' tongue meet. He sot dar an' got it all fixed out
w'at he wus a gwineter do.

W'en de nex' eatin time come 'roun; bofe Brer Cat an' Brer Dog come
to Mr. Man's plate at his call. Brer Cat sot down, an' 'gun to nibble liddle
bites, an' chaw, an' put on aires lak he wus been a doin' all de time befo';
but ole Brer Dog, he come up, he do; an' he alter all his style-buisness.
He pick up one big mouf-full atter anudder; an' he swaller it down whole.
Wid Brer Dog's progrance a tumblin along; Brer Cat quit off his eatin' mo'
hongry dan he 'gin.

W'en Brer Dog up an' do lak dis; Brer Cat ax 'im w'at in de world wus
done gone an' happen, dat he wus tore up all his manners an' throwed
'em away.

W'en he axed Brer Dog lak dat; he sorter tromped heard on de corners of his sore toe. So Brer Dog make answer dat he wus a gwineter eat lak he innerpenunt please; none o' de cat-tails haint got no kind o' sense to say w'at good manners is no way! Furdermo', if he say w'at he say ag'in; he'll give him a sound trouncin' dat will leave him as sore as a bile fer a mont'.

Brer Cat tell 'im to trounce his greatgrandaddies' uncles' paws!—De law say fer folkses to fight fair "fist an' skull"; an' let de best man whup! If he'll fight 'cordin' to law, dat he'll give him setch a thashin dat dere wont be nothin lef' of him but straw.

Dey wus out un'er a big tree; an' Brer Dog drawed a ring aroun' it, an' tol' Brer Cat dat "fair fist an' skull" suited him.—Come on into de ring an' show dat he can fight as big as he talk!

Brer Cat step in; an' him an' Brer Dog 'gin to swap licks. Brer Dog retched in an' bopped Brer Cat on de jaws wid his fist shet. But ole Brer Cat give him in turn a long swipe lick wid his fist half open; an' de way Brer Dog's ha'r flew offn him wus a sin!

Den ole Brer Dog got as mad as a whole nest of dug-up yaller-jackets. He clean fergit offn his mind dat de law wus to fight "fair fist an' skull". So he opened his mouf, showed his tushes, an' made a lunge fer Brer Cat.

W'en old Brer Dog wus done dis; ole Brer cat darted up de tree an' spit down in his face, caze he wus de fust man fer to break de law of de "fair fist an' skull" fight. From dat day clean down to dis one; Brer Cat's folkses an' Brer Dog's folkses has been inimies. W'en Brer Dog's folkses sees Brer Cat's folkses, dey ricomembers 'bout de ha'r w'at wus pulled offn deir relation away back yon'er; an' dey opens deir moufs an' takes out atter 'em. W'en Brer Cat's folkses sees Brer Dog's folkses a comin' atter 'em; dey runs up a tree an' spits down on 'em, caze dey ricomembers dat deir relation away back yon'er wus de fust man fer to break de law of de fair fist an' skull' fight."

When Aunt Ritter had finished this explanation as to how the cat and the dog had become enemies; little Fernie looked up half bewildered and said: "Law, Mammy! I haint never hearn tell of dat befo' in all my new born days."

To this came the prompt response: "Honey, deres a whole heaps of things dat you'll learn befo' you's been a bruisin aroun' in dese Low Grounds of Sorrow as long as I is. Let's git up an' wash de dishes down an' perhaps I'll tell you some mo' some time."

They arouse and went cheerily together to perform tasks not so agreeable as telling and listening to Traditions.

THE DOG'S HABITS, ORIGIN OF
❄

A few days after Ferinie had been told by her mother, Aunt Ritter Motty, how the cat and the dog had become enemies, the two found themselves out by a branch of clear running water, doing the week's washing of a wealthy white family which lived about a mile away. Their dogs were with them. All these dogs, save one, lay lazily panting on the ground in the shade near the water's edge. This dog—a young one—seemed just surcharged with a superfluous amount of animal energy and activity. Therefore, while the other dogs rested, this dog ran with a lightning-like rapidity, inscribing circle after circle on the surface of the ground.

Aunt Ritter, in accord with a common Negro custom, was singing while she labored over the wash-board, rubbing the clothes to a snowy whiteness. At first she sang the more joyous themes of the Negro melodies. As however she grew more and more weary from her labors, she sang the sadder strains, which speak more of the burdens and hardships of life than of the bright hopes which should spring eternally in the human heart.

At last she began to sing the Negro funeral dirge; "We are passing away to the Great Judgment Day"—a great favorite among Negro Christians about a half century ago. When she had sung a few lines of this song, the dog scampering around in a circle suddenly brought his swiftly moving form to a halt. He fell upon the ground, rolled over on his back, stretched his feet towards the blue of the heavens, and uttered a low long piteous howl.

The other dogs, hitherto lying listlessly upon the grounds, raised their heads, and carefully scanned the sky in all directions with inquiring glances. Then the racing dog quickly arose, and ran around again inscribing another and yet another circle on the ground. Suddenly bringing his act to a close, he once more uttered his low mournful howl.

When the dog had thus howled a second time, Aunt Ritter murmured in a low voice to herself: "Laws a Mussy! Who's dat now a walkin' in de col' streams of Jurdon?"

She had not intended these words for the ears of another; but they did not escape the ever attentive listening Ferinie who promptly asked: "Mammy, didn' you say dat somebody wus dead?"

"No, not zacky," replied the mother, "but w'en you sees a dog runnin' aroun', an' a ackin' lak dat one; eider somebody is dead or somebody is a gwineter die mighty soon. W'en dogs makes a circle once an' turns on deir backs wid deir footses to de sky an' howls; somebody is a gwineter die in a week. If dey circles twice an' turns up an' howls; somebody is a gwineter die in two weeks. So w'en dey turns on deir backs an' howls lak dat, somebody is sho a gwineter die; an' if you counts de circles dat dey

makes befo' dey howls, you'll know how many weeks it'll be befo' dat
somebody die.—W'en dey runs aroun' an' looks up an' howls at de moon;
dat's diffunt. W'en dey does dat; dey jes see Sam in de moon an' thinks
dat it wus some of deir Mossers an' dey wants to go to 'em. [For a full
account of this; read "The Negro Slave in The Moon", found elsewhere in
this volume.]

"Mammy," said Ferinie, "I no uner'stan' w'at you's a talkin' 'bout. Caint
you please splain to me 'bout it so as I can know?"

"Ferinie," responded the mother, "dat 'ar same great-granmammy of
mine wus de one w'at tol' me;—de one w'at tol' me how de cat an' de
dog git to be inimies. She mix up so much cu'ious loration wid de facts
dat you couldn' scacely tell w'en she wus a talkin wid de bark on; an'
w'en she wus a jokin'. How-some-be-ever, I thinks dat she wus a givin de
natchul bawn facts w'en she tol' me dem cu'ious things 'bout dogs. Now,
you keep de fire pushed up aroun' de clo'es pot so as to keep 'em a b'ilin;
an' I'll try to splain it all to you as bes' I can."

Ferinie, after "pushing up" the fire, announced to her mother that she was
ready to hear the explanation concerning dogs baying the moon, barking &c.

Aunt Ritter gave her account as follows: "Away back yon'er one time,
befo' Brer Cat an' Brer Dog wus comed to live wid Mr. Man; Brer Dog, he
howl all de time caze he dont know nothin' 'bout barkin'. W'en de dogs in
dem times holler to onenudder sumpin, dey holler it wid a howl; an' w'en
dey answers onenudder, dey answers wid a howl. Dey jine in all deir
confabs wid howls.

In dem days, ole Brer Rabbit wus de big man 'mongst de critters. He
wus powerful liddle; but he wus got setch a big pull in de head dat dem
tother beastes jes natchully couldn' git up in hollerin distance of him. He
wus might 'nigh always a playin' off pranks on dem tothers; but him an'
Brer Dog wus setch good friends dat he haint never yit played off no
pranks on him. Of co'se, atter he play dis here fust prank, w'at I's a
gwineter tell you 'bout; he took Brer Dogs new pair of shoes off right
befo' his face; an' dat wus w'at make 'em fall out an' git clean 'part, so dat
Brer Dog now run him an' all his folkses on sight.

But befo' all dis las' big fallin' out took place, so dat dey dont speak
to onenudder no mo' in peace; dey had a liddle rucus about one o' ole
Brer Rabbit's pranks. It come about in dis way:

One day, ole Brer Rabbit come 'long by ole Brer Dog's house a
whistlin'. He wus jes a whistlin' away! Dis wus w'at he whistle:

Ole Brer Dog wus a settin out in his front yard wid his ole 'oman; an' she tell 'em to jes listen at Brer Rabbit a whistlin; dat he whistle mo' samer an' mo' pruttier dan a mockin bird.

Her ole man say dat he wus jes a lissenin an' he blieve dat he'll call 'em by, an' l'arn how he do it. So he holler out: "Oh, Brer Rabbit!" an' Brer Rabbit make answer: "Whoo—!" Den Brer Dog say: "Come by! I's got some of de mos' nices' 'simmon beer dat you's ever tasted. Come by, an' take a swaller!"

Brer Rabbit holler back dat he dont care if he do; an' he turned hisself outn de trail an' come on up through de bushes to de house. W'en he git dar, ole Brer Dog pass him out de 'simmon beer; an' ole Brer Rabbit gulp it down, clear his th'oat, an' tell 'em dat it wus heaps finer dan dat w'at dey all have over at de corn-shuckin' de tother night whar dey all go home a wobblin in de knees caze dey wus light in de head. Brer Rabbit, he drink one gourd-full atter anudder; ontel atter while he git sorter tipsy, an' he feel mo' fuller of devilment dan a red-eyed mule w'en he's a gittin ready fer to shoot you his behime foot.

Ole Brer Dog, he look at ole Brer Rabbit, he do; an' he lissen to his tongue a rattlin lak it wus tied in de middle an' loose at bofe ends. Bymeby he make up his mind dat ole Brer Rabbit wus three shakes in de wind; an' wus got jes 'bout 'nough swimmin' in de head fer to let his mouf spill out de answer to w'atsome-ever he mought ax him an' den some mo' besides. Ole Brer Rabbit wus a liddle tipsy; but he wus got all his senses 'bout him, an' wus ready to fix up all de fun fer hisself dat he can. De two of 'em talk togedder lak dis:

"Dat wus some powerful fine whis'lin' you wus a doin' jes befo' you come up here to de house; Brer Rabbit!"

"Oh, it wus jes a liddle chune w'at I wus maked up fer to sing to my ole 'oman. She wus been so good an' nice to me, a cookin' up big fine pots of greasy greens, dat I wus l'arnt her how fer to smoke a pipe. To-day she cooked me setch a fine pot of mud-pusly dat I thought dat I'd go down to town an' git her a seegyar fer a liddle extra puffin' to put on aires wid. I wus lakwise maked up dat liddle song fer to sing to her w'at you wus heared me a whis'lin'; as I wus done already done tol' you. I wus done maked up lots of de "calls" fer de song; [For the explanation of "calls", read *The Study* found in Negro Folk Rhymes, by the writer] but I haint fixed no last "call" fer it yit. so whilst I wus a gwine along to town, I wus a tryin fer to git dis here last "call" togedder; so whilst I wus a thinkin', I kep up de whis'lin' so dat de chune an' de "call" would slip one into de tother."

"Humph!" put in ole Miss Dog. "Ole man, you haint never maked up no song fer me; an' w'at's mo' an' besides, you haint never larn't in no ways how to whistle."

"Oh!" say ole Brer Rabbit, sayes he; "Onless you gits yo' mouf all fixed up fer it; you caint whistle in no ways! I dont think dat yo' ole man would lak to go to all de trouble dat he'd need to fer to git so dat he could whistle. He'll hafter fix up sumpin else fer to do fer you w'at haint so turble much bother fer to do."

"Now, ole man", say ole Miss Dog, "you mus' show Brer Rabbit dat you thinks as much of yo' fambly as any of de mens 'bout here. I thinks dat you mought p'int out to Brer Rabbit dat dere haint nobody dat'll go deir lengt' a fixin' up fer deir folks mo' dan you!"

Den ole Brer Dog sorter snap her off by sayin' "Sho! Sho!—Brer Rabbit; we always wus been big friends wid 'simmon beer an' ev'rything else. Now I wants you fer to help me fer liddle. I wants to hear dat song of yourn; so as I can fix up one lak it fer my ole 'oman. Den I wants you to show me how fer to fix my mouf so dat I can whistle too. By de time I gits my song all fixed up, an' wus l'arnt how to whistle; dere'll be a whole rain-bar'l full of sogrum-skimmins beer up here at my house, an' all you's got to do is to come up an' git de gourd from my ole 'oman, an' onkiver de bar'l an' tank yo'self up full."

Ole Brer Rabbit tell him: Now he wus a talkin' a liddle wid de bark on ["talking with the bark on" ordinarily meant, among ex-slaves, dealing with the facts; thus, as here used, it is only a play on words]; an' if he wouldn' tell nobody an' lissen to him, he'd git him to talkin' altogedder "wid de bark on".

Ole Brer Dog make answer to ole Brer Rabbit dat he dont zackly know w'at he mean by dat high-folutin langridge of "talkin wid de bark on"; but he dont care nothin' 'bout dat so long as it p'int de way to makin' de song an' gittin fixed up fer to whistle.

Brer Rabbit tell him; All right, he'll give him de calls of de song w'at he wus done got fixed up; an' by de nex' time dat he come over fer to see him, he'll have de last "Call" an' de "Sponse" all put togedder, den he'll give him dem too. So ole Brer Rabbit hand out to ole Brer Dog de copy of de "Calls" w'at he wus been a whis'lin'. Dey goes lak dis:

Ole Molly Har',
W'at's you doin dar?
'I's settin in de fence corner, smokin' seegyar'.
Ole Molly Har',
W'at's you doin dar?
"I's a pickin out a br'ar, settin on a prickly-p'ar'.
Ole Molly Har',
W'at's you doin dar?
"I's a gwine cross de Cotton-patch, hard as I can t'ar'.
Molly Har to—day,
So dey all say,
Got 'er pipe o' clay, jes to smoke de time away."

W'en ole Brer Rabbit wus got through wid de "Calls" of his song, ole Miss Dog make a great miration an' wonderment over 'em; an' she tell her ole man dat he mus' buckle right down to it, an' fix her up a song jes zackly 'cordin to Brer Rabbit's copy.

Brer Dog sorter order her to hush up an' not to bother 'im; whilst Brer Rabbit wus a gittin ready fer to tell 'im how fer to pucker up his mouf fer to whistle.

De ole 'oman didn' want to drap no Spider in de song dumplins; ["Drop a Spider in dumplings" means to poison and to kill off] so she dried up an' wus jes as ca'm as a lam'. Any udder time, she mought a maked him splain ontel he wus hoarse befo' he miss ketchin de end of de broom handle; but right den she wus got her head mo' fixed on a song dan on a "scrap".

Brer Rabbit den up an' say, says he: "Oh, Brer Dog, de reason why you caint whistle haint caze you caint pucker up yo' mouf; but it's caze yo' mouf is all shaped up wrong. Yo' mouf, Brer Dog (if you'll jes notice) jes run straight 'cross yo' face an' stop; whilst my mouf is split up de sides, back up towards my (y)ears an' eyes. You caint never whistle onless you gits you' mouf shaped up lak mine.

Brer Dog step out in de yard an' take a look at hisself in de big rain-bar'l full of water, out in de sun; an' he see dat his mouf run straight 'cross, jes lak Brer Rabbit say. In dem times de dog's mouf wusnt split up de sides lak dey is now-a-days.

Brer Dog den come back in on de pieizzer an' axed Brer Rabbit how he wus managed fer to git a split mouf fer to whistle wid.

Brer Rabbit make answer: Dat wus easy. He wus jes got ole Molly Har', his olo 'oman, fer to take de butcher knife an' split his mouf back; den he took de butcher knife an' split her mouf back; an' so, dey bofe could whistle.

Brer Dog thank him for all he say; an' say dat he bet dat de nex' time he wus come to his house dat he'd find de whole fambly a whis'lin'.

Wid dat much fixed up, an' ev'rybody tickled to death; ole Brer Rabbit up an' tell 'em good-by, an' leave. W'en Brer Rabbit git outn sight; Brer Dog tell his ole 'oman dat he blieve dat he'll 'gin to make up his song.

Ole Miss Dog, his ole 'oman, tell 'im: If he'll jes notice, dat Brer Rabbit wus got down de thing in whis'lin' fust; an' den he make up de words to de song. She think dat he'd better copy right straight atter Brer Rabbit, if he want to be shore fer to not git no nothin wrong.

Brer Dog sot aroun' fer a long time, an' he rummage de whole thing over fer a long time in his mind; caze he dont want to make no failin's in his ole 'omans song. At las' he make up his head dat his ole 'oman mus' be 'bout right—dat de mouf fixin' should oughter come fust. So he tell ole Miss Dog fer to git him de butcher knife out de cupboard so dat he can git it all whetted up good an' keen.

By de time he wus got de knife all good sharpened up on de grindin'-stone, an' ready; ole Brer Rabbit wus done been home an' brung back his ole 'oman (Miss Molly Har'), to hide out in de weeds away off from de house, an' to see de fun.

Ole Brer Dog hand de butcher knife to his ole 'oman; an' tell her he's ready fer de splittin'. He open up his mouf an' ole Sister Dog give him one o' dese here saveigus licks right in de side of de mouf! She hit 'im sorter gawky-lak: an' she cut off de tops of all his toofs on dat side of his mouf 'cep' two of 'em, one right above de tother, close up to de front. So he didn' have but two of his long "dog-toofs" lef' on dat side of his mouf.

Ole Brer Dog jump an' give one o' dese here (y)ear splittin' howls w'at sound lak a world full o' wagons, a screakin all at one time, w'at haint had no smell o' axle grease 'bout 'em fer a year or mo'.

Ole Brer Rabbit an' his ole 'oman, out in de weeds, bust right out in a great big laugh; an' olo Brer Dog mought a heared 'em, if his ole 'oman hadn a kicked up setch a big racket a scoldin' him 'bout actin' so much "lak a great big baby". she tell him dat he wus de most chicken-heartedest w'at-'is-name dat she wus laid her two eyes on since de woods wus burnt over.—Dar wus Brer Rabbit an' Miss Molly Har', dey wus bofe done git deir moufs split back. W'at wus mo' dan dat; dey wusnt maked no noise 'bout it, an' dere wusnt nobody 'roun' dar in dem diggins w'at know how it git done.—Dar he wus, a gwine around whis'lin' an' a singin'; an' no-body from nowhars haint in no ways found out how dey git all fixed up fer doin' it! She go on an' she lowrate Brer Dog so much lak dis 'bout bein' a big "cry-baby" dat he wus jes bleedged to shet up.

She den tell 'im to open up on de tother side of his head, so dat she can finish up fixin' dat side of de whis'lin' mouf fer him. Brer Dog, he open up sorter slow, he do. His ole 'oman git half tired an' mad 'bout waitin' on 'im. So she hauled off an' bopped him in de side of de mouf dis time befo' he git it good wide open. De practice from a hittin' him wrong on de fust side of de mouf make her hit him puffect wrong on de tother side. Beance de mouf wus half shet, she hit de toofs ag'in; an' didn't leave him but two long "dog-toofs", one right above de tother, on dat side. (Dat's de reason dogs haint got but four long "dog-toofs" clean down to dis day.)

Dis time, ole Brer Dog grit his toofs so hard to keep from a hollerin; de long "dog-toofs" bend out, an' de short cut off ones come down smack togedder. He whine a liddle but he dont do no cryin'. His ole 'oman den tell him: Now he wus a actin' lak he wus made outn genuwine good stuff; an' not outn common mud! Furdermo', he look to her lak he mought now git to whistle mo' samer dan Brer Rabbit.

Brer Dog answer his ole 'oman: All right; but he spec now dat he'd oughter better fix her up so dat she can whistle 'long wid 'em lak Miss Molly Har' do wid her ole man.

Ole Miss Dog tell him: All right. An' she open up wid flint-rock grit.

Ole Brer Dog was mighty handy wid tools; an' he mought a done a good job, if his eyes hadn' a been so filled up wid water from de mouf a hurtin' dat he couldn' see good. So he maked two awky-gawky licks in his mouf splittin' job too; an' didn't leave his ole 'oman but four long "dog-toofs" neider. His ole 'oman tumbled down on de ground, an' jes rolled over whinin' to keep from a hollerin'; an' Brer Rabbit an' Miss Molly Har' hafter git up outn de woods an' leave, to keep deir laughin from a comin' to de notice of ole Brer Dog's 'tention.

Ole Miss Dog 'buse her old man right smartually. She tell him dat she believe dat he hit her toofs on purpose; but he jes declar' to Gracious dat he didnt. Atter while she say dat de off licks sorter leave 'em bofe a lookin' alike, so she reckin dat it wus all right; an' dey gits a liddle peace patched up 'tween 'em.

Fer a long time deir moufs wus so sore an' stiff dat dey couldn' hardly open 'em. Dey couldn' chew nothin an' so dey wus bleedged to stick out deir tongues an' lick up deir water an' sumpin' t'eat . Dat wus de time w'en de Dog fambly 'gin its lickin-up ways; an' it keep on a keepin' 'em up still.

Atter so long a time deir moufs git well; an' Brer Dog an' his ole 'oman go out on deir pieizzer to 'gin deir practicin up of deir whis'lin'. But Law, Chile! W'en dey opened up deir moufs fer to whistle, dey didn' do nothin but bark! Dey tries an' dey tries fer to whistle; but, nothin but bark! Dey tries an' dey tries fer to whistle; but, wid deir split moufs, dey dont do nothin but bark, bark, bark!

Dey sot dar an' looked at onenudder; an atter while it sorter crope across deir minds dat ole Brer Rabbit wus done gone an' played off one of his tricks on 'em. Of co'se, once dey couldn' do nothin but howl, an' now dey could bofe howl an' bark; but dat dont keep 'em from a bein' awful mad 'bout ole Brer Rabbit a foolin' 'em.

Ole Brer Rabbit hear 'em a barkin'; an' he laugh fit to kill hisself. Atter while he make up his mind to go 'round an' have some mo' fun offn 'em. He daresant go whar dey can see 'im; caze he know w'at end of de shovel in de fireplace git hot fust, eben w'en bofe ends is black. He go an' hide out in de bushes jes in hearin' distance of ole Brer Dog's house; an' he give him de "Sponse" to dat song lak he wus promused him an' ole Miss Dog w'en dey wus seed him last at deir house. De "Sponse" run lak dis:

"De dogs say 'boo!'
An' dey barks too.
I haint got no time fer to talk to you."

He sing dis here "Sponse" to de balunce of de chune dat he wus been a makin' up. Fust he would sing de part of de chune dat he wus whistled fer 'em; an' den he would add on de balunce. All of it put togedder make dat 'ar liddle fiddle song of "Ole Molly Har'" w'at de Niggers picks an' plays on deir banjers an' fiddles. Dis was de way he sing it:

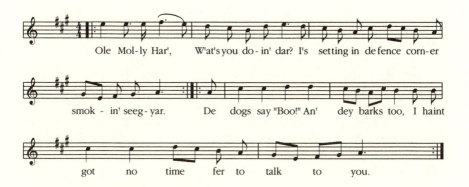

Ole Mol-ly Har', W'at's you do-in' dar? I's setting in de fence corn-er smok-in' seeg-yar. De dogs say "Boo!" An' dey barks too, I haint got no time fer to talk to you.

Ole Brer Dog an' his ole 'oman hear him a singin', away over in de bushes; an' dey say some things w'at haint fitten fer to tell nobody! Him an' his ole 'oman go out a smellin de ground tryin' to track Brer Rabbit up; but dere haint no use. Brer Rabbit jes keep on a gwine away from 'em an' a leadin' 'em through all de brier-patches an' bramble' bushes in dem parts; an' he have a whole heaps mo' fun offn 'em a gittin deir clo'es tore 'up. Atter dat, it take ole Miss Dog a whole mont' fer to git her ole man's britches patched up good 'nough fer him to w'ar outn de house ag'in.

Atter while dey hafter give outn de notion of huntin' him down; an all dem tother animuls in dem diggins rig 'em so much 'bout de trick, dat dey wus bleedged to laugh wid 'em an' git over it or move outn de neighbor-hood to keep from bein' plagued to death. Atter so long a time, w'en dey gits sorter cooled off; Brer Rabbit sont 'em over a big ham of meat, an' sont word along wid it w'at fine folks Brer Dog an' his olo 'oman wus; an' he managed to git it all fixed up ontel he took off Brer Dog's new pair of shoes right befo' his face. Of co'se Brer Dog run him den; an' he keep on a runnin' him clean down to dis day an' a hollerin: "Shoes! Shoes! Come-back! Come-back!" [All this matter concerning the taking of the shoes has reference to the Negro story concerning Why Mr. Dog Runs Brother Rab-bit recorded by Joel Chandler Harris].

A long time atter dis; dere git to be a whole heaps of dogs. De Dog Fambly git on fin; an' keep up bofe deir barkin' an' deir howlin', case dey thinks dat two tricks is always mo' better dan one. Dere wus rich dogs an' dere wus poo' dogs; dere wus big dogs an' dere wus liddle dogs. De ole sayin' sayes dat de big dogs took all de meat, an' dey wus rich an' dey dont leave nothin' but bones fer de liddle dogs, so dey wus poo'.

Dere wus liddle dogs an' dere wus big dogs; an' de big dogs wus powerful overbearin' an' imposin', so dat de liddle dogs have to live an' ketch as ketch can. One day, one of dem 'ar liddle dogs do sumpin dat one of dem 'ar big dogs didn' lak; so he jump on him, whup him, bite him, an' beat him all up. He wouldn' eben hardly stop w'en de liddle poo' dog holler out "'nough!"

W'en dis big dog git gone; de liddle dog up an' study how he wus a gwineter git eben wid 'im. Bymeby he hit on dis here plan: He would go out an' find a bone, an' bring it home an' bury it; den he would go out an' find anudder bone, an' bring it in an' bury it. He keep dis up ontel he git a whole lots of bones buried aroun' his house. Den he go out an' ax all de tother liddle dogs fer to come over an' take dinner wid 'im. He lakwise ax dis here big dog, w'at whup him so, fer to come over an' eat wid 'im at de same time.

Dey all come but de liddle dogs all got dar fust. W'en de liddle dogs wus all got over dar; he telled 'em all 'bout how de big dog wus done lit in an' bit him all up. Den dey all scussed how mean all de big dogs wus a actin'. At las' dey all maked up deir minds an' tetched an' 'greed dat sumpin mus' be done 'bout it. So dey fixed it all up dat dey wus a gwineter give dis here big dog a good beatin' an' bitin' w'en he come over to dinner.

Bymeby de big dog come a struttin' up wid his tail all heisted, an' his nose a snuffin de air lak he wus smelt sumpin. Honey! I reckins dat he wush dat he had a smelt w'at wus a comin' to 'im befo' he git away from dar; caze all dem liddle dogs jumped on him an' almos' e't him up alive. Dey give him de wust beatin an' bitin' dat he wus ever drempt of. W'en he did manage to git loose; he tucked his tall 'tween his legs an' split de wind a makin tracks away from dar.

Den de liddle dog, w'at de tothers wus helped out, gived 'em all dinner. Atter dinner he go out an' dig up all de bones w'at he wus buried; an' give 'em all one apiece fer helpin' 'im out. W'en de tothers liddle dogs ax him w'at make him do dis; he say to dem: "One good turn deserves anudder". Dey wus turned down de big dog; an' he wus turned up de big bone.

W'en he say dis, one of de tother liddle dogs make a speech an' say dat de word "One good turn deserves anudder" wus setch a fine one dat dey all should oughter think 'bout it always befo' dey lays down to go to sleep. Dey all 'gree wid 'im; but dey say dey dont see no way how dey can keep from fergittin it sometimes. Den dis liddle dog subgest dat dey always tune aroun' w'en dey goes to lie down to sleep. Dis would put 'em in de mind of "One good turn deserves anudder". Dey all 'gree to dis; an' Brer Dog's folkses keeps up dis turnin' aroun' befo' dey lies down eben down to dis very day.

You knows, Ferinie, dat I telled you a few days ago 'bout Brer Dog a gwine over along wid Brer Cat to live wid Mr. Man; an' how dey fall out. Dis here man git so many dogs atter while dat he pass 'em over to de tother mens. So all de folkses git so dey wus got dogs.

De mens an' de dogs git to be setch big podners, dat w'en de mens dies dey fixes it all up to take deir dogs 'long wid 'em to Heaben. *So dere git to be heaps an' heaps of dogs up dar in de "Good Place".*

Atter while de mens git some Nigger slaves too. One time, one of dese here slaves (I fergits his name) wus got a wife w'at he git to be a fool over jes lak Sam w'at git to be de Nigger slave in de moon [This refers to "The Negro Slave in The Moon" found elsewhere in this volume]. De white folks sol' dis here fellers wife to anudder man w'at live on a planta-tion five or six mile away. So dis here Nigger—I blieves his name wus Tank—So dis here Nigger Tank wus got a great habit of slippin' off of nights; an' a gwine to see his wife. Her name wus Suze.

De white folks wus awful tight on Tank: an' w'en dey cotched on to his slippin off, dey watch him so close dat dey makes his cakes all dough. One time, he wus been a makin' up sossages fer his Missus an' Mosser up at de Big House. De white folks grind up great big hams an' hunks of lean meat; an' dey flavor it all up wid pepper, an' sage, an' salt ontel its good scent would call you to eat it w'en it wus a cookin' a mile away.

Tank, he want some of dem 'ar good ole sossages to eat; but he know dat his white folk dont never give him none of dem 'ar kind of good fixins. Atter Suze wus sol' away from 'im, she wus his day's study an' his night's dreams; an' he want some of dem 'ar good ole sossages fer to slip off an' take to her in de dead hours of de night. He useter beslong to de church. W'en he heared de white folks a talkin' 'bout seelin' Suze, he prayed fer her not to git sold; but dey sold her. W'en dey sold Suze, he got powerful wicked ag'in; an' he do all sorts of things which he should not oughter do. So w'en he dont see no way fer to git none of dem 'ar good ole sossages fer him an' Suze; he jes steal some. He put 'em in a big water-gourd tied to a string; an' hung 'em down in a ole well, away off down in de corn-field.

He steal go much of de sossages dat de white folks miss 'em; so dey keeps a eye on him mo' closer dan a hawk a watchin' a chicken. Dey watch him so close dat he caint git no chance fer to slip off dem five or six mile to Suze, on de fust night dat he wus got 'em.

De dogs all smelt dem 'ar good ole sossages an' wus a wantin' 'em; so dey hangs aroun' dat well off down dar in de corn-field whar Tank wus hid 'em. Dey hangs aroun' dar all dat night, an' all de nex' day ontel it 'gin to git about good dark. Den dey gits so hongry dat dey leaves an' goes home to git a liddle sumpin t'eat. Dey stays aroun' home a pickin' up de scraps ontel it git sorter late in de night; den dey goes back down in de field to watch aroun' de well, a hopin' somehow to git holt of some of dem 'ar good ole sossages.

W'en dese here dogs gits to de well; dey looks up an' sees Tank about a hunderd yards away, a slippin' off wid de sossages fer to take dem to Suze. So dey falls in, an' follers right 'long behin' him widout sayin' a mumblin' word.

Tank, he dont go down de big road; caze he wus skeard dat de Patterrollers mought ketch him an' whup him. He go by de cow-paths w'at lead through de woods; but he sorter go close to de folkses' houses on de way so as to keep from a gittin' so lonesome. Ev'ry time he go' to pass by de folkses' houses; de dogs ketch de scent of dem 'ar good ole sossages, an' dey comes out an' goes a lookin' aroun' fer 'em. Atter while dey sees Tank; an' dey sees de tother dogs a follerin him fer to git some of dem 'ar good ole sossages. So dey falls in line along behin' de tothers dogs already a follerin him; an' dey lakwise follers him wid de hope of gittin holt of some of dem 'ar good ole sossages. He pass by mo' an' mo' houses; an' mo' an' mo' dogs falls in behin' him an' follers him.

Tank go on, ontel he wus might 'nigh up to Suze's house, widout lookin back; caze he wus always heared all his life dat it 'twus bad luck fer to look back w'en you wus a gwine aroun' at night. An' besides dat; if you looks back over yo' left shoulder at night, you is lierbul fer to see hants! But Tank, once in a while, keep on a thinkin dat he half-way hear sumpin a creepin' 'long behin' 'im. He wus skeared fer to look back; caze it mought be hants; an' he wus skeared not to look back; caze dere wus heaps of wild-cats, an' wolfs, an' b'ars, an' (y)other varmints out in de woods in dem days. At las' he make up his mind: Beance dat you sees hants by lookin' over de lef' shoulder, dat he'd resk de takin' of jes one peep back over de right shoulder.

Tank look back, he do. He see de great big long string of dogs a follerin him! De line wus so long dat he couldn' see, in de dark, to de end of it. He think right off dat dey wus a great big pack o' wolfs atter him. Tank wus some runner' He could go so fast dat all de folkses say dat he go lak a blue streak of lightnin'; an' w'en he git good a gwine on de run, he hafter run a thousan' mile on de tother side of nowhere befo' he could stop hisself. He outrun de whole pack of dogs; an' lef' 'em some distance behin' 'im, all 'cep' one big dog w'at keep mighty close up wid 'im.

Tank look back whilst he wus a runnin' for to see how de gang of "wolfs" wus a comin' on. He feel mighty good w'en he see jes one; an' he thins to hisself dat he can soon give him 'nough "leg-ball" to git hisself outn jail. But w'en folkses looks back'ards, dey haint a lookin' whar dey's a gwine; an' dar's whars dis here feller miss his footin'. He runned into a great big tree w'at knocked him senseless, an' sent him a sprawlin' on de ground in one direction; whilst de bundle of sossages go a tumblin' off in anudder one.

Whilst he wus a lyin' dar outn his head; de big dog, away in front of de tothers, git up wid him fust. He jes grabbed up de bundle of sossages;

an' kep' on a gwine off in de woods. Atter while, de whole pack of dogs ketched up wid him a lyin' dar on de ground outn his head. De dogs 'gin to pulls an' t'ar him an' his clo'es all to pieces. a guess dat dey think dat he wus de sossages. He wusnt de sossages; but befo' de dogs see deir mistake, he wus mighty much lak de sossages. Dey jes tore him all up!

Nex' mawnin, Tank's Mosser git up an' fine him gone: caze he wusnt able fer to walk home atter he wus come back to his senses. But Tank's Mosser maked up his mind, dat Tank wus done gone an' runned away; caze he wus sold his ole 'oman, Suze. So Tank's Mosser say to his ole Missus: "De early bird ketch de worm"; an' he go straight on off an' hire some blood-hounds fer to track him up befo' de trail git cold.

He git de hounds an' dey start off. De hounds track Tank lak a blaze in a storm caze de trail wus hot. De Mosser an' de white mens w'at wus a follerin' 'em couldn' keep up wid 'em. But dey follers away behin', an' hollers to 'em: "Huoy! Git him up, Bullies!"

Bymeby de hounds come up on Tank. He wus got all his senses; but he wusnt able to do nothin fer to help hisself ag'inst de dogs. De hounds jes fairly e't him up alive! He wus turble wicked; an' de white mens w'at wus a follerin away behin' de hounds git dar jes in time fer to hear him cuss an' say befo' he die, dat he wus a gwineter git eben wid dem dogs, eben if he die an' git rammed an' crammed an' jammed down in de Devil's Hell.

De white mens dug out a hole an' throwed w'at dere wus lef' of him in it; an' shoveled a liddle dirt over him an' went on home.

Atter de dogs, w'at wus runned Tank on de night befo' to git de sossages, didn' find none on him; dey helt a meetin' to scuss it. Dey say dat dey smelt de sossages. some say dat dey seed Tank start off wid 'em, an' heaps of 'em claim dat dey seed de sossages in de bundle un'er his arm, whilst he wus a totin' it along in front of 'em.

At las' dey all sayes dat some dog or (y)other got dem 'ar good ole sossages; an' whoever it wus dat wus mean enough to git 'em an' gobble 'em all down, widout splittin 'em up fa'r an' squar', mus' have a good whuppin. Dey makes up deir minds dat whoever it wus dat e't all dem sossages wus bleedged to smell lak sossages. So dey hits on dis plan: W'en dey meets up wid a strange dog, dey'll smell 'im; an' if be smell lak sossages, dey'll know dat he's de rogue w'at git de sossages and run off wid 'em. Any man w'at find anudder man a smellin' lak sossages mus' give him a good whuppin or git outn de dog push.

De dog w'at stole de sossages hear tell of de big Pot of Crow w'at de tothers wus got cooked up fer him; so he take his ole 'oman an' move away off in de sticks [sticks = a backwoods locality] so dat de tothers caint find him. Though dem tother dogs couldn' find him; dey jes kep' on a smellin every dog dat dey met, a lookin' for him.

Atter while de dog, w'at stole de sossages w'at Tank dropped, have a whole pack of chilluns in his fambly. Dese here chilluns all smell lak sossages caze deir daddy wus stuffed hisself so full of sossages dat he give de scent of dem to de whole fambly. He didn' tell his chilluns no nothin 'bout his not 'vidin' up de sossages; caze he wus shamed of w'at he wus done gone an' done.

So atter de olo man wus dead; dese here chilluns go a sharadin deirselfs 'mongst de tother dogs, a courtin'. W'en dese here tother dogs sees dese hear chilluns—bein' strangers—dey walks up to 'em an' smells 'em, Dey smells lak de sossages; an' dem tother dogs jumps on 'em an' bites 'em from top to bottom, from side to side, an' den dey turns an' bites 'em catawampus! Dey whups 'em an' bites 'em all over.

De bitin' an' whuppin of dese here chilluns didn' satisfy de dog compoodle; so, clean down to dis day, de dogs keeps on a gwine aroun', an' a smellin 'mongst de chilluns' chilluns fer to find out all of dem w'at had de sossage-stealin' dog fer a great-grandaddy. W'en dey comes 'cross dem w'at haint no kin to 'im, dey wags deir tails an' makes friends wid 'em; but w'en dey finds one, w'at's his kin, dey fights him an' tries to eat him up.

W'en Tank die an' go down to de Devil whar he beslong, caze he cuss so hard; de Devil look at him all tore up, an' he feel sorter sorry fer him. He ax him w'at he wus a doin' all tore up lak dat; an' Tank make answer an' tell 'im all 'bout de dogs. He den allow to de Bad Man dat he dont care w'at he do to 'im; if he'll jes give him a liddle chance fer to git eben wid dat lowdowned Nigger-runnin Dog-fambly.

De Devil put in wid Tank, dat de white mens wus got it all fixed up fer de dogs to go to Heaben wid 'em; so he dont see noways nowhars dat he can git a lick at 'em.

Tank den tell de Bad Man dat he wus got a plan all in his head, if he would lend him a liddle hand in carryin' it out.

De Devil promus right off dat he'll help 'im; an' say if he wus got up a plan w'at he could 'sturb de 'rangements of de Good Place up dar wid, he'll give him a job fer to stay at home in de house an' not burn him to boot.

Tank make answer to de Devil dat it wus "a go". He den tell him dat dis wus de plan: De Devil, fer his part, mus' fix up a whole pack of Imps w'at'll look jes zackly lak de dogs w'at go up to Heaben. Den dey mus' send de Imps up an' have dem to make deir road into de Good Place fer dogs. W'en de Imps git in; dey can go 'roun' an' make~ noises an' raise rucuses. W'en de 'sturbances gits a gwine; dey'll all know, up dar, dat sumpin is went wrong. Dey'll lakwise know dat de noises is a comin' from de dog-side of de house. Den dey'll have to put all de dogs outn Heaben, w'at's up dar, so as to git so 'sturbances out; an' dey wont let no mo' come in. Dey caint let no mo' dogs come in; caze, if dey does, de Imps can go in fer dogs an' bust it all up an' git 'em all out ag'in.

De Devil slap Tank on de back, an' "Wha! Wha!" an' tell him dat his plan wus jes fine. Dere haint no fire fer him! His job wus jes to set up in de Imp's house; an' let 'em out an' in, atter dey wus all git made.

De Devil make de Imps; an' dey git all de dogs outn Heaben.

—De Devil make de Imps,
An' de Imps make trouble;
De dogs tumbled out,
An' ole Tank, he paid 'em double!

W'en de dogs git tumbled outn Heaben; deir hants go in a dream an' tell de tother dogs, w'at wus still a livin', 'bout w'at wus done gone an' took place. So all de livin' dogs, atter dat, know dat dey caint never go to Heaben no mo'; caze deir great-grandaddies befo' 'em wus fust robbed Tank of de sossages, an' den kilt him.

Eben now w'en somebody is a gwineter die; de dogs howls an' cries, caze dey thinks 'bout how much dey misses; an' dey mourns, caze dey caint go along wit 'em to Heaben. Some say dat de dog-hants tells 'em w'en folkses a gwineter die; an' some sayes dey dont. Some sayes one thing an' some anudder; but, how-some-ever dat may be, dey knows w'en somebody is a gwineter die, an' dey howls an' cries.

Atter dis anudder Nigger, named Sam, w'at wus a bigger fool 'bout his wife dan Tank, got to be de slave in de moon. (If yo' mammy haint never telled you 'bout him; den she will one o' dese days.)

Sam is so fur off up dar on de moon dat de dogs caint zackly see whedder he's black or whedder he's white. So some of de dogs, clean down to dis dey, sees him up dar on de moon; an' thinks dat he's deir Mosser. W'en dey sees him; dey howls an' cries, a lookin' up dar at him all de time. Dey hopes somehow dat he'll come down, an' git 'em, an' take 'em up dar to live wid him. Dat's de reason you sometimes sees dogs a howlin' an' a whinin' an' barkin' at de moon.

With these words, the primitive mother closed her account of the origin of the habits of the dog. The child only looked at her in admiration and said. "Mammy, I sho does lak to hear you talk; caze you knows so much more an' de tother folkses aroun' here bout setch things. You mus' tell me some mo' 'bout 'em right now, jes as soon as you gits rested up a liddle from talkin'."

THE DEVIL'S DAUGHTERS OR
WHY THE FISH HAVE FINS
❄

If one journeys southward from Shelbyville, Tennessee, on a pike that leads over Skull-camp bridge which spans Duck River, looking toward the west, on the south side of the stream as he crosses, he will see a level fertile field. Nearly a half century ago, on one of the early days of the month of July, this field was ladened with a crop of golden waving bearded wheat awaiting the keen blades of the harvesters. It was a time when the reaping machine was a comparative stranger to the Southland. Negroes with old-fashioned mowing blades, known as cradles, followed by deft hands which bound the ripened grain into sheaves and set them into shocks, were the efficient harvesters of this crop.

The reapers were a jolly crowd and; as they moved from one side of the field to the other, multitudinous jokes, showers of song, and peals of laughter accompanied them. They were joyous; first because, for reasons apparent to those who know about a farm, they received a wage for this work about double that received for ordinary farm labor; second, because the dinners spread under the shade of the trees for those who reaped were, from the viewpoint of these impoverished laborers, always sumptuous affairs. The menu would not be considered attractive by men of the present day. It commonly included two or three meats, and every sort of garden vegetable then ordinarily raised. The meal was usually "topped off" with fruit cobblers, pies, gingerbread, and cider. Thus as these black men worked, they were happy. I can hear them now as they sang to the little boy with whom I am well acquainted and whose duty it was to bring them water to quench their thirst.— Yes, they made the welkin ring as they sang:

Fetch a lid - dle mo' wat - er, Bud-die! I needs a

lid-dle mo' wat - er on de wheel. Fetch a lid-dle mo' wat-er,

Bud-die, 'Way down in de ole wheat - fiel'!

When the noonday came on, the dinner was spread upon cloths on the ground, underneath ancient giant sycamores, then growing by the riverside; and the tired hungry men seated themselves around it for an hour of feasting and fun. White fleecy clouds had lazily floated over the clear blue of the skies all the morning; and as the men sat there, eating, one of these clouds drifted slowly overhead without obscuring to any marked degree the bright rays of the sun. As it passed overhead, it turned loose a veritable shower of raindrops which seemed to descend from a clear sky.

When this took place one of the men, known as Uncle Jake Smart, looking upward cried out: "You Tobe! You stop dat 'ar whuppin o' Dinah! We's done wuked ontel we's wet wid sweat; an' we dont want no water a fallin outn no 'oman's eyes fer to make us mo' wetter!"

"Oh come off, Uncle Jake!" said Sib, one of the younger men of the crowd. "W'at's dis you's a tryin' fer to give us anyhows?"

"Haint a tryin' fer to give you nothin' but de natchul bawn facts"; answered Uncle Jake. "Leasewise dat's w'at I wus tol' w'en I wus a liddle shaver of a boy."

"W'at's all dis now, you's been tol'?" asked a number of voices, in rapid succession, from the crowd, in almost identically the same words.

"Humph!" replied Uncle Jake. "You all mus' a been brung up away back in de backwoods lak ole Aunt Jemima! [See "Aunt Jemima" and "Old man Know-all" in Negro Folk Rhymes, complied by the writer.] An' if you dont know no mo' an' dat, I specs you'd better stump yo' toe lak her an' fall clean back in de backwoods an' stay dar!"

"Oh you needn' cut setch a hobbin dash 'bout w'at you knows; caze we knows all 'bout dat too!" answered three or four of the older men in concert, as if some one had already told them what Uncle Jake wus going to say, and had drilled them to give their reply as if uttered by a single voice.

"Well!" responded Uncle Jake, "I draws in my water-tarrapin head whar deres so many axes in de air a lookin' down fer de neck; caze w'en de poo' tarrapin leave his head out whar deres sharp folkses, his head mos' in ginerally drap off an' he set in de plate at de dinner table! W'en it comes to dat 'ar part of de progrance; I wants to set in de chair. I draps it all!

"Please dont drap dat, Uncle Jake"; entreated the younger men. "We wants to hear all about it."

"Yes, go on Jake an' splain it all to 'em", said Uncle Harry Ledbetter, one of the older men who had just claimed that they knew all about it. "We uns jes helt you up a liddle; caze we didn' want no "Ole Man Know-alls" around here a eatin' wid us. De loration 'bout Tobe a whuppin Dinah'll make de dinner-grub taste so good dat we'll all wush our th'oats wus a mile long, feel so good go down".

"Now if you all feels dat a way, I dont care if I does tell it"; replied Uncle Jake, glad of an opportunity to become the center of attraction at the dinner part.

"Well, befo' you 'gins to tell us", said Ben—one of the younger men, "I wants to know whedder w'at you's a gwineter tell is de troof, or whedder it's jes a tale."

Uncle Jake sat quietly for a moment, then said: "Boys, w'en de tale wus fust told, I lef' jest befo' dey got through wid it; an' atterwards some of de folkses w'at stayed an' heared it all sayed it wus de troof, an' some sayed dat it wusnt. So I didn' know zackly which to believe!"

The crowd greeted this explanation of Uncle Jake with a hearty good laugh. Then all was quiet until Uncle Harry Ledbetter broke the silence by saying: "Well, go on Jake wid yo' splavercations on Tobe an' Dinah. I thinks dat all de questions is been axed an' answered."

"All right den!" replied Uncle Jake with an air of importance. "De loration, or de tale, or de troof, or w'at-some-ever it mought be called, go lak dis:

'Way back yon'er one time, dere wus a Nigger man named Tobe w'at wus jes full o' devilment, an' wus de bigges' Conj'er in de world. His ole 'oman wus named Dinah; an' de couple had three chilluns w'at wus all gals. De gals wus named Missy, Sissy, and Prissy. De ole 'woman l'arnt all de ole man's conj'er tricks to de gals onbeknowance to him. Dis make ole man Tobe so mad dat he still whups her now an' den behin' de doo' of his cabin away up in de sky. An' w'en he whup her, she cry so much dat 'nough water drap outn her eyes to make it look lak it's a rainin' whilst de sun is still a shinin'. So w'ensoever you sees it look lak it's a rainin' w'en de sun's a shinin'; it's jes Tobe a whuppin Dinah behin' de doo', an' de water a runnin' outn her eyes."

"Oh pshaw! Uncle Jake!" ventured Ben to interrupt once more. "I haint never hearn no tale 'bout it;' but I's always heared dat it wus de Devil a whuppin his wife behin' de doo', an' I haint never hearn tell of no Tobe a doin' dat."

"Law', Sonny!" protested Uncle Jake. "You mus' a got sont to de College to git a head full o' knowledge; den up an' clean fergit offn yo' mind w'at you git sont dar fer. If you mought jes hold yo' hot sweet-taters fer a while, I mought could git some of de natchul bawn facts befo' you."

"Scuse me!" said Ben apologetically. "I didn' mean no harm; an' if you'll jes go an' tell us all 'bout Tobe, I wont bust in an' bother no mo'".

"All right!" replied Uncle Jake. "But I wants de crowd dat, de nex' time I's stopped, I's corked! an' de tale's finished. So now I'll try to go on, if nobody dont turn in an' head me off.

—Dis here Tobe wus setch a big Con'jer dat de folkses in dem times git so dey wus skeard to go about 'im; an' dey takes to de woods w'en dey sees him a comin'.

He could jes make hisself, his ole 'oman, an' his chilluns put in deir dispearunce w'en he git ready; den he could turn 'roun' an' bring 'em all back ag'in. He could make de big things liddle an' de liddle things big; de sweet things sour an' de sour things sweet. He could jes throw spells on folkses an' make 'em do w'at he want 'em to do.

De folkses all keep away from 'im all dey can; but he could git about so fast wid his tricks dat he keep close behin' 'em. He keep so much devilment a gwine on dat de folkses 'gin to call him de Devil. So he git his name, Devil, from de devilment he do; an' heaps of folkses, w'at dont know his ole name Tobe, calls him de Devil. Setch folkses as dese says dat de Devil is a whuppin his wife, instid o' Tobe; w'en de water draps outn de clear sky.

De folkses keep away so good from Tobe, or de Devil, or w'at-some-ever you mought call 'im; dat he make up his mind to throw a spell on his house an' land of a kind dat would keep it hid an' up in de sky all de time. Atter dis he growed fer hisself some hawns an' hoofs an' snaggle toofs.

His three gals wus monstus good lookin'; an' he wus always a lettin' 'em put in deir pearunce here an' dar an' ev'rywhar. W'en de boys come across, dese her prutty gals; it make deir hearts go pitty-pat an' deir heads go whirly-gig. Dey jes natchully go clean crazy over 'em. Of co'se, whilst de boys wus a tryin fer to court dese gals; de Devil, wid his hawns an' hoofs an' snaggle toofs, git a holt no 'em, an' he make use of 'em lak he want to.

Dis here thing of a Devil a gittin holt of all de boys through his gals, an' a usin 'em lak he want to, go on right well fer a long time. But you all knows dat a 'oman'll be a 'oman, dont care w'at you do; an' de Devils three gals wus jes lak de best of 'em. Atter while dey sees a boy apiece dat dey loves an' wants to marry;—Dar's whar de rub come w'at make de sore un'er de hoss's collar dat stop him a pullin'.

De Devil's gals wusnt none of dese here bashful set. So dey goes an' git deir mammy off by herself an' tells her all 'bout deir lovin' de boys an de boys a lovin' dem; an' all 'bout deir wantin fer to jump de broomstick an' git married. Den dey lakwise call to Dinah's membunce dat dey wus jes broke de lookin-glass a few days befo' dat; an' dat of itself would jes natchully make seben years of bad luck onless dey all gits married befo' de end of de year. If dey dont git married in dis time; den whilst de seben years is a gwine off, all three of de gals'll git to be ole maids. An' if dey gits de back luck of de broke lookin' glass an' three ole maids in de fambly all at de same time; den dey'll hall have lebenty times seben years of back luck. Dey subgests to deir mammy dat de onliest way fer to head off all dis bad luck wus fer to tell ' em all deir daddy's conj'er tricks so dat dey can git away an' marry in wid de boys.

Deir mammy tell 'em dat Tobe, de Devil, wus done maked her cross her heart an' hope she may drap dead, if she tell anybody 'bout his conj'er tricks; an' darfo' she wus skeared fer to tell 'em, caze all de conj'er-house riggins wus so sot dat she'd kick de bucket an' pass over Jurdon if she

start to do it. But she say she'll do dis: She'll go into de cabin whar de
Devil is got all his tricks barred up outn sight; she'll put de conj'er tricks,
one by one, behin' de doo'; She'll crack de doo' a liddle bit ev'ry time de
sun shine out bright; w'en she crack de doo', de sun'll shine in 'twixt de
doo' an' de doo'-facin' an' light up, a conj'er-trick; de gals can set away off
from de house an' look at de lit-up conj'er tricks one atter anudder 'tween
de doo' an' de doo'-facin'; den w'en dey wus seed de tricks, dey can practice up on 'em; an' practice'll make puffect. Dis wus all 'greed upon' an' so
de gals l'arn all deir daddy's conj'er-tricks.

De gals all go away off out in de woods fer to practice up de conj'er-
tricks so as to do 'em up in good fashion. Whilst dey wus a practicin' de
tricks; de youngest gal, named Prissy, l'arnt a while lots of new conj'er-tricks
w'at eben her old daddy dont know. W'en dey git through wid practicin an'
l'arnin' new tricks; dey all 'gree to let Prissy push her marryin' projick fust,
caze she wus l'arnt a lots of new tricks wid which she can match de Devil.

Dey all goes home; an' w'en dey wus got dar, deir mammy wus got
supper a waitin' fer 'em all to eat. Whilst dey wus a eatin; de Devil praise
up Dinah's supper, an' ax her how she wus a feelin'. She tell him dat she
wus jes a feelin' sorter tolerbul. She wus done gone an' wuked so hard a
cookin' dat she wus jes 'bout worried out.

De Devil make answer wid his hawns an' hoofs an' snaggle toofs, he
do, dat dis wus a natchful bawn shame whar dere wus three big strappin
grown gals a livin' in de house. So he tells de gals dat dey mus' git up an'
cook Breakfus ev'ry mawnin an' let deir mammy lay in de bed an' rest.

Dis here progrance jes suit de gals. Dey gits up nex' mawnin an'
cooks Breakfus an' jes strews deir daddy's victuals full of Love Powders
w'at dey wus maked up out in de woods.

W'en de Devil wus e't his Breakfus, an' wus stuffed full o' Love Powders; he couldn' say "no" to nothin' w'at de gals ax him fer, eben though
he'd druther be dead dan to say "yes". So w'en he git all bloated up wid
Love Powders; Prissy tell him dat she want to git married to Jack.

De Devil knowed right away which a way de wind wus a blowin' an'
wus been blowed. He hem an' he haw, but he caint say "no"; so he wus
bleedged to say "yes". But he telled Prissy dat she wus got to git Jack fer
to make his road all de way from de open world up to his big hid conj'er-
plantation away up in de sky, all by hisself. Den he laid back in his chair,
an' wunk his off eye at de tother two gals an' give 'em one of dese here
jolly-whopper laughs; caze he think dat nobody don know how to git
folkses from de open world to de Devil-plantation 'cep' him. You see, he
didn't know dat Prissy wus done l'arnt all his tricks an' den some mo'
besides. Den he tell her dat eben if she manage fer to git Jack up dar; he'll
have to do all he tell him fer a week, so dat dey can all be shore dat he'll
make a fit-in wid de fambly.

W'en de Devil git through wid his layin' down de 'greements wid Prissy;

he look aroun' an' see dat Dinah wusnt yit got up outn de bed an' comed in. So he say: "Boo—! Boo—! I knows dat Dinah is done gone an' showed you all de trick of makin' Love Powders behin' de Trick Cabin doo'. I's a gwineter go an' git her outn bed, an' whup her right behin' dat same doo'; whilst de sun is a shinin' lak it wus w'en she sowed you de Trick!" So he go an' git Dinah outn de bed, an' whup her behin' de doo'; an' de water drap outn her eyes, an' make rain right out in de bright sun-shine. Ever since dat time, he wus been a keepin de whuppin up once in a while.

Atter dis; de Devil, wid his hawns an' hoofs, an snaggle toofs, take Prissy an' bring her from his plantation in de skies down to de open world; an' dey goes togedder to see Jack. W'en dey finds Jack; Tobe—de Devil wid his hawns an' hoofs an' snaggle toofs—tells him dat he wus done l'arnt dat him an' Prissy wants to jump de broom-stick an' git hitched, jined, an' married. He say to him dat dis wus all right; dat he can have her, vidin he can make his way up to de plantation in a week, an' do some liddle odd jobs w'at'll make it look lak he sorter beslongs in "Tobe's" fambly. He say if Jack haint dar in a week; den he'll jes go out an' shake de death-rattles tree, an' dat'll bring him by de plantation as he go a bulgin down to de Hot Hole. Den he looked at 'im; an' give him one of dese here sickenin' death grins, wid his hawns an' hoofs an' snaggle toofs, caze he wus shore dat he wus got de bidder sale of him, soul an' body, in a week.

Atter he wus sayed all dis; he called one of de big black oxes w'at he keep fer to ride aroun' on his plantation. De ox heared him away off up dar on de Conj'er-plantation; an' he come jes a bellerin an' a bug-jumpin. He beller so coarse an' rough dat he sound lak de rumblin thunder; an' he bug-jump so hard an' high dat he shake de (y)earth. Jack, he jes stan' dar an' look, wid his eyes all bucked an' his knees a shakin, as de ox come a caperin' up. W'en he git dar; de Devil mount up, ride off, an' soon git clean gone.

Atter her daddy git outn sight an' outn hearin'; Prissy take Jack away off to one side, an' whisper in his (y)ears, an' tell 'im 'bout her a knowin' of de Conj'er-tricks. She say to 'im dat she would tell 'im all of 'em; but dere wus so many of 'em dat she wus skeard dat he'd fergit w'ich an' w'at to use w'en de time come fer to use 'em. She beg him not to be skeard; an' say w'at-some-ever de Devil ax him to do, to jes tell him dat he'll do it; she'll come to him an' push over de job. But he mus' be shore to do jes lak she tell him all de time—dat way; dey can beat Devil, daddy, an' all; an' git married.

Jack promus her fer to do all dis; but he ax Prissy how in de world is he a gwineter make his way from de open world to de big hid Conj'er-plantation in a week. It look to him lak it mought take a week of lifetimes fer to git up dar.

Prissy make answer to 'im dat dis wus all easy. She wus a gwineter fix it up fer him to git up to de Devil's plantation by de nex' mawnin!

Jack allow dat he he dont see no way how dat can be done.

Prissy order him to shet up his doubtin' mouf; an' open up his head a doin 'jes zackly lak she tell 'im! W'at wus furdermo'; he mus' jes keep on a shettin up an' keep on a doin' w'at she tell 'im, onless he want to tumble head over heels into her daddy's Hot Hole. Jack make promus dat he'll jes keep on a shettin up an' jes keep on a doin'.

Wid dat much all fixed up; Prissy tell Jack dat he mus' go an' ketch a yearlin' calf, kill, clean it, an' quarter it dat evenin' befo' de sun go down. He mus' take dis here calf's quarters along wid him as he travel de road to de big hid Conj'er plantation.

Den she splain to him dat dere wus some big red-headed, red-eyed, scorch-feddered buzzards; w'at live up dar on her daddy's plantation, close by de Hot Hole whar dey puts all de bad folkses. She tells him dat one of dese here buzzards'll come to him jes atter sundown. W'en it come he musn' be skeard. He mus' mount up on its back an' take de four quarters of calf meat along wid 'im.

De big buzzard will fly off wid him to de Devil's plantation. W'en he 'pear to be a gittin tired from flyin', from time to time, on de way wid him to de plantation; she say dat he mus retch aroun' an' stick a quarter of de calf-meat in his mouf. De buzzard'll swaller de meat; an' dat'll make him stout 'nough fer to keep on a flyin' an' a gwine. De four quarters'll make de buzzard stout 'nough to tote Jack all de way to de Devil's Land.

W'en he git dar, an' de Devil ax him how he git dar; he mus' jes make answer: "Dat's fer jack to know, an' fer de Devil to find out." He mus' always be shore fer to say dis very same thing; w'en de Devil ax him 'bout anything w'at-some-ever w'at he may do, atter he git up dar. Atter Prissy tell him all dis; she leave him an' go home.

Dat night w'en Prissy an' de tother gals got home; de Devil axed her w'en she wus a lookin fer Jack to call up to see her.

Prissy sorter whimper up, she do, lak she wus 'bout to cry; an' she say to 'im dat he wus knowed dat no Jack couldn' git up dar inside of no week. She knowed at fust dat he wus a gwineter be hard on Jack; but she wouldn' a thought dat he'd a fixed up fer to kill him dat quick.

De Devil give a wide grin, wid his hawns an' hoofs an' snaggle toofs; an' den he allow dat Jack looked lak dat he mought make right fair kindlin' wood fer de fire down in de Hot Hole. He subgest dat de nex' time dat she want to git married; she mought come aroun' an' start wid her ole daddy instid of her mammy.

Law, Chilluns! But Prissy wus got de Devil all fooled up; caze, at dat very time, he wus a talkin' to her, de big red-headed red-eyed scorch-feddered buzzard wus a lightin' in de place whar Jack wus got de yearlin' calf killed, cleaned, cut, an' quartered.

As soon as de big buzzard lit; Jack took de four quarters of de calf an' tied 'em togedder wid strips of hick'ry bark, he den took some mo' strips of hick'ry bark, to lash hisself on to de back of de buzzard, he den took a ladder an' clumb up on top of his fine big new flyin' hoss. He tied hisself an' de meat up dar all good an' hard an' fast. He den clucked to de big flyin' hoss dat he wus ready.

De big red-headed, red-eyed, scorch-feddered buzzard riz; an' he sailed aroun' in one circle atter anudder. As he circle aroun', a flyin', he go up higher an' higher; an' git closer an' closer to de Devil's plantation. He fly so fast dat heaps of times he leave de breezes clean behin' him; an' it look lak Jack wus a gwineter smother to death, caze he couldn' ketch his wind. But de buzzard, atter while, 'gin to git a liddle tired a sailin' so fast; an' he slow down. W'en he slow down; Jack sorter ketch his wind ag'in.

Atter Jack ketch his wind rail good; he think 'bout Prissy an' how he wus 'bout to sprise de Devil, an' he feel bigger dan all out-of-doors. Den he cut a loose a quarter of de yearlin', an' retched aroun', an' stuck it in de big buzzard's mouf. He swaller it all down at one gulp. De drappin of de meat down de buzzard's th'oat change him up lak hot grease poured on a dyin' fire change it up into wild fire.—Mon! he sailed so fast dat Jack couldn' see which a way he wus a gwine! But atter while he slow down ag'in; an' Jack ketch his wind, an' shove anudder quarter o' meat into his mouf. He keep dis up; and soon atter de big buzzard swaller de las' quarter, he light right down in one corner of de Devil's plantation wid 'im.

He git dar a good while befo' daybreak; so he lie down an' take a nap an' res' his weary bones. W'en daylight come on; he wake up, an' go a walkin' up to de Devil's house jes as dey wus all about ready fer to set down to Breakfus. He walk up an' knock on de doo'; an' de Devil come, wid his hawns an' hoofs an' snaggle toofs, an' open it—Chile! he wus jus so stonished dat his mouf drap open; an' he couldn' git it close 'nough togedder fer to say nothin'.

W'en de Devil stan' dar a sayin' nothin'; his wife, Dinah, up an' go to de doo' to see w'at wus done gone an' happen. She look; an' she wus so stonished dat her mouf freeze up mo' wusser dan de Devil's. Den de gals come a bulgin to de doo' fer to git a eye on w'at wus done gone an' happen. W'en dey git dar an' see Jack; dey have to git behin' de ole man's back, an' stuff deir big red pocket-hankchers in deir moufs to keep from a laughin right out. Atter dey gits deir sides sorter pushed back in; dey takes de red hankchers outn deir moufs, an' comes aroun' an' makes a great miration 'bout Jack a bein' dar.

W'en de Devil manage to git his jaw so dat he could wuk it ag'in, he say to Jack: "How'd you git up here, Sah?" Den Jack make answer lak he wus been tol' to do by Prissy; an' say, "Dat's fer Jack to know an' fer de Devil to find out!"

Well, de Devil hemmed an' hawed aroun' fer a while, wid his hawns an hoofs an' snaggle toofs; den he tell Jack dat he'll have to do a week's wuk fer him, so as to show dat he's fitten to be counted 'mongst deir kin;

he can den blow on his horn dat he's de fust to git a gal an' jump de
broom-stick wid her on de shiftin' sands of a Conj'er-plantation.

Jack tell him all right, dat he'll do de week's wuk; but he wouldn' care
if he'd let Prissy give him a liddle bit to eat, caze he feel a liddle sorter
hongry atter walkin' so fur.

It sorter git de Devil's time w'en he hear tell o' Jack a walkin' all de way
from de open world clean up to de Conj'er-plantation in one night, an' he ax
if he moughtn't zamine his footses; but Jack tell him dat dis haint in de bargain. But befo' de Devil can git in anudder word; he say to him dat de eatin'
wus bleedged to be in de bargain, caze wukin an' eatin' always goes togedder.

De Devil look at him, wid his hawns an' hoofs an' snaggle toofs, an'
say dat he reckin dat wus right; but he caint let him eat at de house at de
table ontel he jump de broom-stick wid Prissy an' git in de fambly. So he
tell him dat he'll give him his fust day's wuk to do, dat he can go out an'
'gin on de wuk; an' dat atter while, Prissy can come an' bring him some
Breakfus fer to eat.

Jack make answer to de Devil: Dat wus "Tetch an' go"; an' dat wus jes
de sorter of man dat he wus a lookin' fer.

So de Devil, wid his hawns an' hoofs an' snaggle toofs, handed out to
Jack de fust day's wuk to be done. De fust day's wuk wus to clear up a
great big field of timber lan'—as big as he could see across, raise a crop of
corn on it, gedder up de corn, put it in de corn-crib, lock up de crib doo',
an' bring him dey key jes befo' sundown.

Jack pick up a ax an' a grubbin'-hoe; an' go on off to de new-groun',
an' start to do de days wuk. W'en he git out dar an' 'gin to wuk; he find
out dat about all de trees wus big iron-woods w'at you couldn' scacely
stick no ax in; an' de un'ergrowth wus dese here big bramble-briars wid
so many thorns an' stickers on 'em dat you caint hardly tetch 'em to git to
de roots to grub 'em up widout gittin yo'self all tore up. An' w'at wus mo',
ev'ry time Jack would cut down one tree or one bush; three mo' would
pop up outn de groun', an' take deir place. W'en he cut off a lim' or pull
off a leaf, three mo' would shoot up an' take deir places. He wus mightly
disheartened; caze he didn't see no way how he wus a gwineter git started
on de clearin' of de field, much less de pitchin' of a crop an' gedderin it.
'Bout dis time Prissy come an' brung Jack his Breakfus. W'en she git dar;
she tell him to come an' eat.

Jack looked at Prissy, an' den drapped his head; an' den de water 'gin to
run outn his eyes lak rain. He say: "Law, Honey! I's gone! Yo' daddy is a
gwineter git me fer de fire to-night! De mo' harder I wuks; de mo' lesser I
clears. Oh, I caint eat; I caint tetch a mouf-full! Jes set down an' see how
hard I loves you by how hard I wuks; befo' de time come fer yo' daddy to
toe me off!

Prissy make answer to him dat he musn' come a talkin' lak dat. She
wus brung him up dar, an' she wus a gwineter take him through; if he'd

do lak she tell him. Den she say: "Jack, dont you ricomember dat I tol'
you dat you mus' do all I say w'en you git up here on de plantation?"

Jack say: "Yes".

Den Prissy sing him a song lak dis:

1. Come un' er! Come un' er! My
2. Come eat den! Come eat den! My
3. He's cotch you fer his pris' ner! My

Hon-ey, my Love, my Heart's a - bove! Caze my heart's gone a
Hon-ey, my Love, my Heart's a - bove! Caze my heart's gone a
Hon-ey, my Love, my Heart's a - bove! Caze my heart's gone a

weep - in, 'way down be - low de trees.
weep - in, 'way down be - low de trees.
weep - in, 'way down be - low de trees.

Atter Jack wus heared Prissy sing dis here song, he come an' sot down
an' e't his Breakfus. Den he tell her dat he mus' git up an' go at de clearin'.

But Prissy tell him dat he musn' do dat yit. He mus' lay his head down
in her lap an' take a nap an' res' hisself awhile befo' he go to wuk.

Jack say: He haint got no time to tarry!

Prissy make answer: But he wus promused fer to do lak she tell him
to do.

Jack say: Yes, dat wus so. So he laid hes head down in her lap, an'
dozed on off to sleep.

W'en Prissy wus got Jack off to sleep; she sing-song off, in a sorter
half whisper, over an' over:

"Liddle mens, liddle mens, busy as de bees!
Liddle mens, liddle mens, come an' cut trees!"

In a liddle of no time; a whole wood's full of liddle mens comes. Dey wus de
Devil's Imps. Prissy wus l'arnt how to call 'em up an' use 'em; by watchin' an
seein' de tricks w'en Dinah showed 'em behin' de Devil's Trick Cabin Doo'.
W'en de Imps all git dar, dey blowed deir hot bref on de woods an' kilt 'em

all. Den dey hit a lick or so apiece; an' dere wus so many of 'em, dat de
trees an' bushes wus all gone an' de big new-ground field wus all cleared.

Den Prissy helt up her hands an' all de Imps stop an' lissen; an' she
sing-song ag'in. She say over an' over:

> Liddle mens! Liddle mens! Liddle mens not bo'n!
> Liddle mens! Liddle mens! Raise an' gedder co'n!

Dere wus a liddle rattlin an clat'rin aroun'; an' de co'n crop wus planted,
raised, geddered, put in de co'n-crib, locked, an' de key brung to Prissy
quicker dan a wink.

Den Prissy waked Jack up. He looked aroun'; an' he seed de woods
all gone. He see dried up co'n-stalks a standin' in de fiel' wid de (y)ears
all pulled offn 'em. He look away ac ross de fiel' at de Devil's co'n-cribs.
He see dem all locked up an' de co'n all a shinin' through de open gable
ends of de roof.

Jack look at Prissy in wonderment an' say: "How'd all dat come 'bout?"

Prissy make answer to 'im: "Nev' mind 'bout 'how'. You jes do w'at I
tells you!" Den she and him de keys an' say; "W'en my daddy come an'
holler out—a callin' 'Jack! Jack!' you mus' answer him an' say: 'So, Mosser
so! De wuk's all done; but Jack's so tired, he's almos' fitten to die!'"

Jack promus dat he'll do dis. But befo' Prissy lef' him, she tol' him dat
she wus done seed in a dream dat her daddy wus a gwineter make him do
one day's wuk right un'er his eyes befo' he wus got through. She wouldn'
have no chance fer to help 'im wid dis. So she give him a liddle teneinchy
tiny red bag wid sumpin in it; an' she tell him to hold dis bag in his lef' hand
w'en he git called to do wuk un'er her daddy's eyes. Dis here bag would make
him able fer to do any one job dat de Devil give him. Prissy den go on off an'
leave him to set down in de cool shade, an' wait fer de Devil to come back.

Along towards sun-down, de Devil come a ridin' home, wid his hawns
an' hoofs an' snaggle toofs, on one of his big bellerin black oxes. W'en he git
almos' dar, he holler out: "Jack! Jack!" an' Jack make answer: "So, Mosser so!
De wuks all done; but Jack's so tired, he's almos' fitten to die!"

De Devil rid up, he did, an' he looked an' he looked; den he axed
Jack how'd he manage to do all dat.

Jack made answer, he do, lak Prissy wus done tol him—"Dat's fer Jack
to know, an' fer de Devil to find out!"

De Devil say: "All right den, to come up tomorrer mawnin; an' he'll
give him his second day's job." Atter dis, Tobe—de Devil—rush on home
befo' de sun go down; an' he take Dinah an' whup her behin' de doo' of
de Conj'er-trick cabin, an' a shower come down from de skies, from de
water a drappin outn her eyes, jes lak while ago 'twus done, out in de
open sun. He done dis; caze he knowed dat she mus' have showed somebody, or anudder, one of his tricks from dar.

Jack git up de nex' mawnin bright an' early; an' he go up to de Devil's house fer to git his second day's job; w'at he mus' do to git Prissy fer a wife. W'en he git up dar; de Devil wus a settin out on his pieizzer, wid his hawns an' hoofs an' snaggle toofs, a waitin fer him to come. He say: "Boo—! Boo—! Mawnin, Son! I's a gwineter give you a big fine job, an' Prissy can come atter while an' bring you yo' Breakfus an' Dinner all in one, w'en you wus been long 'nough fer to relish it. I specs dat you mought need at least de two meals befo' you gits all de wuk done. It's a big fine job!—I wants you to clean out my whole big flock o' stables whar I keeps my big flock of big black bellerin oxes.—It's a fine job! You see: I's got it so fixed up dat all de rubbish from all de stables down in de open world will come up an' take de place of my oxes' rubbish jes as fast as you throws it out. So w'en you gits through wid de cleanin' of my flock of stables; all de stables in de open world will lakwise be cleaned out! I wants you to help de whole world whilst you's a helpin' me, caze I wants you to help me in hinderin' de whole world. No man, w'at caint help de whole world caint hinder no whole world. I knows you wont mind to do dis", say de Devil wid his sickly grin an' hawns an' hoofs an' snaggle toofs' "caze a man w'at can clean up a new-ground fiel' as big as he can see across an' bring in a crop from it in a day, should oughter clean de whole worl' in a day, if he wus a mind to".

Jack pick up his spade an' go on off to de flock of stables. De Devil e't his Breakfus an' mounted a big black ox an' rid on off fer de day.

W'en Jack wus been a wukin an' a throwin' out filth from one of de stables fer about a couple of hours; Prissy come an' brung him his Breakfus an' Dinner, all in one. W'en she git dar; Jack wus done throwed out mo' rubbish dan a eight-ox wagin could haul off in a day. Yit he wusnt got out 'nough fer to git over de doo'-sill of de fust stable.

Prissy tell him to come on an' eat his Breakfus.

Jack look at her; an' as de water come pourin' outn his eyes; he say he dont want no Breakfus, caze he dont see no way fer to de wuk an' her daddy wus shore a gwineter git him fer kindlin'-wood dat night.

But Prissy call to his membunce dat he wus promused fer to do w'at she tell him. So Jack come an' sot down an' e't his Breakfus. Atter he git through wid his eatin'; she tell 'im: If he'll hold up his right hand, an' promus not to git skeared an' holler out so dat her daddy'll come to see w'at's de matter; she'll clean out de stable right befo' his eyes.

Jack helt up his hand an' maked de promus.

Den Prissy sing-songed an' sayed over an' over:

"Liddle mens! Liddle mens! w'at eats from my daddy's tables!
Liddle mens! Liddle mens, come clean out dese here stables!"

W'en she called lak dis, de Imps come up lak ants; an' ev'ry one of 'em wus a totin a pitchfork in deir hot claw hands. Jack wus might 'nigh skeared to death; but Prissy pulled out a big red pocket-hankcher, an' slapped dat over his mouf, an' tied it, to make shore dat dere wusnt a gwineter be no promuses fer to git broke.

Well; de Imps soon git all de Devil's stables cleaned out, wid all de stable rubbish of de open world throwed in fer good measure. It make so much litter dat it kiver up half of de Devil's plantation. De scent from de pile wus sumpin awful; so Prissy throwed a spell over it w'at would make it blow down de road a leadin' from de Hot Hole of de Bad Place up to Tobe's plantation. Dis wus de road dat de Devil wus bleedged to travel up dat evenin' [The Antebellum Negro used the word evening for the afternoon.] w'en he go to come home. W'en Prissy git it all fixed, she tell Jack to be shore to give de answers to her daddy's questions, dat evenin', w'at she wus already tol' him. Den she leaves him.

Dat evenin, de Devil wus a comin' from de Hot Hole of de Bad Place, wid his hawns an' hoofs an' snaggle toofs; an' he ketch de stench! He fust git sick, an' den he git wusser. He wus done set all his megs fer to live always; but he git so powerful sick dat he wus skeared dat it wus all a gwineter fail him, an' he mought die! W'en he think 'bout diein', he shake all over; caze he wus skeared dat his ole 'oman mought time him hand an' foot, an' dump him over into de Hot Hole of de Bad Place wid his conj'er tricks all took away from him! But at las', he manage to git home by de hardes'. W'en he got dar, he didn' go a huntin' an' a hollerin fer Jack. He maked a bee-line fer his Conj'er-trick cabin so as to git hisself chuored up an' so as to make de turble scents from de rubbish pile go off straight up in de air an' keep on a gwine.

He git to de Trick cabin; but by de time he git hisself an' de turble scents all fixed up, de sun wus a gwine down. So he didn't git no time fer to whup Dinah in de sunshine an ' no time fer to look at de stables befo' dark. He ramshack his mind an' he dont know 'w'at to do! But at las' he call out offn de Trick-cabin steps: "Jack—! Jack—!" an' Jack make answer away off down in de ox-lot: "So, Mosser so! De wuk's done; but Jack's so tired, he's almos' fitten to die."

De Devil holler back down though de dark: "How, in de thunder, did you manage to do dat?"

Jack, he holler back to 'im: "Dat's fer Jack to know; an' fer de Devil to find out".

Den ole Tobe, de Devil, holler back: "All right, Sah! Come up tomorrer mawnin."

W'en de Devil leave de Trick cabin an' go in de house, he wus as tetchous an' stingy as a prickly-pear; but Dinah wus jes as sweet as peaches, caze she knowed w'at side her bread wus buttered on. So she axed him right in to a pipin' hot Supper. He make answer dat he dont want no nothin' fer to eat, dat his stomach wus jes a liddle bit turned; but he'll come in an' set down an' jaw her an' de gals whilst dey wus a puttin' away deir sumpin t'eat.

W'en she git him in to de table; Dinah pass him over a big red-cedar piggin, full of mint julip. He turned dis up an' drunk it dry at one gulp. W'en de whisky an' mint git down him; de mint sorter settle his stomach, an' de whisky make him feel mo' better an' loosen up his tongue.

He sot dar a eatin an' a drinkin' mo' an' mo' mint julip; an' he feel mo' better an' mo better wid his hawns an' hoofs an' snaggle toofs. Atter while, w'en he git a liddle sorter tipsy, he open up an' say: "Boo—! Boo—! Well Dinah, w'en I wus fixed up de plantation fer us to live on; I jes fixed it up wid room 'nough on it fer four famblies. Me an' you makes one of de famblies. An' I wus thinked maybe some day, w'en I wus got about as much of de folkses in de Hot Hole of de Bad Place as I wus wanted, I mought let de gals git married; an' den, dey an' deir mens would make de tother three famblies. But—Boo—! Boo—! Dinah, half of de plantation is know kivered over an' piled up wid Jack's stable cleanin's; an' dere's jes 'nough room now lef' fer two famblies. So I reckins dat we'll have to let two of de gals go down an' marry an' live in de open world."

W'en de Devil say dis, Prissy jes grin all over; caze she wus thought dat her an' Jack mought now git away an' jump de broom-stick, an' live happy togedder in de open world.

Den de Devil, he look at her; an' he grin some all on his own hook, wid his hawns an' hoofs an' snaggle toofs. An' he say: "Boo—! Boo—! You knows—Dinah—dat it's good, high, an' proper fer de oldest gals to git deir mens fust, amongst de 'Big-to-do'; so we'll jes foller up dat away of doin' things. Tomorrer mawnin, we'll let Missie an' Sissie sail down to de open worl' on one of our big rid-headed red-eyed scorch-feddered buzzards; an' git deir mens, an' marry 'em, an' stay dar. We'll jes keep Prissie an' Jack up here. I's a gwineter give him four mo' days of wuk' caze he think dat he wus jes natchully a June-sweetener. [June-sweetener = one who can change the nature of things.] If he fall through wid de wuk; den we can use him fer kindlin', an' go an' git Missie an' her man fer to come back an' be de tother fambly on de Conj'er plantation. We can den keep Prissy fer de ole maid to take care of de bad luck from de lookin'-glass w'at de gals wus broke. But an' if Jack git through wid all de wuk; I reckin dat we'll have to sorter somehow manage to stomach him in de fambly as de man fer Prissy, an' take over de care of de broke-lookin-glass bad luck fer ourselves!

Boo—! Boo—! Dinah, I put Jack to clean up lan' on a Monday, I put him to clean up de flock of stables wid all de rubbish of de open worl' on a Chuesday, an' I wus at fust fixed up a whole week's prorgance of cleanin' fer him; but I's a gwineter change dat prorgance. I's sorter skeared dat if I keeps up de cleanin' prorgance, an' dont git Jack fer no kindlin';

dat our whole plantation will git so filled up, dat we'll git clean scrouged [Scrouged = crowded] out an' dere wont be no room lef' up here fer us! Den we'll have to go an' live aroun' de Hot Hole of de Bad Place; so as to git elbow-room!"

—0—

"Wus dem tother two gals a marryin' down in de worl' de occasion fer some folkses a havin' de Devil in 'em?" Uncle Harry Ledbetter interrupted the narrator, Uncle Jake, to ask.

"Yes", replied Uncle Jake, "an' dat's de reason dat heaps of folkses is got de devil in 'em. Dat's lakwise de reason why heaps of folkses is got daddies an' mammies w'at can conjer, an' is fore-knowin', an' can tell fortunes."

—0—

The interruption over, and the question apparently philosophically answered; Uncle Jake again continued his narrative as follows: "Nex' mawnin, de Devil got up befo' day wid his hawns an' hoofs an' snaggle toofs; an' sot aroun' an' figgered out a new progrance of wuk fer Jack. He sont Missie an' Sissie off at day-break to de open worl' to git married; an' den he go to find Jack, as de sun riz, fer to give him his Wednesday's job to do.

W'en he find Jack, he showed him one of de big red-headed red-eyed scorch-feddered buzzards' nests out on top of a big tall slick rock, out in de middle of a big lake filled up wid black b'ilin' stewin' water. He tell him to go out dar an' git de aigs fer him; an' brings 'em up to de house to 'im dat evenin' befo' sun-down. Den he mounted one of his big long-hawned coal-black big-bellerin oxes; an' rid on off fer de day.

Jack look at de Devil an' he look at de nes'; an' he dont say nothin'. Atter de Devil git gone; he go an' git a foot-adds. [Foot-adds = adz.] He wus made up his mind to cut down a big tree; an' make a dug-out to git in an' go an' git de aigs. He 'gin to chop one de tree fer to chop it down; but ev'ry time he would knock out a chip, de tree would git growed bigger. He wus outn heart w'en Prissy come to bring him his Breakfus; caze he didn' see no way in de worl' fer to git no dug-out at de rate dat he wus a gwine.

Prissy tell Jack to eat his Breakfus; an' he do it. Den she tell him to lay down his head on her lap an' go to sleep. He tell her dat he dont want to go to sleep, dat he want to see dat dug-out as it git made. Prissy maked answer to him dat she wus skeared dat lookin'; at it a gittin made mought make him buckeyed. If his eyes git bucked; den her daddy would ketch on to her doins, an' dat would break up ev'rything an' ruin 'em bofe. Wid dat much sayed, he layed down his head in her lap an' went on to sleep.

W'en he 'gin to doze, Prissy 'gin to call de Devil's Imps. She sing-song off:

"Liddle mens! Liddle mens! come on through!
Liddle mens! Liddle mens, burn canoe!"

De Imps come up all wropped up in sheets of fire, an' wid red-hot pokers in deir hands. Dey burnt de tree in two close down to de roots; dey burnt all de limbs off; den dey hollered it out wid fire, an' dar wus yo' dug-out! Dey nex' pushed de dug-out into de aidge of de smokin' water of de lake; an' den waved "good-bye" to Prissy wid deir blazin' red-hot pokers.

Prissy den woke Jack up; an' dey bofe got in de dug-out, an' went out fer to git de aigs of de big-red-headed red-eyed scorch-feddered buzzard, fer de Devil. W'en dey got to de rock; de big scorch-feddered buzzard come a sailin over fer to spit on Jack an' kill him; but Prissy helt up some sort of a liddle red bag in her hand, an' he flew on off widout pesterin' 'em. So Jack got de aigs; an' him an' Prissy go on back to de land. Den she leave him.

Late dat evenin', jes befo' de sun git down, de Devil wus back wid his hawns an' hoofs an' snaggle toofs; an' wus a settin out on his pieizzer, a waitin fer Jack to come. He wus shore dat he wus a gwineter git him fer kindlin' wood dis time! Jes as de sun wus a sinkin', he looked up an' seed Jack out at de front gate of de yard; but he dont see him wid no aigs.

He holler out to 'im: "Boo—! Boo—! —Son or kindlin'-wood? Jack—! Jack—!"

Jack den hand de answer back to 'im: "So! Mosser, so! De wuk's done; but Jack's so tired, he's almos' fittin to die!"

But de Devil say: "Boo—! Boo—! Me see no aigs! Seein' is blievin!"

Den Jack retched in his two pockets an' took out de two aigs in his two hands; an' helt 'em up befo' de Devil's eyes, an' handed 'em over to 'im.

De Devil sorter look 'em over, an' den he say: "How, in de Sam-hill, did you git dese?"

De answer come back to ' im: "Dat's fer Jack to know an' fer de Devil to find out!"

"All right", sayed de Devil, "tomorrer is Thursday ; an' I has a thunderin good job fer you. I'll come down bright an' early into de ox-paster fer to git it to you. You can meet me down dar by de well whar we draws up water fer to water de oxes wid."

Jack make answer "all-right"; an' den dey bofe goes off fer to sleep fer de night.

So de Devil meets Jack down by de well, de nex' mawnin, wid his hawns an' hoofs an' snaggle toofs. He say to 'im: "Mawnin, Jack! Boo—! Boo—!" Den he pull out his keys an' drap 'em all down in de well. Dere wus a bucker down dar, wid a ole rotten rope, fer to draw water wid; an' he say to Jack: "Boo—! Boo—! You can jes draw all de water outn dis well, den draw out de keys an' bring 'em to me dis evenin; an' dat'll do fer yo' day's wuk fer today". Wid dat much sayed, he go on off.

Jack, he 'gin to draw de water, he do; but he find out dat de well wus done conjered. Ev'rytime he'd draw out bucket of water; two mo' buckets would come in an' take deir places. So dat 'ar well git mo' fuller instid o' mo' emptier from de drawin' of de water. Bymeby w'en it wus riz almos' chug full of water from de drawin'; de ole rotten rope broke, an' de bucket rumbled back down an' sunk to de bottom.

Jack, he stan' dar an' look at de water in de well. W'en he didn' see no way fer to do no mo' drawin'; his heart sorter fail him, an' de water 'gin to drap outn his eyes. One of de draps of water from his eyes tumbled into de well; an' it swelled up right away ontel it git to be a whole bar'l-full. So Jack had to dry up his eyes, an' walk away from de well.

About dis time, Prissy come a bringin him his breakfus an' his dinner all in one. She call him an' tell him to set down an' eat.

He tell her dat he'd druther see dem keys fust an' den set down an' eat.

But Prissy tell him dat he mus' mind w'at she say. So he sot down an' managed to swaller down a mouf-full or so somehow.

W'en he wus got through; Prissy telled him fer to take her fan, an' fan her hand all de time whilst she is a drawin' de water up outn de well;' caze de water an' de keys wus all hot. Dey bofe takes deir stand by de side of de well. Prissy helt her hand out over it wid sumpin in it w'at looked lak a liddle whit gravel. Den she sing-song over an' over:

"Come up water!
Come up water!
Come up water!
Come up water!"

Chile! Dat smokin'-hot water runned up from outn dat 'ar well lak dere wus a river cut loose from de bottom of it. De smoke from it would a burnt Prissy's han', if Jack hadn' a fanned it so hard. De well wus dry in a liddle o' no time. Den Prissy sing-songed off an' over:

"Come up bucker, bring de keys!
Come up bucket, if you please.
Come up bucket, bring de keys!
Come up bucket, if you please.

W'en she wus done sayed dis fer a liddle while; de bucket comed up an' tumbled out on de groun' wid de keys in it. Prissy den blowed her bref on de keys to cool 'em; an' passed 'em over to Jack. She nex' tied de broke rotten rope back togedder, an' put it back on de bucket. She den walked off an' waved her hand to him "good-bye".

Dat evenin', w'en it wus about time fer de Devil to come home; Jack go off a liddle piece an' hide hisself behin' a tree. Bymeby, ole Tobe come. He come home by de well; an' he seed de bucket an' de rope a settin dar by de well. Den he peeped over de aidge into de well' an' he seed dat it wus as dry as a chip, an' de keys wus all gone.

So he hollered out: "Boo—! Boo—! Jack! Jack!" but no Jack dont make no answer. De Devil den call ag'in, an' he call so loud dat he fairly shake his plantation all over; but Jack he lay low an' he dont say nothin'. Den de Devil 'gin to talk to hisself sorter lak he wus a half loon, [loon = idiot.] an' he say: "I railly do believe widout a doubt dat 'dat lowdowned Slick-slickum' wus done gone an' runned off to de open world, an' took all my keys wid 'im. Boo—! Boo—! I's jes ruint! How is I a gwineter open an' shet all de doo's to de Bad Place fer to put de folkses w'at I ketches in dar? I's moved de bar from my Trick-cabin doo', an' locked it up!—Boo—! Boo—! How is I a gwineter git in dar an' git my Conjer-tricks? Oh! How's I a gwineter keep de worl' a movin' widout dem keys? Boo—! Boo—! I's ruint! I's ruint!"

Den he called Jack ag'in lak claps of thunder: "Jack—! Jack—!" So Jack maked answer: "So, Mosser! So! De wuk's done; but Jack's so tired, he's almos' fitten to die!" Jack den splain to de Devil dat he wus so tired dat he wus drapped off into a liddle nap—though he wusnt git de wuk finished up fer mo' dan a minute befo' he wus come fer to look it over. He den put in dat he wus in hopes dat he didn't have to call him mo' dan once; an' handed him over his keys.

De Devil took de keys widout sayin' nothin'; an' turned 'em over in his hands an' zamined 'em. Den he rubbed his eyes fer to clean dem up; an;' to make shore dat he wus a lookin' wid dem, an' not wid some conjer trick w'at Jack wus managed fer to stick up in his head onbeknowance to him.—Well, at las', he sorter half way make up his mind dat dey wusnt w'at dey wusnt. So he say to Jack: "Boo—! Boo—! If you'd jes tell me, Jack, how you wus managed fer to git de water an' de keys outn de well; I mought quit off eben, an' take you in to de fambly right now".

But Jack, he make answer an' say: "Dat's fer Jack to know, an' fer de Devil to find out".

De Devil say to 'im: "All right, den. Tomorrer is Friday—bad-luck day. Come up; an' I'll give you a job w'at'll fit in wid de day. We'll git to see who's de most onluckiest; Jack or de Devil!" So dye leaves onenudder ontel nex' day.

Nex' mawnin, Jack meet de Devil out on his plantation wid his hawns an' hoofs an' snaggle toofs. Ole Tobe say: "Boo—! Boo—! Mawnin, Jack!—Does you see w'at dem is a flyin' an' a gwine down de big road by my plantation to de Hot Hole of de Bad Place?"

Jack make answer: "So! Mosser, so! I sees oudles [oudles = a countless number] an' oudles of jaybirds a totin moufs full of sand down to de burnin pit fer you to heat up hot, an' throw on de folkses w'at you gits down dar in de fire."

"Boo—! Boo—!" say de Devil. "You's mighty zackly right! All de jaybirds is up here in de hid worl' of my beslongins today whilst all de tother birds is down in de open worl'; caze dis day is Friday.

Since you comes all de way from de open worl' up here, in one night; I wus thought dat, in a pinch, you mought do a good job in bofe worlds, all in a single day. Now, if you's good an' soupple [soupple = supple] 'nough to go down dar an' back, an' do wuk in bofe places all in one single day; den you's might-'nigh up wid me, an' it mought make me think dat you's almos' good 'nough to claim kin wid de fambly.

De job are dis: Go down in de open world, an' git one fedder offn' ev'ry kind of wild bird dere is down dere; an' put dem in a bag. Den come on back up here an' git a fedder offn ev'ry jaybird w'at's come up here from de open worl'; an' put dem in dat 'ar same bag. Brink 'em to me dis evenin befo' sundown; fer to make a fedder-bed; so dat de bed w'at de Devil lie on here in his hell, wont be hard no mo' an' he wont have to turn over 'cep' aş he want to fer to rest hisself.

I's a gwineter stay all day aroun' 'mongst my big red-headed red-eyed scorch-feddered buzzards; so dat, if you does all dis, you caint steal no chance fer to do it wid dem! Yes, bring de fedders in befo' sundown; caze I wants to see 'nough of 'em on dis day, bofe fer my use now, an' 'nough fer my chilluns' chilluns to boot!"

W'en Jack hear all dis, an' know dat de Devil wus a gwineter spend de day aroun' 'mongst de big buzzards w'at toted him over de road befo'; it look to him lak his time wus come to grease up de embers in de Hot Hole fire. He wus so powerful down in de mouf, dat he couldn' say nothin; an' de Devil, widout sayin no mo', go on off, wid his hawns an' hoofs an' snaggle toofs, to de Buzzard-lot, an' leave him dar.

Jack 'gin to make bird-traps jes as fast as he know how. He didn' have no hopes of ketchin no fedders in de traps, but he say to hisself; Jes any thing fer to keep him from a thinkin' 'bout de Devil; a ketchin, an' a quarterin, an' a burnin' him wid he he't-up sand w'at de jaybirds wus brung him.

W'en Prissy wus come fer to bring his Breakfus; she found him jes a puffin an' a blowin' an' a sweatin' over his trap-makin'. She tell him fer to stop an' come an' eat Breakfus; but he tell her dat he jes caint stop fer dat! He ax her fer to come dar an' stan' by him; so dat he can tell her w'at wus done gone an' took place, whilst he keep on a makin' bird-traps. Prissy go over to 'im; an' he tell her all 'bout de fedders w'at he's bleedged to bring, or burn. Darfo' she caint fix up on buzzard fer him to ride. W'en he tell her 'bout de loss of de buzzards; he fall down on de groun', an' 'gin to cry.

Prissy go to him an' put her hand on his head; an' she tell him dat he mus' do w'at she tell 'im, or all wus lost. He must fust eat his Breakfus.

At las' Jack e't a bite or so; den Prissy tell him to put his head in her lap an' go to sleep. Jack lie down jes lak she tell him; but it look lak dat he jes couldn' git to no sleep. Prissy rub his head sorter sof'-lak wid her hand; an', at las', he drap off in to a kind of a cat-nap snooze.

W'en he git 'bout half way to sleep; Prissy reach in un'er her big cotton apron, an' pull out a big stretchy bag w'at she wus got hid up un'er dar. She took outn dis bad some liddle white powders; an' she strowed 'em in de air an' sing-songed off:

"Fedders! Fedders, hear dese words!
Fedders, come from offn de birds!
Fedders come down in de baggie;
Pick dat crow wid ole Tobe, Aggie!"

Whilst Prissy wus a sing-songin dis off; de air jes git alive wid fedders. Dey comed down jes a windin' deirselves into de big stretchy bag. Ev'ry sort of fedders dat you's ever hearn tell of, mixed up half an' half wid jaybird fedders, blowed deirselves into dat bag!

W'en Prissy wus got de bag all stretched an' puffed out as big as two or three hills wid all kinds of fedders; she shaked Jack outn his noddin', an' showed 'em to him. She conjered a string aroun' de mouf of de bag into a knot so as to fasten de fedders up; an' den she went off an' lef' him. Atter a few minutes she come back jes to say dat she want to say to him: She dont want to never see no mo' water a comin' outn his eyes, nor hear no mo' blubberin a comin' outn his mouf. She want him fer to always keep in his mind dat, w'en her daddy wus got a crow fer to pick wid him, she wus always got a bag fer to hold de fedders. Den she lef' him fer good, dat day.

Dat evenin'; de Devil come home, a whis'lin, an' a dancin', an' prancin', wid his hawns an' hoofs an' snaggle toofs. He wus shore he wus got Jack dis time. W'en he wus got up to his yard gate; he looked down towards de well, an' he seed a great big bag—as big as two or three hills—an' it look lak it wus all conjered up so dat it could walk! An' w'at wus mo' dan dat; Dat bag look lak it wus in a notion of walkin' right to him! As he look at de bag; he 'gin to feel sorter jubous! So he holler out: "Jack!! Jack!!"

Den he hear de answer; "So! Mosser, so! De wuk's done; but Jack's so tired, he's almos' fittin to die!"

De Devil look an' he look' but he caint see no Jack. He caint see no nothin' but a big stuffed bag of fedders wid a liddle pair of footses un'er it, a totin it along. De Devil den 'gin to wonder how Jack wus managed to conjer hisself over into a bag of fedders. He lakwise 'gin to wonder whedder or not dat he'd be willin fer to sleep on Jack fer a bed-tick, all puffed up an' bloated up an' feddered up lak dat! Bymeby de bag git sorter close up to 'im. It make a low bow an' tumble right over lak it was a gwineter fall on him. De Devil jumped to one side to dodge it, sorter lak a silver bullett [The tradition went among ex-slaves that conjurers and witches might be shot with silver bullets only.] wus tetched him! He wusnt eben shore dat he want to tetch Jack, all conjered up into a bag of fedders lak dat.

At las' he walk sorter careful lak aroun' towards de end of de bag. He peeped behin' it; an' who should he see a stan'in' dar but Jack, big as life an' twice as natchul?

De Devil look at him wid his hawns' an hoofs an' snaggle toofs an' wid his mouf wide open. Den he stutter off, lak he wus been struck wid de 'ralysis: "De—e—e! Great—! Geeminie! Jack! W'at in de worl' did you do to git dem fedders?"

De answer come a rollin' back to 'im: "Dat's fer Jack to know; an' fer de Devil to find out!"

De Devil den rattle his hawns an' hoofs an' snaggle toofs an' say: "Ve'y well, Jack! But you's got to do one mo' day's wuk an' I's a gwineter have you do dat job right un'er my eyes! Tomorrer is Sadday. It's de las' day of de week; de las' day dat'll tell whedder it be Jack or de Devil lose! So come up in de mawnin. De job wont be long; an' we'll bofe know whedder it be a Sad fer Jack or a Sad day fer de Devil". Dey lef' onenudder.

De Devil didn do no good a sleepin' dat night; caze it look to him lak dat Jack wus about to win de gal fa'r an' squar'. He spize de ve'y groun' dat Jack walk on; an' he never wus had no notion of takin' him into de fambly. Den, he love Prissy; caze she wus his baby. He say to hisself dat he'd druther crawl on his belly an' eat dirt dan to give her to him!

Fust of all' he rolled aroun' on his pallet on de floo' ontel he maked up his mind 'bout w'at kind of a job he wus gwineter give Jack. He ricomember dat he wus jes promused fer to give Prissy's hand to Jack. So he maked up his mind, if de wust come to de wust, dat he's jes give her hand to 'im. W'en he do dis; it sorter 'gin to crawl 'cross his mind dat Prissy's hand should not oughter go whar her whole body wusnt due to foller. Atter he git his head all twisted up lak dis; he drap it all, an' say to hisself dat he wus a gwineter use dis fer a plan: If wust come to wust an' Jack win wid de wuk; he'll stand Prissy up behind a big white hung-up sheet, an' two dead womens along by de side of her. Den he'll make Prissy an' de dead womens stick deir hands, through hole sin de sheet, all mixed up togedder. He'll den have Jack to go up an' pick out de hand dat he want. If he's lucky duck 'nough to git Prissy's hand; den he'll fix her all up in grave clo'es, an' kiver her face, an' stan' her an' de dead womens up in a line. Den he'll make Jack walk up an' pick out de body he want. If he choose de body right once; he'll make him choose twice. If he choose de body right twice, den he'll make him choose three times; caze de ole sayin' sayes: "De third time is de charm". But if Jack is a big 'nough Conjer fer to git Prissy in spite of all dis; he say to hisself dat he reckin dat he'll have to take 'im into de fambly long 'nought fer to git a chance to kill 'im on de sly. W'en he got dis all planned out; he turned over fer to take a liddle snooze.

Prissy wus a lyin' awake too. In her practicin' up wid de conj'er doins; she wus l'arnt a whole heaps of tricks w'at her daddy dont know nothin' 'bout. One of dese tricks w'at she wus l'arnt wus how to hear w'at de Devil wus a thinkin'. So she know w'at crow he wus a gwineter pick wid Jack; an', by dis time, she wus got a bag whupped togedder fer to hold all de fedders.

So she git up, she do; whilst de Devil wus sound asleep; an' she go out to whar de dead womens wus, w'at her daddy wus stopped, fer a few days, on de way to de bad place, so dat he mought fool Jack wid 'em if he need to. She clipped a liddle bit of de tips offn deir liddle fingers; an' den she slipped on off down to whar Jack wus a sleepin; an' waked him up.

She tell him to be shore to bring de liddle red bag, w'at she give him, along wid 'im w'en he come in de mawnin fer to do his las' day's wuk. W'en her daddy give him dis las' job; he can do it widout no trouble, if he'll jes keep dat bag in his hand. She lakwise telled him how her daddy wus a gwineter make him choose fust her hand an' den her body. She let him know how she wus done clipped de liddle finger tip so as to let him see which wus de hands of de dead womens. Den she tell him how she wus a gwineter do; so dat he could pick her out from 'mongst de dead womens, all wropped up in a windin' sheet an' her face all kivered up. She den slip back into Tobe's house an' go on back to sleep.

Nex' mawnin, de Devil rousted de fambly up at daylight, wid his hawns an' hoofs an' snaggle toofs; an' maked 'em eat Breakfus befo' sun-up. He tell 'em dat he want all de time he can git fer to split up Jack into kindlin' wood; w'en he git fell through wid de job dat he wus a fixin' fer to give him.

Sadday—sooner in de mawnin—as de sun git cut loose from behin' de hills; Jack come a mozeyin sorter slow hoky-poky up to de Devil's house fer to git his las' job.

W'en he git dar, de Devil say: "Boo—! Boo—! Jack! Jack! You mus' do yo' las' job of wuk befo' you eats a mouffull; caze, if you wins, you den sets down at my right han' to be my son an' to eat dinner wid me at my table. Boo—! Boo—! Jack! Dis las' job is so liddle—so liddle dat it haint no job at 'tall. De liddle piece of wuk is dis: Jes go down de hill dar to whar you sees dat 'ar runnin' gugglin spring; pull it up by de roots, an' bring it up here an' hol' it up to my mouf fer me to drink water outn.

Jack drapped his head lak he wus been cotched at las'. He walk off down to de spring wid his fedders all a hangin' droppy lak wus got de limber-neck.

De Devil look at 'im as he go off down towards de springs; an' den he give him one of dese here hoss-laughs an' say: "Dat's it Jackie Kindlin! You's de bully boy! Bring it on up!" You see, de Devil make shore dat he wus got him dis time.

'Bout de time he git dis hollered off, Jack git to de spring. He retched down wid Prissy's red bag in his han', stopped de spring a runnin', picked it up; an' come a trottin' up to de house, an' a bringin' it fer de Devil to drink outn. W'en he got nearly up to whar Tobe wus, he holler out; "So! Mosser, so! De wuk's done, but Jack's so tired, he's almos' fitten to die! Drink quick, Mosser. It's a gittin hot an' heavy; an' I mus' run back wid it befo' it scald my hands!"

De Devil look at Jack a holdin' up dat conjered spring, already a gitin smokin hot, an' he wus jes natchully skeared fer to drink outn it. So he say: "Jack, you beats de Devil! Take de spring back an' set it down in its place; an' I'll lay a spell on all water so dat nobody caint never no mo' pull it up by de roots outn de groun'; an' dere caint never be no mo' Jacks lak dis Jack so long as de worl' stand.

Hurry an' come back! You mus' git de han' an' body of Prissy by knowin' an' choosin' 'em; caze a man mus' always be able fer to know de 'oman w'at's his own from all de tother womens, w'atever way she git fixed up.

Jack took de spring an' planted it back in its place; den he come on back up fer to choose Prissy's han' an' body.

De Devil say to 'im: "Boo—! Boo—! Jack, you mus' now choose; an' you mus' live whar de 'oman is bound to live forever, on account of de life she wus done already lived. You mus' choose from three; caze dat's de rule. Prissy will make one. Some mo' womens is here on deir way to de Hot Hole of de Bad Place; dey'll make tow an' dey'll make three. All of 'em togedder'll make three. Dese dead womens is dead; an' yit dey lives w'en I wants 'em to live! If you chooses two or chooses three; you'll live in de Hot Hole. De bed of embers, on which you'll lie, will be bristlin red; an' dey'll give you bofe life so's you'll never die!

You mus' choose Prissy from 'mongst de dead; caze dead womens come by de plantation ev'ry day on de way to de Hot Hole. If you couldn' tell her from dem; den it 'twouldn' be no time befo' you'd foller one of 'em off by mistake, an' my gal would be left a grass-widder. De Devil caint never let it come aroun' dat he'll have grass-widders in his fambly. If

you chooses Prissy's hand; de hand is yourn. You mought live wid her
down in de cabin by de road; w'at lead to de Hot Hole on de one end,
an' to de open world on de tother. You'll be safe dar; if you always knows
Prissy, so as not to foller no other womens off by mistake

—But come Jack! Whar deres three womens, a man should oughter
have three choices; a' de Devil hisself wont be mean 'nough fer to take
dese away from you. Choose!! If you gits Prissy; you gits a hand on de
whole worl' wid her; dat's *one* choosin. Choose!! If you gits a dead
'oman; you goes to de Hot Hole; dat's *two* choosins, dat's *three* choosins.
But Jack; since you's wuked so good an' wuked so hard, if you'll leave off
de choosin' an' go back to de open worl'; if you'll give up de idee of
havin Prissy fer a wife; den we'll shake hands an' call it eben. Come! W'at
sayes you, Jack?"

Jack say to all dis: "So, Mosser, so! De wuk's done; but Jack's so tired,
he's almos' fitten to die! If he go back to de open world widout Prissy;
den dat world'll be a Hot Hole for him. If he choose a dead 'oman; dat
lakwise give him a Hot Hole fer a home. Jack is a gwineter choose!!"

W'en Jack say dis, it make de Devil so mad dat it git blue all aroun'
him; an' he tell Jack dat de scuffle wus on. He take him to de steps of de
cabin whar he wus got Prissy an' de dead womens fastened up, ready fer
de choosin'. He hand a sheet in front of de doo'; den reach behin' an'
push it open. He nex' hit his conj'er stick down on de groun, wid his
hawns an' hoofs an' snaggle toofs, ontel it strike fire; den he hol' it up an'
say:

"Dead womens walk,
Dead womens talk,
Dead womens move; dont me no balk."

Prissy, an' de dead womens den walk from de cabin behin' de sheet;
an' stick deir hands through de six holes w'at de Devil wus made in it fer
dat purpose.

De Devil den look at Jack wid his hawns an' hoofs an' snaggle toofs;
an' growl of to him: "Go choose!"

Jack walked up to de sheet; an' he seed w'at hands wus got liddle
fingers w'at haint never nowhars been tetched wid no knife. He choose
dese hands an' win his fust round in his tussle wid de Devil. Dat give him
Prissy's hands.

De Devil sorter drap his fedders an' his eyes fill up wid water; caze he
look lak he wus about to lose his stake, an' he haint never been got clean
beat befo'. He say to Jack: "You's got de hands all at one clip; caze dey
wus in de bargain at fust. But it's de best three outn three fer de body;
caze de bargain fer dat come now.

Den he holler in de house to Prissy fer to wrop herself up in grave-clo'es, an' kiver up head an' (y)ears, an' git ready fer to come out on de pieizzer wid de dead womens fer Jack to choose out her body.

W'en Prissy git herself fixed; de Devil hold up his conj'er stick again an' say:

"Dead womens walk,
Dead womens talk,
Dead womens move; dont make no balk!"

De womens come a walkin' out on de pieizzer—dead ones an' all—an' stan' deirselves up in a line. De Devil look at Jack, an' open de corner of his mouf, an' show his long white tushes, an' say: "Go choose!"

Jack step up an' look at de womens. De dead womens caint move no mo'; caze de Devil wus said: "Dont make no balk!" Prissy jes sorter tilted hear head jes a leedle, leedle bit; an' Jack knowed her an' picked her out.

Dis pinched de Devil in a tender place, an' he squalled out:

"Boo—! Boo—!
Dat wont do!
Go back; swap clo'es wid onenudder too!"

Prissy an' de dead womens go back in de house an' swap clo'es. Den de Devil holler out, a holdin' high his conj'er stick:

"Dead womens walk,
Dead womens talk,
Dead womens move; dont make no balk!"

De womens come a walkin out—dead ones an' all. De Devil den look at Jack sorter puzzled-lak an' say: "Go Choose!"

Jack walk up ag'in, he do' an' he look at de womens all wropped up an' hid. Of co'se de dead womens still caint move no mo', atter dey gits in line; caze de Devil wus put in "Dont make no balk". Prissy sorter raised up her heel jes a leedle, leedle bit, an' put it back down on de ground; lak she telled Jack she wus a gwineter do, on de night befo', w'en she go to him. Jack, he know her an' pick her out.

De Devil beller out:

"Boo—! Boo—!
Dat wont do!
Go back; swap clo'es through an' through!"

Whilst de womens wus a swappin' deir windin' sheets an' clo'es with onenudder, de Devil say: "Boo—! Boo—! Jack! De third time's de charm. If you gits de body dis time; den Prissy's yourn!"

Prissy hear w'at her daddy say away in de house; an' she have to stuff a grave-handcher in her mouf to keep from a laughin' right out, an' Jack have to stick his hands in his pockets an' pinch hisself so as to git hisself stopped form one of dese here wide grins w'at reach from (y)ear to (y)ear.

W'en ev'rything git fixed; de Devil hold high his conj'er stick an' say:

"Dead womens walk,
Dead womens talk,
Dead womens move; dont make no balk!"

De womens all come a walkin' out, an' stan' up in a line; an' de Devil sorter look at Jack lak he wus already don fixed up fer losin' an' say: "Go choose!"

Whilst Jack wus a walkin' up; Prissy moved de sheet aroun' her jes a tiny bit, an' Jack cotch holt on her an' pult her outn de line.

De tother womens flewed off down de road to de Hot Hole; De Devil den comed up an' helt a broom-stick behin' Jack an' Prissy. Dey jumped over it back'ards, a holdin' hands togedder, an' dey wus man an' wife. He give 'em a cabin by de road a leadin' to de Hot Hole to live in. He tell 'em dat a plenty good victuals an' a plenty good clo'es would always be in deir cabin; caze he wus got ev'rything so conjered up, dat, w'en dere wus a need any whars on his plantation, de stuff in de open world would jes natchully come up ontel dere wus mo' dan a plenty an' 'nough.

He say to Jack dat he'll let him have ev'rything 'cep' heaps of money. He caint let him have no mo' dan a liddle bit of dis; caze he need it all, all de time, to git folkses to do devilment in de open worl'.

Atter Jack an Prissy move into deir cabin; de Devil pass by dar ev'ry mawnin, a ridin' one of his big black oxes; an' a drivin' dead folkses down to de Hot Hole. He holler in to 'em: "Boo—! Boo—! My son Jack! How's my son an' daughter?"

Dey'd make answer to him: "We's fine an' fat an' sassy! Come down tonight, an' let's have some fun".

So wen de Devil's day's wuk wus done; he'd go down to de cabin, an' cut up, an' dance, an' drink whisky, an' frolic, an' raise san' aroun' along wid Jack an' Prissy. Dis here raisin' Old Ned ev'ry night go on fer some years.

Atter while Jack tell de Devil dat he think dat a liddle game of chyards mought give a good liddle change fer 'em; an' de Devil say dat he speck so too. So dey plays "Seben-up" an' has heaps of fun. Den Jack make offer fer to bet a liddle on de game; an' de Devil 'gree to meet him half-way. So dey 'gun to bet; an' it 'twusnt no time befo de Devil git stripped by Jack of all his money.

W'en Jack git all de money fer hisn; de Devil have to borry from him so as to carry out all his projicks on de open worl'. He have to hang aroun' Jack an' eat umble pie. Jack hisself wus a fair conj'er; but he couldn' a beat de Devil by hisself. You see: Prissy wus de one. She knowed mo' conjer-tricks dan her daddy; an' she wuked 'em fer Jack ag'in him.

Wid de money rations runned short; de Devil wusnt a ketchin so many folkses wid his hawns an' hoofs an' snaggle toofs; an' de Imps all vex him by keepin' on a axin fer why he didn' bring down mo' folkses fer to throw hot sand on.

Bymeby, somehow, it sorter leaked out 'bout Jack an' Prissy a havin' all de money, an' a bein' de "Big Bosses". Dem 'ar Imps wus jes full of devilment. So dey maked up a song an' sung it fer to git a big laugh on deir Mosser. Dis wus de song:

2. O, I wush I wus de Devil, wid his hawns an' hoofs an' shovel;
   Den I'd han' down to de Imps a liddle burden.
   Put de Niggers in a huddle, lak de ducks all in a puddle;
   An' den lan' 'em on de tother side of Jurdon.

3. Oh, ole Missus an' ole Mosser wus got heaps of kinds of meat.
   It wus sheep an' ham an' lam' an' hog an' mutton.
   Black Jack step'd up to de house, stuffed a ham down in his mouf;
   Den he brung away de balunce jes' a struttin'.

W'en de Devil hear dis here song; it ketch him whar de wool wus short, an' pull it hard. So he maked up his mind dat he wus a gwineter kill Jack an' Prissy bofe. He go home an' twis' up his conjer sticks so dat he'd know w'en Jack an' Prissy go to bed dat night. He aimed to go down to de cabin jes befo' day, de nex' mawnin, an' draw down lightnin, an' kill 'em bofe in bed. But, as I wus done tol' you; W'en Prissy wus a l'arnin' new tricks, she l'arnt one trick by which she could hear her daddy think. So she know jes zackly w'at de Devil wus up to.

She telled Jack, dat night, w'at her daddy wus up to; an' she say dat deir onliest chance fer life wus to git away an' go back down to de open world an' hide deirselves. Dey can hide deirselves by gwine somewhars, whar de Devil caint go; an' a sayin' de Blessin' three times a day, w'en dey eats—lettin' dis be de Blessin;"

"Lawd, bless us an' bind us,
Take his eyes from behind us,
An' keep us whar de Devil caint find us.

She speshully say to him dat whilst dey wus a gittin away; he musn' never fergit to do jes zackly lak she say, or dey'll bofe git kilt an' toted off down by deir own cabin to de Hot Hole of de Bad Place.

Jack make answer dat he wus ready fer to foller her to de Jumpin' Off Place an' jump off wid her. [Jumping Off Place is an expression brought down from olden days when men thought the earth was disc-like in shape. Thus at its edge one might jump off into space—thus "a jumping off place."]

She den tell him to come an' slip wid her up to de Devil's house; Dat he wus done fell off into a snooze fer de fust part of de night an' dere wus some things up dar dat she mus' git fer 'em.

W'en she gits up dar she stands Jack out by de winder; whilst she conjers it open an' goes in whar her daddy is a sleepin'. She fust brings a knife an' a fo'k an' hands dem outside to Jack. She den go back an' git two pairs of hill-high Tom-walkers, [Tom-walkers = stilts] w'at de Devil use to conjer up, ontel dey's as high as de hills, an' walk aroun' in 'em w'en he want to step from one place to anudder in de open worl' to look atter de folkses. She comes on out wid dese an' conjers de winder back togedder.

Dey takes a pair apiece of de hill-high Tom-walkers an' goes on back down to deir cabin. Dey wus got in mind to take dese along wid 'em so as to outrun de Devil in gittin away, w'en dey gits down in de open worl'. W'en dey wus got back down to deir cabin; Prissy put de knife an' fo'k, w'at she wus took from her daddy's house, in deir bed, side by side. Jack ax her w'at she wus a doin' dat fer. She splain to him dat de fo'k always stan' fer a man, caze it git an' tote all de provisions fer de eatin; dat de knife stan' fer de 'oman, caze it fix up de provisions fer eatin. Dis bein' de case, de knife an' de fo'k a bein' in de bed would so fix up de Devil's instriments dat dey'd keep on a tellin' him dere wus a man an' a 'oman in deir bed w'en dere wusnt; if he happen to wake up in de night an' zamine 'em to see w'at wus w'at, whilst dey wus a journeyin' to de open worl'.

Den Jack an' Prissy take meat an' de two pairs of high-hill Tom-walkers; an' goes out an' mounts a big red-headed red-eyed scorch-feddered buzzard apiece, an' dey sails away to de open worl' to git away from ole Tobe—her daddy. Whilst de Devil wus a sleepin'; dey wus a flyin'.

Along jes befo' day w'en Jack an' Prissy wus a landin' in de open worl'; de Devil wake up, an' git up, an' go down to de cabin by de road w'at lead to de Hot Hole. He want to do w'at he call a "Gittin good riddance of bad rubbish". W'en he got dar, he raised up his conjer stick an' hit it down on de groun'. As he do dis, it flash fire; an' de lightnin come down outn de sky an' hit Jack an' Prissy's bed—"Bang! Boo—oo—oo—!"

De Devil stan' still fer a minute wid his hawns an' hoofs an' snaggle toofs, an' lissen. W'en he dont hear nothin'; he break out in a great big laugh, an' call de Imps.

"Liddle mens, liddle mens, liddle mens wid jokes!
Liddle mens, liddle mens, come an' git yo' folks!"

De Imps, down at de Hot Hole, hear deir Mosser a callin' 'em; an' dey come, jes a tiltin'. Dey went into Jack an' Prissy's cabin, an' turned back de kiver on de bed fer to git 'em; but dey dont see no nothin' dar 'cep' a knife an' a fo'k. So dey comes back out an' tells deir Mosser dat de lightnin' mus' a burnt 'em up; caze dey wus bofe gone.

Den de Devil, hisself, go in; an' look in de bed. He see de knife an' de fo'k a lyin' dar in it; an' it come across his mind dat Jack an' Prissy wus done gone an' fooled him once mo'.

He send de Imps on away; but as he hear 'em a gwine down de road to de Hot Hole, a gigglin' 'bout deir Mosser a bein' fooled; it make him git as mad as Brinjer. He walk back up to his house, a cussin' an' a sw'arin dat he wus a gwineter git Jack an' Prissy, if it's de las ac'.

De Devil den go to git his hill-high Tom-walkers so dat he can step nearly a mile at a clip; an' soon ketch up wid Jack an' Prissy. But w'en he look in de house fer 'em; dey wus all gone! But de Devil wusnt to be outdone dat way. He go an onlock his cedar chist, an' take out his sky-high Tom-walkers wid which he step mo' dan a mile at a clip w'en he git 'em conjered up right good. Dese here wus his Sunday-go-to-meetin Tom-walkers. He use dese on a Sundays; caze on dat day, w'en de folkses haint a doin' nothin, dey gits into a heaps of devilment; an' de Devil wus bleedged to have dese here high Tom-walkers to git 'roun' 'mongst 'em fast 'nough to look atter 'em. In de week time; he wus used to use his hill-high Tom-walkers, befo' Jack an' Prissy stole 'em, from him.

W'en he git on his sky-high Tom-walkers, he sorter stomped his footses aroun' in 'em on de floo' an' say: "I reckin, w'en deres some good mens in front a steppin' along lak de wind in hill-high Tom-walkers, an' deres some better mens behin' a steppin' along lak lightnin' in sky-high Tom-walkers; dey should oughter git togedder sometime somewhars". Wid dis much sayed; he start off atter Jack an' Prissy.

He looked aroun' an' he seed de direction dat de big red-headed red-eyed scorch-feddered buzzards wus a comin from; so he knowed zackly whar Jack an' Prissy wus landed in de open worl'. He maked a bee-line fer dat spot; an' w'en he git landed, he 'gin to pursue atter 'em.

Atter he wus been a walkin fer some time; he 'gin to git up in sight of 'em. Jack look back, he do; an' he see de Devil a comin', wid his hawns an' hoofs an' snaggle toofs. Whilst him an' Prissy wus a pullin' away on deir hill-high Tom-walkers, Jack say to her: "Law', Honey! Yonner he come! De Devil on Tom-walkers! He's a gwineter ketch us on dem Sky-high Tom-walkers; an' tote us back an' dump us in de Hot Hole!"

Prissy make answer to him: "Dry up! Put mo' foot on yo' hill-high Tom-walkers, an' less mouf on de wind!"

"But he's a gittin might 'nigh close 'nough now fer to retch down an' nab us!" sayed Jack, says he.

Prissy hand Jack a liddle piece of glass, an' say: "Take dat an' throw it back'ards over yo' lef' shoulder!"

Jack took de piece of glass an' throwed it back'ards over his lef' shoulder; an' it turned into a great big slick glass wall, w'at wus taller dat de sky. Dis sorter helt de Devil up; caze he couldn' step over it to pursue on atter 'em.

De Devil stopped an' shook his fistes at 'em; an' hollered out to 'em: "Nev' mind! Dere haint no glass conjer wall w'at can stop me!"

He wus brung his sledge hammer along wid him so as to knock de run-aways in de head w'en he ketch up wid 'em. So he took dis here hammer an' give de big high slick glass wall a lick wid it; an' he busted it all to flinders. But w'en it fall down, it pile up de fine pieces of glass so high dat he couldn' walk through 'em wid his sky-high Tom-walkers; caze he wus skeared dat he mought trip an' fall in de glass an' git his footses all riddled up. He couldn' git down offn his sky-high Tom-walkers, an' walk over; caze den he'd lakwise git his footses all riddled up by de glass. De wall of fine glass wus so long dat it reach clear 'cross de worl'; so, he couldn' walk aroun' it. Dar he wus—him a stan'in' still an' Jack an' Prissy a gwine on wid a wall of powdered glass to bar off de Devil!

Ole Tobe study a liddle while; an' he dont see but one way out. So he go all de way back to de Hot Hole fer to git de Imps to come an' tote de pieces of glass away, one by one; an' make a road through fer him. Dis took so long dat it look lak dat Jack an' Prissy should oughter be fur 'nough ahead of him to sow wheat, raise it, cut it, an' thash it; an' den git away befo' he could ketch up. But de Devil wus up in dem 'ar sky-high Tom-walkers; an' 'sides dat, he wus some runner to boot! So atter so long a time; he git up in sight of Jack an' Prissy ag'in.

Jack look back an' see him a comin'. He say to Prissy: "Law' , Honey! De Devil on Tom-walkers! Yonner he come mo' faster dan he wus ever come befo'! W'at in de open worl' is we a gwineter do?"

Prissy looked back an' seed her daddy; an' she turned an' spit a big gob of spit behin' her an' de spit turned into a big conjer lake dat de Devil daresant [daresant = did not dare] try to cross. He git to de conjer lake an' look at it. He try all kinds of conjer tricks on it; but he caint in no way dry it up. So he go back home an' git his flock of big black bellerin oxes w'at he ride aroun' on an' he brung dem down to de conjer lake. W'en he git 'em down dar, he say: "Drink, oxes!—Drink, oxes! Drink!"

Dem 'ar oxes, dey drunk an' dey drunk; an' den dey drunk some mo'! Bymeby dey drinks de conjer lake dry; an' de Devil sont 'em back home so bloated up dat dere wusnt scacely no room up dar on his plantation fer 'em. Den he pursue on atter de run-aways.

Atter while he git up in sight of Jack an' Prissy ag'in. Dey wus a runnin some on deir won hooks; but de Devil jes natchully ketch up wid 'em w'en he git up in dem big fine sky-high Tom-walkers, whilst dey wus jes only a steppin' along in de hill-high Tom-walkers.

Jack look back an' see him a comin' an' say: "Law', Prissy! Honey! W'at's we a gwineter do? De Devil on Tom-walkers; an' he's about to ketch us!"

Prissy Looked back an' seed her daddy a comin'. She up an' pulled a strand of hair outn her head; an' throwed it down 'twixt her an' her daddy. It turned into a big wall of iron w'at de Devil caint cross.

De Devil runned up to de big iron wall, wid his hawns an' hoofs an' snaggle toofs; an' he hit it wid his big sludge hammer. But de iron wall jes make a soun' w'at deefen him; an' stay dar, an' dont budge. At las' he didn' see no way 'cep' to go back home an' git all his tools. So he go an' git dem. Den he cut, an' he gash, an' he slash, an' he mash; ontel at las' he git a big 'nough gully cut through it to let him pass on.

No sooner wus he got through de iron wall; dan he jes go a tiltin' atter Jack an' Prissy. Jack look back an' see him a comin' an' say: "Law' Honey! De Devil on Tom-walkers! He's got me! Dere haint no use in yo' usin' no mo' conjer tricks on him; caze I's so tired an' broke down dat I caint run no furder. De furder I runs; de mo' deeper he'll stick me down in de Hot Hole of de Bad Place w'en he gits me! You can go on an' jump off at de Jumpin' Off Place, an' keep on a gwine; caze you can run on an' on lak yo' daddy forever. Good-bye! I loves you! An' w'en I thinks 'bout yo' being' safe; it wont go so hard wid me fer to roast in de embers an' toast in de fire."

"I caint in no ways leave you, Jack!" sayed Prissy. As she sayed dis; dey wus jes reached to de banks of de big deep sea. She stopped an' throwed a spell over him an' herself; an' dey bofe git made over into mare-maids. [mare-maids = mermaids] Dey jumped in, head-foremost, an' dived down to de bottom of de sea whar dey could live safe from de Devil. You see: De Devil is uster livin' in de fire; an' it would jes natchully kill him if he git in de water much. Water an' fire dont go togedder.

De Devil come up to de banks of de sea wid his hawns an' hoofs an' snaggle toofs. He wus jes bleedged to stop; an' he git so mad dat he wus jes fit to pop open. Atter while he go back an' git a lot of his Imps. He take dem an' string dem out all along de banks of de sea; an' along de banks of all de water courses. Den he go back home an' pick out anudder pack of Imps; an' set dem to wuk, a makin' hatchets. He tell dem dat deir job wus to keep on a makin' hatchets forever. Den he pick out a flock of Imps; an' set dem to totin' down de hatchets to de Imps all strung out along de water courses; an' he tell dem dat deir job wus to keep on a totin' down hatchets forever. Den he go back down to de Imps strung out along de water courses; an' he tell dem dat dey mus' throw hatchets into de water forever, so as to be shore to kill Jack an' Prissy.

But Prissy still hear her daddy a thinkin' down dar on de bottom of de sea whar she an' Jack is. So she conjer up de fishes; so dat dey'll always swim between de hatchets, an' her an' Jack. Dat way, de hatchets sticks in de fishes, an' turns into fins; an' dat's de way dat fishes 'gin to have fins, an' dey wus been a havin' 'em ev'ry since. Atter dat, w'en de folkses in de open world ketch de fishes, an' git sticked wid deir fins; dey holler out: "Whew! De Devil on Tom-walkers!"

De Devil, wid his hawns an' hoofs an' snaggle toofs, still think once in a while 'bout Dinah a showin' de tricks to Prissy; which fixed it so dat Jack could beat de Ole Boy Tobe. So he take her behin' de doo' w'en de sun is a shinin' an whup her ontel de water run outn her eyes an' fall lak rain."

When Uncle Jack had finished his story, the noon hour for the rest had more than passed; and all arose with renewed strength and zest for the work of harvesting the grain. Uncle Jake was the hero of the hour as he accompanied them humming a tune in a low voice to the words:

"Did you ever see de Devil, wid his iron handled shovel,
A scrapin' up de san' in his ole tin pan?
He cuts up mighty funny, he steals all yo money,
He blinds you wid his san'. He's a tryin' to git you man!"

Why White Overseers of
Negro Slaves Had Little Sense
❄

When the dark clouds of the American Civil war blew over, and the Negroes were left in the dawning light of Freedom, few of them had a place which they might call home. Few white men, of the South, of the land-owning class, were willing to sell their lands to the "one-time" slave.

In Bedford County, Tennessee, there was a Southern man, of "the blue-blood type", who had been connected with the Andrew Johnson presidential administration. He was one among the very few Southern white men who had the vision, at that time, that the Negro must ultimately have all the ordinary civil rights belonging to other American citizens. This man, whom we shall call Mr. Ed, was therefore willing to sell and began to sell small farms to Negroes, on the partial payment plan. He was at that time much loved by these Freedmen; and, in their humble minds, almost took rank along with the "men in blue" who had poured out their life's blood for their liberation.

These Negroes who purchased for themselves these first little humble homes, just after the Civil War, were not wanting, you may be sure, in their sense of self esteem. Perhaps they had much more than their righteous share of it. Though they associated rather freely with all, they were inclined to form themselves into a little Class. And why should they not? Had they not seen the white people, the dominating Class, divide themselves into social strata galore? They were imitating, as they thought, the very best.

Two Negro women—heads of homes of this early land-owning Class—were visiting with each other. Aunt Dilsie Hightop was paying a call at the home of Aunt Donie Gooden. They were sitting in a little open hall-way between the two rooms of the little log-cabin home, chatting rather aimlessly, when Miss Sookie Bigun—one of the poorer Class of the Southern whites—came in.

Miss Sookie was on quite friendly terms with Aunt Donie; but she and Auth Dilsie were only on such terms as enabled them to "pass de time o' day wid onenudder", as the estranged Negro women expressed it. There being no large mutual ground of close friendship for the three, the general conversation immediately died into silence.

Thus the circumstances forced Miss Sookie to come to the point of her mission at once; and, she said, with a rather characteristic local drawl: "Aunt Doenee; I wanter borry er leetle meat, an' er leetle meal, an' er leetle bit er coughee. Mheester Bigun is gone ter town to geet t'e things; an' I'll bring 'em back in 'e moreen. Mheester Bigun is swapped off our ole hoss Ishum, whut wus one-eyed, fer anuther hoss whut's named Baalum, an' he's moon-eyed. Thes morneen, he hitched up Baalum weeth our blin' hoss Seelum; an' tuck a beeg load o' wood to town fer which he's a goin' to geet a dollar!—Oh, I'll jes have plenty an' to spare to breeng ev'rything you let me have all back in 'e morneen!"

Aunt Donie listened quitely to the request; then silently arose, and took a small piece of bacon from a small container on a shelf in the hall, and wrapped it in a small piece of old newspaper. She then opened a second small container on this same shelf, and poured out its contents—about a quart of meal—on a second piece of old newspaper and carefully wrapped it up. A third container on this same shelf, with about a half tea-cupfull of coffee, was in like manner emptied and the contents wrapped. The three packages were then handed to Miss Sookie; and she departed.

When Miss Sookie was well out of sight and out of hearing; Aunt Dilsie renewed the conversation in a rather different vein from the one which had preceded it between the two. She began as follows:

"Law, Donie! If I wus you, I wouldn' fool wid dat 'ar low-downed Nigger-overseein white trash. Dar is ole Miss Sookie' dere haint no harm much to her, caze she haint scacely got no sense at 'tall nohows. But deres ole Jim Bigun, her ole man, he haint got no sense neider; but he's so mean dat I thinks dat de Devil'll have to hitch him off by hisself to a iron stake down in de Bad Place, w'en he git down what he beslong, so as to keep him from a killin off de bad Niggers down dar, befo' he git a chance fer to burn 'em.

Now deres de big rich white folks, lak Mr. Ed, dey's all right. Dey could borry my whole plantation, wid de shoats an' all throwed in, if dey want 'em. But done give me none o' dat 'ar lowdowned trash, w'at haint got no sense, an' wat got deir livin' in slavery days by overseein' an' whoopin Niggers!"

"You's zackly right, Dilsie"; interrupted Aunt Donie, then the conversation proceeded further between the two.

"Well, Donie you sayes dat, but you goes right on a loanin dem 'ar poo' white crazies jes de same.—Den Chile; dey's so dirty wid deir things; I dont see how you eats w'at dey brings back, atter dey borries it an' brings it back."

To this semi-upbraiding came the reply; "Me an' my folks dont never eat nothin w'at dem 'ar poo' Crackers brings back, Donie! W'en dey brings sumpin back w'at dey wus borried; I jes puts it up dar on de shelf in dem liddle buckets by deirselves. Den w'en dey comes to borry ag'in; I jes loans 'em w'at dey wus brung back befo'. W'at I loaned ole Sookie today is jes dat same stuff w'at she wus brung back a week ago. I jes keeps deir 'borryins' an' deir 'payin's up dar; an' loans it to 'em over an' over ag'in. Of co'se dere haint no use a talkin' 'bout Mr. Ed , an' dem sort of folks along by de side of ole Jim Bigun' caze folks lak dem 'ar Roperses is made outn

Heaben-dust, an' de Lawd didn' pick up nothin but de commones' kind o' dirty mud w'en he go to make de white trash w'at overseed de Niggers in slavery days."

"Well, Donie, I jes tells dat Nigger-overseein class dat 'I haint got none'; w'en dey comes to borry from me", said Aunt Dilsie.

"W'y, Dilsie! You's a chuch member; and I dont see no ways how you can say dat, w'en ev'rybody knows dat you's always got a plenty of ev'rything"; answered Aunt Donie, in a somewhat disappointed tone.

"Oh, I haint a tellin' no story!" explained Aunt Dilsie. "You see: I jes means dat I haint got none fer dem; an' w'en dey haint got sense 'nough fer to un'erstan', I haint in no way to blame fer dat."

"Well", replied Aunt Donie with a new 'moral' viewpoint: "I guess dat's so; caze it haint none of yo' fault about some folks a totin gourds aroun' fer heads. I's always wondered how it come about dat all dat poo' white Nigger-overseein class haint got no sense anyhows!"

"Donie", said Aunt Dilsie, "W'en you wonders lak dat; it put me in de mind of one of de cu'iousest lorations I almos' ever heared of. My grandaddy tol' me 'bout it 'way back yonder w'en I wus a liddle gal".

"I so do wish dat you'd tell me how it come about", anxiously insisted Aunt Donie.

"It'll take too long, Donie."

"Oh, no it wont! Go on wid it, Dilsie."

"Well, is you got time to set up here an' listen to a poo' conbersationer fer a half hour?"

"Yes, an' longer dan dat too. It dont make no diffunce 'bout de time. All of my folks is fed full, an' gone a huntin'; an' dey wont git back befo' night. So I haint got nothin else to do, but to set 'roun' here an' lissen to you."

"All right! Dis wus de loration, w'at wus tol' me by my grandaddy, a splainin how it come about dat de white over-seers of Nigger slaves haint got no sense;" said Aunt Dilsie.

"Away back yonder—I thinks from w'at dey sayes; it mus' have been Bargro Times, [Bargro Times—The time of the passing of the Embargo Act in Colonial days] or eben befo' dat—Away back dar; dere wus a young white Overseer w'at play big, w'en liddle become him. He wus one of de Class of Overseers w'at wus sposed to have a liddle sense. He wus de Overseer on de bigges' plantation in dem diggins; [Diggins—locality] an' w'en he go out a spo'tin' an' a co'tin', all de half-strainer poo' white gals wid Nigger-overseein' daddies w'at wusnt got no sense, wus a settin' deir caps fer him wid a hair trigger. His name was Mistah Phil Highstepper; an' all de poo' white daddies an mammies wus a hopin fer to git his name mixed up wid deir fambly tree.

"Dere wus, in dem same times, a fambly of Overseer w'at wunt got no sense, by de name of Tryups. Dey wus got a acre of groun', all of deir own. Dey had a one-room house on it; an' lived in dar. None of de tother

white overseein' famblies aroun' dar wus got no place w'at wus deirn. So
de Tryups wus looked on, aroun dar, as de top of de pot 'mongst de poo'
overseein' class w'at wusnt got no sense. Dey wus got jes one chile—a gal
by de name of Jerushy. She wus right goodlookin' fer a poo' white gal. Of
co'se her neck was a liddle long an' stringy, an' her nose wus almos' as
long as yo' ole man's Sunday walkin'-stick; but de young white mens
fergit all 'bout dis w'en dey go home wid her an' see dat acre of groun'
wid a one-room house on it w'at beslong to her daddy.

Miss Jerushy Tryup was kermilious-lak, [Kermilious-lak = affable.] an' so
she wus de pick an' choice of all de poo' whit gals aroun' dar; an' of co'se
Mr. Phil Highstepper go over to claim an' pull de watermillion, if he can.
Ev'ry night, atter he git through a weighin' up de cotton an a beatin' up all
de Nigger slaves w'at haint picked no hundred an' fifty pound o' cotton
enjorin de day, he go over fer to see Miss Jerushy Tryup. He go over dar;
day in, an' day out! He go so much; dat he make de road so muddy w'at
lead up to ole man Tryup's house, dat de ole man wus skeared dat no
hosses wouldn be able fer to pull no winter wood fer him up dat road to de
house; an' dey all mought git frez up to death w'en it go to git col'.

Mistah Phil Highstepper go over dar fer to see de gal enough; but he
wus sorter bashful, an' he sot away off from her across de room. Heaps of
times he dont say nothin'; an' w'en he do talk, he dont say nothin dat he
should oughter say, so as to git de gal to marry him. Miss Jerushy wus one o'
dem 'ar kind too w'at turn red in de face lak a beet; if she hear somebody
say sumpin lak 'love' or 'co't'. So de most of de time w'en Mr. Phil wus over
dar; him an' de gal jes sot off an' looked at onenudder, an' didn' say nothin.

At las', Mr Phil git off one Sunday mawnin, an' go over to see her.
W'en he git dar, he find dat de ole folks wus before gone off to meetin,
[Meetin = church] an' wus lef' de gal at home fer to cook dinner.

De gal tell him to come in an' res' his hat. Mr. Phil go in an' pitch his
hat over on de bed; an' set down in a chair in de house by de side of de
front doo'. Miss Jerushy, she go on wid her cookin', she do; an' neider
one of 'em dont say nothin to de tother one.

Bymeby Miss Jerushy finish up de cookin' of de dinner. De one-room
house wus got a front doo' an' a back doo'. Mr. Phil wus a settin in de
room at de front doo'; so w'en Miss Jerushy git through wid her cookin,
she take her chair an' set down in de room at de back doo'. Dar dey sot—
one at de front doo' an' de tother at de back doo'; an' neider one of 'em
dont say nothin' to de tother one! Dey sot dar a makin dem honey-Jerusa-
lem faces at onenudder; whar one say: "I wish you would"; and de tother
one say: "I wish I could widout doin' it."

Bymeby Phil sorter hitch up his chair a niche or so over towards
Jerushy; den dey befo sot right still fer a minute. Terreckly Jerushy hitch
her chair a niche or so over towards Phil. Den Phil, he grin, he do; an'

hitch his chair a liddle mo' over towards Jerushy.—Den Jerushy hitch her chair over towards Phil! Phil hitch, an' Jerushy hitch, ontel at las' deir chairs slap togedder right out in de middle of de floo' between de two doo's. Der dey sot; a grinnin' at onenudder!

At las' Phil, he open up; an' 'gin to talk. Dey talks lak dis:

(he) I's a good min' to bite chyer!
(she)   W'at chyer wanter bite me fer?
(he) Caze yer wont haive me!
(she)   Caze yer haint axed me!
(he) Now I axes yer!
(she)   Now I has yer!

About dis time Phil looked outn de doo', an' he sed ole man Tryup an' his ole 'oman a comin in at de front gate; an' he grabbed up his chair an' snatched it off about ten foot from de gal. Den he sot down on it so tight dat he looked lak he was glued dar.

De ole folks come on in; an' de ole man say "Howdee-doo, Meester Highstepper!—I caint see fer de life of me w'at make you an Jerushy so distant wid onenudder. Set up togedder an' talk lak you wusnt skeared of onenudder!" Den ole Miss Tryup she bust in sorter fopper-lak: "Yas! Yas! Yas!—So! So!" (You see: She hear dat aroun' dar 'mongst de big white folks whar her ole man wus been a overseein. So she talk fopper-lak lak dem.)

Den Phil, he up an' say highfolutin lak de big whitefolks too: "Oh Sah an' Madam! We's been a gitin on might 'nigh as snug as a bug in a rug".—Whar-upon befo ole Miss Tryup an' ole man Tryup say dat dey wus awful glad to hear of it. But Jerushy she sot dar, she did; an' chawed one corner of her pocket-hankcher.

Bymeby ole man Tryup up an' say: "Ole 'oman, sorter rush aroun'; an' put de pot of chicken an' dumplins, an' de peach-cobbler w'at Jerushy wus maked on de table; so dat Meester Highstepper can have a liddle bite wid us befo' he leave. I wants him to see w'at a fine cook Jerushy is."

De ole 'oman tell him all right; she wus already got dat in mind, an' wus jes about to sen' Jerushy to git a lim' fer a fan de flies offn de table wid. So she 'gin to put de grub on de table; an' she sen' Jerushy off atter de lim'.

Jerushy go out; an' instid o' goin atter de lim' fer to fan de flies off wid, sh go aroun' in de chimbly corner outside of de house an' she holler out: "O Maw!" an' ole Miss Tryup holler back: "W'at yer want?" Den Jerushy make answer: I fergit if offn my mind fer to tell yer dat Meester Highstepper wus maked me say 'yes' to marryin him!" Den she runned clean off down in de woods.

Mr. Highstepper wus so shame-faced w'en she wus hollered dis into de house to de ole folks, dat he drap his head an' face clean down 'tween his knees; but ole man Tryup an' ole Miss Tryup gits aroun' him, an' honey an' sugar him all up ontel dey gits him all right. Den de ole 'oman go down in de woods an' find de gal a tryin fer to hide in a ole holler rotten stump. She git her out, an' pet her up, an' tell her dat Meester Highstepper jes suit her an' de ole man, an' she mus' go right straight on back to de house. De gal go wid her an' pull a leafy lim' offn a tree on de way back fer to keep off de flies wid whilst dey wus a eatin' de dinner.

W'en dey gits back to de house; de ole 'oman goes on to puttin de dinner on de table. W'en she wus jes about ready fer to ax 'em to set down to de dinner, ole man Tryup say, says he: "Ole man I thinks you'd better go outdoors an' go down un'er de house in de cellar an' draw a big jug full of cider from our big bar'l of it down dar. I wants Meester Highstepper to see w'at kind of good swallers'll run down his th'oat w'en he sho 'nough jine in wid de fambly."

Well, it wus tetch an' go wid 'em; so de ole 'oman grab up jug, an' go out, an' go down in de cellar fer to git de cider. W'en she git down dar; she set de jug down on de dirt floo' un'er de bung of de bar'l, an' open it, an' de cider it 'gin to run into de jut. Whilst she wus a stan'in' dar a drawin de cider; she 'gin to think 'bout dat dey didn' have but de one room to de house, an' her an' her ole man an' Jerushy wus a livin in dat room wid a big bed, wid a trundle bed un'er dat big bed, wid a table, wid four box-chairs, wid a kittle, wid a wash board, wid a pot, wid a skillet, wid a lid, wid a wash pan, wid a towel, wid clo'es, wid shoes, wid stockins, wid four cups, wid six saucers, wid five plates, wid a oven, wid six knives, wid six fo'ks, wid six big tin spoons, wid two liddle pewter spoons, wid a cubbard, wid a meal bar'l, wid a tray, an' wid so-on. She stan' dar an' she think an' she wonder how in de worl' dey wus a gwineter make room fer dis here Highstepper w'en he marry Jerushy an' come to live wid 'em. Whilst she wus a stan'in' dar, a wonderin an' a wonderin' w'at dey wus gwineter do; de cider bar'l fill up de jug, run it over, an' 'gin to run de cider out on de cellar dirt floo'. De ole 'oman stan' dar, an' think, an' fergit de cider; an' de cider run out on de dirt floo', an' make mud, an' fergit de ole 'oman! As de ole sayin' sayes:

"De ole 'oman stan' dar an' wonder an' wonder!
(Dere is setch a thing as a filled-up jug.)
De dirt floo' all down dar git muddier an' muddier;

Bymeby, ole man Tryup, up dar wid Jerushy an' Mister Highstepper, say to 'em: "De ole 'oman is a takin' a turble long time fer to draw dat jug of cider. It mus' a smelt so good to her dat she take to drinkin' an' a drawin' all at de same time. De dinner is all a gittin' col'; an' I specs I'd better go out an' go down an' push up de drawin' end a liddle bit!"

So ole man Tryup git up an' leave de young folks, an' go out an' go down in de cellar. W'en he git dar; he step in through de half shet slab doo', an' it wus so dark dat he couldn' see good w'at wus a gwine on. An' befo' his eyes git fixed up good fer seein' down dar; he sorter half whisper to ole Miss Tryup: "Ole 'oman, we's all a waitin fer you in de house! W'at in de worl' is a keepin' you down here so long?"

Den de ole 'oman go through; an' splain to him all 'bout how she wus been a rackin her brains, a tryin' to make out some way how dey was a gwineter git 'nough room fer Mr. Highstepper w'en he wus come to live wid 'em. She name off all dey wus got in de house; an' den she say dat it look to her lak dat w'en Mr. Highstepper comed to live wid 'em, dey'd all git "scrouged out! [Scrouged = crowded]—All dis time; de cider jes keep on a runnin' outn de bar'l on de dirt floo' of de cellar; an' it make mo' an' mo' mud!

Atter ole man Tryup hear w'at his ole 'oman say: he tell her dat he haint never done thinked 'bout dat neider! So he stan' dar wid his ole 'oman; an' he think, an' he think, an' he think!—All dis time, de cider jes keep on a runnin an' a makin' up mud.

Bymeby Miss Jerushy say to Mr. Highstepper dat she jes caint see w'at in de worl' wus got into mammy an' daddy; dat de dinner was a gittin col', an' it wouldn' be fitten fer nobody to eat. An' 'sides all dat; she wus done fanned de flies offn de table already ontel she wus a acheing all over. So she tell him to make hisself at home ontel she step down in de cellar an' git 'em.

She step out, an' go down into de cellar through de half shet doo', a sayin as she go in: "Mammy, why in de name of goodness dont you an' daddy hurry on; an' come on up to dinner?"

Den her mammy an' daddy splain w'at wus a keepin' 'em down dar; an' she up an' say, sayes she: "I haint never done thinked 'bout dat befo' at no time!" So she stan' up in dar along by de side of her daddy an' mammy; an' she think, an' she think, an' she think; whilst de cider, it run an' it run out on de dirt floo' an' make mo' mud an' mo' mud!

Mr. Highstepper, he sot up dar in de room; an' he wait an' he wait. But dere dont nobody come back. He wait an' he wait ontel he 'gin to git lonesome.—(De cider, it jes keep on a runnin!) Bymeby he maked up his mind dat he'd better go an' see w'at wus done gone an' become of 'em all. So he go out an' go down. W'en he git to de slab doo' of de cellar, he pull it wide open an' look in; an' he see de ole 'oman an' de ole man an' de gal all a standin up dar in loblolly of mud w'at de cider wus don maked, an' a sayin nothin! He peep in, he do, an' he say: "W'at in de name of common sense is you all a doin' a stanin up dar in de mud a sayin nothin?"

De ole 'oman squall back to him, sorter mad-lak; "Haint no name o' common sense 'bout it! Here we is a tryin fer to study how we's a gwineter git you into de house outn de col;' an' dar you is a axin: 'W'at in de name o' common sense!'"

De young man say to her: "Dat wus powerful cu'ious kind o' common sense—to be a stanin up dar in de mud-hole, an' a sayin nothin'."

About dat time ole man Tryup come a pullin up outn de cellar wid de mud a drappin offn him; an' he splain to Mr. Highstepper all 'bout how dey wus a tryin fer to look ahead, an' fin' a place fer him in deir house; an' he axes him if he wont come down an' jine in wid 'em in tryin to fix up a plan.

Mr. Highstepper tell him dat dey'll please scuse him; caze he dont think he want to marry in wid no fambly w'at wusnt got no sense, or w'at wus got dat kind o' sense—which-some-ever dey mought call it.

Ole man Tryup make answer to 'im: "Humph! Folks w'at dont never look ahead, dey dont never have nothin an' dey's always bumpin' deir heads; so he'd sorter 'vise him to stick to de fambly w'at wus foresighted, caze dey wus always de goodest provisioners."

Mr. Highstepper say to de ole man dat he dont jes zackly see it dat way. So he tell 'em all dat he wus a gwine away a co'tin' aroun' 'mongst de tother Overseein famblies. If he ever come across as much as three mo' famblies w'at wusnt got no mo' sense dan de Tryup fambly; den he'd come back an' wouldn' marry nobody else fer de worl' 'cep' Jerushy Tryup.

So Mr. Highstepper leave an' go on off to de Capn of de plantation whar he wus hired fer de Overseer. He tell him dat he want to take a few days off; so as to take a liddle look aroun' fer to git hisself a wife. De Capn tell him dat dis wus all right. He wusnt by his Niggers no ways lak a heaps of de white folks w'at jes believe in wukin' 'em to death, an' not a bodderin 'long wid deir ailments, an' killin 'em out, an' a buyin' new ones. Since his way of carryin-on was jes to flog 'em an' to git all he could outn 'em, but to sorter take care of 'em; de whoppin w'at dey needs can sorter be laid up fer 'em ontel he git back. Wid de business all fixed up dis way; Mr. Highstepper go on off a co'tin' bright an' early Monday mawnin.

He step over about ten mile to a Overseer's house w'at wus got a gal by de name of Tildy. W'en he git up in sight of de house; he see dis here Tildy gal a stanin an' a holdin de doo' to de house shet tight! Terreckly she would open de doo' right quick; an' her mammy would rush outn de house a rollin a empty wheelbar, an' Tildy would shet de doo' ag'in right quick an' hol' it togedder tight behin' her. De ole 'oman would den run aroun' de house right fast two or three times wid de empty wheelbar, den run to de doo'; an' Tildy would open it an' let her in right quick, an' den shet de doo' togedder: "kerblam!!" an' hol' it togedder. Terreckly de doo' open ag'in; an de ole 'oman rush out an' run aroun' de house an' go back in ag'in; whilst de gal slam de doo' togedder an' keep it tight w'en she haint a passin through. All

de time whilst Mr. Highstepper wus a gwine up to de house; he watch de
ole 'oman a runnin in an' outn de house an' de doo' a "blamin!" an' he dont
know w'at to make of her an' her empty wheelbar.

Bymeby, once, while de ole 'oman wus in de house, she peep out
through a crack 'tween de logs of de cabin; an' she see Mr. Highstepper a
comin. So she run out an' sot a bench out up un'er a tree in front of de
house; an' as he come up she say to him: "Oh Meester Highstepper, we's
so glad to see you! You an' Tildy come here an' jes set down on dis here
bench in de cool shade un'er de tree; an' 'joy you'selves."

Den Mr. Highstepper up an' 'spon': "You railly mus' scuse my comin'
over here on a week days. I wus jes got to studyin' 'bout Miss Tildy; an' I
jes had to come over an' git a look at her. I notice dat you wus awful
busy; an' so I'll jes drap in a few words wid Miss Tildy an' den I'll be a
gwine.—It are changin de conbersation a liddle; but I notice, whilst I wus
a comin up, dat you git sorter shamed fer to load up yo' wheelbar an'
fetch in an' outn de house de things w'at you wants fer to git moved. I
seed you a gwine in wid it an' a comin' out wid it empty; all caze you
didn't want to wheel things in an' out befo' me. Now you musn' be lak
dat! Sides; If you'll jes tell me w'at you wants took in an' outn de house,
I'll do dat fer you befo' I has my confab wid Miss Tildy."

"Good sakes o' life, man!" de ole 'oman say. "You dont look lak dat
you un'erstan's nothin! I wus jes scoured de house out inside; an' so, you
see, I wus jes a rollin de sun in, in de wheelbar, so as to dry it out, whilst
Tildy wus a keepin' de doo' shet, so as to keep it from a rollin out as fast
as I roll it in!"

Mr. Highstepper stan' dar a minute an' look at de ole 'oman an' Tildy;
den he say to hisself: "Dar be fools number one—heaps bigger fools dan
dem Tryups." Den he tell 'em dat he spec dat he'd better be a gwine so as
to git back home befo' night; an' went on 'way.

Along about sundown, on his road home, he pass by de Tryup's
house; an' he holler over to 'em: "Say! I's done foun' one fambly w'at's
heaps bigger fools dan you all is; an' I mought come over in a day or so
to tell you 'bout em!"

De Tryups hollers back an' makes answer to 'im: "Bully fer you! Come
over almos' any time!" An' he go on home.

He lay awake dat night a studyin' whar he'd go de nex' day. At one of
de big Camp Meetins, he wus got a knockin-down [knockin-down = intro-
duction] to Miss Samanthy Lucy Jane Philpot, w'at live about fifteen or
twenty mile back in de sticks. Her daddy wus one o' dem 'ar no-sense
Overseers w'at couldn' keep no job hardly nowhars caze he kilt off de
Niggers so fast; but he wus managed aroun' some way fer to git a liddle
place back out dar in de backwoods. He wus built dis a one-room house
wid a stoop. He wus got hisself a cow an' a calf; an' he wus managed fer

to raise a liddle crop of corn by hand. He didn' have no hawgs; caze he ketch all de wild hawgs up dar dat he want; an' he didn't need no chickens, caze he ketch all de birds up dar dat he want wid traps. Dey took de place of chickens an' he say dat dey tas'e mo' better. Ole man Philpot e't so much wild meat dat he sorter looked wild; an' de folkses wus all nicknamed him: "Coon". Well, Mr. Highstepper maked up his mind dat he wus a gwine up to see dis here gal Samanthy Lucy Jane. He den drap off to sleep fer a hour or so; an' den he git up three or four hours befo' day so as to walk up to whar he was a gwine by a liddle befo' dinner time.

He git up dar w'en de sun was about four hours high; an' w'en he git in sight of de house, he see ole man "Coon" a doin sumpin w'at look sorter cu'ious, an' he stop and look a liddle bit befo' he go up to de house.

Dar wus a great big shade tree right in front of de doo' of de house w'at wus got on it a long lim' w'at reach out over de top of de roof. Ole man "Coon" Philpot wus got a great long rope throwed over dat lim' w'at reach out over de top of de roof of de house. He wus got a hold on one end of dis rope; an' he had his ca'f tied around de neck to de tother end of it. He would set to wuk, an' pull on his end of de rope, an' he hang de ca'f up in de air jes a kickin an' a bawlin' an' a bellerin! But de calf would kick an' scuffle so hard dat atter while he'd have to let it ack down on de groun'. He look lak he wus a gwineter butcher de ca'f fer beef by hangin' it.

Mr. Highstepper say to hisself dat ole man Philpot sho wus got powerful barbous from a eatin' wild meat! He guess he'd better rush up dar, an' try to git him to kill his beef by knockin' it in de head instid of by hangin' it. So he runned up to him an' sayed: "Mawnin, Meester Philpot! Let me help you kill yo' beef! Dont hang it; Jes let me take yo ax an' knock it in de head. Den you can stick it an' bleed it; an' it'll be all hunky."

Ole man Philpot look at Mr. Highstepper lak he wus stonished, an' he say: "Look here, boy! Has you done gone raven stracted? Has you los' all yo' senses? I wouldn' take a prutty fer da 'ar ca'f! It's de fines' thing dat I's laid eyes on in lebenteen years!"

Mr. Highstepper look at him mighty much puzzled an' ax him: "W'at wus you a tryin' to do den; if you wusnt a tryin' to hang de calf?"

Ole man "Coon" p'int to de roof of his cabin an' say: "Fer Heaben sakes, man! Caint you see dat fine long moss a growin' up dar on top of de house? I wus jes a tryin' fer to pull de calf wid de rope, so as to put it to paster on it!"

"Humph!" say Mr. Highstepper, "Why didn' you go up dar yo'self an' pull off de moss an' throw it down to de calf?"

"Oh, I haint never done thinked about dat!" answered up ole man "Coon."

Mr. Highstepper say to hisself: "Well, here's fambly number two w'at's a heap bigger fools dan de Tryups!" Den he say to de ole man: "I believes if you'll give me a drink of water, dat I'll sorter knock on home."

Ole man "Coon" maked answer to dis: "Well, we dont keep no

drinkin water in de house now. We drapped our big water gourd about a week ago an' busted it; an' de ole 'oman haint took time yit fer to clean out an' bile out anudder one. But you can jes stop down dar at de spring as you goes back down de cow-path to de big road an' git down on yo' knees an' drink yo' fill."

Mr. Highstepper go on off; an' it wus so late w'en he git home, dat w'en he git to sleep he didn' wake up ontel dinner time de nex' day. W'en he git out, it look to him lak it wus too late fer him to git out an' do much co'tin' dat day. But dat evenin' he walk off about a mile to talk wid anudder young man by de name of Pill Fishback, w'at wus a tryin to look hisself up a gal an' git married too. He got dar about sundown. He find Pill a settin out on de fence un'er a tree, a whittlin' a stick; so he got hisself a cedar stick to whittle on too, an' den sot down to talk wid 'im to see if he's hearn tell of some tony gal w'at he can give him a riccommen to.

Fust he tell Pill sumpin 'bout all dis here hard luck w'at he wus been a havin'. He tell him dat he wus done got a gal fer to say "yes" by sayin' sof' things an' a rollin' sheep eyes at her; but her an' her folks wus all setch big fools dat he make up his mind dat he wusnt a gwineter marry her onless dat de happen to find out dat der wus three mo' famblies w'at wus bigger fools dan dey wus. If some-how-be-ever he find three mo' famblies w'at wus bigger fools dan de Tryups, since three make a rule; he would den know dat dis Tryup fambly wus de smart fambly, an' dat all de tother famblies wus bigger fools as a rule. In dis case he say he wus a gwine back an' marry Jerushy Tryup. He den ax Pill, if he dont know of some gal w'at wus got smart folks.

Pill make answer to him: Yes, of co'se he do. He say: Dar wus Gillie Jane Wisener w'at wus as sharp as a razzer, an' as keen as a briar—not only her but all her folkses. He tell Mr. Highstepper fer to stay all night wid him; an' he'll take him over to see de gal de nex' day. Mr. Highstepper tank him; an' tell him dat he'll stay.

Den Pill tell him 'bout dat he wus a co'tin' too; but he wus got a diffunt sort of trouble, an' maybe he mought help him out since he know how fer to git de gals to say "yes". He say dat his onliest trouble wus dat he couldn' git his gal to say "yes"; an' if he can jes tell him how to git her to do dis, it'll fix him up all right.

Mr. Highstepper say to him: "Oh, dat's dead easy! You jes say sof' things; an' roll sheep-eyes at her lak I don wid Jerushy Tryup; an' she'll say "yes" right off."

Pill tell him dat he wus mighty much arbleedged to 'im; an' maybe, by gitin his own mammy an' daddy to help him an' lend him a han', he can git his gal to say "yes" to marryin' him right away.

So he leave Mr. Highstepper a settin out dar, an' go an' see his mammy an' daddy, an' tell 'em w'at it would take fer to git a gal at dat time fer to say "yes".

His mammy an' daddy talk it all over wid 'im; an' dey say dat dey wants him fer to git married, if he want to. Dat bein' de case, dey say: "W'at's bleedged to be done wus bleedged to be done." So dey tells him to do down in de sheep pen an' ketch one of de sheeps an' git its eyes out; an' whilst he wus gone, dey'd git de sof' things all fixed up fer him to say.

Pill go down in de pen an' knock a sheep in de head an' cut de eyes out an put 'em in his pocket an' come on back to de house. W'en he git back, de ole folks wus done b'iled him up some tunnups an' taters; an' wus mashed 'em up an' put 'em in two diffunt rags. Dey hands dese here two bundles of stuff over to 'im.

Den Pill go out an' say to Mr. Highstepper, w'at wus still a settin out dar un'er de tree, dat he wus now a gwine over fer to git his gal to say "yes"; an' he would be back terreckly, an' den dey would go to bed.

W'en Pill git gone; his mammy an' daddy ax Mr. Highstepper fer to come in an' et an' talk wid dem ontel deir son git back from his liddle "co'tin' bee". Dey say dey wus got some ginger-cakes w'at dey wus saved over from deir las' big Camp Meetin' basket dinner of a mont' or so ago; an' dey would pass him out some of dese wid a big gourd-full of 'simmon beer so as to make his stay seem mo' shorter to 'im. Mr. Highstepper come in; an' go to eatin', an' a drinkin', an' a talkin.

Whilst all dis wus a gwine on; Pill git over to de gal's house, an' she come in de room whar he wus a waitin fer to see her. She wus all bucked up in a white dress; all starched, an' ironed, an' puffed, an' fluted, an' pluted! Dey sot down, dey did, an' talked 'bout fust one thing an' den de tother.

Atter while Pill think it wus 'bout time fer to git his gal fer to say "yes" to marryin' him. So he say over to hisself: "Now, w'at wus it dat Mr. Highstepper say?"—"Say sof' things to her an roll sheep-eyes at her!" Den he look at de gal, a grinnin'-lak, an' take de liddle rag bundles from outn his pockets, an' onroll one, an' say: "Tunnups!" Den he dash de mashed tunnups over on her dress!

Chile, dat gal sho did git mad! She wus puffed an' fluted an' pluted, w'en she come in; but she git riffled all over w'en dat throwin' took place. She say to him: "you ole ugly mud-turkle, you!"

About dat time, Pill say right quick: "Taters!" An' he whirled over de mashed taters on her. Den she say: "You ole slushy-sloshy dirty mud-puddle, you!" An' she riz to run. As she riz to run; Pill throwed de bloody sheep-eyes on her wid a sort of a rollin' motion; an' she let out one of dem 'ar hallelujah hollers w'at brung her mammy an' daddy a tiltin' into de room. W'en she holler, Pill hear de Angels answer, a callin' him home; an' his footses couldn' tote him dar fast 'nough to suit him.

W'en de gal show de ole folks w'at wus done gone an' happen; de ole man grabbed his ax an' de ole 'oman de shovel, an' dey takes out atter him. De gal foller 'long 'hind 'em wid de broom wid de hopes of gittin a crack at his head wid de handle. Pill look away back through de moonlight; an' he see 'em a comin'. Mon! You'd jes oughter a seed him! He jes flewed!

He git home a long ways in front of his gal an' her folks. He run'd in de room whar his mammy an' daddy an' Mr. Highstepper wus a settin; an' he drapped down on de floo' an rolled up un'er de bed. W'en he git un'er dar an' ketch a few mouf-full's of win', he holler out: "Shet an' bar de doo' quick! Dey's a comin' fer to kill me!"

His daddy jump an' bar de doo', an' peep out through a crack; an' see de gal an' her folks a comin' wid a ax. Den he 'gin to question Pill 'bout w'at wus done gone an' happen.

Pill splain to 'em: Dat he jes say "sof" things an' "roll sheep eyes at her" lak Mr. Highstepper wus told him to do; an' dey all look lak dey wus ben on butcherin' him up 'bout it; an' maybe eben dey look lak dey mought git taken wid a notion fer to kill him by mistake!

Mr. Highstepper den tell 'em all dat he didn' mean nothin' lak dat! W'en he say dis; Pill's daddy an' mammy git fightin-mad. Dey tells him: He haint got no, business a sayin w'at he dont mean' an' a gittin folks in pecks of trouble! If dey hadn' been skeared dat de gal an' her folks mought git in; dey mought a opened de doo' an' a pitched him out on his head.

Mr. Highstepper splain it all as bes' he can on de inside; whilst dem w'at wus on de outside keep up a rip-rarin an' a tryin fer to git in. At fust de mo' Mr. Highstepper splain, de mo' hotter Pill's mammy an' daddy got! Dey say a man w'at caint talk no mo' plainer dan dat should oughter git his tongue split lak a pet crow; but de folkses outside cut up an' raise setch a hullabaloo dat dey makes up deir minds dat maybe dey'd better patch up a liddle peace wid him. So dey tells Mr. Highstepper: Dey reckins dey'll hafter look over him an' charge it up to his ignancy dis time.

Pill's daddy holler out through de cracks 'twixt de logs of de house to de gal an' her folks: De whole thing wus jes a liddle mistake in tellin an' un'erstan'in'. Dey mus ricomember dat mistakes sometimes happens 'mongst de smartest of de "Big Boys". He tells 'em dat his ole 'oman'll wash up de dress; an' Pill'll polergize an' perfess, an' never come a botherin along wid de gal no mo'.

W'en de ole man say all dis; de gal's folks thinks maybe dis wus about as good as dey could fix it up atter Pill wus outrunned 'em, so dey all goes on off home.

W'en dey gits off a liddle piece; Mr. Highstepper tell Pill an' his folks dat he wus done clean gone an' fergit offn his mind dat dere wus sumpin at home a callin him so dat he couldn' in no wise think 'bout stayin' all night. He say he wus a burnin' some ole fence rails fer wood; an' dey wus too long fer to go in his fire-lace. He didn' git time fer to cut 'em up; so he jes stuck de ends of de rails in de fire-place, an' lef' de tother ends a stickin' out on de floo'. Dis bein' de case: He wus awful skeared dat de rails would burn out ontel dey reach de floo', an' set his house on fire. So he mus' be a gwine home. Pill an' dem let him out; an' he slid off home mo' samer dan a black-racer snake w'en he see you a comin' wid a stick. As he slid along de road, a splittin' de wind; he say to hisself: "Three, it make de rule!—Dere sho be's three famblies w'at's heaps bigger fools dan de Tryups!—I's a shore a gwineter fix it up tomorrer fer to marry Jerushy Tryup.

Well, Mr. Highstepper manage to snatch a liddle sleep dat night; an' de nex' mawnin, bright an' early, find him at de Tryup's. Dey wus mighty glad fer to see him; an' dey ax him in fer to eat a bite of Breakfus wid 'em. He set down to de table, he do, an' he tell 'em his spearunces, an' he telled 'em dat he wus done maked up his mind: Dere never wus no fool whar dere wusnt a bigger fool. So he wus come over fer to ax 'em to let him an' Jerushy hand one-nudder de meal an' bacon; an' 'gin to be man an wife on de nex' Sunday. He polergize an' perfess to 'em dat he wouldn' a been in no mind fer to rush 'em so, an' he would a waited ontel de nex' day to come over an' ax for Jerushy; but dat day would a been Friday, an' dey knows dat Friday was bad-luck day. He mought a waited ontel de nex' day atter dis; but dat would a been Sadday, an' dat wus almos' de onlies' day dat de Jedge go to town fer to sell folkses pairs of licenses fer to git married. So he wus jes bleedged fer to go to town on dat day. Den he want to git Parson Greenholler fer to marry him; an' he'd hafter go to git him to look up de ceremony on a Sadday so as to git ontwisted togedder fer Sunday.

Ole man Tryup an' his ole 'oman tell him dat ev'rything wus all right an' 'greeable jes so long as he wus a gwineter marry Jerushy; an' fer him to go right ahead wid his rat-ketchin an' his cat-killin'.

So Mr. Highstepper go on back home an' lie up an' res' all day Friday, caze it was bad-luck day; an' he go down to de Jedge on a Saddy an' git a pair of licenses fer to marry wid. He come back by Parson Greenholler's wid his pair of licenses a stickin outn befo of his jacket-pockets, an' he tell him dat he want him to come over tomorrer an' hitch him an' Jerushy in de bounds of matteramonie; caze he wus don l'arnt: *Dere never wus no fool whar dere wusnt a bigger fool.*

De Parson maked answer: All right; he'd sho be dar widout fail, if nothin' dont happen.

Den Mr. Highstepper ax him how much he wus a gwineter charge him fer yokin' him an' Jerushy up togedder.

De Parson say dat he charge fer common a quarter an' a quart of 'simmon beer; but, beance he wus so smart, dat he wus found out: Dere never wus no fool whar dere wusnt a bigger fool, he think dat he'd hafter hitch him up fer nothin.

Ole man Tryup—de gal's daddy—spen' all of Saddy night a gwine aroun' an' a wakin' up all de Overseein' famblies an' a axin 'em in to see Jerushy an' Mr. Highstepper git jined togedder de nex' day at de 'p'inted time.

W'en de preacher git through wid marryin' Miss Jerushy an' Mr. Highstepper, he make a big speech to de crowd wharin he praise up de pony. [In order to fully appreciate this semi-sarcastic expression one needs to read the Negro story: "Mr. Rabbit grossly deceives Mr. Fox", recorded by Joel Chandler Harris. In the story the rabbit makes the fox his riding horse and then proceeds to "praise up the pony."] He tell 'em all w'at a fine thing Mr. Highstepper wus done gone an' fin' out. De fine thing wus: *Dere never wus no fool whar dere wusnt a bigger fool.* He say he hope dey would all keep dis in deir membunce clean down 'mongst deir chilluns' chilluns.

Atter dis: *Dere never wus no fool whar dere wusnt a bigger fool* got to be de word ["De word" means a proverb] 'mongst de poo' Nigger-overseein' white folks. W'en dis git to be de word amongst 'em' dem w'at wus got a liddle sense git all married up 'mongst dem w'at wusnt got no sense; an', atter while, dey all git so dey wusnt got no sense. Leaswise dat's de way my grandaddy tell it to me; an' splain how white Overseers of Niggers come not to have no sense, an' beat up de slaves an' kill 'em up so;" concluded Aunt Dilsie.

"Well, Dilsie, dat sho dont look at 'tall onreasonable"; said Aunt Donie by way of keeping the conversation a going. "I thinks dat I'll hafter set it down fer so; onless I finds out sumpin w'at's a heaps better."

"I mus' be knockin' along home," said Aunt Dilsie, arising from her chair. "Now, you mus' come over an' jaw me tomorrer".

"I will, Dilsie; but you musn' fergit dat we's too good a friends to be a markin' down visits".

"I haint a gwineter do dat, Donie!—Good-bye".

"Good-bye, Dilsie. Come over any time you're amind to".

"I will".

They parted.

RIDDLE THEM RIGHT

❄

During the great American Civil War, when the Northern army made near approaches to certain localities in the South, some slave-holders sold many of their slaves whom they thought they might lose through their running away to that army and to Freedom. Pos Simmons was a slave thus sold. His wife—"Aunt" Jane Simmons—and his children were retained by their owners. Pos was carried to the far South. Just where he was sold, he never seemed to know. When asked where he was carried, after being sold, he commonly answered: "Away down dar somewhars in Possum Trot".

But when Freedom came, he had not forgotten the dusky wife and children whom he had left behind and still dearly loved. When informed that he was free, without waiting one day, he tied his little belongings into a bundle, placed them on the end of a stick thrown over his shoulder and turned his face northward to find all that was dear to him. After about six weeks of continuous walking (according to his story) he turned up unexpectedly in the presence of his wife and children on a mid-autumn afternoon. There was crying and weeping there, but it was not the wail called forth by death; it was the gladsome tear shed over the resurrection.

When over-joy had given way to reason, the wife and children at once busied themselves to prepare food to refresh the returned weary hungry father. It was ready in a short time. The family had not been through with its dinner so very long, but the father insisted that he could not eat unless they also partook of food along with him. So the mother and children were seated for a second dinner. There was little eating however; joy had banished all desire for food.

After the meal was over, the few remaining moments of daylight were spent in listening to the hard and bitter experiences through which the father had passed since they had seen him last. The outline of his story was finished just as night came on. As the darkness gently settled, he expressed the feeling that he could retire more happily for the night, if the family would join in an hour of fun-making like that in which they commonly indulged daily before he was sold away from them.

To suggest his remotest desire was for him to have it gratified so far as it lay in the power of his household. They brought a few ears of green corn and some sweet potatoes, opened up a place in the live coals of fire in the spacious fire-place, placed them therein, and covered them, up to be roasted for use as a final lunch before retiring for the night. Then they gathered themselves into a semi-circle about the fire to engage in such amusements as they knew.

First, they sang. The selections were the Jubilee songs: "No mo' peck o' corn fer me. No mo' !", "I want to be a soldier and the Lord will set me free", and others of this same general type. They were rejoicing in their newly found freedom. It was a Christian Negro family; and thus the banjo, the "fiddle", and dancing were tabooed.

After singing; they played "Club Fist", "Chickamee Crany Crow", and other little simple Negro plays. Finally, they began to propound riddles to each other. As they sat in their semi-circle, each one gave his riddle to the others in his turn.

> "Long legs, spotted thighs,
> Rusty back an 'bullet eyes' cried number one.
> "A frog", answered the others almost in unison.
> Then followed many other riddles with their answers,

such as:

> "Runs all aroun' de house;
> An' w'en it git back.
> You caint see nothin',
> 'Cep its jes one track."—A wheelbarrow.
> "Rusty back an 'bullet eyes,
> Bal' head an' no eyes."—A shovel with a riveted handle.

> "Goes wid you all day,
> Comes home at night,
> Sets in de chimbly corner,
> Licks its tongue out right."—Your shoe.

> "I jes swore by my flipti-flapti,
> If I jes had my ticti-tacti,
> I'd make ole Roy lay down Mirandi."—I swore by my old hat,
> If I had my gun,
> I'd make the fox
> lay down my goose.

The flow of the riddles was continuous; and the stock supply of the children seemed so inexhaustable that the mother suggested that they cease to propound them. She feared lest the father should grow tired, and yet refrain from mentioning it, because of his tender regard for them. As she expressed it: "Too much seasonin' sometime spile de Puddin'".

Turning to her husband, she said: "Law, Pos! dese here chilluns

knows so many of dem 'ar riddles; an' de tother Niggers aroun' here
knows so many mo' dan dese 'blackbirds' of mine; I sho do wonder heaps
o' times whar all dem so many riddles come from".

"Jane, Honey!" replied the husband, "Dem 'ar Niggers, away down
Souf, whar I's been; w'at dont know nothin' but a liddle piece o' mutton,
an' dey dont know dat; wus a set w'at wus ready to tell you whar
ev'rything come from 'cep' deirselves. One of 'em, one day, eben tried fer
to tell me whar riddles come from. Yes sah! Dese here riddles w'at you's
all been a givin' out, an' you's been a wonderin' whar dey all come from
puts me in de mind of a great long rig-a-ma-role loration w'at one of dem
'ar Bargro-Guinea-Niggers telled me. He had a great long tale 'bout folkses
a co'tin' in riddles, talkin' in riddles, gittin outn jail wid riddles, an' a
whole passel of stuff w'at nobody couldn' never ricomember.

W'en he git through, I axed him jes fer fun whar folkses comed from;
an' he say right offn de handle: De Lawd made 'em outn mud an' sot 'em
up side of a rail-fence to dry. Atter dat, I kep' on a stickin' questions un'er
him; ontel it git so hot fer him dat he went off a whistlin'.

"Dont ax me no questions,
An' I wont tell you no lies;
But bring me dem apples,
An' I'll make you some pies."

"Well," interrupted the mother, seconded by the children, "We dont
wish dat we'd a done been took an' sol' off down to Possum Trot; but we
sho do wish dat we mought a heared de tale."

"Of cose," said the father,"I caint ricomember much of it an' I haint no
hand fer to tell no tales no hows; but if you wants to hear setch as I can
wobble off, I'll try an' do de bes' I can fer you."

"Wobble away "' answered the family almost in unison.

"Well," said the father, "it go sumpin lak dis: Away back yon'er one
time, de free Niggers got deir victuals an' clo'es by huntin'. Dey all loved
one-nudder an' lived togedder lak two peas in a pod. W'en de boys an'
gals 'gin to git grown; de ole folks do de marryin' of de gals off. But w'en
dey wus been got married off once, an' de ole 'oman lose her ole man;
she mought go an' court 'roun' 'mongst de tother widders lak folks does
now-a-days. It wus de rule in dem times dat ev'rybody mus' treat
ev'rybody else right. An' if a somebody want to kill a somebody else: dey
slapped him in jail an' rolled a big rock on top of de doo'. Den atter dat
dey took dat somebody out an' maked him set up in a pizen tree; an'
drink pizen ontel he drap out an' fall on de groun' dead. Lakwise it wus
de rule in dem days dat w'at-some-ever folkses wus got to eat an' w'ar;
dey wus bleedged to use up or give it away to dem w' at wusnt got none.
Nobody wusnt 'lowed to throw nothin away.

Dis here loration ' bout riddles wus 'bout three boys w'at lived in dem times. Dese here boys wus named Horn, Rab, an' Codger; an' dey wus a castin' aroun' so as to manage somehow to git hitched, jined, an' married.

Dere wus a prutty coffee-colored gal, named Hun, w'at dey all see sometimes w'en dey pass by de house, an' w'at dey all love so much dat dey wus almos' clean stock crazy 'bout her.

Almos' all de Niggers wus free in dem times. Dis gal an' her mammy an' daddy wus free. De free Niggers jes marry in wid de free Niggers in dem times; an' no slave Niggers didn' have no show of couplin' up wid 'em.

Horn an' Rab an' Codger wus one time been slave Niggers; so w'en dey went to Hun's daddy to ax him deir chances fer marryin' her, he sing out to 'em:

"I ax pretty Lize fer to marry me;
She say she's a lookin' fer a Nigger dat's free."

But Horn, an' Rab, an' Codger say to 'im dat dey wus done gone already an' got free.

Her daddy den tell 'em; if dat was de case, he didn' care. He'd druther his gal would marry a free Nigger w'at wus once been a slave; case he'd stir aroun' an' keep de pot on de pot-rack a b'ilin' mo' better. Dem 'ar free Niggers git deir livin' by huntin'; an' heaps o' times almos' instid o' grub to keep 'em a cuttin an' a charvin, dey wus settin 'roun' starvin'.

But Hun's daddy allow to 'em dat he want so know from ev'ry one of 'em how dey wus managed fer to git free; befo' he go any furder wid 'em. So he say he'll fust call on Codger to tell 'im how he git free.

Codger say dat he git free from his Mosser by givin' him a riddle dat he couldn' onravel. His Mosser make offer fer to set him free if he could do dis. But de Mosser lay it down dat de riddle mus' be about sumpin whar he can make his livin atter he git free. So Codger give him dis riddle:

"Worl' stuffed chug full,
Caint git yo' han' full.
Dat riddle's a gwineter stay in me,
Ontel I gits whar I's been free."

Codger say dat his Mosser study an' study, an' guess an' guess; but he caint git no answer, so he give it up. Den he onwind de riddle an' string it out befo' him. Dis was de answers

"De worl' wus full of air
You caint git yo' han'ful of it.
It stay inside you ontel you dies,
An' all dead mens is free".

W'en he tell his Mosser de answer wus "de air"; he wus set free wid de greements dat he'd git his livin' a stayin' 'roun' in de air. So Codger say dat he wus gittin' his livin' 'cordin' to de greements by livin' 'roun' out in de air. Now dat he wus free; he want to marry Hun.

Nex' de gal's daddy want to know from Rab how he wus managed fer to git free.

Rab lakwise say dat he wus had one of dem 'ar "smart" Mossers w'at offer to set him free fer a riddle dat he couldn' ontangle. So he handed him out dis one:

"He lie low!
Oh, my Mosser! Put on yo' cryin' Jack!
Run'd upstairs, run'd downstairs;
Maked no noise wid two sharp pairs.
See bald Tommy dough Jack,
Or say so."

De Mosser, he runned up stairs an' he runned down stairs; but he didn't see no nothin' 'tall nowhars. He sot down an' scratched his head an' addled his brains; but he couldn' see no sense in de riddle. Den he took down his lead pencil from behin' his (y)ears; an' he tried to figger it out; but his answers all come out hind-parts befo'. At las' he give it up.

Den Rab splain it. He ax him: Dont he ricomember, about a year ago, dat de ole Tom-cat cotch de Missus' parrot w'at wus named Jack?

His Mosser say dat he ricomember dat.

Den he axed him: W'en de cat cotch an' e't de parrot; wusnt his 'cakes all dough?'

De Mosser say: Yes, he guess dey wus!

Well (Rab tell him) dat wus 'Tommy dough Jack.'

His Mosser say: "Yes".

Den Rab go on to ax him: Didn' he ricomember dat de Missus tol' him fer to kill de cat?

His Mosser say: "Yes".

Den he ax him: Didn' he ricomember; w'en he kilt dat cat; dat he skint him an' kep' de hide an' skull so as not to have no bad luck from de cat-killin'?

De Mosser say: "Yes".

"Well den;" Rab tell him; "de cat wus bal' headed w'en he skint him, an' de whole riddle run lak dis:

"De Tom-cat is dead,
Oh Mosser, put on yo' new boots'
He useter run up stairs an' run down stairs;

Widout makin' no noise wid his two pairs of sharp claws.
Look at de skinned head he got fer makin' Jack's cakes all dough.
Guess it, or set me free!'"

Rab's Mosser hem an' haw, but at las' he say: All right, dat he wus frees but he musn' never fergit dat he mus' live on cats, or come back an' be a slave 'cordin to de greements; caze de answer to de riddle wus "A cat".

Rab tell his Mosser: Dat wus all right; but, of co'se, he wus got to feed his cats. An' since de cats e't rats; he wus jes bleedged to raise heaps of corn an' meat, so as to make de rats come aroun', so as his cats could git deir livin'. An' den, since it wus de law dat de folks couldn' throw no vict-uals away; he would have to eat up w'at de rats didn' git so as to keep de laws lak good free folks should oughter. So Rab walked on off free, an' lef' his Mosser a sayin': De nex' time he do sumpin lak dat; he wus a gwineter put it in de bargain, dat dere wusnt to be no Nigger-slave-made riddles about it.

De gal's daddy tell Rab dat he sho wus "some punkin"; den he ax Horn to tell how he git free.

Horn, he up an' say dat he git free lakwise by his Mosser offerin' to set him free; if he could give 'im a riddle w'at he couldn' onravel.

Horn tell dat he wus out in de cornfiel', a wukin along wid de tother slaves; an' he handed out dis here riddle to his Mosser:

"No use a talkin!! No use a talkin!!
Dont dey think dey's some?
W'en he come, he no come;
W'en he no come, he come".

Horn say dat his Mosser chaw on dat 'ar riddle day an' night; but he couldn' make no mark on de hull, much less crack it open. So his Mosser make up his mind dat he wus jes one Nigger short; an' give de riddle up.

Den Horn tell 'im dat de riddle run lak dis: "Dere wusnt no use in ogifyin 'bout de p'int dat be black-bird an' de corn wus bofe to be studied 'bout; caze in you draps de corn in plantin' time an' de black-bird come an' git it, it no come up; but if de black-bird no come in plantin' time, den de corn, he come up an' grow."

Horn say dat his Mosser wus one of dem 'ar big mens w'at maked de laws. So he tell him to go free; but de nex' time he go to town, to set dem laws fer folkses down, dat he wus a gwineter bring it 'roun' to kill all dem—bofe good an' soun'—w'at hands out Nigger riddles, dey's done foun'.

Hun's daddy look at de boys; an' tell 'em dat wus w'at he called "Riddlin 'em Right!" So he dont see no reason 'g'inst takin 'em all in de

fambly; 'cep' dat he haint got but de one gal. He wus jes tickled to death
dat dey all knowed how to wuk in de cornfiel' an' have a plenty fer to
w'en it wus starvation times wid de huntin' free Niggers. He tell 'em w'en
deir crops wus laid by; dey could whirl in an' hunt lak de tother free
Niggers, an' wid it all put togedder dey'd git to be de bigges' dogs in de
bone-yard.

All dis bofe make de boys feel good an' didn' make 'em feel good;
caze dey knows dere haint no room fer mo' dan one of 'em in de fambly.
Dey knows dat somebody wus bleedged to git sacked; so dey axes de ole
man which one of 'em he wus a gwineter give de gal to.

De gal's daddy sot aroun' an' scratched his head; an' sayed dat he
didn hardly scacely know. He allow dat he lak 'em all; so he guess he'll
hafter sorter take de case to Hun, an' see which a way de wind blow.

Dis wus de way dat he wus a gwineter take de matter to Hun. Of
co'se, dey wus all bleedged fer to hunt, eben if dey did raise crops; so dat
dey could git to be put along in de Class wid de tother free Niggers. He
allows: W'en de free Niggers goes to hunt; dey dont hunt ev'rything. Some
hunts possums, some coons, some hunts one thing an' some anudder. So
dey mus' make up deir minds w'at dey wus a gwineter hunt, an' keep on
a huntin'; so dat dey can be put along in de Class wid de quality folkses.
Den dey mus' all give him a riddle apiece, wid w'at dey hunt fer de answer to it. Nex', he'll take dese here riddles to Hun. W'en Hun wus got de
riddles onraveled, an' knowed w'at each man wus a gwineter hunt, an'
knowed how good he could make up riddles; den she could say which
one she want, an' dat one can have her.

But an' if Hun caint make up her mind from de riddles; den she mus'
ax 'em all to do sumpin else so dat she can make up her mind which one
she want. Den her daddy close up de contrack by sayin': So as to treat
'em all fa'r an' squar'; dat w'at-some-ever she ax one to do, he'll make her
ax all of 'em to do.

De boys all holds up deir right hands an' crosses deir hearts so as to
sign de greements; den dey goes off an' takes a day to make up deir
minds w'at dey's a gwineter hunt an' keep on a huntin' so as to fix up deir
riddles fer de gal. De nex' day dey all comed back an' forked over deir
riddles to de ole man.

W'en Hun's daddy git de riddles; he go in an' tell her dat he wus got
three fine Nigger-bucks whar she can have de pick of 'em fer her ole man.
He gun out to her de names: Codger, Rab, an' Horn. But he tell her dat he
haint a gwineter p'int out to her who's named w'at. Yit an' still, she mus'
pick out her ole man by name. He say dat he want to give her a good
chance at 'em; so he wus a gwineter give her, along wid de names, a
riddle w'at wus got in it w'at each man hunt. In dis way; she can ravel out
de name, in onravelin de riddle.

De fust riddle he give over to her wus dis:

"Bucked out eyes, switch all white.
Runs all day, stays home at night."

Dis wus Rab's riddle; an' de answer wus "Rabbit". Rab say to Hun's daddy
dat he love rabbits, he ketch heaps of 'em, an' so he'll keep on a huntin'
rabbits.

De nex' riddle dat he dumped out to de gal wus:

"Wid its top so liddle de bush caint spread;
It run through de woods, wid a tree on its head."

Dis wus Horn's riddle an' it mean "A deer". Horn wus sayed to Hun's
daddy he wus done managed fer to kill heaps of deers; an' so he wus a
gwineter keep on a tryin' his hand wid dem.

De las' riddle dat Hun's daddy hand over to her wus:

"Eyes lak a barn doo',
Teef sharp, not flat;
Some can kill all dem tother things,
W'at caint kill dat."

Dis wus Codger's riddle; an' it mean "A pant'er". Codger wus tol' Hun's
daddy dat he wus done fought wid a pant'er an' kilt him single-handed.
Since dat time, he wus done l'art how to outsharp 'em w'en he git ready;
so he was maked up his mind fer to keep on a huntin' pant'ers.

W'en Hun's daddy git through a givin' her de riddles, she see w'at dey
all means in a liddle of no time. In dem days, de boys an' de gals wusnt
allowed to go 'roun' 'mongst one-nudder. Since Hun haint never yit had no
talk wid none of de boys, she dont know none of deir names; but she wus
done long ago cotch de scent of w'at wus in de air. She knowed de boys
wusnt a comin' fer to see her daddy, caze dey love him; an' she knowed dey
wust a comin' dar so much fer nothin'. She wus been a peepin' out through
de chinks in de cracks 'tween de logs of de walls of de cabin at 'em. She
wus crazy over de looks of Codger; but she dont know which one of de
names wus hisn w'at she wus done found in de riddles. So de nex' day w'en
her daddy comes an' axes her w'at name in de riddles she wus picked out;
she make answer dat he haint picked out none yit. She say he mus' give her
mo' time fer to onwind it all an' git lt straight.

Bymeby, de fust day of May come on; an' Hun took de lookin'-glass,
an' slipped off down to de well in de middle of de day fer to look in dar
an' see de man dat she should oughter marry. W'en she git to de well, she

hold de lookin'-glass behin' an' above her head; an' in dis way she manage to throw de light clean down to de bottom of de water in de well. Den she look in; an' who should she see but Codger'

Now, she knowed w'en you sees de one you's to marry; dey'll put in deir dispearunce, if you calls deir names. So Hun 'gin to call off de names of de three boys w'at she wus got outn de riddles; An' w'en she say "Codger", de man in de well fade away an' go out. Den Hun know dat de boy dat she want wus named "Codger".

Four mont's or such a matter atter dis, Hun's daddy say to her dat she take a mighty long time to choose which one of de boys dat she want fer her ole man from de riddles. So he think dat she'd better oughter tell him sumpin.

Hun allowed to her daddy: She dont blieve in none o' dis here puttin' of jes a liddle bit of de dinner on de table at a time, an' a eatin' it up bite by bite lak de white folks. She blieve in puttin' all de grub on de table at one clip, an' a sorter sayin': "Pass it lak you pleases"

Her daddy ax her fer to splain herself.

Hun den tell him dat she mean lak dis: Dat w'en she go to hand out de answer; she wus a spectin to pick de one she want by name, by riddle, an' by ev'rything else—all at one mouf-full. She say: Of co'se she wus got de names an' de riddles to pick from; but she think dat he should oughter let her hear all de boys talk a liddle, caze she want her ole man to be a good conbersationer; an' she want to put dat in de pickin'. She dont want no man w'at talk so sildom, dat de winter come on an' freeze up de words befo' he can git 'em outn his mouf.

Hun's daddy allows to her dat he dont know 'bout dat. But he wus a gwineter take her mammy, an' go on a visit to her Uncle Si; an' whilst he wus up dar, he wus a gwineter talk dat over wid him. He say dat her Uncle Si wus done gone an' raised ten gals an' married 'em all off; so he should oughter know w'at wus best in ginerally to be done in setch cases. Atter he come back from talkin' wid her Uncle Si; he'll let her know 'bout hearin' de boys.

De nex' day, Hun's daddy go an' git anudder free gal by de name of Babe to come an stay all night wid her; whilst he an' her mammy go up an' stay all night wid her Uncle Si. Babe come over about dinner time, dat day, atter Hun's mammy an' daddy wus gone.

W'en Babe git dar, Hun up an' tell her all 'bout how her daddy wus got her a choosin a ole man fer herself by means of a riddle. She tell her how she wus found out de names of de one she lak by lookin' in de well on de fust day of May. But she dont know w'at riddle beslongs to Codger; an' she want her to subgest some way fer her to find dat out.

Babe subgest fust one thing an' den de tother; but nothin' dont look to 'em lak it mought wuk good. But at las' she look out an' see de new moon;

an' den she tell Hun she wus got a plan w'at would give her de riddle w'at Codger sont in. She say dey mus' git up "A Dumb Supper", dat night.

Hun say: "Yes, dat soun' jes fine' But dey caint have no Dumb Supper onless dey can git five folkses to set de table. It take a big crowd an' a odd number fer to set a Dumb Supper. "Two's comp'ny an' three's a crowd"; more dan three is a big crowd; an' five is de fust odd lot to count up to a crowd bigger dan a crowd. So it make a big crowd.

Babe den say she dont know nowhars whar dey can git three mo' gals so as to sit 'nough to fix up de love feast.

Hun allows to Babe dat maybe dey can fix it up so ss to git three mo' gals by gittin some slave gals. Dey can go over to Kyernel Jackson Snapper's house, tell de Missus up dar dat dey wus sorter skeard to stay at home all night by deirselves, pitch in an' help de slave gals to git through wid deir wuk in de Big House, an' den ax fer 'em to come an' stay all night wid 'em.

Babe an' Hun do dis, an' Missus Jackson Snapper let 'em have de three slave gals fer comp'ny; beance Hun's mammy and daddy wus gone off fer de night. So all five of de gals go over to Hun's house; an' on de way over, Hun tell de slave gals 'bout de Dumb Supper dat she want to make so as to l'arn w'at riddle Codger wus sont in. Dey wus all ig [eager] fer de supper too; caze all of 'em wus got sumpin dat dey want to know lakwise. De slave gals wus named May, June, an' Sooky.

In de Dumb Supper, nobody caint say no nothin whilst it's a gittin fixed; an' atter it wus git fixed, dey mus' set down in a row on de floo', on de side of de room whar de moon rise, sine deir hands, an' set dar a sayin' nothin'. Den along 'bout midnight, de one w'at a gal is a gwineter marry will come in an' set down at de plate w'at de gal wus done put on de table. De doo' to de cabin, whar dey gives de Dumb Supper, mus' be lef' open; so dat de sweethearts'll know dat dey're welcome, or dey wont come in. If some of dem, w'at is a givin' de Dumb Supper, haint a gwineter git married; den sumpin else 'sides a man will come in, an' set down at de plate, an' den go out. If some of de gals, w'at is a givin de Dumb Supper, is already married; den sumpin will come to de plate w'at will show w'at changes is a gwineter take place, if deres a gwineter be changes.

De gals give de Supper dis way: Dey fust jined deir hands an' lifted 'em up an' down togedder five times, caze dere wus five of 'em. Den dey all goes out to make a wush to de new moon 'bout w'at dey wants fer to come to deir plate; widout utterin' one mumblin word. All dese gals wush to de moon dat de one w'at dey wus to marry mought come to deir plate—all 'cep' June. June—one of de slave gals—wus already jumped de broomstick; an' she jes want to know her chances fer keepin' her ole man, caze she wus skeard dat de white folks wus a gwineter sell him. De ole Missus an' ole Mosser wus got so dat dey didn' fancy him much; caze he dont want to let his liddle bitsy Missuses an' Mossers (de white folkses' liddle chilluns) whoop him.

So dey all maked deir wushes to de moon, den dey spit on a chip as' throwed it back'ards over de right shoulder widout lookin' to see whar it fall; an' walked on away so as to make de wush come true. Hun make de wush dat de one, she love an' should oughter marry, mought come in wid de skin of de varmint, w'at wus in his riddle, throwed across his shoulders. In dat way, she hope to l'arn which wus Codger's riddle.

Atter dey makes deir wishes; dey goes about fixin' de Dumb Supper. Fust dey took off deir shoes an' got in deir stockin' feets, so dat deir walkin couldn' make no noise. Den dey goes out in de gyardin an' pulls some pop-corn, an' brings it up to de cabin an' shells it; widout sayin' one word an' widout makin' no noise.

All de settins on de table have to be white. Dey darfo' takes a big white sheet an' so puts it on de table as to kiver it clean down to de floo'. Den dey went out to de wood-pile an' got some liddle pieces of white ash wood. Dey den whittled from dese here pieces of white wood, a knife apiece an' a sharp-p'inted stick fer a fork. Dey put dese at de plates fer white knives an' forks.

Nex', dey pops de pop-corn nice an' white. Den dey took some nice white rags an' maked a lamp-wick, an' put white lard on it, on a white saucer, wid a white rock close to de end of de wick to make it not burn nowhars 'cep' on de end. Dey lit dis here light an' sot it on de middle of de table; an' maked a low bow to it widout sayin' nothin. Dey lit a white candle, w'at de slave gals wus brung wid 'em from de white folkses house; an' sot it on a board stuck in 'twixt de logs of de cabin, so as to make shore fer to keep de lights a gwine. W'en dis wus all done, each one of de gals took a plate, put some white pop-corn on it, an' sot it on de table wid de white wood knife an' fork a lyin' on de plate. Den each one took a chair an' sot to de plate w'at she wus done put on de table.

At las' dey all sot down on de floo', side by side, on de side o' de cabin whar de moon wus riz. Den dey jined hands, an' sot dar widout sayin' nothin'; an' waited to see w'at dey'd see. Dey all grit deir teef so as not to make no noise, caze it's a life-time bad luck to make a noise atter de table's done been sot fer a Dumb Supper. Dem w'at set de Supper is bleedged fer to keep still ontel sumpin come to de plates; or ontel de day break de nex' mawnin.

Dey all sot dar. Once in a while dey could hear sumpin a hissin', whilst de wind wus a blowin' through de tree-tops outside, lak somebody a hushin' up deir chilluns w'en dey wants 'em to keep still. —"Sh—'. Sh—!" Den dey hears sumpin rattle lak somebody wus a walkin' 'roun' un'er de house. Once in a while, de doo', w'at wus a a stan'in' open, would sorter move an' crack, lak sumpin dat you couldn' see wus a wantin' to shet it. De gals sot dar an' kep' still.

Bymeby, a big gush o' wind come in de doo'. De candle an' de lamp flickered lak dey wus a gwineter go out; an' de knife an' fork rattle an' jump aroun' on June's plate (de gal w'at wus married) lak dey wus a gwineter jump offn de table. Whilst de knife an' de fork wus a cuttin up deir capers on June's plate; de ole rooster, out in de hen-house, w'at wus a settin' in front of de cabin doo', he crow out three times, he do: "Koo-Kookoo-koo—! Koo-Kookoo-koo—! Koo-Kookoo-koo—!"

Dis make 'em all feel mighty bad. Dey sot dar an' dey caint say nothin'; but dey all ricomembers de sayin' of de ole Witch 'oman w'at wus de fust to l'arn how fer to set a Dumb Supper. De ole Which say:

> "W'en de rooster crow,
> In front o' de doo';
> Her ole man's gwineter be no mo'!"

Dey wus all powerful sorry fer poo' June; caze dey knows dat de white folks is a gwineter sell her ole man, or he wus a gwineter die.

De wind blow a liddle mo'; an' sumpin outdoors say: "Sh—! Sh—!" It sound lak somebody a hushin' up deir chilluns. Den, a blackish big-moufed bird fly in an' peck at May's plate; an' turn right aroun' an' fly out!

All deir eyes git filled up wid water; an' dey helt May's hands tighter, caze dey knowed dat dey wusnt a gwineter have her aroun' 'mongst 'em much longer. De ole Witch 'oman w'at sot de fust Dumb Supper sayed:

> "W'en de bird flies in, an' picks at de plate;
> She's soon a gwineter leave ole Mosser's gate."

Poo' June wush dat she mought a set May's plate too, 'sides her own; caze den she think, w'en de white folks sell her ole man, she mongst a got sol' along wid 'im.

Terreckly, sumpin a flyin' aroun' in de wind talk ag'in an' say: "Sh—' Sh—" Den in come a great big black bob-tailed dog! He r'ared up, an' smelt Sooky's plate; den he turned aroun' an' trotted out widout makin' no noise wid his footses. Poo' Sooky drapped her head down on May's lap; an' stuffed her big checked apron into her mouf to keep from a makin' a noise an' a havin' bad luck w'at liddle time she wus got to live! She wus already got de grave-yard cough. One day she wus out in de woods a nursin' her Mosser's chilluns an' a givin' 'em fresh air. A big rain come up; an' she took off her top-clo'es fer to wrop 'em up in so as to keep 'em from a gittin' wet. She herself got soaked an' drenched; an' she wus been a coughin' wid de grave-yard cough [tuberculosis] ever since. Dey all calls to deir membunce de words of de ole Which 'oman, w'at maked de fust Dumb Supper. She say:

"W'en de black dog come by de light of de moon;
You's a gwineter be a lyin' in a black box soon'."

But dey all sot dar an' kep' still.

Bymeby, sumpin hiss ag'in: "Sh—! Sh—!" Den a big yaller cat wid big yaller eyes walk in de doo" It step along widout makin' no noise an' sump right up on Babe's plate. It sot dar fer a good while; den drapped down on de floo' widout makin no noise lak a bunch of cotton, an' passed on out lak a shadder!

W'en dey all seed de cat, dey well-nigh fergit offn deir minds all de bad things dat dey wus done seed; an' dey hafter pinch deirselves to keep from a laughin' whilst de Supper wus a gwine on, caze in dat way dey would bring awful bad luck on deirselves.

You sees: Babe wus one of dem 'ar gals w'at wus always a dotin an' a braggin' 'bout her fellers. Dat ole Which 'oman w'at maked de fust Dumb Supper wus lakwise left some words fer Babe's plate. Dey goes lak dis:

"An' de yaller cat sot by de plate an' stayed?
Well, she's a gwineter be dat ugly ole maid!"

W'en dey sorter sot settled down ag'in; dey sot dar anxious an' a waitin' fer to see w'at wus a gwineter come to de las' plate, which wus Hun's plate. At las' sumpin' make de hush-up sound ag'in outside. It talk it out three times instid o' two: "Sh—! Sh—! Sh—!" A liddle while atter dis, sumpin lak a liddle white cloud look lak it come in through de doo'. It move across de room to Hun's plate; an' it stan' dar. Atter a little while it 'gin to take on de shape of a man. Terreckly de dimness all leave; an' dar stood Codger wid a pant'er's skin throwed aroun' his shoulders.

Den Hun knowed dat de riddle, w'at her daddy wus brung her from de boys, w'at mean "Pant'er" beslonged to him. In a minute or so de haziness 'gin to come back; an' terreckly dere wus a cloud at de plate ag'in. Den dis cloud drift outn de doo' an' go on away jes lak it wus comed. It lef' Hun a feelin' as chipper as a mockin'-bird; caze she want to marry Codger; an' now she knowed bofe de name an' de riddle to choose from her daddy so as to git him.

Whilst dey wus all a lookin' at dar 'ar randsome tantsome good-lookin stick-a-ma-stew [an individual of importance] a setin' at Hun's plate, dey ricomembers de words lef' by de ole Which 'oman fer dis sort of thing, w'en she wus sot dat fust Dumb Supper. De words go:

"Ringlum-tinglum; shine new moon'!
He's a gwinter marry dat gal soon."

W'en de las' one of de comp'ny to de Dumb Supper git gone; de gals sot up offn de floo', an' put deir hands up an' down fogedder five times. Den de Dumb Supper wus over.

It wus almos' day-break; an' so de gals makes up deir minds not to go to bed. Dey shets de doo' to de cabin, an' clears ev'rything away; den Hun begin to cook sumpin fer deir breakfus. Whilst she wus a cookin' de tothers talk a liddle over de Dumb Supper. June say dat she git sick at heart w'en de rooster fust crow, caze she knowed dat her ole man wus bound fer to be sold; but she wus been thought it all over, an' she feel all right now. She now see dat de bes' of friends mus' part. She wus some time ago talked de partin' over wid her ole man. Dey wus done promused one-nudder not never to marry no mo'; so dat dey could jine hands togedder ag'in in Heaben never to part no mo'. Dat make it all right.

May say: Well, it dont make no diffunce no way much 'bout her bein' sold; caze she haint got no folks nowhars fer to grieve over on her part, nor none nowhars fer to grieve atter her atter she's gone. She haint never had no mammy an' daddy as she knows of; an', de tother day, she wus heared a smart white man a tellin' her Missus dat Niggers wusnt got no souls no ways; so now she wus all right, caze she wus now in hopes dat w'en she die, dat would be de las' of her. All she want was to git dead right quick so dat it wouldn' hurt too much. She end her palaver by sayin'; dat de bein' sol' dont bother her no mo'.

W'en May sit through wid her big talk; Sooky (w'at wus sick) shame her 'bout w'at she say. She tell her dat it wus bad 'nough fer to be a slave; but it wus a heaps wusser to die an' go down to de "Bad Place". She jes should oughter a been at de Meetin' House las' Sunday night; an' a heared de Parson a tellin' 'bout de Devil a burnin' de wicked folkses an' a turnin' 'em over in de red-hot embers wid his blazin' pitch-fork' She tell May dat she'd better leave off her wicked ways an' try fer to git to de "Good Place".

She den say to 'em all: W'en she drapped her head in May's lap, an' stuffed her apron in her mouf; it wus to stop up de stream of shoutin', an' not to shet off de drops of tears. She wus a Heaben-born soldier; an', though she dont want no bad luck from a makin' a noise at a Dumb Supper, she haint skeared to die. She wus a gwineter sleep away easy; caze de Lawd wus done died fer her. She close her talk by sayin': She hate to leave de liddle white chilluns; caze deir mammy, w'at wus her Missus, didn' never pay no 'tention to 'em 'cep' to kiss 'em once atter she wus cleaned 'em up. She wus awful skeard dat dey'd go aroun' all de time all stuffed up full o' colds, and sick.

Babe tell 'em dat she wusnt a carin' much if she do git to be a ole maid; if she can jes keep on a havin Hun fer a friend. Den Hun break in, an' say dat her bein' a friend ontel doomsday wus all fixed; an' dat wus de end of dat!

Dey all axed Hun who wus dat feller w'at wus comed to her plate?

She tell 'em fer to wait an' see; she's a gwineter ax 'em all in, w'en she git married. By dis time de Breakfus wus ready. Dey all sot down, an' e't togedder, an' den went on off home.

Along about Dinner time, Hun's mammy an' daddy come home from her Uncle Si's house. W'en dey got dar; Hun wus got de dinner all ready; an' she tell 'em to come in an' have sumpin t'eat, whilst she give bofe de riddle an' de name of de boy w'at she want to marry.

De ole man wus sorter sprised; an' he tell Hun dat he wus skeared dat she wus been a stealin' a peep in on 'im an' a seein' de boys.

Hun raise up her han' an' cross her heart an' hope she may drop dead dat dis wusnt so.

Den her daddy tell her; he think it wus best, atter talkin it all over wid her Uncle Si, to let each one of de boys come in an' tell her a tale lak she wus axed fer. Atter she wus heared de tales; she can choose her ole man from de riddles, tales, an' all. If she git 'em all put togedder right, she can marry de boy w'at dey happens to hit; but if she mix 'em all up, she caint marry nobody. So he tell her to git ready to hear de boys de nex' day; but he's a gwineter stay in de room all de time w'en dey come, so as to see to it dat none of 'em dont tell her deir names or deir riddles.

W'en de nex' say come, de ole man sot in de room wid Hun whar de boys wus to come in; an' de ole 'oman stayed outs-side to send de boys in, one at de time. De fust one to git sont in wus Codger. Though he wus a great big strappin boy; w'en he git in; he wus dat shame-faced dat he drapped his hat. Hun, she picked up de hat an' handed it to 'im; an' axed him to have a chair.

W'en Hun's daddy see dis; he telled de young gemmun fer to jes wait a minute, caze he mus' see de gal in de tother room a liddle while. W'en he git her in de tother room; he tell her dat she should not oughter a never picked up de young gemmun's hat, w'en he wus drapped it; caze dat mean dat she want to marry him. He ax her haint she never done heared de ole sayin' dat "So-an'-so" would marry "So-an'-so" at de drap of his hat? Hun say: "Yes". He tell her: Well, in de ole days, dat wus de way dat de women folkses tell de mens dat wants to marry 'em. W'en de man drap his hats de 'oman pick it up.

Hun allow to 'im dat she haint never hearn tell of dat befo'.

Her daddy tell her dat he wus awful sorry fer dis. She mus' now go back into de room, an' ax de young gemmun fer to rest his hat; an' take it an' lay it on de bed botom-side up'ards, so as to let him know dat she jes pick up de hat fer perliteness. Dey den goes back into de room; an' Hun do all her daddy wus told her.

W'en dey sits all settled down good; her daddy tell de young gemmuns dat he wus made up his mind fer to let Hun hear 'em all talk a liddle befo' she pick 'em by de riddles an' names which she dont know. He think dat de bes' way wus fer so let each an' all of 'em tell some sort of a liddle huntin' tale.

Codger up an' 'spon': Well, here it comes! One time he went out a huntin'; an' he met up wid a pant'er w'at hat had her liddle baby pant'er along wid her. Of co'se, de ole pant'er wus skeard dat he wus a gwineter git her baby; so she come at his wid her claws an' mouf stretched! He runned aroun' an' aroun' a tree wid de pant'er right atter him. He keep on a runnin' an' de pant'er keep on a follerin'. Atter while he git his sharp keen butcher-knife outn its case. Den he runned a liddle faster aroun' de tree. Terreckly he gain 'nough on her in de runnin' of de circle fer to ketch her by de tail. He cotched de tail, throwed it over a low swingin' lim', jerked de ole pant'er up a swingin' offn de groun', stuck in de knife behin' de fore shoulder an' dar she wus as dead as a doo' nail.

He skint her an' took de baby pant'er on home wid him an' put it in a chicken coop in de house fer to raise. Dat night ole man pant'er come a trailin' up to his house; an' a lookin' fer hie ole 'oman an' his baby. At dat time he wusnt got no setch dogs as he wus den got. He didn't have nothin' but a liddle feist-dog; an' he wus bleedged fer to take it into de house to keep de pant'ers from a ketchin it. Dis here dog wus jes skeard to death w'en-so-ever it hear or see a pant'er; an' it jes runned wid its tail tucked 'tween its legs an' shivered all over.

Ole man pant'er would come ev'ry night; an' since he didn' hand de baby pant'er outside to him, he would jes take a chicken or so an' a pig fer spite an' den go on away. Dis here grabbin' an' nabbin by ole man pant'er look lak it wus a gwineter break up all his prospects; so he sot down to think how he mought keep de ole feller from hoakin him outn house an' home.

He go an' dig a hole in de groun' about as big as a liddle wash kittle; an' he tied up his liddle dog by de side of dis here hole. Nex' he sot a wood-flatform over de hole wid a trigger un'er it lak a dead-fall; an' he tied a long string to de trigger. Den he go to de house an' git ole lady pant'er's skin an' wrop up in it. Atter dat he come out wid his face all kivered; an' make a noise lak a pant'er. He holler out: "Hoo—! wee—!"

W'en de liddle dog looked up an' seed de pant'er skin, he almos' took a fit. Of co'se he wus tied an' couldn' git away. So at las' he jumped down in de hole; an' he (Codger) pulled de trigger, an' de wood flatform fall an' kiver de dog up. He keep dis up ontel de dog would sump right in de hole, de minute he see a pant'er skin.

Atter dis w'en night come on; he took away de wood flatform, an' sot a big rock dead-fall over de hole whar he wus got de dog tied. He den took de end of de string tied to de trigger through a crack to de inside of his cabin; an' sot down to watch.

Bymeby, ole Mr. Pant'er come. He see de liddle dog an' start fer 'im. De dog dart down in de holes an' jes as de pant'er git his head un'er de rock a gwine atter him, he (Codger) pulled de trigger an' dar laid Mr. Pant'er wid his head mashed off! He skint him an' took de skin to de house, an' wus got it dar now.

Codger say: He den took de baby pant'er an' raised it ontel it got to be a great big grown one. At las', one day, a frien' of hisn comed along wid his big dog; an' offer to bet his whole plantation dat his dog could whoop his pant'er. Now Codger say he wus jes been a figgerin all along on only gittin a extra pant'er skin fer all his troubles wid de baby; but he maked up his mind dat a whole pant'er skin wusnt wo'th nigh so much to him as a good plantation. So he bet him.

Dey put up deir plantations—de man to take de extra plantation w'at win. Dey den dug a big hole in de groun' an' kivered it over; den dey put de dog an' de pant'er down in de hole an' kivered 'em over fer to fight it out.

Setch anudder fightin' you haint never hearn tell of in all yo' born days! Bofe mens sot aroun' a lissenin at de bitin an' de scratchin' ontel atter while ev'rything git still an' dey dont hear nothin'. W'en dey knowed dat de fight wus all over an' de plantation won; dey onkivered de hole, to look in an' see w'at man wus de lucky duck. W'en dey wus looked in; dey didn' see nothin. —Bofe of 'em wus done e't one-nudder up' So Codger end up his tale by sayin: He jes farm an' hunt now. He dont never bet no mo', caze he wus done los' a whole good pant'er skin a doin' dat.

W'en Codger riz fer to go outn de room; de ole man telled him dat he wus a genuwine race-hoss a switchin' a mighty fine tail; but he reckin dat he'll hafter let him go an' bring in some wheel-hosses so as to see how hard dey can pull a totin a straight tail un'er de crack of de whup.

Codger thank him, an' tell him dat dis dont worry him none; caze w'en de hosses wus called dey dont never come 'cordin' to runnin' an' pullin' but 'cordin' to deir names; an' he wus a hopin' dat Hun would call de right name.

W'en Codger go out; de ole 'oman nex' sen' Rab in. De ole man tol' Rab dat he wus called him in to tell a tale; so as to git de gal in good sperits fer to choose de one w'at she want to marry from de riddles an' de names. So he ax him to crack away wid his tale.

Rab say: One day, he went out a rabbit huntin'. He took his big rabbit-dogs an' his liddle feist-dog along wid 'im. De dogs jumped up one of dese here ole long-legged gray grave-yard rabbits. Now, w'en a grave-yard rabbit git in de grave-yard; he jes put in his dispearunce lak any udder hant. So he knowed dat he wus got to keep him outn de grave-yard if he want to ketch him at 'tall. So he put his big dogs atter de rabbit; an' he hung aroun' de grave-yard wid de liddle feist dog fer to head him off from dar.

Ev'ry once in a while, de grave-yard rabbit would take out fer de grave-yard; but him an' de feist dog would head him off. De rabbit keep on a tryin' fer to git into de grave-yard an' de feist keep on a headin him off. Bymeby de big dogs git de rabbit about runned down; an' he crawled up inside of a holler log an' curled up in dar. De big dogs tracked him up an' treed him. So he (Rab) go to de log whar de big dogs wus got de rabbit hemmed up. W'en he wus got dar, he cut hisself a long, pronged hick'ry wythe to twis' him out wid. He got de twis' on him an' pulled him out. So dar he stood wid his grave-yard rabbit!

Now, dat he wus got him; he knowed de bes' thing to do, so as to keep him, wus to kill him right den an' dar. So he hopped up on top of de log, an' hit de rabbit's ag'in' it so as to kill him. W'en he lammed de head ag'in de log; it flew off a hunderd yards an' kilt seben pattridges! W'en he looked down at de rabbit, de body wus all gone; an' dere wusnt nothin' lef' of him cep de right behime foot in his hand. So he went an' picked up de seben dead pattridges; an' sticked de rabbit's foot in his jacket pocket fer good luck an' went on home.

Whilst Rab wus a tellin' dis part of de tale; he pult de foot of de grave-yard rabbit outn his pocket, an' showed it to 'em. W'en he do dis, de ole man tell him dat he think dat he'd better stop; caze w'en de chicken wus good seasoned, it wouldn' do to add no mo' pepper an' salt. Rab thank him; an' bow hisself outn de room lak de quality white folkses.

De ole 'oman sont Horn in las' fer to tell his tale. Horn say: Well, he plant him a corn-patch, an' put him up a big tall picket fence all aroun' it so as to keep de deers outn it. But de deers, dey keep on a pushin an' a breakin in at de gate.

Dere wus a great big tree a stan'in' by de gate. So he got him a great big rock an' clum up in de tree; an' hid hisself. Bymeby Mr. Deer come to break in de corn-patch as fer common. He drapped de big rock down, an' it butted Mr. Deer in de head an' kilt him. He skint dis one; an' took him home fer grub.

Den, atter dis, de deers jes keep on a comin'; an' he jes keep' on a killin' ontel he wus got mo' meat dan Chyarter wus got oats. Bymeby it come to de p'int dat he haint got no use fer no mo' meat; an' he git tired of killin' 'em. So he clumb up an' hid in de top of de tree wid his pockets chug-full of peach-seeds. Atter dis, w'en de deers would come; he would throw an' knock 'em in de head wid two peach seeds. He throwed de peach seeds so hard dat dey sticked in de heads of de deers w'at come: so dis make 'em all run off wid deir heads planted wid a peach seeds.

Nex' Spring dese here peach .seeds all sprouted an growed up peach trees on de heads of all de deers. Dese peach trees on de deers' heads dont never have no leaves on 'em: caze de leaves wus all got knocked off from de deers a runnin' through de woods.

W'en Horn git to dis p'int in de tale; de gal's daddy stop him an' tell him dat'll do. He say: W'en a man show dat he wus made de animuls over, he think he wus close 'nough up wid de Lawd to stop.

Horn allow dat he mus' railly scuse him; he didn' mean to git up in de Lawd's seat; he wus jes aimed fer to git up high 'nough to make him an' de gal want him.

Hun's daddy tell him dat dis make ev'rything all right; but de gal wusnt a gwineter choose neider high up nor low down; she wus a gwineter choose her ole man by de riddles an' by de names. So Horn lef.

De nex' week, de gal's daddy give a big dance; an' w'en he han' out de invite he tell 'em all: Hun wus a gwineter choose her ole man by de riddles, an' by de names at de end of de party. De three boys wus to be dar; an' if de guess wus right fer one of 'em, dey wus to git married dar an' den an' de boy wus to take her on off home wid him.

De dance come off at de 'p'inted time. Dey danced reels, jigs, break-downs, an' all dem tother things ontel de chickens 'gin to crow fer day-light nex' mawnin. Den Hun's daddy make all de folkses form a circle wid him an' Hun an' de preacher in de middle, an' de three boys on de out-side. W'en dey wus got de circle all fixed up, Hun's daddy holler out:

"Ridlum, ridlum, ridlum, right'
Choose yo' man fer life to-night"'

Den Hun answer: "Pant'er!—Codger!"

W'en dey all finds out dat Hun wus got all de answers in one, an' all right; dey tells Horn an' Rab to pick up Codger an' bring him into de middle of de ring, which wus 'cordin' to de ways of dem times. You sees: It wus de rule in dem days dat; w'en heaps of boys want to marry de same gal, an' one of 'em git her; de tothers mus' pick him up, an' tote him into de middle of de ring to show dey wus all still good friends widout no bad feelings 'mongst 'em.

Horn an' Rab lugged Codger into de ring an' sot him down by de side of Hun. Den dey bowed to 'em bofe; an' went an' took deir places in de circle wid de tothers.

Den all dem w'at wus in de circle danced an' sung:

"It's hard to love, yes indeed 'tis.
It's hard to be broke up in mind.
You's all lugged up in somebody's heart;
But you haint a gwineter lug up in mine".

Atter dis, Hun an' Codger j'ined hands an' jumped de broomstick back'ards; an' de preacher tell 'em dat dey wus hitched, j'ined, an' mar-ried. De party broke up an' dey all went home.

Hun an' Codger lakwise go home to deir cabin; an' beance dey wus some of de "Big-to-do", Codger whirl in an' throw up anudder room to de house. So dey lived in a big fine house wid two rooms to it. A liddle atter dis; Codger took a notion dat de dirt floo' in de house wusnt good 'nough fer Hun. So he pitched in an' split some prutty long straight logs into pun-

cheons. Den he got him a draw knife an' shmoved de flat side of de pun-
cheons off; an' put down a nice shmove puncheon floo' instid of a dirt
floo'. Mon! It wus a "Joe-darter!"'

W'en deir chilluns git up to be a liddle of no size; dey combed deir
heads, fixed 'em up, an' put clo'es on 'em all over. (—Of co'se dey
mought a gone bar'-footed a liddle w'en it wus warm wedder.) Ev'rything
move along wid de fambly as shmove an' as sweet as honey.

Horn an' Rab play big lak dey wusnt hurt. (Maybe dey wus, an'
maybe dey wusnt.) But bofe of 'em turn out to be ole bachelors; an' live
off in a house togedder by deirselves.

One day atter all o' Codger's crops wus laid by; he went out a huntin'.
He dispear, dat day; an' nobody haint never seed him no mo' from dat day
clean down to dis one. Dey looked from de swamps to de hills, an' from de
hills to de mud-holes an' sink-holes; but he wusnt nowhars to be found. At
fust, Hun an' her chilluns wus almos' 'stracted; but atter while dey managed
fer to pull deir minds togedder. De neighbors wus all mighty good to 'em;
an' dey went in an' sot up wid 'em ev'ry night ontel bed-time. Horn an' Rab
went an' sot up an' talked wid de fambly along wid de tother neighbors.

Atter Codger wus been gone fer about a year, de neighbors prutty
well nigh quit a gwine an' a settin up wid de fambly at night; but Horn an'
Rab sorter keep de path, a leadin' up dat way, worked into a liddle slushy
loblolly. How-some-ever dey quit off a walkin' along dat muddy path
togedder; w'en dey fix up an' go over to see Hun. Bofe of 'em 'gin to set
up to Hun an' try to court her. Dis time, dere wusnt no riddles an' no
daddy in de way; caze Hun wus been married an' wus her own 'oman.

She caint make up her mind dat Codger wus clean gone; so she dont
know 'bout lakin Horn an' Rab too much. So w'en dey drives up deir
fowls fer sale; she sorter put 'em off a liddle while longer fer de coops to
git a liddle mo' emptier.

Bofe of 'em, at las', make up deir minds dat it was jes a matter of
who'd be smart 'nough fer to ax her straight out to have him fust. So bofe
of 'em maked up deir minds onbeknowance to de tother one to go over
an' ax her fer to marry him.

W'en night come on, Horn tell Rab dat he wus a gwineter go over an'
pay his 'spects to de Widder, Miss Hun.

Rab say: Dat wus all right . De house wus good 'nough fer him. So
Horn go on off to see her. W'en he got dar she axed him in, an' took his
hat, an' tol' him to set down by de fire. She sot down dar wid ' em an' dey
'gun to talk.

Jes atter Horn leave home, Rab s lipped off an' went to Hun's house too;
an' he hid outside in de chimbly corner fer to lissen to 'em talk. Hun an'
Horn sot up dar an' runned on wid one-nudder an' had mo' fun dan you
could shake a stick at. Rab, he lay low in de chimbly corner an' lissen.

Bymeby Horn think 'twus 'bout time fer him to ax Hun to marry him. Fust, he sorter halt talkin a liddle while, den he open up: "Is you a flyin' lark or a settin dove?"

But Hun, instid o' answerin' "Is a flyin' lark, my Honey, Love!" lak folkses answers fer common w'en dey wants to marry;up an' say: "I's a mournin' dove fer my Honey, Love!"

Well dis here answer sorter hol' up Horn fer a liddle, an' make him know dat he caint git to marry her den; but he want to see if he wus got any hopes of gittin her. So he push his question a liddle furder an' say: "Is you a bird o' one fedder or a bird o' two?"

Den Hun give a answer ag'in w'at put him off; but lef' him wid hopes. She say: "W'en it be two fedders, it mought be you." Atter dat Horn say: He reckin it wus 'bout time dat he wus a gwine.

Rab hear all dis out-side in de chimbly corner; an' he lit out lak a streak fer home. He got dar some time befo' Horn; an' went on to bed. Horn come in atter he git through "Moonin", [Moonin' = courting] an' go to bed too.

Nex' night, Rab tell Horn dat he reckin dat he'd better go up an' talk wid Codger's widder for a liddle while. Horn say: All right; he'll stay in de shack, an' see to it dat de rats dont come in an' tote it off whilst he's gone.

So Rab go on off to Hun's house; but he wusnt more 'an got settled down dar good wid her by de fire, befo' Horn wus dar outside in de chimbly corner a lissenin to 'em. Rab an' Hun talk along about ole times; an' look lak dey wus enjoyin' deirselves monstus well.

Terreckly Rab tell Hun dat de times right den mought go on jes as good as de ole times, if she wus a mind fer to "go a fishin"; ["Go a fishin" = set out in search for a husband] den he ax her if she wus a fishin. She make answer to 'im: No, not zackly; but she wus got de pole an' line, an' she mought bait it fer de right kind of man. Den he tell her dat he wus skeard dat she wus a fishin' fer Horn. Hun say to him: Oh no, mussy' Horn wus one of dem 'ar sucker fishes w'at dont bite fer to git cotched. If she go a fishin', she wus a gwineter fish fer cat-fish w'at take a hold on de bait lak dey means sumpin, lak somebody w'at wusnt so fur away.

When Hun tell Rab dis; he hafter retch down an' pinch hisself to see whedder dat it wus him or somebody else w'at wus dar. Den he say to her: If she'll jes holler out "Fishin!" dat he know somebody w'at would holler out "Cotched"! befo' she wus able fer to git de word out good.

Hun tell him: She caint holler it out right den; but fer him to keep on a comin' back to see her, an' he mought git sprised sometime befo' he knowed it.

Well, Horn hear all dis palaver; an' he pick hisself up outn de chimbly corner outside an' mozey on off home to bed. He wus blue mad'

Atter while w'en de chickens 'gin to crow fer day; Rab mope on off home too. It wus so late w'en he got dar dat he didn' go to bed; he jes sot up an' napped by de fire ontel daylight.

W'en day wus got good broke, Horn got up; an' him an' Rab rushed aroun' an' got up a liddle Breakfus for deirselves. Dey den sot down to eat. Whilst dey wus a settin' dar an' a boltin' deir victuals; Horn, he sorter open up liddle by liddle. He tell Rab dat dey wus always been friends; an' friends mus' be friends. Den he give 'way how he wus been out in de chimbly corner; an' w'at he hear him an' Hun say.

W'en Horn git through; Rab open up an' tell him 'bout his gwine to dat ve'y same chimbly corner on de night befo', an' w'at all he wus heared. Den dey bofe look at one-nudder an' git taken wid de dry-grins.

W'en dey wus managed fer to git shed of deir dry-grins; Horn open up ag'in. He talk an' he talk, he splain an' he splain lak one of dese here Philermerdelphy lawyers. At las' he ax Rab how it 'twus dat he didn ' see whilst Hun wus a gabbin wid 'im dat she wus jes a tryin fer to make a fool outn bofe of 'em.

Rab tell Horn dat he wus jes zackly right; but he jes natchully love dat 'oman so much, at dat time, caze she suit him so, dat he didn' neider see nor know nothin'. Bofe of 'em den jine togedder in sayin' dat Hun wus de meanest w'at-'is-name dat ever crawled de top o' dirt! She wus done already socked 'em bofe an' wus got married to somebody else, w'en dey wus all boys. Now, she wus a prankin'; an' a tryin' fer to make gooses outn 'em atter dey wus got ole. Dey jes bofe declar's befo' Gracious dat dey spizes an' hates de groun' dat she walk on!

Nex' day dey bofe talks it over some mo' wid one-nudder. Dey sayes dat dey thinks dat it'll pizen 'em fer to ketch deir bref in de same air whar she live. At las' dey makes up deir minds dat dey's a gwineter kill her.

Horn say he wus got de plan all fixed out. He'll go over an' tell Hun dat dey wus a gwineter give her a big moonlight watermillion eat. He'll tell her dat he wus done axed her friend, May, fer to come wid 'em; so dat dere'll be two couples. Dey'll have de big eat down in de woods-lot un'er de big chinquapin tree. He'll tell Hun dat dey caint have it at her house, an' dey wus bleedged to have it down in de woods-lot; caze de white folks mought miss May, an' sen' de patterrollers to her house a lookin fer her. He'll make her see dat de woods-lot is de onliest safe place; an' de house haint.

Rab tell Horn dat de plan suit him; an' fer him to go over an' fix it all up. Of co'se dey haint got no notion of axin May over to no meetin'. How-some-be-ever Horn go over an' lay out de progrance, an' 'suade Hun to come to de big watermillion eatin'; so dat dey can kill her an' bury her down dar in de dark an' de night.

So dat evenin', befo' de tothers wus yit comed, an' w'en it wus a gittin dark; Hun went down to de chinquapin tree. W'en she wus got dar, nobody wusnt yit comed. As she stan' dar a waitin fer de tothers; she 'gin to feel sorter skittish an' skeard of de varmints, an' all setch things as run aroun' at night. So she clum away up in dis here chinquapin tree; an' hid herself from de varmints in 'mongst de leaves. She wait up dar fer de tothers to come on over to de watermillion party.

Atter while Hun peep out through de leaves from de top of de tree; an' she see two mens a comin'. She say to herself dat dis wusnt her crowd; caze her crowd wus a crowd of three wid a 'oman put in fer one to boot. She sot up dar mighty still 'mongst de leaves, as she sees de strange mens a comin' towards her hidin' place. W'en dey gits a liddle closer; she sees dat one of 'em wus got a spade an' a pick, an' de tother one wus got a ax. W'en dey wus got still closer, she sees dat it wus Horn an' Rab; an' dey wusnt got neider no 'oman nor no watermillions wid 'em! So Hun sot up dar as still as death.

W'en dey wus got up un'er de tree; dey marked off her grave, an' 'gun to dig it whilst dey wus a waitin' fer her to come' Hun sot up dar an' looked an' looked at 'em. Dey dug away an' talked to one-nudder about how low-downed Hun wus. As dey shovels de dirt out, dey allows; whilst ev'ry dog wus got his own day, some dogs wus got deir night.

Bymeby dey got de grave dug; but "No Hun yit!" Dey sot dar; an' dey wainted an' dey wainted, but no Hun dont come'. At las' Horn say to Rab dat Hun wus jes played one mo' nasty dirty trick on 'em. He say to him fer to come on an' let's fill up de grave. He'll try fer to set his "dead fall" a liddle mo' better nex' time. He wus a gwineter ax her over to deir cabin to dinner, an' go atter her an' bring her; an' he think den dat dey can manage fer to make her "git lost" on de way home(?) Dat would sorter make things eben.

Dey filled up de grave an' lef'. Atter dey wus been gone long ' nough fer to be home two or three times; Hun slipped down de tree an ' runned home as fast as her footses could tote her an' barred de doo'. She shiver all over herself w'en she git dar; but she pull herself togedder an' make up her mind fer to stan' her groun' ag'inst Horn, Rab, an' all deir kind.

Nex' mawnin Horn go over to Hun's house fer to ax her to go over to his house to take dinner. Hun make answer dat she'll go; if he'll come over bright an' early an' take Breakfus wid her on de mawnin of de same day befo' she wus to go.

Horn tell her: All right, he'll come; but he want to know fust fer why she didn' come over to de big watermillion feast w'at dey wus gived fer her las' night. Dey all had a big time a bustin' open dem big red ripe striped fellers an' stuffin 'em down; an' dey wushed mighty much dat she mought a been dar an' a e't her po'tion.

Hun make answer dat she railly couldn' come. He railly mus' scuse her; an' she'll splain it all to 'im, w'en he come to Breakfus.

W'en Horn leave, Hun go over an' see de Big Jedge of de folkses in dem times; an' she tells him all 'bout Horn an' Rab a planin' up fer to kill her. She call to de Jedge's 'membunce dat de law call fer him to make all de folkses w'at plan fer to kill somebody, set up in de Pizen tree an' drink pizen ontel dey draps out dead. She lorate 'bout Horn an' Rab from beginnin' to end.

De Jedge tell her dat he wus willin' fer to do w'at he should oughter do; but she mus' prove it by somebody befo' he can act. Hun den promus dat she'll git de proofs; an' de Jedge say, if she do dis, he'll do de res'.

So Hun leave de Jedge an' go over fer to see her frien', Babe. She tell her all 'bout Horn an' Rab a tryin' fer to git to kill her. She want her to git anudder 'oman; an' bofe of 'em to come over an' hide un'er her table to hear her talk wid Horn at Breakfus. She wus a gwineter woolgether him at de Breakfus-table; an' make him say dat he wus a fixin' fer to kill her. W'en dis take place; she wus a gwineter call fer 'em lak dey wus hants, an' dey mus' pop out from un'er de table a lookin' lak de wus come outn coffins.

Babe tell her: All right; she'll go an' git it all fixed up wid anudder 'oman, an' dey'll be on hand.

Nex' mawnin, Babe an' de tother 'oman go, bright an' early, to Hun's house befo' Horn git dar. Hun had a great big table; an' she sot it dat mawnin fer Breakfus wid a great big table-cloth w'at comed clean down to de floo'. She wropped up de two womens in big white windin' sheets lak dey wus dead folkses; an' hid 'em up un'er de table at one end. Den she sot de plates at de tother end of de table fer her an' Horn to eat Breakfus togedder.

W'en Horn got dar, she had de Breakfus all ready, an' put on de table; an' axed him in. Mon! She had fried chicken, hot chittlins, cracklin bread, an' ev'rything good! Dey sot down; an' w'en Horn seed all dem good ole sweet taters an' chicken-fixins, he didn' feel so mean, an' he think to hisself maybe dere wus sumpin he didn' know wharfo' Hun wusnt so turble bad after all.

He praise up de good eatins, an' 'gin to hide 'em in his big mouf; an' in 'twixt de sputterin' of de grub aroun' in dar, he ax Hun ag'in fer why she didn' come over to de big watermillion eatin' by de light of de moon.

Hun make answer: Fer him to do no worry 'bout dat; caze she wus a gwineter splain it all, befo' dey goes over to his house to Dinner. Fer de present: She jes want him to he'p hisself an' injoy w'at her shelf wus able fer to set befo' him. She fust want to run over wid 'im de good ole times w'at useter be w'en dey wus boys an' gals an' rolled sheep eyes at one-nudder through de cracks 'tween de logs of her daddy's cabin. She ax him do he ricomember how dey useter send riddles to one-nudder.

Horn answer: Yes; an' he'd jes almos' give de whole worl' to lissen to a whole heaps of riddles ag'in.

Well, Hun tell Horn dat she want ev'rything to make him feel good; an' so, whilst he's a eatin, she's a gwineter tell him a tale an' put in a riddle, here an' dar, fer him to answer, so dat dey'll bofe be a tellin' de tale whilst one of 'em is a hearin it.

Horn make answer: Dat wus jes fine. Fer her to go ahead wid de riddles an' he'll go ahead wid de onravelin' of 'em. He's death on riddles.

Hun say; all right, here come de tale: "Once dere wus a 'oman an' lakwise dere wus two mens w'at wus in de riddle:

"In de chimbly corner, or up on de shelf;
Dont never hear nothin' good 'bout deirself?"

"Eaves-drappers dat didn hear nothin good 'bout deir-selves!" put in Horn, a answerin' de riddle, whilst de good Breakfus wus a skeetin down his red lane an' he wusnt payin' no 'tention to which a way de wind wus a blowin'.

Den Hun go on wid de tale: Dese two mens tell her fer to meet 'em at a:

'Look-look, look-look, look-look up!
Body all naked, an' head kivered up!'

"Tree", spoke up Horn a answerin' de riddle; an' Hun follered it up wid de words: "in a woods-lot whar dey wus to have a jolly big time". Den she say:

'As I went 'cross de big corn-fiel',
I met ole granny Gray.
I cut her open an' e't de meat;
An' throwed her skin away'."

"Watermillion", hollered out Horn a answerin' de riddle.
Den Hun go on wid de tale, a sayin: "an' injoy:

"As went down de ole dirt road,
I met my gal.—She didn' keer!
I pulled her head off, sucked her blood,
An' lef' her body a stan'in' dere'."

"A jug o' 'simmon beer!" put in Horn, a answerin' de riddle.
Den Hun pick up de thread of de tale: "De 'oman wus skeard dat she would be late. So she got up in a on-chyart w'at you mought say wus:

"Bigger towards de sky.
Bigger towards de groun'.
De furder it go up;
De furder it go down'."

Dis here riddle sorter stump Horn an' he hafter stop his gulpin down de good eats a liddle, so as to onravel it. W'en he see w'at de riddle means; he speak up sorter slow-lak: "A—tree."

"Hol' on dar a minute, Hun! "say Horn. "I wants to turn dis here thing over in my mind a liddle. I hardly knows whedder I's got de riddle straight or no!"—You sees, Chile, Horn wus sorter a ketchin de direction de storm wus a comin' from; an' he ax his stomach fer to stop an' give him a liddle time to find out how fur he wus from a shelter. Horn's 'membunce sorter runned over de tale w'at he wus done helped Hun to make lak dis: "Once dere wus a 'oman; an' dere wus two mens along wid her w'at wus eaves-drappers dat didn' hear nothin' good 'bout deirselves. Dese here two mens told her fer to meet 'em at a tree down in a woods-lot whar dey wus to have a jolly big time an' eat watermillions an' drink down a whole jug of 'simmon beer. De 'oman wus skeard dat she would be late; an' she went down an' clum up in a tree".—W'en Horn's mind git to dis part of de tale; his face turned right ashy'

Den Hun busted in wid anudder riddle:

"Ridlum, ridlum, ridlum right!
Whar wus I las' Friday night?
Dat night whilst I wus a settin high,
A lookin fer three, jes two come by.
It maked my poo' heart shiver an' shake,
To see w'at a hole dem foxes make!'—
Answer de riddle, Suh! Answer de riddle, Suh!"

Horn look at her sorter lak one o' dese here sheepkillin' dogs w'en he see a man a comin' wid a stick. He holler out: "I haint a gwineter do it! I haint a gwineter answer no riddle w'at'll make up a tale outn my own mouf to git me killed by de Big Jedge!"

But Hun cut loose ag'in:

"'Ridlum, ridlum, ridlum right!
Whar wus I on Friday night?
De grave, it show down from below;
By stars in Heaben w'at struck a leben!
Fall, Fox, down on yo' knee'
Pity! Pity! Bury me?"

Den Horn speak up big, he do, an' say: "I dont keer if you does know dat I wus a fixin up fer to kill you! You caint prove it; an' it dont make no diffunce! Go on an' tell de Big Jedge!

"Tell 'er, an' smell 'er, an' kick 'er down de cellar!
Let him stay down dar till he's good an' sof' an' meller!
W'en you gits 'im back; you wont never be no weller!"

Den Hun open up an' hand 'im back dis answer: "Yes, I can prove it! De hants w'at walks outn deir coffins at night hears you now, down in deir graves whar dey sleeps. An' w'en dey hears of a man w'at's ready fer to kill a 'oman dey shakes off deir dreamin' an' comes up in de broad-open 'em time fer to fix up riddles to save 'em.—At de end of dat time; dey mus' come an' stump ev'rybody wid riddles or take deir dose.

Dey git turned out. Den w'en de time wus passed an' comed, dey wus got deir riddles all fixed.

At de 'p'inted time; all de folkses comed togedder. (Back enjorin de year; Horn wus got him a calf w'at he wus named "Love". He kilt it an' skint it one nights an' buried some of it un'er de Pizen tree so dat de roots would take up some of dis calf. Nex' he chuore de skin wid salt an' dry it in de Hun. Den he make hisself some shoes an' mittens outn de hide. Atter dat, he sont word to de Big Jedge dat he wus ready wid his riddle.)

All de folkses wus dar fer de trial. Horn an' Rab wus lakwise dar befo' de Big Jedge. Dey all takes 'em down to de Pizen tree; caze if some W'at-'is-name guess deir riddles, dey wus got to drink de pizen an' die.

W'en de folkses wus got 'em down dar fer de trial by de Pizen tree; Horn wus already put on de shoes an' de mittens w'at he wus maked outn de hide of his calf, Love. None of de folkses didn' know why nor how he wus got 'em. Some sayed dat he wus put 'em on; so dat if he mus' drink de pizen an' de Imps git him an' start him to walkin' through hot embers down in De Bad Place, de embers wont burn him much. De tothers sayed he wus jes a puttin' on, an' a playin' big.

De Big Jedge called on Horn fer to climb de Pizen tree fust; an' to set up dar an' glve his riddle. He clumb de tree; an' sot down an' den stood up in de forks of it; an' den he give 'em out dis fer a riddle:

"Lose I set,
Love I stan',
Love I holds in my right han'."

As de folkses lissen at Horn a talkin' 'bout love, w'en he wus a hatin' folks bad 'nough to kill 'em; dey wus all puzzled an' bumfuzzled. Dey didn' know w'at to make outn him. Dey guessed an' dey guessed; but dey couldn' ontangle de riddle. So dey wus jes bleedged to give it up.

Horn den onfold it an' splain it to 'em. He splain to 'em how he wus done long ago put his calf, Love, un'er de Pizen trees so dat she wus done been took up an' wus in de tree. So, w'en he sot down on de fork of de tree; he wus sot down on Love. W'en he stan' up in de fork of de tree; he stan' on Love. 'Sides all dis; his shoes wus maked outn de hide of Love. So, he stan' on Love all de time.

At dis p'int of Horn's splavercations de folkses all busted in an' hollered out: "But none o' dat haint a holdin' no Love in yo' right hand!"

Den Horn jes sorter grinned an' helt up his right hand wid de mitten on it made outn de same thing as de shoes.

Dey all den say dat Horn wus got away wid his life. De Big Jedge tell him dat he can stan' to one side; an' wait fer de riddle w'at'll tell him w'at he mus' do fer to make his wrong right.

De Big Jedge den called on Rab to come up an' give his riddle to try fer to save his life. Rab walked up sorter keerless-lak, an' looked at Horn; an' say to 'em all dat he'll hafter try to ride free on Horn's back since he wus already turned free. Den he turned to 'em an' sayed: "Onravel dis,

'Brudders an' sisters—I haint got none.
But dis man's daddy is my daddy's son.
If you guesses dat riddle;
You can kill me fer fun!'

Well, dey all stayed dar putnigh all day; a tryin' fer to make out what kin Rab an' Horn wus. Dat 'ar brudder—buisness riddle upthripped 'em an' floored 'em all. Atter rackin deir brains almos' outn deir heads dey wus bleedged to give it us.

Rab den splain to 'em dat, of co'se, he wus a gwineter ride free on Horn; but Horn wusnt in de riddle. He onravel de riddle to 'em on dis wise: He (de one w'at wus a sayin' de riddle to 'em.) wus de "Dis man" in de riddle dat he wus a handin' out. He say he haint got neider no sisters nor no brudders; so, "Brudders an' sisters—I haint got none". Since he wus de "Dis man", an' wus his own daddy's son; den, "Dis man's daddy is my daddy's son".

De Jedge tell Rab dat he reckin dat he wus flewed outn de Pizen tree too; down safe an' soun' on de groun'.

De Jedge den call fer Hun to come up an' give bofe Horn an' Rab a riddle; de answer to which will tell 'em w'at dey mus' do to make deir wrong right; if dey caint onravel it. If dey onravels it; den dey's free from all.

Hun den stepped up an' handed 'em out dis riddle:

"I's been all aroun' in de whirly-whicky-whackum,
An' I's seed dem tackum;
So I tol' dem tackum,
Fer to drive dem tackum outn' whirly-whicky-whackum."

Horn an' Rab bite down hard an' gnaw on de riddle; but dey caint crack it open an' git out de kernel, so, dey had to give it up.

De Big Jedge den called on Hun to ontie de riddle; so dat Horn an' Rab would know w'at all de folkses wus a gwineter see to it dat dey done so as to make deir wrong right. She ontie de riddle lak dis:

"I's been all about in de worl',
I's seed dem w'at 'tack folkses.
So I's tol' folkses w'at 'tack folkses,
Fer to drive folkses w'at 'tack folkses outn de worl'."

De Big Jedge den call up Horn an' Rab; an' tell 'em dat dey mus' leave, an' keep on a gwine, ontel dey drives one-nudder clean out de world. So dey lef' dat country fer to keep on a gwine an' a keep on a gwine forever.

De Nigger w'at telled dis here loration to me, away down yon'er in Possum Trot, say dat all dis here riddle tellin' commenced away back dar in de times of Hun, Babe, Horn, Rab, an' Codger. But w'en dere git to be a whole heaps of riddles, an' all de folkses git to riddlin on deir own hooks; dey do so much devilment wid deir riddles an' git outn so much devilment wid 'em, dat dey wus bleedged to make it de rule dat no mo' folkses couldn' talk wid no riddles befo' no Jedges 'cep dey gits to be Philermerdelphy lawyers. How-some-be-ever de folkses keeps on a lakin' de riddles an' dey keeps on a tellin' em fer fun. *So, dar's whar all yo' riddles an' all yo' riddlin' come from!"* said Pos—the returned husband.

"Well", responded the happy wife, "we sho has enjoyed de loration; an', bes of all, we's awful glad fer to have you back here to tell it to us."

"Yes, daddy!" chimed in the children. "We wants you to tell us some mo' of de things dat you wus done gone an' l'arnt down dar in Possum Trot, in de Mawnin."

With the story finished, and the evening's entertainment over, the corn and the potatoes were drawn from the embers of the dying fire in the spacious fire-place. All hastily partook sparingly of the crudely prepared lunch; and lay themselves down to pleasant dreams and sleep.

SELECTED AFRICAN-AMERICAN FOLK MOTIFS IN *THE NEGRO TRADITIONS*

❄

DE WULL-ER-DE-WUST
  Mammy kilt me! Daddy eat me!
    Bird's song of indictment
  I'll Take Dis One
    Counting souls
  Jack-O-Lantern
    Transformation ritual
  Wait Till Phoebe Comes
    Haunted house

COTTON-EYED JOE or THE ORIGIN
OF THE WEEPING WILLOW
  Big Feard and Little Feard
    Imitative monkey
  Brer Rabbit and Brer Bear
    Meeting Mr. Man
  The Weeping Willow
    Transformation/Origin
  Haunted House
    Endurance Test

WHY THE JAYBIRD GOES TO SEE
THE "BAD MAN" ON FRIDAY
  Friday as Bad Luck
  Jaybird/Mockingbird Carrying Sand to
  the Devil
  The Smell Test

THE HEADLESS MAN
  Servants Obey Your Masters
    Sermon
  Sheephead Boiling out of the Pot
  What Did Paul Say?
  Servant Overheard in Prayer for
  Death and Tricked
  The Woodpecker
    Transformation/Origin
  Origin of the Headless Horseman

WHY THE BUZZARD IS BLACK
  Wait on the Lord
    Trickster Buzzard
  Origin of the Buzzard's Baldness
  Origin of the Buzzard's Black
  Feathers
  Bird Debate/Parliament

THE NEGRO SLAVE IN THE MOON
  Haunted House/Black Cat Hant
  Praying Slave Tricked by Master
  Gullible Slave Curses Master
  Talking Tarrapin/You Talk Too Much
  Liar's Contest/Riddle: Shot Three With
  One Bullet
  Angels and Devil's Imps Negotiate for
  Souls

HOW THE BEAR LOST HIS JUDGESHIP
  Bear as Nursemaid
  Mother's Song Imitated
  Origin of Milksnake

WHY THE IRISHMAN IS A RAILROAD
SECTION BOSS
  Irishman and Mosquitoes/Lightning
  Bugs/Fireflies
  Irishman and Mule Eggs/Pumpkins
  Irishman and Watch/Turtle
  Irishman and Frog's Advice
  Irishman and Fishing/Flood
  Irishman and Quicksand
  Irishman and Game-Cock/Blue Game
  Eggs
  Irishman and Bear Hunt: Prayer that
  the Lord not help Bear

WHY THE PREACHER DRESSES
IN BLACK
> The Foolish Boy
> What the Fowl Said/Guinea Hen
> (Ideophones)
> Origin of Whites

THE PARROT OVERSEER
> Parrot Tells on Slaves
> Parrot and Hot Biscuits
> Parrot and Buying Wood
> Parrot and the Hawk
> Parrot loses its Feathers
> Parrot and Nightclub Scenario
> Jaybird Soup
> John as Trickster
> Imitative Monkey

THE COURTING OLD WOMAN
> The Frigid Old Maid
> The Near-Sighted Old Lady

WHY THE CAT AND THE DOG ARE
ENEMIES
> Buzzard Reads Message on Rock
> *Hidden Gold*
> Animals Build a House Together
> *A Meeting/Council*

THE DOG'S HABITS, Origin of
> The Dog's Habit of Smelling
> *The Smell Test*
> Rabbit Trickster: Splits Dog's Mouth to
> Sing/Court
> Ole Molly Hare

THE DEVIL'S DAUGHTERS OR WHY
THE FISH HAVE FINS
> The Devil Beats His Wife
> Jack Beats the Devil/Gambles: Trickster
> Jack Accomplishes Impossible Tasks
>> Clears one hundred acres of
>> timber; plants, harvests, stores
>> corn
>> Cleans stables
>> Gathers egg from remote place
>> Plucks feathers for mattress
>> Dips dry a well and retrieves
>> object from bottom
>> Uproots spring
>> Chooses fiancée concealed
>> among dead women
> The Obstacle Flight
> The Transformation

WHY WHITE OVERSEERS OF NEGRO
SLAVES HAD LITTLE SENSE
> The Biggest Fool
> The Cow Grazes on the Roof
> Carrying Sunlight in a Wheelbarrow

RIDDLE THEM RIGHT
> Riddle to Gain Freedom from Slavery
> Riddle to Win a Wife
> Riddle to Identify a Suitor
> The Dumb Supper
> The Lucky Shot
> The Riddle of Self-incrimination
> The Neck Riddle
> Peach Pits and the Deer's Antlers

BIBLIOGRAPHY

Aarne, Antti, and Stith Thompson. *The Types of the Folktale*. Folklore Fellows Communications. No. 184. Helsinki: Academia Scientarium Fennica, 1964.

Abrahams, Roger D., ed. *Afro-American Folktales: Stories from Black Tradition in the New World*. New York: Pantheon Books, 1985.

———. *Deep Down in the Jungle: Negro Narrative Folklore from the Streets of Philadelphia*. Chicago: Aldine Pub. Co., 1971.

Adams, Edward C. L. *Tales of the Congaree*. [1927–28.] Ed. Robert G. O'Meally. Chapel Hill: Univ. of North Carolina Press, 1987.

Aswell, James R. *God Bless The Devil: The Liars' Bench Tales*. [1940.] Ed. Charles K. Wolfe. Knoxville: Univ. of Tennessee Press, 1985.

Backus, Emma M. "Animal Tales from North Carolina." *Journal of American Folklore*. 11 (1898): 288–89.

Baer, Florence E. *Sources and Analogues of the Uncle Remus Tales*. Helsinki: Academia Scientarium Fennica, 1980.

Baughman, Ernest W. *Type and Motif Index of the Folktales of England and North America*. The Hague: Mouton, 1966.

Botkin, B. A., ed. *Lay My Burden Down: A Folk History of Slavery*. [1945.] Athens: Univ. of Georgia Press, 1989.

Brewer, J. Mason. *American Negro Folklore*. Chicago: Quadrangle Books, 1968.

———. *Dog Ghosts and Other Texan Negro Folk Tales*. Austin: Univ. of Texas Press, 1958.

———. "John Tales." *Publications of the Texas Folklore Society* 21 (1946): 81–104.

———. "Juneteenth." *Publications of the Texas Folklore Society* 10 (1932): 9–54.

———. *The Word on the Brazos: Negro Preacher Tales from the Brazos Bottoms of Texas*. Austin: Univ. of Texas Press, 1958.

———, ed. *Worser Days and Better Times: The Folklore of the North Carolina Negro*. Chicago: Quadrangle, 1965.

Browne, Ray B. "Negro Tales from Alabama." *Southern Folklore Quarterly* 18 (1954): 129–34.

Brunner, Theodore. "Thirteen Tales from Houston County." *Publications of the Texas Folklore Society* 13 (1962): 8– 22.

Carawan, Guy and Candie. *Ain't I Got a Right to the Tree of Life? The Peoples of John's Island: Their Faces, Their Words, and Their Songs*. Athens: Univ. of Georgia Press, 1989.

Chesnutt, Charles Waddell. *Collected Stories of Charles W. Chesnutt*. [1899.] Ed. William L. Andrews. New York: Mentor, 1992.

Courlander, Harold. *A Treasury of Afro-American Folklore*. New York: Crown, 1976.

Cox, John Harrington. "Negro Tales from West Virginia." *Journal of American Folklore* 47 (1934): 341–57.

Crowley, Daniel J., ed. *African Folklore in the New World.* Austin: Univ. of Texas Press, 1977.

Dance, Daryl Cumber. *Shuckin' and Jivin': Folklore from Contemporary Black Americans.* Bloomington: Indiana Univ. Press, 1978.

Davis, Daniel Webster. "Echoes from a Plantation Party." *Southern Workman* 28 (1899): 54.

Davis, Gerald. *I Got the Word in Me and I Can Say It, You Know.* Philadelphia: Univ. of Pennsylvania Press, 1985.

Dillard, J., ed. *Perspectives on Black English.* The Hague: Mouton, 1975.

Dillard, J. L. *Black English: Its History and Usage in the United States.* New York: Vintage Books, 1972.

Dorson, Richard M. *American Negro Folktales.* Greenwich, Conn.: Fawcett Publishers, 1967.

———. *Negro Tales from Pine Bluff, Arkansas, and Calvin, Michigan.*
Bloomington: Indiana University Folklore Series No. 12. New York: Kraus, 1975.

Dundes, Alan. *Mother-Wit from the Laughing Barrel.* [1973.] Jackson: Univ. Press of Mississippi, 1990.

Faulkner, William J. *The Days When the Animals Talked: Black American Folktales and How They Came to Be.* Chicago: Follett Publishing Co., 1977.

Fauset, Arthur Huff. "Negro Folk Tales from the South (Alabama, Mississippi, Louisiana)." *Journal of American Folklore* 40 (1927): 213–303.

———. "Tales and Riddles Collected in Philadelphia." *Journal of American Folklore* 41 (1928): 529–57.

"Folktales from Students in the Georgia State College." *Journal of American Folklore* 32 (1919): 401–5.

"Folktales from Students in Tuskegee Institute, Alabama." *Journal of American Folklore* 32 (1919): 397–401.

Frye, Gladys-Marie. *Night Riders in Black Folk History.* Knoxville: Univ. of Tennessee Press, 1975.

Genovese, Eugene D. *Roll, Jordan, Roll: The World the Slaves Made.* New York: Vintage Books, 1976.

Gonzales, Ambrose E. *The Black Border, Gullah Stories of the Carolina Coast.* Columbia, S.C., 1923.

———. *With Aesop Along the Black Border.* 1924.

Goss, Linda, and Marian E. Barnes, eds. *Talk That Talk: An Anthology of African American Storytelling.* New York: Simon and Schuster, 1989.

Hamilton, Virginia. *The People Could Fly: American Black Folktales.* New York: Knopf, 1985.

Harris, Joel Chandler. *Uncle Remus: His Songs and His Sayings.* [1880.] Ed. Robert Hemenway. New York: Penguin, 1982.

Hermance, Belinda, ed. *Before Freedom.* New York: Mentor, 1990.

Holloway, Gary. *Saints, Demons, and Asses: Southern Preacher Anecdotes.* Bloomington: Indiana Univ. Press, 1989.

Hughes, Langston. *The Book of Negro Humor.* New York: Dodd, Mead, 1966.

———, and Arna Bontemps, eds. *The Book of Negro Folklore.* New York: Dodd, Mead, 1958.

Hurston, Zora Neale. *Mules and Men.* New York: Harper and Row, 1935.

———. *The Sanctified Church.* Berkeley: Turtle Island, 1981.

Jackson, Bruce. *Get Your Ass in the Water and Swim Like Me: Narrative Poetry from Black Oral Tradition.* Cambridge, Mass.: Harvard Univ. Press, 1974.

———. *The Negro and His Folklore in Nineteenth Century Periodicals.* Publications of the American Folklore Society, Bibliographical and Special Series, vol. 18. Austin: Univ. of Texas Press, 1967.

Jarmon, Laura C. "Metaphoric Forms in Thomas W. Talley's 'De Wull er de Wust.'" *Tennessee Folklore Society Bulletin* 56 (1993): 1–13.

———. *Way Back in Time: West Tennessee Narrative and Song in African American Tradition.* Audiotape. Rec. Sum. 1989. Middle Tennessee State University, Murfreesboro, Tennessee Folklore Society, 1993.

Johnson, Guy B. *Folk Culture from St. Helena Island, South Carolina.* North Carolina: Chapel Hill, 1930.

Jones, Bessie, and Bess Lomax Hawes. *Step It Down: Games, Plays, and Stories from the Afro-American Heritage.* Athens: Univ. of Georgia Press, 1985.

Jones, Charles C., Jr. *Negro Myths from the Georgia Coast.* Boston, 1888.

Jones-Jackson, Patricia. *When Roots Die: Endangered Traditions on the Sea Islands.* Athens: Univ. of Georgia Press, 1987.

Kane, Elisha K. "The Negro Dialects Along the Savannah River." *Dialect Notes* 5 (1925): 354.

Kochman, Thomas, ed. *Rappin' and Stylin' Out.* Urbana: Univ. of Illinois Press, 1972.

Labov, William. *Language in the Inner City: Studies in the Black English Vernacular.* Philadelphia: Univ. of Pennsylvania Press, 1972.

Lester, Julius. *Black Folktales.* New York: Grove Press, 1969.

Levine, Lawrence W. *Black Culture and Black Consciousness: Afro American Folk Thought From Slavery to Freedom.* Oxford: Oxford Univ. Press, 1977.

Parsons, Elsie Clews. *Folk-lore of the Sea Islands, South Carolina.* [1923.] Rpt. Chicago: Afro American Press, 1969.

Puckett, Newbell Niles. *Folk Beliefs of the Southern Negro.* [1926.] New York: Negro Univ. Press, 1968.

Roberts, John W. *From Trickster to Badman: The Black Folk Hero in Slavery and Freedom.* Philadelphia: Univ. of Pennsylvania Press, 1989.

Rosenberg, Bruce. *Can these Bones Live?: The Art of the American Folk Preacher.* New York: Oxford Univ. Press, 1988.

Schneider, Edgar W. *American Earlier Black English: Morphological and Syntactic Variables.* Tuscaloosa: Univ. of Alabama Press, 1989.

334 / The Negro Traditions

Smiley, Portia. "Folklore from Virginia, South Carolina, Georgia, Alabama, and Florida." *Journal of American Folklore* 32 (1919): 357–83.

Smitherman, Geneva. *Talkin and Testifyin: The Language of Black America.* [1977.] Detroit: Wayne State University Press, 1986.

Spalding, Henry D., ed. *Encyclopedia of Black Folklore and Humor.* New York: Jonathan David Publishers, 1972.

Talley, Thomas W. "De Wull er de Wust (The Will o' the Wisp)." *Tennessee Folklore Society Bulletin* 21.3 (1955): 57–78.

———. "The Origin of Negro Traditions." *Phylon* 3.4 (1942): 371–76.

———. "The Origin of Negro Traditions, Part II." *Phylon* 4.1 (1943): 30–38.

———. *Thomas W. Talley's Negro Folk Rhymes.* [1922.] Ed. Charles K. Wolfe. Knoxville: Univ. of Tennessee Press, 1991.

Thompson, Stith. *Motif-Index of Folk-Literature.* 6 vols. Bloomington: Indiana Univ. Press, 1955–58.

Trabasso, T., and D. Sears, eds. *Black English: A Seminar.* New Jersey: Lawrence Erlbaum Assoc., 1976.

Turner, Lorenzo Dow. *Africanisms in the Gullah Dialect.* Illinois: Univ. of Chicago Press, 1948.

Waugh, Butler H. "Negro Tales of John Kendry from Indianapolis." *Midwest Folklore* 8 (1958): 132.

Williams, Girlene Marie. "Negro Stories from the Colorado Valley." *Publications of the Texas Folklore Society* 29 (1959): 161–69.

Williamson, Juanita, and Virginia M. Burke. *A Various Language: Perspectives on American Dialects.* New York: Holt, Rinehart and Winston, 1971.